THE MASTERS AND THE SLAVES

THE MASTERS

AND THE SLAVES

[CASA-GRANDE & SENZALA]

A Study in the Development of Brazilian Civilization

BY

Gilberto Freyre

TRANSLATED FROM THE PORTUGUESE BY
SAMUEL PUTNAM

[Second English-Language Edition, Revised]

Introduction to the Paperback Edition by

DAVID H. P. MAYBURY-LEWIS

UNIVERSITY OF CALIFORNIA PRESS
Berkeley   Los Angeles   London

University of California Press
Berkeley and Los Angeles, California

University of California Press, Ltd.
London, England

Library of Congress Cataloging in Publication Data

Freyre, Gilberto, 1900–
    The masters and the slaves = Casa-grande & senzala.

    Bibliography: p.
    Includes indexes.
    1. Brazil—Social life and customs.   2. Brazil—Civilization—African influences.
3. Slavery—Brazil—History.   4. Blacks—Brazil—History.   5. Indians of South
America—Brazil—History.   6. Family—Brazil—History.   I. Title.   II. Title:
Casa-grande & sensala.   III. Title: Casa-grande e senzala.
F2510.F7522   1986   981   86-19197
ISBN 0-520-05665-5 (pbk. : alk. paper)

Printed in the United States of America

1 2 3 4 5 6 7 8 9

In Memory of My Grandparents

ALFREDO ALVES DA SILVA FREIRE

MARIA RAYMUNDA DA ROCHA WANDERLEY

ULYSSES PERNAMBUCANO DE MELLO

FRANCISCA DA CUNHA TEIXEIRA DE MELLO

CONTENTS

PREFACE TO
THE FIRST ENGLISH-LANGUAGE EDITION OF
THE MASTERS AND THE SLAVES

THIS essay is the first of a series in which I have undertaken to study the formation and disintegration of patriarchal society in Brazil, a society that grew up around the first sugar-mills or sugar plantations established by Europeans in our country, in the sixteenth century. It was upon this basis that the society in question developed: the production of sugar by means of a socio-economic system that represented, in a way, a revival of European feudalism in the American tropics. In the nineteenth century the system was to undergo an alteration that was not so much one of form or sociological characteristics as of economic content or cultural substance, through the substitution of coffee for sugar as the mainstay of the regime.

Sociologically matured through an experience of three centuries, the tropical feudalism of Brazil has conditioned the expression of life and culture and the relations of man with nature in this part of the Americas down to our own time, and its disintegration is a process that today may still be studied in a living form; for its survivals constitute the most typical elements of the Brazilian landscape, physical as well as social. The majority of our countrymen are the near descendants either of masters or of slaves, and many of them have sprung from the union of slave-owners with slave women. The visiting foreigner cannot be said to have seen Brazil unless he has been in the old Big House of some sugar or coffee plantation, with what is left of its family silver, its rosewood, its porcelain, its ancestral portraits, its garden, its slave quarters, and its chapel filled with images of the saints and the mortal remains of former inmates. These Big Houses, slave quarters, and plantation chapels blend harmoniously with the fields of sugar-cane, the coffee groves, the palm trees, the mangoes, the breadfruit trees; with the hills and plains, the tropical or semi-tropical forest, the rivers and waterfalls; with the horse-teams of the former masters and the oxen that were the companions in labor of the slaves. They likewise blend with those descendants of the white or near-white masters and of the Negro, mulatto, or *cafuso* [1] slaves who out of inertia have remained rooted in these old places where their grandfathers held aristocratic sway or engaged in servile toil.

---

[1] Offspring of Indian and Negro. (Translator.)

So perfect is this fusion that, even though they are now all but life-
less, these old elements, or mere fragments, of the patriarchal regime
in Brazil are still the best integrated of any with their environment
and, to all appearances, the best adapted to the climate. As a result,
the curious observer of today has the impression that they have grown
up together fraternally, and that, rather than being mutually hostile
by reason of their antagonisms, they complement one another with
their differences. Men, animals, houses, vegetables, techniques, values,
symbols, some of remote derivation, others native—all of these today,
now that the conflict between modes of life and the at times bitter
clash of interests have subsided, tend to form one of the most harmonious unions of culture with nature and of one culture with another
that the lands of this hemisphere have ever known.

If we speak of a union of cultures, it is for the reason that the most
diverse ethnic factors have contributed to this picture, bringing with
them cultural heritages that were widely different and even opposed:
the Portuguese "old Christian," [2] the Jew, the Spaniard, the Dutch,
the French, the Negro, the Amerindian, the descendant of the Moor.
As for the Jew, there is evidence to the effect that he was one of the
most active agents in the winning of a market for the sugar-producers
of Brazil, a function that, during the first century of colonization, he
fulfilled to the great advantage of this part of the Americas. He would
appear to have been the most efficient of those technicians responsible
for setting up the first sugar-mills. The history of patriarchal society
in Brazil is, for this reason, inseparable from the history of the Jew in
America. In speaking of his economic activity in the post-Columbian
world, the fact should be stressed that among the Portuguese of the
continent theological hatreds and violent racial antipathies or prejudices were rarely manifested. The same is true of the relations between whites and blacks: those hatreds due to class or caste, extended,
and at times disguised, in the form of race hatred, such as marked the
history of other slave-holding areas in the Americas, were seldom
carried to any such extreme in Brazil. The absence of violent rancors
due to race constitutes one of the peculiarities of the feudal system
in the tropics, a system that, in a manner of speaking, had been softened by the hot climate and by the effects of a miscegenation that
tended to dissolve such prejudices. This was the system that, in our
country, grew up around the sugar-mills and, later, the coffee plantations.

---

[2] As distinguished from the "new-Christian," the latter being a euphemism for a Jew who had accepted Christian baptism, the implication being, frequently, that he still clung to his old faith. (Translator.)

To be sure, the social distance between masters and slaves under this system, corresponding to differences in color, was an enormous one, the whites being really or officially the masters and the blacks really or officially the slaves.[3] The Portuguese, however, were a people who had experienced the rule of the Moors, a dark-skinned race but one that was superior to the white race in various aspects of its moral and material culture; and accordingly, though they themselves might be white and even of a pronounced blond type, they had long since formed the habit of discovering in colored peoples—or, as "old Christians," in the people of Israel and Mohammedans as well—persons, human beings, who were brothers, creatures and children of God with whom it was possible to fraternize, and with whom, as a matter of fact, their forebears had had fraternal relations. And all of this, from the very first years of colonization, tended to mitigate the system. It was this habit that led the Portuguese readily to adopt the foodstuffs, standards of feminine beauty, and modes of life of peoples that by other Europeans were looked upon as being absolutely inferior; and to this liberal attitude certain students of the subject have given the name "Lusitanian Franciscanism." [4]

It is a known fact that, in some of the best Portuguese families at the time of the colonization of Brazil there was Jewish, Moorish, or Indian blood, and this in no wise detracted from the prestige of the families in question when these strains were of socially illustrious origin. The same thing happened in America, where one of the first Brazilian colonists, a man of noble birth, was married to the daughter of an Indian chief. They had many descendants who became outstanding figures among the agrarian aristocracy and in the field of politics, literature, the magistracy, and the colonial clergy, a state of affairs that continued under the Empire and down to our own day. It was one of these descendants who became South America's first Cardinal.

It thereby becomes possible to interpret the formation of Brazilian society in the light of a "synthetic principle"—to make use of an expression consecrated by usage—such as, perhaps, could not be applied with a like degree of appropriateness to any other society. So viewed, our social history, despite the grievous and persisting imprint left

---

[3] The color line between master and slave, as is brought out later (see p. xxi–xxii), was far from being always distinct. The master might be a *brancarão*, or light-skinned mulatto, and the slave very often was partly white. (Translator.)

[4] The allusion, of course, is to the teachings or general attitude of St. Francis of Assisi and the Franciscan Order. (Translator.)

upon it by the experiences of a feudal economic system, is undergoing a process whose direction is that of a broad democratization. A democratization of interhuman relationships, of interpersonal relations, of relations between groups and between regions. The fact of the matter is that miscegenation and the interpenetration of cultures —chiefly European, Amerindian, and African culture—together with the possibilities and opportunities for rising in the social scale that in the past have been open to slaves, individuals of the colored races, and even heretics: the possibility and the opportunity of becoming free men and, in the official sense, whites and Christians (if not theologically sound, at any rate sociologically valid ones)—the fact is that all these things, from an early period, have tended to mollify the interclass and interracial antagonisms developed under an aristocratic economy.

Accepting this interpretation of Brazilian history as a march toward social democracy, a march that has on various occasions been interrupted and frequently has been disturbed and rendered difficult, we are unable to conceive of a society with tendencies more opposed to those of the Germanic *Weltanschauung*. What we have here is a society whose national direction is inspired not by the blood-stream of families, much less that of a race, as the expression of a biological reality, nor, on the other hand, by an all-powerful State or Church; it is, rather, one of diverse ethnic origins with varying cultural heritages which a feudal economic system maintained throughout whole centuries in a relative degree of order, without being able, meanwhile, to destroy the potential of the subordinated cultures by bringing about the triumph of the master-class culture to the exclusion of the others.

The sentiment of nationality in the Brazilian has been deeply affected by the fact that the feudal system did not here permit of a State that was wholly dominant or a Church that was omnipotent, as well as by the circumstance of miscegenation as practiced under the wing of that system and at the same time practiced against it, thus rendering less easy the absolute identification of the ruling class with the pure or quasi-pure European stock of the principal conquerors, the Portuguese. The result is a national sentiment tempered by a sympathy for the foreigner that is so broad as to become, practically, universalism. It would, indeed, be impossible to conceive of a people marching onward toward social democracy that in place of being universal in its tendencies should be narrowly exclusive or ethnocentric.

It would, truly enough, be ridiculous to pretend that the long period, ever since colonial times, during which a large part of Brazil had lived under a system of feudal organization had predisposed its people to the practice of political democracy, which recently underwent a crisis among us under a dictatorship that was at once near-fascist [5] in its ideology and Brazilian and paternalistic in fact. The major effort that is being put forth by the apologists of the present dictator is in the direction of popularizing him as the "Father" of his people, the "Father" of the workers or of the poor. It seems to me, meanwhile, that no student of Luso-American society can fail to recognize the fact that—as a consequence of the weakness rather than the virtue of the slave-holders and landowners—what I have here called Brazilian feudalism was in reality a combination of aristocracy, democracy, and even anarchy. And this union of opposites would appear to be serving as the basis for the development in Brazil of a society that is democratic in its ethnic, social, and cultural composition and, at the same time, aristocratic in its cult of superior individuals and superior families, and in the tolerance that it accords to differing personalities.

Hence a certain fondness that the Brazilian has for honoring differences. In Brazil individuals of the most widely varied social origins and personalities, differing likewise in race or religion, or by the fact that some are the descendants of Negro slaves while others are of white European or *caboclo* [6] ancestry, have risen to the highest positions. Some have been the sons of black women, like the one-time Archbishop of Mariana, Dom Silverio. Another, like the ex-Chancellor Lauro Muller, may be the son of an impoverished German immigrant. Still another may be the son of a non-Portuguese Jew, like David Campista, who was for some time Minister of Finance, and who in 1910 was practically President of the Republic. The most divergent types, in short, have been the object of the Brazilian's admiration and of his confidence. We Brazilians—and this, paradoxical as it may appear, is due to the effect of our "feudalism," which was at once aristocratic, democratic, and anarchistic in tendency—do not possess that cult of uniformity and horror of individual, family, and regional differences which are the accompaniments of the equalitarian spirit throughout so large a part of English-speaking America.

There are men in the public life of our country today, descendants of old and feudal families, of whom everyone knows just what service to the nation or to the community is to be expected, so marked are the characteristics and the differences of each one of these families. The Andradas of São Paulo, for example, are known for their stern ideal-

---

[5] *"Para-fascista"* is Freyre's word. (Translator.)   [6] American Indian or Indian-white mixture. (Translator.)

ism; the Calmons are noted for their suavity and spirit of conciliation; the Prados are realistic conservatives, the Mendes de Almeidas conservative idealists. This, to cite but a few. Yet such is our respect for individual differences that no one would be surprised to see a Prado a Communist leader in politics or a Mendes de Almeida a Surrealist in poetry or in art. We have seen the son of one old feudal family embarking for India and turning fakir; another, in Paris, became an airplane-inventor; a third, back in the days of slavery, became an abolitionist agitator; a fourth was a Protestant leader and terribly antipapist. And none of these was regarded as a madman. On the contrary, all were admired by their fellow countrymen; for the latter love and esteem those individuals who stand out by reason of their superior talents, knowledge, or virtue.

One word more, with regard to the title of the present essay in the original. That title does not mean that I have undertaken to trace the history of domestic architecture in patriarchal Brazil, with added commentaries of a sociological nature. The two expressions that make up the title—the Portuguese *casa-grande* (that is, big house or mansion in English) and the African *senzala* (slave quarters)—have here a symbolic intention, the purpose being to suggest the cultural antagonism and social distance between masters and slaves, whites and blacks, Europeans and Africans, as marked by the residence of each group in Brazil from the sixteenth to the nineteenth century. An antagonism and a distance that conditioned the evolvement of the patriarchal-agrarian or, simply, the feudal complex [7] in Portuguese America, and which were in their turn conditioned by other influences: that of the physical environment and those deriving from the antecedents of the Portuguese colonizer, of the Negro, and of the native or *caboclo*. Without for a moment forgetting the fact that the antagonism and distance of which we are speaking had their force broken by the interpenetration of cultures and by miscegenation—the democratizing factors of a society that otherwise would have remained divided into two irreconcilable groups—we cannot view with indifference the aristocratic effect of those interpersonal and interregional relations symbolized by the Big-House-and-Slave-Quarters complex in the history of Brazilian society and Brazilian culture.

Availing myself, then, of this symbolism (which since the first appearance of this essay, in 1933, has been utilized by other students of our history, sociology, and economy), my purpose has been to "evoke

---

[7] The author employs this term in the sociological sense; see p. 133, note 172. (Translator.)

that clear-cut image" which, as a distinguished Hispanic-American historian—a disciple, it may be, of Hans Freyer—observed not so long ago, is the recourse open to historical sociologists, confronted as they often are with the impossibility of reducing "the characteristics of a historical process to the precision of a concept," or of subjecting them to "hard and fast limitations."

GILBERTO FREYRE

Recife, July 1945

PREFACE TO
THE SECOND ENGLISH-LANGUAGE EDITION OF
THE MASTERS AND THE SLAVES

Rather than preserve here all the prefaces written for the several Portuguese editions of *Casa-Grande & Senzala,* I have decided to keep only the Preface written especially for the First English-Language Edition, and to fuse the others into this single synthetic Preface.

Accomplishing this was not easy. Prefaces for new editions, now as always being written by the calendar, I faced a problem of time. Also, there was something journalistic about the Portuguese Prefaces which makes them valuable only in relation to their dates. Nevertheless, some of the tentative ideas set forth in a preface may have both a chronological time-value and a psychological value in relation to a book that does not die in its first, second, or third edition. Such ideas and their possible psychological time-values are the ones I have included in this synthetic Preface. In doing this I have tried to fuse the several Portuguese Prefaces in the light of Dr. Johnson's generalization: "In contemplation we easily contract the time of real actions, and therefore willingly permit it to be contracted when we only see their imitation."

When I wrote the long Preface to the First Portuguese-Language Edition of my first long essay on the patriarchal society of Brazil—from the days when Brazil was a colony of the king of Portugal to the first period of the equally patriarchal and almost equally colonial national monarchy—and when I wrote the long Preface to the Second Portuguese-Language Edition, I was performing a sort of pioneering work which necessitated justification of some of my unorthodox methods. Those methods were somewhat more scandalous to some academic minds then than they are today—in fact, they were almost pure heresy.

Now that in the English-speaking world a writer like Mr. David Riesman has won recognition for books that (according to a favorable criticism of them) "cut across the social sciences," here picking a method of treatment from anthropology and using it to handle history, there mingling ideas from psychoanalysis and economics and "enriching the result"—as a critic has pointed out—"with literary references" (from Tolstoy, Samuel Butler, Virginia Woolf, Franz Kafka, St. Augustine, Nietzsche, Cervantes, Joyce, etc.) and, besides this, presenting himself "relatively free of academic jargon," it is no longer shocking for a Brazilian author to have done precisely that years before *The Lonely Crowd* was published.

Remembering some of the sharp or sarcastic remarks of strictly academic critics (English-speaking and Brazilian) about my pioneering work, I can now neutralize their poison—for they meant to kill what they considered to be an absurd book—with the generous understanding that I have met more recently not only in Europe (especially France), but also in the two Americas. This generous understanding has been coming more and more from such orthodox or conservative academic centers as the Sorbonne, the University of Strasbourg, Heidelberg, Rome, Coimbra, and—in the United States—such universities as Virginia, Princeton, Harvard, Northwestern, and Columbia. It was at Columbia, years ago, that I did graduate work with a scholar who was one of the first to think my experimental work not entirely worthless: Franz Boas. Another who found some worth in my scandalous book soon after its appearance was Señor José Ortega y Gasset; a third was the Swiss anthropologist Alfred Métraux.

Another significant change tending to prove that time has much to do with the fate of books has occurred in the attitude of some of the conservative groups that at first, through a few of their most representative voices, considered the present book hostile to them—some of the Jesuits, for example, and some Jewish leaders who went so far as to see "anti-Semitism" in my book. Now a better understanding is evident in both groups. *Études,* the well-known publication of the Paris Jesuits, regretted—in a book review published in 1952—that this book had not been translated sooner into French. Some outstanding Jewish leaders in Europe, the United States, and Latin America have publicly acknowledged my work as an endeavor to do justice to the Jewish contribution to Iberian civilization. In recent years also, the Communists, who at first took the attitude that this book was written from an "unprogressive" point of view, being too nostalgic over a past that should be repudiated by those who believe in "social progress," have become more tolerant of my ideas and my methods.

The fact is, of course, that I never meant to be anti-Jesuit or anti-Semitic. I admire the Jesuits, and I have always pointed out that Iberian and Ibero-American populations and cultures owe much to both Jewish and Moorish elements and values. Nor did I intend to oppose to "progressive" Communism, of Russian or some other style, a systematic or sentimental apology for the Luso-Brazilian "feudalistic" past. What I wanted to save from conventionally narrow points of view was a number of such Luso-Brazilian achievements as miscegenation and the fusion of cultural values which pseudosocial scientists like Gustave Le Bon have represented as absolutely disgraceful or harmful to so-called human progress. Those achievements are now being seen by other, technically more progressive peoples as culturally and politically valuable anticipations of what some modern thinkers, social anthropologists, and statesmen now consider to be adequate European behavior in tropical areas, areas in which European civilization enters into close relations with a non-European physical milieu and non-European races and cultures.

Thanks to my English-language publisher, Mr. Alfred A. Knopf, this book reappears in English not as a mere expression of a Latin American writer endeavoring to consider a Latin American situation through purely Latin American eyes, but as of possible human interest exceeding and transcending its regional significance and regional material. It was thus treated by European critics when presented in the French translation published by Gallimard in Paris—an edition which, appearing in 1952, has already been reprinted seven times. A French critic said that a book can be at once regional and universal in the perspective it tries to open up, in a pioneering way, with regard to primarily human matters needing to be considered whenever possible as human wholes or complexes within their regional configurations (in this case a Latin American configuration). Such wholes or complexes should not be sacrificed entirely to the treatment generally given them by rigid specialists in one or another branch of the social sciences, social history, or human geography, a treatment tending to deal with them as dry, dead fragments of wholes that on being dealt with in this anatomical way immediately cease to be living realities.

As I said above, since the first publication of this book in Portuguese in Rio de Janeiro in December 1933, books with this inter-related, integrative point of view have appeared in the United States and have been well treated even by academic critics. But in 1933 a book of this adventurous, experimental sort was considered to be violently opposed to the dominant academic orthodoxy in the United States and other countries. For excessive academic specialization had perverted social studies with extremes of pedantic purity. Aiming to separate such studies entirely from literature and other humanities, such specialization succeeded only in making most social studies caricatures of the biological or physical sciences.

Changes in attitude in the relations between social sciences and the humanities have been such in the United States and Europe during the past decade that university teachers of sociology, psychology, and other social sciences frankly admit that the social problems confronting the modern world challenge everyone to seek greater social insight. They admit that awareness and understanding of human values and relationships may be increased in students of social subjects if to the purely scientific analysis of these subjects are added other approaches, including disciplines from history, literature, philosophy, the humanities. This explains the publication in English for the use of students of social sciences—particularly of social anthropology—of books in which short stories and novels are employed to increase that awareness and that understanding. This interrelationistic or—as some would prefer to call it—integrative point of view dominates the area studies that have been introduced in a number of Anglo-American universities since the Second World War. Those studies have had valuable consequences for the study of social and cultural problems as regional wholes or complexes. The value of literary and folkloric approaches should not be disregarded or thought unworthy of contributing, alongside scientific analysis of their inter-relationships, to a deeper, more comprehensive interpretation of such regional complexes.

In writing on the patriarchal society of Brazil an essay that was also an attempt to analyze and interpret the meeting in a tropical area of a European civilization and at least two primitive cultures, as well as other non-European influences such as those brought to Brazil from the Orient by the Portuguese, I was trying to accomplish a pale equivalent of what Picasso has masterfully accomplished in plastic art: the merging of the analytic and the organic approaches to man: what one of his critics has called "a creative image." By doing that, the same critic said, Picasso promoted the intrusion of scientific dissection into art, thus showing by his action an accord with some aspects of modern science. But in this attempt to define the organic bases of form in all their possible virgin condition—through intuitive as well as concrete study of the Negro and the Polynesian—Picasso linked himself with the rebellion against some aspects of modern academic science. His aim, however, having been to express new potentialities of integration that might resolve contradictions, his pioneering work may be considered an example (as some of his critics have pointed out) of the way by which the union of images, ideas, and forms drawn partly from science and partly from anthropological material artistically apprehended may become an expression of what one of these penetrating critics, the Englishman J. Lindsay, considers "the unitary trend which is emerging in all really creative work of our period. . . ."

For, as Mr. Lindsay points out in his very intelligent pages on the present status of anthropology in relation to art, only a unitary methodology in anthropological studies "can make the whole human tradition a vital part of common experience," thus overcoming "the deadening and disintegrative forces of an industrialism based on mechanist science," disintegrative forces that have radically separated technically successful types of culture from the subdued or technically dominated ones, breaking the unity of man into at least two antagonistic types. The truth really seems to be that only "within" the living whole of human development can the relations between what is arbitrarily considered rationality and irrationality in human behavior, or between different human cultures, be fully understood. Consequently, one is justified in associating anthropology with history, folklore with literature, when one has to deal, as in the case of Brazil, with a human development in which "rational" and "irrational," "civilized" and "primitive" elements have mingled intimately, all contributing to the process of adaptation to life in a tropical and quasi-tropical area of a new type of society and a new harmony among otherwise antagonistic men—white and black, European and brown, civilized and primitive.

In attempting to do this, I was reminded more than once of the words of Henry James concerning the novel as vital literature. The novel to him was indeed "a living thing, all one and continuous . . . in each of the parts there is something of each of the other parts."

Of a history like the one outlined in this book—part history, part anthropology, part genetic or psychological sociology—with time-values that are also modified by differences of approach—the anthropological and the historical—I might say that, within modest limits, it was history attempted also as "a living thing, all one and continuous . . ." with something from one past always present in the other pasts. My aim has been to reach what Mr. Lindsay calls "a creative image." Hence the literary character of this anthropological-historical essay, which has been pointed out by some of the ablest French, Italian, German, and British critics in their generous comments, and irrespective of their "Existentialist" or "Sartrist" views of literature and of their Roman Catholic or Marxist or post-Marxist ideology. This literary character, not sacrificing its possible scientific structure—a structure maintained by a combination of several scientific approaches—was most clearly pointed out in *Le Figaro Littéraire*, by M. André Rousseaux, and by the critic of *The Economist* (London).

Some writers have compared the "creative image" aimed at in this essay, as it tries to fuse the historical and anthropological past and their mixture with the present, with the Proustian technique of recapturing the past. In both cases there is a study of human figures and social situations in which the apprehension of those realities by the scientific observer's eyes, as space-forms, is completed by the apprehension of the same realities by the observer's participant mind, as time-formations. This technique is illustrated by Proust's conception of the Duchesse de Guermantes as "a collective name . . . not merely in history, by the accumulation of all the women who have successively borne it, but also in the course of my own short life, which has already seen, in this single Duchesse de Guermantes, so many different women superimpose themselves, each one vanishing as soon as the next has acquired sufficient consistency."

In writing this book, which deals also with barons and baronesses, with captains and captains' wives from the colonial and imperial days of Brazil—men and women whose names were also collective, and whose succession in Brazilian life also was sociological as well as historical, in the sense that some of them were always masters in relation to slaves—I did indeed try to follow them as time-formations and, at the same time, as regional space-forms. I have tried to do this from a historical-sociological or historical-anthropological point of view, perhaps aided in some instances by a literary intrusion of my own person as participating in a social and psychological present still pregnant with the past, a historical past mainly European, and an anthropological past mainly Amerindian and African. The latter was represented by the influence of native women upon conquerors somewhat lost in the tropical wilderness, of slaves upon the minds, culture, and sometimes the bodies of the masters.

A modern Anglo-American sociologist has written that where Freud abstracts the libido, sociologists might abstract status. In relation to the Brazilian past, as in relation to other national and regional pasts, perhaps both libido and status should be abstracted. The sociological treatment of history should be supplemented with a psychological treatment. To do that was my aim in this book.

It is now generally admitted by anthropologists and sociologists that social science has become less intolerant than it was twenty years ago of what was then considered subjective psychology. Recesses of the mind—individual and collective, present and past—not to be visited easily by objective sociologists or anthropologists are now admitted to exist by an increasing number of students of human behavior and the human past, some of whom recognize the possibility of exploring those recesses by not entirely objective techniques and methods.

Now a few words as to how this essay was conceived and written, how it developed into an unorthodox book under both academic and extra-academic influences that led me to a new and adventurous treatment of a complex subject.

In October 1930 I embarked upon the adventure of exile, going to Bahia and Portugal, with Africa as a port of call—the ideal journey for the studious interests reflected in this book. I was secretary to the governor of Pernambuco when the 1930 revolution broke out there with un-Brazilian violence. People died on both sides, and seventeen residences were burned in the city of Recife, that of my own family included. Although non-partisan, I suffered the effects of partisan violence and, to my surprise and that of others, became a political *émigré* in Portugal, the United States, and Germany.

While in Portugal I unexpectedly received, in February 1931, an invitation from Stanford University to be one of its visiting professors in the spring of that year. With nostalgic regret I left Lisbon, where this time, in the course of a few months of leisure, I had been able to familiarize myself with the National Library, with the collections in the Ethnological Museum, with novel vintages of port, and with new varieties of codfish and sweetmeats. Added to this had been the pleasure of viewing Cintra and the Estories once again and of greeting distinguished acquaintances, among them the admirable scholar João Lúcio de Azevedo.

A similar opportunity had been mine in Bahia—known to me of old, but only from brief visits. Residing in Salvador, I could take my time in becoming acquainted not only with the collections in the Nina Rodrigues Museum of Afro-Bahian antiquities, with the art of apparel of the Negro women confectionery workers, and that art which they employ in the decoration of their cakes and cake-trays,[1] but also with certain more intimate delights of the Bahian kitchen and sweetmeat shop that escape the observation of the ordinary tourist, representing the more refined culinary tastes of the old Big House that have found in the hearths and cake-boards of Bahia their last stronghold and, God grant, an invincible one. I here must express my thanks to the Calmon, Freire de Carvalho, and Costa Pinto families, as well as to Professor Bernadino de Sousa of the Historical Institute, to Brother Philotheu, superior of the Franciscan Monastery, and to the Negro woman Maria Inácia, who provided me with interesting data on the dress of the Bahian women and the decoration of sweetmeat-trays. "*Une cuisine et une politesse! Oui, les deux signes de vieille*

---

[1] A separate study might well be made of the decorative and possibly mystical motives employed by these women in Bahia, in Pernambuco, and in Rio de Janeiro in the cutting of paper—blue, carnation-colored, yellow, etc.—for the garnishing of their trays and the packing of the sweets, and the forms that they give to their cakes, sugar-pastes, sugar-plums, and the like. The decoration of the trays is a true art of lacework in the medium of paper, executed practically without a pattern.

civilisation," I recall having learned in a French book. And that is precisely what I remember best about Bahia: its courtesy and its cooking, two expressions of patriarchal civilization that today are to be met with there as in no other part of Brazil. It was Bahia that gave us some of our major statesmen and diplomats under the Empire; and similarly in no other region are the most savory dishes of the Brazilian cuisine prepared so well as in the old houses of Salvador and the Reconcavo.[2]

Having given the courses that, on the suggestion of Professor Percy Alvin Martin, had been entrusted to me at Stanford University—one a course of lectures, the other a seminar, courses that brought me into contact with a group of young men and women students animated by a lively intellectual curiosity—I returned from California to New York by a route new to me: across Arizona, New Mexico, and Texas, an entire region that, in its wildest stretches, reminds one who comes from northern Brazil of our own backlands or Sertão, bristling with mandacarús and xique-xiques.[3] Desert wastes in which the vegetation has the appearance of enormous bottlenecks, of a crude and at times sinister green in color, thrust down into the arid sand.

No sooner has one crossed the New Mexico state line, however, than one begins to lose the feeling of a Brazilian backlands *paysage*, the place of which is now taken by the landscape of the old slave-holding South. This impression reaches a peak as the transcontinental express enters the canebrakes and swamps of Louisiana. Louisiana, Alabama, Mississippi, the Carolinas, Virginia—the so-called "deep South," a region where a patriarchal economy created almost the same type of aristocrat and of Big House, almost the same type of slave and of slave quarters, as in the north of Brazil and in certain portions of our own south; the same taste for the settee, the rocking-chair, good cooking, women, horses, and gambling; a region that has suffered and preserved the scars (when they are not open and still bleeding wounds) of the same devastating regime of agrarian exploitation: fire and ax, the felling of the forests and the burning over of the land, the "parasitic husbandry of nature," as Monteiro Baena puts it with

---

[2] The Reconcavo is a strip of land outside the city of Salvador (Bahia), bordering All Saints Bay. It is some sixty miles long and varies in breadth up to thirty miles. It was formerly the seat of the landowning and slave-holding rural aristocracy. (Translator.)

[3] The mandacarú is a variety of fig tree, this being the vernacular name in Brazil for a species of *Cereus* in general. Euclides da Cunha (*Os Sertões*, 16th edition, p. 43) identifies it as the *Cereus jaramacarú*. The xique-xique, also spelled chique-chique, is identified by Cunha (ibid.) as the *Cactus peruvianus;* it would appear to be the *Opuntia brasiliensis*, or the *Opuntia* in general. (Translator.)

reference to Brazil.[4] Every student of the patriarchal regime and the economy of slave-holding Brazil ought to become acquainted with the "deep South." The same influences deriving from the technique of production and of labor—that is to say, the one-crop system and slavery—have combined here in this English-settled portion of North America, as in the Antilles and Jamaica, to produce social results similar to those that are to be observed in our country. At times, indeed, they are so similar that the only variants to be found are in the accessory features: the differences of language, race, and forms of religion.

I had the good fortune to make the greater part of this journey through the Southern states of the Union in the company of two former colleagues of Columbia University, Ruediger Bilden and Francis Butler Simkins. The former was specializing, with all the rigorous detachment of his Germanic cultural background, in the study of slavery in the Americas, particularly in Brazil. The latter was engaged in studying the effects of abolition in the Carolinas, a subject on which he has since written a most interesting book in collaboration with Robert Hilliard Woody: *South Carolina during Reconstruction* (Chapel Hill, 1932). To these two friends, and especially to Ruediger Bilden, I am indebted for valuable suggestions in connection with the present work; and to these names I should add that of another colleague, Ernest Weaver, the companion of my studies in anthropology in the course given by Professor Franz Boas.

The scholarly figure of Professor Boas is the one that to this day makes the deepest impression upon me. I became acquainted with him when I first went to Columbia. I do not believe that any Russian student among the romantics of the nineteenth century was more intensely preoccupied with the destiny of Russia than was I with that of Brazil at the time that I knew Boas. It was as if everything was dependent upon me and those of my generation, upon the manner in which we succeeded in solving age-old questions.[5] And of all the problems confronting Brazil there was none that gave me so much anxiety as that of miscegenation. Once upon a time, after three straight years of absence from my country, I caught sight of a group of Brazilian seamen—mulattoes and *cafusos*—crossing Brooklyn

---

[4] Antônio Ladislau Monteiro Baena: *Ensaio chorográphico sobre a província do Pará (Chorographic Essay on the Province of Pará)* (Pará, 1839).

[5] Freyre has given an admirable picture of his generation in his book *Região e tradição (Region and Tradi-*

tion) (Rio de Janeiro, 1941). See especially his paper: "*Apologia pro generatione sua,*" in which he has some extremely interesting things to say about Randolph Bourne as well as Charles Péguy and Ernest Psichari. (Translator.)

Bridge. I no longer remember whether they were from São Paulo or from Minas, but I know that they impressed me as being the caricatures of men, and there came to mind a phrase from a book on Brazil written by an American traveler: "the fearfully mongrel aspect of the population." That was the sort of thing to which miscegenation led. I ought to have had some one to tell me then what Roquette Pinto had told the Aryanizers of the Brazilian Eugenics Congress in 1929: that these individuals whom I looked upon as representative of Brazil were not simply mulattoes or *cafusos* but *sickly* ones.[6]

It was my studies in anthropology under the direction of Professor Boas that first revealed to me the Negro and the mulatto for what they are—with the effects of environment or cultural experience separated from racial characteristics. I learned to regard as fundamental the difference between *race* and *culture*, to discriminate between the effects of purely genetic relationships and those resulting from social influences, the cultural heritage and the milieu. It is upon this criterion of the basic differentiation between race and culture that the entire plan of this essay rests, as well as upon the distinction to be made between racial and family heredity.

However little inclined we may be to historical materialism, which is so often exaggerated in its generalizations—chiefly in works by sectarians and fanatics—we must admit the considerable influence, even though not always a preponderant one, exerted by the technique of economic production upon the structure of societies and upon the features of their moral physiognomies. It is an influence subject to the reaction of other influences, yet powerful as no other in its ability to make aristocracies or democracies out of societies and to determine tendencies toward polygamy or monogamy, toward stratification or mobility. Studies in eugenics and cacogenics are still in a state of flux, and much of what is supposed to be the result of hereditary characteristics or tares ought rather to be ascribed to the persistence for generations of economic and social conditions favorable or unfavorable to human development. It is Franz Boas who, admitting the possibility

---

[6] Roquette Pinto, an anthropologist who died in 1954, was one of Brazil's most distinguished scientists. "Aryanization" has a special meaning in Brazil, with allusion to the absorption of the "inferior" races by the "superior" one (i.e., the white race), and the gradual shedding of the characteristics of the hybrid type. This view is set forth by J. F. de Oliveira Vianna, among others, in his book, *Populações meridionaes do Brasil* (3rd edition, São Paulo, 1933); see in particular p. 154. There is, however, a wide difference of opinion on the subject. See Donald Pierson: *Negroes in Brazil* (University of Chicago Press, 1942), Chapter viii, "Racial Ideology and Racial Attitudes." (Translator.)

that eugenics may be able to eliminate the undesirable elements of a society, reminds us that eugenic selection should concern itself with suppressing the conditions responsible for the creation of poverty-stricken proletarians, sickly and ill-nourished; and he further reminds us that so long as such conditions exist, the result can only be the creation of more proletarians of the same sort.[7]

In Brazil the relations between the white and colored races from

[7] Boas stresses the fact that in those classes where the economic conditions of life are unfavorable, individuals evolve slowly and are low in stature in comparison with the wealthy classes. Among the poorer classes a low stature would appear to be hereditary, but capable none the less of modification once the economic conditions are modified. Bodily proportions, Boas tells us, are in some cases determined by occupation and are seemingly handed down from father to son when the son follows the same occupation as the father.—Franz Boas: *Anthropology and Modern Life* (New York and London, 1929). See also the researches of H. P. Bouditch: "The Growth of Children," *Eighth Annual Report of the State Bureau of Health of Massachusetts*. In Russia, as a result of the famine of 1921-2, a famine due not only to the bad organization of the first Soviet administrations but also to the blockade of the new Republic by the capitalist governments, there was found to be a considerable decrease in the stature of the population.—I. Ivanovsky: "Physical Modifications of the Population of Russia under Famine," *American Journal of Physical Anthropology*, No. 4, 1923. On the other hand the studies of the North American population made by Hrdlička show an increase of stature.—Ales Hrdlička: *The Old Americans* (Baltimore, 1925). On the differences in stature and other physical and mental characteristics between one social group and another, see the classic work of A. Niceforo: *Les Classes pauvres* (Paris, 1905); and among more recent studies, that of Pitirim Sorokin: *Social Mobility* (New York, 1927). As to the correlation between intelligence and social class, see the notable work by Professor L. M. Terman of Stanford University: *Genetic Studies of Genius*, 1925-30. The interesting thing in connection with these differences —the exceptional case naturally being excluded—is to determine to what point they are hereditary or genetic and at what point they cease to be, becoming instead the reflection of a favorable or unfavorable succession of economic conditions—that is to say, a reflection of the social milieu and the diet of rich and poor. Or—looking at the problem from another point of view—we may ask: what are the possibilities of qualities acquired and cultivated for generations becoming transmissible by heredity? Dendy stresses the observation of Oliver Wendell Holmes to the effect that an intellectual and social aristocracy had been formed in New England through the repetition of the same influences for generation after generation.—Arthur Dendy: *The Biological Foundation of Society* (London, 1924). On this point see also J. A. Detlefsen: *Our Present Knowledge of Heredity* (Philadelphia, 1925); H. S. Jennings: *Prometheus* (New York, 1925); C. M. Child: *Physiological Foundations of Behavior* (New York, 1924); A. J. Herrick: *Neurological Foundations of Animal Behavior* (New York, 1924); F. B. Davenport: *Heredity in Relation to Eugenics* (New York, 1911); A. Myerson: *The Inheritance of Mental Disorders* (Baltimore, 1925).

the first half of the sixteenth century were conditioned on the one hand by the system of economic production—monoculture and latifundia—and on the other hand by the scarcity of white women among the conquerors. Sugar-raising not only stifled the democratic industries represented by the trade in brazilwood and hides; it sterilized the land for the forces of diversified farming and herding for a broad expanse around the plantations. It called for an enormous number of slaves. Cattle-raising, meanwhile, with the possibilities it afforded for a democratic way of life, was relegated to the backlands. In the agrarian zone, along with a monoculture that absorbed other forms of production, there developed a semi-feudal society, with a minority of whites and light-skinned mulattoes dominating, patriarchally and polygamously, from their Big Houses of stone and mortar, not only the slaves that were bred so prolifically in the senzalas, but the sharecroppers as well, the tenants or retainers, those who dwelt in the huts of mud and straw, vassals of the Big House in the strictest meaning of the word.[8]

Conquerors, in the military and technical sense, of the indigenous populations, the absolute rulers of the Negroes imported from Africa for the hard labor of the *bagaceira*,[9] the Europeans and their descendants meanwhile had to compromise with the Indians and the Africans in the matter of genetic and social relations. The scarcity of white women created zones of fraternization between conquerors and conquered, between masters and slaves. While these relations between white men and colored women did not cease to be those of "superiors" with "inferiors," and in the majority of cases those of disillusioned and sadistic gentlemen with passive slave girls, they were mitigated by the need that was felt by many colonists of founding a family under such circumstances and upon such a basis as this. A widely practiced miscegenation here tended to modify the enormous social distance that otherwise would have been preserved between Big House and tropical forest, between Big House and slave hut. What a latifundiary monoculture based upon slavery accomplished in the way of creating an aristocracy, by dividing Brazilian society into two extremes, of

---

[8] On the relation between building materials and the formation of aristocratic societies, see George Plekhanov: *Introduction à l'histoire sociale de la Russie* (translation) (Paris, 1926).

[9] The *bagaceira* was the place where the bagasse, or refuse of the sugarcane after the juice had been pressed from it ("cane trash"), was stored.

The word in Brazil comes to mean the general life and atmosphere of the sugar plantation. A famous modern novel by José Américo de Almeida is entitled *A Bagaceira* (Rio de Janeiro, 1928); this work is looked upon as the beginning of the school of social fiction of the 1930's and the present day. (Translator.)

gentry and slaves, with a thin and insignificant remnant of free men sandwiched in between, was in good part offset by the social effects of miscegenation. The Indian woman and the *"mina,"* [10] or Negro woman, in the beginning, and later the mulatto, the *cabrocha*,[11] the quadroon, and the octoroon, becoming domestics, concubines, and even the lawful wives of their white masters, exerted a powerful influence for social democracy in Brazil. A considerable portion of the big landed estates was divided among the mestizo sons, legitimate or illegitimate, procreated by these white fathers, and this tended to break up the feudal allotments and latifundia that were small kingdoms in themselves.

Bound up with a latifundiary monoculture were deep-rooted evils that for generations impaired the robustness and efficiency of the Brazilian population, whose unstable health, uncertain capacity for work, apathy, and disturbances of growth are so frequently attributed to miscegenation. Among other things, there was the poor supply of fresh food, subjecting the major part of the population to a deficient diet, marked by the overuse of dried fish and manihot flour (and later of jerked beef), or to an incomplete and dangerous one of foodstuffs imported under the worst conditions of transport, such as those that preceded the steamboat and the employment in recent years of refrigerator compartments on ships. The importance of the factor of hyponutrition, stressed by Armitage,[12] McCollum and Simmonds,[13] and of late by Escudero,[14] a chronic hunger that comes not so much from a diet reduced in quantity as from its defective quality, throws a new light on those problems vaguely referred to as due to racial

---

[10] Name given to highly respected Negro women of Bahia who became "friends," concubines, and "housewives" (*donas de casa*) of their white masters. The name is derived from Forte de el Mina on the west coast of Africa, one of the places from which the Portuguese imported their slaves. The *"minas"* were light-skinned, with features that resembled those of a white person, and were looked upon as "excellent companions." They were probably the first Negro women to be legally married to Europeans. See Donald Pierson: *Negroes in Brazil*, pp. 145–6. (Translator.)

[11] A dark-skinned mestizo type. (Translator.)

[12] F. P. Armitage: *Diet and Race* (London and New York, 1922).

[13] E. V. McCollum and Nina Simmonds: *The Newer Knowledge of Nutrition: the Use of Foods for the Preservation of Vitality and Health* (New York, 1929).

[14] Pedro Escudero: "Influencia de la alimentación sobre la raza," *La Prensa* (Buenos Aires), March 27, 1933. The articles of the Argentine professor are interesting, even though they add little that is original to the studies of North American and European physiologists: Armitage, McCollum, Simmonds, Lusk, Benedict, McCay, Nitti.

"decadence" or "inferiority" and, thank God, offers greater possibilities of a solution. Prominent among the effects of hyponutrition are: a decrease in stature, weight, and chest measurement; deformities of the bony structure; decalcification of the teeth; thyroid insufficiency, pituitary and gonadial, leading to premature old age, a generally impoverished fertility, apathy, and, not infrequently, infecundity. It is precisely these characteristics of sterility and an inferior physique that are commonly associated with the execrated blood-stream of the so called "inferior races." Nor should we forget other influences that developed along with the patriarchal and slave-holding system of colonization: syphilis, for example, which is responsible for so many of those "sickly mulattoes" of whom Roquette Pinto speaks and to whom Ruediger Bilden attributes a great importance in his study of the formation of Brazilian society.

The formative patriarchal phase of that society, in its virtues as well as in its shortcomings, is to be explained less in terms of "race" and "religion" than in those of economics, cultural experience, and family organization; for the family here was the colonizing unit. This was an economy and a social organization that at times ran counter not only to Catholic sexual morality but to the Semite tendencies of the Portuguese adventurer toward trade and barter as well.

Spengler stresses the point that a race does not migrate from one continent to another; for that it would be necessary to transport along with it the physical environment. In this connection he alludes to the results of the studies of Gould and Baxter and those of Boas, which show that individuals of varying origin brought together under the same conditions of physical environment tend to a certain uniform development with regard to stature and even, perhaps, bodily structure and shape of the head.[15] The modifications, possibly due to environment, to be found in the descendants of immigrants—as in the case of the Sicilian and German Jews studied by Boas in the United States [16]—would appear to be the result chiefly of what Wissler calls the influence of the biochemical content.[17] Indeed, the study of such modifications in a new climate or milieu is acquiring an ever greater importance. The rapid alterations that occur would seem to be due to the iodine that the environment contains, which

---

[15] Oswald Spengler: *The Decline of the West* (translation). (New York, 1926, 1928), Vol. II, p. 119.

[16] Franz Boas: "Changes in Bodily Forms of Descendants of Immigrants," *Senate Documents* (Washington, 1910–11).

[17] Clark Wissler: *Man and Culture* (New York, 1923).

acts upon the secretions of the thyroid gland. And diet is likewise of considerable importance in the differentiation of the physical and mental characteristics of the descendants of immigrants.

Admitting the tendency of the physical environment, and especially of the biochemical content, to re-create in its own image those individuals who come to it from various places, we still must not forget the action exerted in a contrary direction by the technical resources of the colonizers: their effect in imposing upon the environment strange cultural forms and accessories such as would permit the preservation of an exotic *race* or *culture*.

The patriarchal system of colonization set up by the Portuguese in Brazil and represented by the Big House was one of plastic compromise between the two tendencies. At the same time that it gave expression to the imperialist imposition of an advanced race upon a backward one, an imposition of European forms (already modified by colonizing experience in Asia and Africa) upon a tropical milieu, it meant a coming to terms with the new conditions of life and environment. The plantation Big House that the colonizer began erecting in Brazil in the sixteenth century—thick walls of mud or of stone and lime, covered with straw or with tile, with a veranda in front and on the sides and with sloping roofs to give the maximum of protection against the strong sun and tropical rains—was by no means a reproduction of Portuguese houses, but a new expression, corresponding to the new physical environment and to a surprising, unlooked-for phase of Portuguese imperialism: its agrarian and sedentary activity in the tropics, its rural, slave-holding patriarchalism. From that moment the Portuguese, while still longing nostalgically for his native realm, a sentiment to which Capistrano de Abreu has given the name of "transoceanism"—from that moment he was a Luso-Brazilian, the founder of a new economic and social order, the creator of a new type of habitation. One has but to compare the plan of a Brazilian Big House of the sixteenth century with that of a Lusitanian manor house (*solar*) of the fifteenth century in order to be able to perceive the enormous difference between the Portuguese of Portugal and the Portuguese of Brazil. After something like a century of patriarchal life and agrarian activity in the tropics, the Brazilians are practically another race, expressing themselves in another type of dwelling. As Spengler observes—and for him the type of habitation has a historical-social value superior to that of race—the energy of the blood-stream that leaves identical traces down the centuries must necessarily be increased by the "mysterious cosmic force that binds together in a single rhythm those who dwell in close proximity to one another."[18] This force in the formation of Brazilian life was exerted from above downward, emanating from the Big Houses that were the center of patriarchal and religious cohesion, the points of support for the organized society of the nation.

The Big House completed by the slave shed represents an entire economic, social, and political system: a system of production (a latifundiary monoculture); a system of labor (slavery); a system of transport (the ox-cart, the *banguê*,[19] the hammock, the horse); a system of religion (a family Catholicism, with the chaplain subordinated to the paterfamilias, with a cult of the dead, etc.); a system of sexual and family life (polygamous patriarchalism); a system of bodily and household hygiene (the "tiger,"[20] the banana stalk, the river bath, the tub bath, the sitting-bath, the foot bath); and a system of politics (*compadrismo*).[21] The Big House was thus at one and the same time a fortress, a bank, a cemetery, a hospital, a school, and a house of charity giving shelter to the aged, the widow, and the orphan. The Big House of the Noruega plantation in Pernambuco, with its many rooms, drawing-rooms, and corridors, its two convent kitchens, its dispensary, its chapel, and its annexes, impresses me as being the sincere and complete expression of the absorptive patriarchalism of colonial times. An expression of the gentle and subdued patriarchalism of the eighteenth century, without the air of a fortress that characterized the first Big Houses of the sixteenth century. "On the plantations it was like being on a field of battle," writes Theodoro Sampaio, with reference to the first century of colonization. "The rich were in the habit of protecting their dwellings and manor houses by a double and powerful row of stakes, in the manner of the natives, and these stockades were manned by domestics, retainers, and Indian slaves and served also as a refuge for the neighbors when they were unexpectedly attacked by savages."[22]

The plantations at the end of the seventeenth century and those of the eighteenth century, on the other hand, more nearly resembled

---

[18] Oswald Spengler, op. cit. The significance of the dwelling-place had already been stressed by G. Schmoller, in the classic pages that he has written on the subject.

[19] In northeastern Brazil the *banguê* was a variety of litter with leather top and curtains. (Translator.)

[20] The *"tigre"* was a vessel for the depositing and carrying away of fecal matter. (Translator.)

[21] *"Compadrismo"* was a system of oligarchic nepotism and patronage; the author refers to it later in this chapter. From *compadre*: literally, a godfather or sponsor, a friend, etc. (Translator.)

[22] Theodoro Sampaio: "*S. Paulo de Piratininga no fim do século XVI*" ("S. Paulo de Piratininga at the End of the Sixteenth century), *Revista do Instituto Histórico de São Paulo*, Vol. II.

a Portuguese convent—a huge estate with the functions of a hospital and a house of charity. The indescribable air of aloofness that characterized the houses at the beginning of the seventeenth century, with their verandas that appeared to have been erected on wooden stilts, was no longer to be met with in these end-of-the-century dwellings and those of the eighteenth and the first half of the nineteenth century; the latter were houses that had been almost wholly demilitarized and, accentuatedly rustic in appearance, offered to strangers an easygoing and expansive hospitality. Even on the cattle ranches of Rio Grande, Nicolão Dreys, at the beginning of the nineteenth century, encountered a custom reminiscent of medieval convents, that of ringing a bell at the dinner hour: "It serves to advise the traveler wandering over the countryside or the destitute of the vicinity that they may come to the lord of the manor's table which is now being spread; and, indeed, whoever cares to do so may and does sit down at that hospitable board. Never does the lord of the manor repel anyone or so much as ask him who he is. . . ." [23]

It seems to me that José Marianno *fils* is not entirely right in saying that our patriarchal architecture did no more than follow the model of religious architecture as developed here by the Jesuits,[24] those terrible enemies of the lords of the plantation. What the architecture of the Big Houses took from the monasteries was, rather, a certain Franciscan gentleness and simplicity, a fact that is to be explained by the identity of functions fulfilled by a plantation manor house and a typical convent of Franciscan friars. There is no doubt (and I here find myself in perfect agreement with José Marianno *fils*) that Jesuit and Church architecture was the highest and most cultured expression of its kind in colonial Brazil, and it certainly had its effect upon the Big House. The latter, however, following a rhythm of its own, its own patriarchal tendency, and conscious of a larger need than that of a purely ecclesiastical adaptation to environment, proceeded to individualize itself and came to take on so great an importance that it ended by dominating the architecture of convent and church, breaking with the lofty Jesuit style and leveling the Spanish verticality, to make of it a gentle, humble, and subservient expression in the form of the plantation chapel, a dependency of the domestic habitation. If the Big House took from the churches and monasteries

[23] Nicolao Dreys: *Notícia Descriptiva da Província do Rio Grande de São Pedro do Sul (Descriptive Account of the Province of Rio Grande de São Pedro do Sul)* (Rio de Janeiro, 1839), p. 174.

[24] José Marianno *fils*: Lecture in the School of Fine Arts of Recife, April 1933.

artistic values and technical resources, the churches likewise assimilated the characteristics of the manor house: the entryway, for example. Nothing is more interesting than certain churches in the interior of Brazil with a veranda in front or along the sides, like a private residence. I am acquainted with a number of them, in Pernambuco, in Paraíba, in São Paulo. Quite characteristic is the Church of São Roque de Serinhaem, and still more so the chapel of the Caieira plantation, in Sergipe, whose aspect at a distance is wholly residential. And in São Paulo there is the little Chapel of São Miguel, which also dates from colonial times.

The Big House in Brazil, in the impulse that it manifested from the very start to be the mistress of the land, overcame the church. It overcame the Jesuit as well, leaving the lord of the manor as almost the sole dominating figure in the colony, the true lord of Brazil, or nearer to being than either the viceroys or the bishops.

For power came to be concentrated in the hands of these country squires. They were the lords of the earth and of men. The lords of women, also. Their houses were the expression of an enormous feudal might. "Ugly and strong." Thick walls. Deep foundations, anointed with whale oil. There is a legend in the northeast to the effect that a certain plantation-owner, more anxious than usual to assure the perpetuity of his dwelling, was not content until he had had a couple of slaves killed and buried beneath the foundation stones. The sweat and at times the blood of Negroes was the oil, rather than that of the whale, that helped to give the Big House foundations their fortress-like consistency.

The ironical part of it is, however, that owing to a failure of the human potential all this arrogant solidity of form and material was very frequently wasted, and in the third or fourth generation enormous houses built to last for centuries would begin crumbling from disuse or lack of proper care, the great-grandsons or even the grandsons being unable to preserve the ancestral heritage. In Pernambuco the ruins of the big country house of the barons of Mercês are still to be seen, and it is evident that even the stables were built like fortresses. But all this pomp has long since turned to dust, and when all is said, it was the churches that survived the Big Houses. At Massangana, the plantation where Nabuco[25] spent his boyhood, the old manor house has disappeared and the *senzala* also has crumbled; only the ancient and diminutive Chapel of São Mateus remains standing, with its saints and its catacombs.

---

[25] Joaquim Nabuco was a famous abolitionist leader and intellectual of the later nineteenth century. (Translator.)

The custom of burying the dead underneath the house—beneath the chapel, which was an annex of the house—is quite characteristic of the patriarchal spirit of family cohesiveness. The dead thus remained under the same roof as the living, amid the saints and the floral offerings of the devout. The saints and the dead were, indeed, a part of the family. In Portuguese and Brazilian cradle songs mothers never hesitated to make of their infant sons the younger brothers of Jesus, with the same rights to Mary's care, to the guardianship of Joseph, and the doting ministrations of St. Anne. St. Joseph was the one who was called upon with the least ceremony to rock the cradle or hammock of the child:

> *Rock, Joseph, rock,*
> *For the Lady, she is out:*
> *She's gone to Belem creek,*
> *To wash the baby's clout.*[26]

As for St. Anne, she was supposed to take the little ones on her lap and cuddle them:

> *Mistress St. Anne, come tend*
> *My little daughter here;*
> *Just see how pretty she is*
> *And what a little dear.*
>
> *This little girl of mine*
> *Does not sleep in a bed;*
> *She sleeps in the blessed lap*
> *Of the good St. Anne instead.*[27]

So much liberty was taken with the saints that to them was entrusted the task of protecting the jars of preserves against the ants:

> *Praise St. Benedict, 'tis a sin*
> *That ants should come here*
> *To enter in.*[28]

Such the inscription that was posted on the pantry door. Another was put up on the windows and house doors:

> *Jesus, Mary, Joseph,*
> *Pray for us, do, who have recourse to you.*[29]

---

[26] *Embala, José, embala,*
que a Senhora logo vem:
foi lavar seu cueirinho
no riacho de Belem.

[27] *Senhora Sant' Ana,*
ninai minha filha;
vede que lindeza
e que maravilha.

Esta menina
não dorme na cama,
dorme no regaço
do Senhora Sant' Ana.

[28] *Em louvor de S. Bento*
que não venham as formigas
cá dentro.

[29] *Jesús, Maria, José,*
rogai por nós que recorremos a vós.

Whenever a thimble, a coin, or object of value was lost, it was St. Anthony who had to account for it. In Brazilian patriarchal society, even more than in Portugal, there never ceased to be this perfect intimacy with the saints. About the only thing the Infant Jesus did not do was to get down on all fours with the children of the household, smear himself with guava jelly, and play with the Negro lads. The Portuguese nuns in their ecstasies would often feel him seated on their laps and playing with their sewing or tasting the sweets that they were preparing.[30]

Beneath the saints and above the living in the patriarchal hierarchy were the dead, who in so far as possible ruled and kept watch over the lives of their children, grandchildren, and great-grandchildren. In many a Big House their portraits were preserved in the sanctuary among the images of the saints, with a right to the same votive lamp and the same flowers. Sometimes also women's braids and the curls of infants were kept. It was, in short, a cult of the dead that puts one in mind of that of the ancient Greeks and Romans.

But the patriarchal Big House was not only a fortress, chapel, school, workshop, house of charity, harem, convent of young women, and hospital; it fulfilled another important function in Brazilian economy: it was also a bank. Within its thick walls, in the ground beneath the bricks or tiles, money was buried and jewels, gold, and other valuable objects were stored. The jewels were sometimes kept in the chapel, being used to adorn the saints; whence all the images of Our Lady, laden down in the Bahian manner with trinkets of all sorts, with *balangandans*,[31] hearts, little horses, little dogs, gold chains, and the like. Thieves in those days were God-fearing and rarely ventured to enter the chapel and rob the sacred images. True, a certain thief did steal the halo and other jewels of

---

[30] The infant Jesus used to come to aid Sister Mariana de Beija in "winding her wool and thread" as she sewed, and the same thing happened to the Venerable Mother Rosa Maria de Sto. St. Anthony would put in an appearance to play with the spinning-wheel, etc.—Gustavo de Matos Sequeira: *Relação de Varios Casos Notaveis e Curiosos Sucedidos em Tempo na Cidade de Lisboa*, etc. (*Account of Various Notable and Curious Happenings in the City of Lisbon*, etc.) (Coimbra, 1925).

[31] Donald Pierson (*Negroes in Bra-*

zil, p. 246) says: "The balangandan . . . consisted of a gold or silver frame on which were hung gold or silver images of animals, birds, fowls, fish, flowers, parts of the human body, houses, household utensils, amulets (including gold or silver balls inclosing soil from a cemetery), bells, medallions with religious significance, angels, suns, moons, etc. It was worn on festive occasions, tied at the waist. . . . A limited number may still be seen among the heirlooms of wealthy Bahians." (Translator.)

São Benedito, but his excuse, one that carried weight in those days, was that "a Negro ought not to be adorned so luxuriously"; and indeed, in colonial times, the use of "ornaments of a certain price" came to be forbidden to blacks.[32]

For safety's sake and as a precaution against pirates, against demagogic excesses, and against the communistic tendencies of the natives and the Africans, the proprietors of the big landed estates in their excessive zeal for private property would bury beneath their houses jewels and gold just as they did their beloved dead. These two motives were always uncannily mingled in the folklore of the Big Houses: with empty rocking-chairs rocking away on loosened tiles and leaving no trace on the morrow; with dishes clattering in the cupboard at night; and with the souls of departed lords of the manor appearing to relatives and even to strangers, begging Our Father's and Hail Mary's as they moaned and groaned and pointed out the places where barrels of money were to be found. This at times was the money of others, of which the owners of the house had illegally possessed themselves, money that friends, widows, and sometimes slaves had entrusted to them for safekeeping. Many of these poor folk were shorn of all they had and ended in utter poverty, owing to the sharp dealing or sudden death of the one with whom they had deposited their treasure. There were certain unscrupulous gentry who, accepting valuable objects in this manner, later pretended to be strangers who knew nothing whatever about the transaction: "Are you crazy? You mean to say you gave me something to keep for you?"[33] Often money that had been buried disappeared mysteriously. Joaquim Nabuco, who had been reared by his godmother in the Big House of Massangana, died without ever knowing what became of the store of gold which the good lady had scraped together for him and which was probably buried in some hole in the wall. When Nabuco was Brazilian Minister in London, an old priest told him of the treasure that Dono Ana Rosa had saved for him, but not a pound of it was ever discovered. In various instances, in Bahia, Olinda, and Pernambuco, in the course of the work of demolition or excavation, kegs of money have been found beneath the houses. This happened in the

---

[32] Letters royal of September 3, 1709, and proclamation of 1740, in Maranhão, cited by Agostinho Marques Perdigão Malheiro: *A Escravidão no Brasil, Ensaio jurídico-histórico-social* (*Slavery in Brazil, a Juridical-Historical-Social Essay*) (Rio de Janeiro, 1866).

[33] J. da Silva Campos: "Tradições baianas" ("Bahian Traditions"), *Revista do Instituto Geográphico e Histórico da Baia*, No. 56.

case of the Pires d'Avila, or Pires de Carvalho, manor in Bahia, where in a corner of the wall there was found "a veritable fortune in gold coins." In other cases all that has been dug up is the bones of slaves, executed by their masters and buried in the garden or inside the house without the authorities knowing anything about it. It is related that the Viscount of Suassuna on his estate at Pombal had caused to be buried in the garden more than one Negro, victim of his patriarchal justice. There is nothing surprising in this, for there were those who even had their own sons put to death. One of these patriarchs, Pedro Vieira, by that time a grandfather, upon discovering that his son was having relations with a favorite slave girl, had him slain by an older brother. "It was that God's will might be done that I had my son killed," he wrote to the father coadjutor of Canavieira after the terrible order had been carried out.[34]

The friars, also, fulfilled the function of bankers in colonial times. Much money was given to them to keep in their monasteries,[35] which were as strong and inaccessible as fortresses. Whence the legends, so common in Brazil, of convent cellars with money still buried there. It was chiefly the Big Houses, however, that served as banks in the colonial economy; and it was almost always the suffering souls of plantation-owners that would appear beseeching Our Fathers and Hail Mary's.

The Big House ghosts are in the habit of making their presence known by apparitions and noises that are practically the same throughout Brazil. A short while before the manor of Megaipe was stupidly demolished by dynamite, I had occasion to collect from the residents of the vicinity ghost stories connected with the old seventeenth-century dwelling. These tales had to do with the clatter of dishes heard in the dining-room; the sound of merry laughter and dance steps from the drawing-room; the rattling of swords; the swish and rustle of feminine silk; lights that were suddenly kindled and extinguished all over the house; moans and the clank of dragging chains; the weeping of a child; and apparitions of the grow-and-shrink variety. Similar ghosts, so I was informed in Rio de Janeiro and in São Paulo, inhabit the ruins of the Big Houses in the valley of

---

[34] Tristão de Alencar Araripe: *"Pater-familias no Brasil dos tempos coloniais"* ("The Paterfamilias in Colonial Brazil"), *Revista do Instituto Histórico e Geográphico Brasileiro*, Vol. LV.

[35] José Vieira Fazenda: *"Antigualhas e memorias do Rio de Janeira"* ("Antiquities and Reminiscences of Rio de Janeiro"), *Revista do Instituto Histórico e Geográphico Brasileiro*, tomo 95, Vol. CXLIX.

the Paraíba.[36] And in Recife I learned from one old inhabitant that every night at midnight there issues forth from the chapel of the Big House that formerly belonged to Bento José da Costa a very pretty young woman clad in white who customarily goes mounted on a donkey like Our Lady. This is possibly the daughter of old Bento, fleeing the patriarchal tyranny of a father who had forbidden her to marry Domingos José Martins. For these ghosts commonly embody all the joys, sorrows, and most characteristic actions of the life of the manor houses.

In contrast to the adventurous nomad life of the *bandeirantes*[37] —the majority of whom were mestizos, part white and part Indian— the Big House gentry represented, in the formation of Brazilian society, the most typical of Portuguese tendencies: namely, settledness, in the sense of a patriarchal stability. A stability based upon sugar (the plantation) and the Negro (the slave hut). Not that I am here suggesting an ethnic interpretation in place of the economic. I would merely set alongside the purely material or Marxist aspect of things or, better, tendencies the psychologic aspect. Or the psycho-physiologic. The studies of Cannon[38] on the one hand, and on the other those of Keith,[39] would seem to indicate that, independently of the economic pressure, societies like individuals are acted upon by psycho-physiologic forces presumably susceptible to control for the benefit of future scientifically formed élites—the forces of pain, fear,

---

[36] Also in Minas. On the abandoned estate of Samangolê, in the municipality of Paracatú, there was until recently a ghostly ball that was held on St. John's Night, attended by people from all over the countryside, who came in carriages and litters, escorted by pages, etc. The orchestras played the whole night long; but at dawn there would be no trace of it all. Of late these apparitions have ceased.

[37] The *bandeirantes* were members of the *bandeiras* or armed bands of the São Paulo region that in the eighteenth century, like our own "forty-niners" the century following, went in search of the gold, silver, diamonds, emeralds, and other hidden wealth of the interior, which had become the subject of legend and fable. (They also sought the Indian to sell as a slave.) The *bandeirantes* were bold, adventurous spirits and by their energy and intrepidity did much to open up the pathways to the backlands, thereby contributing to the expanding national consciousness and pride. For a colorful work on this subject, the reader of Portuguese may be referred to the volume by the artist Belmonte: *No Tempo dos Bandeirantes* (São Paulo, 1939). For comparatively recent and learned studies, see *Vida e Morte do Bandeirante*, by Professor Alcantara Machado (São Paulo, 1930); and *História Geral das Bandeiras Paulistas*, by Professor Affonso d'E. Taunay. (Translator.)

[38] Walter B. Cannon: *Bodily Changes in Pain, Hunger, Fear and Rage* (New York and London, 1929).

[39] Arthur Keith: "On Certain Factors Concerned in the Evolution of Human Races," *Journal of the Royal Anthropological Institute*, London, Vol. XLVI.

anger, alongside the emotions of hunger, thirst, and sex—forces that are possessed of a great intensity of repercussion. Thus Islamism, in its imperialist fury and in its formidable achievements, in its mystic exaltation of the sensual pleasures, would be the expression not simply of economic motives, but of psychological forces that have developed in a special manner among the populations of North Africa. And the same may be said of the activity of the *bandeiras*, with the generalized emotions of fear and anger asserted through reactions marked by a high degree of combativeness. The purer type of Portuguese, who came to settle as lord of the plantation, being dependent upon the Negro rather than upon the Indian, represents, it may be, in his tendency toward stability a psychologic specialization in contrast to the tendency manifested by the Indian and the mestizo (mixture of Indian with Portuguese) toward mobility. This is not to overlook the fact that in Pernambuco and in the Reconcavo the soil is exceptionally favorable to the intensive cultivation of sugar as well as to an agrarian, patriarchal, and stable existence.

The truth of the matter is that around the plantation-owners was created the most stable type of civilization to be found in Hispanic America, a type that is illustrated by the squat, horizontal architecture of the Big Houses: enormous kitchens; vast dining-rooms; numerous rooms for the sons and guests; a chapel; annexes for the accommodation of married sons; small chambers in the center for the all but monastic seclusion of unmarried daughters; a gynæceum; an entry-way; a slave hut. The style of these Big Houses—style in the Spenglerian sense—might be a borrowed one, but its architecture was honest and authentic. Brazilian as a jungle plant. It had a soul. It was a sincere expression of the needs, interests, and the broad rhythm of a patriarchal life rendered possible by the income from sugar and the efficient labor of Negro slaves.

This honesty, this expansiveness without luxurious display, was sensed by various foreign travelers, from Dampier to Maria Graham, who visited colonial Brazil. Maria Graham was enchanted with the residences in the vicinity of Recife and with the plantation houses in the province of Rio de Janeiro. The only bad impression that she got was due to the excessive number of bird and parrot cages hung up everywhere. But these parrot cages merely served to confer upon family life a bit of what today would be called local color. As for the parrots themselves, they were so well trained, Mrs. Graham adds, that they rarely screamed at the same time.[40] So far as that goes, d'As-

---

[40] Maria Graham: *Journal of a Voyage to Brazil and Residence There during the Years 1821, 1822, 1823* (London, 1824), p. 127.

sier notes a still more significant instance: that of monkeys receiving the benediction from Negro lads, just as the lads received it from the aged blacks, who in turn were blessed by their white masters.[41] The hierarchy of the Big Houses was extended even to parrots and monkeys.

The Big House, although associated particularly with the sugar plantation and the patriarchal life of the northeast, is not to be looked upon as exclusively the result of sugar-raising, but rather as the effect of a slave-holding and latifundiary monoculture in general. In the south it was created by coffee, in the north by sugar; and it is as Brazilian in the one case as in the other. In traveling through the old coffee-plantation zone of the Rio Grande and São Paulo region, one sees the ruins of former mansions with the land round about bleeding still from the wounds of the ax and the processes of latifundiary labor, and one realizes that they are the expression of the same economic impulse that in Pernambuco created the Big Houses of Megaipe, of Anjos, of Noruega, of Monjope, of Gaipió, of Morenos, laying waste a considerable part of the region known as *"mata,"* or jungle forest. It is true that certain variations are to be noted, some of them due to a difference in climate, others to psychological contrasts, and to the fact that, in São Paulo at least, a latifundiary monoculture was a regime imposed at the end of the eighteenth century upon a system of small ownership.[42] In passing we should not overlook the fact that "while the inhabitants of the north sought out for their habitations

---

[41] Adolphe d'Assier: *Le Brésil con-temporain — Races — Mœurs — Institu-tions — Paysages* (Paris, 1867), p. 89.

[42] Alfredo Ellis, Jr., in *Raça de Gigantes* (*Race of Giants*), basing his statements upon the old *Inventories* and *Allotments* of colonial days, asserts that down to the end of the eighteenth century a small-property regime was the dominant one in São Paulo, the dwelling-houses being no more than stucco-walled structures, originally covered with sapé. "They ordinarily had three rooms with a garden and were very badly furnished. . . ." They were, however, very large, with enormous dining-rooms, and already had a "house for Negroes," or *senzala*. In the seventeenth-century house of Francisco Mariano da Cunha the same writer

found sixteen rooms of huge dimensions and a dining-room 13 meters by 5.4 [about 43 feet by 18]. Oliveira Vianna, in his *Populações Meridionais do Brasil* (*Southern Populations of Brazil*), stresses the contrast between the São Paulo plantations prior to the century (the nineteenth) in which coffee was introduced—"diminutive estates measured in cubits, the majority of them being a league in circumference"—and "the estates of Minas and the Rio Grande region, which are latifundia of 10,000 alquiers or more." But the real latifundia were those of Pernambuco and Bahia, of the type of the Garcia d'Avila plantation.

[The alquier (alqueire) is a land measure varying in extent from 24.2 to 48.4 square meters. (Translator.)]

elevated sites, on the mountain slopes, the Paulistas commonly preferred the lowlands, the depressions of the earth, as the place to erect their dwellings. . . ." [43] These latter houses were "always built on a steeply inclined slope as a protection against the south wind, in such a manner that on the lower side the house had a ground floor that gave it the appearance of a two-story edifice." The southern mansions have more of a closed-in, aloof air than do the houses of the north; but the "terrace from which the planter with his gaze could take in the entire organism of rural life" is the same as in the north, a terrace that is pleasing, hospitable, and patriarchal in character. Coming down the river from Santos to Rio in a small steamer that puts in at all the ports along the way, one has a glimpse at the water's edge—in Ubatuba, São Sebastião, Angra dos Reis—of town houses that recall the patriarchal dwellings of Rio Formoso. And at times, as in the north, one encounters churches with a porch in front—gently inviting and typically Brazilian.

The social history of the Big House is the intimate history of practically every Brazilian: the history of his domestic and conjugal life under a slave-holding and polygamous patriarchal regime; the history of his life as a child; the history of his Christianity, reduced to the form of a family religion and influenced by the superstitions of the slave hut. The study of the intimate history of a people has in it something of Proustian introspection—the Goncourts had a name for it: "*ce roman vrai*." The architect Lúcio Costa has given us his impression in the presence of the old mansions of Sabará, São João d'El-Rei, Ouro Preto, and Mariana, the old Big Houses of Minas: "How one meets oneself here. . . . And one remembers things one never knew but which were there inside one all the while; I do not know how to put it—it would take a Proust to explain it." [44]

It is in the Big Houses that, down to this day, the Brazilian character has found its best expression, the expression of our social continuity. In the study of their intimate history, all that political and military history has to offer in the way of striking events holds little meaning in comparison with a mode of life that is almost routine; but it is in that routine that the character of a people is most readily to be discerned. In studying the domestic life of our ancestors we feel that we are completing ourselves: it is another method of search-

---

[43] João Vampré: "*Fatos e festas na tradição*" ("Facts and Festivals as Handed Down by Tradition"), in the *Revista do Instituto Histórico de São Paulo*, Vol. XIII.

[44] Lúcio Costa: "*O Aleijadinho e a Arquitetura Tradicional*" ("Aleijadinho and Traditional Architecture"), *O Jornal*, Rio de Janeiro, special Minas Geraes edition.

ing for the *"temps perdu,"* another means of finding ourselves in others, in those who lived before us and whose life anticipates our own. The past awakens many strings and has a bearing on the life of each and every one of us; and the study of this past is more than mere research and a rummaging in the archives: it is an adventure in sensitivity.

This becomes clear when we succeed in penetrating the past's intimate secrets, in discovering its true tendencies in its homely, unaffected aspects and most sincere forms of expression. All of which is not an easy thing in a country like Brazil, where the confessional absorbs personal and family secrets and provides an outlet for that passion for self-revelation on the part of men, and especially of women, which the student of history meets with in Protestant countries in all the intimate diaries, confessions, letters, memoirs, autobiographies, and autobiographical novels that are at his disposal. I do not believe that in Brazil there has ever been a single diary written by a woman. Our grandmothers, so many of them illiterate even when they happened to be baronesses and viscountesses, were content to tell their secrets to their father confessor or to their favorite slave girl, and their propensities to gossip were almost wholly satisfied by conversations with their black-skinned maids on rainy afternoons or in the depressing heat of scorching noontides. In vain would one look for the gossip-filled diary of a mistress of the house of the sort to be encountered among the British and North Americans of colonial times.[45]

---

[45] There do exist *"livros de assentos,"* or memoranda books kept by plantation-owners. Thanks to the kindness of an aged relative of mine, Dona Maria (Iaiá) Cavalcanti de Albuquerque Mello, I was permitted to inspect the "book of special memoranda" that was begun in Olinda on March 1, 1843 by her father, Felix Cavalcanti de Albuquerque Mello (1821–1901), containing not only matters of interest to the family of Francisco Casado de Hollanda Cavalcanti de Albuquerque (1776–1832), former owner of the Jundiá plantation, which was sold in 1832, and to the families of his sons and sons-in-law, but items of general interest as well—a cholera epidemic, a riot

against the Portuguese, the hecatomb of Vitória, etc.

[Selections from the *"livro de assento"* in question have since been edited by Freyre under the title *Memórias de um Cavalcanti* (São Paulo, 1940). The anti-Portuguese riot, or *"mata-mata-marinheiro,"* referred to occurred on June 26–7, 1847, when Brazilians rose up against the Portuguese merchants and traders of the city of Recife, with much consequent bloodshed. The Brazilians or "liberals" objected to the fact that retail trade was being monopolized by the Portuguese. The term *mata-mata-marinheiro* comes from the cry used by the Brazilians in the course of the rioting, *marinheiro* (literally, a

On the other hand, the Inquisition kept its enormous and watchful eye trained upon the intimate life of the colonial era, upon the bedrooms and the beds (usually, it would appear, made of leather) that creaked beneath the weight of adulteries and forbidden intercourse; upon the small chambers and the rooms occupied by the saints; upon the relations of the white masters with their slaves. The confessions and denunciations resulting from the visitation of the Holy Office to Brazil [46] afford precious material for the study of Brazilian sexual and family life in the sixteenth and seventeenth centuries. They show us, among other things: the age at which young girls married—from twelve to fourteen; the principal pastime of the colonists—the game of backgammon; and the dramatic pomp of the religious processions —with men clad as Christ and other figures of the Passion and with the devout carrying sweetmeat boxes from which to feed the penitents. They enable us to behold the heresies of the new-Christians and the "Holiness" sects, their mingling of Christianity and witchcraft, their roguish festivals inside the churches, with merrymakers seated on the altars singing *trovas* [47] and playing the guitar; and along with all this, irregularities in the domestic and moral life of the Christian family: married men marrying a second time with mulatto women; others sinning against nature with effeminates of the country or from Guinea; still others committing with women the lewd act that in modern scientific language as well as in the classics is known as *felatio,* and which the denunciations describe in minute detail; foul-mouthed individuals swearing by the "Virgin's muff"; [48] mothers-in-law planning to poison their sons-in-law; new-Christians plac-

---

sailor) being roughly equivalent to *gringo*—"kill-kill-the-gringo."—"The hecatomb of Vitória" is an allusion to the heavy toll of life taken by the cholera epidemic in that city. (Translator.)]

[46] *Primeira Visitação do Santo Ofício as Partes do Brasil, pelo licenciado Heitor Furtado de Mendonça—Confissões da Baía—1591–92 (First Visitation of the Holy Office to the Regions of Brazil, by the Licentiate Heitor Furtado de Mendonça—Confessions of Bahia, etc.)* (São Paulo, 1922). *Primeira Visitação do Santo Ofício as Partes do Brasil, etc.—Denunciações da Baía—1591–1593 (First Visitation, etc.—Denunciations of

Bahia) (São Paulo, 1925). *Primeira Visitação do Santo Ofício as Partes do Brasil,* etc.—*Denunciações de Pernambuco (First Visitation, etc.—Denunciations of Pernambuco)* (São Paulo, 1929). These documents form a part of the Eduardo Prado series, published by Paulo Prado; the first two volumes bear introductions by Capistrano de Abreu; the third has an introduction by Rodolfo Garcia.

[47] The *trova* is a poetic form that stems from the love songs of the medieval troubadours of the Iberian Peninsula. (Translator.)

[48] "*Pelo 'pentelho da Virgem.'*" The pubic hair. (Translator.)

ing crucifixes beneath the bodies of women at the moment of copula-
tion or tossing them into urinals; lords of the manor having pregnant
slave girls burned alive in the plantation ovens, the unborn offspring
crackling in the heat of the flames.

There were also—this was in the eighteenth and nineteenth centuries—certain dandies, shabby versions of Mr. Pepys, who had the
habit of methodically collecting in notebooks bits of spicy gossip
and who were known as "gatherers of facts." Manuel Querino mentions them in connection with Bahia; Arrojado Lisboa, in a conversation that I had with him, told me of some of them having to do with
Minas; [49] and in Pernambuco, in the old rural region, I have met with
traces of them. Some of these "gatherers of facts" anticipated the
authors of the pasquinades by collecting shameful incidents that, at
the opportune moment, might serve to cast a blot upon respectable
names or escutcheons. As a rule they exploited cases where the possession of white and noble blood was assumed, by digging up some
remote female ancestor who had been a slave or a *"mina,"* some uncle
who had served a prison sentence, some grandfather who had fled
the Inquisition. The moral and sexual irregularities of ancestors were
all duly chronicled, including those of the ladies.

There are other documents that are of assistance to the student of
the intimate history of the Brazilian family: inventories, such as
those that the former President of Brazil, Washington Luis, caused
to be published in São Paulo; letters of allotment; wills; court cor-

---

[49] I had the good fortune to come
upon these notebooks in the course
of a recent journey to Minas. Some
were found in Caeté, others in Belo
Horizonte, in the hands of a private
individual who kindly permitted me
to read them. They represent the
patient and, everything would indicate, the scrupulous labors, not of a
mere talebearer, but of an old municipal archivist who died years ago: Luis
Pinto. Pinto spent his life rummaging
among the archives, the legal documents, marriage and birth records,
wills, etc., in the genealogical collections of some of the most important
Minas families. By means of these
data I had the pleasure of verifying
some of the generalizations that I had
ventured to set forth in the first edition of this work regarding the formation of the family in those regions
of Brazil where there was the greatest
scarcity of white women. Thus, Jacintha de Siqueira, "the celebrated
African woman who at the end of
the seventeenth or beginning of the
eighteenth century came with various
bandeirantes from Bahia," and "to
whom is due the credit for the discovery of gold in the Quatro Vintens
ravine and the founding of the settlement at Villa Nova do Principe in
1714," is seen to be identified with the
matriarchal trunk, so to speak, of a
whole group of illustrious families in
our country. "The fathers of all the
sons of Jacintha de Siqueira," adds
the genealogist, "were rich and important individuals, and many of them
were prominent in the government.
. . ." Among others there was a major-
general.

respondence and royal decrees such as those that exist in manuscript form in the Library of the State of Pernambuco or are scattered about in old registry offices and family archives; the pastoral letters and reports of the bishops, such as that most interesting one by Friar Luis de Santa Thereza which, written in Latin and copied out in a fine ecclesiastical hand, lies yellowing in the archives of the Cathedral of Olinda; the proceedings of the tertiary orders, confraternities, and religious houses as preserved in the archives of the Tertiary Order of St. Francis in Recife, where they are inaccessible and useless (they have reference to the eighteenth century); the *Interesting Documents for the History and Customs of São Paulo*,[50] of which Affonso de E. Taunay made so much use in his notable studies of colonial life in São Paulo; the *Acts* and the *General Registry of the Chamber of São Paulo*;[51] the registry-books of baptisms, deaths, and marriages of freedmen and slaves and those containing the roll of families and the proceedings in matrimonial cases such as are preserved in ecclesiastical archives; the genealogical studies of Pedro de Taques in São Paulo and of Borges da Fonseca in Pernambuco; the reports of hygiene committees; parliamentary documents; medical studies and theses, including doctoral theses submitted to the faculties of Rio de Janeiro and Bahia; the documents published by the National Archives,[52] by the National Library, by the Brazilian Historical Institute in its *Review*, and those published by the Institutes of São Paulo, Pernambuco, and Bahia. I myself not only had the good fortune to come upon various letters from the Paranhos family which had been kindly placed at my disposal by my friend Pedro Paranhos; I also had access to another important family collection, unfortunately greatly damaged by moths and humidity but containing documents dating from colonial times: that of the Noruega plantation, which for long years was the property of Commander Manoel Thomé de Jesus and which was handed down to his descendants. It is highly desirable that what is left of these old collections belonging to private individuals be

---

[50] *Documentos interessantes para a história e costumes de São Paulo.*

[51] *Atas* and *Registro Geral da Camara de São Paulo.*

[52] Among others, documents having to do with the land. In his preface to "*Synopsis das Sismarias Registradas nos Livros Existentes no Archivo da Thesouraria da Fazenda da Bahia*" ("Synopsis of the Acts of Allotment Registered in the Books Existent in the Exchequer of the Plantation of Bahia"), *Publicações do Arquivo Nacional*, XXVII, Alcides Bezerra stresses the interest these documents hold for the sociologist, the anthropo-sociologist, and the simple genealogist. They constitute, indeed, a "foundation stone for Brazilian territorial history," and any interpretation of our social development must be based upon an acquaintance with them.

brought together in libraries or museums, and that the ecclesiastical archives and those of the tertiary orders be conveniently catalogued. Various documents that are still in manuscript form in the archives and libraries ought to be published as soon as possible. I may perhaps be permitted to remark that it is regrettable that some of our historical reviews should devote page after page to the publication of patriotic addresses and literary gossip while so much material of strictly historical interest remains unknown or is difficult of access to students.

For a knowledge of the social history of Brazil no source is more dependable than the travel books written by foreigners—although it is necessary to exercise great discrimination betweeen superficial writers or those whose work, though suggestive or informative, is vitiated by preconceptions (the Thévets, Expillys, Dabadies) and the good and honest ones like Léry, Hans Staden, Koster, Saint-Hilaire, Rendu, Spix, Martius, Burton, Tollenare, Gardner, Mawe, Maria Graham, Kidder, and Fletcher.[53] I have drawn largely upon these writers,

---

[53] Most of the authors mentioned are famous in their field. Jean de Léry, French Huguenot and a shoemaker by trade, has been called "the Montaigne of travelers." He was the author of a *Histoire d'un voyage faict en la terre du Brésil* (new edition, with Introduction and Notes by Paul Gaffarel, Paris, 1770). A Portuguese translation of this work, *Viagem á terra do Brasil* (*Voyage to the Land of Brazil*), by the distinguished contemporary writer and scholar Sergio Milliet, was published at São Paulo in 1941. Hans Staden was the author of the first book published on Brazil, a famous work commonly known as the *True History* (*Wahrhaftige Historia*), first published at Marburg in 1557, and since translated into many languages. There is an English version: *Hans Staden: The True History of His Captivity, 1557, Translated and Edited by Malcolm Letts* (London, 1928; New York, 1929). For a Portuguese rendering, see *Hans Staden: Meu Captiveiro entre os Selvagens do Brasil*, edited by Monteiro Lobato (Rio de Janeiro, 1925). Henry Koster was the author of *Travels in Brazil* (London, 1816). Auguste de Saint-Hilaire wrote *Voyages dans l'intérieur du Brésil* (1852). A. Rendu's *Études sur le Brésil* was published at Paris in 1848. J. B. von Spix and C. F. P. von Martius were the authors of *Reise in Brasilien* (Munich, 1823–31); an English translation, *Travels in Brazil, 1817–1820*, was published at London in 1924. Richard F. Burton's *Explorations of the Highlands of the Brazil* appeared at London in 1869. L. F. Tollenare was a French traveler who left manuscript notes on his residence in Brazil that have been published in Portuguese under the title: "*Notas Dominicais Tomadas durante uma Residência no Brasil, 1816–1818*" ("Dominical Notes Made during a Residence in Brazil," etc.); these notes appeared in part in the *Revista do Instituto Arqueológico e Geográphico Pernambucano*, No. 61 (1905), the portion referring to Pernambuco being translated by Alfredo de Carvalho. George Gardner: *Travels in the Interior of Brazil, Principally through the Northern Provinces* (London, 1846). John Mawe: *Travels in the Interior of Brazil* (Philadelphia, 1816). Maria Graham's work has been referred to; see note 40 above. The North Americans, Daniel P. Kidder and J. C. Fletcher, are the authors of

putting to use here a familiarity, dating from my student days, with this species of—I shall not say literature, for most of these books [54] are very badly written, even though they display at times a delightful and almost childlike candor. I had occasion to explore this field in connection with the research work for my master's thesis, *Social Life in Brazil in the Middle of the 19th Century*, submitted in 1923 to the Faculty of Political and Social Sciences of Columbia University. This study Henry L. Mencken did me the honor to read, and it was he who advised me to expand it into a book. The book in question, which is the present one, is accordingly indebted for this word of encouragement to the most antiacademic of critics.

To come back to the question of sources, mention must be made of the valuable data to be encountered in the letters of the Jesuits. Already a large amount of this material has been published; but a note from João Lúcio de Azevedo, an authority on the subject, reminds me that there must still be in the archives of the order a great deal that has not been printed. The Jesuits were not only great letter-writers, many of their letters touching on the intimate details of the social life of the colonists; they also sought to develop in their pupils, the *caboclos* and *mamelucos*,[55] a taste for the epistolary art. Writing from Bahia in 1552, the Jesuit Francisco Pires, in speaking of the pilgrimages made by his young wards to the backlands, has this to say: ". . . I shall not undertake a description, for the reason that the Father has directed them to write to the young of Lisbon, and it may be that you will have seen their letters. . . ." It would be interesting to come upon these communications and see what the Brazilian

---

a well-known work: *Brazil and the Brazilians* (Boston, 1879). See also D. P. Kidder's *Sketches of Residence and Travel in Brazil* (Philadelphia, 1845). On Thevet, see Chapter ii, note 115, p. 103. (Translator.)

[54] I have also at times, in transcribing passages from well-known travel accounts, made use of existing Portuguese translations, but have been careful always to check them with the original, correcting them in certain instances where I disagree with the translators. The texts of the oldest travel books—those of the fifteenth, sixteenth, seventeenth, and eighteenth centuries and the early part of the nineteenth century—have been transcribed, where they are kept in the original, with all their archaisms. The same is true of the texts of the ancient Portuguese and Brazilian chronicles, treatises, and documents. Those works, looked upon as principal sources, have been indicated in this book where quotations from them appear.

[55] A mameluco is the offspring of white and Indian. It is sometimes employed as a generic term, embracing all varieties of mestizo, including the offspring of Negro and white, of Negro and Indian, etc. (Translator.)

caboclos of the sixteenth century had to say to Lisbon. The letters of the Jesuits frequently contain valuable bits of information concerning social life in the first century of colonization and the contact of European culture with that of the native and the African. Thus, Father Antônio Pires, in a letter written in 1552, describes for us a procession of Guinea Negroes in Pernambuco who had already been organized into a confraternity. They were all very orderly as they marched "one after another with their hands constantly upraised, as they all repeated: *Ora pro nobis*." The same Father Antônio Pires, in a letter from Pernambuco dated August 2, 1551, alludes to the settlers on the land of Duarte Coelho as "the best folk to be found in all the *capitânias*." [56] Another letter informs us that the Indians at first "were embarrassed in pronouncing *Santa Jooçaba*, which in our language means: 'by the Sign of the Holy Cross'; for this impressed them as being a kind of foolish dumb show." [57] As for Anchieta, [58] he mentions the many poisonous insects that made life miserable for these first settlers, with jararacas [59] crawling through the houses and dropping from the roofs upon the beds. "And when people awake they find them coiled around their necks or their legs, and when they go to put on their shoes in the morning they discover them there." Both Anchieta and Nobrega [60] lay stress upon the sexual irregularities of the colonists, their relations with the Indians and the Negroes; and they mention the fact that the foodstuffs derived from the land were of poor quality, costing all of "three times what they do in Portugal." In connection with the natives, Anchieta had occasion to repeat the lament of Camões with respect to the Portuguese, speaking of their "lack of wit"—that is to say, of intelligence—a condition rendered worse by the fact that they would not apply themselves to study but were always ready for festivals, singing, and merrymaking. He also emphasizes the abundance of sweets and dainty

---

[56] "The country was divided, rather empirically, into several provinces called *capitânias*, which were donated as fiefs to bankrupt Portuguese fidalgos who were to rule them as their captains." Erico Verissimo: *Brazilian Literature: An Outline* (New York: The Macmillan Company; 1945), p. 6. (Translator.)

[57] *Cartas Jesuíticas (1550–1568)* (*Jesuit Letters*) (Rio de Janeiro, 1887), p. 41.

[58] The Jesuit missionary José de An-chieta (1530–97) is one of the first outstanding names in the literature of Brazil. (Translator.)

[59] The jararaca is a poisonous snake of Brazil (the *Bothrops jararaca*), brownish in color with red and black spots. (Translator.)

[60] Manoel de Nobrega is another important name in the early literature; his *Cartas do Brasil* (*Letters from Brazil*), 1549–60, were published at Rio de Janeiro in 1886. (Translator.)

repasts, orangeade, preserved squash, preserved marmelo, etc., all made with sugar.[61] These are realistic and honest details such as are to be gathered in large number from the letters written by the padres, amid other data that is of purely religious or devotional interest. They are details that have a light to throw on those aspects of colonial life that are generally neglected by other chroniclers. Nor have we any cause to complain of laymen, who, in chronicles like those of Pero Magalhães de Gandavo and Gabriel Soares de Souza, also have afforded us significant and lively glimpses of the intimate life of the early colonists. Gabriel Soares even goes into details regarding the revenues of the plantation-owners, the material of which their houses and chapels were built, the food they ate, the confections and sweet-meats of the Big House kitchen, and the clothing that the ladies wore. A bit more of this sort of thing and he would have been a gossip like Pepys.

There are other sources that will afford information or, simply, offer suggestions to the student of the intimate life and sexual morality of Brazilians in the days of slavery: the rural folklore in those regions where slave labor has left its deepest imprint; manuscript notebooks containing popular songs and cake recipes;[62] newspaper files; books of etiquette; and, finally, the Brazilian novel, which in the pages of some of our best writers affords many interesting details having to do with the life and customs of the old patriarchal family. One may mention: Machado de Assis in *Helena*, the *Posthumous Memoirs of Braz Cubas*,[63] *Iaiá Garcia*, *Dom Casmurro*, and other of his novels and volumes of short stories; Joaquim Manuel de Macedo in *Cruel Victims*,[64] *The Brunette*,[65] *The Blond Lad*,[66] and *Women of the Mantilla*,[67] all of these being romances that are filled with

---

[61] Joseph de Anchieta: *Informações e Fragmentos Históricos* (*Historical Data and Fragments*) (Rio de Janeiro, 1886), p. 37.

[62] I possess one of these notebooks that belonged to Gerôncio Dias de Arruda Falcão, for some time master of the Noruega plantation and a great gourmet. Seated in his rocking-chair, old Gerôncio would sometimes supervise the preparation of the finest of ragouts or desserts. I also have a song book that was formerly the property of my great-uncle Cicero Brasileiro de Mello.

[63] *Memórias Póstumas de Braz Cubas.*

[64] *Vítimas Algozes.*

[65] *A Moreninha.*

[66] *O Moço Louro. A Moreninha* and *O Moço Louro* have delighted generations of Brazilians and have gone through numerous reprints. A new edition of *A Moreninha* was published at Rio de Janeiro in 1943. It is the custom of hyper-æsthetes to drop a sneer at Manuel de Macedo, but he was in many ways a true writer of the people. (Translator.)

[67] *As Mulheres de Mantilha.*

"*sinhazinhas*," "*iaiás*," and "*mucamas*";[68] José de Alencar in *Mother*,[69] *Lucíola, Senhora, Familiar Demon*,[70] *Ipê Trunk*,[71] *Golden Dreams*,[72] and *Gazelle's Hoof*;[73] Francisco Pinheiro Guimarães in the *Story of a Rich Girl*[74] and *Punishment*;[75] Manuel de Almeida in the *Memoirs of a Militia Sergeant*;[76] Raul Pompéia in *The Athenæum*;[77] and Júlio Ribeiro in *Flesh*.[78] In addition there are Franklin Tavora, Agrário de Menezes, Martins Penna, Américo Werneck, and França Júnior, novelists, folklorists, or writers for the theater who with a greater or less degree of realism have set down characteristic aspects of the Brazilian's domestic and sexual life,[79] having to do with the relations between master and slave, the work on the plantations, the festivals and processions, etc. The same thing was done in his own way—that is to say, through caricature—by the seventeenth-century satiric poet Gregório de Matos. In the field of memoirs and reminiscences the Viscount Taunay, Vieira Fazenda, and the two Mello Moraes have provided us with valuable data.[80] There are in existence novels by foreigners undertaking to portray Brazilian life in the days of slav-

[68] Terms expressive of the familiar and affectionate relations between master (or mistress) and slave. Compare our Southern "honey," "mammy," etc. *Sinhazinha*—diminutive of *sinha*, which the slaves used for *senhora*—was employed in addressing the daughter of the house. *Iaiá* (*yaya*) was the form of address for girls and young ladies generally. *Mucama* (*mucamba*) was the term for a favorite slave girl who served as housemaid, personal attendant, and sometimes as wet-nurse. (Translator.)

[69] *Mãe*.

[70] *Demônio Familiar*.

[71] *Tronco de Ipê*.

[72] *Sonhos de Ouro*.

[73] *Pata de Gazela*. José de Alencar was Brazil's great romantic novelist. He has been compared to Sir Walter Scott and to James Fenimore Cooper. (Translator.)

[74] *História de uma Moça Rica*.

[75] *Punição*.

[76] *Memórias de um Sargento de Milícias*. Manuel de Almeida, who died prematurely, leaving this one masterpiece behind him, has been seen as a potential Brazilian Balzac cut off by death. (Translator.)

[77] *O Ateneu*.

[78] *A Carne*.

[79] A vivacious account of practically all the writers mentioned by Freyre in this passage will be found in Érico Verissimo's *Brazilian Literature: An Outline* (New York, 1945). See the preface that Freyre wrote for the volume by Olívio Montenegro: *O Romance Brasileiro: As Suas Origens e Tendências* (*The Brazilian Novel: Its Origins and Tendencies*) (Rio de Janeiro, 1938). (Translator.)

[80] Alfredo d'Escragnolle (Visconde de) Taunay is one of the best known and most mature of nineteenth-century Brazilian novelists. His novel *Inocência* is the most widely translated of Brazilian books. Among his collections of essays is *Céos e Terras do Brasil* (*Heavens and Earths of Brazil*) (Rio de Janeiro, 1882). Vieira Fazenda, Mello Moraes, and Mello Moraes *fils* were end-of-the-century publicists and memoir-writers. (Translator.)

ery,[81] but none of them is of any great worth from the point of view of social history. As to the iconography of slavery and patriarchal life, that has been masterfully executed by artists of the order of Franz Post, Zacharias Wagner, Debret, Rugendas, not to speak of lesser and even untutored ones—draughtsmen, lithographers, engravers, watercolorists, and painters of ex-votos—who from the sixteenth century on (many of them being illustrators of travel books) have reproduced and preserved for us, with emotional power or realistic exactness, intimate household scenes, the life of the street, and the work of the fields, the plantations and manor houses, and ladies, slaves, and mestizos of various types.[82] Out of the last fifty years of slavery there have come down to us, in addition to portraits in oil, daguerreotypes and photographs showing the aristocratic profiles of plantation-owners in their old-fashioned cravats; *sinhá-donas* and *sinhá-moças*[83] with little church-bonnets on their high-combed hair; young girls on the day of their first communion, all of them clad in white, with gloves, garland, veil, prayerbook, and rosary; and large patriarchal family groups, showing grandparents and grandchildren, young lads in the cassocks of seminary students, and small lasses smothered in the silks of full-grown ladies.

But I must not extend this preface any further, having already wandered sufficiently far afield from my original purpose, which was

---

[81] Among others, the novel by Adrien Delpech: *Roman Brésilien,* and Saint Martial's *Au Brésil;* there is also Mme Julie Delafage-Brehier's book, *Les Portugais d'Amérique* (*Souvenirs historiques de la Guerre du Brésil en 1635*) (Paris, 1847). Senhor Agrippino Grieco, in a critical article upon this present work, recalls the novel written by the Spaniard, Juan Valera: *Genio y Figura,* "where there are scenes that have much to tell us about Rio in the middle of the Second Empire."

[82] Among the albums may be mentioned: the *Album Brésilien* (aquatints) of Ludwig and Briggs on Rio de Janeiro and the *Memória de Pernambuco* (lithographs by F. H. Carls and drawings by L. Schlappriz). In addition, there are various collections of watercolors and engravings, among

which may be noticed: the Oliveira Lima collection of Brasiliana at present in the Catholic University of America, in Washington, D. C.; the collection of the old Baltar Museum, which, thanks to the happy initiative of its former director Estácio Coimbra, has been acquired by the Museum of the State of Pernambuco, under the direction of Annibal Fernandes; and the collections of the Historical Museum and the National Library in Rio de Janeiro. Also of historical interest are the ex-voto tablets scattered through the sacristies of old churches, plantation chapels, etc. Rotting away in the little church of Sitio da Capela, near Recife, are some very interesting ones.

[83] Terms applied to the ladies and young women of the Big House. (Translator.)

merely to give a general idea of the plan and method of the essay that follows and the conditions under which it was written. An essay in genetic sociology and social history, with the object of determining and at times interpreting some of the more significant aspects of the formation of the Brazilian family. Unfortunately, I was not able to realize my intention of condensing the entire work into a single volume. The material overflowed, exceeding the reasonable limits of a one-volume book. The study of certain aspects of the subject accordingly had to be reserved for Volume II., and, for that matter, these could be developed still more extensively.

The turn-of-the-century period in Brazil, for example, remains to be interpreted—the attitudes, tendencies, and prejudices of the first generation to follow the Law of Free Birth [84] and the debacle of 1888; a study should be made of the anti-monarchist reactions of the propertied class, its bureaucratic inclinations, the tendency of many of its members to embark upon liberal careers by becoming State functionaries and obtaining republican sinecures—sinecures that prolonged the life of ease of the sons of ruined gentlemen and did away with the degrading necessity of engaging in manual labor for the sons of slaves anxious to put as great a distance as possible between themselves and the slave hut; in short, the entire bureaucratic and non-productive regime that, in the agrarian Brazil of old, with the exception of those regions that benefited more intensively from European immigration, followed the abolition of slave labor—all this should be related to slavery and to the one-crop system, which still continue to influence the conduct, ideas, attitudes, and sexual morality of Brazilians. So far as that is concerned, a latifundiary monoculture even after the abolition of slavery found a means of subsisting in certain parts of the country, with more absorptive and sterilizing effect than under the old regime and with abuses that were still more feudal in character, through the creation of a proletariat under conditions of life less favorable than those of the mass of slaves. Roy Nash was astonished to find in the hands of a single individual in Brazil landholdings that exceeded the whole of Portugal in size, while he learned that in the Amazon region the Costa Ferreiras were the owners of an estate whose area was greater than that of England, Scotland, and Ireland combined.[85] In Pernambuco and Alagoas, along with the development of sugar factories, large-scale property has increased these last few

---

[84] *Lei de Ventre Livre,* passed in 1871, giving freedom to children born in slavery (although sometimes they remained slaves until the age of twenty-one). (Translator.)

[85] Roy Nash: *The Conquest of Brazil* (New York, 1926).

years, bringing with it in its wake, and as the result of monoculture, an irregularity and deficiency in the supply of foodstuffs such as meat, milk, eggs, and vegetables. In Pernambuco, in Alagoas, in Bahia, they continue to consume the same bad meat as in colonial days. Bad, and dear in price.[86] It may be said, then, that from the point of view of the general welfare and that of the working classes in particular, the worst features of the old economic order persist, and have persisted since 1888, when the patriarchal system was abolished that up to then had sheltered the slaves, fed them with a certain liberality, cared for them in sickness and old age, and provided their sons with an opportunity to rise in the social scale. The slave's place was taken by the pariah of the factory, the slave hut was replaced by the slums, and the plantation master by the factory-owner and absentee capitalist. Many Big Houses remained closed, with the big estate-owners roaming about in automobiles from city to city, living in Swiss chalets and Norman villas, and finding diversion in Paris with ladies of easy virtue.

I must express my thanks to all those who have aided me either in the work of research or in the preparation of the manuscript and reading of the proofs of this essay. In connection with the proofreading I am chiefly indebted to Manuel Bandeira. Another friend, Luis Jardim, has aided me in cleaning up the manuscript, which had left for Rio full of erasures and corrections. I wish to thank them

---

[86] According to official statistics— *Annuário Estatístico de Pernambuco* (*Statistical Yearbook of Pernambuco*) (Recife, 1929–30)—the zone that in Pernambuco is sacrificed to monoculture embraces an area of 1,200,000 hectares [2,965,200 acres], with only 138,000 [340,998 acres] under cultivation. In an address delivered before the Rotary Club of Recife, Senhor André Bezerra, representing the Land-Lease and Cattle Corporation of that city, stressed the fact that 88.5 per cent of the zone in question was completely uncultivated, while 20 per cent of the total, or 240,000 hectares [593,040 acres], had been "transformed into pasture land, seeded with selected grasses and conveniently divided into enclosures, with adequate water supply, sanitary baths, etc., to maintain a herd of 240,-000 head, which, on the basis of 10 per cent being utilizable for the purpose, would furnish 24,000 head for the slaughter pens. . . ." (*Diário de Pernambuco*, April 2, 1933.) This is a subject that I propose to treat in greater detail in a forthcoming work. In passing I would remark that it is hard to understand the obstacles that are raised in Pernambuco to the importation of frozen meat from Rio Grande do Sul and São Paulo, which would improve the quality of foodstuffs and bring down the price, while at the same time no better use is made, from the point of view of the general welfare, of those lands that are sacrificed to a latifundiary monoculture— unless it is that governments act the way they do under pressure from the so-called "silent interests."

both for their intelligent assistance, as well as those who so kindly helped me in translating from the Latin, the German, and the Dutch passages in old documents, and those who facilitated my library and folklore research: my father, Dr. Alfredo Freyre; my cousin José Antônio Gonsalves de Mello (Neto); my friends Júlio de Albuquerque Bello and Sérgio Buarque de Hollanda; Maria Bernarda, who gave me a quite satisfactory schooling in culinary traditions; the former slaves and old plantation servants Luiz Mulatinho, Maria Curinga, Jovina, Bernarda. Sérgio Buarque translated from the German for me practically the entire essay of Wätjen.[87] Júlio Bello on his Queimadas plantation brought together for me interesting folklore data concerning the relations of master and slave. Alone or in the company of Pedro Paranhos and Cicero Dias, I made excursions for folklore research, or for obtaining an acquaintance with the typical Big Houses, through various portions of the old aristocratic region of Pernambuco, and I must here thank all those who extended to me their hospitality on these occasions: Alfredo Machado on the Noruega plantation; André Dias de Arruda Falcão at Mupã; Gerôncio Dias de Arruda Falcão at Dois Leões; Júlio Bello at Queimadas; the Baronesa de Contendas at Contendas; Domingos de Albuquerque at Ipojuca; Edgar Domingues at Raiz—a true old people's home, where I encountered four survivors of the plantation *senzalas*, one of them a centenarian, the others octogenarians. The oldest of this group, Luiz Mulatinho, had a marvelous memory. In connection with other regions that I visited and which are now well known to me, I must recall the kindness of a number of persons: Joaquim Cavalcanti; Júlio Maranhão; Pedro Paranhos Ferreira, owner of Japaranduba, grandson of the Viscount and nephew of the Baron of Rio Branco; Estácio Coimbra; José Nunes da Cunha; the Lyra family in Alagoas; the Pessôa de Mello family in North Pernambuco; the relatives of my friend José Lins do Rego [88] in South Paraíba; my own relatives, the Sousa e Mellos, on the São Severino dos Ramos plantation, in Pau d'Alho—the first plantation that I ever knew, which always awakens personal memories when I revisit it. My thanks to Paulo Prado, who

---

[87] E. Hermann Wätjen: *"Das Judentum und die Anfänge der Modernen Kolonisation,"* in *Das holländische Kolonialreich in Brasilien* (Gotha, 1921). (Translator.)

[88] José Lins do Rego, one of Brazil's most distinguished novelists, is the author of the "Sugar-Cane Cycle" (*Ciclo da Cana de Assucar*), a novel-

sequence in which he describes, with a melancholy Thomas Hardy touch, the rapidly disappearing life of the old sugar plantations. Lins do Rego has also written one of the best essays on Gilberto Freyre, in his preface to Freyre's *Region and Tradition* (see note 5, above). (Translator.)

arranged such an interesting excursion for me through the old slave-holding region that extends from the state of Rio to São Paulo, offering me hospitality afterwards, he and Luiz Prado, at the coffee plantation of São Martinho. I wish to thank him also for his advice to return from São Paulo to Rio by sea, in a small steamer putting in at the old colonial ports, a bit of advice that Capistrano de Abreu used to give my friend. The author of the *Portrait of Brazil*,[89] the truth is, distrustful and fond of his ease, never put into practice the old *caboclo's* advice, possibly because he foresaw the horrors to which those innocent ones who entrusted themselves to boats of the *Iratí* make would be subjected in their laborious effort to become acquainted with this portion of our Brazilian physiognomy, which is such an expressive one.

I must extend my thanks, also, for the courteous treatment shown me in libraries, archives, and museums in the course of my researches: at the National Library of Lisbon; at the Portuguese Ethnological Museum, organized and directed by the scholarly Leite de Vasconcellos; at the Library of Congress in Washington, especially in the documents section; at the Catholic University of America, whose Oliveira Lima Collection is so rich in rare travel books on Portuguese America; at Stanford University, whose John Casper Branner Collection similarly specializes in books on Brazil by foreign scientists— scientists who, like Saint-Hilaire, Koster, Maria Graham, Spix, Martius, Gardner, Mawe, and Prince Maximilian, were often keen observers of the social and family life of Brazilians; in the documentary section of the Stanford Library, where I made use of the valuable collection of diplomatic reports and British parliamentary documents[90] on the life of slaves on Brazilian plantations; at the National Library of Rio de Janeiro, at present directed by my friend and teacher Rudolfo Garcia; at the library of the Brazilian Historical Institute, where I was always so graciously received by Max Fleiuss; at the Archæological Institute of Pernambuco; at the Nina Rodrigues Museum in Bahia; in the documentary section of the Library of the State of Pernambuco; at the Registry Office of Ipojuca, whose nineteenth-century inventories afford interesting documentation for the study of the old slave-holding economy and patriarchal family

[89] The *Retrato do Brasil* is a famous work by Paulo Prado. Capistrano de Abreu, the "old *caboclo*," fine scholar and historian of the turn-of-the-century era, was an authority on Indian dialects. (Translator.)

[90] *British and Foreign State Papers, 1825–1841* (London); and *Parliamentary Papers* (London), especially, Reports from Committees, Sugar and Coffee Planting, House of Commons, Session 1847–8.

life; and, finally, at the Cathedral of Olinda, whose archives contain the manuscripts of pastoral letters and bishops' reports touching on fashions, sexual morality, the relations of master and slave, etc.— manuscripts which the canon, Carmo Baratta, kindly placed at my disposal for purposes of study. I thank my good friends André and Gerôncio Dias de Arruda Falcão and Alfredo Machado for having thrown open to me their family archives at the Noruega plantation, with virgin documents dating from the time of Commander Manoel Thomé de Jesus, while others are of the epoch of the Baron of Jundiá —some of these are of lively interest for the study of the social life of plantation-owners and their relations with their slaves. To José Maria Carneiro de Albuquerque e Mello, director of the Library of the State of Pernambuco, my thanks for the excellent reproductions from Piso, Barleus, and Henderson, which at my request were prepared for use as illustrations, in this book. Thanks also to Cicero Dias and to the architect Carlos Pacheco Leão for plans of the Big House of Noruega. There is one other name that must be associated with this essay: that of my friend Rodrigo M. F. de Andrade. He it was who chiefly inspired me to write and publish it.

I am not unaware of those defects of construction in this essay which various critics have emphasized. Some of these I have undertaken to correct, but there remains throughout this book that lack of cohesion of subject-matter which a foreign critic, even though a most friendly one, has taken occasion to lament in connection with these pages, which have in them so little that is French in their technique and, it may be, little that is Latin in their manner of presentation, which is somewhat loose and informal. It should be remarked, however, that this essay pretends to be not so much a conventional literary work as a piece of research and an attempt at a fresh interpretation of a determined group of facts having to do with the formation of Brazilian society.

With regard to the method of interpreting my material, I have endeavored to be almost entirely objective, but at certain points an objective-introspective method has been employed, somewhat in the manner of certain Spanish studies in which there is to be seen an extension of the technique of introspective analysis to the task of recapturing the past and the life of a people—the concentration of the *Spiritual Exercises* applied to the more intimate facts of history until one is able to feel the life lived by our ancestors in all its, so to speak, sensual fullness of outline. It is also the Proustian method extended to social history after having been Romain Rolland's technique of making his characters lose their present-day identity in the successive "several times" of their forefathers. Jean-Christophe, as readers of Rolland will recall, sometimes felt that what was now was not now, but some other time. There seems to be no social history when the past is not re-captured in this way until it becomes as alive as the present and the present seems to be some other time of the re-captured past.

It is said of Michelet that he tried to re-capture the past of medieval France by re-peopling its great churches: through architecture. It seems that in the Brazilian past, as in some other pasts, the equivalent of great churches or castles or kings' palaces was the big patriarchal houses that were at the center of the community's life during its formative years. To re-capture that life, one has to attempt to re-people those houses. And no attempt of this sort can be valid without what some modern historians know as "imaginative sympathy." That is why one modern historian, following suggestions from Herder, has said that "we ourselves are Time, inasmuch as we live."

With this notion of Time the past ceases to be dead in contrast with the present as the only living reality. Historical periods are now considered by some students of man to be as valid for a genuine division of mankind as races and nations—rather than societies and cultures that sociologically do not seem ever to die entirely, but appear to combine in new forms.

As to the absence of didactic qualities in this book, stressed by one critic, I am fully aware of it; but the truth is that I have no pedagogic intention. Similarly, my purpose is not to *draw conclusions*, much less to *judge*. Taking as my point of departure new hypotheses, ideas, and even at times highly personal intuitions, I have limited myself to the effort to determine certain aspects of the patriarchal influence in the formation of the Brazilian family, though I do at times venture upon interpretations of this influence on present-day Brazil. To those thinkers who are wholly uninterested in historical and sociological research I leave the task, a loftier and more brilliant one, to be sure, of formulating conclusions independent of historical research. What will be found here is simply a group of facts that, by reason of their constant social significance and the novel manner in which they are presented and interpreted, may possibly give pause for thought in a direction contrary to the opinions advanced by those improvisers who are not always very exact in the conclusions they reach through a process of pure sociological divination. I have attempted a study of Brazilian patriarchal society and culture in which the social reality is

seen as a constant flow of the past and the present into the future—a
constant flow of time that never stops to allow for definitive sociological conclusions about rigid "historical periods."

Still other critics have noted that there are few references in this
work to the great names among the historians of my country—Handelmann, for example, Southey, Varnhagen, Capistrano, Oliveira
Lima, Rocha Pombo, João Ribeiro, Joaquim Nabuco, some of whom
have written memorable pages on the subjects treated here—slavery,
for instance.[91] This apparent lack of devotion to the masters on the
part of a beginner is partly to be explained by the fact that one of
my chief concerns has been a direct contact with my sources, so
often cited in these pages: the manuscripts to be found in family
archives and churches; the letters of the Jesuits; wills; allotments;
diaries; travel books written by foreigners; royal decrees and regulations; the correspondence of colonial governors with the court; newspapers; pastoral letters; doctoral theses; physicians' reports; acts in
chamber; etc. It is upon such material as this and upon researches
made in the field that this essay is in reality based, and not upon the
books of recognized historians and their use and interpretation of
those sources.

It would be impossible to reply here to those who have criticized
the language of this essay—a language that represents a reaction, possibly exaggerated, to the pedantries of scientific erudition, technical
terminology, grammatical correctness, and style. By a critic more
orthodox in his notions of propriety I have been accused of being
"anecdotical," while my language is "lacking in dignity" for "so
serious a work"—it is even "vulgar" and "anything but technical."

With respect to the last point, I would merely remind my readers

---

[91] H. Handelmann is the author of
a history of Brazil, translated from
the German and published in Portuguese (*História do Brasil*) at Rio de
Janeiro in 1931. Robert Southey's
History of Brazil (London, 1810–19)
is well known. The nineteenth-century historian Adolpho de Varnhagen
wrote an *História Geral do Brasil*
(*General History of Brazil*), an *História das luctas contra os hollandezes*
(*History of the Struggles against the
Dutch*), an *História da Independencia*
(*History of Independence*), etc. Capistrano de Abreu's works include:
Brasil no seculo XVI (*Brazil in the*

Sixteenth Century); *O Descobrimento do Brasil* (*The Discovery of
Brazil*); and *Capitulos de história
colonial* (*Chapters of Colonial History*). Oliveira Lima's *Memórias*
(*Memoirs*) appeared at Rio de Janeiro
in 1937; there are many passages in
his earlier writings dealing with Brazilian history. He was a statesman,
diplomat, and historian. Rocha Pombo
is the author of an *História do Brasil*,
as is João Ribeiro. Joaquim Nabuco
is the author of several historical essays, one of them—*O Abolicionismo*
(London, 1883)—on the abolition
movement. (Translator.)

that in sociological, anthropological, and historical-social studies the criterion of the worth of facts is every day coming more and more to take its place alongside the criterion of pure materiality, tending to break the rigidity of the latter, to humanize it. In connection with such studies the time is past for imitating that difficult and inhuman idiom in which certain scientists, chiefly technicians, take a delight. This for the very reason that the situation in the social sciences is different from that in the other sciences. As MacIver says, in his great sociological work, *Community*,[92] there are no chemically good or evil results and combinations, just as there are no geologically good or evil types of rocks. For the student of the social sciences, on the other hand, things—even the most elementary of things—in their relations with societies undergo a prolongation into values and *are* good or bad, rich or poor, depending upon the human interests involved. To deprive sociology of this human aspect would be to deform it; and all this, to quote MacIver's works, "in a vain attempt to ape the so-called natural sciences."

The sociological, anthropological, and historical-social essay has a language of its own; it is not obliged to limit itself to an exact terminology as conceived by other sciences that are not concerned with human values. Its language may at times resemble the language of the novel or the literary essay.

I do not know how to answer, without the risk of appearing pedantic, all the misrepresentations of my points of view by literary critics and journalists, of the "Right" as of the "Left," who possess as yet little familiarity with the technique, method, and terminology of genetic sociology and social history, anthropology, and social psychology. This terminology has been employed only when strictly necessary. I have preferred to address myself to the intelligent reader rather than to the initiate. It is to be hoped, however, that with the progress of instruction in these branches in my country—the University of Brazil and the universities of São Paulo, Bahia, Recife, Porto Alegre, and Minas Gerais are hastening such progress—those critics who are none too familiar with the sociological meaning of such expressions as "culture," "complex" (sociological or anthropological), "social mobility," and "genetic sociology" will acquire a little scientific humility in their criticisms. In the case of some, one wishes this for the sake of their own intellectual and personal reputations; in the case of others, for the sake, also, of the ideologies that they so emphatically defend. There is no doubt that, with the

---

[92] R. C. MacIver: *Community, A Sociological Study* (New York, 1928).

progress of such instruction, the idea will soon disappear in Brazil that sociological or anthropological culture—as necessary for creative works as it is essential for critical studies—is something that can readily be improvised.

There have been, meanwhile, not a few intelligent criticisms, among them the painstaking and penetrating analysis by Professor Almir de Andrade—and also certain suggestions technically well considered, some of which were embodied in the second edition— criticisms and suggestions that the author of *Casa-Grande & Senzala* has received not only from foreign specialists, but also from scholars at home, and which are always to be expected in the case of a work as daring as this, accomplished in so short a time, a work that undertakes to reconstruct and interpret the most intimate aspects of our nation's past while endeavoring to probe the racial and, above all, the cultural antecedents of Brazilian society, so profoundly agrarian-patriarchal in its formation. The truth of the matter is: a degree of boldness, above all else, was required for the undertaking of so complex a task; and boldness at times may have a renovating and even creative effect, but at the cost of numerous imperfections and deficiencies such as are wholly avoided by only the most captious of historical and scientific miniaturists.

Certain criticisms, even among the most authoritative ones, the author has received as the differing and eminently to be respected opinions of specialists and masters, without for that reason feeling obliged to modify his own points of view. This may be said of the observations of Professor Coornaert of the Sorbonne and of Professor Martin of Stanford—in articles otherwise very friendly to the author—regarding what they considered an excessive preoccupation with the sexual elements in the interpretation of some of the most characteristic aspects of our social evolution. But these criticisms appeared before the publication in the English language of the now famous Kinsey Reports. Then there were the reservations of Professor Sylvio Rabello—one of the ablest of our specialists in the field of pedagogy and social psychology—with respect to the excessive importance attributed to the formative influence of environment upon the Brazilian living within a patriarchal slave-holding economy.

Some of the most substantial criticisms of *Casa-Grande & Senzala* came from an old-time conscientious investigator of the indigenous cultures of northern Brazil: Carlos Estevão de Oliveira, for some time director of the Goeldi Museum, who devoted to the second edition of this book a long, minute, and at the same time extremely sympathetic analysis from the point of view of his favorite studies.

According to this scholar, the masculine sex among Brazilian Indians—at least, among the tribes of his acquaintance—has not perceptibly diminished as a result of agricultural labor, which with them is woman's specialty. But it is possible that the tribes known and studied by Senhor Estevão de Oliveira over a period of twenty years had been directly or indirectly influenced by European colonization and by European patterns of the sexual division of labor. As to the interpretation that he suggests, of "sympathetic magic applied to the sowing of grain," it impresses me as one of the most lucid to have been advanced, there being, moreover, no discrepancy between it and those patterns of the sexual division of labor which, according to some of the best students of the subject, were followed by the natives of Brazil at the time the Portuguese arrived.

Worthy of consideration also is a suggestion from the same source that the "list of fruit trees cultivated [by the natives of Brazil, that is to say] and handed down to us" should include "the guava tree, the pupunha tree,[93] the genip tree,[94] the cacao, and the cashew." The areas dominated or influenced by these cultures should be determined as soon as possible in order that the sociologist or social historian may be able to make use of such data in interpreting and reconstructing those facts having to do with the formation of Brazilian society which have been most affected by the influence of American Indian culture on that of the foreign-comers, and particularly the influence exerted upon the culture of the Portuguese colonists who set up their patriarchal regime in Brazil as large-scale agriculturists. It is these latter who are the object of study in *Casa-Grande & Senzala;* for to this writer, in his work, about the only elements of interest in connection with the indigenous and Negro cultures were those absorbed by the type of agrarian-patriarchal colonization that is represented economically, in the first two centuries of Brazilian life, by the sugar plantation and socially by the Big House and the slave hut.

As to the other objections of Carlos Estevão de Oliveira—such as what he has to say with regard to the interpretation of the form of family organization among the aborigines of Brazil, the position of woman, that of bisexuals, the possible stimuli resulting from the seg-

---

[93] The *pupunheira*, a tall prickly palm of the genus *Guilielma* (*Guilielma speciosa Mart.*), also known as *pupunha verde-amarela* (greenish-yellow *pupunha*), the *pupunha* being the fruit of the *pupunheira*). (Translator.)

[94] The *jenipapeiro*, a tree of the *Rubiaceæ* family (*Gen. americana Lin.*). The tree is known in English as genip (or genip tree), its fruit as genipap. The fruit is "the size of an orange, oval, with greenish-white rind, dark purple-blue juice, and a somewhat acrid flavor."—*Standard Dictionary.* (Translator.)

regation of men for homosexual practices, the significance of urucú painting,[95] and the like—some of these have to do with controverted questions of cultural anthropology which still are in flux, while others involve the variations to be found between tribes, variations which, from the point of view of the influence of the more or less general traces of native culture upon the formation of an agrarian-patriarchal society in Brazil, render it difficult to separate the representative or typical from the exceptional case, the exceptional being often assimilated in place of the typical. To undertake to resolve these points would have meant a possibly endless discussion between critic and author, in which, it is obvious, the former would always have had the advantage of his direct, living knowledge of the present specialized forms of indigenous culture in northern Brazil. The late director of the Goeldi Museum, it seems to me, was under the obligation to treat this subject in an essay, one that would have been looked forward to with interest, not to say impatience, by those who knew him well and knew how assured and accurate a knowledge he possessed of Brazilian ethnography. Unfortunately, he died without having written such an essay.

Another critic raised another controversial question. This had to do with the extension of communism—that is to say, of communism sociologically considered—among American societies. There appears to be no doubt that there was a greater tendency in that direction than toward individualism, though a fondness for private property was not foreign to certain groups, and under forms that at times are surprising. This inclination, however, was never strong enough to lead them to adapt themselves readily or immediately to the European concept of private ownership.

A subject that is treated in *Casa-Grande & Senzala* and which Carlos Estevão de Oliveira courageously attacks in the course of his patient analysis is the "clash of European with native culture" and "the effects of the Jesuit catechism upon the Brazilian tribes." Carlos Estevão recognizes the considerable importance of this problem: "Had the study embraced only these two themes, the author would have given us a worth-while work, in view of the fact that, at least so far as I am aware, no one to this day has analyzed them so photographically." For the illustrious student of Brazil's native culture, or, better, cultures, "the conquistadores . . . and the Jesuits" were in

---

[95] The urucú or (in English) arnotto is a small tropical American dye-yielding tree of the *Bixaceæ* or Indian plum family (*Bixa orellana*). It produces the annatto of commerce. The Indians used it extensively for dyeing purposes and body decoration. (Translator.)

fact "the initiators of its decadence" (that is, the decadence of those cultures). This is a fact that I emphasized without meaning to assert thereby that the Amerindian societies should have been idyllically preserved from all Europeanization and, much less, all Christianization. The methods of Europeanization employed by the sugar-planters and the *bandeirantes* and the methods of Christianization used by the Jesuits were not always the most intelligent, the most Christian, or the most humane ones. This is true, at least, from the point of view of the better use that might have been made of the native peoples and their culture in the formation of Brazilian society. Brazil owes much to the Jesuits, some of whom are heroic figures who will always be associated with the difficult beginnings of civilization in the tropical region of the Americas, a fact that has been proclaimed by some of the major voices in our literature: by Joaquim Nabuco, by Eduardo Prado, by Oliveira Lima, by Capistrano himself, who was so hard to please in his enthusiasms. It is simply that we must have the courage not to be content with a unilateral and piously conventional interpretation of Brazil's past, for the voluptuous use of apologists for the missionary work of the Society of Jesus. It would be banal to repeat here that the life of any institution is full of ups and downs, while none has a past that is altogether glorious.[96]

It is precisely this aspect of the analysis that I made, or undertook to make, of the work of the Jesuits in Brazil, in one of the chapters of *Casa-Grande & Senzala*, which forms the subject of a paper by Father J. Alves Correia, a venerable Portuguese missionary who has made a special study of the activities and contemporary tendencies of various Catholic missions conducted by his countrymen. In his paper, Father Alves Correia agrees with the criticism made by the present writer of the "exaggerated academicism in the education of the native" by the Jesuits; and this leads the erudite historian Father Serafim Leite of the Society of Jesus, also a Portuguese, to take up the cudgels in an article published in the review *Broteria*. According to Father Leite, the author of *Casa-Grande & Senzala* is an enemy not only of the Society, but, as it appears, of the Church itself: an enemy "cloaked in *Casa-Grande & Senzala* and . . . unmasked in *Sobrados e Mucam-*

---

[96] Euclides da Cunha, in his famous work *Os Sertões* (published in English as *Rebellion in the Backlands*, University of Chicago Press, 1944), similarly wrestled with the problem of the Jesuits; and it may be of interest to compare Freyre's remarks on this subject in his essay *Atualidade* *de Euclides da Cunha* (*Contemporaneity of Euclides da Cunha*) (Rio de Janeiro, 1941). Freyre speaks of Da Cunha's ultimate "reconciliation" with the Jesuits—it would be better to say with Jesuit history in Brazil—through his admiration for the lyric figure of Anchieta. (Translator.)

bos." [97] In this the scholarly cleric, ordinarily so unperturbed, was being a bit extreme. It was Father Alves Correia who felt obliged to defend the author against the charge of sectarianism, of being prejudiced against the Catholic clergy in general and the Society of Jesus in particular. He wrote that "so far as sectarianism is concerned," it would take "a magnifying glass to discover it" in the descriptions contained in these two essays—descriptions that he has the kindness to describe as "taken from the life"—of the "methods employed by the Jesuits in their schools." "To tell the truth," he says, "we do not find that Gilberto Freyre is an enemy of the Society of Jesus. He could have been more of an enemy than he is; or he could [on the other hand] have been a fervent admirer [of the Society], blind to or worshipping its defects, which are those of an era rather than of the Jesuit pedagogues themselves." Meanwhile, Father Serafim's words aroused an echo in Brazil among the members of the Jesuit right wing of Catholicism, one of whom demanded for *Casa-Grande & Senzala* the extreme punishment of *auto-da-fe*, insisting that both the book and its author be burned. Nor did he mean burned in effigy or in oil portrait; he was employing the word in the most realistic sense, an attitude that has not met with the approval of the Jesuits of *Études* (Paris), so generous in their treatment of the French translation of this book.

A word as to the criticism made of this book, among extremely courteous references to its author, by the eminent scholar in the field of historical research in our country, Professor Affonso d'E. Taunay: to the effect that it is concerned almost exclusively with the northeast and neglects the social landscape of the south. But this essay, as it happens, is one that deals with genetic sociology rather than with history in the conventional sense—though it frequently has recourse to historical chronology and even to anecdotal history—and the author's task accordingly has been to make a study of the patriarchal system based upon a latifundiary and slave-holding monoculture in that part of the country where the system found its most characteristic and forceful expression. Only in the eighteenth century—which is studied sociologically, in some of its aspects, in *Sobrados e Mucambos*—does the patriarchal family regime attain some prominence in the Minas region, a prominence diminished by the greater power of the crown there and by the influence of the Minas cities, more autonomous than those in the north. As for Rio de Janeiro, it was, one might say, an exceptional blot—a northeastern blot—upon the south-

---

[97] Freyre's *Sobrados e Mucambos* (São Paulo, 1936) is the sequel to the present work. The title means "town houses and slums." It will shortly appear in English, French, Italian, and Spanish.

ern landscape; for in São Paulo and other portions of the south it is an exception to find large-scale property and monoculture developing to any extent.

To be sure, in nineteenth-century São Paulo the agrarian-patriarchal regime was to be revived in a new form, that of a slave-holding monoculture based not upon sugar, but upon coffee, which, along with the advantages offered by the climate, was to permit the development of immigration to that province from Italy and other European countries, thereby stimulating various tendencies to social transition in Brazilian life, including that trend toward a republic which was so marked among Paulistas of the second half of the nineteenth century. But these more recent aspects of the disorganization of the colonial patriarchal system in Brazil and of the organization in a certain more accentuatedly national direction of economic and family life in our country are precisely the subject of a study in the next and final essay of the series begun with *Casa-Grande & Senzala,* to be entitled *Ordem e Progresso.*[98]

A word, also, to the Portuguese journalist who felt a trifle offended by the comparison, in *Casa-Grande & Senzala,* of the figure of the Lusitanian colonist—whom the author greatly admired—with the Negro, the point being that the latter should rather have been included among the purely physical elements and resources that contributed to the agrarian organization of Brazil—such as horses, oxen, beasts of burden. The observation is an interesting one. It happens, however, that in sociology and cultural anthropology it is customary to separate man from the animals by the capacity peculiar to man (or, at any rate, enormously greater in man) of becoming a creator of culture. Upon the basis of this criterion—an erroneous one, if you will—it is necessary to include the Negro with the human element. The author does not feel that he is invested with the authority or possessed of the boldness requisite to undertaking to revolutionize the social sciences in so important a respect as this.

In collecting the data for this book I did not follow a rigorously geographical or historical criterion, though I was always faithful to the regional one based upon the area in which the historical-social formation of Brazilian society sociologically began, with its greatest vigor: the Northeast. Within this criterion—which is at once genetic and regional—I could not fail to give prominence, at times great prominence, to sugar and, as a consequence, to northeastern group-

---

[98] *Ordem e Progresso* (Order and Progress) is the national motto of Brazil. (Translator.)

ings in the development of the patriarchal (agrarian and slave-holding) family in our country. The influence of this technique of production and of the societies that developed on the basis of it—in Maranhão, Bahia, Pernambuco, and Rio de Janeiro—was so strong that for a long period sugar gave to Brazilian society, taken as a whole and seen simply for what it was, its most characteristic traits, by creating the conditions most favorable to economic and social stability and organized family life. It was the two economies, sugar and coffee, that conditioned the development of our agrarian-patriarchal system, at least in its essential features; and I believe that no serious study of the formation of Brazilian social life can be separated from that system, for it is under its influence or in opposition to it that the formation is to be perceived taking place. Such was the case with the *bandeirante* movement, with which, possibly, may be associated the formation, not alone of a society based upon the exploitation of gold—in Minas Gerais—but of pastoral groupings that to this day are antagonistic, in their interests, their style of living, and their culture, to those groups of purely agrarian origin whose interests were for so long a time economically and politically dominant in Brazil. Whence the Brazilian—and not merely the Pernambucan, Bahian, or northeastern—character of interpretations based upon material gathered in those centers where an agrarian and patriarchal society took shape. Gathered in those centers, to be sure, but without any geographic exclusiveness and indifference to the marginal areas or to those areas antagonistic to the sugar and coffee zones: the pastoral, the diversified farming, and mining regions. The trips that I made for purposes of study and observation through those areas of Brazil which are less agrarian in background than the northeast—being wholly pastoral or semi-industrialized, as are certain neo-Brazilian areas in the southern part of the country—have merely confirmed me in the ideas and interpretations outlined in this book. The subject is one that I propose to treat in greater detail in *Ordem e Progresso*.

This book continues to call forth contradictory criticisms. "He reaches no conclusions," some say, repeating the word of the great scholar João Ribeiro. "He draws too many conclusions," others say. Senhor Miguel Reale finds the work cold and, so to speak, lacking in soul; but a foreign critic, while making use (without indicating its source) of the historical-sociological material presented by me, terms the book "emotional" and "impassioned." Even if I were more optimistic than I am with regard to my own efforts, I still would be content with the fact that this book had aroused mental and sentimental reactions so diverse in kind. I am also pleased with the fact that documents recently published in Brazil furnish new evidence in favor of my suggestions. These documents confirm the sociological fact that the Big House complex, considered in its architectonic expression—so significant from the historical and social point of view—presents essentially the same aspect in the oldest agrarian regions of Brazil, whether northern or southern. Diversities of a topographical nature or those caused by regional climatic conditions do not alter it with respect to the essential human or social ecology involved. The complex has its peculiarities in the south and center of the country, and these call for special study; but everything goes to indicate that the sociological process operates in practically the same manner as in the north in those areas which are less intensely agrarian and latifundiary —the intensity having reference now to the time factor, now to the spatial one, and again to both.

Keeping my distance from a so-called ethnic determinism, I continue to incline toward a cultural and historical interpretation of the facts having to do with the social formation of a people as the one best corresponding to the complexity of the facts themselves. But a cultural interpretation completed by the psychological and, in some cases, by the functional one, without any rigidly exclusive tendency to substitute a cultural for a racial determinism.

Preceding recent books published in English, this book—written in Portuguese, and published in Rio de Janeiro as long ago as 1933—has been, since its appearance, a modest pioneer attempt to add to a social-historical approach to the study of the past-present of a half-European, half-primitive society and culture a multi-anthropological approach: sociological, cultural, functional, ecological, and psychological. So psychological that sometimes it is less the strictly psychological approach of academic psychologists than that of novelists who have found it necessary to add a psychological time to the conventional chronological one, in novels otherwise historical in their substance—as in Balzac's analysis of French bourgeois society—and ultra-historical or intra-historical only in form or dimension—as in some of Unamuno's interpretations, through a partly fictional literature, of Spanish life and character.

Perhaps it may be admitted, in a study like this one, where the chronologically historical approach had to be completed by the sociological-anthropological one, that a psychological time is sometimes to be made the predominant one for the more vivid presentation of relations among events and among human beings artificially separated by conventional historical time. For the sociological interpretation of the Brazilian social past it means little, almost nothing, that in

1822 Brazil ceased to be a colony in the purely political sense. Other political changes, so prominent in chronological history, are insignificant from the same point of view. Hence the greater importance given to a sort of psychological-sociological time.

For the Brazilian past here sought for has been almost exclusively the past that the French call *histoire intime* and the Spaniards sometimes describe as *intra-historia*. When the Goncourts wrote of an *histoire intime* that it was a *roman vrai* and would eventually become *la vraie histoire humaine*, they had a vision of a modern development in both history and literature.

GILBERTO FREYRE

Lisbon-Stratford-Berlin-Rio de Janeiro-Recife
1933–1955

TRANSLATOR'S ACKNOWLEDGMENTS

For invaluable assistance in connection with Brazilianisms I am indebted to Mr. Arthur Coelho of New York City. I must also express my obligation to Dr. Lewis Hanke, head of the Hispanic Foundation of the Library of Congress; to Dr. Robert C. Smith of Sweet Briar College, Virginia; to Dr. Paul Russell, Associate Botanist, the United States Department of Agriculture, Washington, D. C.; to Miss Sylvia Leão of the Pan American School, Richmond, Virginia; to Dr. Bernhard J. Stern of Columbia University; to Senhor Erico Verissimo, novelist and historian of Brazilian literature; to Dr. Aluísio Napoleão, Brazilian cultural attaché, Washington, D. C.; to Professor D. Vittorini of the Romance Languages Department of the University of Pennsylvania; to Mr. J. Gordon Leahy of New York City; to Mr. Albert Mordell of Philadelphia, and to my son, Mr. Hilary Whitehall Putnam. All of these individuals have been most kind in connection with the labor of research or in helping to clear up obscure points in the text.

S. P.

AUTHOR'S PREFACE TO THE
PAPERBACK EDITION

IT HAS not been long since that the primitiveness of the illiterate, of the man of little learning, of the uncivilized man, was given a new positive value in art, first by Gauguin, then by Picasso. This greater value can arise only out of the intuition and imagination of an artist in close touch with his immediate surroundings.

Modern "regionalisms" are conspicuous for their spontaneous vigor. In Brazil, European and Europeanizing commandos, fanning out from the big plantation houses, were met by matching creative spontaneities issuing from the slaves' quarters.

In connection with the regionalism emerging in Brazil during the nineteen-twenties, it might be mentioned that the much traveled Blaise Centrars was then in São Paulo, that exalted propaganda center for the Semana de Arte, where he was courted by its champions. But after careful examination of the movement, he, so to speak, transferred his interest and intellectual esteem from the absolute Brazilian modernists and their impatience for introducing European novelties into our land, to the regionalists of the Pernambuco capital, although these latter were traditionalists and, only in their own special way, modernists. As a result, Cendrars, impressed by the originality of the book *Casa-Grande e Senzala* [*The Masters and the Slaves*], especially in its Dionysiac aspects, singled it out as a new way of writing a human history, through emphases on everyday occurrences and regional peculiarities among common folk, among illiterates, among slaves, in their daily life, sex, cookery, and a Christian religion that was more Dionysiac than Apollonian.

Concerning the traditionalist regionalism that began to appear during the twenties, one should emphasize that it anticipated in the Occident the actual emergence, in various parts of the world, of regionalisms and traditionalisms, or of their resurgence. It signalized a Brazilian tendency toward psychosociocultural pioneering. It was also significant for an outpouring of Brazilian works that were something between scientific and literary; although innovative and even revolutionary under various of their cultural aspects, still they served to give a positive value, in their presentation of Brazil's development, to singularities of manner characteristic of relations between masters of the Big Houses and slaves from the *senzalas*. This relationship imparted to the Big Houses religious, culinary, and sexual spontaneities arising out of the slaves' quarters.

The recognition of mixed values arising from the slaves' quarters and assimilated by the Big Houses has resulted in the bringing to light of hidden values and the rejection of evaluations based on the application of imperialist European criteria, according to which the *casas-grandes* represented an absolute superiority over the senzalas. The conditioning of Brazil's sociocultural future upon its ecology, in large part tropical, may be said to have favored the senzalas. The mixture of races, accompanied by a fecund interpenetration of cultures—European, Amerindian, Afro-Negro—pointed up the advantages of the Big-House-and-slave-quarters complex. Although this situation was considered by French Le Bons and Argentine Ingenieroses as totally negative, their judgments were reduced to insignificance both by in-depth scientific sociological reexamination and by conclusions concurring with that reexamination, independently arrived at by competent foreign observers, men of the stature of the two French Bastides, Arbousse and Roger, and Jean Duvignaud, the German Konrad Guenther, the Italian Roberto Rossellini, the Englishmen Aldous Huxley, Asa Briggs, and Arnold Toynbee. In the end the Le Bons and Ingenieroses served only to confer prestige upon the miscegenetic action of the process represented by the interpenetration of opposites as found in Brazil.

The above conclusions were anticipated in books of applied social science, among them the pioneering *Casa-Grande e Senzala*, a work by a Brazilian author whose education in foreign universities had been completed by his telluric origin as a native of the tropics of his own country. His opinions also appeared in serious studies from a Brazilian perspective of social and anthropologically social concepts, such as his *Problemas Brasileiros de Antropologia* [*Brazilian Problems in Anthropology*] and *Sociologia, Introdução ao Estudo dos seus Princípios* [*Sociology: An Introduction to the Study of Its Principles*], but above all in that book of pioneering par excellence, *Casa-Grande e Senzala*.

When one says of the Portuguese member of the trans-European expansion that he showed himself to be more Christiano-centric than ethnocentric, there is no intention of investing him with virtues or praiseworthy religious attributes and thus recognize in him a departure from ethnocentrically imperialist tendencies, that is, tendencies among certain trans-Europeans to consider themselves ethnocentric and, as such, ethnically and culturally superior to non-Europeans.

Perhaps he felt that he was more likely to be recognized as a member of a prestigious group if he called himself Christian rather than Portuguese, because as a Portuguese he felt less secure than other Europeans of both his ethnic and cultural superiority. By giving himself the title "Christian" he would compensate for that insecurity. According to the chroniclers, it used to be said that such a Portuguese man spoke, not Portuguese, but Christian. He was, it seems, a European who perceived that his national language lacked recognition for cultural values present in other national languages of the trans-European expansions beginning in the sixteenth century, such as Spanish, French, and English. Thus, wrapping himself in the prestige of the title "Christian" by giving that designation to his style of speech, he would be defining himself as Christiano-centric rather than ethnocentric. This definition of expressing himself in Christian speech distinguished him and served to confer dignity upon a conduct that was more given to miscegenation than that of other Europeans in the trans-European expansion. It was as if the accident of speech accentuated his disparagement of his biocultural group and its identification with the practice of biological confraternization with colored people. His attitude was political, but it also had something about it at once ethically and mythically Christian.

It must be remembered that from remote times Portuguese kings and their bishops had begun to entrust to miscegenates of Amerindian or Afro-Negro blood important posts in the colonial administration and in the Catholic hierarchy. Such men received titles of nobility like the *Dom* bestowed upon the Amerindian Brazilian Felipe Camarão for his bravery during the expulsion of the Dutch from Brazil, and they held posts of honor, not only religious but also political, like the one conferred upon the not entirely Aryan Antônio Vieira in the seventeenth century.

The Big-House-and-slave-quarters complex represents a symbiosis, with the slave influencing the master within a patriarchal familial system, the Catholic church being annexed after a fashion to that complex. And the complex was an expression of private initiative, something that caused the Portuguese colonization of Brazil to more nearly resemble the English colonization of what was to become the United States of North America than the colonization of Spanish America conducted by the royal metropolitan power and by theocratic power.

The familial complex, of which the Big House in conjunction with the slaves' quarters was the expression, included, in its socioeconomic power, accretions to its basic role as residence of the patriarchal family—accretions in the form of a church, a bank, a school, and centers not only for spiritual assistance but also for social welfare, not only for slaves but also for small farmers and for dependents, the latter being a species of poor relations attached to the Big Houses as, so to speak, sociological members of the principal family. This system grew out of the most patriarchal institution imaginable, in a Brazil with a patriarchal society based on slavery. The institution was the *compadrio*, a shared paternity, an intimacy between godparents and natural parents. With the blessing of the Catholic church, the owners of a typical Big House were, by dint of noblesse oblige, godfather and godmother to the children of small farmers, to the children of dependents, and, above all, to the slaves' offspring, some of whom took the patriarch's family name. To be a *compadre* of these patriarchs, that is, to have them as godparents to one's child, was more than an honor; it meant the acquiring of rights to patriarchal protection. To be their godchild was to grow up with special rights to such protection.

For these reasons, not a few sons of slave mothers or fathers, or sons of dependents living in the Big Houses, received, when sufficiently intelligent, the same education as the young masters of the house. They too were taught by the family priest, were sent to study in schools of higher learning, and were favored in their advancement as professionals by government administrations attentive to requests by influential patriarchs. All this was an extension of the patriarchal family's power over the psychosociocultural whole.

Thus are explained the accounts of godsons of Afro-Negro origin, sons of slave mothers or fathers who, with patriarchal support for their superior intelligence, graduated with degrees from institutions of higher learning. Among these accounts we may single out the remarkable example of Teodoro Sampaio, who, though born of a slave mother, attained an eminent position and profound influence in the society and culture of nineteenth-century Brazil. Nor did he fail to achieve recognition for his superior intelligence; a civil engineer, he was a graduate of Rio de Janeiro's Polytechnic School—a difficult course—and filled important posts in both the professional and public life of Brazil. Hence it may be concluded that the Big-House-slave-quarters-chapel system or complex favored, in its own special way, the utilization of the supremely gifted sons of slaves for the improvement of Brazilian culture and the democratization of Brazilian society, and not only the sons of slaves but also the sons of tenants and small farmers.

It is interesting that the dramatist Eugene Ionesco, famous for his quick wit, noticed the sociologically Christiano-centric spirit present in not a few expressions of Brazilian social development. He got this idea from reading the book *Casa-Grande e Senzala* and discussing it with its author. One of Ionesco's observations was that almost the same thing that had already taken place in such countries of Europe as Rumania and Hungary had been repeated in Brazil. For the Latin Rumanian, though not for the Slavic Rumanian like himself, Christianization, he felt, must have restrained ethnocentric cultural excesses, which in the absence of a Christian culturally comprehensive Europeanness would have tended to be nationalistic.

In the Brazilian, Christianization gave rise to a super-European consciousness that was above political state nationalism and found its most effective instrument for symbiotic action in the reciprocity functioning within the Big-House-and-slave-quarters complex.

It may perhaps be said that not a few of the eyes today reading *The Masters and the Slaves* are mouths rather than eyes—mouths repeating the words read with the sensuous enjoyment of one who repeats them for the pleasure of tasting them, savoring them, almost masticating them at times without bothering to completely understand their exact scientific meaning.

The Masters and the Slaves is a book in which the author's scientific learning performs the role of servant to his intuition or his musically verbal art rather than to a display of merely scientific knowledge. The author has read Spencer, read Comte, studied Darwin and evolution. He was a pupil of Boas and Giddings at Columbia University, of Lucien Febvre in Paris. But he arrived at a point where, like one who plays music by ear, his scientific idiom was blended with the language of a metascience in large part intuitive and existential.

Some such thing may have occurred to a certain extent with Euclydes da Cunha. In *The Masters and the Slaves*, however, it was through a kind of musical equivalent that was more Wagnerian than classical, consisting of sounds at times discordant rather than quite harmonically correct. Its literary music may perhaps be said to be a distant relative, so to speak, of Stravinsky's, with a soupçon of Villa-Lobos.

For these reasons, the author has felt obliged to emphasize once again the standard by which he sought, some years ago, to develop his plan for reconstructing and interpreting the Brazilian patriarchal society or tutelary family. It was his intention to study, in its different types and styles of habitation, the reflections of diverse types and styles of life and culture as well as expressions and conditions of the living together as a family and the resultant interpenetration and synthesization of values. Although synthesization and interpenetration did take place under the patriarchal system or organization, it was at the cost of its purity and finally of its integrity.

Within this system there was close communication—not merely separation or differentiation—between the Big House and slave quarters, and only later between the mansions and the shanties of the cities. There was synthesis, not just antithesis; affective complement, not merely the antagonism of economic diversification. In no other way can one explain the growing importance among us of hybrid manifestations not only of culture but also of physical types. The original system scarcely appears above the ocean of crossbreeding that overwhelms it, and within which absolutely pure values of one origin or another—European or Amerindian, Lusitanian or African, civilized or primitive, seignorial or servile—survive only in the form of tiny islands every day more insignificant, ethnographic, ethnic, or aesthetic curiosities rather than sociological realities. They are floating fragments broken away from a disintegrating continent or archipelago rather than terra firma capable of resisting, even in a reduced form, the triumphant flood. Out of this sea is emerging a new superficies, a new configuration of culture, new forms of society characterized principally by human beings of different sex, origin, age, and profession, living together as a family that merits the qualifier "democratic." It is a society characterized by an inceptive generalization in type of man and in type of house. The type is not unique, however, for it retains certain individual characteristics of race and class, but it is much less differentiated than formerly by extremes of social position or situation in the social space.

In the Brazilian cities of today one rarely finds stately houses tenanted only by wealthy individuals or patriarchal families. Instead there are many collective habitations, as already mentioned: hotels, boardinghouses, hospitals and private sanatoriums, asylums, military headquarters, private schools, apartment buildings, and workmen's cooperative lodgings. There are a great many average single houses, neither very large nor extremely small for the physicosocial space they occupy: a middle term between the former town house replete with rooms of large and small dimension and the one- and two-room shacks that are still abundant in the cities and in the country—abundant and overflowing with occupants. The most noticeable change in the Brazilian landscape is the decrease in city mansions, big plantation houses, and ancestral estates occupied by individuals or by patriarchal families.

This alteration in architectonic volume and in the space occupied by it marks the final disintegration of the patriarchy in our society and in our society as reorganized on a new basis, although this new society is still impregnated with patriarchal survivals. This aspect of Brazilian social development is taken up in a subsequent essay, *Order and Progress*, dedicated mainly to the analysis of our transition from slave labor to free labor. That transition coincided with the abandonment of the monarchical form of government for the republican, on behalf of which Brazilians of São Paulo and other states, and principally the positivists of Maranhão, Rio de Janeiro, and Rio Grande do Sul, had begun to work actively as far back as 1870.

These republicans, some of them masters of casas-grandes, were Brazilians of a most progressive type, but the majority of them would have rejected a republic that was incapable of assuring the nation the order necessary for material development of the cities and for mechanization of industry and farming, forms of progress they ardently desired for Brazil. Hence, the positivist motto adopted by the republic, founded in 1889, would have answered the aspirations of these republicans of ours, even ones ideologically far removed from Comte's philosophy and its adherents. It is not without significance that, after the founding of the republic, various of its principal leaders—some of mixed race but with aristocratic blood, some of plebeian origin who had been made aristocratic by means of academic instruction or by reason of marriage with the young daughter from a Big House or with a town house girl—should have distinguished themselves as particularly energetic chieftains in defense of *Order*. *Order* was now middle class but still patriarchal and constituted the security of the Brazilian society of those days. One of these leaders, handsome and powerful, the very picture of a highborn Moor, confronted with unusual force a crowd in Rio de Janeiro which was the perfect picture of the *capoeira*, a mass expression of the free Negro's hatred and the poor, free mulatto's hatred for the rich white man, the native's hatred for the European, the shanty crowd's hatred for those who dwelt in fine city houses. That knife-wielding riffraff had distinguished themselves by their defense of the throne under the name "Black Guard" during the days when the monarchy found itself rejected and spurned by so many illustrious gentlemen of Big House and city mansion, of general headquarters and bishop's palace—gentlemen disappointed, some with the emperor's abolitionist excesses, others with his exaggerated patrician or royalist ways. It was then that the monarchy, in the person of Isabel, was acclaimed "savior" and found sympathy and even dedication among stalwart *cabras* of mingled African, Indian, and white blood, Negroes, and scapegrace young mulattoes from the city shanties. Many of these were runaway slaves or descendants of runaway slaves and, though despairing of their relations as "sons" with "fathers" on plantations or in other patriarchal establishments, they still felt the need of "fathers" or symbolic "mothers" or ideals that would protect them, if not actually in the manner of their neglectful or mean fathers, at least in a mystical or symbolic manner.

In this regard, it only remains to add the following footnote: Just as there has been an increase in medium-size one-story houses, habitations of a middle class into which many an old wealthy casa-grande family had been fragmented and there joined by many a mulatto and free Negro who had elevated himself through mechanical skills, in like manner the city mansion, after succeeding the big plantation house as the expression of the patriarchal system's domination of the Brazilian landscape, with the decline or weakening of that domination, experienced the degeneration of its former stately residences into collective habitations—slum tenements, brothels, boardinghouses, hotels, asylums, and the like—or their transformation, with complete loss of character, into government ministries, embassies, consulates, clubs, newspaper offices, private sanatoriums, Masonic lodges, theaters, stores, and so on.

Corresponding to the decline of the wealthy individual's political power with its seat in a Big House of the most aristocratic, most prestigious, or most markedly patriarchal character, was the increasing public political power lodged in judicial, police, military, or simply bureaucratic agencies of the monarchic government and, later, of the republican. Not infrequently these agencies were installed in former patriarchal residences as though in the ruins of forts captured from a powerful enemy; even in their conquered state these made-over ruins were conspicuous for the survival or the look of their former power. For example, the Catete Palace and the Itamarati Palace, in Rio de Janeiro, even today recall to the eyes of Brazilian and foreigner alike the patrician elegance of patriarchal Brazil; so opulent was it, especially in the Rio de Janeiro area, that the statesmen of the republic of 1889 found in the residences of former barons of the empire better palaces in which to install the principal organs of the republican government than in the very residences of the former emperors and princes. The patriarchal casa-grande in the two signal instances cited above impressed the conquering heroes of '89 by the solidity of its architectonic nobility. This nobility, adapted to the land and the milieu, threw into contrast the badly proportioned, uncouth architecture of edifices specially built by the republican governments to house state offices.

The same may be said of the edifices erected by the last governments of the monarchy; their dignity does not equal that of the private mansions built by barons still of the patriarchal class, a sign that the Brazilian patriarchal system succeeded in expressing itself in types of private residence which surpassed the architecture of officialdom in authenticity, in ecological qualities of adaptation to the milieu and domination of the landscape, and even in nobility of construction and style. Such buildings demonstrate that the patriarchal system in more than one aspect created values that were characteristically Brazilian as well as characteristically patriarchal, or "tutelary," as Professor Zimmermann would say. He rejected the expression "patriarchal" because it seemed to attribute absolute power to the individual patriarch, whereas that power resided with the family, involved as it was in tutelary functions, rather than with its head. Patriarchal or tutelary, it is certain that the Brazilian family with its centers of authority in big plantation houses and city mansions created among us an architecture representative or characteristic of its power.

It follows, then, that not all enthusiasts of the old-time architecture of patriarchal, or tutelary, residences are simple or perverse amateurs of the archaic, clinging with the fond love of the antiquarian to relics of a social system that expressed itself in those houses, which were at times ugly but by the same token sturdy, like the Portuguese mothers within. And there are qualities in those houses, as in the women, which often compensate for their lack of physical beauty with, for example, a hospitable gentleness, an honesty, or a dignity tempered by simplicity.

It is plain that, once the old system expired, its type of residence should not be capriciously or arbitrarily perpetuated in a society that was becoming collectivist on the one hand and, on the other, individualist in opposition to the private nature of the economic system or of the patriarchal organization, which was at once individualist and communist, given the absorption of the individual in the family and the subordination of the state to the nobleman. Nonetheless one must not fail to recognize in the Brazilian patriarchal casa-grande a source of valuable suggestions for the architect who wishes to create for Brazil collectivist architecture that will also be individualized and, at the same time, in conformity with the teaching of the Brazilian experience; it should not be inspired by political passion or aesthetic partisanship, which are regularly in conflict with that experience, nor should it be created in a vacuum.

In Brazil, what found its expression in types of residence, which harmonized with the land and the milieu, like the Big House or even the slave's shanty, was not only an economic system or a familial or cultural system; it was also the human being. It was the Brazilian, the man of various origins, who had to conquer the hostility of the tropics to those higher forms of Christian and Mussulman civilization brought from Portugal to the American colony, not only by Europeans but also, to a much lesser degree, by Africans. These higher forms of civilization, it is true, here turned soft or corrupt. But it is extraordinary how many of them got spread, though in a weakened and impure state, over a space physically so extensive and socially so arid as the Brazil of the early days of colonization.

From that dissemination of higher forms of civilization in so vast a tropical land resulted the first great modern civilization in the tropics: the Brazilian. And tremendous as was the work of the missionaries—Carmelite, Benedictine, Jesuit, Franciscan—and of agents of the Crown or the government, the truth is, the aforesaid dissemination seems to have been brought about principally by the Big Houses and their chapels, and only to a lesser extent by the regular convents or cathedrals, or by the palaces and other establishments belonging to the king and, after Brazil's independence, to His Majesty the Emperor.

Recife   Gilberto Freyre
1986

INTRODUCTION TO THE
PAPERBACK EDITION

A READER who opens *The Masters and the Slaves* for the first time in 1986 might well be puzzled by the book. This "essay" (as its author called it) on the development of Brazilian civilization is in fact an unashamedly digressive treatise on the elements that went to make up Brazilian colonial society and the Brazilian national character. Its nearly five hundred pages are divided into five chapters, dealing respectively with the Portuguese colonization of Brazil, with the Indians, the Portuguese, and the blacks (who get two chapters). Even so the book ends abruptly and idiosyncratically with a long list of diseases acquired by black slaves in colonial Brazilian households, giving the impression that the author is by no means talked out on his topic. The impression is quite correct. *The Masters and the Slaves* was the first major treatise to set out the central theme of Gilberto Freyre's lifework, namely to describe and account for the nature of Portuguese civilization in the tropics, particularly Brazil. He returns to this theme explicitly in his later books, *The Mansions and the Shanties* and *Order and Progress*, and it is implicit in much of his other work. Yet *The Masters and the Slaves*, for all its idiosyncrasies, is his best-known book and the one that established his reputation.

It was first published well over fifty years ago at a time when Gilberto Freyre had just returned to Brazil after completing his studies in the United States. There he had studied anthropology with Franz Boas, among other people, at Columbia University. Boas was then leading the fight against theories of racial causation in anthropology and marshaling the evidence necessary to combat racism not only in the academy but beyond it. Within anthropology it was still quite common to explain social and cultural phenomena by the racial characteristics of the populations among whom they were found. The proponents of such biosocial views defended them fiercely against the "unscientific" theories of Boas and his disciples, who insisted that cultural phenomena be explained in cultural terms. The struggle within anthropology was bitter, but for Boas it was anything but academic. He was acutely conscious of European anti-Semitism and of the intimate link between racism and the rising tide of fascism, so that in combating racial determinism he saw himself as using the science of anthropology for a noble purpose, in the service of a higher tolerance that was essential to liberal democracy.

Gilberto Freyre used his Boasian training to reanalyze his native Brazil and particularly to revise the explanations that were conventionally advanced to account for its backwardness. These pointed to miscegenation as the primary factor. According to the prevailing theories of the time it was believed that racially mixed populations were physically and culturally inferior to unmixed ones (or at least to unmixed white ones) and that the racial mingling that had so characterized the history of Brazil was therefore the cause of its problems. Gilberto Freyre took direct aim at this thesis in *The Masters and the Slaves*, where many of his digressions are for the purpose of marshaling evidence to show that physical, cultural, or psychological disabilities that had previously been attributed to racial mixture could in fact be explained in terms of malnutrition, disease, or the social pathology of the great slave plantations. At the same time he argued eloquently that miscegenation (and particularly the cultural mixing that went with it) was not the shame and encumbrance of Brazil but, on the contrary, its great strength. It was through this genius for physical and cultural synthesis that the Portuguese had succeeded in the difficult task of creating a civilization in the tropics.

It is one of the little ironies of history that this thesis came out in *The Masters and the Slaves* in 1933, the very year that Hitler came to power in Germany. Although racist theory, and certainly racist practice, seemed to be in the ascendancy in Europe, this was a propitious moment for Gilberto Freyre's argument in Brazil. That country had passed through a period of political turmoil in the 1920s, occasioned by a growing self-consciousness and a growing awareness of the nation's shortcomings, coupled with an ardent and spreading desire to see them eliminated through modernization. *The Masters and the Slaves* appeared therefore at a time of national debate concerning the causes of and the cures for the country's ills, and it changed the terms of that debate. The shift in scientific thinking about race and culture was already evident in the writings of certain Brazilian scholars, notably Roquette-Pinto, but it was Gilberto Freyre's book that started Brazilians thinking that they might have something to be proud rather than ashamed of in their history.

Not that the book was universally acclaimed in Brazil. Gilberto Freyre's intimate portrait of the Portuguese in the great houses of colonial Brazil was not particularly flattering. He described them as lascivious, domineering, and syphilitic, as much given to harboring criminals as to maintaining priests, both of whom were treated like family retainers. In particular, his detailed discussions of family life in colonial Brazil and of the unbridled lusts of the masters, growing up as they did in the tropics, surrounded by available slaves, titillated some readers and shocked many. Freyre's book was attacked in some quarters as a caricature and even denounced as pornography.

In spite of this response, its main arguments were quickly accepted. Brazilians discovered that modern scientific evidence showed that no particular social or physical harm came from racial mixture. On the other hand, a great deal of good could result from cultural synthesis. Moreover, Brazil needed no longer to be ashamed of its colonial past, because the slaveholding, patriarchal society that Gilberto Freyre described could be seen in historical perspective to have had some virtues. Compared with the other imperialists of the time the Portuguese appeared as more tolerant of other races and cultures, more ready to adopt their customs and even adapt to their ways. Even slavery under the Portuguese, while hardly pleasant (and Freyre goes into gruesome detail over some of its nastier aspects), was a milder form of bondage than that experienced by those who labored under the yoke of the Anglo-Saxons or suffered at the hands of the Spaniards.

The reasons for this were complex. The Portuguese had lived since time immemorial at the margins of the warring civilizations of Christian Europe and Islamic North Africa. This experience had made them a cosmopolitan and practical people, given to compromise. They had moreover experienced centuries of Moorish rule, so that they did not instinctively look down on dark-skinned people, even when the tables were turned and the Moorish populations of Christian Portugal were reduced to helot status after the reconquest. In any event the Portuguese taste for Moorish beauties, implanted when the Moors were their overlords, endured through centuries of warfare and coexistence and induced later generations of colonists to mate enthusiastically with the dark, long-haired Indians of Brazil and later with the even darker Africans they brought over to work the plantations. There was practicality as well as pleasure in this policy. Metropolitan Portugal had a tiny population (not much more than a million by some accounts) at the time when it embarked on its imperial adventures. The Portuguese could seize a worldwide empire, if that meant no more than defending their trading monopolies along the coasts of Africa and Asia, but they could not people it from the mother country. In Brazil, therefore, where the Portuguese established settlements on a large scale, there was a chronic shortage of colonists, and particularly of Portuguese women. Miscegenation was thus both a pleasure and a solution.

As for slavery, Freyre suggested that its horrors were mitigated in Brazil by the influence of the Catholic church and the effects of Portuguese law. The Portuguese legislated savagely against heretics but were prepared to accept all races on equal terms provided that they professed Catholicism. Furthermore, the church insisted that slaves had souls and thus protected their right to certain minimal considerations—baptism, marriage, the integrity of their families, and treatment as human beings (albeit enslaved ones)—rather than as chattels or mere pieces of property. Slaves also received some protection under the law, since Portuguese law, unlike the codes of the northern European slaving nations, derived from Roman law, which recognized the status of the slave and guaranteed certain minimal rights to persons occupying it.

Brazilians thus discovered with pleasant surprise that they need no longer be ashamed of their mestizo heritage or of their colonial past. On the contrary, they had no *leyenda negra* (the record of cruelties of which the Spaniards stood accused in their empire) to live down. Instead they could take some comfort from the fact that their ancestors were now reported to have been the least cruel of the European slavers and could take positive pride in the fact that they were supposed to have acted in this way out of an absence of racial prejudice and a willingness to live and let live where other peoples and cultures were concerned.

It is small wonder that *The Masters and the Slaves* was also enthusiastically received when it first appeared in English in 1946. Its publication in the United States, two years after the appearance of Gunnar Myrdal's *An American Dilemma*, once again had the effect of telling a troubled public something that it wanted to hear. At a time when the horrors of World War II were still fresh in people's minds and the international conscience was still trying to come to terms with the ghastly evidence of the Nazi holocaust against the Jews, the treatment of blacks in the United States was anomalous in the extreme. Myrdal had exhaustively analyzed this American dilemma, showing how the United States, which had taken a leading part in the war against racism and totalitarianism in Europe, still tolerated institutionalized racism at home which mocked the ideals it had fought for and undermined its democratic pretensions. By contrast Gilberto Freyre's book showed that things did not have to be this way. Brazil is, after all, a country that shares many of the characteristics of the United States. It is equally large. It had relatively small Indian populations which have been exterminated or marginalized over the centuries. It brought in large numbers of black slaves to work on its plantations. Indeed, its northeastern region is in many ways analagous to the American South. Yet slavery was not so cruel there, miscegenation was encouraged, and racial prejudice was nonexistent (or muted). No wonder Manuel Cardozo wrote that *The Masters and the Slaves* had an important lesson to teach all Americans. The lesson was one of racial and cultural tolerance. This soon became part of the Brazilian national self-image as well as something that the Portuguese of the mother country could take pride in; and people beyond the Lusitanian world took heart from the thought that the cancer of racial prejudice could be eliminated even in societies where whites once lorded it over enslaved blacks.

The Masters and the Slaves is also a veritable treasure chest of Brazilian folklore. In it Gilberto Freyre expatiates lovingly on foods, plants, dances, clothes, charms, folktales, hygienic habits, architecture, aphrodisiacs, and a host of other topics, tracing them back to their Indian, African, and Portuguese origins in such a way as to give Brazilian readers a fresh appreciation of their own culture. At the same time its focus on patriarchal institutions and their connection with the Brazilian family gave Brazilians new insights into their own domestic lives and the formation of their own personalities. It was a book that offered Brazilians a fresh understanding of themselves, of their culture and its roots. Now, half a century later, it has to be admitted that some of the most influential theses of *The Masters and the Slaves* no longer seem so convincing. Consider the lack of racial prejudice among the Portuguese, the comparative mildness of slavery in Brazil, and the consequent harmoniousness of race relations in that country. A comparative examination of the historical evidence does not support the conclusion that the Portuguese were markedly less racially prejudice than the people of other imperialist nations. Moreover, they systematically enslaved blacks for centuries and came to hold that they were justifiably enslavable, which indicates some prejudice against them.

The comparative mildness of Brazilian slavery would therefore have to depend on the presumed influence of the church and the law, but these are equally dubious. It is not clear why the church should have been more effective in protecting slaves in Brazil than in the Spanish colonies, or indeed why the teaching of the church or the letter of the law should have benefited slaves very much in a country where, as Freyre showed, real power was exercised by slave owners on whom the church depended and who interpreted or ignored the laws as they saw fit.

Nor is it clear that race relations in Brazil since the days of slavery have been as harmonious as some of Freyre's suggestions might lead one to expect. It seems that those writers who paint a rosy picture of the racial situation in Brazil are usually comparing it implicitly or explicitly with what is happening elsewhere. They tend therefore to be using Brazil as an object lesson rather than as an object of analysis. On the other hand, sociological studies of race relations in Brazil have shown that racial stereotypes in that country are unfavorable to blacks and that blacks are kept in the lowest socioeconomic strata precisely because they are black.

The other major theme of *The Masters and the Slaves*—the analysis (one might almost say the psychoanalysis) of the character of the Portuguese and the Brazilians—is also criticizable. It is not helped by the style of the book which has been so widely praised and which makes it so readable. Freyre has all along insisted that the sociological, anthropological, and historicosocial essay should have a language of its own and that it is not obliged to limit itself to the exact terminologies of other sciences that are not concerned with human values. This meant in practice that his analyses of national character were literary and evocative but also imprecise to a fault. He makes generalizations about the Portuguese at all times and places. He speaks of the "vegetable contractility" of the Indians and makes the surprising and implausible assertion that Brazil is still struggling to find a "point of fixation" between Amerindian communism and the European notion of private property. He constructs a black ethos out of scraps of information taken from the days of slavery and juxtaposed with observations of modern blacks. In fact, he is curiously lax about the normal scholarly procedures, be they historical, anthropological, or psychological.

It is also noteworthy that Gilberto Freyre, who became one of the leading figures in the regionalist movement of Brazil's northeast, pays little attention to regional differences when he generalizes about Brazil. As a result, he presents a view of Brazil from a northeastern perspective, one that downplays the differences in the composition of the population and the local ethos to be found elsewhere, notably in the south. Consequently there is a tendency in his writings to focus on the seigneurial side of Brazil, which has led critics to attack them as conservative. At the same time his enthusiasm for the accomplishments of the Portuguese in the tropics led his work to be used to defend the pretensions of Portuguese imperialism, at the time when Portugal was trying to hang onto its last colonies and justifying this policy by its peculiar genius for establishing tropical civilizations.

The most serious of all these criticisms are the scholarly ones. Gilberto Freyre is an extraordinarily gifted writer with an uncanny knack for evoking the spirit of the colonial northeast and for delving into Brazilian society and the Brazilian psyche. Yet if his arguments are to be taken seriously, they have to be couched in terms that are specific as well as evocative so that they can be evaluated in terms of scholarship dealing with particular times and places.

Nevertheless these reservations hardly apply to *The Masters and the Slaves*. It was a pioneering book and deservedly acclaimed as such. It contains a rich harvest of ideas and, if some of them have to be modified in the light of subsequent work, it is equally true that others are as important now as they were when Gilberto Freyre sat down to write. Race relations in Brazil may not be as harmonious as apologists have claimed, and the existence of racial prejudice in that country is easy to document, yet there is something different and remarkable about the way in which Brazilians deal with the issue. Formal racial discrimination has never been sanctioned either by law or by public opinion and informal discrimination is neither automatic nor irrevocable. There is a certain flexibility within the system which can be seen as admirable or inadequate, depending on what the standard of comparison is. This flexibility may not be derived from any Portuguese tradition of tolerance, but it is a characteristic feature of all spheres of Brazilian social life and it is to Gilberto Freyre's credit that he was the first writer to attempt an extended analysis of it.

Similarly his analysis of the patriarchal organization of Brazilian society and of its effects on family life and on the personalities of the people raised in such a system is more than merely evocative. It suggests a series of important and interrelated truths about Brazilian history and contemporary Brazilian society which still repay further investigation. It is surely hyperbole to suggest, as Gilberto Freyre did, that the social history of the Big House is the intimate history of practically every Brazilian. Yet his provocative phrase suggests connections among the plantation systems of colonial Brazil, the regional political bosses that ran the country in the time of the Old Republic, and the patron client systems of more recent times. It suggests furthermore that there is a strain of authoritarianism in Brazilian life and in the Brazilian family which we would do well to recognize and to understand.

Today it is, in a sense, immaterial whether the arguments put forward in *The Masters and the Slaves* are right or wrong. What is clear is that the book marked a watershed in Brazilian social thought. After its appearance, discussions of Brazilian history and Brazilian society could never be the same again, and that is the measure of its importance.

David H. P. Maybury-Lewis

THE MASTERS AND THE SLAVES

I

GENERAL CHARACTERISTICS
OF THE PORTUGUESE COLONIZATION OF
BRAZIL: FORMATION OF AN AGRARIAN,
SLAVE-HOLDING, AND HYBRID
SOCIETY

W HEN, in 1532, the economic and civil organization of Brazilian society was effected,[1] the Portuguese already for an entire century had been in contact with the tropics and had demonstrated, in India and in Africa, their aptitude for living in those regions. The definitive proof of this aptitude is to be found in the change of direction that Portuguese colonization underwent in São Vicente and in Pernambuco, from an easy-going mercantile way of life to an agricultural existence, with colonial society in Brazil now organized upon a more solid basis and under more stable conditions than it had been in India or on the African plantations. The basis was agriculture, and the conditions were a patriarchal stability of family life; the regularization of labor by means of slavery; and the union of the Portuguese male with the Indian woman, who was thus incorporated into the economic and social culture of the invader.

In tropical America there was formed a society agrarian in structure, slave-holding in its technique of economic exploitation, and hybrid in composition, with an admixture of the Indian and later of the Negro. This was a society that in its evolution was protected less by a consciousness of race, which was practically non-existent in the cosmopolitan and plastic-minded Portuguese, than it was by a religious exclusiveness given expression in a system of social and political prophylaxis; less by official action than by the arm and sword of the

---

[1] "Martin Afonso de Souza . . . set up in January, 1532, the first substantial Portuguese settlement at São Vicente, near the present port of Santos. This event, the real birth of Brazil, is commemorated by a monument which stands today on the spot where the founder set foot upon the shore."— F. A. Kirkpatrick: *Latin America: A Brief History* (New York: The Macmillan Company; 1939), p. 35. (Translator.)

individual. All this, however, was subordinated to a spirit of political, economic, and juridical realism that here as in Portugal,[2] from the first century on, was the decisive element in the forming of the nation. What we had in our country was great landowning and autonomous families, lords of the plantation, with an altar and a chaplain in the house and Indians armed with bow and arrow or Negroes armed with muskets at their command; and from their seats in the municipal council chamber these masters of the earth and of the slaves that tilled it always spoke up boldly to the representatives of the crown, while through the liberal-toned voices of their sons who were priests or doctors of the law they cried out against every species of abuse on the part of the Metropolis and of Mother Church itself. In this they were quite different from the rich *criollos*[3] and learned bachelors of Spanish America, who for so long were inert in the dominant shadow of the cathedrals and the palaces of the viceroys, or who, when gathered in *cabildos*,"[4] did little more than serve as a laughingstock for the all-powerful lords of the realm.

The singular predisposition of the Portuguese to the hybrid, slave-exploiting colonization of the tropics is to be explained in large part by the ethnic or, better, the cultural past of a people existing indeterminately between Europe and Africa and belonging uncompromisingly to neither one nor the other of the two continents; with the African influence seething beneath the European and giving a sharp relish to sexual life, to alimentation, and to religion; with Moorish or Negro blood running throughout a great light-skinned mulatto population, when it is not the predominant strain, in regions that to this day are inhabited by a dark-skinned people;[5] and with the hot and

---

[2] This was true of Portugal, as we shall see further on, but it came about there through the maritime bourgeoisie, which soon developed into the dominant force, rather than through the will or action of the rural nobility. The latter, following the death of D. Fernando, in 1383, came to favor the reunion of Portugal with Castile, against which the bourgeoisie rose up, selecting as the occupant of the throne the Master of Avis. The followers of the Master of Avis, so Antônio Sérgio tells us (*A Sketch of the History of Portugal*, Lisbon, 1928), were "in the minority but they had the favor . . . or the money of the middle class."

[The work by Antônio Sérgio is an English version, by Constantino José dos Santos, of his *Bosquejo da História de Portugal* (Lisbon, 1923). (Translator.)]

[3] Creoles, in the sense of one of Spanish descent born and reared in the colonies. (Translator.)

[4] ". . . the town councils (*cabildos*) . . . exercised, each over a wide area, administrative and even, in some degree, legislative authority."—Kirkpatrick. op. cit., p. 23. (Translator.)

[5] In Beira Baixa are to be found in abundance "localizations of a small dolichocephalic race of the Mugem type," just as in Alentejo there is a predominance of "tall statures, possibly due to the influence of a meso-

oleous air of Africa mitigating the Germanic harshness of institutions and cultural forms, corrupting the doctrinal and moral rigidity of the medieval Church, drawing the bones from Christianity, feudalism, Gothic architecture, canonic discipline, Visigoth law, the Latin tongue, and the very character of the people. It was Europe reigning without governing: it was Africa that governed.

Correcting up to a certain point the great influence exerted by an enervating climate, the always tense and vibrant conditions of human contact between Europe and Africa acted upon the Portuguese character, rendering it more firm. There might be a constant state of warfare (which, incidentally, does not by any means exclude miscegenation or a sexual attraction between the two races, much less an intercourse between the two cultures),[6] but the victor would find relaxation from the intensity of his military exertions by falling back upon the agricultural and industrial labor of war captives, the enslavement or semi-enslavement of the vanquished. Hegemonies and states of servitude, these, which were never perpetuated, but which tended always to alternate,[7] as in the incident of the bells of Santiago de Compostela: the Moors had had them borne to the mosque of Córdoba on the backs of Christians, and the latter, centuries later, had them returned to Galicia on the backs of Moors.

As to what is looked upon as the autochthonous base of a population that is so shifting a one, it is to be found in a persistent mass of dark-brown dolichocephalic individuals[8] whose color Arabian and

cephalic Arabic race," while in Algarve as in other sections of the littoral there are to be encountered numerous representatives of a "Semito-Phœnician type, of medium stature."—Mendes Corrêa: *Os Criminosos portugueses (Portuguese Criminals)* (Lisbon, 1914). See also Fonseca Cardoso on "Portuguese Anthropology" in *Notas sobre Portugal (Notes on Portugal)* (Lisbon, 1908). In the Municipality of Alcacer do Sul mulatto families are numerous, according to Leite de Vasconcellos, cited by Mendes Corrêa: *Os Povos primitivos da Lusitania (The Primitive Peoples of Lusitania)* (Porto, 1924).

[6] Rafael Altamira, in his *Filosofía de la Historia y Teoría de la Civilización* (Madrid, 1915), observes that reciprocal influences operate "between enemy peoples, separated by hatreds," and he cites the example of the Moslems and the Christians, "who in spite of their wars continue to influence each other to a high degree."

[7] Freeman stresses "the general law by which, in almost all periods, either the masters of Spain have borne rule in Africa or the masters of Africa have borne rule in Spain."—E. A. Freeman: *Historical Geography of Europe* (London, 1882). But it is above all in Portugal that this alternation of rule between the continents, with a constant adjustment and readjustment of cultural values and racial preponderance, is to be observed.

[8] This, according to the craniometric and osteometric researches of Paula e Oliveira. Two other Portuguese anthropologists, Silva Bastos and Fonseca Cardoso, have encountered in the mountainous regions of Beira Alta,

even Negro Africa have more than once come to enliven with traces of the mulatto and the black as they overflowed large portions of the peninsula—it was as if they felt this people to be their own by remote affinities, merely grown a trifle paler, that is all, and as if they did not wish to see the stock obliterated by superimposed Nordic layers or transmuted by a series of Europeanizing cultures: all that invasion of Celts, Germans, Romans, Normans, the Anglo-Scandinavian, the *H. Europæus L.*, feudalism, Christianity, Roman law, monogamy—it all suffered a restriction or refraction in a Portugal influenced by Africa, conditioned by the African climate, and undermined by the sensual mysticism of Islam.

"It is in vain that one would look for a unified physical type," Count Hermann Keyserling recently observed, in speaking of Portugal. What he did note was elements as diverse and opposed to one another as could be, "individuals with an air of the Scandinavian about them and Negroid types" living together in what impressed him as being a "state of profound unity." "Race here does not play a decisive role," concludes this astute observer.[9] Previously, Alexandre Herculano had described Mozarabic society as consisting of an "indeterminate population in the midst of two contending groups (the Nazarenes and the Mohammedans), half-Christian, half-Saracen, with relatives and friends in both groups, and having sympathies with both of them on the grounds of belief and customs."[10]

This portrait of historic Portugal as drawn by Herculano might possibly be extended to the prehistoric and proto-historic eras, which are shown by archæology and anthropology to have been quite as vague and indeterminate in character as the historical epoch. Before the Arabs and the Berbers: the Capsitanians, the Libyo-Phœnicians, the most remote of African elements. The *H. taganus*.[11] Semitic and Negro, or Negroid, waves breaking against those from the north.

Trás-os-Montes, and Beira Baixa, "in a state of relative purity, representatives of the dolichocephalic race of Mugem (Beaunes-Chaudes type) who constitute," says Mendes Corrêa, "the anthropological base of the Portuguese people." See Mendes Corrêa: *Os Criminosos portugueses*, and Fonseca Cardoso, loc. cit. See also the paper by Costa Ferreira: "*La Capacité du crâne chez les portugais,*" *Bulletins et Mémoires de la Société d'Anthropologie de Paris*, Série V, Vol. IV; and Ferraz de Macedo: *Bosquejos de*

Antropologia Criminal (Outlines of Criminal Anthropology) (Lisbon, 1900).

[9] Count Hermann Keyserling: "Portugal" (translated from the German by Herta Oppenheimer and Osório de Oliveira), in *Descobrimento*, No. 2 (Lisbon, 1931).

[10] Alexandre Herculano: *História de Portugal (History of Portugal)* (Lisbon, 1853).

[11] Mendes Corrêa: *Os Povos primitivos da Lusitania*.

In its ethnic and cultural indeterminateness between Europe and Africa Portugal appears to have been always the same as other portions of the peninsula. A species of bi-continentalism that, in a population so vague and ill defined, corresponds to bisexuality in the individual. It would be difficult to imagine a people more fluctuating than the Portuguese, the feeble balance of antagonisms being reflected in everything that pertains to them, conferring upon them an easy and relaxed flexibility that is at times disturbed by grievous hesitations,[12] along with a special wealth of aptitudes that are frequently discrepant and hard to reconcile for the purpose of a useful expression or practical initiative.

Ferraz de Macedo, whom his patriotically sensitive fellow countrymen will not pardon for the unpleasant character of some of his just conclusions, amid a number that are grossly exaggerated, in undertaking to define the normal type of Portuguese is brought face to face with the basic difficulty: the absence of a definite dynamic type. What he encountered was customs, aspirations, interests, temperaments, vices, and virtues of the most varied sort and of diverse origins —ethnic origins, he would say; cultural would perhaps be more scientifically exact. Among others, he discovered the following widely varying traits: "violence in sexual relations" and a "taste for erotic stories," "high spirits, frankness, loyalty," little of individual initiative, a "vibrant patriotism," "improvidence," "intelligence," "fatalism," and "an aptitude for skillful imitation."[13]

The astonishment he felt at the wealth of contradictions in the Portuguese character was given superb expression by the novelist Eça de Queiroz. His Gonçalo, in The Illustrious House of Ramires,[14] is more than a synthesis of the fidalgo; it is a synthesis of the Portuguese of any class or condition. Whether one thinks of Ceuta, of India, or of the discovery and colonization of Brazil, the Portuguese has ever been, like Gonçalo Ramires, "full of big plans and enthusiasms that end by going up in smoke," yet hard and persistent "when he attaches

---

[12] This is that incapacity for forming quick resolutions which Theóphilo Braga holds responsible for the "lack of initiative" on the part of the Portuguese.—O Povo Português (The Portuguese People) (Lisbon, 1885).

[13] Ferraz de Macedo, op. cit.

[14] Eça de Queiroz: A Ilustre Casa de Ramires (Lisbon). The opinion expressed here is that of Antônio, Arroyo, writing on "The Portuguese People," in Notas sobre Portugal (Notes on Portugal) (Lisbon, 1908). Meanwhile, in the pages of Eça de Queiroz, following the description of Gonçalo, we find this passage:

"Taken by and large, the good with the bad, do you know what he reminds me of?"

"What?"

"Portugal."

himself to an idea." His is "an imagination that carries him away . . . leading him to exaggerate to the point of lying," while at the same time he is possessed of "a practical mind, always attentive to reality and the useful." He exhibits "vanity" and "scruples touching his honor," he has a "taste for decking himself out in pomp and finery" that occasionally makes him ridiculous, but he is also capable of a great "simplicity." He is at once melancholy and "talkative, sociable"; he is generous, negligent, a scatterbrain in business matters, lively and easy-going when it comes to "understanding things." Always waiting for "some miracle, for some Golden Fleece that will solve all his difficulties," he "lacks confidence in himself, is cowardly, shrinking, until one day he decides to show himself a hero." [15] These are opposite-tending extremes of introversion and extroversion, representing, as we would say in scientific language, the alternations of syntony and schizophrenia.

Considered as a whole, the Portuguese character gives us, above all else, the impression of being "vague, unprecise," in the opinion of the English critic and historian Aubrey Bell; and it is this lack of preciseness that permits the Portuguese to unite within himself so many contrasts that are impossible of adjustment in the hard and angular Castilian, whose aspect is more definitely Gothic and European.[16] The Portuguese character, Bell goes on to say, is like a river that flows along very calmly and then of a sudden hurls itself over waterfalls. It is capable of passing from "fatalism" to "outbursts of heroic effort," from "apathy" to "bursts of energy in private and revolutions in public life," from "docility" to "outbreaks of harshness and arrogance"; it is a character that is "indifferent yet with fugitive enthusiasms," one marked by a "love of progress and change," one that exhibits sudden spurts and, in the intervals between impulses, delights in a voluptuous indolence that is very Oriental, in nostalgic longings, romantic ballads, and *laus perenne*. "Mystical and poetical" the Portuguese still are, according to Bell (the Englishman who, after Beck-

---

[15] Eça de Queiroz, op. cit. The author mentions other characteristics.

[16] I do not know on what it is Waldo Frank bases his opinion when he writes: "The Portuguese is more European than the Spaniard; he possesses a Semitic lineage that is weaker, a Gothic lineage that is stronger."— "La Selva," in *Sur*, No. 1 (Buenos Aires, 1931). I believe that the exact opposite is the case: that the Portuguese, being more cosmopolitan than the Spaniard, is probably the less Gothic and the more Semitic, the less European and the more African of the two; in any case, less definitely the one thing or the other. The more vague and unprecise as an expression of the continental European character. The more extra-European. The more Atlantic.

ford, has best sensed and understood the people and the life of Portugal), "with intervals of intense utilitarianism . . . falling from idle dreams to a keen relish for immediate profit, from the heights of rapture to depths of melancholy and suicidal despair," combining "vanity with . . . pessimism" and "indolence with love of sport and adventure." [17]

Within this antecedent factor of a general nature—the bi-continentalism or, better, the dualism of culture and of race—there are other, subordinate factors that call for our special attention. One of these is the presence among the elements that united to form the Portuguese nation of individuals of Semitic origin, or stock,[18] individuals endowed with a mobility, a plasticity, and adaptability social as well as physical that are easily to be made out in the Portuguese navigator and cosmopolitan of the fifteenth century.[19] Hereditarily predisposed to

---

[17] Aubrey F. G. Bell: *Portugal of the Portuguese* (London, 1915). This author, whose observations on the lyrical element in the Portuguese character coincide with those of Unamuno (*Por Tierras de Portugal y España*) and more recent essayists, stresses other contrasts.

[18] [Freyre uses the English word. (Translator.)]

Fonseca Cardoso (op. cit.) verifies anthropologically the presence of the Semito-Phœnician element in the populations of present-day Portugal, and Professor Mendes Corrêa, emphasizing the ethnogenic role of the Jews in the formation of Portuguese society, states that it was already a factor of great importance in the time of the Visigoths.—*Raça e Nacionalidade* (*Race and Nationality*) (Porto, 1919). From the point of view of social history, the definitive study of the Israelite infiltration into Portugal is that by J. Lúcio de Azevedo: *História dos Cristãos-Novos Portugueses* (*History of Portuguese New-Christians*) (Lisbon, 1915).

[19] D. G. Dalgado, in his study *The Climate of Portugal* (Lisbon, 1914), lays emphasis on the fact that the Portuguese "acclimatize themselves in various parts of the world better than almost all the other European races."

Possibly—and this is the opinion of many persons as gathered by Dalgado —the explanation lies in "the great admixture of the people of the country with the Semitic race." Emile Béringer, in his *Studies of the Climate and Mortality in the Capital of Pernambuco* (translated by Manuel Duarte Pereira, Pernambuco, 1891), states that "the Portuguese race appears to be endowed with a temperament that permits it to adapt itself more easily than other races to climates that are different from that of the mother country. This quality is to be attributed not only to the crossing of the Portuguese with the Israelites who had found domicile in Portugal after their expulsion and who possessed a notable aptitude for acclimatization; it is to be attributed also to the persisting influence of Negro blood, which was widely diffused in Portugal during the period when, in our own country, the slave trade was flourishing." Writing of "*Das Judentum und die Anfänge der modernen Kolonisation*," in *Das holländische Kolonialreich in Brasilien* (Gotha, 1921), E. Hermann Wätjen stresses the point that the strong feeling of the Dutch against the Jews in Pernambuco (which practically amounted to anti-Semitism) was in

a life in the tropics by a long tropical habitat, it was the Semitic element, mobile and adaptable as no other, that was to confer upon the Portuguese colonizer of Brazil some of the chief physical and psychic conditions for success and for resistance—including that economic realism which from an early date tended to correct the excesses of the military and religious spirit in the formation of Brazilian society.

This mobility was one of the secrets of the Portuguese victory. Without it, it is not to be explained how a country that was practically uninhabited,[20] with a population that was numerically insignificant as a result of all the epidemics, famines, and especially wars that had afflicted the peninsula in the Middle Ages, should have succeeded in virilely besprinkling with what was left of its blood and culture populations so diverse and at so great a distance from one another: in Asia, in Africa, in America, and in the numerous islands and archipelagoes. The scarcity of man-power was made up for by the Portuguese through mobility and miscibility, by dominating enormous spaces and, wherever they might settle, in Africa or in America, taking wives and begetting offspring with a procreative fervor that was due as much to violent instincts on the part of the in-

---

part due to the fact that the Israelites acclimated themselves with an astonishing facility, whereas it was extremely difficult for the Flemish to adapt themselves to the life of the tropics.

[20] It is impossible to state definitely what was the size of the reduced population of Portugal in the fifteenth and sixteenth centuries. Historians are not agreed on the point. Rebello Silva thinks that in the fifteenth century it possibly did not exceed 1,010,000.— *Memória sobre a População e Agricultura em Portugal desde a Fundação da Monarquia até 1865* (*Memoir on the Population and Agriculture in Portugal from the Founding of the Monarchy to 1865*) (Lisbon, 1868). Two writers closer to the era in question who may be consulted on this subject are: Manuel de Severim de Fária: *Notícias de Portugal* (*Tidings of Portugal*) (Lisbon, 1655); and Duarte Nunes de Leão: *Descripção Geral do Reino de Portugal* (*General De-scription of the Realm of Portugal*) (1610). Among the moderns, see the figures given by Adrien Balbi: *Essai statistique sur le Portugal* (Paris, 1822); Gama Barros: *História da Administração Pública em Portugal nos Séculos XV a XVI* (*History of Public Administration in Portugal in the Fifteenth and Sixteenth Centuries*) (Lisbon, 1896); Costa Lobo: *A História da Sociedade em Portugal no Século XV* (*History of Portuguese Society in the Fifteenth Century*) (Lisbon, 1904); Oliveira Martins: *A História de Portugal* (*History of Portugal*) (Porto, 1882). See also J. Lúcio de Azevedo on "Economic Organization" in *História de Portugal*, 27, II; and J. J. Soares de Barros: "Memoirs on the Causes of the Differences in the Population of Portugal at Different Periods of the Portuguese Monarchy," in *Memórias Econômicas da Academia Real das Ciências* (2nd edition, Lisbon, 1885).

dividual as it was to a calculated policy stimulated by the State for obvious economic and political reasons.

Individuals of worth, warriors, administrators, technicians, were shifted about by the colonial administration in Lisbon like pieces on a backgammon board: from Asia to America and from there to Africa, depending upon the exigencies of the moment or of the region. To Duarte Coelho, grown rich from his stay in India, John III intrusts the new *capitânia* of Pernambuco. His sons, trained in fighting the American Indians, are summoned to the more difficult wars in Africa. From Madeira technicians in the manufacture of sugar are sent to the plantations of northern Brazil. Ships employed in trade with the Indies are made use of for commerce with the American colony. From Africa whole nations, almost, of Negroes are transported for agricultural labor in Brazil. An astounding mobility. An imperial domain achieved by an all but ridiculous number of Europeans running from one end to another of the known world as in a formidable game of puss-in-the-corner.[21]

As to their miscibility, no colonizing people in modern times has exceeded or so much as equaled the Portuguese in this regard. From their first contact with women of color, they mingled with them and procreated mestizo sons; and the result was that a few thousand daring males succeeded in establishing themselves firmly in possession of a vast territory and were able to compete with great and numerous peoples in the extension of their colonial domain and in the efficiency of their colonizing activity. Miscibility rather than mobility was the process by which the Portuguese made up for their deficiency in human mass or volume in the large-scale colonization of extensive areas. For this they had been prepared by the intimate terms of social and sexual intercourse on which they had lived with the colored races that had invaded their peninsula or were close neighbors to it, one of which, of the Mohammedan faith, was technically more highly skilled and possessed an intellectual and artistic culture superior to that of the blond Christians.[22]

---

[21] If the Portuguese were able to achieve so great a mobility, this was owing to the near perfection (considering the era) which the technique of maritime transport had attained in that country. Perfection, and an abundance of vessels. "In compensation for the scant human material," notes C. Malheiro Dias, "Portugal possessed as did no other nation in the first decades of the sixteenth century abundant means of maritime transport."— *História da Colonização Portuguesa do Brasil* (*History of the Portuguese Colonization of Brazil*), Introduction, Vol. I (Lisbon, 1924).

[22] Roy Nash, in *The Conquest of Brazil* (New York, 1926), stresses the

Long contact with the Saracens had left with the Portuguese the idealized figure of the "enchanted Moorish woman," a charming type, brown-skinned, black-eyed,[23] enveloped in sexual mysticism, roseate in hue,[24] and always engaged in combing out her hair or bathing in rivers or in the waters of haunted fountains;[25] and the Brazilian colonizers were to encounter practically a counterpart of this type in the naked Indian women with their loose-flowing hair. These latter also had dark tresses and dark eyes and bodies painted red,[26] and, like the Moorish Nereids, were extravagantly fond of a river bath to refresh their ardent nudity, and were fond, too, of combing their hair.[27]

---

fact that the Brazilian colonizer, before exerting an imperial sway over colored races, had in his own turn experienced the domination of a dark-skinned people superior to the Hispano-Goths in organization and in technique. "Under such circumstances," writes Nash, "it would be deemed an honor for the white to marry or mate with the governing class, the brown man, instead of the reverse." Ruediger Bilden ("Brazil, Laboratory of Civilization," in the *Nation,* New York, 1929) likewise emphasizes the fact that the relations of the Portuguese with colored peoples had been begun under circumstances unfavorable to the whites. He is referring, obviously, to the historical phase of the matter.

[23] Luiz Chaves: *Lendas de Portugal* (*Legends of Portugal*) (Porto, 1924).

[24] "It is red . . . that the Portuguese sees in everything that is marvelous, from the romantic garments of the Enchanted Moorish Women. . . ."—Luiz Chaves: *Paginas Folclóricas* (*Pages from Folklore*) (Lisbon, 1920).

[25] To the "Enchanted Moorish Women" in Portugal, as Leits de Vasconcellos points out, is ascribed "the role of divinity of the waters."— *Tradições Populares de Portugal* (*Popular Traditions of Portugal*) (Porto, 1882). According to the studies of this eminent investigator and those of Consigliere Pedroso in *As Mouras Encantadas* (*The Enchanted*

Moorish Women) and Luiz Chaves in *Lendas de Portugal,* the belief was common among the people that these creatures put in an appearance almost always by the side of fountains and were to be seen combing their hair, sometimes with "golden combs." There is similarly a common belief to the effect that the Moorish women not only went clad in roseate garments but were in the habit of drawing near to those who showed them a "red kerchief" or "something red." (Leite de Vasconcellos, op. cit.) All of these circumstances would appear to confirm the assumption that these women were an expression of sexual or erotic mysticism, a species of cult of the colored woman or of the dusky Venus among the Portuguese.

[26] Among the natives of Brazil red was perhaps the erotic color *par excellence,* in addition to its mystic and prophylactic significance. On this subject, which I shall have more to say later on; see the study by Professor Rafael Karsten: *The Civilization of the South American Indians* (New York, 1920).

[27] Speaking of the Indian women of Brazil, Ives d'Evreux (*Voyage au Nord du Brésil*) notes that "they often combed their hair." As to the frequency with which they bathed, this is stressed by practically all the observers of native customs in the sixteenth and seventeenth centuries— among others, Pero Vaz de Caminha, companion of Pedro Alvarez Cabral,

What was more, they were fat like the Moorish women. Only, they were a little less coy and for some trinket or other or a bit of broken mirror would give themselves, with legs spread far apart, to the "*caraibas*," [28] who were so gluttonous for a woman.

In opposition to the legend of the "enchanted Moorish woman," although it never attained the same prestige, there evolved that of the "Moorish hag," representing, it may be, an outlet for the blonde woman's sexual jealousy toward her colored sister. Then, there were outbreaks of religious hatred, with the blond Christians from the north pitted against the dark-skinned infidels, a hatred that was later to result in the idealization throughout Europe of the blond type as identified with angelic and divine personages, to the detriment of the brunet type, which was associated with evil and fallen angels, with the wicked, and with traitors.[29] One thing we know is that in the fifteenth century, when ambassadors were sent by the Republic of Venice to the two Spains, bearing greetings to King Philip II, the envoys noted that in Portugal certain women of the upper classes were in the habit of dyeing their hair a "blond color," while both there and in Spain a number of them "painted their faces a white and red tint" by way of "rendering their skin, which is a trifle swarthy—which is, indeed, quite swarthy—more fair and rosy, being persuaded that all swarthy-skinned women are ugly." [30]

Meanwhile, it may be stated that the brown-skinned woman was preferred by the Portuguese for purposes of love, at least for purposes of physical love. The fashions of the blonde woman—limited, for that matter, to the upper classes—were the reflection of influences coming from abroad rather than a genuine expression of the national taste. With reference to Brazil, as an old saying has it: "White woman for marriage, mulatto woman for f—, Negro woman for work," [31] a saying in which, alongside the social convention of the superiority of the white woman and the inferiority of the black, is to be discerned

---

in a letter written May 1, 1500, to be found in Manuel Ayres de Casal: *Chorographia Brasilica* (2nd edition, Rio de Janeiro, 1833), Vol. I, p. 10.

[28] Term applied by the Indians to Europeans. *Caraiba* commonly refers to the linguistic stock to which many Brazilian tribes belonged: the Caribs, or first Indians to be discovered by the Spanish, found in the West Indies, Central America, and the northern part of South America. (Translator.)

[29] Madison Grant: *The Passing of the Great Race* (New York, 1916).

[30] "*Viagem a Portugal dos Cavaleiros Trom e Lippomani*" ("Voyage to Portugal of the Cavaliers Trom and Pippomani), translated by Alexandre Herculano, in *Opusculos* (Lisbon, 1897).

[31] This adage is reported by H. Handelmann in his *História do Brasil* (translation, Rio, 1931).

a sexual preference for the mulatto.[32] Moreover, in our national lyricism there is no tendency more clearly revealed than one toward a glorification of the mulatto woman, the *cabocla* or Indian woman, the brown-skin or brunette type, celebrated for the beauty of her eyes, the whiteness of her teeth, for her wiles and languishments and witching ways, far more than are the "pale virgins" and the "blonde damsels." These latter, it is true, appear here and there in a sonnet or popular song (*modinha*) of the eighteenth or the nineteenth century, but they do not stand out as the others do.

Another circumstance or condition that favored the Portuguese as much as did miscibility and mobility in the conquest of the land and the domination of the tropical peoples was their acclimatability. With respect to physical conditions of soil and temperature, Portugal is Africa rather than Europe. The so-called "Portuguese climate" of Martonne, unique in Europe, is one that approximates the African. Thus, the Portuguese was predisposed by his own mesology to a victorious encounter with the tropics; his removal to the torrid regions of America was not to bring with it the grave disturbances associated with adaptation nor the profound difficulties of acclimatization that were experienced by colonizers coming from cold climates.

While Gregory [33] may insist upon denying that the tropical climate *per se* has a tendency to produce in the north European the effects of degeneration, and while it may be recalled that Elkington in 1922 found in the Dutch colony of Kissav, founded in 1783, conditions

---

[32] See Gilberto Freyre: *Sobrados e Mucambos* (1936). See also Donald Pierson: *Negroes in Brazil* (1942). Pierson (pp. 172–3), quoting the adage cited here, speaks of "the myth of the sexual potency of the hybrid," and observes that "the sexual attraction which the mulatto male exerted upon daughters of rich and influential European families led quite often to the elopement or, occasionally and increasingly, to marriage with parental consent." See also what he has to say (pp. 136–7) of the "*morena*," or brown-skinned type, as the "ideal type" of femininity at Bahia. ("The *morena* may or may not have African blood. But at least in Bahia this category includes many individuals of partial African descent.") "The *morena* has the reputation of being more desirable than lighter Brazilian women;

she is commonly described as 'more *ardente*' (passionate), 'more *adstringente*' (clinging)." The distinguished Brazilian anthropologist Arthur Ramos (letter quoted by Pierson) admits that "the charms of the morena exert a profound sexual attraction" and that the preference for her "has a sexual basis in the Freudian sense," but points out that the attitude in question "grew out of the enthusiasm and sentimentalism of the abolition campaign," and adds: "The *morena* expresses in a symbolic way the union of the two races —the black and the white—and the absence of (caste) prejudice." (Pierson, op. cit., p. 137.) In general, see in Pierson the chapters on "Race Mixture and the Color Line" and "Intermarriage." (Translator.)

[33] J. W. Gregory: *The Menace of Color* (Philadelphia, 1925).

that were satisfactory as regards health and prosperity, and with no "obvious evidence of physical degeneration" among the fair-featured colonists,[34] there is on the other hand a large mass of evidence that would seem to favor the opposite point of view, to the effect that the Nordic in the tropics shows a low degree of acclimatability or none at all. Professor Oliveira Vianna not long ago, brushing aside with extreme partiality findings such as those of Elkington and Gregory, to whom he does not even refer, proceeded to bring together the testimony of some of the best modern specialists in the fields of climatology and anthropo-geography—men like Taylor, Glenn Trewartha, Huntington, and Karl Sapper—by way of contradicting the asserted capacity of Nordics to adapt themselves to tropical climates. The Brazilian sociologist quotes Sapper's forceful opinion with regard to the colonizing activities of north Europeans in the tropical zone: "The north Europeans on the tropical highlands have never succeeded in setting up anything more than temporary establishments. They have attempted to organize in those regions a permanent society based upon agriculture, with the colonist living by his own manual labor; but in all these efforts they have failed." [35] But of the anthropologists, it is Taylor,[36] perhaps, whose conclusions most forcefully and with present-day pertinence contradict those of Gregory. Prior to the studies made by Taylor and Huntington in anthropo-geography and cultural anthropology and those of Dexter in climatology, Benjamin Kidd, in speaking of the acclimatization of north Europeans in the tropics, had observed that all the experiences of this sort had been vain and futile attempts, foredoomed to failure.[37] And Mayo Smith, from the point of view of statistics applied to sociology, concludes that, while our statistics are not sufficiently exact to indicate that it is impossible for the European permanently to acclimate himself in the tropics, they show this to be extremely difficult.[38]

---

[34] Quatrefages had previously mentioned a number of notable cases of acclimatability: of the French in Corsica, of the fugitives from the Edict of Nantes in Cape Colony. And Hintze, in a study made of the descendants of white settlers in the island of Sabá, colonized in 1640, a pure-blooded population, without mestizos, found no effects of degeneration. (A. Balfour: "Sojourners in the Tropics," the *Lancet*, 1923, Vol. I, p. 1329.) But no case is so impressive as that of the Dutch in Kissav, cited by Gregory.

[35] Karl Sapper, in Oliveira Vianna: *Raça e Assimilação* (*Race and Assimilation*) (São Paulo, 1932).

[36] Griffith Taylor: *Environment and Race* (Oxford, 1926).

[37] Benjamin Kidd: *The Control of the Tropics* (London, 1898).

[38] Mayo Smith: *Statistics and Sociology* (New York, 1907). A friend calls attention to the reseaches of A. Ozório de Almeida on "the basal metabolism of tropical man of the white race," an inquiry the first results of which were published in 1919, in the

Over against this apparent incapacity of the Nordics is the fact that the Portuguese have displayed so notable an aptitude for acclimating themselves in the tropical regions. Certain it is that, owing to a much greater degree of miscibility than other Europeans possess, the colonial societies of Portuguese origin have all been hybrid, some of them more so, others less. In Brazil, at São Paulo as at Pernambuco—the two great foci of creative energy in the first centuries of colonization, the Paulistas operating in a horizontal, the Pernambucans in a vertical direction [39]—the society that was capable of such notable undertakings

Journal de physiologie et de pathologie générale. In ten white residents of Rio de Janeiro Ozório found that their basal metabolism was inferior to European and American standards. The same thing was later found to be true in the case of Negroes, also residents of Rio. Upon the basis of these researches the noted Brazilian scientist considers "this reduction as a basic feature of acclimatization in hot countries," believing that "acclimatization consists essentially in a slow and progressive modification of the basal metabolism to the point of fixation in a value compatible with the new climatic conditions in which the individual finds himself." "The theory of acclimatization of A. Ozório de Almeida," writes O. B. de Couto e Silva, "will clear up many points that until now have been wholly obscure. Thus, it explains the inferiority of the European in his struggle with the tropical climate." —See the thesis by O. B. de Couto e Silva: *Sôbre a Lei de Rubner-Richet (On Rubner-Richet's Law)* (Rio, 1926). The subject is one that has been notably enriched these last few years with scientific papers and studies.

[39] The terms *horizontal* and *vertical* are not here employed in the pure and restricted sociological sense that is attributed to them in the recent book by Professor Pitirim Sorokin, *Social Mobility* (New York, 1927). In speaking of the vertical activity of the Pernambucans, I have reference not so much to the change of economic activity, followed by social and political changes, in accordance with Sorokin's concept, as to the regional concentration of effort in the establishment of sugar-raising and the sugar industry, the consolidation of a slave-holding and agrarian society, and the expulsion of the Dutch, who disturbed this effort and this process of forming an aristocracy. This is in contrast to the activity of the Paulistas, or rather, as Sorokin would say, the horizontal mobility of the slave-hunters and gold-seekers, the founders of the backland cattle-ranches, and the missionaries. It may be noted, however, that in the special sense of Sorokin's terminology, Brazilian society was mobile in both a horizontal and a vertical direction—in the changes, at times abrupt, that occurred, especially in the south, in the position of the individual in the economic and social scale. This phenomenon is expressed by the old proverb: "Father a tavern-keeper, son a gentleman, grandson a beggar." The truth is that in Brazil, even where colonization was the most aristocratic in character, as in Pernambuco, the patriarchal system was never absolute, nor could it be with "the more or less general custom of parceling out inheritances and estates," to which Sylvio Romero alludes in a letter to E. Demolins in *Provocações e Debates (Polemics and Debates)* (Porto, 1916). Primogeniture was the exception, as in the case of the Paes Barreto family, at Cabo, in Pernambuco; such cases were rare.

as the *bandeiras*, the catechizing of the natives, the founding and consolidating of tropical agriculture, and the wars against the French in Maranhão and against the Dutch in Pernambuco was one that was constituted with a small number of white women and a broad and profound admixture of native blood. In view of this, it becomes difficult in the case of the Portuguese to distinguish between acclimatability on the part of the white colonizer—whose own ethnic purity is so greatly in doubt, while his European quality is a conventional assumption rather than genuine—and the capacity of the mestizo who has been formed from the earliest times through a union of the unscrupulous foreign-comer, lacking in race consciousness, with women of vigorous native stock.

In any event, it is a known fact that the Portuguese triumphed where other Europeans failed; and the first modern society formed in the tropics with national characteristics and qualities of permanence was one of Portuguese origin. These were qualities that in Brazil came early in stead of late as in the tropical possessions of the English, the French, and the Dutch.

Other Europeans, those pure white, dolichocephalic inhabitants of a cold climate, upon first contact with equatorial America would succumb or would lose their colonizing energy, their moral tension, physical health itself. This was true of the most rigid of them, such as the Puritan colonizers of Old Providence, who, made of the same fiber as the New England pioneers, upon the tropical island became soft, flabby, and dissolute.[40]

The results were no different in the case of the British loyalists who emigrated from Georgia and other new states of the American Union for the Bahama Islands—hardened Englishmen whom the tropical climate in less than a hundred years turned into "poor white trash."[41] The same thing probably would have happened to the French Calvinists who in the sixteenth century very proudly and triumphantly sought to establish in Brazil a colony that should be exclusively white, and who retired from the scene without leaving any traces of their colonizing activities—unless it was traces on the sands of the shore or on the reefs where the more persistent of Villegaignon's companions were to founder before they definitely abandoned the Brazilian coast.[42]

----

[40] On the Puritans in the tropics, see A. P. Newton: *The Colonizing Activities of the English Puritans* (New Haven, 1914).

[41] E. Huntington: *Civilization and Climate* (New Haven, 1915).

[42] It was on one of these reefs near Olinda that a Frenchman set down the bitter observation preserved for us by Sebastião da Rocha Pitta: *"Le monde*

Nor should we forget that the French who since 1715 have been established in the islands of Réunion and Mauritius are today obviously inferior in energy and efficiency to those of the first generations.[43]

Not three or four, but two generations were sufficient to enervate the Anglo-Americans who set themselves up in Hawaii.[44] And Semple reminds us that the researches carried out in 1900 by the International Harvester Company show a diminishment of German energy in southern Brazil, which, as it happens, is not a tropical but a subtropical region.[45]

This was not true of the Portuguese colonist. Thanks to all the fortunate predispositions of race, mesology, and culture of which I have spoken, he not only succeeded in overcoming those conditions of climate and soil that were unfavorable to the settlement of Europeans in the tropics; he also, through unions with colored women, made up for the extremely small number of whites available for the task of colonization. Through intercourse with the Indian or the Negro woman the colonizer propagated a vigorous and ductile mestizo population that was still more adaptable than he himself to the tropical climate. The lack of man-power from which he suffered more than any other colonist and which compelled him to immediate miscegenation—against which, moreover, he had no racial scruples and but few religious prejudices [46]—was for the Portuguese an advantage in the conquest and colonization of the tropics. An advantage so far as his better social, if not his biological, adaptation was concerned.

Semple denies to the movements of European peoples in the tropical regions of Asia, Australia, Africa, and the Americas, and that of Americans in the Philippines, the character of a genuine ethnic ex-

---

va de pi ampis" (*sic*). See Rocha Pitta: *História da América Portuguesa* (*History of Portuguese America*) (Lisbon, 1730). With regard to the activity of the French in Brazil in the sixteenth century, read the book by Paul Gaffarel: *Histoire du Brésil français au seizième siècle* (Paris, 1878).

[43] C. Keller: *Madagascar, Mauritius and Other East African Islands* (London, 1901).

[44] Ellen Churchill Semple: *Influences of Geographic Environment* (New York, 1911).

[45] Semple, op. cit. Gregory, on the other hand, sees the German colonists settled in southern Brazil since 1847 as proving the acclimatability of Europeans in the tropics. (J. W. Gregory, op. cit.) On this general subject, see A. G. Price: *White Settlers in the Tropics* (New York, 1939).

[46] Donald Pierson (op. cit., p. 113): "Even the church came to recognize *de juras* marriage, if consummated by sexual intercourse." Freyre, later on, has something to say of these *de juras* ceremonies. On the general attitude of the Church and the Jesuits, see Pierson, pp. 115, 117–18. (Translator.)

pansion; as she sees it, down to this day European and Anglo-American colonization of the tropics has been a matter of economic exploitation or political domination: [47] colonization of the type represented by the 76,000 Englishmen who with gloved hands, so to speak, and preserved from more intimate contact with the natives by the prophylactic of the bottle, direct the commercial and political affairs of India. But Semple makes an exception in the case of the Portuguese, who through hybridization [48] really succeeded in colonizing Brazil, overcoming, in doing so, the adverse conditions of climate.

Although no one any longer looks upon climate as the almighty being of old, it is impossible to deny the influence that it exerts upon the formation and development of societies: if not a direct influence, through its immediate effects upon man, an indirect one through its relation to the productivity of the earth, the sources of nutrition, and the means of economic exploitation available to the settler.

The so-called "tropical diseases" are now half-discredited; yet it cannot be denied that climate *per se*, through social or economic factors conditioned by it, predisposes the inhabitants of hot countries to diseases that are unknown or rare in countries with a cold climate,[49]

---

[47] Semple, op. cit.

[48] Ibid.

[49] The ancients believed that diseases came from "miasmas" or "winds"—a belief that is prolonged in the form of an indiscriminate attribution of "tropical diseases" to the effects of climate. There is no doubt that, indirectly, various diseases are associated with climatic conditions—malaria, among others. To quote the generalization of Professor Carl Kelsey in his book *The Physical Basis of Society* (New York and London, 1928): "bacterial diseases are likely to be more numerous in the warmer and moister regions of the earth and to be least in evidence in high mountain countries and polar regions." Dalgado (op. cit.), in studying the effects of climate upon the Portuguese population, establishes the fact that in the hot region (the south) diarrhea, enteritis, etc., are common, the higher disease-rate in this region than in the north corresponding to the general results obtained by Adolphe Quetelet (*Physique sociale*, Brussels, 1869) in his investigation of conditions in northern as compared with southern Europe. Recognizing the pathologic influence of a hot climate, as shown by the statistics of disease, crime, and suicide and those relative to economic efficiency and labor capacity (see E. Huntington: *Civilization and Climate;* Huntington and Williams: *Business Geography;* Robert de Courcy Ward: *Climate Considered Especially in Relation to Man*, New York, 1908; and Edwin Grant Dexter: *Weather Influences*, New York, 1904)—recognizing all this, such influences still should not be exaggerated, as is the tendency with those who would confuse the effect of climate *per se* with social and economic causes, such as poverty, want, ignorance, syphilis, and inefficient sanitary protection. Sanitary protection not only so far as man is concerned (against germs that attack him directly), but protection, as well, of the animal and vegetable sources of nutrition and man's drinking-water. Semple insists (op. cit.) that we rigorously discriminate

that it diminishes their capacity for labor,[50] and excites to crimes against the person.[51] Similarly it would appear to be demonstrated that some races show more resistance than others to those pathogenic influences that, in character or intensity, are peculiar to the climate of the tropics.[52]

The importance of climate is being reduced as those elements that are in some degree susceptible to the domination or modifying influence of man are dissociated from it. It would appear to have been demonstrated by recent experiments that it is possible for us to modify the nature of certain soils through drainage, thus influencing the sources of atmospheric humidity; to alter the temperature through the irrigation of parched lands; to break the force of winds or change their direction by huge masses of trees conveniently planted. This is not to speak of the victories that are being achieved, one after another, over "tropical diseases," which are being tamed when not subjugated by hygiene and sanitary engineering.

Man, in short, is no longer the plaything of climate that he once was. His capacity for labor, his economic efficiency, his metabolism

---

between the direct and the indirect effects of climate, between the transient and the permanent effects, between the physiologic and the psychologic ones. As she sees it, a number of the supposed direct effects are as yet imperfectly established. Meanwhile she recognizes the fact that climate does modify many of the physiological processes in individuals, affecting their immunity to certain diseases, their susceptibility to others, their energy, their capacity for sustained or intermittent effort, determining thereby their efficiency as economic and political agents. In general, see the conclusions of Julius Hann: *Handbuch der Klimatologie* (Stuttgart, 1897); of E. Huntington: *Civilization and Climate;* of Griffith Taylor: *Environment and Race;* of Robert de Courcy Ward: *Climate Considered Especially in Relation to Man;* of M. R. Thorpe and collaborators: *Organic Adaptation to Environment* (New York, 1918); of Jean Brunhes: *La Géographie humaine* (Paris, 1912); of Robert Russel: *At-mosphere in Relation to Human Life and Health* (Smithsonian Institution, *Miscellaneous Collection,* Vol. XXXIX. For climate and its influence on Brazilian life, see the *Bibliografia do Clima Brasílico* (*Bibliography of Works on the Brazilian Climate*), by Tancredo de Barros Paiva (Rio de Janeiro, 1929), where the principal Brazilian and foreign works on the subject are indicated.

[50] Huntington and Williams, op. cit.

[51] Dexter, op. cit. The influence of a hot climate or high temperature on crimes against the person is generally accepted, but a doubt was recently raised by Professor Todd, who attributes such crimes to the greater contact between individuals that is permitted by such climates or temperatures. The direct cause, he says, is social.

[52] ". . . diseases attack some races more than others. Whether this is due to some original quality of the body or to some immunity acquired by long contact with the disease involved is disputed." (Kelsey, op. cit.)

undergo less of a change where hygiene and sanitation, diet, and the adaptation of clothing and habitation to new circumstances create for him conditions of life that are in accord with his physical surroundings and the temperature of the region. The very systems of modern communication—easy, rapid, and hygienic—change the aspect of what was until now a most important problem, bound up with physical conditions of soil and climate: namely, the quality and to a certain extent the quantity of the means of alimentation at the disposal of any people. Ward stresses the importance of the development of steam navigation, more rapid and regular than that by sailing-ships, and he sees the tropical populations benefiting greatly from this.[53] The same may be said of the processes of preserving and refrigerating foodstuffs. By means of these processes and the modern technique of transportation man is triumphing over that absolute dependence upon regional sources of nutrition to which colonial populations in the tropics were formerly subject.

In this essay, however, climate is to be looked upon as the rude and practically all-powerful agent that it was for the Portuguese in 1500: an irregular, swampy climate, leading to disturbances of the digestive tract; a climate that, in its relation to the soil, was unfavorable to agriculture, especially of the European variety, since it permitted neither a traditional form of labor regulated by the four seasons of the year nor the profitable cultivation of those alimentary plants to which the European had been accustomed for so many centuries.[54]

The Portuguese colonist in Brazil had to alter quite radically his system of alimentation, whose base now had to be changed, with a perceptible deficit, from wheat to manihot flour; and this was true also of his system of labor, which, in view of the physical and chemical conditions of the soil, as well as the meteorological conditions, could not be the same as the easy-going mode of tillage in the Portuguese homeland. In this respect the English colonizer in the United States had a decided advantage over the Portuguese in Brazil, for the former in America met with physical conditions of life and sources of nutrition similar to those in the mother country. In Brazil there was necessarily a certain lack of balance that affected the morphology as well as the efficiency of the European, owing to the lack, immedi-

---

[53] Ward, op. cit.
[54] The first letters written by the Jesuits speak of processions motivated by droughts or floods. Father Manuel de Nobrega refers to one in which the people came out "beseeching rain, by reason of the great drought that there was, as a result of which the means of subsistence dried up."— *Cartas do Brasil (Letters from Brazil),* 1549–60 (Rio de Janeiro, 1931), p. 182.

ately felt, of those chemical means of alimentation that he had known
in his own country. This lack, along with the difference in the
meteorological and geological conditions under which agricultural
labor, performed by Negroes but directed by him, had to be performed, gave to the colonizing activities of the Portuguese an original,
creative character such as neither the English in North America nor
the Spaniards in Argentina could claim for their efforts.[55]

Although the Portuguese came nearer than any other European
colonizer of the Americas to being familiar with the climate and conditions of the tropics, it was, all the same, a rude change that he underwent in removing to Brazil. Within the new circumstances of
his physical life he found his economic and social life also compromised.

Everything here in this new land was in a state of disequilibrium,
marked by great excesses and great deficiencies. The soil, leaving aside
certain patches of black or reddish earth of exceptional fertility, was
far from being suited to the planting of everything one might desire,
as the earliest chronicler had pictured it in his enthusiasm. Rugged, in-
tractable, impermeable, it was in good part rebellious to the discipline
of agriculture. The rivers were another enemy of regularized agricultural effort and a stable family life. Death-dealing floods and
sterilizing droughts—that was what the waters brought with them.
And in addition to the land and jungles that were so difficult to cultivate, in addition to the rivers which it was impossible to utilize for
the purposes of an agricultural or industrial economy or even for the
regular transport of products—in addition to all this, there were the
swarms of larvæ, the multitude of insects and worms, harmful to man.
Especially to the one engaged in agriculture, who, the moment he
began setting out his plantations, was afflicted on all sides by "ants
that do much damage" (to his crops) and by the "caterpillar of the
fields"—curses that the Indian witch-doctors defied the padres to
exorcise with their prayers and the ringing of their bells.[56]

Contrast these conditions with those that the English found in

---

[55] Alberto Torres had already observed, in *O Problema Nacional
Brasileiro* (*The Brazilian National
Problem*) (Rio de Janeiro, 1914), that
"The United States and, in good part,
Argentina as well are lands similar to,
if not identical with, those that the
European colonizers had inhabited. In
climate and the nature of the soil they
do not differ from the mother country. . . . Colonization is merely a
change of dwelling, from an old house
to a new one." Professor Konrad
Günther in a recent book, *Das Antlitz
Brasiliens* (Leipzig, 1927), stresses the
similarity between the vegetation of
North America and that of Europe.

[56] See the correspondence of Father
Nobrega, *Cartas do Brasil* (1549–60).

North America. To begin with the temperature: it was substantially the same as in western Europe (a year-round average of 56 degrees Fahrenheit), a temperature considered the most favorable for economic progress and a European type of civilization. For this reason the generalizations of Professor Bogart concerning what he vaguely refers to as the "Latin-American race" do not appear to fit the case as regards Brazil. According to this economist, the people in question, even though surrounded by great "natural resources," were incapable of attaining the same conditions of agricultural and industrial progress as the Anglo-Americans, and this incapacity he attributes to their being "a weak ease-loving race" and not "a virile, energetic people" like the North Americans, who "devoted themselves to the exploitation of the natural resources with wonderful success." [57] Yet these latter were the same stock, so virile and energetic, that had come to grief in Old Providence and in the Bahamas.

The Portuguese colonist found in tropical America a land that apparently offered an easy way of life; but it was in truth a most difficult life for one who wanted to organize there some permanent or advanced form of economy or of society. If it be true that in hot countries man can live without effort off the spontaneous abundance of products, it must not be forgotten on the other hand that in these countries the pernicious forms of animal and vegetable life, the enemies of all organized agriculture and of all systematic and regular labor, are to be found in equal luxuriance. Man and the seed that he plants, the houses that he builds, the animals that he breeds for his use or subsistence, the archives and libraries that he founds for his intellectual culture, the useful or beautiful products that he fashions with his hands—all this is at the mercy of the larvæ, worms, and insects, gnawing, boring, corrupting. Grain, fruit, wood, paper, flesh, muscles, lymphatic glands, intestines, the white of the eyes, the toes of the feet, all are a prey to these terrible enemies.

It was under physical conditions so adverse as these that the civilizing activities of the Portuguese were carried on in the tropics. Had those conditions been the mild and easy ones of which the panegyrists of our landscape speak, then, in contrasting the difficult triumph of the Lusitanian in Brazil with the rapid and sensational success of the English in that part of America which enjoys a stimulating climate, a balanced flora, and a fauna that is an aid to man rather than his enemy, along with favorable agrological and geological conditions—

---

[57] Ernest Ludlow Bogart: *The Economic History of the United States* (New York, 1913).

in making such a contrast the sociologists and economists would be right in concluding that the fair-featured colonizer was superior to the brown-skinned one.

Before the Portuguese succeeded in colonizing Brazil, Europeans were familiar with no other type of domination in tropical regions than that represented by the commercial exploitation of large-scale plantations or the simple extraction of mineral wealth. In no case did they seriously consider the extension of the European way of life or the adaptation of its material and moral values to an environment and climate so diverse, so enervating and dissolvent in its effects. The Portuguese in Brazil was the first among modern colonizers to shift the basis of such activity in the tropics from the mere extraction of mineral, vegetable, or animal wealth—gold, silver, wood, amber, ivory —to the creation of wealth upon the scene, a wealth created, under the pressure of circumstances in America, at the expense of slave labor and bearing the mark of that perversion of the economic instinct which quickly distracts the Portuguese from the activity of producing values to that of exploiting, transporting, and acquiring them.

A similar shift, although imperfectly carried out, was to lead to a new phase and a new type of colonization: the "plantation settlement," based upon agriculture and with the colonist remaining permanently upon the land, in place of a mere chance contact on his part with the environment and the native folk. It was in Brazil that the Portuguese began a large-scale colonization of the tropics by means of an economic technique and a social policy that were entirely new, having been no more than foreshadowed in the subtropical islands of the Atlantic. The technique consisted in the utilization and development of vegetable resources through private capital and initiative: agriculture, the parceling out of land, and large-scale farming with slave labor. The social policy consisted in the utilization of the natives, chiefly the women, not merely as instruments of labor but as elements in the formation of the family. Such a policy was quite different from that of extermination or segregation followed for so long in Mexico and Peru by the Spanish exploiters of the mines, and, in a loose way, by the English in North America.

Colonial society in Brazil, principally in Pernambuco and in the Reconcavo of Bahia, evolved patriarchally and aristocratically, not at random and in unstable groups, but in the shadow of the great sugar plantations; in Big Houses built of clay or of stone and mortar, and not in the thatched huts of adventurers. Oliveira Martins observes that the colonial population in Brazil, "especially in the north, was aristocratically constituted; that is to say, the Portuguese houses (families) sent branches overseas, and from the very beginning the colony presented an aspect that was quite different from the scene created by the turbulent Spanish immigrants in central and western America." [58] And Southey previously had told us that in the plantation houses of Pernambuco, in the first centuries of colonization, were to be found refinements and comfort such as one would have looked for in vain among the populations of Paraguay and the River Plata region. [59]

In Brazil, as in the tobacco-, cotton-, and rice-growing colonies of North America, the big plantations were the result not of a colonizing effort on the part of the State, which in Portugal was always niggardly in this respect, but of courageous private initiative. It is to such initiative, on the part of such individuals as Martim Affonso in the south and, above all, Duarte Coelho in the north, [60] that we owe the first substantial colonists, the first mothers of families, the first sowings, the first herds, the first transport animals, alimentary plants, agricultural implements, Jewish mechanics for the sugar factories, and African slaves for the labor of the *bagaceira* and other work (for which the indolent and undependable natives had demonstrated their incapacity). It was private initiative that, in connection with the allotments, held itself in readiness when the need arose to defend with military means the many leagues of uncultivated land that Negro labor was to render fertile. As Payne points out in his *History of European Colonies*, the Portuguese in Brazil were the first Europeans really to settle in colonies, and with this end in view they sold what-

---

[58] Oliveira Martins, op. cit.

[59] Robert Southey: *History of Brazil*.

[60] It was in the south, where, for that matter, colonists of the type of Ramalho and the Bachelor of Cananéia were already flourishing by their own unaided efforts, with a large mestizo progeny and hundreds of slaves in their service—it was there that the colony of São Vicente was officially founded, in 1532, at the expense of the crown (as later at Bahia), "which bore all the expenses of the fleet and the installation, contrary to what happened in the other *capitânias*, where colonization was accomplished wholly at the expense of the proprietors." —C. Malheiro Dias on "The Feudal Regime of the Proprietors Prior to the Institution of a Governor-General," in *História da Colonização Portuguesa do Brasil* (*History of the Portuguese Colonization of Brazil*), Vol. III. It was in Pernambuco that, in the first century of colonization, the spirit of private initiative, depending upon the individual effort of the inhabitants, shone most brilliantly, which leads to the belief that these were economically the most capable of the Portuguese who came to Brazil in the sixteenth century. They were a people endowed with greater resources and a greater aptitude for the task of agrarian colonization.

ever they possessed in the land of their origin, transporting their families and their fortunes to the tropics.[61]

Leroy-Beaulieu [62] believes that one of the advantages that Portuguese colonists in tropical America enjoyed, at least during the first two centuries, was "the complete absence of a regular and complicated system of administration" and that "freedom of action" (*"la liberté d'action que l'on trouvait dans ce pays peu gouverné"*) which was characteristic of Brazilian life in its beginnings. *"L'organisation coloniale ne précède pas, elle suivit le développement de la colonisation,"* the French economist observes in his study of modern colonization.

And Ruediger Bilden remarks, with admirable critical sense, that in Brazil it was private colonizing effort to a far greater extent than official action that promoted the mixture of races, a latifundiary agriculture, and slavery, thereby rendering possible, upon such bases, the founding and development of a large and stable agricultural colony in the tropics. This in addition to the fact that it greatly enlarged our territory to the west, something that officialdom would have been incapable of accomplishing, beset as it was by the compromises of international politics.[63]

From 1532 on, Portuguese colonization in Brazil, like that of the English in North America and unlike that of the Spanish and the French in both the Americas, was marked by the almost exclusive domination of the rural or semi-rural family, a domination that only the Church could challenge, through the activity—at times hostile to that of the family—of the fathers of the Society of Jesus.

The family and not the individual, much less the State or any commercial company, was from the sixteenth century the great colonizing factor in Brazil, the productive unit, the capital that cleared the land, founded plantations, purchased slaves, oxen, implements; and in politics it was the social force that set itself up as the

---

[61] J. Payne: *History of European Colonies* (London, 1878).

[62] Paul Leroy-Beaulieu: *De la colonisation chez les peuples modernes* (Paris, 1891). On this subject I may mention here a basic work that was recommended to me by Professor Leo Waibel, a colleague at the summer school of the University of Michigan, in 1939: Georg Friederici's *Die europäische Eroberung und Kolonisation Americas* (Vol. I, Stuttgart, 1930; Vols. II and III, Stuttgart, 1937).

[63] Reference here is to a forthcoming book of Bilden's on the economic and social development of Brazil, the manuscript of which I have been permitted to read. Sérgio Buarque de Hollanda is preparing an interesting paper on Brazilian expansion to the west. On this subject see *Marcha para Oeste* (*Westward March*), by Cassiano Ricardo (Rio de Janeiro, 1939).

most powerful colonial aristocracy in the Americas. Over it the King of Portugal may be said, practically, to have reigned without ruling. The representatives in the municipal council, the political expression of these families, quickly limited the power of the kings and later that of imperialism itself, or, better, the economic parasitism that sought to extend its absorbing tentacles from the Kingdom to the colonies.

Colonization through soldiers of fortune, adventurers, exiles, "new-Christians" fleeing religious persecution, shipwreck victims, slave-dealers, and traffickers in parrots and lumber left practically no trace on the economic life of Brazil. This irregular and haphazard mode of settling the land was so superficial and lasted so short a while that politically and economically it never reached the point of becoming a clearly defined system of colonization. Its purely genetic aspect, on the other hand, should not be lost sight of by the historian of Brazilian society. From this point of view, there are those who look upon it as an "initial ethnic flaw" and who discover "among the features of the Brazilian people's collective physiognomy the traces of hereditary stigmata left there by those patriarchs who have little to commend them from the standpoint of nationality." It is Azevedo Amaral who makes this observation, and I am willing to accept two generalizations of his regarding the period under discussion: first, that this period, by reason of its "racial heterogeneity," was not a Portuguese but a promiscuous one, the Portuguese imprint having been left upon the prevalent ethnic confusion merely because of the predominance of the language; and, second, that the period constituted a species of "prehistoric epoch for the nation." "To eliminate," says this author, "the first fifty years during which, without any political supervision whatsoever and even beyond the bounds of civilization, Brazil received the first complex alluvia of settlers—to do this would be equivalent to suppressing a basic element in the shaping of our national life, one whose influence, as projected down the centuries following, we may safely infer from those positive facts which modern biological research has sufficiently demonstrated. If we like, we may put this period in a category by itself, as a prehistoric epoch in the life of our nation." [64]

Where Azevedo Amaral appears to me to be guilty of a lamentable exaggeration (seeing that he admits that "the available information . . . is so scant and so precarious") is in viewing all these settlers as a lot of "degenerates, criminals, and semi-madmen." [65] He is referring

---

[64] Azevedo Amaral: *Ensaios Brasileiros* (*Brazilian Essays*) (Rio de Janeiro, 1930).   [65] Ibid.

chiefly to the exiles; but, on the other hand, there is no good reason to doubt that many of them had been banished upon the flimsiest of excuses, for in those days some of the best subjects in the realm were thus sent out to the wilderness. The standards that in the fifteenth and sixteenth centuries still guided the Portuguese in their criminal jurisprudence were exceedingly strict ones. In their penal law mysticism, still aflame from the war against the Moors, gave a disproportionate aspect to offenses. C. Malheiro Dias asserts that "there did not exist in contemporary legislation a code that was comparable in severity to Book V of the Statutes of Emanuel," and he adds that "according to its provisions, around two hundred offenses were to be punished with banishment." [66]

General Morais Sarmento tells us that the law of Dom Diniz, of January 7, 1453, "decreed that those who disbelieved in God or who offered an affront to God or to the saints should have their tongues drawn from their throats and be burned alive"; while for the employment of witchcraft "that one person might love or hate another," [67] as for other mystic or imaginary crimes, the Portuguese subject in the sixteenth and seventeenth centuries was to be "banished forever to Brazil." [68] For in a country whose formative background was religious rather than ethnocentric, these were high crimes, and the criminological perspective was quite different from the modern one and from that in countries whose background was less religious in character. In the meanwhile whoever offered an affront to the saints had his tongue drawn from his throat and whoever engaged in amorous witchcraft was banished to the wilds of Africa or America; whereas for the crime of killing his neighbor, dishonoring a woman, or defiling his daughter the delinquent frequently was liable to no penalty more severe than that of "paying a fine of one hen" or of "paying fifteen hundred bushels." [69] And there was always the possibility of fleeing to one of the numerous "cities of refuge."

These places made no mystery of their function, which was that of protecting homicides, adulterers, and fugitive servants; they even proclaimed it openly. "Let it not be thought," says Gama Barros, "that those lands where the sovereign had decreed that criminals might enjoy immunity felt themselves dishonored by the granting of

[66] *História da Colonização Portuguesa do Brasil*, Introduction, Vol. III, p. 315.

[67] Morais Sarmento: *D. Pedro l e sua Epoca* (*Dom Pedro l and His Epoch*) (Porto, 1924).

[68] *Ordenações Filipinas* (*Decrees of Philip*), Book V, tit. III.

[69] Mendes Corrêa: *A Nova Antropologia Criminal* (*The New Criminal Anthropology*) (Porto, 1931).

such a privilege." [70] And Professor Mendes Corrêa informs us that Sabugal in 1369 petitioned that "more guarantees be given the refugees in this city," while in Azurara "immunity was carried to the point where a grave punishment was meted out to those who had pursued the fugitive criminal within the bounds of the city." [71] One gets the impression that the underpopulated portions of the realm disputed for the granting of the privilege, and that those who found refuge in these havens, along with the large number of fugitive servants, were individuals guilty of the crimes of murder and of rape, while those who came to Brazil were, rather, the ones charged with slight or imaginary misdemeanors that the Portuguese, with the criminological outlook of their era, had distorted into heinous offenses equal to those of the real criminals. These latter, however, must have come to the American colony in numbers that were by no means insignificant; or otherwise the landed proprietor Duarte Coelho would not have been so vehemently concerned with them as he is in one of the many letters that he wrote in his role of stern and scrupulous administrator—a letter in which he beseeches His Majesty not to send him any more such exiles as these, because they are worse than poison. [72]

It is possible that, with the genetic interests of the population in view, certain individuals were deliberately sent to Brazil whom we know to have been expatriated for irregularities or excesses in their sexual life: for hugging and kissing, for employing witchcraft to induce love or hatred, for bestiality, effeminacy, procuring, and the like. [73] To the wilderness, so underpopulated, with a bare sprinkling of whites, came these oversexed ones, there to give extraordinarily free rein to their passions; and the results, it may be, were advantageous to the interests of Portugal in Brazil. Attracted by the possibilities of a free and untrammeled life, with a host of nude women all around them, many Europeans of the type that Paulo Prado has described for us with such forceful realism [74] proceeded to settle here out of predilection or of their own free will. Unbridled stallions is what they were. Others, like the cabin-boys that fled Cabral's

---

[70] Gama Barros, op. cit., II.

[71] Mendes Corrêa, op. cit. In the study by this distinguished anthropologist other privileged cities of refuge are cited: Monforte de Rio Livre, Segura, Nondal, Marvão, Miranda, Penha, and Caminha, which was a "city of maritime fugitives."

[72] Letter of Duarte Coelho to His Majesty, *História da Colonização Portuguesa do Brasil.*

[73] *Jornal de Timon* (*Log Book*), in the *Works* (*Obras*) of João Francisco Lisboa, edited by Luiz Carlos Pereira de Castro and Dr. A. Henriques Leal (São Luiz de Maranhão, 1864).

[74] Paulo Prado: *Retrato do Brasil* (*Portrait of Brazil*) (São Paulo, 1928).

fleet, going up into the jungles, may have remained there out of a taste for adventure or "youthful audacity." [75] And the unions that many of these exiles entered into—unions of Norman "interpreters," shipwrecked mariners, and new-Christians, Europeans all of them, in the prime of life and the best of health, young and full of masculine vigor, "adventurous and ardent youths, brimming with strength" [76] —the unions that they formed with native women, who were possibly equally clean and physically wholesome, need not always have belonged to the category of those "unhygienic matings" of which Azevedo Amaral speaks. Quite the contrary. Such unions may have served as a "true process of sexual selection" [77] if one takes into account the liberty that the European had of choosing a mate from among dozens of Indian women. Sexual intercourse under such conditions could only have resulted in good healthy animals, even though bad Christians or individuals of unprepossessing character.

To the advantages already pointed out that the Portuguese of the fifteenth century enjoyed over contemporary peoples who were also engaged in colonizing activity may be added their sexual morality, which was Mozarabic in character: Catholic morality rendered supple by contact with the Mohammedan, and more easy-going, more relaxed, than among the northern peoples. Nor was their religion the hard and rigid system of the Reformed countries of the north, or even the dramatic Catholicism of Castile itself; theirs was a liturgy social rather than religious, a softened, lyric Christianity with many phallic and animistic reminiscences of the pagan cults. The only thing that was lacking was for the saints and angels to take on fleshly form and step down from the altars on feast-days to disport themselves with the populace. As it was, one might have seen oxen entering the churches to be blessed by the priests; mothers lulling their little ones with the same hymns of praise that were addressed to the Infant Jesus; sterile women with upraised petticoats rubbing themselves against the legs of São Gonçalo do Amarante; married men, fearful of infidelity on the part of their wives, going to interrogate the "cuckold rocks," while marriageable young girls addressed themselves to the "marriage rocks"; and finally our Lady of Expectancy [78] being worshipped in the guise of a pregnant woman.

In the case of Brazil (we are here dealing with a seventeenth-century phenomenon), the Portuguese colonizer had in his and the

---

[75] Ibid.
[76] Ibid.
[77] Roy Nash: *The Conquest of Brazil.*

[78] "*Nossa Senhora do Ó.*" A feast that was celebrated in Portugal in honor of the Virgin's expectation of her delivery. (Translator.)

colony's favor all the wealth and the extraordinary variety of experiences that had been accumulated during the fifteenth century, in Asia and in Africa, in Madeira and in Cape Verde, among these experiences being a knowledge of useful plants, good to eat and pleasing to the palate, which were to be successfully transplanted to Brazil; certain advantages of the Asiatic mode of building that were adaptable to the American tropics; and the ascertained capacity of the Negro for agricultural labor.

All of these elements, beginning with a Christianity that was lyrically social, a cult of the family rather than a religion of the church or cathedral—and the Portuguese, incidentally, never erected great and dominant church edifices of the type to be found at Toledo or at Burgos, just as in Brazil such structures were never to attain the importance and prestige that they had in Spanish America—all these elements and advantages, to repeat, were to favor a colonization that in Portuguese America, as in the "proprietary colonies" of the English in North America, was to rest upon the institution of the slave-holding family, the Big House, the patriarchal family, the only difference being that in our country the family was to be enlarged by a far greater number of bastards and dependents, gathered round the patriarchs, who were more given to women and possibly a little more loose in their sexual code than the North Americans were.

The true formative process of our society, as has been said, is to be viewed from 1532 on, with the rural or semi-rural family as the unit, whether it was a matter of married couples who had come from the homeland or of families that had been set up here through the union of colonists with Indian women, with orphan girls, or even with women whom matchmaking fathers had sent over at random from Portugal.

The lively and absorbing organ for the formation of Brazilian society, the colonial family, upon the economic base of agricultural wealth and slave labor combined a variety of social and economic functions, including one at which I have already hinted: political command, in the form of an oligarchy or nepotism that made its appearance early here and that already in the middle of the sixteenth century is to be seen clashing with the clericalism of the Society of Jesus.[79] In opposition to the interests of colonial society in Brazil,

---

[79] Clericalism as represented by the priests of the Society was then colliding with the oligarchy that was forming in Pernambuco around the person of Duarte Coelho and that of his brother-in-law the patriarch Jeronymo de Albuquerque. It similarly came into collision with the patriarchalism of Ramalho.

the priests of this order wished to found a holy republic of "Indians domesticated by Jesus," like those of Paraguay: seraphic *caboclos* obedient only to the ministers of the Lord and laboring only in His gardens and plantations, with no individuality and without any autonomy, either personal or of the family, all of them with the exception of the chief being clad in garments that resembled an infant's nightgown in an orphan-asylum or boarding-school, with the men indistinguishable, so far as their raiment was concerned, from the women and children.

It was owing to the presence of so strong and weighty an element as the rural or, better, the big landowning family that Portuguese colonization in Brazil very quickly took on social aspects quite different from the theocracy idealized by the Jesuits—and later realized by them in Paraguay—one like that of the Spaniards and the French. It is obvious that the family would not have been able to assert itself in this fashion if colonization with us, as with the English in Virginia and the Carolinas, had not rested upon an agricultural base. "Established in the islands of the Atlantic," says Manuel Bomfim, in speaking of the Portuguese colonist, "and not finding there any form of activity or possibility of acquiring wealth other than the steady exploitation and regular settlement of the land, he proceeded to accomplish these tasks and in doing so proved to be an excellent colonizer, better than any other people in medieval Europe, inasmuch as to the qualities of the pioneer he added those of one who founds a regular and agricultural mode of life in lands that are new." [80]

The truth of the matter is that many of the colonists who here became big rural proprietors had no love for the land and no taste for its cultivation. For centuries in Portugal a bourgeois and Semitic mercantilism on the one hand and, on the other, Moorish slavery followed by Negro slavery had turned an ancient people of husbandmen-kings into the most commercial and least rural of any in Europe. In the sixteenth century the king himself gives audience not in any Gothic castle surrounded by pine groves, but from his warehouses on the river bank; for both he and every great lord of the realm were enriching themselves by the trade in Asiatic spices. All that was left of a rural way of life for the Portuguese of that century was an easygoing horticulture and a mild and pastoral existence; for with them, as with the Israelites before them, it was the culture of the olive and the vine alone that flourished. Curious, therefore, that the success of

---

[80] Manuel Bomfim: *O Brasil na América* (*Brazil in the Americas*) (Rio de Janeiro, 1929).

their colonizing effort in Brazil should have been based precisely upon agriculture.

Taking the Portuguese colonizers in the mass and leaving aside the exceptional cases like that of Duarte Coelho—the perfect type of large-scale agriculturist—it may be said that the rural mode of life in Brazil was not spontaneous with them, but was forced upon them by circumstances; it was something to which they had to become used. The ideal for them would have been not a plantation colony, but another India, with which they might, in the manner of the Israelites, carry on a trade in spices and precious stones; or a Mexico or Peru, from which they might extract gold and silver. A Semitic ideal. It was circumstances in America that made of this colonizing people who were the least rural of any in their tendencies, or whose agrarian direction, in any case, had been perverted by mercantilism, the most rural of all in the end; the same people that India had transformed into the most parasitic now became the most creative.

Under such circumstances as these the quality and physical conditions of the land and the material and moral conditions attendant upon the life and culture of its inhabitants become exceedingly important.

Both the earth and man were in a crude state, and their lack of cultivation did not afford the Portuguese an advantageous opportunity for commercial intercourse of a kind that would supplement or extend that which they maintained with the Orient. The discoverers of Brazil encountered neither kings of Kananor (Cananore) nor chieftains of Sofala with whom they might trade and barter. Nothing but *"murubixabas,"* *"bugres."* [81] Savages, wild men, running about naked, sleeping here and there, in hammocks or on the ground, and feeding on manihot flour, jungle fruit, and game or fish, devoured raw or roasted in the embers of a fire. On their hands gleamed no pearls of Cipango nor rubies of Pegú; neither the gold of Sumatra nor the silks of Kata embellished their copper-colored bodies, however bedecked with feathers they might be, and in place of Persian rugs their feet trod the uncarpeted sands. They possessed no domestic animal to serve them, and their agriculture consisted merely of a few

---

[81] The *murubixaba* (*morubixaba*) was the temporal chief of an Indian tribe, while the *pajé*, or, in general, medicine-man (discussed later in Chapter ii; see p. 110, 119), was the spiritual leader. *Bugre* is our "bug-ger," and is explained by the belief that the Portuguese came to acquire that all Indians were addicted to sodomy (see Chapter ii, p. 124 f.). (Translator.)

scattered plantations of manihot or *midubi* (peanuts) [82] or some fruit or other. Viana is right when he observes that between the Indies, "with a marvelous accumulation of wealth and a long tradition of trade with the peoples of the Orient and the Occident," and Brazil, "with a population of aborigines still in the polished stone age," there was an essential difference. "This absence of organized wealth, this lack of a base for the permanent organization of trade," adds the author of *Evolution of the Brazilian People*,[83] "is the thing that led the men of the peninsula, transplanted here, to devote themselves to agricultural exploitation."

Cloves, pepper, amber, sandalwood, cinnamon, ginger, ivory—none of these nor any vegetable or animal substance whatsoever of recognized value in satisfying the needs and tastes of aristocratic or bourgeois Europe did the Portuguese find in the American tropics. This is not to speak of gold and silver, more sought after than anything else, and which as yet eluded the explorers of the new land. The melancholy conclusion of Vespucci sums up the bitter disappointment that they all felt: "an infinite number of brazilwood trees and pipe-reeds. . . ."[84] "Groves everywhere" and "many waters," notes the astute chronicler of the discovery, Pero Vaz de Caminha.[85]

Enormous masses of water, that is certain, conferred a grandeur upon this land covered with dense jungles. They gave it drama. But it was a grandeur without economic possibilities suited to the technique and the knowledge of the age. On the contrary, so far as the needs of the men who created Brazil were concerned, these formidable masses of rivers and waterfalls only in part, never wholly, lent themselves to the civilizing functions of regular communication and utilization for purposes of power. When one of these great rivers overflowed its banks in the rainy season, it would inundate everything, covering cane fields and killing cattle and even the inhabitants. It brought destruction and devastation. Agriculture and cattle-raising upon its banks were almost out of the question, for if it was easy to initiate such an undertaking, destruction by the flood-waters

---

[82] *Midubi* is the *amendoim* (peanut), a plant of the *Leguminosæ* family. (*Arachnis hipogæa Lin.*) (Translator.)

[83] *Evolução do Povo Brasileiro* (Rio de Janeiro, 1929).

[84] Letter of Amerigo Vespucci, cited by Capistrano de Abreu: *O Descobrimento do Brasil* (*The Discovery of Brazil*) (Rio de Janeiro).

[85] ". . . a land . . . very full of groves of trees everywhere . . . waters . . . many and endless."—Letter of Pero (or Pedro) Vaz de Caminha, published by Manuel Ayres de Cazal: *Chorographia Brasilica* (*Brazilian Chorography*) (2nd edition, Rio de Janeiro, 1845), Vol. I, p. 10.

was sure to follow and herds would be decimated or their pasture-grounds ruined. In place of benefiting the plantations, therefore, these huge bodies of water destroyed them completely or in large part.

Without any balanced volume or regularity of course, varying extremely as to conditions of navigability and utility, the great rivers were undependable collaborators—if we may call them that—of the agriculturist engaged in shaping the economic and social life of our country. Agrarian Brazil owes much, on the other hand, to the lesser but more regular streams, where these submissively lent themselves to the work of grinding the cane, irrigating the river plains, bringing verdure to the fields, and transporting sugar, lumber, and, later, coffee to serve the interests and needs of the settled populations, human and animal, along their banks. Here it was that large-scale tillage flourished, a latifundiary agriculture prospered, and cattle-raising expanded. Rivers like the Mamanguape, the Una, the Pitanga, the Paranamirim, the Serinhaem, the Iguaçú, the Cotindiba, the Pirapama, the Ipojuca, the Mundaú, the Paraíba, neither running dry nor overflowing their banks, were valuable and regular collaborators in the organization of our agrarian economy and the slave-holding society that developed around it. Of the Paraíba Alberto Rangel writes that in the days of slave labor it was "the paradisiacal river, the Euphrates of the *senzalas*, with Taubaté for metropolis." [86] In brief, the more regular and balanced was the water supply afforded by the rivers and river sources, the richer was the rural life of our country, from the sixteenth to the nineteenth century, in the qualities and conditions that make for permanence.

If the great Brazilian rivers have been glorified by monuments and hymned in a celebrated poem to the Paulo Afonso Falls [87] (which to this day are of purely æsthetic, not to say scenographic, interest in our national life), the lesser streams that are so much more serviceable are surely deserving of a study that shall determine the important civilizing role they played in the formation of our society; for they are bound up with traditions of stability, whereas the others—more romantic, it may be, but not more Brazilian—are associated with traditions of mobility, dynamism, the backlands expansion of the *bandeirantes* and the padres, the search for gold, for slaves, and for souls for Our Lord Jesus Christ. The great rivers were, *par excel-*

[86] Alberto Rangel: *Rumos e Perspectivas* (*Directions and Perspectives*) (Rio de Janeiro, 1914).

[87] Castro Alves, the romantic and abolitionist poet of the mid-nine-teenth century—"the poet of the slaves," as he is known—has a famous poem entitled "Paulo Afonso Falls" ("*Cachoeira de Paulo Afonso*"). (Translator.)

lence, those of the *bandeirante* and the missionary, who in making their way up them had to overcome the difficulties presented by cataracts and by the irregular courses of these streams.[88] The small rivers, by contrast, belonged to the plantation-owner, to the rancher, and to the transport of the products of the land. The great ones dispersed the colonizer, the small ones kept him settled by rendering possible a sedentary life in the rural regions.

Having as a physical base the waters of the great rivers, even though these were strewn with waterfalls, the Brazilian continued to display the tendency manifested by the Portuguese colonist: to scatter out, in place of settling down in compact groups. The *bandeirante* in particular, from the end of the sixteenth century on, became a founder of sub-colonies. Though not the owner of the land on which he was born, but a mere colonial, he made himself master of the lands of others and exhibited in doing so an imperialist impulse that was as daring as it was precocious. With the *bandeirante* Brazil went through a process of self-colonization. Pedro Dantas had noted this constant in our history, represented by the tendency to spread out over the surface instead of evolving "in density and depth"[89] — the same dispersive tendency that was characteristic of Portuguese colonial expansion. In Brazil this tendency—coming from far back and possibly of Semitic origin[90]—was prolonged, and took the form

---

[88] On the role of the great rivers in Brazilian history, it may be of interest to compare Euclides da Cunha: *Os Sertões* (16th edition, Rio de Janeiro, 1942), p. 82 f.; for English version, see *Rebellion in the Backlands* (University of Chicago Press, 1944), p. 64 f. (Translator.)

[89] Pedro Dantas: *"Perspectivas"* ("Perspectives"), in *Revista Nova*, No. 4 (São Paulo, 1931).

[90] São Paulo was probably the nucleus of the Brazilian population with the largest strain of Semitic blood. The tentacles of the Holy Office had not reached as far as that, although they were already closing upon Bahia and Pernambuco, where all that was lacking was for the bonfires to be prepared. This circumstance Capistrano de Abreu, in the course of conversations (so we are informed by his intimate friend and constant companion Paulo Prado), was accustomed to attribute to the fact that São Paulo had become the preferred haven of new-Christians. "The fact is that no other populated locality in our colonial territory gave the immigrant Jew a better reception," writes Paulo Prado in *Paulística* (2nd edition, Rio de Janeiro, 1934). And he adds: "In São Paulo they were not persecuted by the formidable instrument of the Inquisition, which never reached as far as the southern *capitânia*." On the Israelitish infiltration into Brazil, read the essay by Solidonio Leite *fils*: *Os Judeus no Brasil* (*The Jews in Brazil*) (Rio de Janeiro, 1923). On this subject see also the all but unknown *Essai historique sur la colonie de Surinan . . . le tout rédigé sur des pièces authentiques y joustes & mis en ordre par les Régens & Représentans de ladite Nation Juive Portugaise*, published at Paramaribo in 1788, where we find it stated that "*ces*

of what impressed Alberto Torres as being our "passion for extending adventurous populations and capitalist enterprises . . . throughout the whole of our territory." A passion that, as he sees it, we should endeavor to offset by a "policy of conserving our natural resources, reclaiming devastated regions, and concentrating our populations in zones that are already open to cultivation, with man being trained to make the most of these regions, to cause them to bear fruit, and get their real worth out of them." [91] This is also precisely what Pedro Dantas would wish for present-day Brazil: "that our development might proceed in density and depth." Such, indeed, was the initial tendency of those same plantation-owners and *fazendeiros* [92] in agrarian Brazil whom Azevedo Amaral criticizes so severely in the pages of *Brazilian Essays.*[93]

If it is an established fact that the furious expansionist movement on the part of the *bandeirantes* won for us real treasures in the form of lands, it is likewise perfectly true that this ardent expansion compromised our economic health, not to say our political unity. Happily, these impulses to dispersion, with the accompanying dangers of differentiation and separatism, were opposed from the beginning of our colonial life by forces that were practically equal to them in aggressiveness and that neutralized them or mitigated their effects. To begin with, there were the physical features of the region, forming an *"ensemble naturel"* which Horace Say, a century or so ago, contrasted with that of Spanish America: *"Aucune limite ne s'élève pour séparer les diverses provinces les unes des autres et c'est là un avantage de plus que les possessions portugaises ont eu sur les possessions espagnoles en Amérique."* [94]

The same dispersive mobility that, from the sixteenth century on, divided us into Paulistas and Pernambucans, or Paulistas and Bahians, at the same time kept us in contact, and even in communion, with one another through the difficult but not for that reason infrequent means of intercommunication in colonial days. "Fluminenses [95] and Paulistas

---

Juifs donc recontrant au Brésil leurs frères . . . ceux de Brésil étoient la plupart des gens de condition & très versés dans le commerce & l'agriculture. . . ."

[91] Alberto Torres: *O Problema Nacional Brasileiro.* See also by the same author: *A Organização Nacional (National Organization)* (Rio de Janeiro, 1914).

[92] *Fazendeiro:* owner of a *fazenda,* a large estate, ranch, or plantation. (Translator.)

[93] Azevedo Amaral: *Ensaios Brasileiros.*

[94] Horace Say: *Histoire des relations commerciales entre la France et le Brésil* (Paris, 1839).

[95] The Fluminenses are the inhabitants of the Rio de Janeiro region. (Translator.)

went to fight at Bahia and Pernambuco, which were engaged in defending themselves against the Dutch," Manuel Bomfim reminds us,
apropos of Euclides da Cunha's assertion that this struggle against the
foreigner in the north was carried on with the southern peoples
"completely divorced" from it all.[96] It was, further, the Paulistas who
"answered the repeated calls from Bahia to help in the defense against
the Aimoré Indians, as well as against the Dutch, just as at Pernambuco they were called in to resolve the affair at Palmares."[97] Later
—and it is still Bomfim who is speaking—"Ceará came to the aid of
Piauí, which was still controlled by Portuguese troops, and together
the Piauienses and the Cearenses went to the assistance of Maranhão."[98] And it was in the same era that the Pernambucans brought
succor to the Bahians, helping the latter to achieve the victory of the
2nd of July.[99]

There were also the Jesuits, with their uniform system of education and morality and the influence which it exerted upon an organism that was still soft and plastic, without bones, one might say, as
our colonial society was in the sixteenth and seventeenth centuries.
As educators they helped to articulate what they themselves as cate-

[96] See *Os Sertões*, 16th edition, pp.
83–4; *Rebellion in the Backlands*, pp.
64–5. (Translator.)

[97] M. Bomfim: *O Brasil na História*
(*Brazil in History*) (Rio de Janeiro,
1931).
[Palmares was the famous republic
set up by runaway slaves in the seventeenth century, which lasted sixty-
seven years (1630–97). (Translator.)]

[98] In contradicting Euclides da
Cunha's assertion, Bomfim bases his
own point of view up the São Paulo
documents (wills, inventories, allotments) among the great and valuable
mass of material that was published
at the instigation of Brazil's former
President, from the state of São Paulo,
Washington Luis—material of which
Professor Alcantara Machado made
use in organizing his interesting book
Vida e Morte do Bandeirante (*Life
and Death of the Bandeirante*) (São
Paulo, 1930), as did Affonso Taunay
in his definitive study of the *bandeiras*.
Pernambucan documents recently examined by me in the manuscript
section of the State Public Library

and in the collection of the Historical
and Archæological Institute of Pernambuco confirm M. Bomfim in the
stand he takes. I am referring to the
books of allotments, where grants of
Pernambucan and São Paulo lands
will be found registered in return for
collaboration in "campaigns against
the Negro uprising in Palmares."
There were the cases of João Paes de
Mendonça Arraide and his father,
Christovão de Mendonça Arraide
(Registry of Allotments and Land
Grants, 1689–1730) and that of
Pascoal Leite de Mendonça, "Captain
of Infantry of the Paulistas," to whom
the captain-general of Pernambuco,
in 1702, granted "three square leagues
of land of those conquered at Palmares," where was situated "the Plantation of Christovão Dias in the river-
mead of Setuba" (manuscript collection of the Pernambucan Institute).

[99] The victory of July 2, 1625,
which routed the Dutch from Bahia;
although they afterwards captured
Pernambuco (1630) and held it for
over twenty years. (Translator.)

chists and missionaries had been responsible for dispersing. The fathers of the Society of Jesus were everywhere, moving from one end to another of the vast colonial domain, establishing a permanent contact between the sporadic foci of colonization and, through the *"lingua geral,"* [100] between the various groups of aborigines as well.[101] Their mobility, like that of the Paulistas, if on the one hand it became dangerously dispersive, on the other hand was salutary and constructive in so far as it tended to that "unionism" in which Professor João Ribeiro sees one of the great social forces of our history.[102]

So far as that goes, we had been prepared for this "unionism" by the singular, the very special situation of the Portuguese people as colonizers. They had come to the shores of America united politically and juridically; and however great might be the real or apparent variety of creeds and ethnic strains, all these were accommodated to the political and juridical organization of the State in union with the Catholic Church. As M. Bomfim observes, "the formation of Portugal was marked by so high a degree of political precocity that the little Kingdom impresses us as being the first completely rounded

---

[100] Literally, the general (common) tongue or language. It is a form of the Tupí-Guaraní language. The author alludes to this a little later on as the creation of the Jesuits. (Translator.)

[101] Father Simão de Vasconcellos, in his *Chrónica da Companhia de Jesus do Estado do Brasil, e do que obraram seus Filhos nesta Parte do Novo Mundo* (*Chronicle of the Society of Jesus of the State of Brazil, and of the work done by its Sons in this Part of the New World*) (2nd edition, Rio de Janeiro, 1864), p. 41, states that such was the haste with which Father Leonardo Nunes ran about from place to place "that they came to give him the name, in the language of Brazil, of *Abaré bebé"*— that is to say, "the flying padre." And in his introduction to the same Chronicle, Canon Fernandes Pinheiro observes, in speaking of the first missionaries, that it might be said of them that they had "solved the problem of ubiquity." Varnhagen remarks that, traveling continuously, the missionaries "established more frequent communication and closer relations between one town and another." By way of generalization it may be said that all the missionaries in Brazil were flying padres. This is surely true of some of them, who traveled in hammocks borne by Indians, and so may be said to have flown.

[102] For João Ribeiro, who always sees so clearly the facts and tendencies in connection with the historical development of Brazil, the "local particularism is distinguished . . . by a higher spirit of unionism. . . ." (*História do Brasil*, advanced school course, Rio de Janeiro, 1900.) For that matter, as M. Bomfim points out, Euclides da Cunha contradicts himself in putting forward the idea that Brazil consists of "groups divorced from one another," when in *Os Sertões* he stresses the importance of the *sertanejo* (man of the backlands)— that same *sertanejo* who radiates northward from Minas to Goiaz and Piauí, to the far bounds of Maranhão and Ceará on the northeast, and to the highland mining region of Bahia on the east.

nation in sixteenth-century Europe." An observation that Stephens had already made in *The Story of Portugal*.[103]

The Portuguese brought with them to Brazil neither political divisions, as the Spaniards did to their American dominions, nor religious differences, as was the case with the English and the French in their colonies. The Maranos [104] in the homeland did not constitute the same intransigent element of differentiation that the Huguenots did in France or the Puritans in England; they were an imperceptible minority, economically odious in some of their characteristics, but they were not aggressive, nor did they tend to disturb national unity. On the contrary, in many respects, no minority was more accommodating and tractable.

The formation of Brazil went forward without the colonizers being concerned with racial unity or racial purity. Throughout practically the whole of the sixteenth century the gates of the colony were open to foreigners; the only thing that mattered to the colonial authorities was that the newcomers be of the Catholic faith or religion. Handelmann notes that, in order to be admitted to Brazil as a colonist during that era, the principal requirement was that one profess the Christian religion: "only Christians"—and in Portugal this meant Catholics—"might acquire allotments." "No restriction, however," the German historian continues, "was laid down as to nationality; and Catholics from foreign countries might accordingly emigrate to Brazil and settle there. . . ." [105] Oliveira Lima emphasizes the fact that during the century in question Portugal tolerated within its possessions many foreigners, the Portuguese policy with regard to colonization and settlement not being one of "rigorous exclusion, as later adopted by Spain." [106]

Throughout certain colonial epochs we may note the custom of having a friar aboard every ship that entered a Brazilian port, that he might be able to examine the conscience, faith, and religion of the new arrival.[107] The thing that barred an immigrant in those days was

[103] H. M. Stephens: *The Story of Portugal* (New York, 1891). For a deeper-going acquaintance with the subject see the work by H. Schäffer: *Geschichte von Portugal* (Hamburg, 1836–54), of which there exists a Portuguese translation.

[104] The Maranos were Jews who, under threat of or torture by the Inquisition, had publicly embraced Christianity, while continuing to

practice their own creed in private. (Translator.)

[105] H. Handelmann: *História do Brasil* (translation, Rio de Janeiro, 1931).

[106] Oliveira Lima: "*A Nova Lusitania*" ("The New Lusitania"), cited in *História da Colonização Portuguesa do Brasil* (op. cit.), Vol. III, p. 297.

[107] See Ritter von Schäffer: *Brasilien als unabhängiges Reich*, (Altona,

heterodoxy: the blot of heresy upon the soul and not any racial brand upon the body. It was a question of religious health; and syphilis, buboes, smallpox, and leprosy might enter freely, being brought in by Europeans and Negroes alike from various places. For the danger lay not in the fact that the individual was a foreigner or that he might be unhygienic or cacogenic; it lay in the possibility of his being a heretic. Let him be able to say the Our Father and the Hail Mary, to recite the Apostles' Creed, and to make the sign of the cross—let him be able to do this, and the foreigner was welcome in colonial Brazil. The friar aboad ship was there to investigate the individual's orthodoxy just as today the immigrant's health and race are investigated. "Whereas," remarks Pedro de Azevedo, "the Anglo-Saxon regards an individual as being of his race only when the latter is of the same physical type as he himself, the Portuguese forgets race and regards as his equal the one who professes the same religion." [108]

The thing that was feared so far as the Catholic immigrant was concerned was the political enemy who might be capable of shattering or of weakening that solidarity which in Portgual had evolved in unison with the Catholic religion. This solidarity was splendidly maintained throughout the whole of our colonial period, serving to unite us against the French Calvinists, the Reformed Dutch, the English Protestants. To such an extent that it would, in truth, be difficult to separate the Brazilian from the Catholic: Catholicism was in reality the cement of our unity.[109]

At the beginning of our colonial era we find uniting with families

---

1824). Concerning this quarantine of heretics, which is what it amounted to, Tristão de Athayde has the following to say: "In 1813 they inquired into one's religious beliefs and passport. Today they inquire into one's passport, luggage, political creed, personal habits, and state of health."—*Estudos (Studies)*, Series I (Rio de Janeiro, 1927). On the friars and priests who in the ports watched over the colony's Catholic orthodoxy, at times with a suavity that is lacking in modern health inspectors and police functionaries connected with the immigration service, see "Certain notes of the voyage to Brazil with the Minion of London . . . in the yere 1580 written by Thomas Grigs Purser of the same ship," in *The*

Principal Navigations Voyages Traffiques & Discoveries of the English Nation . . . by Richard Hakluyt (London, 1927), Vol. VIII, pp. 13–14.

[108] Pedro de Azeuedo: "*Os Primeiros Donatários*" ("The First Proprietors"), cited in *História da Colonização Portuguesa do Brasil*, Vol. III, p. 194.

[109] In Brazil the unbeliever Fustel de Coulanges, even more than in France—which since the Revolution had been divided into the Black and the Red—felt himself under the necessity of being a Catholic out of a sentiment of nationalism. This, moreover, was the attitude of Oliveira Lima, who, lacking a more ardent religious ideal, once declared himself to be a "historic Catholic."

of Portuguese origin foreigners from various lands, some of them being from Reformed countries or those tainted with heresy; and we come upon such names as Arzam, Bandemborg, Bentinck, Lins, Cavalcanti, Doria, Hollanda, Accioly, Furquim, Novilher, Barewell, Lems, and later, in the seventeenth century, Van der Lei.[110] Still others of the same sort were dissolved into Portuguese names. Those persons who came from Protestant countries were already Catholics or else were converted here; and this sufficed for them to be received on intimate terms into our social and even our political life. They might here set up a family and marry with the best of the land, acquiring agricultural property, influence, and prestige.

Sylvio Romero, Brazilian sociologist and historian, observes that in Brazil the Jesuit catechism and the ordinances of the Realm "guaranteed from the earliest times the unity of religion and the law." [111]

As for the mechanism of colonial administration, marked by feudal tendencies in the beginning, it was lacking in the severity displayed by the Spaniards; it was slack and weak, leaving the colonies and in many respects the proprietors to their own free will. When later it was rendered more rigid through the creation of the office of governor-general, this was by way of assuring the union of certain of the *Capitânias*, by keeping them under the same moral guardianship, under the same governor-general, the same Ultramarine Council, the same Tribunal of Conscience,[112] while still maintaining a separation between them in so far as it was possible to subject each one of them to special treatment by the Metropolis. The object in view was to prevent a national consciousness (which would inevitably arise out of a uniformity of treatment and administrative regime) from overshadowing the regional one; but this prophylactic measure against the peril of nationalism in the colony was not carried to the point of sacrificing to it the colony's essential unity, assured by the catechism and by the Ordinances, by the Catholic liturgy, and by the Portuguese language, aided by that "general" tongue which the Jesuits had created.

Physical conditions in Brazil, which might have contributed to the deepening of regional divergencies to dangerous extremes, were not

---

[110] This is not to take into account the numerous colonists from other parts of the Iberian Peninsula who are here not distinguished from those of Portuguese origin. Among other names we find Bueno, Camargo, Aguirre, Lara y Ordones, Freyre, Bonilha. Not to speak of the colonists of Hebraic origin joined to the Catholic communion.

[111] Sylvio Romero, op. cit.

[112] *The Mesa de Conciencia*, a tribunal in Lisbon instituted by King John III to decide matters of conscience. (Translator.)

merely something to be put up with, but were even turned to advantage in assuring to a colony so extensive as this one the comparative degree of political well-being that it always enjoyed. The influence of the physical factors, of the considerable though not dominant differences in climate and in the physical and chemical quality of the soil, in the system of alimentation and the forms of agriculture, was but weakly exerted in the direction of separatism. Such conditions, it may rather be asserted, in Brazil contributed to the preservation of unity within the bonds of consanguinity and a solidarity assured by the tendencies and processes of Portuguese colonization, which in their effect were regionalist but not separatist, unionist in the best sense of the term—that sense which precisely coincided with the interests of the Catholic catechism.

A climate that from north to south, from the maximum altitude to the minimum, did not vary sufficiently to create profound differences in the mode of colonial life, or variations in the physical and chemical quality of the soil such as would stimulate the development of two societies basically antagonistic in their economic and social interests, was at the same time the factor that overcame the tendency to uniformity. Despite the astonishing mobility of the *bandeirantes* and the missionaries, this was an influence that made itself felt from the first century of settlement and territorial expansion.

The cultivation of the sugar-cane was begun at São Vicente and in Pernambuco, being later extended to Bahia and to Maranhão. In those regions where it attained success—a mediocre one as at São Vicente or a maximum one as in Pernambuco, the Reconcavo, and Maranhão— there grew up a society and a mode of life whose tendencies were those of a slave-holding aristocracy, with a consequent similarity of economic interests. Economic antagonism was to show its head later, when it sprang up between those individuals who, possessing more capital, were able to meet the costs of the cultivation and manufacture of sugar and those less favored ones who were obliged to scatter out through the backlands in quest of slaves—a species of living capital— or else to settle there as cattle-raisers. This was an antagonism that a land so vast was in a position to support without any shock to the economic balance of things; but out of it was to result a Brazil that was anti-slavery or indifferent to the interests of the slave-owners, represented in particular by Ceará and in general by the *sertanejo* and the *vaqueiro*.[113]

The identity of agrarian and slave-holding interests that during the

---

[113] *Sertanejo*: man of the *sertão*, or backlands. *Vaqueiro*: a cowboy or cattle-man of the backlands region of northeastern Brazil. (Translator.)

sixteenth and seventeenth centuries prevailed in a colony wholly devoted, with a greater or less degree of intensity, to the raising of sugar was not so profoundly disturbed as at first sight might appear to be the case by the discovery of the mines or the introduction of the coffee tree. If the economic point of support of the colonial aristocracy was shifted from the sugar-cane to gold, and later to coffee, its instrument of exploitation, the arm of the slave, was still retained. The very divergency of interests that now became defined—the difference in the technique of economic exploitation between the northeast, which persisted in the cultivation of sugar, and the *capitânia* of Minas Geraes, and between these two regions and coffee-growing São Paulo—was in a manner compensated in its separatist effects by the human migration that the economic phenomenon in itself induced. By dividing between the sugar-raising zone, the mining region, and the coffee zone to the south an ethnic element, the slave of African origin, which had been preserved *en bloc* in the northeast (up to then the section that, by reason of the excellence of its soil for sugar-growing, was the most inclined of the three to slavery), the phenomenon in question was to result in profound regional differences in the sphere of human culture.

For the needs of alimentation during the first centuries of colonial life practically the same native or imported plants were cultivated from north to south. The basis of our system of nutrition became manihot flour, and in addition Indian corn was cultivated. Practically the same colonial table was to be found everywhere, the only variations being certain regional specialties in the form of fruit and greens. In certain places a dash of local color was afforded or local taste was reflected in the greater influence exerted by the native, while elsewhere a lively exotic coloring was provided by the proximity of Africa. It was in Pernambuco that, by reason of its being the point closest to Europe, a balance was struck between the three influences: the native, the African, and the Portuguese.

Upon the São Paulo plateau—where the barely compensatory results of the cultivation of the sugar-cane led the settlers to divert their agricultural efforts to other crops, thus initiating something like a salutary tendency to diversified farming—a relatively successful attempt was made at the regular cultivation of wheat in the first century of colonization. Had the attempt wholly succeeded, diversified farming, which had been no more than begun, might have been carried further and these two factors would have resulted in a profound differentiation of regional life and the regional type. Relative as they were, they made themselves powerfully felt in the greater efficiency and higher eugenic standard of the Paulista as compared with the Brazilians of other regions, with a similar background of agrarian slavery and ethnic hybridism, but who, as a result in large part of the conditions referred to, enjoyed less of the advantages of a balanced diet. "The dietetic regime of the Paulistas was not, then, the least of those factors which contributed to the prosperity of the people of the plateau," concludes Alfredo Ellis, Jr., in the suggestive chapter which, in his *Race of Giants*,[114] he devotes to the eugenic development of the inhabitants of this region. Generally speaking, it may be said that wherever agriculture flourished, the system of big landownership prevailed in slave-holding Brazil, a system that was to deprive the colonial population of a balanced and constant supply of fresh and wholesome foodstuffs. Much of the physical inferiority of the Brazilian, commonly attributed to race or vaguely and with Mussulman fatalism to climate, is due to the bad management of our natural resources in the matter of nutrition, resources that, while not the richest in the world, might have provided, within the system of slavery and big landownership, a more varied and healthful diet than that which the first colonists and their descendants knew.

It is an illusion to suppose that the majority of individuals in colonial society were well nourished. As to quantity, there were in general two extremes: the whites of the Big Houses and the Negroes of the slave quarters, the big landed proprietors and the blacks who were their slaves and who had need of the food that was given them to enable them to endure the hard labor of the *bagaceira*. What happened was that the sugar-planters, "since they lived solely on what they gained with the labor of so many slaves" (those from Guinea), practically never employed their Negroes—"not a single one of them" —at anything that did not have to do with "the husbandry that they professed."[115] From this—so concludes the author of the *Dialogues on the Grandeurs of Brazil*, who set down his notes at the beginning of the seventeenth century—"from this results the lack and scarcity of things."[116]

The conditions of climate and soil being unfavorable to the cultivation of wheat, the fathers of the Society of Jesus were practically the only ones who insisted upon raising it, for the preparation of the

---

[114] Alfredo Ellis, Jr.: *Raça de Gigantes* (São Paulo, 1926).

[115] *Diálogos das Grandezas do Brasil* (Rio de Janeiro, 1930), p. 33. [The *Dialogues* are attributed to Bento Teixeira Pinto, one of the most important of Brazil's colonial writers, author of the well-known epic *Prosopopéa*. (Translator.)]

[116] The chronicler is referring (op. cit.) to fruits, vegetables, and beef.

Sacred Host. As for manihot, employed in place of wheat, the sugar-cane planters abandoned it to the undependable *caboclos*. The upshot of it all was that the almost complete absence of wheat from the list of our natural resources, or possibilities, in the realm of nutrition led to the lowering of the alimentary standards of the Portuguese colonizer, and the lack of stability in the cultivation of manihot—left to those haphazard agriculturists, the Indians—resulted in a corresponding instability in our diet. To this must be added the lack of fresh meat, of milk, eggs, and even vegetables in various agrarian, slave-holding regions, possibly in all of them with a single exception, and that a relative one: the São Paulo plateau.

And so, admitting the influence of the individual's diet, an influence that is possibly exaggerated by certain modern authorities,[117] upon the physical and economic development of populations, we must recognize the fact that the Brazilian's method of food supply, within the organizational framework of that system of agrarian slavery which so largely shaped our national life, was an exceedingly deficient and unstable one; and this possibly will go to explain certain important somatic and psychic differences between the European and the Brazilian which ordinarily are attributed exclusively to miscegenation and to climate.

Certain it is that, in the stressing of such differences, by shifting the responsibility from climate or miscegenation to diet we are not thereby giving the first mentioned a clean bill of health; for when all is said, it is upon climate and upon the chemical qualities of the soil that the alimentary regime that is followed by the population in large part depends. What are the conditions, if not these (the physical and chemical qualities of the soil, and climate), that go to determine the character of the spontaneous vegetation and the possibilities of agriculture, and through them the character and possibilities of man himself?

In the case of Brazilian society what happened was that, owing to the pressure of an economic-social influence—monoculture—the deficiencies of the natural sources of nutrition were accentuated, where diversified farming might possibly have attenuated or even have corrected and suppressed them through the regular and systematic application of agricultural effort. Many of these sources were, so to speak, perverted, while others were held in check by monoculture, by a slave-holding and latifundiary regime that, in place of encouraging

---

[117] F. P. Armitage: *Diet and Race* (London and New York, 1922); E. V. McCollum and Nina Simmonds: *The Newer Knowledge of Nutrition—the Use of Foods for the Preservation of Vitality and Health* (New York, 1929).

their evolution, choked them and dried them up, destroying their freshness and spontaneity. For nothing so disturbs the equilibrium of nature as monoculture, above all when the plant that is to dominate the region is of extraneous origin—so notes Professor Konrad Günther.[118] This was precisely the case with Brazil.

In the formation of our society the bad system of alimentation, deriving from monoculture on the one hand and from lack of adaptation to the climate [119] on the other, had its effect upon the physical development and economic efficiency of the Brazilian in the same way as would a depressing climate and a chemically poor soil. The same latifundiary, slave-holding economy that rendered possible the economic development of Brazil, giving it a relative stability in contrast to the turbulent neighboring countries, was the one that poisoned and perverted its sources of nutrition, the sources of life itself.

The best nourished, let us repeat, in this society based upon slavery were the two extremes: the whites of the Big Houses and the Negroes of the slave huts. It is natural that the strongest and healthiest elements of our population should have descended from the slaves. The

---

[118] Konrad Günther: *Das Antlitz Brasiliens* (op. cit.).

[119] In an interesting article, *"Fundamentos Científicos da Alimentação Racional nos Climas Quentes"* ("Scientific Bases of a Rational Diet in Hot Climates"), *Brasil Médico*, Rio de Janeiro, ano XLV, No. 40, the physician Sinval Lins recently took up this subject. As he sees it, the Brazilian remains, so far as his diet is concerned, an individual who is unadapted to his climate. "He eats too many sweets . . . in midsummer, when everything invites him to protect himself from the heat; he indulges in too many greasy dishes and, at times, alcoholic beverages as well . . . he takes too many liquids at mealtime without observing that the more he drinks, the greater his . . . taste for spicy foods . . . he almost never eats any leguminous vegetables. . . . The consequences of such errors," the hygienist adds, "have long since made themselves felt. Our teeth are weak and rotting from lack of calcium—that is to say, of vegetables. . . ." Other organs that suffer are "the skin, the kidneys, the stomach." Sinval Lins lays stress upon the Brazilian's "postprandial sluggishness," attributing to it "that fatigue of which so many of us complain," another cause for which he finds in "the autointoxication resulting from an abuse of nitrates and that constipation which is so very common among us and which is due to a lack of fruit and vegetables in our diet. . . ." Climate, he believes, is unjustly held responsible for this fatigue. Similarly Dr. Araujo Lima, in studying the diet of the populations in the far north of Brazil, insists upon the importance of the factor of alimentation in interpreting that "legendary indolence of individuals in these parts, of which so much is heard to their discredit."— J. F. de Araujo Lima: *"Ligeira contribuição ao estudo do problema alimentar das populações rurais do Amazonas"* ("Slight Contribution to the Study of the Problem of Alimentation among the Rural Populations of the Amazon"), *Boletim Sanitário*, Rio de Janeiro, 1923, ano 2, No. 4.

athletes, the *capoeiras*,[120] the "cabras," [121] the deep-sea sailors. It is likewise natural that from the middle classes, free but poverty-stricken in their conditions of life, should have come many of the worst elements, the weakest and most incapable. It was chiefly these latter who, owing to the lack of vigor that is induced by under-nourishment, fell a prey to paludic anemia, beriberi, worms, and buboes. And when all this practically useless population of *caboclos* and light-skinned mulattoes, worth more as clinical material than they are as an economic force, is discovered in the state of physical wretchedness and non-productive inertia in which Miguel Pereira and Belisário Penna [122] found them living—in such a case those who lament our lack of racial purity and the fact that Brazil is not a temperate climate at once see in this wretchedness and inertia the result of intercourse, forever damned, between white men and black women, between Portuguese males and Indian women. In other words, the inertia and the indolence are a matter of race. Or else it is the climate, which is suited only to the Negro. And thus is death-sentence passed upon the Brazilian for the reason that he happens to be a mestizo and Brazil in large part chances to lie within the torrid zone.

All of which means little to this particular school of sociology, which is more alarmed by the stigmata of miscegenation than it is by those of syphilis, which is more concerned with the effects of climate than it is with social causes that are susceptible to control or rectification; nor does it take into account the influence exerted upon mestizo populations—above all, the free ones—by the scarcity of foodstuffs resulting from monoculture and a system of slave labor; it disregards likewise the chemical poverty of the traditional foods that these peoples, or rather all Brazilians, with a regional exception here and there, have for more than three centuries consumed; it overlooks the irregularity of food supply and the prevailing lack of hygiene in the conservation and distribution of such products. There are still populations today—or, better, there are more today than there were in colonial times—that are very badly nourished. The researches of Araujo Lima lead to the conclusion that the greater part of our northern *caboclos*—lyrically looked upon by the naïve as a huge

---

[120] *Capoeira* is an untranslatable Brazilian term, signifying here an individual who engages in the athletic pastime of the same name, in which the participant, "armed with a razor or a knife, with rapid and characteristic gestures goes through the motions of criminal acts" (Lima and Barroso: *Pequeno Dicionário Brasileiro da Lingua Portuguesa*). (Translator.)

[121] A *cabra* is a brave mestizo of African-white or African-white-Indian ancestry. (Translator.)

[122] See note following. (Translator).

reserve of Brazilian vitality—have been reduced to a "state of organic inferiority . . . which at times amounts to an open breakdown." Speaking of the *caboclo*, this hygienist writes: ". . . his economic and social value is annulled by a nutritional insufficiency that, abetted by alcoholism and by the double dystrophic action of swamp fever and worms, must be recognized as one of the factors of his physical and mental inferiority." [123]

---

[123] J. F. de Araujo Lima, (article cited in note 119 above). This observation regarding the *caboclo* of the far north might be applied in general, with certain regional restrictions here and there, to the poor Brazilian in the other rural sections. In certain regions of the lower Amazon Araujo Lima met workers from the great cotton plantations who lived exclusively on a single meal of manihot paste with rice, taken in the morning. A *xibé*, whose base is flour and water, so poor in vitamins, constitutes very frequently an individual's sole nourishment in twenty-four hours." Azevedo Pimentel had previously discovered practically the same conditions among the inhabitants of central Brazil, where the "lack of a balanced diet and the perversions of organic nutrition" due to "unsuitable alimentary substances containing little nourishment" have proved more devastating in their effects than syphilis and other venereal diseases. The one who threw into relief the situation existing among our rural populations, badly nourished and the ready victims of a macabre series of afflictions— swamp fever, beriberi, ancylostomiasis, dysentery, leprosy, syphilis—was Miguel Pereira, whose findings were ratified by Belisário Penna. With reference to the rural and backlands populations of Paraíba, José Américo de Almeida has this to say: "The organic suffering brought about by the lack of vitality and insufficiency of diet is a field made ready for invasion by the ordinary means of infection."— *A Paraíba e Seus Problemas* (*Paraíba and Its Problems*) (Paraíba, 1924). On this subject see also the replies made in the course of the investigation carried out in 1778 by the Senate of Rio de Janeiro, regarding the climate and healthfulness of that city (*Annais Brasilienses de Medicina*, Vol. II, ano 2, No. 5). See the *Discurso* delivered at the anniversary session of the Imperial Academy of Medicine, July 30, 1847, by Roberto Jorge Haddock Lobo (Rio de Janeiro, 1848). See, in addition: J. F. X. Sigaud: *Du climat et des maladies du Brésil* (Paris, 1844); A. Hendu: *Études sur le Brésil* (Paris, 1848); J. A. B. Imbert: *Ensaio Hygiénico e Médico sobre o Clima do Rio de Janeiro e o Regime Alimentar de Seus Habitantes* (*Hygienic and Medical Treatise on the Climate of Rio de Janeiro and the Diet of Its Inhabitants*) (Rio de Janeiro, 1837); José Martins da Cruz Jobim: *Discurso sobre as Molestias que Mais Affligem a Classe Pobre do Rio de Janeiro . . .* (*Discourse on the Ailments That Most Afflict the Poorer Class of Rio de Janeiro . . .*) (Rio de Janeiro, 1835); Azevedo Pimentel: *Subsidios para o Estudo da Hygiene do Rio de Janeiro* (*Aids to the Study of the Hygiene of Rio de Janeiro*) (Rio de Janeiro, 1890); Azevedo Pimentel: *O Brasil Central* (*Central Brazil*) (Rio de Janeiro, 1907); Louis Couty: "*L'Alimentation au Brésil et dans les pays voisins,*" *Revue d'hygiène de Paris*, 1881; Eduardo Magalhães: *Higiene Alimentar* (*Alimentary Hygiene*) (Rio de Janeiro, 1908); Alfredo Antônio de Andrade: "*Alimentos Brasileiros*" ("Brazilian Foodstuffs"), *Annais da Faculdade de Medicinado*

It was not only the great mass of free men—free, however wretched —that must have been affected by this alimentary insufficiency, but those extremes of our population as well: the big landowning families and the slaves of the *senzalas*, the two classes in whom Couty was to encounter, in the absence of a "people," the only social realities to be found in Brazil.[124] If we regard the lords of the manor and their slaves as being well nourished—the latter, in a certain sense, better

Rio de Janeiro, Vol. VI (1922); Alberto da Cunha: "*Higiene Alimentar*," *Arquivos de Higiene*, No. 11, Rio de Janeiro; Manuel Querino: *A Arte Culinária na Baía* (*Culinary Art in Bahia*) (Bahia, 1928); Theodoro Peckholt: *História das Plantas Alimentares e de Gozo do Brasil* (*History of Alimentary and Palatable Plants of Brazil*) (Rio de Janeiro, 1871). The student may also be referred to the following doctoral theses: Antônio José de Sousa: *Do Regimen das Classes Pobres e dos Escravos na Cidade do Rio de Janeiro em Seus Alimentos e Bebidas* (*On the Diet of the Poor and the Slaves in the City of Rio de Janeiro, Their Food and Drinks*) (Medical Faculty of Rio de Janeiro, 1851); José Maria Regadas: *Do Regimen das Classes Abastadas no Rio de Janeiro* (*Diet of the Well-to-do Classes in Rio de Janeiro*) (Rio de Janeiro, 1852); José Rodrigues de Lima Duarte: *Ensaio sobre a Hygiene da Escravatura no Brasil* (*Treatise on the Hygiene of Slavery in Brazil*) (Rio de Janeiro, 1849); Antônio Corrêa de Sousa Costa: *Qual a Alimentação de que Vive a Classe Pobre do Rio de Janeiro e Sua Influência sobre a Mesma Classe* (*The Diet of the Poorer Class in Rio de Janeiro and Its Influence upon That Class*) (Rio de Janeiro, 1865); Francisco Fernandes Padilha: *Qual o Regimen das Classes Pobres do Rio de Janeiro?* (*What Is the Diet of the Poor in Rio de Janeiro?*) (Rio de Janeiro, 1852); Francisco Antonio dos Santos Sousa: *Alimentação na Baía* (*Diet in*

Bahia) (Faculty of Medicine of Bahia, 1909); Renato Souza Lopes: *Regimen Alimentar nos Climas Tropicaias* (*Diet in Tropical Countries*) (Rio de Janeiro, 1909).

Numerous Brazilian works have been published recently on the problem of alimentation in our country. Among them may be mentioned those by the physicians Silva Mello, Sinval Lins, Josué de Castro, Ruy Coutinho, Gama e Sousa, Peregrino Júnior, and Dante Costa. The preceding bibliography, published in the first edition of this essay, has been widely transcribed and cited by a number of these authors.

[124] Louis Couty: *L'Esclavage au Bresil* (Paris, 1881), p. 87. This is likewise the opinion of the clearest of our political thinkers, Professor Gilberto Amado, in the study that he has made of our slave-holding society from the political point of view: "*As Instituções Políticas e o Meio Social do Brasil*" ("Political Institutions and Social Milieu in Brazil"), in *Grão de Areia* (*Grain of Sand*) (Rio de Janeiro, 1919). Dom Luiz de Souza Botelho, Governor of the *capitânia* of São Paulo during the second half of the eighteenth century, had written: "In this land there is no people, and for that reason none to serve the State; with the exception of a very few mulattoes who fulfill its functions, the majority are gentry or slaves who serve the gentry." (Paulo Prado: *Paulistica*, 2nd edition, Rio de Janeiro, 1934).

nourished than the former [125]—it is merely in relation to the back-woodsmen, the inhabitants of the open country, the Indians, retainers, and impoverished *sertanejos*.[126] These are, by Couty's count, those six million useless beings out of a population of twelve million constituting that enormous void which to him appeared to exist in Brazil between the plantation-owner and the Negroes of the huts. "*La situation fonctionnelle de cette population peut se résumer d'un mot: le Brésil n'a pas de peuple*": so writes Couty;[127] and the French scientist's words were to be repeated two years later by Joaquim Nabuco. "There are millions," wrote Nabuco in 1883, "who find themselves in this intermediate condition which is neither that of a slave nor that of a citizen. . . ." Useless pariahs living in straw huts, sleeping in hammocks or on the highway, a water-jug and a pot for cooking their only utensils, their diet consisting of meal with codfish or salt beef, and "with a guitar alongside a holy image to complete the picture." [128]

From reading the chronicles of Cardim and Soares [129] we are accustomed to think of the plantation-owners as a lot of gluttons amid a rich variety of ripe fruits, fresh greens, and excellent loins of beef, seated at the groaning board and eating like mad in the company of their families, dependants, friends, and guests; yet the truth is that

---

[125] Theodoro Pecholt (op. cit., note 123, above) arrives at the conclusion that the European laborer of the era was "less well nourished" than the Brazilian slave. "Thus the slave in Brazil, and the plantation laborer in general," he writes, "has from a remote period been given a good and nourishing diet, based upon experience and not upon scientific calculation." He is referring to the laborer under the patriarchal regime; it was to the proprietor's interest to supply the worker with good food.

[126] The author here makes use of a number of rather vague, or general, Brazilian terms, such as: *matutos* (backwoodsmen); *caipiras* (inhabitants of the *campo*, or open country); *caboclos* (Indians); and *sertanejos* (inhabitants of the *sertao*, or backlands). (Translator.)

[127] Loc. cit.

[128] Joaquim Nabuco: *O Abolicion-* *ismo* (London, 1883). Herbert S. Smith also speaks of this intermediate class of useless pariahs, which he encountered on his journeys into the interior of Brazil at the end of the nineteenth century.—*Do Rio de Janeiro a Cuiabá (From Rio de Janeiro to Cuiabá)* (São Paulo, Caieiras, Rio de Janeiro, 1922). He attributes the poverty and economic incapacity of the backwoodsmen (*matutos*) to the fact that they are a mixture of Indian and Negro, forgetting that if he were to take a trip in his own country through the old slave-holding south and the Kentucky and Carolina mountains, he would encounter the same human detritus—in this case white: the "poor whites."

[129] Father Fernão Cardim and Gabriel Soares de Sousa, sixteenth-century chroniclers and letter-writers. (Translator.)

the lords of the manor, of Pernambuco and Bahia, were insufficiently nourished, their diet consisting principally of a bad quality of beef with only now and then a few worm-eaten fruits, rarely any vegetables. Such abundance or high quality of food as might be found in any particular instance would be the exception and not the rule among these large estate-owners. They were foolish enough to import a good part of their food supplies from Portugal and the Islands, and the result was that their victuals were often badly preserved, with meats, cereals, and even dried fruits losing their nutritive values when they did not still further deteriorate owing to faulty packing and the circumstances of slow and irregular transport. However strange it may seem, the table of our colonial aristocracy was lacking in fresh vegetables, fresh meat, and milk; and to this fact, surely, is to be ascribed the numerous ailments of the digestive tract common in that era, which by many an old-time doctor were attributed to the "bad vapors."

As a result of the antagonism that speedily sprang up in Brazil between large-scale agriculture, or, better, the absorptive monoculture of the littoral, and the cattle-raising industry of the backlands, which was in its turn equally exclusive—each of them keeping as great a distance as possible between itself and the other—the agricultural population, including even the wealthy owners of leagues of land, found itself deprived of a constant and regular supply of fresh foodstuffs. Cowan is right when he sees the historical development of most peoples as being conditioned by the antagonism between nomadic and agricultural pursuits.[130] In our country, from the earliest times, this factor had its effect upon the Brazilian's social evolution, acting upon it favorably in certain respects, but so far as alimentation is concerned, unfavorably.

Bahia was quite typical of a latifundiary agriculture on the one hand and, on the other hand, of an absorptive cattle industry, to such an extent that the vast majority of its lands came to belong to two families: that of the Senhor da Torre, and that of the lord of the open country, Antônio Guedes de Britto. The former possessed "260 leagues of land along the São Francisco River, upstream on the right-hand side, then southward," and "then along the said river to the north—80 leagues." The latter family held "160 leagues . . . from the hill known as Morro dos Chapéus to the source of the Rio das Velhas." [131] And it is a known fact that in Bahia, with its latfundia,

---

[130] Andrew Reid Cowan: *Master Clues in World History* (London, 1914).

[131] André João Antonil: *Cultura e Opulência do Brasil por Suas Drogas e Minas* (*Culture and Wealth of Bra-*

the big landed proprietors, in order not to suffer damage to their crops (sugar or tobacco), were in the habit of avoiding domestic animals, "sheep and goats being looked upon as useless creatures," [132] while hogs were hard to raise for the reason that they became wild when allowed to run loose, and the herds of cattle were insufficient for "the provisioning of the plantations, the expenses of slaughtering, and the supplying of the ships." [133]

So great was the neglect of any other crop than sugar or tobacco throughout the agricultural zone that eighteenth-century Bahia, with all its show of luxury, came to suffer "an extraordinary lack of flour." As a result, in 1788 the governors of the *capitânia* had a clause inserted in the land grants requiring the proprietor to plant "a thousand mounds of manihot for each slave that he possesses, employed in the cultivation of the land." [134] This was a kind of precaution that had been taken by the Count of Nassau with regard to the plantation-owners and farmers of Pernambuco in the seventeenth century.[135]

---

zil, *Its Drugs and Mines*), with a bio-bibliographical study by Affonso de E. Taunay (São Paulo and Rio de Janeiro, 1943), p. 264.

[132] "In order that the agriculturists may not suffer damage to their crops, domestic animals are everywhere scarce," says Ayres de Cazal, in his work already cited: *Chorographia Brasilica.*

[133] Ayres de Cazal, op. cit., II, p. 119.—Cazal attributes this fact to the circumstance that the pasture-grounds were not good as a rule, while there was "prevailingly . . . a lack of water." But this is not to lose sight of the social cause: "that the agriculturists may not suffer damage to their crops." Referring to the absence of cattle, Capistrano de Abreu observes that this was to "protect the cane fields and other plantations from their inroads."—*Diálogos das Grandezas do Brasil*, with an Introduction by Capistrano de Abreu and notes by Rodolfo Garcia (edition of the Brazilian Academy of Letters, Rio de Janeiro, 1930), p. 13. [On the *Diálogos*, see note 115 above. (Translator.)]

[134] "Fragments of a Memoir on the Plantings of Bahia" (copy of a manuscript that appears to have belonged to the library of the late Marques de Aguiar, and which is possibly from his pen), to be found in the *Livro das Terras ou Collecção da Lei, Regulamentos e Ordens Expedidos a Respeito desta Matéria até ao Presente . . . (Book of the Lands, or Collection of the Laws, Regulations, and Ordinances with Respect to This Matter, down to the Present Time . . .*) (2nd edition, Rio de Janeiro, 1860), p. 24.

[135] Hermann Wätjen, op. cit.— Among the documents in the Royal Archives of The Hague, relating to Brazil and published in the *Revista do Instituto Arqueológico e Geográfico de Pernambuco*, No. 33 (Recife, 1887), are to be found a number of decrees of this sort. For that matter, as far back as the sixteenth century we come upon evidence of governmental intervention with the object of regularizing the cultivation of those foodstuffs sacrificed to the growing of sugar. In the Acts of the Chamber of São Paulo (1562–1601),

It is true that Padre Fernão Cardim, in his *Treatises*, is always speaking of the abundance of meat, game, and even of fruit and greens that he met with everywhere in sixteenth-century Brazil among the rich and in the schools kept by the priests.[136] But we must bear in mind that Cardim was a visiting cleric and as such was received on the plantations and in the schools with exceptional feasts and repasts. He was a personage for whom the most that the colonists could do was little enough. The good impression produced by the laden tables and soft beds of the big slave-owners might possibly do away with the very bad impression that was conveyed by the dissolute life that they all led on the sugar plantations: "the sins that are committed there [on the plantations] are without number; practically all live in a state of fornication, by reason of the many opportunities that are afforded; full of sins, they have an easy time of it in view of all that they do; great is the patience of God, who suffers all this." [137]

These huge feasts and banquets, all this ostentatious hospitality and abundance of food, do not enable us to form any precise idea of the diet of the big estate-owners, much less of the usual diet of the majority of the inhabitants. Commenting upon the description of a colonial feast in eighteenth-century Boston—a special banquet, on a festive occasion, with plum pudding, pork, chicken, bacon, beef, mutton, roast turkey, sauce, cakes, pies, cheese, etc. (all representing an excess of animal protein)—Professor Percy Goldthwait Stiles of

---

Taunay found a requisition of the Governor-General of Brazil for 800 alquiers of flour, destined for Pernambuco, a *capitânia* that, because it was the most exclusively devoted to sugar, would accordingly be the most exposed to a dearth of local foodstuffs. This requisition, however, was beyond the capacity of the Paulistas; had they furnished all that flour to Pernambuco, they themselves would have been left in penury. "The Chamber," writes Taunay, "resolved to publish abroad, so that all the inhabitants of the town and district might know it, a decree in which the residents were called upon to furnish flour, in obedience to a provision of the commander-in-chief (*capitão-mor*) and the judge (*ouvidor*) of the *capitânia* of São Vicente. All this un-

der penalty of a fine of fifty cruzados and two years of banishment to the inhospitable regions of the Strait of Magellan. This great concern for the supplying of flour shows us plainly enough how irregular was the output of agriculture."—Affonso de E. Taunay: *São Paulo nos Primeiros Tempos* (*São Paulo in the Early Days*) (Tours, 1920).

[The Brazilian alquier is roughly equal to our bushel. The cruzado is worth 400 reis. (Translator.)]

[136] Fernão Cardim: *Tratados da Terra e Gente do Brasil* (*Treatises on the Land and People of Brazil*), with an Introduction and Notes by Baptista Caetano, Capistrano de Abreu, and Rodolfo Garcia (Rio de Janeiro, 1925).

[137] Ibid., p. 321.

Harvard University very sensibly observes that such an abundance was perhaps not typical of the ordinary everyday diet of the New England colonists; and he adds that such feasts were possibly compensated by fastings.[138] It would seem that this might be applied with literal exactitude to the colonial banquets in Brazil, spaced as these were by periods of parsimonious eating, not to speak of the fasts and abstinences whose observance was enjoined by Holy Mother Church; for the matriarchal shadow of the Church, then a much more powerful and dominant influence, was projected over the intimate and domestic life of the faithful to a far greater degree than it is today.

From Father Cardim's descriptions of the old-time feasts and the allusions of Soares one is by no means justified in drawing the conclusion that the daily diet of the colonists was always an abundant, nourishing, and varied one, or that Brazil during the first centuries of colonization was any such "land of Cockaigne" as Capistrano de Abreu, who is being a bit too literary for once, would imply that it was.[139] Even in Cardim himself we come upon this striking bit of realism: "In the school of Bahia there is never lacking a little glass of the wine of Portugal, without which it would be impossible for nature to sustain itself, the earth being left to lie so unproductive and the sources of nourishment being so poor." [140] It may be noted in passing that it was in this same wine of Portugal that the New England Puritans drowned their sorrows.[141]

Land of Cockaigne—nothing of the sort. Brazil during its three centuries of colonial life was a land of uncertain alimentation and difficult sustenance. The shadow of a sterilizing monoculture lay over all. The rural gentry were always in debt, and termites, floods, and droughts seriously interfered with the food supply for the majority of the population. That Asiatic luxury which many imagine to have been general in the sugar-raising north was confined to the privileged families of Pernambuco and Bahia, and even there it was but a partial luxury of an unwholesome sort, being marked by an excess of certain things (at the cost of going into debt) [142] and a scarcity of other things. Silk-lined palanquins, but in the Big Houses bare-tiled roofs with vermin dropping into the inmates' beds.

In Pará in the seventeenth century "the families of certain noblemen" were unable to go to the city for the Christmas festivities (1661) "for the reason that the young ladies, their daughters, had

---

[138] Percy Goldthwait Stiles: *Nutritional Physiology* (Philadelphia and Boston, 1931).

[139] Op. cit., note 136 above, Appendix, p. 433.
[140] Ibid., p. 299.
[141] Stiles, op. cit.
[142] Cardim, op. cit., p. 334.

nothing to wear to Mass."[143] From João Lúcio de Azevedo we learn that Antônio Vieira,[144] when he reproved the Chamber of Pará for not having any slaughter-pen or grazing-ground in the city, met with the reply that it was impossible to remedy this condition "inasmuch as payment for ordinary food was out of the question." And the author adds: "The common diet of game and fish, which were abundant in the early days, grew rare in proportion as the number of inhabitants increased. . . . The lands, left untilled or without intelligent cultivation, lost their primitive fertility, and the inhabitants transferred their homes and labor to other regions."[145] Writing from Maranhão, Father Vieira stresses the fact that in his day there was throughout the state "neither slaughter-pen nor grazing-ground nor kitchen garden nor shops where ordinary edibles were for sale."[146] And speaking of the whole of Brazil, Father Anchieta tells us that the sixteenth-century colonists, even "the richest and most honored ones" and the missionaries, were accustomed to going barefoot in the manner of the Indians,[147] a custom that would appear to have been handed down to the seventeenth century and the fidalgos of Olinda — those same ones of the silken beds for the hospitable entertainment of the visiting padres and the silver knives and forks for feast-day banquets. Their finery, it may be, served only for state occasions. From a dinner that Maria Graham attended in Pernambuco early in the nineteenth century,[148] it would seem that our gentry of that era were in the habit of using silver forks — by way of impressing the English (though the English are rarely deceived by the glitter of gold and silver) with their dainty table manners. Nor should we forget that formidable contrast which existed in the life of the plantation-owners: fine gentlemen on horseback, silver stirrups and all, but inside the house they were so many barefooted Franciscans, clad in cotton nightgowns and at times merely in their drawers. As for the colonial dames, rich silks and a display of jewels and trinkets in church, but in the privacy of the home a chemise, a petticoat, house-slippers, and stockingless legs.[149] This airy costume was partly due to

[143] Berredo, in J. Lúcio de Azevedo: *Os Jesuitas no Grão-Pará* (*The Jesuits in Grão-Pará*) (2nd edition, Coimbra, 1930).

[144] Seventeenth-century missionary and writer, renowned for the eloquence of his style, one of the outstanding figures in early Brazilian literature. (Translator.)

[145] J. Lúcio de Azevedo, op. cit.

[146] Father Antonio Vieira, in J. Lúcio de Azevedo, op. cit.

[147] *Informações e Fragmentos Históricos do Padre Joseph de Anchieta, S.J.,* 1584-6 (*Historical Data and Fragments by Father Joseph de Anchieta, S.J.*) (Rio de Janeiro, 1886), p. 47.

[148] Maria Graham: *Journal* (op. cit.)

[149] On the negligence of dress

the climate, but it was at the same time an expression of colonial Franciscanism as reflected in the everyday garb as well as the diet of many a gentleman of the time.

Salvador da Bahia [150] itself, when it was the city of the viceroys, inhabited by many rich Portuguese, in a land full of fidalgos and friars, won a reputation for its very bad and deficient food-supply. Everything was lacking: fresh beef, fowls, vegetables, fruit; and what there was to be had was of extremely poor quality or almost in a state of putrefaction. There was an abundance only of sweets, jellies, and pastries, made by the nuns in the convents; and it was these that rounded out the girth of the brothers of the monastery and the lady of the house.

Such was the state of alimentation in Brazilian society in the six-teenth, seventeenth, and eighteenth centuries: bad upon the planta-tions and very bad in the cities—not only bad, but scarce. The Bishop of Tucumán, visiting Brazil in the seventeenth century, observed that in the cities he would "send out to buy a young cock, four eggs, and a fish, and they would bring nothing back, for the reason that nothing was to be found in the market place or at the butcher's." He accord-ingly had to make the rounds of the private houses of the rich.[151] Father Nobrega's letters speak of the "lack of edibles," [152] and from the letters of Anchieta we learn that there was not a slaughterhouse in the town, the fathers of the school being obliged to raise a few head of cattle: "if they had not done so, they would have had nothing to eat." And he adds: "All are poorly nourished, despite their labor, for things here are very dear, costing three times what they do in Portugal." [153] We further learn that the beef was deficient in fat: "not very fat for the reason that the land was not fertile in pasturage." [154]

---

among the people of colonial times, even the most illustrious, see James Henderson: *A History of the Brazil* (London, 1821); and John Luccock: *Notes on Rio de Janeiro and the Southern Parts of Brazil* (London, 1820). The latter work was recently published in Brazil in Portuguese translation.

[150] The city of Bahia, capital of the province (now the state) of the same name, today known as Salvador. (Translator.)

[151] *História do Brasil*, by Frei Vicente do Salvador, edition revised by Capistrano de Abreu (São Paulo and Rio de Janeiro, 1918), pp. 16–17.

[Frei Vicente do Salvador was a notable historian and prose-writer of the later sixteenth and early seven-teenth century. (Translator.)]

[152] Nobrega: *Cartas* (op. cit.), p. 162.

[153] See the work of Anchieta cited in note 147 above, to be found in *Materiaes e Achegas para a História e Geographia por Ordem do Ministério da Fazenda* (*Materials and Aids for History and Geography, by Order of the Minister of Finance*) (Rio de Janeiro, 1886), No. 1, p. 34.

[154] Anchieta, op. cit., p. 50.

And once more it is Father Anchieta who informs us: "Some of the rich eat wheat-flour bread of Portugal, especially in Pernambuco and Bahia, and from Portugal also come wine, olive oil, vinegar, olives, cheese, preserves, and other things to eat." [155]

Such was the diet in Bahia of the viceroys, with its fidalgos and its rich burghers, clad always in the silk of Genoa, the linens and cotton cloth of Holland and of England, and even in gold cloth imported from Paris and Lyon. It was a diet in which the lack of meat was made up for by an overuse of fish, the ichthyophagous menu being varied with salt meat and cheese from the Kingdom, imported from Europe along with other articles of food." [156] "One never sees a sheep and rarely a herd of cattle," says the Abbé Reynal in speaking of Bahia.[157] Neither beef nor mutton nor even chicken was to be had. Neither fruits nor vegetables. Vegetables were extremely rare, and fruit when it reached the table was already worm-eaten or else had been plucked while still green to save it from the birds, the worms, and the insects. Such beef as was to be found was lean, the cattle coming from far away in the backlands, with no pasturage to refresh them after their arduous journey; for the great sugar and tobacco plantations would not permit pasture-grounds for steers coming from the backland regions and destined for the slaughter-pen. Those oxen and cows that were not employed in agricultural service were looked upon as damned by the owners of the big estates.

As for milk-cows, it is known that there were few of these on colonial plantations; almost no butter or cheese was made, and it was only now and then that beef was eaten. This is explained by Capistrano de Abreu as being due to "the difficulty of raising herds in places unsuited to their propagation." As a result of this difficulty, the number of cattle was limited to those necessary for plantation

[155] Ibid., p. 41.

[156] "*Il y a quantité de Bœufs, de Cochons, de Moutons, de Volailles & de Gibier; mais tout y est extrémement cher. La Flote qui y vient tous les ans de Portugal apporte des vins, des farines, de l'huile, du fromage. . . .*" So we read in the *Relation du voyage autour du monde de Mr. de Gennes au Détroit de Magellan, par le Sr. Froger* (Amsterdam, 1699), p. 81. See also La Barbinais: *Nouveau Voyage autour du monde* (Paris, 1728-9).

[157] "*On n'y voit point de moutons; la volaille y est rare & le bœuf maivais. Les fourmis y désolent, comme dans le reste de la colonie, les fruits et les légumes. D'un autre coté, les vins, les farines, tous les vivres qu'on apporte d'Europe, n'arrivent pas toujours bien conservés. Ce qui a échappé à la corruption est d'une cherté prodigieuse.*"—*Histoire philosophique et politique des établissements & du commerce des Européens dans les deux Indes* (Geneva, 1775), Vol. III, p. 91.

work.[158] It was the shadow of monoculture projecting itself for leagues round about the sugar-factories, sterilizing and stifling everything save the cane fields and the men and cattle in its service.

Not only at Bahia, Pernambuco, and Maranhão, but at Sergipe d'El-Rei and Rio de Janeiro as well this phenomenon, with greater or less intensity, was to be found existing—the phenomenon, so disturbing to the eugenics of Brazilian life, of the scarcity of fresh food, whether animal or vegetable. But possibly nowhere was it so acutely felt as at Pernambuco.[159] This was the *capitânia* that, *par excellence*, was given over to sugar-raising and large estates; and at the end of the eighteenth and the beginning of the nineteenth century it was reckoned to be the best land for agricultural purposes, situated as it was near the sea and under the control of eight or ten plantation-owners among some two hundred inhabitants of the region—"among two hundred inhabitants, eight or ten proprietors"—proprietors who ordinarily permitted their tenants to "plant cane and keep the half of it." [160] It was here that the lack of those foods that are of prime necessity made itself most painfully felt at times. It was in vain that the Count of Nassau, in the seventeenth century, had undertaken to correct this unbalanced condition in the economic life of the great sugar-growing *capitânia*. And as in Bahia and Pernambuco, so in Rio de Janeiro the cattle never arrived for "the consumption of the butchers and the provisioning of the plantations." [161] Indeed, the presence of cattle on the sugar-cane plantations, or even near them, was shunned; and furthermore, as in the northern *capitânias*, the lands in the province of Rio de Janeiro were concentrated in the hands of a few: the great sugar-planters—including the friars of the Monastery

---

[158] Capistrano de Abreu: Introduction to the *Diálogos das Grandezas do Brasil* (op. cit.).

[159] The reader may be referred to a sixteenth-century document that is almost unknown in Brazil: "A discourse of the West Indies and South Sea written by Lopez Vaz a Portugal borne in the citie of Elvas continued unto the yere 1587," etc., included in Richard Hakluyt's *Voyages* (op. cit.), Vol. VIII, p. 172. In this work we read of Pernambuco in the sixteenth century, so opulent in sugar plantations: ". . . yet are they in great want of victuals that come either from Portugal or from some places upon the coast of Brazil." The scarcity extended even to flour: "of which there is ordinarily a dearth," we are told by Ayres de Cazal (op. cit.).—On the social background of Rio de Janeiro see Alberto Lamego: *A Terra Goitacá* (*The Land of the Goitacá Indians*) (Rio de Janeiro, 1913–25); see also Alberto Lamego fils: *Planicie do Solar e da Senzala* (*Plain of the Country House and Slave Hut*) (Rio de Janeiro, 1933).

[160] Ayres de Cazal, op. cit., Vol. II, p. 146.

[161] Ibid., p. 45.

of St. Benedict. Under a similar regime of monoculture, big land-ownership, and slave labor, the population never enjoyed an abundance of cereals and green vegetables.

In short, the nutrition of the Brazilian colonial family, that of the plantations and notably that of the cities, astonishes us by its bad quality, its obvious poverty of animal proteins [162] and possibly of albuminoids in general, its lack of vitamins, of calcium and other mineral salts, and, on the other hand, its comparative richness in toxins. The Brazilian of good rural stock would find it hard to follow the example of the Englishman by tracing his ancestry back over a long period with the certainty of coming upon ten or a dozen generations of forebears who had been well nourished on beefsteak, vegetables, milk and eggs, oatmeal, and fruits, a diet that assured a prolonged eugenic development, sturdy health, and a physical robustness such as would not readily be disturbed or affected by other, social influences where a nutritional hygiene was the predominant factor.

If, contrary to the extremists—those who believe that everything is to be explained by diet [163]—the quantity and composition of foods are not enough in themselves to determine differences in morphology and psychology, the degree of economic capacity and of resistance to disease in human societies, their importance is none the less considerable, as is being shown by researches and investigations in this field. An attempt today is being made to rectify the anthropo-geography of those who, oblivious of diet, would attribute everything to the factors of *race* and *climate;* and in this work of rectification Brazilian society must be included, for it is the example of which alarmists make so much use in crying about the mixture of races and the malignity of the tropics in support of their thesis that man's degeneration is the effect of climate or of miscegenation. Ours is a society that historical investigation shows to have been, throughout a broad phase

---

[162] Proteins of animal origin, of high biologic value, or "proteins of the first class," to distinguish them from those of vegetable origin. For the most modern criticism with respect to the classification of proteins, see *Report of Committee on Nutrition,* by E. K. Le Fleming and others, supplement to the *British Medical Journal,* Vol. II (1933).

[163] E. V. McCollum and Nina Simmonds, in their work *The Newer Knowledge of Nutrition* (New York, 1929), oppose to Huntington's crite-rion that of diet. By it they explain, among other things attributed to the influence of climate or of race, the difference that within a few generations is to be found in Englishmen of the same *stock*: those that emigrated from Georgia at the end of the eighteenth century, some for Canada, others for the Bahama Islands. The diet of the former was milk, vegetables, meat, and an abundance of wheat; that of the latter, one resembling the diet of Brazilians.

of its development, one of the most lacking in eugenic prestige of all modern peoples, one of those whose economic capacity has been to the largest extent compromised by a deficiency of nutrition. Moreover, carried still further, back to the ancestors of the European colonizer of Brazil—those of even the most outstanding among the colonists— such investigation will reveal in the peninsula of the fifteenth and sixteenth centuries, as we shall see a little later on, a people whose physical vigor and hygiene had been profoundly disturbed by a pernicious combination of economic and social influences. One of these was of a religious nature: the abuse of fasts.

It is possible now to make certain generalizations regarding the sources of the Brazilian's food supply and his nutritional regime. As to the sources—vegetation and waters—they reflect the chemical poverty of the soil, which over a large area has little calcium.[164] As to the diet, when it is not deficient in quality as well as in quantity, it always shows a lack of balance.[165] This latter condition is general, among the well-to-do classes as well as others. This deficiency in quality and in quantity, this alimentary parsimony, has been the lot of the greater part of the population—a parsimony that is at times disguised to give an illusion of abundance such as is produced by manihot flour diluted with water.[166]

---

[164] In a study of the nutritive value of Brazilian foods, Alfredo Antônio de Andrade stresses the fact that calcium "is thinly distributed in the soil of Brazil, being concentrated in very rich deposits at certain points in our territory." Plants "do not commonly contain it in a high degree." This practically amounts to a death-sentence, in the light of modern research, which indicates that "the defense of the organism revolves about calcium, especially so far as resistance to infection and dyscratic diseases is concerned; it is upon calcium that all the phenomena subordinate to the activity of the muscles, nerves, and glands depend, taken in proper proportions with the ions, sodium, potassium, and magnesium. Unfortunately, this scarcity is to be found also in our waters. . . ."—Alfredo Antônio de Andrade: *Alimentos Brasileiros* (op. cit.). It is doubtful if calcium in water has the importance that Andrade attributes to

it. At any rate, the results of researches carried on among the inhabitants of the Alps, in a region in which the drinking-water is particularly rich in calcium, run counter to his opinion. Rickets was found there just as in regions relatively poor in calcium. See A. F. Hess: *Rickets, Including Osteomalacia and Tetany*, (London: Henry Kimpton, 1930), p. 51, cited by Ruy Coutinho: *Valor Social da Alimentação (Social Value of Alimentation)* (São Paulo, 1935).

[165] Antônio Martins do Azevedo Pimentel: *Subsidios para o Estudo da Higiene do Rio de Janeiro* (op. cit. note 123 above).

[166] Flour—a carbohydrate food with second-class protein, and poor in vitamins and mineral salts—has little nutritional value. Even when taken in its natural state, or dry, as a student of Bahian diet picturesquely observed in 1909, "it doubles in volume, strongly distending the walls of the

The poverty of the Brazilian soil in calcium is something that eludes all social control or rectification by man; but an explanation for the other two factors will be found in the social and economic history of our people: in monoculture and in the system of slave labor and big estates, responsible for the reduced consumption of milk, eggs, and vegetables among the majority of the population of Brazil.[167] These factors do admit of correction and control.

If I exclude the São Paulo populations from our generalization regarding the effect of alimentary deficiency upon the formation of Brazilian society, it is for the reason that the conditions to which they were subject were a little different from those that prevailed in the province of Rio de Janeiro and in the north: geological and metero-

---

intestines . . ." and may give rise to "abnormal fermentations." In addition, owing to the "presence of ligneous fibers of manihot root," it contributes to "the formation of hardened fecal cakes, constituting true *fecalomas,* capable of resisting the strongest enemas and the most energetic purgatives. . . ."—Francisco Antônio dos Santos Sousa: *Alimentação na Bahia* (*Alimentation in Bahia*), thesis presented to the Faculty of Medicine of Bahia (Bahia, 1909). There was recently in Brazil a kind of mystic exaltation of manihot flour, based in part upon conclusions that would appear to have been precipitated by the researches of São Paulo specialists; but the investigations later made by Dr. Antenor Machado at the Institute of Chemical Agriculture of the Ministry of Agriculture indicate that ordinary manihot flour does not contain vitamin B, while the coarse variety shows only traces of that vitamin.

[167] In his work *O Problema Fisiológico da Alimentação Brasileira* (*The Physiological Problem of Alimentation in Brazil*), Josué de Castro, from the physiological point of view and that of the most recent technique in his own specialized field, arrives at the same general conclusions as mine by taking a sociological criterion and sounding the Brazilian's antecedents:

to the effect that "many of the unwholesome consequences for which the unfavorable effects of our climate are blamed are the result of the small amount of attention that is paid to the basic problems of diet." As I see it, however, he is wholly in error when he considers those foods that are rich in carbohydrates as being "cheaply and readily obtainable by reason of their natural abundance in an agricultural country such as ours." "The habitual and instinctive diet of the poorer, working classes," he goes on to say, "is in this respect in accord with basic physiological principles." This essay endeavors to bring out precisely the contrary: that monoculture in our country always renders difficult the cultivation of vegetables destined for alimentary purposes. To this day the effect is to be perceived in the diet of Brazilians—that of the rich and especially that of the poor. In this diet vegetables are rare; some fruit or other, a sugar-bar or bit of molasses, a little fresh fish or game—this may, God willing, break the monotony of the poor man's diet, which commonly consists of meal, jerked beef, and codfish. Even beans are a luxury. And meal oftentimes is lacking. In colonial days there were successive "meal crises," and these were also experienced in the period of independence.

logical conditions favoring a diversified agriculture, including even the cultivation, though not to any great extent, of wheat; the probably superior chemical composition of the soil, resulting in a greater wealth of products for purposes of nutrition; the social and economic background of the first settlers, who possessed neither the traditions and tendencies nor the pecuniary resources of the colonizers of Pernambuco, but who were for the most part blacksmiths, carpenters, tailors, stonemasons, and weavers, and who were more given to a semi-rural and gregarious life than they were to monoculture and big estates; and finally—another economic cause—the fact that on the São Paulo plateau the two activities, agricultural and pastoral,[168] were concentrated and there did not exist that Balkan division, as one might almost term it, between separate and, so to speak, inimical forces such as conditioned the development of Bahia, Maranhão, Pernambuco, and Rio de Janeiro.

The generalizations of Professor Oliveira Vianna, who depicts for us in such glowing colors a São Paulo population of landed proprietors and opulent rural squires, have been recently corrected and their false gold and azure hues have been toned down by investigators who are more realistic and better documented than the illustrious sociologist who wrote *Southern Populations of Brazil*.[169] Reference is to such writers as Affonso de E. Taunay,[170] Alfredo Ellis, Jr.,[171] Paulo

---

[168] In his *Informação da Provincia do Brasil para Nosso Padre* (*Information Concerning the Province of Brazil for the Benefit of Our Father*), a work published in 1585, Anchieta (p. 45) tells us that in Piratininga the land consisted "of great prairies, very fertile in many pasture-grounds and herds," a statement that corresponds with another one, also made in the sixteenth century, as transcribed by Professor Taunay in *Non Ducor, Duco* (São Paulo, 1924). The author of this latter statement was Father Balthazar Fernandes, who wrote from Piratininga in 1569 that there "is much pasturage in the open country . . . belonging to anyone who wants it," in addition to "good food" and "much cattle."

[169] *Populações Meridionais do Brasil*. Vianna is also the author of *Evolução do Povo Brasileiro* (*Evolution*

of the Brazilian People*) (Rio de Janeiro, 1929), and *Raça e Assimilação* (*Race and Assimilation*) (São Paulo, 1932). He is the exponent of the "Aryanization" of the Brazilian people through assimilation (absorption) by the white race. (Translator.)

[170] Professor Affonso de E. Taunay's researches, which may be described as embodying a profound historical realism, are among the most extensive in this field. To him we are indebted for important revisions and corrections in the social and economic history of our country. Prominent among his works is a definitive study of the *bandeiras* of São Paulo: *História Geral das Bandeiras Paulistas* (São Paulo, 1924-9), which is perhaps the most serious bit of specialized historical investigation that has ever been undertaken in Brazil.

[171] *Raça de Gigantes* (op. cit.).

Prado,[172] and Alcantara Machado.[173] Basing ourselves upon these authors and upon the exceedingly rich documentation published at the behest of Washington Luis,[174] we must take issue with the conception that São Paulo was quite as aristocratic in its social development, quite as much given to large-scale landownership, as were the sugar-growing *capitânias* of the north. The contrary is the case: notwithstanding the deep disturbances occasioned by the *bandeirantes*, this was perhaps the society whose development proceeded with the greatest equilibrium. Especially so far as alimentation was concerned.

Writing of the São Paulo settlers, Alfredo Ellis, Jr., says: "Their nutrition during the first centuries, in addition to being abundant, must have been very well balanced as to its chemical elements." In making this statement he is relying upon the data contained in the *Inventories and Wills*. "They had, moreover," he goes on to say, "not only an abundance of meat protein from their herds of cattle, but also pork, which is rich in fats of great value. They were, accordingly, carnivorous, even though they had a copious variety of cereal-yielding plants and other vegetables, such as wheat, manihot, corn, beans, etc., which were planted all over the countryside and which contain a high percentage of carbohydrates that are very rich in calories." Again it is Alfredo Ellis, Jr., who reminds us of the observation of Martius [175] concerning the São Paulo populations: to the effect that diseases in São Paulo differ considerably in character from pathological conditions noted in Rio.[176] Martius attributes this fact to the dif-

---

[172] *Paulistica* (2nd edition, Rio de Janeiro, 1934).

[173] *Vida e Morte do Bandeirante* (op. cit.).

[174] Especially the *Inventários e Testamentos* (*Inventories and Wills*), Archives of the State of São Paulo, 1920-1. [On the previously mentioned publication of these documents at the instigation of Washington Luis, former President of Brazil, see p. xxxviii.) (Translator.)]

[175] C. F. P. von Martius, early nineteenth-century German explorer and geographer, author with J. B. von Spix of *Reise in Brasilien* (Munich, 1823-31; published in English translation as *Travels in Brazil, 1817-1820* (London, 1924). (Translator.)

[176] Writing from São Paulo (Ellis, op. cit.), Martius says: "There occur here with greater frequency rheumatic diseases and inflammatory states, chiefly of the eyes, chest, and throat, with subsequent pulmonary and tracheal phthisis, etc. On the other hand, gastric diseases are more rare, and there is not that general weakness of the digestive system, along with heartburn, which is frequent among the inhabitants of regions nearest the equator, affections that appear to increase in proportion to the heat." Ruediger Bilden would place the responsibility for the principal defects in our social, economic, and moral development upon slavery rather than upon climate and miscegenation, where I am inclined to put the blame upon monoculture and the

ference in climate—for it was then the mode to exalt this factor—
and, vaguely, to differences in constitution of the inhabitants. Had
he carried his diagnosis further, he undoubtedly would have arrived
at the important social cause or fact that goes to determine this
difference in pathological conditions between populations that are so
near to one another. The cause in question is the difference in the two
systems of nutrition: one marked by deficiency, with populations
stifled in their eugenic and economic development by monoculture;
the other a balanced system, by virtue of a greater division of the
land and a better co-ordination of activities—agricultural and pastoral
—among the Paulistas.[177] Whence the economic health which was
later to be transmitted to the inhabitants of Minas, who, once the
turbulent gold-and-diamond-rush phase was over, were to settle down
and become the most stable, the best-balanced, and possibly the best-
nourished people in Brazil.

I believe it may be stated that, from the point of view of nutrition,
the most salutary influence in the Brazilian's development has been
that of the African Negro, both with respect to the valuable food
products that through him have come to us from the land of his
origin, and with respect to his own diet, which was better balanced
than that of the white man—at least in this country, under slavery.
If I make this qualification, it is because the plantation-owners in
Brazil had their own variety of Taylorism, by which they endeavored
to obtain from the Negro slave, purchased at a dear price, the maximum of useful effort and not merely a maximum of labor for their
money. For many of the big landowners soon learned that the energy
of the African in their service, when abused or subjected to strain,
paid less dividends than when it was well conserved; and from there
they went on to exploit the slave with the object of getting as much
out of him as possible without impairing his normal efficiency. It was
to the master's interest to preserve that efficiency, for the Negro was

---

latifundia, while not overlooking for
a moment or undertaking to diminish
the tremendous importance of slavery.
It is merely that, if we had to condition or subordinate one to the other,
we should subordinate slavery to
monoculture and the system of big
estates.

[177] At the end of the colonial epoch
the Swedish physician Gustav Beyer,
as well as the Jesuit chroniclers of the

sixteenth century, laid emphasis upon
"the enormous abundance of victuals
in the markets" of São Paulo: fruits
and vegetables, cereals and tuberous
plants, game and slaughterhouse animals. And he added that nowhere else
did the population present so fine an
appearance as in São Paulo, and in no
other place had he seen so few crip-
ples. —See Affonso de E. Taunay:
Non Ducor, Duco (op. cit.).

his capital, his work-machine, a part of himself; which accounts for the plentiful and nourishing food that Peckholt saw the owners passing out to their slaves in Brazil.[178] The diet of the Negro on Brazilian plantations may not have been marked by any culinary niceties, but it was an unfailing source of nourishment; the abundance of corn, salt pork, and beans that it contained commends it as being suited to the hard labor demanded of an agricultural slave.

The Negro slave in Brazil appears to us to have been, with all his alimentary deficiencies, the best-nourished element in our society; owing in large part to *diet*—I repeat—many of the finest expressions of vigor and physical beauty in our country will be found to be of African origin: the mulattoes, the creoles,[179] the quadroons, and, above all, the octoroons;[180] the plantation *cabras;*[181] the sailors in our navy

---

[178] Peckholt adds, with regard to the diet of the slaves: "the planter provided out of his own means for the replacement of the material consumed."

[179] The term *creole* has here not the Spanish-American sense of one of Spanish descent born and reared in the colonies; it means a Negro slave born in America, and comes to be applied today to Negroes in general. (Translator.)

[180] Sylvio Romero: *História da literatura brasileira* (Rio de Janeiro, 1888).

[181] José Américo de Almeida, in his study of the Paraiban populations, referring to the Negroid character of the "ancient centers of slavery" in the marshlands, says: "this individual [the man of the marshlands], ill-nourished and ill-clad, bent over his hoe, labors incessantly from sun to sun and throughout the rigors of the winter season, with an indefatigability of which no other would be capable. . . . Despite this life of privations and physical exhaustion, the type is not one of the most abject; on the contrary, it affords examples of a robust constitution—Herculean *cabras* who endure the most back-breaking toil, such as that of the *bagaceira*" (op. cit.). Lafcadio Hearn makes a similar observation with respect to the mes-

tizo populations (mulattoes, quadroons, octoroons, etc.) of the French West Indies: "Without fear of exaggerating facts, I can venture to say that the muscular development of the working-men here is something which must be seen in order to be believed; —to study fine displays of it, one should watch the blacks and half-breeds working naked to the waist— on the landings, in the gas-houses and slaughter-houses or in the nearest plantations." —*Two Years in the French West Indies* (New York and London, 1923). In response to the allegation that he is merely a writer and not a scientist, Hearn might have replied that he discovered more as a writer than many a sociologist. Moreover, he has to bear him out the statement of J. J. Cornilli, who in his medical study *Recherches chronologiques et historiques sur l'origine et la propagation de la fièvre jaune aux Antilles* stresses the robustness and physical vigor of the mestizo of Martinique.

[For a vivid portrayal of the life and function of plantation *cabras*, see Jorge Amado's *Terras do Sem Fim* (São Paulo, 1943), published in English under the title *The Violent Land* (New York: Alfred A. Knopf; 1945). (Translator.)]

and our naval guners; [182] the *capoeiras;* the capangas; [183] the ath-letes; [184] the stevedores of Recife and Salvador; many of the *jagunços* [185] of the Bahian backlands and the *cangaceiros* [186] of the northeast. The lyric exaltation of the *caboclo*—that is to say, of the native Indian, which is common among us, or of the cross between Indian and white, a type in which certain persons would discover the purest exponent of the physical capacity, beauty, and even the moral resistance of the Brazilian racial strain [187]—all this does not corre-

---

[182] At the beginning of the nine-teenth century the Englishman Henry Koster, traveling in Pernambuco, contrasted the regiments of militia made up exclusively of blacks and mulattoes with those regiments of the line made up of Portuguese, con-cluding that the colored men pre-sented the better physical appear-ance.—*Travels in Brazil* (London, 1816). A Portuguese translation of Koster's book, made by Senhor Luis da Camara Cascudo, has just been published. [One of the best-known and best paintings by Brazil's great contempo-rary artist Cândido Portinari is *The Naval Gunner's Family.* (Transla-tor.)]

[183] *Capanga* means a professionally brave man, often a bodyguard. (Translator.)

[184] Those who exhibited their prowess at fairs, on feast-days, etc. (Translator.)

[185] Originally, back-county ruffians; the term comes to be practically syn-onymous with *sertanejo,* or inhabitant of the backlands. (Translator.)

[186] A *cangacerio* is a bandit, one who is laden with the *cangaço,* or bundle of weapons that bandits carry in northeastern Brazil. For colorful details on the *cangaceiros,* see the work by Luis da Camara Cascudo: *Vaqueiros e Cantadores (Cowboys and Singers)* (Porto Alegre, 1939), pp. 116–20. —Such terms as *cabra, capoeira, capanga, jagunço, canga-ceiro,* etc., by reason of their shades of meaning and connotation, are prac-tically untranslatable, or dangerous to translate. (Translator.)

[187] To call anyone a *"caboclo"* in Brazil is almost always a tribute to his character or his capacity for phys-ical and moral endurance. This is in contrast to "mulatto," "Negro," *"moleque"* ("black boy"), "creole," *"pardo"* (mulatto), *"pardavasco"* (off-spring of Negro and mulatto), and *"sarará"* (light-colored Negro with red or sandy hair), which in general carry a derogatory implication with respect to the individual's morals, cul-ture, or social position. Many a Bra-zilian mulatto of high social or politi-cal standing makes a point of referring to himself as a *caboclo:* "we *caboclos,*" "if I were not a *caboclo,*" etc. And Júlio Bello tells us that old Sebastião de Rosário, the well-known Pernam-bucan planter of the nineteenth cen-tury, a pure Wanderley by descent, coming from the best branch of the family, that of Serinhaem—almost all the members having the rubicund complexion of Europeans, blue eyes, and reddish hair—was in the habit at great banquets, when he was feeling at peace with the world, of praising himself falsely as being a *"caboclo."* The one thing that no one wanted to be at such moments as this was a Negro or an individual with a trace of Negro blood. The exceptions were exceedingly rare. [Euclides da Cunha described him-self in a verse couplet as "this *caboclo,* this tame *jagunço,* mixture of Celt, of Tapuia (Indian), and of Greek." (Translator.)]

spond to reality. On this point the distinguished scholar Roquette Pinto hints at the necessity of correcting Euclides da Cunha, who is not always accurate in his generalizations. Much of what Euclides extols as the strength of the indigenous race, or sub-race formed by the union of white with Indian, is due to virtues coming from an admixture of the three races, and not from that of Indian and white alone; or in any event, as much of it is due to the Negro as to the Indian or the Portuguese. "Racial admixture," says Roquette Pinto, "produced the mameluco, but the *jagunço* is not a mameluco, offspring of white and Indian. Euclides studied him in Bahia,[188] and Bahia and Minas are the two states of the Union in which the African is most widely dispersed." [189]

The Brazilian anthropologist stresses the point that "it is a big mistake to believe that in the great central *sertão* and the Amazonian lowlands the *sertanejo* is exclusively the *caboclo*. In the rolling highlands of the northeast as in the rubber forests," he goes on to say, "there are *cafusos* or *caborés*, of part-Negro descent." And he underlines the fact that many a Negro had left the coast or the sugar-raising zone to take refuge in a *quilombo*, or fugitive-slave settlement, in the backlands: "Many slaves fled to the *quilombos* in the forests, in the vicinity of the Indian tribes. Inasmuch as it was difficult for their own women to flee, the rape of Indian women was widely practiced by the black *quilombolas*." [190]

Previously, in his study *Rondônia*,[191] Roquette Pinto had published some interesting documents, which he had found in the archives of

---

[188] See *Os sertões* (*Rebellion in the Backlands*), *passim*, but especially the chapter on "Man" (Chapter ii). (Translator.)

[189] E. Roquette Pinto: *Seixos Rolados* (*Rolled Pebbles*) (Rio de Janeiro, 1927). "However," adds Roquette Pinto, "elements are not lacking in the book *Os Sertões* to prove that those individuals who were 'above all robust' had a large drop of Negro blood in their veins. One has but to reread the description of the rabble of Canudos: 'all ages, all types, all colors . . . Creole women with their dyed and battered mops of hair; the straight smooth hair of the *caboclas;* the outlandish topknots of the African women; the light-colored and brown hair of pure-blooded white women; their heads all jumbled together, with-out a ribbon, a hairpin, a flower, without covering or ornament of the meanest sort." [For the complete passage of da Cunha, see *Os Sertões*, 16th revised edition, p. 199; see *Rebellion in the Backlands*, pp. 136–7. (Translator.)]

[190] Roquette Pinto, op. cit. [For a fascinating account of the *quilombos*, see an article by the internationally known Brazilian anthropologist Arthur Ramos: "*O Espírito Associativo do Negro Brasileiro*" "The Associative Spirit of the Brazilian Negro"), in the *Revista do Arquivo Municipal* of São Paulo, Vol. XLVII, pp. 105–26 (May 1938). (Translator.)]

[191] Roquette Pinto: *Rondônia* (Rio de Janeiro, 1917).

the Brazilian Historical Institute, concerning the *caborés* of the Serra do Norte, in the very heart of Brazil, showing that they were the hybrid offspring of Negro fugitives from the mines and Indian women who had been raped by them. The victims of these rapes committed by the Negroes of the *quilombos* were not merely, as Ulysses Brandão puts it,[192] "black Sabines . . . of the plantations"; the greater part of them were Indian women. In traveling recently through lower Cuminá, Gastão Cruls came upon various remains of the old *mucambos* or *quilombos*;[193] that is to say, of the fugitive-slave settlements founded by Negroes from the plantations and the ranches. "What is more," he writes, "these slave refuges were to be found along nearly all the rivers of the Amazon region; and even on the upper Içá, Crevaux discovered the thatched hut of an old black woman."[194] Wherever one turns, even in places where it is supposed that Amerindian blood or that of the Portuguese-Indian hybrid is preserved in its purest state, it will be found that the African has been there: in the very heart of the Amazon region, on the Serra do Norte, and in the backlands.

The *sertanejo's* supposed absolute freedom from African blood or influence will not withstand a thorough examination. If pure whites are numerous in certain backland regions, African traces will be found in others. It would be most interesting to make a study with the object of locating the sites of the old slave strongholds, which must have stained with black, a black that today has grown paler, many a region of central Brazil. These concentrations of pure Negroes must necessarily correspond to the Negroid patches in the bosom of populations far removed from the centers of slavery. Women of their own color being scarce among the fugitives, they would have had recourse, in supplying the lack, "to the rape of Indian women," or the *caboclas* of the nearest towns and settlements; and thus they would have dispersed their blood through much of the region that was later to be looked upon as being virginally pure from Negro influence. For this activity of the fugitive Negroes in the backland regions and along the Amazon River represents an impulse that is almost equal to that of the São Paulo *bandeirantes* or the settlers of Ceará.

---

[192] Ulysses Brandão: *A Confederação do Equador* (*The Confederation of Ecuador*) (Pernambuco, 1924).

[193] According to Ramos (loc. cit., note 190 above), the *mucambo* was a hut in a *quilombo;* but the two terms are commonly used as synonymous. (Translator.)

[194] Gastão Cruls: *A Amazônia que Eu Vi* (*The Amazon Region As I Saw It*) (Rio de Janeiro, 1930). [In addition to being a physician and man of science, Gastão Cruls is a prominent novelist and literary figure in contemporary Brazil. (Translator.)]

Mulatto in composition, or a mixture of white and Indian and, in lesser proportion, of three races, the greater part of the free population, which in our slave-holding society corresponded to the "poor white trash" of the English colonies in North America, was an element that was comparatively exempt from African coloring or influence; and it was at the same time the one that was subject to the most devastating effects of paludic anemia, beriberi,[195] and worms, affections that, following abolition, which in this respect came as a calamity, were extended to those Negroes and mulattoes who had been abandoned by the Big Houses and deprived of the patriarchal assistance of their former masters and the diet of the slave quarters. The Negro slaves enjoyed, as the *caboclos* and free mulattoes did not, the advantage of living-conditions that were preservative rather than depreciative from the point of view of eugenics; they were in a better position to resist pathogenic and social influences and those deriving from their physical environment, and so were able to propagate descendants who were healthier and more vigorous.

The same cannot be said with regard to the effects of syphilis, which was, *par excellence*, the disease of the Big Houses and the *senzalas*. The son of the plantation-owner would contract it almost as he played with the Negro and mulatto girls, acquiring precociously his first sexual experience at the age of twelve or thirteen; for from that time on, the lad was already a young gentleman who was subject to ridicule for not having had carnal knowledge of a woman and who would be the butt of jests if he could not show the scars of syphilis on his body. Such scars, Martius notes, the Brazilian would display as he might those of war;[196] and half a century after his time, a French observer, Émile Béringer, while denying the preponderant influence of the climate of northern Brazil upon the disease-rate of the region, was to emphasize the truly tragic importance of syphilis: "Syphilis works great havoc. The major portion of the inhabitants do not look upon it as a shameful disease and do not pay much attention to it. Aside from its influence upon the development of numerous special affections, it accounts for ten deaths in every thousand." [197]

The advantage of miscegenation in Brazil ran parallel to the tre-

---

[195] Especially beriberi, an avitaminosis resulting from a lack of vitamin B, and not an infection. At least, this is the conclusion of profound students of the subject: Sherman, Mendel, Aykroyd, Cowgill, Sure. On beriberi in Brazil, see the study by V. Baptista: *Vitaminas e Avitaminoses* (*Vitamins and Avitaminoses*) (São Paulo, 1934). Also the work of Ruy Coutinho, previously cited.

[196] Spix and Martius, op. cit.

[197] Émile Béringer, op. cit. So sensitive to the perfections of sanitary technique and the general comforts of life does the disease-rate of north-

mendous disadvantage of syphilis. These two factors began operating at the same time: one to form the Brazilian, the ideal type of modern man for the tropics, a European with Negro or Indian blood to revive his energy; the other to deform him. Out of this there arises a certain confusion of thought on the subject of responsibilities, many attributing to miscegenation effects that are chiefly due to syphilis, the Negro or the Amerindian or even the Portuguese race being held responsible for the "ugliness" and "ignorance" [198] of those of our backland populations who have been most affected by syphilis or eaten with worms, whereas the truth is that each one of these races, in a pure or uncrossed state, is exhausted with producing admirable examples of beauty and physical robustness.

Of all the social influences, perhaps syphilis has been, next to bad nutrition, plastically the most deforming in its effects, the one that has to the greatest extent drained the economic energy of the Brazilian mestizo. It would appear to have come from the first unions of Europeans, wandering aimlessly along our shores, with those Indian women who offered themselves to the white man's sexual embrace. That "initial ethnic tare" of which Azevedo Amaral speaks was first of all a syphilitic tare.

It is customary to say that civilization and syphilis go hand in hand, but Brazil would appear to have been syphilized before it was civilized. The first Europeans to come here were swallowed up in the aboriginal mass without leaving upon the latter any traces of their origin other than those of syphilis and racial hybridism. They did not bring civilization, but there is evidence to show that they did bring the venereal plague to the population that absorbed them.

It is precisely from the twofold point of view of miscegenation and

---

ern Brazil seem to Béringer to be that he is led to conclude from his studies in Pernambucan climatology that "with the progress of hygiene and civilization, many of the causes will disappear. Already today the death-rate is lower among the better-to-do white inhabitants, who are more prudent, more appreciative of their own well-being, than are the mulattoes or the blacks." Thus does Béringer respond to the question that, in this same era, came from the pen of Capistrano de Abreu: ". . . what, after all, do we know of the action of that ardent climate which is held respon-sible for so many of our defects?"— Preface to *Geografia Geral do Brasil* (*General Geography of Brazil*), by A. W. Sellin (translated from the German, Rio de Janeiro, 1889). It was as if the perspicacious historian had attained the modern attitude of anthropo-geography toward the factor of climate: a tendency to diminish its responsibilities.

[198] A. Carneiro Leâo: *Oliveira Lima* (Recife, 1913); Paulo de Moraes Barros: *Impressões do Nordeste* (*Impressions of the Northeast*) (São Paulo, 1923).

of syphilis that the first phase of settlement impresses us as being so extremely important a one. With regard to the former, it was the first random settlers who prepared the way for the only colonizing process that would have been possible in Brazil: the formation of a hybrid society through polygamy—the Europeans being so few in number. Paulo Prado, in writing of figures like Diogo Alvares, of João Ramalho, and, somewhat inappropriately, of Jeronymo de Albuquerque (who belongs to another phase of settlement), observes that they "were widely prolific in offspring, as if to indicate the solution of the problem of colonization and racial formation in our country." [199] The fact of the matter is that out of their contact with the Amerindian population there resulted the first hybrid layers, constituting, it may be, the point of easiest penetration for the second lot of Europeans; and when the regular settlers arrived, they were to encounter among the dark reddish-skinned native masses these traces of a lighter stock. Even though they were without definite European characteristics, the mestizos, as if by very reason of the fact that their color was closer to that of the whites and they possessed one vestige or another of that moral or material culture which they had acquired from European lands, must have served as a wedge or fleshly lining to cushion the violent shock of contact with females who were so wholly different from the European type, for those Portuguese colonists—and there must, surely, have been many of them, coming from northern Portugal—who were still virgins so far as such exotic experiences were concerned.

Many of the first settlers did no more than lose themselves in the midst of the native population. There were few of those "true chieftains" [200] of whom Paulo Prado speaks: great white patriarchs who, living alone among the Indians, succeeded in subjecting to their will as Europeans sizable bands of the native folk. But even those who lost themselves in the darkness of native life, without leaving so much as a name behind them, are none the less forced upon the attention of one who is concerned with the genetic and social history of Brazilian society. For good or ill, they were the forebears of that society; it was they who were responsible for contaminating it with some of its most persistent vices and characteristics: ethnic tares, as Azevedo Amaral would assert; social tares, I should prefer to say.

The syphilization of Brazil, it would seem, resulted from the first contacts along our shores—chance contacts, some of them— of Euro-

---

[199] Paulo Prado, op. cit.   [200] Ibid.

peans with Indian women. Not only the Portuguese, but the French and Spaniards as well; but chiefly the Portuguese and the French. Exiles, new-Christians, Norman dyewood traders who had remained here and who, having been left behind by their own people, had gone to live with the natives – these individuals frequently ended by acquiring a taste for this disordered way of life, with women of easy virtue all about them, to be had in the shade of the cashew and guava trees.[201]

Oscar da Silva Araujo, to whom we are indebted for valuable data on the appearance of syphilis in Brazil, associates it principally with the contact of native women with the French. "In the sixteenth century," the Brazilian scientist reminds us, "there broke out in France the great epidemic of syphilis; and in the accounts left by the contraband traders of this era we find references to the existence among them of venereal diseases that sometimes decimated the populations. And it is to be presumed that these French adventurers who dealt with our natives were likewise infected, and that it was, indeed, they who had first introduced and spread the disease." [202]

The Portuguese could have been no less infected, for they were an even more mobile and sensual people than were the French. "The disease that laid waste the Old World at the end of the fifteenth century," says Oscar da Silva Araujo in one of his works, "was spread throughout the Orient, having been carried there by the Portuguese. The investigations of Okamura, Dohi, and Susuky, in Japan and in China, and those of Jolly and others in India, show that syphilis appeared in these countries only after they had come into contact with Europeans. In India it made its appearance after the arrival of Vasco da Gama, in 1498, who had sailed from Portugal the year before. Gaspar Corrêa, in his *Lendas da India* (*Legends of India*) tells us that "in Cacotorá, in the year 1507, the people began to fall ill of the bad vapors and bad food, and especially as the result of intercourse with women, of which they died." [203] Silva Araujo goes on to remind us of Engelbert Kömpfer's assertion, cited by Astruc, to the effect that the Japanese term *mambakassam*, with its literal meaning of "disease of the Portuguese," is the one by which syphilis is known in

---

[201] The guava tree (*araça*) belongs to the Myrtaceæ or myrtle family (*Psidium araça Raddi*). (Translator.)

[202] Oscar da Silva Araujo: *Alguns Comentários sobre o Sífilis no Rio de Janeiro* (*Some Comments on Syphilis in Rio de Janeiro*) (Rio de Janeiro, 1928).

[203] Oscar da Silva Araujo: *Subsídios ao Estudo da Framboesia Tropical* (*Contributions to the study of Buboes*) (Rio de Janeiro, 1928).

Japan. And even to our day, he adds, in many Oriental countries the two expressions are synonymous. In the Indian, Japanese, and Chinese languages there are no names for the disease." [204]

Although a number of authorities on the tropics, some of whom, like Sigaud, have made a special study of Brazil, are inclined to look upon syphilis as autochthonous,[205] the evidence gathered by Oscar da Silva Araujo leads us to a different conclusion. "Physicians who have most recently traveled among the natives," the Brazilian author tells us, "and who have studied the diseases to be found among those of our Indians who have not yet come into contact with civilization— among others, Dr. Roquette Pinto, Dr. Murillo de Campos, and Dr. Olympio da Fonseca *fils*—report that they have never observed syphilis among these tribes, notwithstanding the fact that they have noted the presence of various skin affections." And he adds: "the first travelers and writers who allude to the climate and diseases of Brazil never mention the existence of this malady among the savages, who up to that time had lived isolated from European contacts. . . ." [206] The same opinion is held by another distinguished investigator, Professor Pirajá da Silva, who regards leprosy and syphilis as having been "introduced into Brazil by European and African colonists." [207] What would appear to have happened is that buboes has been widely confused with syphilis.

Not only was sexual intercourse between the European conqueror and the Indian woman disturbed by syphilis and other highly contagious venereal diseases of European origin; it also took place, after relations between masters and their female Negro slaves became widespread, under circumstances that were otherwise unfavorable to the woman. A species of sadism on the part of the white man and of

---

[204] Ibid.

[205] "*La syphilis*," writes Sigaud, "*fait beaucoup de ravages dans les populations nomades, et bien que certains observateurs pensent qu'elle se soit propagée davantage après la conquête des portugais, a été constaté que la maladie existait déjà chez les indigènes qui n'avaient eu aucum rapport avec les Européens. Le voyageur Ribeiro de Sampaio, dans sa relation publiée en 1775, pags, 9, 24, dit avoir recontré des tribus avec des symptômes évidents de maladie vénérienne.*"
—J. F. X. Sigaud: *Du climat et des*

maladies du Brésil (Paris, 1844). Professor Milton T. Rosenau of Harvard University says that the study of bones found in pre-Columbian burial-grounds points to the American origin of syphilis. (Milton T. Rosenau: *Preventive Medicine and Hygiene*, 5th edition, New York and London.) The subject, however, continues to be a controversial one.

[206] Oscar da Silva Araujo: *Comentários*, etc. (op. cit.).

[207] *Diálogos das Grandezas do Brasil* (op. cit.), note 12 to the Second Dialogue.

masochism on the part of his Indian companion must have been the predominant feature in the sexual as in the social relations of the European with the women of those races that were subject to his rule. The furious passions of the Portuguese must have been vented upon victims who did not always share his sexual tastes, although we know of cases where the sadism of the white conqueror was offset by the masochism of his native or Negro partner. So much for the sadistic impulses of the man toward woman—which not infrequently derived from the relations of the master toward the Negro slave boy who had been his playmate in youth. Through the submission of the black boy in the games that they played together, and especially the one known as *leva-pancadas* ("take a drubbing"), the white lad was often initiated into the mysteries of physical love. As for the lad who took the drubbing, it may be said of him that, among the great slave-holding families of Brazil, he fulfilled the same passive functions toward his young master as did the adolescent slave under the Roman Empire who had been chosen to be the companion of a youthful aristocrat: he was a species of victim, as well as a comrade in those games in which the *"premiers élans génésiques"* of the son of the family found outlet.[208]

Moll stresses the fact that the first direction taken by the sexual impulse in childhood—sadism, masochism, bestiality, or fetishism—is dependent largely upon opportunity or chance—that is to say, upon external social influences—rather than upon predisposition or innate perversion.[209] The author of *The Sexual Life of the Child* speaks of a period of "sexual indifferentiation"—through which, according to Penta and Max Dessoir,[210] every individual passes—as being one that is particularly sensitive to such influences. It was in this period of indifferentiation that the social influences about him (his position as a master surrounded by docile slaves and animals) acted upon the son of the slave-holding family in Brazil, inducing him to bestiality or to sadism. Even when his sexual impulses later underwent a change, he not infrequently preserved, in various manifestations of life and in his social activities as an individual, that "sexual undertone" which, according to Pfister, "is never lacking to well-marked sadistic pleas-

---

[208] F. Buret: *La Syphilis aujourd'hui et chez les anciens* (Paris, 1890).

[209] Albert Moll: *The Sexual Life of the Child* (translation, New York, 1924).

[210] Pascale Penta: *I Pervertimenti Sessuali* (Naples, 1893); Max Dessoir: *"Zur Psychologie der Vita Sexualis,"* in *Allgemeine Zeitschrift für psychischgerichtliche Medicin,* cited by Westermarck: *The Origin and Development of Moral Ideas* (London, 1926).

ure." [211] The sadism of the small boy and the adolescent was transformed into a taste for administering thrashings, for having them pull out the teeth of the Negro who had stolen his sugar-cane, for having *capoeiras*, cocks, and male canaries fight in his presence—tastes that were frequently manifested by the plantation-owner after he had become a grown man. It would also come out in his passion for giving violent or perverse commands, either as lord of the manor or as the university-educated son occupying an elevated political or public administrative position. Or else it would show, purely and simply, in that fondness for ordering people about which is characteristic of every Brazilian born and reared in a plantation Big House. This tendency is often to be met with refined into a grave sense of authority and of duty, as in a Dom Vital, or brutalized into a crude authoritarianism as in a Floriano Peixoto.

One result of the persistent action of this sadism, a sadism of the conqueror toward the conquered, of the master toward the slave, is a fact that appears to me to be linked naturally with the economic circumstances that shaped our patriarchal society: the fact that the woman in Brazil is so often the helpless victim of the male's domination or abuse.[212] a creature sexually and socially repressed, who lives within the shadow of her father or her husband. Meanwhile we should not forget that feminine variety of sadism, when the woman has become a great lady, which is shown toward slaves, especially toward the mulatto girls, in which case there enters an element of envy or sexual jealousy.

But this sadism of the master and the corresponding masochism of the slave, exceeding the sphere of sexual and domestic life, makes itself felt throughout our history in a broader, social and political domain. It is my opinion that it is to be met with in our political life,

---

[211] Oscar Pfister: *Love in Children and Its Aberrations* (translation, London, 1924).

[212] The fact should not pass without mention that in a country where for long centuries slaves and women have been trodden underfoot by extreme masculine pressure, the dominant cult among the Catholic majority is the masochistic, sentimental one of the Sacred Heart of Jesus. An exhibitionism of the suffering heart is likewise common among our poets. Our amorous as well as our devotional and mystical literature is filled with hearts bleeding voluptuously, or else bruised, grieving, wounded, embittered, lacerated, flaming, etc., etc.

[A vivid picture of the masculine sequestration and domination of women in nineteenth-century Brazil may be had from Escragnolle Taunay's novel *Inocência*, translated by Henriqueta Chamberlain (New York: The Macmillan Company; 1945). In the Preface to the First Edition (see p. 33), Freyre alludes to the "small chambers . . . for the all but monastic seclusion of unmarried daughters." (Translator.)]

where the passion for command has always found victims upon whom to vent itself with refinements that are at times sadistic in character, while at other times what we have is old nostalgias transformed into civic cults, like that of the so-called "Iron Marshal." [213] Our revolutionary, liberal, demagogic tradition is limited to foci that readily admit of political prophylaxis; for when we come down to it, what the majority of those who may be called the Brazilian people are still experiencing is the pressure exerted upon them by a government that is masculine and boldly autocratic. Even in the case of sincere individual self-expressions—not at all uncommon in this kind of American Russia that is our Brazil [214]—expressions of a revolutionary mysticism, a Messianic faith, of the identification of the redeemer with the masses to be redeemed, through the sacrifice of life or of personal liberty—even in such cases as these there is to be sensed a masochistic taint or residue, representing not so much the will to reform or correct certain definite vices of our political or economic system as the pure enjoyment of suffering, of being the victim, of sacrificing oneself.

On the other hand, the conservative tradition in Brazil has always been sustained by the sadism of command, disguised as the "principle of authority" or the "defense of order." Between the opposing mysticisms, that of Order and that of Liberty, that of Authority and that of Democracy, our political life after we had precociously emerged from the regime of master and slave has ever sought a balance. The truth is that the balance continues to lie between certain traditional and profound realities: sadists and masochists; masters and slaves; those with a doctor's degree and the illiterates; individuals of a culture that is predominantly European and others whose culture is chiefly African and Amerindian. All this is not without its advantages, the advantages of a duality that is not wholly prejudicial to our culture in process of formation, enriched on the one hand by the spontaneity, the freshness of imagination and emotion of the many, and on the other hand by a contact through the élites with the science, the

---

[213] A term applied, by those who would make a cult of him, to Floriano Peixoto, the iron-fisted dictator who (following Deodoro Fonseca) ruled Brazil during the greater part of the interregnum between the overthrow of the monarchy and the final establishment of the Republic (1889–94). (Translator.)

[214] The expression "American Russia" impresses one critic who has graciously concerned himself with this essay as being "an antiquated formula after Vicente Licínio Cardoso and Senhor Octávio da Fária." But possibly this critic is mistaken, at least in part. The expression in question was used by me for the first time more than ten years ago, in a paper, *"Vida Social no Nordeste"* ("Social Life in the Northeast"), published in the First Centenary edition of the *Diário de Pernambuco* (1925).

technique, and the advanced thought of Europe. Perhaps nowhere else is the meeting, intercommunication, and harmonious fusion of diverse or, even, antagonistic cultural traditions occurring in so liberal a way as it is in Brazil. Meanwhile the vacuum between the two extremes is still enormous, the intercommunication between the cultural traditions being in many respects deficient; but in any event, the Brazilian regime cannot be accused of rigidity or, as Sorokin would put it, of a lack of vertical mobility, and in a number of social directions it is one of the most democratic, flexible, and plastic regimes to be found anywhere.

A significant circumstance remains to be noted in connection with the formation of Brazilian society, and that is the fact that our progress has not been purely in the direction of Europeanization. In place of a hard and dry, grinding effort at adaptation to conditions wholly strange, the contact of European culture with that of the aborigines was smoothed by the oil of African mediation. The Jesuit system itself—possibly the most efficient force for technical Europeanization and intellectual and moral culture in its effect upon the natives—obtained its greatest success in Brazil during the first centuries on the mystic, devotional, and festive side of the Catholic religion: in the Christianization of the Indians through music, through song, through liturgy, through processions, feasts, religious dances, mysteries, comedies; through the distribution of veronicas with the Agnus Dei, which the *caboclos* might hang about their necks, along with chains, ribbons, rosaries, and the like; and through the adoration of the relics of the Holy Wood and the heads of the Eleven Thousand Virgins. And all of these elements, while they served the cause of Europeanization and Christianization, were impregnated with animistic or fetishistic influence that well may have come from Africa.

For it would appear that even the *Spiritual Exercises* were assimilated by Loyola from African sources; they are in any event the product of the same mystic or religious climate as the manifestations of voluptuous mysticism to be found among the Arabs. The Jesuit heaven, purgatory, and hell, whose delights or horrors the devout one who practiced the *Exercises* would end by seeing, smelling, and tasting as he listened to the canticles of joy of the blessed or the despairing Jesus-save-me of the damned—that heaven, that purgatory, and that hell, brought down to the plane of the senses by means of an admirable technique, are very close, so a comparative study of religions would indicate, to the ancient and mystical teachings of the Mohammedans. Hermann Müller in his book on the origins of the Society of Jesus concludes, a bit hastily perhaps, that the Mussulman technique was imitated by St. Ignatius de Loyola. And Chamberlain, in his interpretation—which is wholly in terms of race, and the Nordic race at that—of the religious culture of modern Europe, absolutely repudiates St. Ignatius for the reason that he has discovered in the latter's system anti-European qualities of imagination, sentiment, and mystical technique—or, as he understands it, anti-mysticism; for Chamberlain does not perceive in Loyola's teachings any mystical perfume, but for him the *Exercises*, when all is said, are merely a "grossly mechanical method, arranged with supreme artistry to excite the individual. . . ." [215]

The possible African origin of the Jesuit system—Chamberlain looks upon it as definitely established—impresses us as being most important in explaining the cultural side of the formation of Brazilian society, which, even where it would seem to be strictly European, as in the case of the Jesuit catechism, must have undergone the softening influence of Africa. African mediation in Brazil has brought the extremes closer to one another; without it, European and Amerindian culture, so strange and antagonistic to each other in many of their tendencies, would hardly have got along so well together.

From a general point of view, the formation of Brazilian society, as I have stressed from the first pages of this essay, has been in reality a process of balancing antagonisms. Economic and cultural antagonisms. Antagonisms between European culture and native culture. Between the African and the native. Between an agrarian and a pastoral economy, between that of the agrarian and that of the mining regions. Between Catholic and heretic. Jesuit and *fazendeiro*. The *bandeirante*

---

[215] Houston Stewart Chamberlain: *The Foundations of the Nineteenth Century* (London, 1911). The Argentine literary critic Senhor Ricardo Sáenz Hayes, in speaking of this passage which I have quoted from Chamberlain regarding Loyola and the *Exercises*, recently observed that "in order to seek the origins of his mysticism," as Chamberlain does, "one would have to be unfamiliar with the Christian sources of Christianity." And he cites as his authority *El Islam Cristianizado*, by A. Palacios (Madrid, 1931).—Introduction to the Spanish edition of *Casa-Grande e Senzala* (Buenos Aires, 1942). But an equally weighty authority is Father Asín Palacios, who wrote *La Es-* catologia Musulmana en la Divina Comedia (Madrid, 1919). If the Christian poetry of Dante is not dishonored by Islamic and African origins, why should this be a mark of dishonor for Loyola and his *Exercises*? With all his Occidentalism, the French Catholic writer M. Legendre, recognizes that "*le sémitisme arabe a mis dans le tempérament spirituel de l'Espagne une forte note d'originalité. . . .*" This is true not only of the Arabic influence, but of the North African as well. And he adds that he looks upon it as "*un signe de pusillanimité chez certains Espagnols . . . répudier cet africanisme.*"—Portrait de l'Espagne (Paris, 1923), p. 51.

and the plantation-owner. The Paulista and the *emboaba*.[216] The Pernambucan and the *mascate*.[217] The landed proprietor and the pariah. The university graduate and the illiterate. But predominant over all these antagonisms was the more general and the deeper one: that between master and slave.

It is true that, acting always upon all these clashing antagonistic forces, deadening the shock or harmonizing them, have been certain conditions peculiar to Brazil that have made for fraternization and vertical mobility: miscegenation; the dispersal of inheritances; the possibility of a frequent and easy change of profession and of residence; frequent and easy access to public office and to elevated political and social positions on the part of mestizos and natural sons; the lyric character of Portuguese Christianity; the spirit of moral tolerance; hospitality to strangers and intercommunication between the different parts of the country. The last mentioned factor has been due less to technical facilities than to physical conditions: the absence of a mountain chain or system of rivers such as would really interfere with Brazilian unity and a cultural and economic reciprocity between the geographic extremes.

---

[216] *Emboaba*: nickname given in colonial times to the Portuguese who came to the backlands in search of gold and precious stones; then applied to the descendants of the São Paulo *bandeirantes;* and finally to the Portuguese in general. (Lima and Barroso: *Pequeno Dicionário Brasileiro da Lingua Portuguêsa.*) (Translator.)

[217] *Mascate*: the word originally meant a peddler. It came to be applied as a nickname to the Portuguese of Recife by the Brazilians who inhabited Olinda. In Pernambuco in 1710 a war between the two peoples broke out, known as the *Guerra dos Mascates,* or War of the Mascates. (Lima and Barroso: *Pequeno Dicionário,* etc.) Cf. the novel (*a roman à clef*) by Brazil's great nineteenth-century romanticist José de Alencar: the *Guerra dos Mascates.* (Translator.)

II

THE NATIVE

IN THE FORMATION OF THE BRAZILIAN

FAMILY

W ITH European intrusion, social and economic life among the aborigines of America was disorganized and the balance in the relations of man to his physical environment was upset. There began then the familiar degradation of a backward race in contact with an advanced one; but this degradation followed differing rhythms: on the one hand conforming to regional differences in human culture or the richness of the soil possessed by the natives—which exhibited a maximum of fertility among the Incas and the Aztecs and a minimum among those tribes at the continental extremes—and on the other hand conforming to the colonizing dispositions and resources of the intruding people or the invader.

Among the Incas, the Aztecs, and the Mayas the Spaniards hastened the dissolution of native values in their fury to destroy a culture that was either in the stage of semi-civilization or undergoing a molting process, and which to them appeared to be dangerous to Christianity and unfavorable to the easy exploitation of the great mineral wealth to be found there. The English did the same among a more backward folk, in the desire to keep themselves immaculate from sexual and social contact with peoples who were repugnant to them by reason of the difference in color and costume and who evoked before their racial consciousness and their Christian conscience the specter of miscegenation and a dissolute paganism.

The Portuguese, in addition to being less ardent in their orthodoxy than the Spaniards and less narrow than the English in their color prejudices and Christian morality, encountered in America not a people already formed into an empire with an established and vigorous system of moral and material culture—with palaces, human sacrifices to the gods, monuments, bridges, irrigation and mining works—but, on the contrary, one of the most backward populations on the continent. What took place here, accordingly, was not a meeting between an exuberantly mature culture and one that was still in the adolescent stage; in this part of America the European colonists were to find, one might almost say, bands of grown-up children with an incipient, unripe culture, or, to vary the figure, a culture that was still cutting its first teeth, without the bony framework, the development, or the resistance of the great American semi-civilizations.

Out of the material and moral values accumulated by the Incas or by the Aztecs and the Mayas was to come a bronze-like quality that refused to take the imprint of European contact, a circumstance that was to lead the Spaniards to shatter this native bronze-work that held out so stubbornly against their rule, in order that amid the fragments they might the more conveniently set up their own colonial system of exploitation and Christianization. But among the aborigines of the dyewood lands resistance to the European took other forms: a resistance that was not mineral but vegetable. Here the invader in his turn was to have to come to terms with the native element, as he made use of the male for the necessities of labor and, above all, those of war, for the conquest of the backlands and the clearing of the virgin forest, and of the woman for purposes of generation and the founding of a family.

The reaction to European rule in that area of Amerindian culture which was invaded by the Portuguese was almost one of pure vegetable sensitivity and contractility, with the Indian withdrawing or shrinking back at civilizing contact with the European, out of an incapacity to accommodate himself to the new economic technique and the new social and moral regime. Even when he became an enemy, the native was still vegetable in his mode of aggression, little more than an auxiliary of the forest. He was not technically nor politically capable of reacting in the manner that had led the white man to adopt the policy of extermination followed by the Spaniards in Mexico and Peru. Thus we may explain—without overlooking other factors—how it is that from the beginning greater profit was had from this impoverished American culture, which was that of the tropical forest, than from the one whose opulence rested upon the wealth of the mines. In the latter case the two semi-civilizations, hard, compact, hieratic, only four centuries later were to reunite their fragments to form a novel whole that was not European but an original creation.

Ruediger Bilden suggestively outlines the differing conditions of racial and cultural amalgamation that, as he sees it, divide into four large groups ("a four-fold division")[1] those ethnic masses and their

---

[1] Ruediger Bilden: "Race Relations in Latin America with Special References to the Development of Indige- ous Culture" (University of Virginia, 1931).

cultures which by many are indiscriminately lumped under the facile but vague term "Latin America."

The first group would be that formed by the white or mulatto republics of the River Plata region and Chile. In these regions, he goes on to observe, "the climate and the physical conditions in general encourage the type of colonization that is most favorable to the development of a predominantly European society." With the exception of the Araucanian Indians in Chile, "the indigenous races were too insignificant in number and too primitive in culture seriously to obstruct the [European] trend of colonization." [2]

The second group would be one "typified by Brazil almost exclusively," a region where the European element never found itself in a "position of absolute and undisputed domination." "However strict," he goes on to say, "may have been their rule over the other ethnic elements, socially and culturally the Portuguese were compelled, by geographic environment and the exigencies of their colonization policy, to compete with the others upon an approximately equal basis."

The third group would be that represented by Mexico and Peru, where the conflict of the European with the indigenous civilizations already evolved, the presence of mineral wealth, and the colonial system of exploitation resulted in a "juxtaposition and antagonism of races" rather than in a "harmonious amalgamation"; it resulted in the "creation of a European superstructure beneath which ran strangely remote and turbulent currents." But sooner or later, he adds, these currents would end by engulfing the "slender and anæmic superstructure and by transmuting those values that were of European origin."

The fourth group would be constituted by Paraguay, Haiti, and "possibly the Dominican Republic." In this group "the European element is at most but a veneer," representing an "incongruous cultural admixture of a substance that is largely Indian or Negroid with badly assimilated fragments or elements of European origin." [3]

Hybrid from the beginning, Brazilian society is, of all those in the Americas, the one most harmoniously constituted so far as racial relations are concerned, within the environment of a practical cultural reciprocity that results in the advanced people deriving the maximum of profit from the values and experiences of the backward ones, and in a maximum of conformity between the foreign and the native cultures, that of the conqueror and that of the conquered. A society was organized that was Christian in superstructure, with the recently

---

[2] Ibid.   [3] Ibid.

baptized native woman as wife and mother of the family, who in her domestic life and economy made use of many of the traditions, experiences, and utensils of the autochthonous folk.

Zacharias Wagner remarked in the seventeenth century that many Portuguese, even the richest of them and even "certain Netherlanders of fiery passions," were in the habit of seeking lawfully wedded wives among the daughters of the *caboclas*.[4] And this union of Europeans with Indian women or their daughters must have been due, not to a scarcity of white or light-skinned women as in the first century of colonization, but rather to a decided sexual preference. Paulo Prado finds "the austere Varnhagen"[5] hinting that the native woman, for her part, "more sensual than the man, as among all primitive peoples . . . in her love affairs gave preference to the European, possibly out of priapic considerations."[6] Capistrano de Abreu, however, suggests that this preference for the European may have been motivated by social rather than sexual considerations: "on the part of the Indian women miscegenation is to be explained by the ambition to bear sons belonging to the superior race, since according to the ideas current among them, it was only parentage on the paternal side that counted."[7]

Added to the "priapic considerations" in the first century was the scarcity, when not an absolute lack, of white women. Even had there not been on the part of the Portuguese an obvious inclination either for a free union with the *caboclas* or for one under the benediction of the Church, they would have been impelled to it by the force of circumstances, whether or not they cared for the exotic type. This was due simply to the fact that there was hardly a single white woman in the land, and without the native one it "would be difficult to control or settle so large a coast as this one," as Diogo de Vasconcellos wrote in a letter to His Majesty in 1612.[8]

Southey observes that the Portuguese colonial system was more fortunate than any other so far as the relations of the European with

---

[4] Alfredo de Carvalho: "O Zoobillion de Zacharias Wagner," *Revista do Instituto Arqueologico, Histórico e Geográfico de Pernambuco*, Vol. XI (1904).

[5] Francisco Adolfo Varnhagen, Visconde de Porto Seguro (1816–78), one of Brazil's outstanding historians, author of a *História Geral do Brasil* (*General History of Brazil*). An ardent defender of the colonial regime,

he was noted for his antipathy to the Indian and his exaltation of the Portuguese element in Brazilian civilization. (Translator.)

[6] Paulo Prado, op. cit.

[7] Capistrano de Abreu: *Capítulos de História Colonial* (*Chapters of Colonial History*) (1924).

[8] Manuel Bomfim: *O Brasil na América* (op. cit.).

the colored races were concerned; but he stresses the point that such a system was the child of necessity rather than the result of any deliberate social or political orientation.[9] This was later to be repeated by that astute observer Koster, in words that the Indiophil Manuel Bomfim is at pains to quote, beneath those of Southey, in the pages of his *Brazil in the Americas.* "This advantage," writes Koster, alluding to the absence of such discrimination on the part of the Portuguese as would tend to degrade the natives, "comes rather from necessity than from a sense of justice."

For the formidable task of colonizing so extensive a tract as Brazil, sixteenth-century Portugal had to avail itself of what man-power was left it after the adventure of India. With such left-overs as these, consisting almost wholly of those who were poor in economic resources,[10] plebeian for the most part, and, in addition, of Mozarabic extraction — which meant that their racial consciousness was even weaker than that of the fidalgos or of the Portuguese from the north — with such material it was hardly possible to establish in America an exclusively white or strictly European regime. A compromise with the native element was imposed by Portuguese colonial policy and was facilitated by circumstances. The lustful inclinations of individuals without family ties and surrounded by Indian women in the nude were to serve powerful reasons of State, by rapidly populating the new land with mestizo offspring. One thing is certain, and that is that the bulk of colonial society throughout the sixteenth and seventeenth centuries was founded and developed upon the basis of a widespread and deep-going mixture of races that only the interference of the Jesuit fathers kept from becoming an open libertinism, by regularizing it to a large extent through the sacrament of Christian marriage.

The milieu in which Brazilian life began was one of sexual intoxication.

No sooner had the European leaped ashore than he found his feet slipping among the naked Indian women, and the very fathers of the Society of Jesus had to take care not to sink into the carnal mire; for many of the clergy did permit themselves to become contaminated with licentiousness. The women were the first to offer themselves to the whites, the more ardent ones going to rub themselves against the legs of these beings whom they supposed to be gods. They would give themselves to the European for a comb or a broken mirror.

"The women go naked and are unable to say no to anyone, but they

---

[9] Robert Southey: *History of Brazil* (op. cit.).

[10] This was the element that, as Alfredo Ellis, Jr., has established, provided São Paulo with its great *bandeirante* figures.

themselves provoke and importune the men, sleeping with them in hammocks; for they hold it to be an honor to sleep with the Xianos." So writes Father Anchieta.[11] And he is speaking of a Brazil that was more or less well ordered, not that of the early days of unbridled libertinism, without the cassocks of the Jesuits to cloak the spontaneity of reactions.

This was a wholly physical love, a taste for the flesh, and from it resulted offspring whose Christian fathers were at little pains to educate them or to bring them up in the European manner, under the wing of the Church. These young ones grew up as best they might, in the forest; and some of them were of so ruddy a complexion, with skins so light, that when they and their progeny were later discovered among the natives by colonists at the end of the sixteenth century, they were readily identified as the descendants of Normans and Bretons. Of these latter, Gabriel Soares wrote in 1587, in his *Log Book of Brazil*,[12] that "many dwelt in fornication in the land, where they died without desiring to return to France, and where they lived like the heathen, with many women; these it is, and those that come every year to Bahia and to the Rio de Sergipe in French boats, who are responsible for filling the land with mamelucos who live and die like pagans; these have today many descendants who are blond, milk-white, and freckled, children borne by women of the Tupinambás,[13] and who are more barbarous than the Indians themselves." [14]

This French contingent in the early settlement of Brazil is not to be overlooked. It was to be found chiefly in Bahia and at all those points along the shore that were the richest in dyewood. Like the first Portuguese, the French gave themselves over to the one form of lust that was possible under the circumstances, in the primitive conditions that accompanied the clearing of the new land, by surrounding themselves with many women. If of their numerous mestizo descendants and those of the Portuguese many were later wholly absorbed by the aboriginal populations, there were others who, one might say, led a life midway between that of the savages and that of the traders and

---

[11] Letter to Laynes, in Paulo Prado: *Retrato do Brasil* (op. cit.).

[12] *Roteiro do Brasil*. Gabriel Soares de Sousa, the sixteenth-century chronicler; see note 14 below. (Translator.)

[13] In Brazil, Tupinambá is the generic designation of various Tupí tribes that in the sixteenth century occupied the coast of Brazil. (Lima

and Barroso: *Pequeno Dicionário Brasileiro da Lingua Portuguêsa*.) (Translator.)

[14] Gabriel Soares de Sousa. *Tratado Descriptivo do Brasil em 1587* (*Descriptive Account of Brazil in 1587*), published by F. A. Varnhagen, *Revista do Instituo Histórico e Geográphico Brasileiro*, Vol. XIV, p. 342.

filibusters, who were somewhat under the European influence deriving from the French ships and Portuguese plantations.

But it is only from the middle of the sixteenth century, Basílio de Magalhães tells us,[15] that we may look upon "the first generation of *mamelucos*" as having been formed—Portuguese-Indian mestizos of a definite demogenic and social significance. As for their predecessors, those produced by the first matings of white and Indian, the interest they hold for us, as already mentioned, is in the fact that they served as a wedge or lining for the great hybrid society that was to be constituted here.

The native woman must be regarded not merely as the physical basis of the Brazilian family, upon whom, drawing strength from her and multiplying itself, rested the energy of a limited number of European settlers; she must also be considered a worth-while cultural element, at least so far as material culture goes, in the formation of Brazilian society. Thanks to her, Brazilian life was enriched, as we shall see further on, with a number of foods that are still in use today, with drugs and household remedies, with traditions that are bound up with the development of the child, with a set of kitchen utensils, and with processes having to do with tropical hygiene—including the frequent or at least daily bath, which must greatly have scandalized the sixteenth-century European, who was so filthy in his own personal habits.

She gave us also the hammock, which still rocks the Brazilian to sleep or serves him as a voluptuous couch. She brought coconut oil for women's hair and a group of domestic animals tamed by her hand.

From the *cunhã*, or Tupí-Guaraní woman, has come the best of our indigenous culture. Personal neatness. Bodily hygiene. Corn. The cashew. *Mingau,* or porridge. The Brazilian of today, a lover of the bath and always with a comb and mirror in his pocket, his hair gleaming with lotion or coconut oil, is reflecting the influence of his remote grandmothers.

But before dwelling at length upon the contribution of the *cunhâ* to the social development of Brazil, let us endeavor to determine that of the Indian male. It was most impressive, but only with regard to the task of invading and conquering the backlands, where he served as guide, canoeist, warrior, hunter, and fisherman.[16] He was

---

[15] Basílio de Magalhães: *O Folclore no Brasil (Folklore in Brazil)* (Rio de Janeiro, 1928). (Translator.)

[16] "*Les Indiens, qui excellent dans la navigation des fleuves, redoutent la pleine mer, et la vie des champs leur est fatale par le contraste de la discipline avec la vie nomade des forêts.*" —Sigaud, op. cit.).

of great assistance to the mameluco turned *bandeirante*, the two of them surpassing the Portuguese in mobility, daring, and warlike ardor. His capacity for activity and for labor failed him, however, when it came to the dreary grind of the cane fields, where only the African's extraordinary reserves of cheerfulness and animal robustness enabled him to endure so well this life of toil. But the Indian, as friend or slave of the Portuguese, made up for his uselessness where steady and continuous exertion was involved by his brilliance and heroism as a soldier, not only in connection with the invasion of the backlands, but in defending the colony against the Spaniards, against enemy bands of Portuguese, and against corsairs.

Indians and mamelucos formed a living, moving wall, engaged in extending Brazil's colonial frontiers in a westerly direction while at the same time, in the sugar-raising zone, protecting the agrarian establishments against the attacks of foreign pirates. Each sugar plantation in the sixteenth and seventeenth centuries was under the necessity of maintaining upon a wartime footing its hundreds, or at any rate dozens, of men, ready to defend against assault by savages or by corsairs the plantation dwelling-house and the riches stored in the warehouses; and these men were almost all of them Indians or *caboclos* armed with bow and arrow.

The hoe never stayed for long in the hand of the Indian or the mameluco, nor did his nomad's foot permit him ever to settle down to a life of patient and rewarding labor. From the native about the only thing that the agrarian colonists took in Brazil was the process known as "*coivara*," or the burning over of the land,[17] one that, unfortunately, was to get a complete grip upon colonial agriculture. As for the knowledge of seeds and roots and other rudimentary agricultural lore, this was transmitted to the Portuguese not so much by the warrior male as by the Indian woman, who in addition to the household work also labored in the fields.

If we are to sift and sum up the collaboration of the Indian with respect to labor that may properly be termed agrarian, we shall have to conclude—contrary to Manuel Bomfim, who is an Indiophile to

---

[17] The *coivara*, properly speaking, is the burning of the piled-up brushwood after the clearing of the woods by fire, which is known as a *queimada*. Euclides da Cunha gives a vivid description of this process and its ill effects. See *Os Sertões*, 16th edition, p. 53 f., "Como se faz um deserto"; for English translation, see *Rebellion in the Backlands*, pp. 43–4. Cf. the observation made by Freyre regarding our own South in comparison with Brazil in this respect, in the Preface to the First Edition, p. xvii. (Translator.)

the roots of his hair [18]—that the native's contribution here was an insignificant one. There is nothing surprising in this, in view of the fact that Amerindian culture at the time of the discovery of America was a nomad culture, a culture of the forest, and not an agricultural one. What little cultivating was done—of manihot, cará,[19] maize, jerimum,[20] peanut, and papaw—by a few tribes that were less backward than the others, was a task disdained by the men, who were hunters, fishermen, and warriors; and it was accordingly relegated to the women, whose household efficiency was as much diminished by this labor in the fields as was the capacity of the men for regular and continuous work by the nomad life that they led. Hence it was that the Indian women did not make such good domestic slaves as did the African ones, who later were advantageously to take the place of the former as cooks and nurses of the young, just as Negro males were to take the place of the Indian men as laborers in the field.

The studies of the tribes of central Brazil that have been made by Martius [21] and by Karl von den Steinen,[22] and Paul Ehrenreich's work on the Indians of the Mato Grosso, Goiás, and Amazon regions;[23] the writings of Whiffen,[24] Roquette Pinto,[25] Koch-Grünberg,[26] Schmidt,[27] Krause,[28] and E. Nordenskiöld;[29] the notes left by travelers and missionaries who found the *caboclos* living a life that was virgin so far as European contacts went—all this lends authority for a generalization on our part to the effect that even the least backward of the indigenous cultures discovered in America by the Portuguese —of which fragments in a crude state still remain—was for the most part inferior to those African cultural areas from which, later, Negroes of pure descent or those who already had become mestizos were to be imported for the colonial sugar plantations. A number of

---

[18] Read his *O Brasil na América* (op. cit.).

[19] Name given to various plants of the *Dioscoreaceæ* or yam family. (Translator.)

[20] Plant of the *Cucurbitaceæ* or gourd family. (Translator.)

[21] C. F. P. von Martius: *Beiträge zur Ethnographie und Sprachenkunde Americas zumal Brasiliens* (Leipzig, 1867).

[22] Karl von den Steinen: *Unter den Indianern Zentral-Brasiliens* (Berlin, 1894). This book has just appeared in Portuguese translation.

[23] Paul Ehrenreich: *Beiträge zur Volkerkunde Brasiliens* (Berlin, 1891).

[24] Thomas Whiffen: *The Northwest Amazon* (London, 1915).

[25] Roquette Pinto: *Rondônia* (1917).

[26] Theodor Kock-Grünberg: *Zwei Jahre unter den Indianern* (Stuttgart, 1908–10).

[27] Max Schmidt: *Indianerstudien in Zentralbrasilien* (Berlin, 1905). This book, also, has just appeared in Portuguese.

[28] Fritz Krause: *In den Wildnissen Brasiliens* (Leipzig, 1911).

[29] Erland Nordenskiöld: *Indianerleben* (Leipzig, 1912).

these African cultural areas have been described, in accordance with
the latest anthropological technique, by Leo Frobenius,[30] while those
of America have been masterfully portrayed by Wissler and Kroeber,
so that we are thus afforded a comparison between the moral and
material values accumulated on the two continents.

The principal cultural traits of the tribes of northeastern Brazil,
many of which traits are to be found throughout practically the
entire country, have been summed up by Whiffen as follows: [31]

hunting, fishing, the cultivation of manihot, tobacco, and the coca-
berry, and to a less extent of maize, yams or cará, the jerimum, and
pepper;
the clearing of fields by fire (the *coivara*) and the furrowing of them
with a digging stick and not with a hoe;
no domestic animal;
all animal life made use of as food;
the use of honey, from bees that had been domesticated to a certain
extent;
the use of manihot flour or cakes and of small game preserved in
spices, as the two basic elements of diet;
the use of manihot wrapped in straw or matting and pressed;
the use of mashed coca-berries and mimosa seeds as snuff;
the use of tobacco only in the form of a beverage and in certain
ceremonies;
the knowledge and use of curare and other poisons;
employment of the bow and arrow, the lance, the oar;
fishing with poison cast upon the water, but also with hook, trap, net,
and pronged spear;
the habit of eating clay;
cannibalism;
signaling by means of drums;
phallic decoration;
use of palm-fiber hammocks;

---

[30] Leo Frobenius: *Ursprung der
Africanischen Kulturen*, cited by Melville J. Herskovits: "A Preliminary
Consideration of the Cultural Areas
of Africa," *American Anthropologist*,
Vol. XXVI (1924).—On the correlation of cultural traits among the various primitive cultures, see the work
by L. T. Hobhouse, G. C. Wheeler,
and M. Ginsberg: *The Material Culture and Social Institutions of the
Simple Peoples* (London, 1915).—On
Herskovits's map Africa is divided in
accordance with the American con-

cept of "cultural area" as defined by
Alexander A. Goldenweiser in "Diffusionism and the American School
of Historical Ethnology," *American
Journal of Sociology*, Vol. XXXI
(1925), and by Clark Wissler in *Man
and Culture*; it is likewise in accord
with the technique applied by Wissler
to his study of the two Americas.

[31] Whiffen, op. cit. The author
mentions other traits in addition to
those that I give here as being the
more characteristic and important
ones.

ceramics and basket-weaving;

no metal; little use of stone; wooden implements;

canoes hollowed out of wood;

uprooting of trees by means of wedges;

large wooden mortars for pounding cocoa, tobacco, and corn;

frequent change of habitation and of crops;

entire communities dwelling in a single big quadrangular thatched house, supported on the inside by four rafters, and without a chimney;

the ground about the house swept clean, but the dwelling hidden away in the heart of the forest and accessible only by confused trails and paths;

no art of apparel, unless it was the tree-bark of which the men made use;

combs for the women made of bits of palm-stalk;

necklaces of human teeth;

decorative bands about the body; piercing of the nose; rattles attached to the legs; elaborate painting of the body;

a kind of conference or conclave, with a black drink made of tobacco as the center of the ceremony, before embarking upon some important undertaking of war or peace;

the couvade;

forbidding of women to take part in the more serious ceremonies or to be present at the initiation of youths into puberty;

the low-voiced pronunciation of the names of persons, while those of mythical characters were barely whispered;

the importance ascribed to witchcraft and the gross frauds that were perpetrated in its name; the sucking-out of diseases by the witch-doctor, whose principal function, incidentally, was to draw out the evil spirits from the body;

two great ceremonies to celebrate the harvest and the ripening of fruit, of the manihot and the pineapple;

the cruel flogging of lads in the ceremonies of puberty;

the trial by biting ants;

the formal presentation of the rancors and grievances of individuals to the group;

a kind of sieve dance; employment of the Panpipe, the flute, castanets, and rattles;

housing of each exogamous group in a single habitation; monogamy; the tracing of descent on the paternal side; a chief and leader for each house, with a council composed of all the adults of masculine sex;

stories that have a resemblance to European folklore; animal tales that are reminiscent of African lore;

worship of the sun and moon;

burial of the dead.

These are widespread characteristics of that culture which Wissler classifies as the "culture of the tropical forest" and which takes in practically the whole of Brazil.

The culture of the Atlantic seaboard—the one with which Europeans in Brazil first came into contact—shows the following additional traits:

the habit of smoking tobacco in a pipe;
settlements surrounded by stockades;
good stone implements;
in place of a simple burial of the dead, the placing of their remains in urns.

On the other hand, the culture of the Gê-Botocudo, or Tapuia of central Brazil, is lacking in some of the traits mentioned: in the little agriculture and weaving and the beginnings of astrology that are to be found among the northern and the coastal tribes; the manufacture and use of stone implements; the use of the hammock for sleeping. In the Gê-Botocudo culture those traits are accentuated which, according to Wissler, relate this people to the Patagonians, indicating a stage of development inferior to that of the Tupís. Among others mentioned is that of cannibalism.[32]

As for domestic animals to be found among either of the two principal groups—the Tupís and the Gê-Botocudos[33]—we should note, contrary to Wissler's generalized statement above, the presence of "a few domesticated birds such as jacamis,[34] of rodents such as the cutia[35] and the paca, and a few monkeys."[36] The truth is that none of these animals was employed either in domestic service or in the carrying of burdens, which were painfully borne upon the native's back, most often that of the woman. Their purpose, it might be said, was simply to keep their owner company and not to furnish him with food—unless we look upon the honey-making bees as serving man, along with those tame birds that Roquette Pinto found being used as dolls by the children of the Nhambiquara tribe.[37]

Theodoro Sampaio, who in his study of the Tupí language has done so much to unveil the intimate life of the aborigines of Brazil, states that round about the dwelling of the savage "and even invading it with the greatest familiarity, there developed a world of domestic

---

[32] Clark Wissler: *The American Indian* (New York, 1922).
[33] As Roquette Pinto says, "we may, in a general way, separate all our tribes into two groups with regard to their stage of culture. . . . This is the primitive division that reasserts itself, no longer from the point of view of linguistics alone, but with the force of a sociological criterion." —*Seixos Rolados* (op. cit.).

[34] The *jacami* or *jacamim*, is a bird of the *Psophiidæ* family, or South American trumpeters. (Translator.)
[35] Rodent of the *Caviidæ* family, which includes the guinea-pigs, etc. (*Dasyprocta aguti* Lin.). (Translator.)
[36] Roquette Pinto, op. cit.
[37] Roquette Pinto: *Rondônia* (op. cit.).

animals to which the name of *mimbaba* was given." But they were all animals that were kept for the owner's pleasure, because he liked them, and not for domestic service or use of other kind: "birds of beautiful plumage such as the flamingo (guará),[38] the arara,[39] the canindé,[40] the toucan, a large number of partridges (ianhambí or iambú), urus,[41] and swans (ipeca), along with animals like the monkey, the coati, the irara,[42] the hart, the cat (pichana), and even tame snakes, were to be found in the most intimate gathering." [43]

Among Amerindians in this part of the country, as among primitive peoples in general, there was a certain fraternity between animals and men, a certain lyricism, even, in their relations. Karsten encountered among the Jibaros a myth to the effect that there once was an age in which the animals talked and acted exactly like men. And to this day, he adds, "the Indian makes no definite distinction between man and animal. He believes that all animals possess a soul of essentially the same kind as that of the human being, that intellectually and morally they are on the same level as man." Whence—independently, even, of totemism, with which we shall concern ourselves later on—whence that (so to speak) lyric intimacy of the inhabitant of Brazil with a numerous group of animals, chiefly birds that have been tamed by him or reared in his house, without any thought on his part of making use of their flesh or eggs as food, or of their energy for domestic or agricultural labor or for draft purposes, or of their blood in religious sacrifices.

As to monogamy, it was never general in those American cultural areas that were invaded by the Portuguese; polygamy had existed and still exists among the tribes that had kept themselves intact from the influence of European morality. And not only the chiefs, but all the braves—those that were able to support a large family—took to themselves many wives.[44]

Nor, in considering the most characteristic traits of those aborigines

[38] The *guará* is a bird of the *Ibides* family (*Eudocismus ruber Lin.*). (Translator.)

[39] Bird of the *Psitaci*, or parrot, family. (Translator.)

[40] Another bird of the *Psitaci* family (*Ara ararauna Lin.*). (Translator.)

[41] Bird of the *Odontophorinæ* family, which includes the American quails (*Odontophorus guiannensis Gm.*). (Translator.)

[42] Carnivorous animal of the *Mus-*telidæ family, which includes weasels, skunks, badgers, etc. (*Tayra barbara Lin.*). (Translator.)

[43] Theodoro Sampaio: *O Tupí na Geografia Nacional* (*The Tupí in National Geography*) (3rd edition, Bahia, 1928).

[44] Rafael Karsten: *Civilization of the South American Indians* (London, 1929). See also Roquette Pinto: *Seixos Rolados* (op. cit.).

to be met with in Brazil, should we underestimate one that Wissler appears to have overlooked: the use of devil and animal masks, which possess a mystical and cultural significance, as stressed by Koch-Grünberg and lately, and notably, by Karsten.[45]

With regard to the moral culture of the early inhabitants of Brazil, we are interested principally, within the limits that we have set ourselves in this essay (those of sexual and family relations), in magic and myths. There are traits that, with great emotional vivacity in the beginning, were communicated to the life and culture of the Portuguese colonizer; and while they have since been dimmed by the greater influence of the African, they still exist in the primitive depths of our social, moral, and religious organization, where they break, or seriously threaten to break, the supposed uniformity of the Catholic or European pattern.

In the middle of the sixteenth century Father Anchieta notes that among the Brazilian aborigines the woman is not annoyed when the man who is her companion takes another woman or other women: "even though he leave her altogether, she is not concerned, for if she is still young, she herself finds another mate." And "if the woman happens to be a strong, masculine type, she in turn may leave her husband and seek another." [46]

This changing of husbands and wives was, naturally, a point upon which Catholic morality, which meant the stern orthodoxy represented by the fathers of the Society of Jesus, could not and did not compromise; the effort made by the Jesuits to enforce the practice of a strict monogamy in the colony must have been a tremendous one, not only with respect to the baptized Indians, but with regard to the Portuguese colonists as well; for the clergy itself, in conflict with the Jesuit padres, facilitated the free union with "Negresses." Already addicted to polygamy through contact with the Moors, the Portuguese found in the sexual code of the Amerindians an opportunity to give free and easy rein to this Mozarabic tendency to live with many women (a tendency that during the last two centuries had been somewhat suppressed and then had broken out again).

The two peoples who first met in this part of America—that is to say, the Portuguese male and the Indian woman—were highly sexed. Contrary to the general impression that it was for the most part the

---

[45] Theodor Koch-Grünberg: *Zwei Jahre unter den Indianern* (op. cit.). Karsten, op. cit.

[46] *"Informação dos Casementos dos Indios do Brasil pelo Padre José d'Anchieta"* ("Data on the Marriages of the Brazilian Indians, by Father José d'Anchieta"), *Revista do Instituto Histórico e Geográphico Brasileiro*, Vol. VIII, p. 105.

African who communicated to the Brazilian his lubricity, it is my belief that the former, as a matter of fact, was sexually the weakest of the three elements that united to form our country, the Portuguese being the most libidinous. In any event, among the Negroes—the pure Negroes, immune from Mussulman influence—erotic dances were more frequent and more ardent than among the Amerindians and the Portuguese, and this would appear to indicate a weaker degree of sexuality. This is the opinion of a number of modern ethnologists and anthropologists, which differs from that held by the older ones; among them may be mentioned Crawley, who devotes some of his finest pages to this subject, and Westermarck,[47] while from the point of view of sexual psychology and genetic sociology, there is Havelock Ellis, who in this field can give lessons to them all.[48]

Fulfilling the functions of an aphrodisiac, that of an excitant or stimulus to sexual activity, such dances point to a lack, and not, as many at first believed and some still do, to an excess of lubricity or libido. Erotic dances such as those witnessed by Koch-Grünberg among the tribes of northeastern Brazil—with the men masked and each one equipped with a formidable *membrum virile*, pretending to be performing the sexual act and spilling semen—would appear to be less frequent among the Amerindians than among the Africans, which leads to the conclusion that the sexuality of the former had less need of a stimulus. Meanwhile, we should note the fact that much of the animal ardor of the nomad Indian warrior of the Americas was absorbed by the necessities of competition before it could be sexualized: by intertribal warfare, migrations, hunting, fishing, and defense against wild animals. He did not possess that surplus of leisure and of

---

[47] "The notion that the Negro race is peculiarly prone to sexual indulgence is due partly to the expansive temperament of the race, and the sexual character of many of their festivals—a fact which indicates rather the contrary and demonstrates the need of artificial excitement."—Ernest Crawley: *Studies of Savages and Sex*, edited by Theorore Besterman (London, 1929). See also on this subject: *The Mystic Rose*, by the same author, edited by Besterman (New York, 1927); and E. A. Westermarck: *The History of Human Marriage* (London, 1921), and *The Origin and Development of Moral Ideas* (London,

1926). The idea, incidentally, of the weak sexuality of primitive peoples is not universally accepted by modern anthropologists; among others who think differently from Crawley, Havelock Ellis, and Westermarck, at least with regard to the Africans, are Leo Frobenius: *Und Africa Sprach; Unter den Unsträflichen Äthiopen* (Charlottenburg, 1913); and Georg Schweinfurth: *Im Herzen von Africa* (3rd edition, Leipzig, 1908). See H. Fehlinger: *Sexual Life of Primitive People* (London, 1921).

[48] Havelock Ellis: *Studies in the Psychology of Sex* (Philadelphia, 1908).

food which Adlez from the biological and Thomas from the sociological point of view see as bound up with the development of the sexual system in man.[49]

Paulo Prado lays emphasis on the meeting here on our shores of the "disorderly way of life of the European conqueror" with the "sensuality of the Indian." Of the Indian woman, to be exact. Those "priapic" *caboclas* who were so foolishly enamored of a white man. The essayist who gave us the *Portrait of Brazil* goes on to remind us of the impressions that the early chroniclers formed of sexual morality among the natives. Impressions of amazement or of horror. Thus we hear Gabriel Soares de Sousa observing that the Tupinambás "are so lustful that there is no sin of lust which they do not commit." There is Father Nobrega, who is alarmed by the number of wives that each native has and the readiness with which he abandons them. And finally there is Vespucci, writing to Lorenzo de' Medici that the Indians "take as many wives as they like, and the son has intercourse with the mother, and the brother with the sister, and the male cousin with the female cousin, and the one who is out walking with the first woman whom he meets." [50]

It was natural that Europeans, surprised at encountering a sexual code so different from their own, should have come to the conclusion that the aborigines were extremely lustful, whereas, of the two peoples, the conqueror himself was perhaps the more lascivious.

As to that prevalence of incestuous relations of which Vespucci speaks in his letter, some ten years later a more accurate observer than the Italian, Father Anchieta, was to give us detailed information. The missionary notes that the aborigines regarded as "true relationship" that which they traced "on the side of the fathers, who are the active agents," the mothers being "no more than so many bags[51] . . . in which children are created," as a result of which attitude they used "their sisters' daughters *ad copulam* without any scruple." [52] He adds

---

[49] Adlez, cited by Crawley: *Studies of Savages and Sex* (op. cit.). W. I. Thomas: *Sex and Society* (Chicago).

[50] Paulo Prado: *Retrato do Brasil* (op. cit.).

[51] It may be of interest to compare the disrespectful slang term "bag" applied to a woman and current in the United States. (Translator.)

[52] Anchieta, loc. cit., note 50 above. —With regard to the distinction that Anchieta makes between those nieces who are the daughters of brothers

and those who are the daughters of sisters, Rodolfo Garcia writes: "The former were respected by the Indians and treated as daughters; they held them in esteem and had no carnal knowledge of them (*neque fornicarie*), for the reason that they believed true blood-relationship to be on the side of the fathers, the latter being the active agents, whereas the mothers were no more than bags in which the children were created; and so it was that they used the daughters

that these latter "now [in the middle of the sixteenth century] are married off by their fathers with their uncles, their mother's brothers, if the parties are content, by reason of the power which they have of disposing of them. . . ." All of which goes to show that, already at the beginning of the colonial period, the sexual morality of the Indians had to some extent come to be affected by Catholic morality and the laws of the Church itself regarding consanguineous marriages.

Moreover, sexual intercourse among the aborigines in this part of America was in general not so unbridled an affair, so free of restrictions, as Vespucci might lead us to believe, nor was life among the natives that endless orgy visualized by the first travelers and missionaries. As Fehlinger observes,[53] laxity of this sort, sexual license, and libertinism are not to be met with among any primitive people; and Baker[54] emphasizes the innocence of certain customs—such as the offering of womenfolk to a guest—which were practiced solely out of an instinct of hospitality. What tends to disfigure these customs is the evil interpretation that has been put upon them by superficial observers. The contrary may today be asserted: that the sexual impulse in the American savage was relatively weak. At least in the man—the more sedentary and regular life of the woman endowing her with a sexuality superior to that of the male, to so disproportionate a degree as will perhaps explain the priapism of many of the women toward white men.

Gabriel Soares alludes to the crude process by which the Tupinambás augment the size of the *membrum virile*, concluding from this that they are exceedingly libidinous. Dissatisfied "with the genital member as nature formed it," the sixteenth-century chronicler tells us, the Tupinambás were in the habit of placing around it "the hide of some poisonous reptile, causing it to swell up most painfully for a period of more than six months, after which, with the lapse of time, the pain goes away, leaving the organ so huge and misshapen that the women are not able to endure it. . . ."[55] Yet even this practice, apparently a bit of pure licentiousness, indicates the necessity that the natives felt of making up for a physical or psychic deficiency with regard to the generative function, rather than dissoluteness or sadistic

---

of sisters *ad copulam* without any scruple and made of them their wives."—*Diálogos das Grandezas do Brasil* (op. cit.), with an Introduction by Capistrano de Abreu and Notes by Rodolfo Garcia, Sixth Dialogue, note 7, p. 316.

[53] Op. cit., note 51 above. (Translator.)

[54] John Baker: *Sex in Man and Animals* (London, 1926). (Translator.)

[55] Gabriel Soares de Sousa, op. cit., p. 317.

masochism. It is indeed a known fact that among primitive peoples the sexual organs are generally less developed than among the civilized;[56] and in addition, as has just been stated, the savages felt the need of saturnalian or orgiastic practices as a compensation, through indirect erethism, for the difficulty they experienced in achieving, without that aphrodisiac oil provided by the sweat of lascivious dances, a state of excitation and erection such as is readily accomplished by the civilized. The latter are always ready for coitus; savages practice it only when pricked by sexual hunger.[57] It would appear that among the more primitive tribes there was even a fixed period for the union of male with female.

Sexual intercourse for the natives of Brazil was not lacking in restrictions; it was only out of ignorance or a tendency to fantasy that sixteenth-century chronicle-writers were led to suppose that love among the *caboclos* was a mere satisfaction of the senses, with the male grasping and subjecting to his virile embrace the first female within the reach of his arms. Exogamy was one restriction observed by all, each group, so to speak, being divided into exogamous halves, which in turn were subdivided into still smaller groups or clans. Father Anchieta has already explained to us why it was the Tupís felt no repugnance at the union of a niece with her maternal uncle: the reason being that the important relationship, the one that restricted sexual intercourse and consequently regulated family life, was that which was traced on the father's side. It is not that the notion of incest or even of consanguinity was wholly absent in the Amerindian, but consanguinity with him was unilateral, and both notions were vague, unprecise. Gabriel Soares notes that among the Tupinambás "the girl called all the relatives on her father's side father, and they called her daughter. . . ." And the author of the *Roteiro* further informs us that "the uncle, brother of the girl's father, does not marry his niece, nor does he touch her when he does as he should do, but looks upon her as a daughter, and she, after her father's death, obeys him as she would her father. . . ."[58] True, the

---

[56] Ploss-Bartels: *Das Weib* (Berlin, 1927).

[57] Westermarck: *The History of Human Marriage* (op. cit.).

[58] Gabriel Soares de Sousa, op. cit. —In his work *Sex in Man and Animals* John Baker of Oxford University makes the point that among primitive societies there is no special word for father or mother; under the terms

father and *mother* are classified, indistinctly, a large number of relationships. Some ethnologists see in this fact an indication of a phase in the sexual life of such societies in which the women of one group were permitted intercourse with any man of the opposite group—of the two great groups into which each society is divided. A similar system of relation-

same chronicler adds that it is not rare among the Tupinambás for a brother to sleep with his sister, but such things were hidden away in the depths of the forest.

In addition to the notion, even though a vague one, of incest and that of a unilateral consanguinity, there was another restriction to sexual intercourse among the aborigines of Brazil, and that was totemism, in accordance with which the individual member of a group that was supposed to be descended from or protected by a certain animal or plant might not form a union with a woman belonging to a group that claimed the same descent or protection. It is known that exogamy as the effect of totemism was extended to groups as distant as possible from one another so far as blood-relationship was concerned. These groups formed mystic alliances, based upon their supposed relationship, or common descent from the wild boar, the jaguar, or the crocodile, avoiding one another as much as would brother and sister or uncle and niece where marriage or sexual union was involved.

With all these restrictions, it may be seen that sexual life among the natives in this part of America was not so dissolute as it has been pictured, but was one bristling with taboos and impediments. These were neither so many nor so keenly felt as those that rendered difficult for Europeans the amorous relations of man with woman; but they did tend to create a social order that was quite different from one marked by promiscuity or debauchery.

It is, for that matter, a mistake, and one of the gravest, to suppose that life among the savages, not only in this respect but in various others, was wholly free and untrammeled. Far from being the unrestrained animal the romantics imagined him to be, the American man of the wilds, utterly naked and a nomad when discovered here, was one who lived in the shadows cast by fear and superstition; and many of these fears and superstitions our mestizo culture was to absorb, cleansing them of their more gross and jumbled ingredients. Thus it is that our notion of *caiporismo*, so bound up with the psychic life of Brazilians today, is derived from the Amerindian belief in the prophetic powers of the *caipora*: a nude little *caboclo* who went on one leg, and whose appearance to the great ones was a certain sign of trouble to come.[59] The *caipora* was swallowed up, leaving in his

---

ships between the sexes, with the children created in common, would have constituted group marriage.

[59] A vivid description of the *caipora* is given by Lima and Barroso

(*Pequeno Dicionário*, etc.): "Name of a mythical being that, varying with different regions, is now represented as a one-legged woman who goes hopping along; now as a child with

place *caiporismo;* just as the *pajés,* or medicine-men, disappeared, leaving behind them first the "Holiness" cults of the sixteenth century,[60] and later various forms of therapeutic and of animism, many of which today are embodied, along with survivals of magic or of

an enormous head; again, as a little Indian who is under an enchanted spell; and yet again, as a man of colossal size, mounted on a peccary *(porco do mato).*" The term is also applied to one who is unfortunate in all his undertakings, or one who can see only the dark side of things. *Caiporismo,* as employed by Freyre, signifies the entire complex that has grown up around this tradition. (Translator.)

[60] In the denunciations of the Holy Office in Brazil, numerous references to the "Holiness" cults (*"santidades"*) are to be met with, among them the following, which indicate that these manifestations, representing a hybrid compound of religion and magic, were possessed of a certain phallic character. Domingos de Oliveira saw Fernão Pires "take from one of the figures of Our Lady or of Christ a bit of clay out of which he fashioned an image of the natural organ of man." *(First Visitation of the Holy Office to the Regions of Brazil—Denunciations of Bahia—1591–1593* [São Paulo, 1925], p. 264.—"Fernão Cabral de Tayde, an aged Christian, in this year of Grace" (August 2, 1591) "upon confessing himself, stated that six years ago, more or less, there arose among the heathen of the backlands a new sect that they called Holiness, having one whom they called Pope and a heathen woman whom they called the Mother of God, and a sacristan; and they had an idol that they called Mary, which was neither man nor woman nor other animal, and this idol they did adore, saying certain prayers with beads, and hanging up in the house that they called their church tablets with a certain writing upon them, saying that these

were holy beads; and thus in their own manner did they counterfeit the divine worship of Christians."—Gonçallo Fernandes, an aged mameluco and a Christian" (January 13, 1592) "upon confessing himself, stated that six years ago, more or less, there arose in the backlands of this *capitânia,* in the direction of Jaguaripe, an erroneous and idolatrous heathen sect supported by pagans and Christians and freedmen and slaves who had fled their masters to take part in the said idolatrous rites, and who, in the said disgraceful and idolatrous company, did counterfeit the ceremonies of the church and pretend to be telling their beads, as they prayed and spoke a certain barbarous tongue that had been invented by them, all the while smoking themselves with the fumes of an herb which they call the Holy Herb and drinking in the said smoke until they fell drunken with it, saying that with this smoke there did enter into them the spirit of holiness; and they have a stone idol before which they perform their ceremonies and which they worship, saying that their God is coming to deliver them from their state of wretchedness and that he will make them the masters of the white folk and that the whites will be their captives, and that whoever does not believe in this disgraceful and idolatrous cult, to which they give the name of Holiness, will be converted into a bird or into beasts of the forest, and thus do they say and do in the said idolatrous cult, and many other unbefitting things."—*First Visitation of the Holy Office to the Regions of Brazil, by the Licentiate Heitor Furtado de Mendonça, Confessions of Bahia* (São Paulo, 1927), pp. 28 and 87.

African religion, in that low-grade spiritualism which, in all the principal cities and throughout the interior of Brazil, competes so strenuously with European medicine and the exorcism of the priests.

In the popular dress of rural and suburban Brazilians—the poor who live in huts or native shacks—as in their diet, their intimate life, their domestic arts, and their attitude toward sickness, the dead, newborn children, plants, animals, minerals, the stars, etc., there remains a large trace of fetishistic, of totemistic influence, of the beginnings of astrology, and Amerindian taboos. At times it exists in almost a pure state; in many cases it has been reinforced and in others offset by the African, while almost always it has been dimmed by the subtle influence of the Catholic Church.

A friend of mine who comes from the same part of the country and has traveled widely through the backlands of Brazil, the Pernambucan physician Dr. Samuel Hardman Cavalcanti, once asked me to what I attributed the frequency of the color red among the women of the interior. This is to be observed in the northeast as well as in the far north and in Bahia, and I have noted it also in the interior of the states of São Paulo and Rio de Janeiro, although in these latter regions it is less frequent than in the former. In the Amazon country, among the pure *caboclos* and the hybrid offspring of *caboclo* and Negro, Gastão Cruls made this observation, which he has set down in his book *The Amazon Region As I Saw It*: "I note in these parts, as I have already observed in connection with the interior districts of the northeast, a decided predilection for scarlet on the part of the women. I do not know if this is merely a matter of taste, or, as they explained to me there, a mimetic attempt to ward off possible vexations on certain days of the month." [61] The same thing was noted in the same region by the physician Samuel Uchôa. [62]

This frequent occurrence of the color scarlet in the popular dress of Brazilian woman, chiefly in the northeast and the Amazon region, is typical of those instances in which the three influences—the Amerindian, the African, and the Portuguese—would appear to have united into a whole without antagonism or attrition. In any event, whatever its origin, by whichever of the three ethnic paths it may have come, we are here dealing with a mystical custom involving the protection or prophylaxis of the individual against spirits or evil influences. But the greater influence seems to have been that of the Indian, for whom

---

[61] Gastão Cruls: *A Amazónia que Eu Vi* (Rio de Janeiro, 1930).
[62] Samuel Uchôa: "*Costumes Amazónicos*" ("Amazonian Customs"), *Boletim Sanitário*, National Department of Public Health (Rio de Janeiro, 1923).

the painting of the body a scarlet hue (with the fruit of the urucú shrub) [63] was never the mere expression of a taste for the bizarre as the first chroniclers thought. We should not underestimate the fact that in painting, or rather anointing, themselves with urucú, the savages apparently, during the hunt or while fishing, were thus protecting themselves from the action of the sun upon the skin, from the bites of mosquitoes and other insects, and from sudden changes in temperature—a custom observed by Professor von den Steinen among the Xingú tribes, by Krause among the Caiarás, and by Crevaux among the Japurás; [64] nevertheless, we still find body-painting among the aborigines of Brazil fulfilling the purely mystical function of a prophylactic against evil spirits, and in a lesser number of cases the erotic one of sexual attraction or exhibition. As a prophylactic against the evil ones, scarlet was the most powerful color, as Karsten's study shows.

As for the Portuguese, it would appear that the mysticism associated with the color red had been communicated to them through the Moors and the African Negroes, and to so intense a degree that in Portugal today red is the dominant hue as in no other country of Europe, not alone in the dress of the women of the people—the fishwives of Lisbon, the *tricanas*, or countrywomen, of Coimbra, Aveiro, and Ilhavo, the women of the port town of Vianna, those of the province of Minho, and the *"ribeiras"* of Leiria—but also as a means of prophylaxis against spiritual ills and in various other expressions of popular life and the domestic arts. Red must be the roof of a house to protect those who dwell beneath it:

> *Red are the tiles of your roof,*
> *Of virtues they hold a wealth;*
> *I pass beneath them, ailing,*
> *And they at once give me health.*[65]

---

[63] The dye-yielding urucú tree (*urucuzeiro*) belongs to the *Bixaceæ* family (*Bixa orellana L.*). (Translator:)

[64] Jules Crevaux: *Voyages dans l'Amerique du Sud* (Paris, 1883).— According to Ozório de Almeida, the employment of urucú dye among the Indians of tropical America is to be regarded "not as a mere adornment, but as an efficacious means of protection against the sun and the tropical heat."—*"A Ação Protetora de Urucú"* ("The Protective Action of Urucú"),

separata of the *Boletim do Museu Nacional*, Vol. VIII, No. 1 (Rio de Janeiro, 1931). Sinval Lins (cited by Gastão Cruls, op. cit.) states that in the interior of Minas it is still the custom to paint with urucú the skin of smallpox sufferers.

[65] *As telhas do teu telhado*
São vermalhas, teem virtude:
Passei por elas doente,
Logo me deram saude.

Pedro Fernandes Thomaz: *Canções Populares da Beira* (*Popular Songs of Beira*) (Lisbon, 1896).

Red is the color that fishing-boats are painted; it is also employed in those popular religious pictures depicting miracles and *souls in purgatory;* it is used on the trappings of mules, in mats, and in the wrappings of various products of Portuguese industry;[66] and, by reason of its miraculous virtues, it is the color of ribbons tied about the necks of animals—donkeys, cows, oxen, goats.[67] Even though the people to a degree have lost the notion of its prophylactic qualities, it is obvious that back of this predilection lie mystical motives. With the Portuguese, red is still the color of love, symbolizing the desire of marriage.[68]

Among the Africans, the mystic red is associated with the chief ceremonies of life, where it shows the same prophylactic characteristics as among the Amerindians. In the various African Xangô [69] sects that I visited in Recife and its suburbs, red is the prevailing color, men clad in scarlet shirts being prominent among the worshippers and most of the women's turbans, skirts, and shawls being of bright red. Ortiz, in his studies of Afro-Cuban mysticism, states that the color scarlet goes with the Xangô cult in Cuba; the women in fulfillment of a *vow,* for a favor asked and received of Xangô, put on red, while for one obtained from Obatala (Virgin of Favors), they clothe themselves in white.[70]

In our carnival dances, the *maracatús* and *reisados,* the king of the Congo or the queen always appears in a red cape, and the banners of the popular carnival clubs, adorned with the heads of animals or the emblems of the various trades, painted or embroidered in gold, are scarlet in hue. In passing we may note the interest that these clubs hold, either as a dissimulated form—within the officially Catholic environment of Brazilian life—of totemism or of African animism (a subject already rather thoroughly treated by Nina Rodrigues), or as a degenerate form of the medieval guilds, perverted by the system of slave labor that was here dominant. These corporations, in Spain at least, were imposed upon or permitted to the Moors and Negroes during the centuries preceding the colonization of America.

---

[66] Luiz Chaves: *Páginas Folklóricas (Pages of Folklore)* (Lisbon, 1929).

[67] Leite de Vasconcellos: *Ensaios Ethnográficos* (op. cit.).

[68] A popular quatrain, cited by Leite de Vasconcellos (op. cit.) runs:

Trazes vermelho no peito,
Sinal de casamento.
Deita o vermelho fora.
Qu'o casar inda tem tempo.

(Red on your bosom you wear,
Sign of marriage, they say;
But there is still time for that;
So throw the red away.)

[69] Fetish cult centering in the African deity Xangô. See Preface to the Third Edition, note 11, p. lxi.

[70] Fernando Ortiz: *Hampa Afro-cubana—Los Negroes Brujos* (Madrid, 1917).

In Brazil that fondness for the color red which we have noted in the dress of women of the people, in the banners of the carnival clubs, in the capes of the queen of the *maracatú*, is to be observed also in other aspects of popular life and domestic art: in the painting of the outside of houses and in their interior decoration; in the painting of tin-plate boxes and various domestic accessories of tin plate or of wood, such as watering-pots, bird and parrot cages, and the like; in the painting of ex-votos; and in the decorating of cake and sweetmeat trays—the erotic interest of which we shall study later on, in connection with a nomenclature that is impregnated with eroticism and which points to that association, common among Brazilians, of the taste of the palate with sexual taste.

The conclusion to be drawn is that the Brazilian's preference for scarlet is a trait that is chiefly Amerindian in origin. As Karsten points out, the savage regards the great enemies of his body as being, not insects and reptiles, but evil spirits.[71] These latter, primitive man imagines, are always on the watch for an opportunity to penetrate his body: through the mouth, through the nostrils, through the eyes, ears, hair. The important thing, accordingly, is to see to it that all these parts, looked upon as being the most critical and vulnerable, shall be especially well guarded from malign influences; whence the piercing of the nose or the lips with rings, bits of stone, and small rods; the use that is made of the bones and teeth of animals for such a purpose; the scraping of the head, which Pero Vaz de Caminha [72] was the first to note among the Indians and the nude Indian women of Brazil; the occasional painting of the teeth black. All this by way of conjuring the evil spirits, keeping them away from man's vulnerable parts. Whence, also, the employment of a species of cosmetic of which various South American tribes, from Tierra del Fuego to Guiana, made use in anointing the hair; this was generally a scarlet-colored ocher, sometimes a blood-red vegetable juice.

Von den Steinen found the Bororós of the River Xingú dyeing their hair scarlet before taking part in funeral dances and ceremonies —on which occasions the Indian feels himself particularly exposed to the malignant action of the spirit of the dead person and that of other spirits as well, all of them evil ones, which the savages believe are let loose or are likely to be provoked at such moments as this.[73] Koch-Grünberg encountered the same custom among the Rio Negro tribes; he saw one whole tribe, with the exception of the medicine-man,

---

[71] Karsten, op. cit.

[72] Vaz de Caminha was clerk to the fleet of Pedro Alvarez Cabral, the discoverer of Brazil (1500). (Translator.)

[73] Von den Steinen, op. cit.

painted red after a funeral. The German ethnologist further noted that, in conjuring dances in which cymbals were employed, the witch-doctors had their faces painted scarlet, presenting a horrible appearance.[74]

Von den Steinen had occasion to witness a ceremony in which the Rio Xingú Indians conjured a meteor, with the *baris*, or medicine-men, gesticulating vehemently and spitting in the air. And before confronting the enemy they had carefully painted their bodies a bright red shade with urucú.

The aborigines of the Rio Negro region painted themselves with the red of the caraiurú plant [75] when one of them fell ill with a cold of the head or chest, the idea being to ward off the evil in time by means of this prophylactic measure. And Koch-Grünberg found that the women of the Kobeuas were accustomed to paint their newborn children scarlet with the same object in view. This custom is one that Léry [76] observed among the Tupís of the seaboard at the time of the discovery, and Spix and Martius [77] met with it among the Coro-ados at the beginning of the nineteenth century.

The Toba women, according to Karsten, were in the habit of painting their bodies an urucú-red while menstruating, a practice that he attributes to prophylaxis, a process of disinfection in warding off those evil spirits which were supposed to assail the woman with especial fury at such a period. Del Campana, for his part, observed that the women of the Chiriguanos would paint themselves scarlet when preparing the *chicha*,[78] or sacred drink, and also after child-birth. Both men and women would do so when convalescing, to give themselves strength. Among the Caraiás, Jibaros, and various other tribes of the Orinoco region, when one member of the tribe sets out to visit another, he must paint his body red before putting in an appearance, and this procedure is repeated when the guest reaches his destination. It is Karsten's opinion that in this case the painting is a prophylactic measure.[79] It is the learned professor of Helsingfors whom we may credit with a real theory for the interpretation of

---

[74] Koch-Grünberg, op. cit.

[75] The Caraiurú (carajurú) is an Amazonian plant of the Bignoneaceæ or trumpet-flower family (*Arribadæa chica Verlot*). It yields a red dye. (Translator.)

[76] Jean de Léry: *Histoire d'un voyage faict en la terre du Brésil* (*nouvelle edition avec une introduc-*

tion et des notes par Paul Gaffarel; Paris, 1880). (Translator.)

[77] *Reise in Brasilien* (*Travels in Brazil*) (op. cit.). (Translator.)

[78] A fermented drink, generally made of corn, but also of fruit kernels, roots, or honey. (Lima and Barroso: *Pequeno Dicionário*, etc.) (Translator.)

[79] Karsten, op. cit.

body-painting among the Amerindians, one that sees in it a prophylactic or magic process in place of a mere decoration designed to exert a purely æsthetic or sensual appeal to the opposite sex.

But for the savages of South America red was not merely, along with black, the prophylactic color, capable of safeguarding the human body against malignant influences; it was not merely one designed to give tone to the body, being possessed of the faculty of invigorating women after childbirth, and convalescents, and of endowing with the power of physical endurance those individuals who were employed at hard or exhausting labor; nor was it simply the good-luck hue, with the magic power of attracting the game to the hunter (with which purpose in mind the Canelos painted even their dogs). It was also the erotic color, of seduction or attraction, not so much out of any consideration of beauty or æsthetic quality as for reasons of magic. It was the color with which the Canelos painted themselves when they wished to seduce a woman, the one of which the Cainguas of the Upper Paraná region made use in attracting into the forest the females they desired or of whom they had need in order to satisfy their sexual hunger, their procedure being one of intimidation rather than of courting.

It is, indeed, not easy to say what was the basic motive that lay behind the American savage's preference for the color red. Possibly it was the fact that red was the color of blood and, for this very reason, enjoyed a mystic prestige among the primitive peoples of America whose life was still permanently devoted to hunting and to war. Some anthropologists have suggested that these peoples may, as a matter of fact, have employed the red of the urucú and other dyes as a substitute for blood.

As we consider, in this essay, the clash of the two cultures, the European and the Amerindian, from the point of view of the social formation of the Brazilian family—where a European and Catholic morality predominated—let us not forget, meanwhile, to note the effect of this contact upon the native from the point of view of his own culture. That contact was dissolvent in effect. Among the native populations of America, dominated by the colonist or the missionary, moral degradation was now complete, as always happens when an advanced culture meets with a backward one.[80] Under the technical

---

[80] "Degeneration probably operates even more actively in the lower than in the higher culture," says Edward B. Tylor: *Primitive Culture* (London, 1929). See also, on this subject, the work by James Bryce: *The Relations of the Advanced and Backward Races of Mankind* (Oxford, 1902).

and moral pressure of the advanced one, that of the backward people is dispersed. The aborigines lose their capacity for evolving autonomously, just as they are incapable of suddenly elevating themselves, through natural or forced imitation, to those standards which the imperialism of the colonizer imposes upon them. Even though the *forms* or *accessories* of the culture may be saved, there is lost what Pitt-Rivers [81] considers the *potential*—that is to say, the constructive—capacity of the culture in question, its *élan*, its rhythm.

The history of the contact of the so-called "superior" races with those looked upon as "inferior" is always the same. Extermination or degradation. Chiefly because the conqueror means to impose upon the subject people the whole of his own culture, in one piece, without any compromise to soften the imposition. From the sixteenth century to the present day the missionary has been the great destroyer of non-European cultures, his activities in this respect having been more dissolvent than those of the layman.

In the case of Brazil, what happened first was the collapse of Catholic morality on the part of a small minority of the colonizers, who in the beginning were intoxicated by the amoral environment created by contact with the indigenous race. Under the influence of the fathers of the Society of Jesus, however, colonization was to take a Puritan turn—even though it was a Puritanism less strictly adhered to in this part of the Americas, by the Portuguese Christians, than it was by the true Puritans, the English ones, in North America. But in any event much of the native spontaneity was stifled, with the Jesuits substituting for the songs of the aborigines, so filled with the flavor of life in the wilds, the dry and mechanical hymns of devotion which they themselves had composed, and which never spoke of love save in such terms as might be applied to Our Lady and the saints. Upon the natural regional differences in speech was superimposed a single tongue, the "general" one; [82] and *caboclos* who had reached the stage of catechumens were now compelled to do away with those dances and festivals that were most impregnated with the instincts, interests, and animal energy of the conquered race, all that was preserved being an occasional childhood dance of some charm.

What is more, the Jesuits sought to destroy, or at least to castrate, every virile expression of religious or artistic culture that was not in agreement with Catholic morality and European conventions. They separated art from life. They laid the foundations in Brazil for an art that should be, not an expression, a prolongation, of the life and the

---

[81] See note 86 below.   [82] See p. 166.

physical and psychic experience of the individual and the social group, but one that consisted in exercises in composition and penmanship.

Whatever was saved of the native, Amerindian culture of Brazil was saved in spite of the Jesuit influence; for if the padres had had their way, only vague and formless phases of that culture would have remained following the Portuguese conquest, and these would have been cleverly adapted by them to Roman theology and European morals. Nor could the outlook of these good and austere soldiers of the Church have been other than what it was; for they more than any others had the vocation of catechists and empire-builders. The economic imperialism of the European bourgeoisie was anticipated by the religious imperialism of the fathers of the Society of Jesus, by the Europeanizing ardor of the great Catholic missionaries of the sixteenth and seventeenth centuries,[83] whose place was later taken by the Presbyterians and the Methodists, who were still more harsh and uncompromising than the Jesuits had been.[84]

With the segregation of the natives into large settlements, the Jesuits fostered in the bosom of the aboriginal populations one of the most deadly and deep-going influences. It was the entire rhythm of social life that was thus altered for the Indians; for peoples accustomed to a scattered and roaming life are always degraded when concentrated into large communities and forced to adopt an absolutely settled mode of existence.

But from the point of view of the Church, I repeat, it must be admitted that the padres acted heroically; they were admirably firm

---

[83] Disagreeing with Max Weber, who in his study *Gesammelte Aufsätze zur Religionsoziologie* (Berlin, 1922) identifies modern capitalism and, consequently, colonizing imperialism with Calvinism and Puritanism, R. H. Tawney stresses the fact that the centers of finance and the capitalistic spirit in the fifteenth century—Florence, Venice, southern Germany, and Flanders—were Catholic and not Protestant.—*Religion and the Rise of Capitalism* (London, 1926). Here, however, I am referring to that religious imperialism which was the predecessor of the economic and of which, in the sixteenth and seventeenth centuries, the Jesuits were the militant exponents. On Weber's

thesis, see W. R. Robertson: *Aspects of the Rise of Capitalism* (Cambridge, 1929); and Amintore Fanfani: *Cattolicismo e Protestantismo nella Formazione Storica del Capitalismo* (Milan, 1934).

[84] Freyre, brought up as a Catholic, spent ten formative years of his life at the Gilreath American School in Recife. At 16 or 17 he went through a religious crisis and became interested in Protestantism, which he later gave up. He has remained on good terms with his former teachers, both Catholic and Protestant. See Lewis Hanke: "Gilberto Freyre: Brazilian Social Historian," *Quarterly Journal of Inter-American Relations*, Vol 1, No. 3 (July 1939), pp. 24–44. (Editor.)

in their orthodoxy, loyal to their ideals; and in connection with any criticism that is made of their interference with native life and culture in America—the first culture to be subtly and systematically degraded —we must take into account this higher religious and moral motive that inspired their activity. Judging them, however, by another criterion—purely as European agents in the disintegration of native values—we must conclude that their influence was a harmful one.[85] Quite as harmful as that of the colonists, their antagonists, who, animated by economic interest or pure sensuality, saw in the Indian only a voluptuous female to be taken or a rebellious slave to be subjugated and exploited for purposes af agriculture.

If we study the picture painted for us by Pitt-Rivers of the deleterious influences—depopulation, degeneration, degradation—which the English anthropologist attributes to the contact of advanced races with backward ones,[86] we shall find that a large if not the major part of these are influences that were operative upon the Brazilian Indian through the catechism or through the moral, pedagogical, and organizational system, with its sexual division of labor, that was imposed by the Jesuits. Of the fifteen influences classified by Pitt-Rivers, it is my opinion that, in striking a balance-sheet of European responsibilities for the racial and cultural degradation of the aborigines in Brazil, we shall find that at least nine are applicable to the Jesuit padres and their civilizing methods:

1. the concentration of the aborigines in large settlements (a measure that the missionaries exerted themselves to enforce);[87]

---

[85] Gonçalves Dias, in his book *O Brasil e a Oceânia* (*Brazil and Oceania*) (São Luiz, 1869), lays emphasis upon the dissolvent effect of the Jesuit system. In speaking of the Jesuit fathers he says: "They loosened family ties, leading children and wives to denounce parents and husbands; they deprived them of their will-power and love of independence, and by means of humiliations, disciplinary measures, and infamous punishments inflicted in the public square—inflicted even upon the tribal chieftains and endured by them as a meritorious act—they stifled and consumed that sense of personal dignity without which no praiseworthy effort is possible on the part of our species."

[86] George Henry Lane and Fox Pitt-Rivers: *The Clash of Cultures and the Contact of Races* (London, 1927).

[87] This point is emphasized by a historian who is extremely sympathetic with the Jesuits, Capistrano de Abreu: "The Jesuits, intelligent and practical observers, had concentrated their efforts upon making of the various native villages one single settlement, ruled over by a sort of bailiff named by the governor, invested with the staff of office, which puffed them up with vanity, and with the means of making themselves obeyed, being able to send people to jail; they had bent their efforts toward this end and toward extinguishing anthropophagy, polygamy, and the drinking of fruit wines, for which the Indians were

2. the dressing of the natives in European garb (another thing that the Jesuits imposed upon their catechumens); [88]

3. segregation on plantations; [89]

4. the raising of obstacles to marriage in the native manner;

5. the application of European penal legislation to supposed crimes of fornication;

6. the abolition of inter-tribal warfare;

7. the abolition of polygamy;

8. the increase of infant mortality due to new conditions of life;

9. the abolition of the communal system and of the authority of the chieftains (and, we may add, that of the *pajés*, or medicine-men, as well, the latter being a special target because of religious rivalry

---

famous."—Appendix to *Tratado da Terra e Gente do Brasil* (op. cit.). And Ayres de Cazal, in his *Choreographia Brasilica* (op. cit.) p. 129, sums up the civilizing methods of the Jesuits as follows: "Within a brief span of years the Jesuits had reduced the various hordes of the nation to a settled life in the great villages known as *Reduções*, the number of which in the 1630's amounted to twenty, with 70,000 inhabitants. . . ." He is referring to the celebrated settlements of the Guaranís in the south, whose mode of life he describes in detail: "Each of the *Reduções*, another name for missions, was a large or fairly large town, and all were of the same pattern, with straight-running streets crossing at right angles; the houses were generally of earth, covered with tile, whitewashed, and with verandas along the sides as a protection against the heat and rains; so that, seeing one of them, one could form a good idea of the others. . . . A vicar and a curate, both Jesuits, were the only ecclesiastics and sufficed to exercise all the parochial functions; they were the inspectors in all matters of civil economy, and under their direction were magistrates (*corregedores*) elected annually, a chief who held office for life, and other officials, each with his own province and jurisdic-

tion. With the exception of these, all individuals of either sex wore trailing robes made of white cotton or some such material. . . . And everything was under the supervision of the *corregedores* or other subordinates." —This was precisely the regime of a boarding-school kept by priests. Or of an orphan-asylum. All dressed alike. An absolutely sedentary existence. A large concentration of people. Stern vigilance and supervision. The nudity of the *caboclos*, men and women, cloaked with ugly robes that resembled children's nightgowns. Uniformity. Young girls segregated from the men. It was, in short, the Jesuit system as it had been refined in Paraguay that, in a milder form, held sway in Brazil. While admirably efficient, it was a regime that was destructive of any animal spirits, freshness and spontaneity, combativeness of mind, or *cultural potential* that the aborigines may have possessed; for these qualities and that potential could not survive the total destruction of the sexual, nomad, and warrior habits that had been forcibly uprooted in the Indians thus gathered together in the great settlements.

[88] Capistrano de Abreu, loc. cit. Ayres de Cazal, op. cit.

[89] Ayres de Cazal, op. cit., I, p. 129.

between them and the padres, for which reason they were more important than the *murubixabas,* or temporal chiefs).[90]

Some of these responsibilities are perhaps to be shared with the colonists: among others, the segregation of the savages on plantations and the sexual division of labor after the European model. And it was the colonists and not the Jesuits who in a large number of instances were the principal dysgenesic agents among the aborigines: for they it was who altered the latter's diet and mode of labor, thereby disturbing their metabolism; and they were also the ones who introduced endemic and epidemic diseases and who communciated to the natives the use of sugar-cane brandy.

It may be seen, meanwhile, that the more systematized it was, the greater in effect was the deadly or harmful influence of the morality, mode of instruction, and technique of economic exploitation employed by the padres. To the colonists, for example, the nudity of slaves or plantation "help" (*administrados*) meant little; it even suited their financial interests. It is known that one rich colonist in the early days went so far as to have himself served at table by naked Indian women,[91] and his case would not appear to have been an isolated one; whereas the good fathers from the first had insisted that the natives should be clad in a manner befitting Christian modesty; at most, they merely tolerated nakedness in the young, or in young and grown-ups alike when there was absolutely no cloth to be had for the making of garments.[92]

---

[90] "The *pajés*," says Affonso d'E. Taunay, "would flee for leagues from the detested *inacianos* (Jesuits), who in turn abominated them; and this was unfortunate, for much might have been learned from the medicine-men."—"*A Fundação de São Paulo*" ("The Founding of São Paulo"), *Revista do Instituto Histórico e Geográphico Brasileiro*, Vol. III, special volume of the First International Congress of American History (Rio de Janeiro, 1927).

[91] The colonist in question was Paschoal Barrufo da Bertioga. The incident is related by Father Simão de Vasconcellos: "At dinner-time they brought in to serve at table some Indian maids, immodestly nude. . . ." It was a dinner at which Jesuits were

present, and they were scandalized.— *Vida do Veneravel Padre Joseph de Anchieta da Companhia Iesu. . . . Composto pello Padre Simão de Vasconcellos . . . (Life of the Venerable Father Joseph de Anchieta of the Society of Jesus. . . . Composed by . . . etc.)* (Lisbon, 1672).—Theodoro Sampaio relates the occurrence, adding that "the Indian slave girls, pretty brunettes, gave rise to many domestic tempests."—"*S. Paulo no Tempo de Anchieta*" ("São Paulo in the Time of Anchieta"), *III Centenario do Veneravel Joseph Anchieta* (*Third Centenary,* etc.) (São Paulo, 1900).

[92] Referring to the first Indians who were Christianized, Capistrano de Abreu (op. cit.) states that "as cloth-

The immediate and profound dysgenic effects of this imposition of European garb upon peoples accustomed to going nude or to covering their bodies merely for purposes of decoration or by way of protecting them from the sun and cold and insect-bites are well known today. This forced use of clothing, it is believed, has played no small part in the development of those skin and pulmonary diseases that have competed with one another in decimating whole populations of savages after the latter had submitted to the rule of the civilized; and these were diseases that in sixteenth- and seventeenth-century Brazil took a terrible toll.[93]

The forcing of clothes upon the natives by European missionaries was to affect the Indian's traditional concepts of morality and hygiene, for which it was difficult to substitute new ones. Thus, there is to be observed in many individuals belonging to tribes that were accustomed to going naked a tendency to take off their European

---

ing did not arrive for all of them, the women went naked." His authority is Father Cardim. The sixteenth-century visiting priest gives us a striking description of the first Indian women who were clothed: "they are so modest, serene, virtuous, and bewildered that they appear to be statues leaning against their male companions; and when they walk, their slippers fall off, for they are not accustomed to wearing them."—Fernão Cardim: *Tratados da Terra e Gente do Brasil*, with Introduction and Notes by Baptista Caetano, Capistrano de Ábreu, and Rodolfo Garcia (Rio de Janeiro, 1925).—From this it may be seen that there was an element of the ridiculous, along with a note of sadness, in this imposition of clothing upon the aborigines of the year 1500. Speaking of the Indians under the influence of the first Christian missionaries, Anchieta tells us: "When they marry, they go to the wedding clothed, and in the afternoon they go out for a walk with only a bonnet on their heads, no other clothing, and they think that they are stepping out right gallantly."—*Informações e Fragmentos Históricos do Padre Joseph de Anchieta* (op. cit.), p. 47.

[93] Simão de Vasconcellos is one of the chroniclers who report these diseases: "There broke out suddenly something like a terrible plague of coughing and deadly catarrh in certain houses of baptized Indians. . . ." —*Chrónica da Companhia de Jesus dos Estados do Brasil (Chronicle of the Society of Jesus of the States of Brazil)* (2nd edition, Rio de Janeiro, 1864), p. 65.—W. D. Hambly attributes to irregularity in the use of clothing by the savage—which frequently happened in Brazil—the responsibility for many of the diseases that decimated the primitive peoples when brought into contact with the civilized.—*Origins of Education among Primitive Peoples* (London, 1926).—Regarding the health and hygiene of the first Indians enslaved by the colonists in Brazil, Theodoro Sampaio generalizes as follows: "The slaves were not healthy. The settled life on the plantations was not good for them, and a large number of them died of pleurisy, hemorrhages, catarrhal affections, and herpes, which were terrible in their effects and very frequent among them."—"*S. Paulo no Fim do Seculo XVI*" ("São Paulo at the End of the Sixteenth Century"), *Revista do Instituto Histórico de São Paulo*.

clothing only when it is ready to fall off them from dirt and grime. Yet these are peoples that, in point of bodily cleanliness and even sexual morality are at times superior to those whom Christian morality loads down with heavy raiment.

As to cleanliness, the natives of Brazil were assuredly superior to those European Christians who arrived in the year 1500. Let us not forget that the latter, in this era, were in the habit of lauding St. Anthony, founder of the monastic life, for having denied himself the vanity of bathing his feet, while the praise given to St. Simeon Stylites was that his stench could have been smelled from afar.[94] And the Portuguese were not the most unclean of European peoples in the sixteenth century, as certain malicious ones, perhaps, would like to picture them. On the contrary, owing to the influence of the Moors, they were among the cleanest.

Of the early chronicle-writers, it is the Frenchmen, Ives d'Évreux [95] and Jean de Léry,[96] who are most astonished by the frequency with which the *caboclos* bathed. And a French hygienist, Sigaud, would attribute to their cold baths the fact that the aborigines of Brazil— already under the influence of European civilization—suffered from disorders of the respiratory tract, running all the way from simple catarrah to acute pleurisy and bronchitis.[97] Cold baths and the habit of going practically naked. were blamed for this. But modern studies in hygiene show the contrary to be the case; they show that these diseases of the respiratory system are developed among savages through the imposition of European clothing and safeguards upon a people accustomed to utter nudity.

The century of the discovery of America—the fifteenth—and the two centuries immediately following, marked by intensive colonization, were for all Europe an epoch marked by a great lowering of the standards of hygiene. At the beginning of the nineteenth century—so we learn from a German writer cited by Lowie—there were still to be met with in Germany persons who in all their lifetime could not remember having taken a single bath.[98] The French in this respect were not superior to their neighbors. Quite the contrary. The author of *Primitive Culture* reminds us that the elegant queen Marguerite of

---

[94] Westermarck: *The Origin and Development of the Moral Ideas* (op. cit.).

[95] Ives d'Évreux: *Voyages dans le nord du Brésil* (Leipzig and Paris, 1864).

[96] Jean de Léry: *Histoire d'un voy-*

age faict en la terre du Brésil (op. cit.).

[97] J. F. X. Sigaud: *Du climat et des maladies du Brésil* (Paris, 1844).

[98] Robert H. Lowie: *Are We Civilized?* (New York and London, 1929).

Navarre would go for an entire week without washing her hands; that when Louis XIV washed his, it was with a little perfumed alcohol, and then he merely sprinkled them; that a French etiquette manual of the seventeenth century advises the reader to bathe his hands and face once a day; while another manual of the century preceding warns the young nobleman that he should not blow his nose with the hand that was holding a piece of meat; that in 1530 Erasmus thought it perfectly decent to blow his nose on the ground in this fashion, stepping upon the mucus with the sole of his shoe; and, finally, that a treatise of the year 1539 gives recipes for protection against lice, which were probably common throughout a large part of Europe.[99]

In Europe, baths in the Roman manner and river baths—at times promiscuous ones, against which for long the voice of the Church had thundered in vain—had almost wholly ceased following the Crusades and the forming of more intimate commercial ties with the Orient. The European was liable to the contagion of syphilis and other transmissible and repugnant diseases; hence his fear of the bath and his horror of nudity.[100] The first Portuguese and Frenchmen to arrive in this part of America, on the other hand, encountered a people that appeared to be without the marks of syphilis and whose greatest pleasure was bathing in the river. The naked aborigines washed themselves constantly from head to foot, by way of keeping their bodies in a state of cleanliness, making use for this purpose of the leaves of trees as the more fastidious Europeans did of towels, in drying their hands, and of pieces of cloth in bathing their young ones; and they would go to the river to wash their soiled linen—that is, their cotton hammocks—a task with which the men were charged.

Even though they urinated within the *ocas*, or huts, the Tupís—Léry observes—". . . *vont néantmoins fort loin faire leurs excremens.*"[101] It is from the Indians that the rural or semi-rural Brazilian appears to have acquired the habit of defecating at a distance from the house, usually in the middle of a banana patch near the river. And in the morning, before bathing. A swallow of rum with cashew nuts and occasionally the sign of the cross to safeguard the body ordinarily preceded this hygienic bath. The cashews to clear the blood-stream. It was, in short, a whole liturgy or sanitary and prophylactic ritual that was thus performed.

With the exception of washing the soiled hammocks, the Indian women were responsible for all the tasks having to do with domestic

---

[99] Lowie, op. cit.

[100] William Graham Sumner: *Folkways* (Boston, 1906).

[101] Léry, op, cit., Vol. II, p. 91.

hygiene, and they were even fonder of the bath and of bodily cleanliness than were the men. They were exceedingly clean, Gabriel
Soares notes.[102] And this—the *cunhã's* greater fondness for water and
hygienic care of the body—according to Léry, is the explanation of
the fact that the women adorned themselves less than did the men,
a circumstance that the chronicler notes *"entre les choses doublement
estranges & vraiment esmerveillables, que i'ay observées en ces
femmes brésiliennes."* If we are to take the word of this scrupulous
Protestant pastor (who shows himself to be possessed of a critical
sense that is out of the ordinary, throughout the whole of his travel
narrative and especially in the opening pages, where, not without a
certain theological odium, he corrects the work of Friar André
Thévet on Brazil)—if we are to take his word, the truth is that it was
the women who offered the greater resistance when the Europeans attempted to impose upon them a garb that was supposed to be moral
in effect but which to them was unhygienic: *"des robbes de frise &
des chemises."* Their excuse was that so much clothing on the body
rendered difficult their custom of bathing freely and frequently—at
times almost hourly, ten or a dozen baths a day. Léry states that *"il n'a
iamais este en nostre puissance de les faire vestir. . . . Elles disoyente
que ce leur seroit trop de peine de se despouiller si souvent. Ne voila
pas une belle & bien pertinente raison?"* [103] Efforts to keep the *cunhãs*

---

[102] Gabriel Soares de Sousa, op. cit.
(Translator.)

[103] Léry, op. cit., Vol. I, p. 136.—
Jean de Léry impresses me as being
one of the two most dependable
chroniclers who have written on sixteenth-century Brazil. The other is
Gabriel Soares de Sousa, of whom
Oliveira Lima is altogether right in
saying: "The Bahian plantation-
owner, as minute in his topographical
as he is meticulous in his ethnographical descriptions, may be looked upon
as one of the safest guides to the
study of rudimentary Tupí psychology. His mind is not beclouded with
exclusive proselytizing tendencies, as
is the case with the fathers of the
Society of Jesus—Simão de Vasconcellos, for example—nor with the il-
lusions of a romantic theology, as in
the case of the French Capuchins of
Maranhão, Claude d'Abbeville and
Ives d'Évreux.—Oliveira Lima: *Aspectos da Literatura Colonial Brasileira, (Aspects of Colonial Brazilian
Literature)* (Leipzig, 1895).—As for
Friar André Thévet, that is a different story. One should read his book—
full of interesting observations—but
as one reads a novel. It is the first
book on Brazil in the French language: *Les Singularitéz de la France
antarctique, autrement nommée
Amérique . . .* par F. André Thévet.
Thévet is the first of the early chroniclers to concern himself, with some
exactitude, with the cashew; his book
has an engraving showing an Indian
climbing a cashew tree and gathering nuts. He praises roast cashew
nuts: *"Quāt au noyau qui est dedãs, il
est tresbon à manger, pourueu qu'il
ait passé legerement par le feu."* Professor A. Métraux makes extensive use
of Thévet in his notable study of the
religion of the Tupinambás, thus beginning the rehabilitation of the in-

clothed in the European manner were systematically frustrated by them in the early days; they might be obliged by the French Calvinists to go clad during the daytime, but at the first sign of nightfall, off would come their petticoats and chemises and they would scatter out along the the shore with delightful abandon. The Protestant pastor tells us that he saw them time and again in this state, concluding that the Indian women "*quant au naturel, ne doivent rien aux autres en beauté.*" He further observes that "*les attiflets, fards, fausses perruques, cheveux tortillez, grands collets fraisez, vertugales, robbes sur robbes, & autres infinies bagatelles dont les femmes & filles de par deçà se contrefont & n'ont iamais assez, sont sans comparaison cause de plus de maux que n'est la nudité ordinaire des femmes sauvages. . . .*"[104] There was something of a Havelock Ellis in the Reverend Jean de Léry.

Thanks to certain of the old chronicle-writers, we are acquainted with many of the intimate details of the day-to-day economic life of the aborigines; their sexual division of labor, for example, the work of the fields being almost wholly assigned to women, along with the care of the house. These facts we find set down with an exactness that has been confirmed by the latest researches of ethnologists. Writing of the Tupinambás, Gabriel Soares informs us that it is the males who "are accustomed to plant the forest, and they also burn it over and clear the land"; it is they who "go to look for wood with which to warm themselves, for they never sleep without a fire alongside their hammocks, which are their beds." This is not to mention the chief responsibility of the men, which was to furnish the *taba*, or Indian village, with meat and fish and to protect it against enemies and wild animals.

There was, however, Léry tells us, no comparison between their labors and the way in which the women worked: "*car excepté quelques matines (& non au chaut du jour) qu'ils coupent & effertent du bois pour faire les jardins, ils* [the men] *ne font gueres autre chose qu'aller à la guerre, à la chasse, à la pescherie fabriquer leurs espées de bois, arcs, fleches, habillements de plume. . . .*"[105] Gabriel Soares, in speaking of the activities of an industrial or artistic character that he encountered among the Tupinambás, does

---

genuous and at times fantastic French Capuchin, who, the truth is, with all his fanciful writing, has given us passages that are indispensable by reason of the information they contain and the suggestions they offer. This work of rehabilitation is being continued by Thévet's Portuguese language translator, Professor Estevão Pinto.

[104] Léry, op. cit., Vol. I, p. 139.
[105] Ibid., Vol. I, p. 125.

not specify the age or sex of those who participated in them; but the "palm-leaf hampers and other containers of the same material, made after their manner and for their use," and the "baskets made of twigs, which they call *samburás*,[106] and other plaited ones, like those of India matting"—these must have represented an art that was due to masculine initiative, but it was an activity in which both sexes and young and old alike must have engaged. The chronicler goes on to mention, as being the exclusive work of women, the cotton-fiber hammocks and "the ribbons like lacework, and some larger ones which they wear in their hair." He goes into further detail: "It is the task of the older women to make the flour which is their sustenance, and they carry the manihot to the house on their backs. And there are many of the old women who are charged with making clay vessels by hand, as these are the jugs in which they make their wines, and they make some of them big enough to hold as much as a couple of hogsheads, and it is in these and in other smaller ones that they ferment the wine they drink. These old women also make pots, drinking-cups, and kneading-bowls for their use, in which they bake the flour, and others in which they store it or out of which they eat, all of them dyed in various colors. This pottery they bake in a hole that they make in the ground, with wood piled over it; and these Indian women hold and believe that if any other person than the one who has made it does the baking, the pottery will burst while in the fire. The same old women also assist in making flour, which they do after their own fashion." [107]

It was also the women who planted the crops and who went to the spring for water; they prepared the food and looked after the young ones. It may be seen that the old woman was a person of no little importance among the aborigines, and the importance of the woman in general was very great. In this category a comparative study of art and industry among primitive peoples authorizes us to place the effeminate male or even the sexual invert, common in various Brazilian tribes.

Hartt makes the point that the art of ceramics among the aborigines of Brazil must have evolved by woman's hand, and this observation of the North American scholar was later confirmed by his disciple, Herbert S. Smith, after the latter had observed the Cadiueus.[108] It has

---

[106] The *samburá* was a basket made of liana or taquara, the latter being a tough-fibered, wild-growing cane resembling bamboo. (Translator.)

[107] Gabriel Soares de Sousa, op. cit., p. 320.

[108] Herbert Smith, op. cit. [The Cadiueus are a group of Guaicuru (Guaycurú) Indians in southern Mato Grosso and Paraguay. (Translator.)]

also been confirmed by the recent researches of Heloisa Alberto Torres, with regard to the ceramics of Marajó.[109] One thing that these studies render certain is that the manufacture of pottery among Brazilian natives came later, being preceded by weaving; since over a long period of time impermeable woven containers were used as vessels for holding liquids; and this must have been a masculine art.

Artistic production that was exclusively or principally the work of men consisted in the making of bows and arrows, musical instruments, and certain ornaments for the body. In the building of the *oca*, or hut, the man's labor was strenuous, as was the effort he put forth in rearing a stockade about the village, a means of defense that the Portuguese were later to adopt in protecting the plantation Big Houses from the attacks of enemies. It was the men, also, who made the canoes, fashioned out of a single log, which likewise were taken over by the early colonists, in their backland raids.[110]

I have already stated, in the opening pages of this chapter, that from the point of view of organized agrarian life, representing the stabilization of the Portuguese colonist in Brazil, the social and economic utility of the native woman was greater than that of the man. The latter almost wholly evaded the efforts of the colonizers, and even the wiles of the priests, designed to make him a part of the new technique of economic exploitation and the new regime of social life. The woman achieved a much better adjustment, a fact that is understandable in view of her technical superiority among primitive peoples and the greater tendency to stability that she manifested among the nomad tribes. Whatever the demands that were made of her in connection with the formation of Brazilian society—that of her body, which she was the first to offer to the white man; that of her domestic and even her agricultural labor; that of stability (a state for which she longed, seeing that her menfolk were still at war with the invader, while she was left to wander aimlessly, a pack on her head and an infant at her bosom or straddling her hips)—whatever the demands, the *cunhã* gave an excellent account of herself.

Among her people the Indian woman was the principal element of economic and technical worth. There was a bit of the beast of burden in her, and a bit of the slave to man. But she was superior to the latter in her capacity for making use of things and producing the necessities for communal life and comfort. Polygamy, among the savages who practiced it—including those who inhabited Brazil—was not merely

---

[109] Heloisa Alberto Torres: "*Cerâmica de Marajó*" (lecture) (Rio de Janeiro, 1929).

[110] The author employs the English word, *raids*. (Translator.)

a fulfillment of sexual desire, so difficult to satisfy in the male who possesses but a single wife; it reflected also the economic interests of the hunter, fisherman, warrior, as he sought to surround himself with those living, creative economic values which women represented.

Thomas tells us that among primitive peoples the man is the active, violent, sporadic element, while woman is the stable, substantial, continuous one.[111] This antagonism is rooted in the physical constitution of the woman, which adapts her to resistance rather than to movement. To agriculture and industry rather than to hunting and war. Hence it is that we almost always find agricultural and industrial activity developing through the woman, as well as the technique that is proper to the habitation, the house; and she is also in good part responsible for the domestication of animals. Even magic and art, if they do not develop chiefly through her, are evolved by the effeminate or bisexual male, who prefers the regular and domestic life of the woman to that of movement and warfare which the man leads. The natives of Brazil at the time of the discovery were still in the stage of relative male parasitism, with a consequent overburdening of the female. In was the *cunhã's* creative hands that were responsible for the regular performance of the principal tasks that had to do with art, industry, and the tilling of the soil.

As to the *pajés*, or medicine-men, it is probable that they were of that effeminate or invert type that was respected and feared by most of the American aborigines, instead of being despised and abhorred.[112] In some cases the effeminacy was due to advanced age, which tends to make certain women more masculine and certain men more feminine; but in other cases perhaps it was due to congenital or acquired perversion. In any event, the fact of the matter is that these bisexual individuals, or individuals bisexualized by age, held in their hands the powers and functions of mystics, healers, *pajés*, and counselors among the various American tribes.

The institution of couvade itself, a cultural complex so characteristic of the Brazilian aborigines, is a case in point: one might venture to interpret it by the criterion of bisexuality. Inasmuch as the custom is found among those peoples who do not despise or ridicule effeminates, but who in general respect them as beings endowed with extraordinary powers and virtues, it is possible that couvade arose from sexually differentiated beings: individuals of great influence and with a mystic power of suggestion over the majority. Wissler observes that certain cultural traits, even though but rarely, may be in-

---

[111] Thomas, op. cit.
[112] Westermarck: *The Origin and Development of the Moral Ideas* (op. cit.).

corporated into the general practice of a tribe or a group through the influence of exceptional individuals who initiate them.[113] It is known that the invert is one in search of creative and painful activities such as will make up to him for the impossibility of femininity and maternity: masochism, flagellation, and the arts of sculpture, painting, calligraphy, and music among the monks of the Middle Ages; the same masochism among the fakirs of India; and according to Silberer, in his work *The Problems of Mysticism and Symbolism,* even alchemy represented a desire of compensation on the part of certain individuals of an introvert type.[114] It is known that in certain diseases, such as tuberculosis and constipation, some introverts appear to find pleasure or compensation.[115]

All these are suggestions that, though they may not be sufficient to carry conviction, perhaps constitute a basis for a possible sexual interpretation of couvade through the criterion of bisexuality. There would seem, indeed, to be present in couvade much of that desire which Faithful notes in the introvert of achieving, through an identification with the woman, the joys of maternity ("to obtain by identification with their mates the joy of motherhood").[116] The effeminates,

---

[113] Wissler: *Man and Culture* (op. cit.).

[114] Theodore Faithful: *Bisexuality* (London, 1927).

[115] Modern scientists believe that certain psychic forms of tuberculosis and constipation are the means by which the introvert compensates himself for the impossibility of satisfying his sexual desires in a feminine manner. Writing on this subject, in his essay referred to above, Theodore Faithful says: "Consumption is a ready means of satisfaction to an introvert who cannot use the libido in artistic or mental creative work, and who either has not a womb to use, or if possessed of one does not wish to use it, or whose desires in that direction are inhibited by attachments to relatives or economic necessity." And, still referring to the means by which an introvert finds compensation for the impossibility of a feminine sexual expression: "Chronic constipation is one of these ways, and is used to satisfy introverted or female desires. . . . In introverted men also

it gives a satisfaction to the psyche unobtainable by the use of their reproductive apparatus. . . . The abnormal laying on of abdominal fat is another means of physical satisfaction to introverted men who are unable to use up the libido in creative work, and in unmarried extroverted women."

[116] Couvade places the man in the position of receiving, as a "patient," attentions that would otherwise be bestowed upon the woman, and in this manner he effects an identification through the special precautions and care with which he is surrounded: "the husband remains lying in the hammock, where he is well covered . . . in which place he is visited by his relatives and friends, and they bring him presents of food and drink, and the woman shows him many endearments. . . ."—Gabriel Soares de Sousa: *Roteiro do Brasil* (op. cit.).— R. R. Schuller explains couvade by "paternal egoism, accompanied by a considerable amount of rivalry with the one who bears the child." "*A*

by their prestige deriving from the practices of sexual magic—an activity that was controlled by them in a number of tribes—would thus have been the initiators of couvade, a cultural complex in which there are so many evidences of that mechanism of compensation of which the invert makes use: repose, precautions, diet, identification of man with woman. For in couvade it was generally the two of them,

---

Couvade," *Boletim do Museu Goeldi*, Vol. VI (1910). This explanation vaguely and distantly approximates the suggestion made here. Sociologically, couvade perhaps represents the first step toward recognizing the biological importance of the father in generation. It is necessary to take into consideration the fact that rarely in the mind of the savage is there an essential connection between sexual intercourse and conception. The notion of paternity or maternity, a notion that is sociological rather than biological in character, by means of which family descent is established among primitive peoples, corresponds in general to a vague and approximate awareness of the interference of one or the other sex in the generative process. Among the various tribes of Brazil the belief was prevalent that the first-born came from the interference of a demon known as "*uauiara*," with—and this is highly significant to a Freudian—the form of a fish, the boto, which is looked upon as the tutelary spirit of the other fishes.— Couto de Magalhães: *O Selvagem* (*The Savage*) (Rio de Janeiro, 1876). —It would seem, however, that the more general notion at the time of the discovery was the one referred to by Anchieta, to the effect that the belly of the woman was a bag in which the man deposited the embryo. A notion more advanced than the other.—Von den Steinen (op. cit.), in carrying further his study of couvade, came upon the belief among the natives of central Brazil that it was the man who left the egg or eggs in the woman's belly and who incubated them during the period of pregnancy. The egg or ovum is identified with the father, to such a degree that the word for *egg* and the word *father* in the Bakairi tongue have the same derivation. The child is looked upon as being no more than a miniature who develops in his mother's belly merely as the seed does in the earth. Hence the belief among savages that evils affecting the father may, through sympathetic magic, affect the newborn child as well. This explains why it is that both father and mother, or the father alone, are commonly safeguarded. On this subject, in addition to the works mentioned by Schuller in the paper referred to above, and others previously cited—especially the one by von den Steinen—see the recent studies of Rafael Karsten, who, in his *Civilization of the South American Indians* (New York, 1920), devotes one of his best chapters to couvade; see also Walter E. Roth's "An Inquiry into the Animism and the Folklore of the Guiana Indians," 13th Annual *Report*, Bureau of American Ethnology (Washington, 1915). In addition, see H. Ring Loth: "On the Significance of the Couvade," *Journal of the Anthropological Institute of England and Ireland*, Vol. XXII (1923). "The sociological problem it involves can hardly be said to have been completely solved," says Karsten in speaking of couvade.

[The fish-demon referred to above, the boto, is a cetacean of the dolphin family (*Stena tucuxi*) which the Amazon Indians believe to be enchanted. (Translator.)]

the man and the woman, and not, as is commonly thought, the man alone who took the precautions and followed the diet.

Goldenweiser [117] from the anthropological, Westermarck from the sociological, and Faithful from the sexological point of view stress the fact that homosexuals or bisexuals not infrequently hold a position of command or influence in primitive societies, a fact that R. Lowe Thompson permits himself to interpret with a boldness that perhaps pure science would not authorize.[118] In his study *Intermediate Types among Primitive Men* Carpenter similarly goes to the extreme of suggesting that many of the most important differentiations of social life may have come from variations of a sexual nature; and he goes on to observe that among primitive peoples culture may have been enriched and activities differentiated as a result of homosexuality or bisexuality. The homosexuals and bisexuals would thereby have fulfilled a valuable creative function by laying the bases of the sciences, arts, and religions. They would have been the prophets, the seers, the healers, the physicians, the priests, and the plastic artists.[119]

This is a theory that perhaps attributes too much importance, in the development of science, religion, and art, to the erratic, the exotic, the romantic, while undervaluing an element that, though unobtrusive, is none the less active and creative: the good sense of the extroverts. Not the "common sense" of every day, but that which is nothing other than equilibrium, intellectual and physical health; the good sense of a Rabelais, a Dr. Johnson, a Cervantes, that of which Marett speaks, identifying it with the experience and the tradition of the majority; a folkloric sense that comes from the people; that of mature nations such as France and of great and ancient churches like

---

[117] "Numerous reports attest the presence in various tribes of effeminate men who avoid male occupations and disregard masculine attire; they dress as women and participate in feminine activities. Not infrequently such men function as magicians and seers." Alexander Goldenweiser, in *Sex and Civilization*, edited by Calverton and Schmalhausen (London, 1929).

[118] As Thompson sees it, effeminate men, "though they may have a poor physique, a less stable mentality and no great love for manly sports or warlike exercises, often have, by reason of their bisexual outlook, a stereoscopic view of life, a quick intelligence, cunning, tenacity, patience, and a power of opportune adaptation, together with a strong desire for self-expression. In fact, they often have an unusually large amount of emulation and emotional energy, which cannot, of course, be expressed in motherhood and may not find an adequate outlook in paternity, since their proper sexual impulses are apt to be weak or confused or restrained by various conventions. They are, indeed, lustful rather than lusty fellows."—R. Lowe Thompson: *The History of the Devil* (London, 1929).

[119] Carpenter, in Goldenweiser, op. cit.

the Roman (which, incidentally, has not hesitated to enrich itself spiritually at the expense of introverts, like St. Theresa, who were all but delirious).

There are, as I have said, numerous evidences of homosexuality [120] among the primitive societies of America; and Westermarck suggests that the warlike rhythm of these societies perhaps favored sexual intercourse between man and man, and even between women. The secret societies of the men, in that sexual and social phase of culture through which many of the Amerindian tribes were passing at the time of the discovery, were possibly an expression, or rather an assertion, of the prestige of the male over the female, of a patronymic as against a matronymic regime, and as such, it may be, were a greater stimulus to pederasty than was the life of a warrior. In connection with the Baitos, a kind of Masonic lodge among the aborigines that was open only to men after a severe initiation, von den Steinen found Bororó youths engaging in sexual intercourse with one another, and this without any sense of guilt, but quite naturally.

As far back as the sixteenth century Gabriel Soares was horrified at seeing the Tupinambás "greatly addicted to the unspeakable sin, which they do not look upon as being a disgrace; he who takes the male's part is held to be a brave, and they regard this kind of bestiality as prowess; and in their villages there are certain of them that keep public shop for those that wish to make use of them as public women." [121]

It is impossible to determine the extent to which homosexuality [122] in America was due to congenital perversion; for the truth is that, among the Amerindians, pederasty was not practiced because the men were deprived of women or because women were scarce. A more potent social influence was the segregation of the youths in houses restricted to males.

At the end of the sixteenth century a number of natives and mamelucos appeared before the visitor of the Holy Office, charged with the crime of sodomy. [123] These were individuals who were only

---

[120] The author's word here, in the original, is *homomixia*. (Translator.)

[121] Gabriel Soares de Sousa, op. cit., p. 313.

[122] *Homomixia*. (Translator.)

[123] Among other cases was that of the Indian, Luiz, a "sodomite who commits the unspeakable sin, playing a passive part and taking the place of the woman, the said one being a

youth around eighteen years of age." —*First Visitation of the Holy Office to the Regions of Brazil—Denunciations of Bahia—1591-1593* (São Paulo, 1925), p. 458.—There was also the Indian Acahuy, against whom Francisco Barbosa lodged a deposition to the effect that he had seen him committing the "unspeakable sin" with one Balthazar de Lomba, "the two of

half-Christianized, and whose Catholicism was still in the crude stage. The Church was in the habit of fulminating against this sin as being one of those from the lower depths—one of the four *clamantia peccata* of medieval theology [124]—but in the sexual morality of these primitive peoples, those savages whom Father Cardim heard confessing themselves with so much candor, it was nothing more than a peccadillo. It seems, meanwhile, that the Portuguese quickly identified the aborigines with the practice of pederasty, a practice that to Christians was so abominable a one.

The term *bugre*, bestowed by the Portuguese upon the Brazilian natives in general and upon a São Paulo tribe in particular, possibly expressed the theological horror felt by Christians who had just emerged from the Middle Ages when brought face to face with the unspeakable sin which for them was associated with a great, indeed with the maximum degree of unbelief and heresy. Just as for the Hebrews the term *gentile* carried the implication of *sodomite*, so for the medieval Christian the term *bugre* was imbued with the same clinging connotation of unclean sin. He who was a heretic was accordingly held to be a sodomite, as if one damnable offense inevitably brought with it the other. "Indeed so closely was sodomy associated with heresy that the same name was applied to both," writes Westermarck. And he adds: "the French *bougre* (from the Latin *Bulgarus*, Bulgarian), as also its English synonym, was originally a name given to a sect of heretics who came from Bulgaria in the eleventh century, and was afterwards applied to other heretics, but at the same time it became the regular expression for a person guilty of unnatural intercourse." [125] And in connection with this subject we find in Léry a passage worthy of note; referring to the Tupís, the chronicler says: "*toutefois, à fin de ne les faire pas assi plus gens de bien qu'ils ne sont, parce que quelquefois en se despitans l'un contre l'autre, ils s'appellent 'Tyvire,' one peut de là coniecturer (car ie n'en afferme rien) que cest abominable pesché se commet entr'eux.*" [126]

---

them being in a hammock, and I heard the hammock creaking and heard them panting as if they were engaged in the unspeakable work, and I heard from the said Negro words of endearment in their tongue."—*First Visitation of the Holy Office to the Regions of Brazil—Denunciations of Pernambuco*—1593-1595 (São Paulo, 1929), p. 399.

[124] St. Thomas Aquinas: *Summa Theologica;* and before him the Apostle Paul, in his First Epistle to the Corinthians (vi, 9, 10): "nor effeminate, nor abusers of themselves with mankind . . . shall . . . inherit the kingdom of God."

[125] Westermarck: *The Origin and Development of the Moral Ideas* (op. cit.).

[126] Léry, op. cit., Vol. II, p. 87.

From the accounts given us by Léry, Gabriel Soares, and Hans Staden, the chronicles of the sixteenth-century Jesuits, and the books of Ives d'Évreux and Claude d'Abbeville, it may be seen that for the Tupí woman married life was one continuous round of toil; she was constantly concerned with her children, with her husband, with the kitchen, and with her small plantations. This is not to mention such domestic duties as the supplying of water and the carrying of burdens. Even when pregnant, the Indian woman was active both within and outside the house, merely ceasing to bear upon her back burdens that were excessively heavy.[127] As a mother she added to her many functions that of becoming a sort of ambulating cradle for her child,[128] which she sometimes nourished at her breast until it was seven years old; she also had to bathe it and to teach the little girls to spin cotton and prepare the meals.

In short, as Léry tells us, she was charged with the management of the entire household: *"toute la charge du mesnage."* [129] The utensils that served for cooking the food, for storing it, for pounding the corn or the fish, for smoking the meat, pressing roots, sifting flour — the earthenware vessels, the wickerwork sieves, the gourd cups, the gourd drinking-vessels, the brooms — all these, many of which were to become a permanent part of the colonial kitchen, were the work of her hands. To this day, amidst the crockery in any Brazilian house in the northern or central part of the country, will be found numerous items of purely indigenous origin or manufacture. No kitchen that prides itself on being truly Brazilian is lacking in a wicker sieve, a mortar, an earthen jar or water-jug. The *cunhãs* not only gave a beautiful form to some of these household utensils, made of clay, of wood, or of animal or fruit shells — the grater being made of oyster shells — but also enlivened them with colored designs: *"mille petites gentillesses,"* as Léry puts it.[130]

Of the dishes prepared by the Indian woman the principal ones were those made from manihot dough or flour. Gabriel Soares saw the natives in the year 1500 scraping the manihot roots until they were gleaming white: "after having washed them, they scrape them with a stone or grater that they have for this purpose; and after [the roots]

---

[127] Ibid.

[128] The cradle of the aborigines in this part of America appears to have been the *tipóia*, or band of cloth that held the child on the mother's back, and the small hammock. On the cradle of the American Indians in general, see O. T. Mason: "Cradles of the American Aborigines," *Report of the United States National Museum* (1886–7).

[129] Léry, op. cit., Vol. II, p. 98.

[130] Ibid., Vol. II, p. 99.

are thoroughly scraped, they press the pulp in a palm-leaf contrivance to which they give the name of *tapitim*, which causes the water to gush forth, leaving the dried pulp behind, out of which they make the flour that they eat, which they cook in an earthen vessel made for this purpose, casting the pulp into the said vessel and heating it over a fire, where an Indian woman stirs it with a half-gourd, as one does when making comfits, until it is quite dry and without any moisture whatsoever, whereupon it remains like couscous, but whiter, and in this manner it is eaten, and very sweet and savory it is." [131]

Manihot flour was adopted by the colonists in place of wheat bread, the rural proprietors preferring it fresh-baked every day. "And," says Gabriel Soares, "I still say that manihot is more wholesome and better for you than good wheat, for the reason that it is more easily digested, and in proof of this I would cite the fact that the governors Thomé de Sousa, D. Duarte, and Mem de Sá did not eat wheat bread in Brazil because they found that it did not agree with them, and many other persons did the same." [132]

Thanks to the native preference, the victory of manihot was complete and it, instead of wheat, became the basis of the colonists' diet (although, contrary to what Gabriel Soares naïvely supposes, it cannot compare with wheat in nutritive value and digestibility). Today manihot is the basic food of Brazilians, and for a good part of our population the technique of its manufacture remains what it was for the aborigines. In the far north, flour made by a process of watering is preferred, and the manner in which it is prepared by the *caboclos* is thus described by H. C. de Sousa Araujo: "After the process of maceration is complete and the manihot has shed its rind, it is then carried away in water-troughs, where it remains for a number of days. When it is quite soft, it is crushed or grated and the dough is placed in long conical *tipitís* [133] made of plaited embira [134] or taquara-cane fiber. These *tipitís* are a yard and a half to two yards or so in length and, after they have been well filled, are suspended from the ridge-pole of the house, being weighted down at the bottom by a large stone. When the manihot water, known as *tucupí*, stops running, they draw off the starchy mass and spread it out in the sun to dry, an operation that ends with drying in the oven. The result is always a coarse flour made up of little hard round lumps that are hard to

---

[131] Gabriel Soares de Sousa, op. cit., p. 164. [132] Ibid., p. 170.
[133] Cf. the "*tapitim*" mentioned by Gabriel Soares de Sousa above. (Translator.)

[134] *Embira* is a term applied to a number of Brazilian plants with fibrous bark of which ropes are made. (Translator.)

masticate." [135] In the northeast the flour commonly manufactured is the dry variety, formerly known as *"de guerra"* (wartime meal); but in this region as in the far north the *tipiti*—that "tubular elastic basket made of palm leaves," as Theodoro Sampaio defines it [136]—continues to characterize the technique of flour-making.

Manihot was put to varied uses by the aborigines in their cooking, and many of the pastries and other dishes formerly prepared from it by the red-skinned hands of the *cunhã* are today the work of white, mulatto, black, and brown hands belonging to the Brazilian woman of widely varying origin and blood-streams. From the Indian woman the latter learned to make a series of delicate confections. Out of fine flour she made for the children the cake known as *carimã*. Out of manihot, also, she made the paste known as *mingau* and the pastries called *mbeiu* or *beijú*. "They were familiar," writes Couto de Magalhães, in speaking of the natives of Brazil, "with processes of fermentation by which they prepared excellent preserves that were very good for weak stomachs; among others, I will mention the '*carimã*' cakes upon which almost all of us were nourished during our infancy." [137]

In connection with the *beijú*, Araujo Lima cites a number of modern Amazonian specialties. In addition to the ordinary *beijú*, known to every Brazilian by that name, or by the name of tapioca [138] —"a cake made of fresh dough, still damp, or of tapioca flour run through a wicker sieve in such a manner as to form lumps that, due to the action of the heat, remain clinging together by reason of the gluten that is in the dough"—in addition to this, there is the *beijú-açú*, [139] "rounded in form, made of the same dough as the *beijú-ticanga*, [140] and baked in the oven"; there is the *beijú-cica*, "made of *macaxeira*, or sweet cassava dough, in very fine lumps"; there is the tapioca cake, "made of moist tapioca, in such a manner that it drops from the sieve in tiny lumps and, when ready, is folded over on itself and buttered"; there is the *beijú-ticanga*, "made of soft manihot dough (*ticanga*) dried in the sun"; there is the *caribé*, which is "the *beijú-açú* put to soak and reduced to a doughy paste, to which more

---

[135] H. C. de Sousa Araujo: "*Costumes Paraenses*" ("Customs of Pará"), *Boletim Sanitário*, ano 2, no. 5 (Rio de Janeiro, 1924).

[136] *O Tupí na Geografia Nacional* (op. cit.).

[137] Couto de Magalhães: *O Selvagem* (op. cit.).

[138] The tapioca of commerce is derived from two species of the genus *Manihot*: the *M. utilissima*, or bitter cassava; and the *M. Aipi*, or sweet cassava. (Translator.)

[139] Lima and Barroso (*Pequeno Dicionário*, etc.) give the spelling *guaçu* for this variety of *beijú*. (Translator.)

[140] Lima and Barroso: *ticuanga*. (Translator.)

water, lukewarm or cold, is added, forming a sort of *mingau*, more or less thin according to taste," a *mingau* that is taken in the morning with lukewarm water and during the day with cold water; and, finally, there is the *curadá*, a large and rather thick *beijú*, made of moist tapioca, with larger lumps than the rolled cake and containing small bits of raw cashew nuts."[141] All this is Indian food that has been adopted by the Brazilian of the far north.

Not only with respect to the *beijú* cake but as regards native food in general, the Amazon region is the Brazilian cultural area that is most saturated with *caboclo* influence. It is as if the tang of the forest had been preserved here; it is wrapped up in the leaf of the palm and the banana tree; it is in the cashew nut, the clay drinking-cup, the powdered *puçanga*[142] made from toasted kurumikáa leaves. The very names are Indian names. All this may seem strange at first, but only at first; for these native delicacies and the names they bear have the familiarity of old acquaintance in the mouth of the Brazilian, a circumstance that does away with any impression of the exotic—it is then that we realize how much that is basically of the forest remains with us, in the tastes of our palate and in the rhythm of our daily speech; it is then that we realize how much we owe to our Tupí and Tapuia[143] ancestors.

The national cuisine—let it be said in passing—would have remained impoverished and its individuality would have been profoundly affected if these delicacies of native origin had not survived; for they give a flavor to the Brazilian diet that neither Lusitanian dishes nor African cookery could supply. But it should be noted that it was in the kitchens of the Big Houses that many of these confections lost their regional and exclusively Indian character to become truly Brazilian.

In the far north they still make out of soft manihot dough a native cake called *macapatá*. "After [the dough] has been pressed in the *tipití*," so Araujo Lima tells us, "and kneaded with turtle fat and bits of raw cashew nuts, it is flattened out in small oblong portions and wrapped in banana leaves, to be baked in the embers." They also make a drink known as *tarubá*, out of *beijús* that, after they have been dipped in water barely enough to moisten them, are laid one by one over curumí (kurumikáa) leaves upon "a bed of banana leaves spread

---

[141] Araujo Lima, op. cit.

[142] The *puçanga* was a remedy prepared by the Indian *pajés*, or medicine-men; it comes to be a term for household remedy. (Translator.)

[143] *Tapuia* (*Tapuya*) is employed as a generic term for Brazilian Indian, commonly referring to a linguistic stock. Cf. *caboclo*. (Translator.)

out in a special rack [144] constructed in the flour-house or in the kitchen," after which they are powdered with *puçanga*, and curumí leaves are spread over them. All the *beijús* are thus covered with the leaves of the curumí or the banana tree, and they let the cakes lie there for three days—when a kind of syrup begins to run. They thereupon dissolve the entire doughy mass in water, run it through the wicker sieve, and let it settle. The result is a delicious beverage that, taken to excess, is inebriating. This is the sweet-perfumed drink called *tarubá*.

The frequent use of the leaf of the São Tomé banana tree in the northeast for wrapping food-preparations made from the coconut, manihot, rice, and corn may possibly be the result of African intrusion, a contagious effect of the Negro complex for the banana plant. It is true that the aborigines did not lack a variety of banana (the caaguaçú, or pacova [145] sororoca), but it is doubtful if the complex we have just mentioned attained with them the degree of development that it did with the Africans, who made an extensive use of the banana and its leaves.

In coconut tapioca, known as "dipped" (*molhada*)—spread out upon an African banana leaf, powdered with cinnamon, and seasoned with salt—is to be perceived the truly Brazilian amalgam of culinary traditions: native manihot, the Asiatic coconut, European salt, all fraternizing in a single and delicious confection upon the same African bed of banana leaves. It is my opinion that the northeast—that is to say, the zone of Pernambucan influence—and, farther to the north, Maranhão are the two points of most intense cultural fraternization, a fraternization that is materialized in the regional cuisine and that finds subtle expression in other spheres where its discovery or differentiation through studies in social psychology, ethnography, folklore, and sociology is rendered more difficult.

Maçoca, of which various cakes in addition to caribé are made, is not restricted to the Amazon region, but may be said to be in general use in northern and central Brazil, although not to so great an extent as *mingau*, Indian-corn *canjica*,[146] and *moqueca*.[147] These last were incorporated into the national diet of Brazilians after what might be termed original or crude products such as the yam, maize, the potato,

---

[144] The *giráo* or *jirau*. (Translator.)

[145] *Pacova* (*pacoba*) is the term for banana in northern Brazil; in the south it is applied to a variety of large banana. The caaguaçú is a plant of the *Eriocaulaceæ* family (*Ericau-* *lon sellowianum Kth.*). (Translator.)

[146] See note 148 below. (Translator.)

[147] See the description below and note 166. (Translator.)

cacao, the peanut, and manihot. *Maçoca* is manihot dough run through the *tipití;* after it has been well pulverized in the pestle and dried in the sun, it is placed in a hamper and is suspended at a certain height above the fire in order to keep it free of moisture.

Out of maize, in addition to flour (*abatiuí*), now used in the making of various cakes, the *cunhãs* prepared: *acanijic,* which today, under the name of *canjica,*[148] has become one of the great national dishes of Brazil; *pamuna,* now known as *pamonha*[149]—a cake that, after being prepared, is wrapped in a corn leaf; popcorn, a term that, according to Theodoro Sampaio, means "cracked epidermis"; and, finally, a fermented drink, the *abati-i.*

Out of fish or meat, pounded and mixed with flour, they made: *paçoka* (*paçoca*),[150] a dish that is still to be found in the north; and *piracuí,*[151] or "fish gravel" (*areia do peixe*), the fish being dressed by hand and then, after the scales have been removed, toasted in the oven, pounded, and breaded. But the most characteristic way of preparing fish, flesh, or fowl among the *cunhãs* was in the form of *mokaen,* which has come down to us under the name of *moquem*[152]—that is to say, with the fish or meat being roasted over the coals, "or upon a wooden gridiron," as Theodoro Sampaio informs us.[153]

As in the case of manihot, so with fish: it is the Amazonian cultural region of Brazil that has come the nearest to preserving the traditions of the aborigines. In the Amazon cuisine the pirarucú[154] occupies a most important place, second only to that of the turtle, which con-

---

[148] "Paste made of grated green corn to which is added sugar, coconut milk, and cinnamon."—Lima and Barroso: *Pequeno Dicionário,* etc. "The pulp of green corn cooked with sugar, salt, and cinnamon to make a dish invariably prepared at Christmas time and for St. João's Day."—*Glossary of Brazilian-Amazonian Terms, Compiled from the Strategic Index of the Americas* (Coordinator of Inter-American Affairs, 1943). (Translator.)

[149] "A kind of cake made of green corn, coconut milk, butter, cinnamon, anise, and sugar, cooked in tubes made of corn leaves fastened at the extremities."—Lima and Barroso: *Pequeno Dicionário,* etc. (Translator.)

[150] "Cashew-nut kernels roasted and pounded in the pestle with flour-water and sugar, the whole being reduced to small grains."—Lima and Barroso, op. cit.

[151] "A flour made from dried fish—especially, the pirarucú and tambaquí—which have been ground with a mortar and pestle; it keeps for a long time and hence is a favorite food for fishermen, hunters, and travellers."—*Glossary of Brazilian-Amazonian Terms, Strategic Index of the Americas.* (Translator.)

[152] "Gridiron made of twigs, for roasting or drying meat or fish."—Lima and Barroso, op. cit.

[153] Theodoro Sampaio, op. cit.

[154] "*Pirarucú:* (Spanish *paiche*)—a very large Amazonian fish (*Arapaima gigas*) of the family Osteoglossidæ." —*Glossary of Brazilian-Amazonian Terms* (op. cit.). (Translator.)

stitutes a culinary complex in itself. Among the rural populations of the far north, the pirarucú at times takes the place of codfish or jerked beef: "it is put up in the form of preserves, being sometimes merely salted down in brine, when it is to be used within the next few days, or, when it is desired to keep it longer for export purposes, it is salted and spread out on blankets in the sun to dry." Other fish much in use in the Amazon region are the tucunaré [155] and the tambaquí.[156] The latter is employed in the characteristically native mode of preserving known as *mixiria*.[157] *Mixiria*, however, is not limited to fish alone, but may also be applied to meat; it consists in roasting the fish or meat in its own fat over a slow fire, after which it is sliced. Thus prepared, the meat, game, or fish, with its fat, is sealed in jars. Formerly, among the aborigines, these were earthenware jars. Today, Araujo Lima tells us, the containers employed are cylindrical tins. In this process of preserving, use is made of the peixe-boi,[158] the turtle, the tambaquí, the tapir, etc.[159]

There is, by the way, a native mode of preparing fish that has become general in Brazil: *pokeka*, "which by corruption becomes *moqueca*," [160] according to Theodoro Sampaio in his Brazilian geographical vocabulary—"and it means a bundle," he adds, the fish being bundled up in leaves. *Moqueca* is fish roasted on the coals and wholly wrapped up in a banana leaf, like a tiny infant in its swaddling-clothes. The *moqueca* that is most appreciated is made of young fish, still transparent and very small: a baby fish. In Bahia and in Pernambuco the *pokeka* was deliciously Africanized, or, better, Brazilianized, in the form of the *moqueca* of the Big House kitchens.

---

[155] "Fish of the *Cyclidæ* family (*Cichla oscellaris*)."—Lima and Barroso, op. cit. (Translator.)

[156] "Various species of fish of the *Caracinidæ* family."—Lima and Barroso, op. cit.—"A fish (*Myletes bidens*) which is a common article of food in Amazonia, found in lakes, *igarapés*, and *igapós*."—*Glossary of Brazilian-Amazonian Terms* (op. cit.). (Translator.)

[157] Lima and Barroso (op. cit.) give the spelling: *mixira*. They define the term as "preserves made from the peixe-boi, the tambaquí, or the young turtle, in the oil of the animal from which they are made." The same word occurs in Spanish. (Translator.)

[158] "Mammifer of the order *Sireni-*

dæ of the *Trichechidæ* family (*Trichechus inunguis*)."—Lima and Barroso, op. cit.—"Manatee . . . a large aquatic mammal."—*Glossary of Brazilian-Amazonian Terms* (op. cit.). (Translator.)

[159] Araujo Lima, loc. cit.—The author mentions another native mode of preparing fish among the rural populations of the Amazon region: *mujica* —"any kind of fish cooked or smoked, sliced into small bits after the scales have been removed, and augmented with its own gravy made with fermented-manihot flour and tapioca dust."

[160] "Ragout of fish or shellfish with oil and pepper."—Lima and Barroso, op. cit. (Translator.)

The turtle, as has been said, constitutes a culinary complex in itself, one of a number that the native has handed down to the Brazilian for his diet. Out of the turtle, in the far north of Brazil, they make a variety of confections, each of which is highly praised by gourmets as being more savory than any other. One of these is *arabú*, made with flour from the yolk of turtle eggs or those of the tracajá [161] –no other ingredients. [162] Yet finer and more delicate is *abunã* –turtle or tracajá eggs "smoked before gestation has been completed," says Araujo Lima, "the small turtle or tortoise having a certain portion of the yolk adhering to its bosom." *Abunã* is eaten with salt and flour. Then there is *mujanguê*, [163] a *mingau* or manihot paste made from the egg-yolks of the turtle or tracajá with fine manihot flour, diluted with water. Some persons Europeanize this dish by adding salt or sugar. And, lastly, there is *paxicá*, a *picado* or ragout made of turtle's liver, seasoned with salt, lemon, and Indian pepper.

The abuse that the aborigines made of pepper is well known, and it is one that is still continued in the Brazilian kitchen of today. [164] In the extreme north there exists *juquitaia*, a hybrid condiment composed of pepper and salt. Boughs of the pepper tree are hung up in the kitchen, and after the pepper has been dried it is run through the oven and is then placed in the mortar to be pounded and mixed with salt. The pepper complex was heightened in Brazil through the influence of African cookery, which was still better adapted than that of the aborigines to excitations of the palate. It is the Afro-Bahian cuisine that is most noted for this abuse. But the native by no means disdained the use of pepper, any more than he disdained the *pijericú*, [165] the

---

[161] "*Tracajá*: (Spanish *terecai*)—a fresh-water tortoise of the genus *Emys*, whose flesh and eggs are considered delicacies."—*Glossary of Brazilian-Amazonian Terms* (op. cit.). (Translator.)

[162] Lima and Barroso (op. cit.) state that *arabú* is "made with turtle eggs, flour, and sugar." (Translator.)

[163] Also written *mujangüê*.—"Dish made from the raw eggs of the turtle, tortoise (*tracajá*), or sea-gull, with sugar and fermented-manihot flour." —Lima and Barroso, op. cit.—"Dish of tortoise eggs, *farinha d'agua*, and sugar."—*Glossary of Brazilian-Amazonian Terms* (op. cit.). (Translator.)

[164] "*L'emploi du piment pour rele-* ver *l'insipidité des aliments*," observes Sigaud (op. cit.), "*s'est introduit depuis lors dans les habitudes au point de constituer aujourd'hui l'indispensable assaisonnement de tous les banquets. . . .*" In Pernambuco, the Barão de Nazareth tells us, one did not go to a banquet without taking condiments along with him, in his coat pocket, from fear that the host, out of European elegance, would not offer them at table.

[165] Lima and Barroso (op. cit.) give the spelling *pijerecu*. "Plant of the *Anonaceæ* family (*Xylopia fructescens*), also known as *coajerucu*."—Ibid. (Translator.)

pixurim,[166] the lemon, and at times, to take the place of salt, the use of ashes. Sigaud states that one of the frequent causes of attacks of dysentery among the Brazilian Indians—attacks of which we learn in the accounts left us by the Jesuits—was the immoderate use of ginger, pepper, and lemon: *"Les Indiens doivent à l'usage immoderé du gingembre, du piment et du limon, de fréquents attaques de dysentérie."*

Peckholt stresses the fact that maize was the only cereal that the Europeans found in Brazil; and he proceeds to mention the other vegetable foods of which the aborigines made use and of which the newcomers availed themselves: manihot; the sweet potato; the yam; the pinhão; [167] cacao; the peanut. Green vegetables were scarce, and the natives attached no importance to those that they possessed. "The green vegetables procured by the Indians were few in number; however, the women did gather for eating purposes certain forest plants, such as various kinds of carurús,[168] the serralha,[169] and especially the palmetto, which, raw as well as cooked, was a favorite edible."[170]

With regard to fruit, the land discovered by Pedro Alvares was more fertile; but so far as those varieties passed on by the natives to Europeans are concerned, there is to be noted only the cultivated mamoeiro, or papaw tree,[171] and the guava. The Indians also transmitted to the Europeans the cashew complex[172]—along with a series of medicinal and culinary applications, especially noteworthy being the use of cashew nuts in the making of a very good wine which today is characteristically Brazilian.

A list of the plants and medicinal herbs with which the Indians

---

[166] "Medicinal plant of the *Lauraceæ* family (*Acrodiclidium puchury-major*), also called *pexorim* and *puxuri.*"—Lima and Barroso, op. cit. (Translator.)

[167] A plant of the *Euphorbiaceæ* family (*Jatropha curcas* L.).—Lima and Barroso, op. cit. (Translator.)

[168] Name given to various plants of the *Amarantaceæ* family.—Lima and Barroso, op. cit.—The *Glossary of Brazilian-Amazonian Terms* (op. cit.) identifies it as the *Amarantus oleracea.* (Translator.)

[169] Plant of the *Compostæ* family (*Sonchus lævis*).—Lima and Barroso, op. cit. (Translator.)

[170] Peckholt, op. cit.

[171] This is the papaya tree (*Carica papaya Lin.*). (Translator.)

[172] The term *complex* is employed throughout this essay in its anthropological or sociological sense, signifying that series of traits or processes which constitutes a sort of cultural constellation. Thus we have the manihot complex, the couvade complex, the milk complex, the exogamic complex, the tobacco complex, etc. As Wissler observes, in *Man and Culture*, this anthropologic usage is not to be confused with the psychopathologic meaning of the word.

were acquainted and of which they made use would be a long one; and Brazilian culture might have taken more advantage of them than it did, had the relations between the first missionaries and the native *pajés* and healers been better than they were. Even so, the Jesuits *"dès le principe de leur établissement s'appliquèrent à recueiller, à étudier les productions locales, et à faire leur profit des connaissances et des observations indigènes,"* writes Sigaud. But the French scientist, to whom Brazilian medicine owes so much, goes on to say: *"Du mélange des pratiques indigènes et des formules copiées des livres de médicine européens, naquit une thérapeutique informe, grossière, extravagante qui se transmit par tradition dans les classes de cultivateurs de sucre et de coton et gardiens de troupeux dans les montagnes ou sertões; et ce mélange primitif, altéré par les arcanes des nègres venus de Guinée et d'Angola, fut dès lors le partage exclusif des hommes qui s'intitulèrent médicins du peuple ou guérisseurs."* [173]

A plantation-owner of the sort mentioned by Sigaud, given to curing the sick by a gross and hybrid therapeutic such as this, but one that at times produced better results than the academic methods of the Europeans, was Gabriel Soares. His *Log Book* is full of recipes that he had learned from the Indians. Among these were the following:

carimã cake soaked in water for children who have worms or the person suffering from poison ("in either case this is a remedy that has been thoroughly tried by the Indians as well as by the Portuguese," he adds);

cooked corn for those suffering from buboes;

cashew juice taken in the morning, before breakfast, for the "conservation of the stomach," and for oral hygiene as well (and, in speaking of cashew nuts, "they give a good breath to the one who eats them in the morning," says Gabriel Soares);

the bud of the embaiba tree [174] for healing wounds and old sores;

gum-mastic plasters for "closing broken flesh";

petume (tobacco) [175] for disease of the sexual organ, and, the smoke of this plant, being sucked in through a straw tube lighted at the tip— indigenous grandfather of the pipe—is excellent for "every man who takes wine."

---

[173] For an excellent creative portrait of this kind of empiric healer in nineteenth-century Brazil, see the novel *Inocência*, by Alfredo d'Escragnolle Taunay, in Henriqueta Chamberlain's translation (New York: The Macmillan Company, 1945). (Translator.)

[174] The *embaiba*, or *umbaúba*, is a tree of the *Moraceæ* family (*Cecropia palmata*). It has a number of other names as well.—Lima and Barroso, op. cit. (Translator.)

[175] *Petum* or *petume* is the Tupí name for tobacco; the forms *petema* and *petima* also occur.—Lima and Barroso, op. cit. (Translator.)

Being possessed like the other plantation-owning colonists of such precious lore, Gabriel Soares did not see the necessity of surgeons from Bahia, "for the reason that every man is a surgeon in his own house." He devotes an entire page of his *Log Book* to the peanut, or midubi, a plant that was not gathered at random by the Indian women in the jungle, but one that was a product of their rudimentary system of agriculture: "the male has nothing to do with this plant and the benefit derived from it; it is the women alone who are accustomed to plant it. . . ." [176]

There was other vegetable lore, useful in domestic economy and the activities of the home, that was transmitted by the indigenous culture to the civilization of the European colonizer, who preserved and developed it, adapting it to his own needs. In connection with this lore, we may mention:

a knowledge of the various fibrous plants of use in weaving and plaiting: cotton, tucum,[177] the wild caraguatá;[178]

the use of peipeçaba[179] for making brooms;

the growing of gourds, to be used as vessels for carrying water and preserving flour, as wash-bowls, and, it would seem, as urinals also;

the method of curing the jerimum[180] by smoking it for an entire year;

a knowledge of the various woods and other vegetable substances of use for building-purposes: liana, timbo,[181] sapé, and pindoba straw,[182] long employed in the roofing of houses;

a knowledge of the animals—birds, fish, shellfish, etc.—that were good to eat and that at the same time lent their shards, feathers, hides, and wool to various uses in the intimate and daily life of the colonial family: for making cups, for constructing shelters, for stuffing bolsters, pillows, mattresses, for the manufacture of hammocks, etc.;

the use of the tabuá reed,[183] an excellent material for mats;

a knowledge of the various-colored dyes now employed in the decoration of house walls, the dyeing of cloth, the painting of women's faces, and the manufacture of inks for writing-purposes: the white of tabatinga

---

[176] Soares, op. cit., p. 151.

[177] "Species of palm (*Bactris setona* Mart.) from whose leaves the best fiber is extracted."—Lima and Barroso, op. cit. (Translator.)

[178] Name given to various plants of the *Bromeliaceæ* family.—Lima and Barroso, op. cit. (Translator.)

[179] The *peipecaba* (*peipetaba*) is a plant generally known in Brazil by the name of "vassourinha," or "little broom" (the *Scoparis dulcis*). (Translator.)

[180] Plant of the *Concurbitaceæ* or gourd family. (Translator.)

[181] A variety of liana. (Translator.)

[182] The *pindoba* is a plant of the *Palmaceæ* family (*Attalea compta* Mart.).—Lima and Barroso, op. cit. (Translator.)

[183] Plant of the *Typhaceæ* family (*Typha domingensis* Pers.), also called *Partazana*, of which mats are made. Lima and Barroso, op. cit. (Translator.)

clay,[184] the carnation hue of the araribá,[185] Brazil-wood, and the urucú, the black of the genipap, the yellow of the tatajuba; [186]
a knowledge of various gums and resins, useful for gluing papers, sealing envelopes in the manner of sealing-wax, etc.

If, in connection with the utilization or adaptation of all this material, European intelligence or technique in the great majority of cases fulfilled something like a creative function, or at least one of transmutation, there were other cases in which a direct transmission of values or acquired knowledge occurred, from one culture to the other—from that of the native to that of the foreign-comer.

A number of these processes and much of this knowledge, it is worth stressing the point once more, were received by the European colonizer from the hands of the native woman—always a more productive element than the man in primitive cultures. She it was who passed on to the Brazilian family valuable methods of infantile and domestic hygiene that deserve to be noted; but first, it is necessary to trace in general outline not only the pedagogical aspect, but the life of the child as a whole among the aborigines. I shall describe, a little farther on, the part played by the child—if not a dramatic role, at any rate a decisive one—as the point of contact between the two cultures, the native and the European, whether as the civilizing vehicle of the Catholic missionary to the heathen or as the conduit through which there flowed a precious portion of the aboriginal culture, from the Indian villages to the missions and from there to the general life of the colonizing race—to the patriarchal Big Houses themselves.

The young Indian was far from being the free child of nature imagined by Jean Jacques Rousseau—created without fear of superstitions. Just as among the civilized, so among the savages we shall encounter numerous abuses with regard to childhood, some of them of a prophylactic intent, corresponding to a fear, on the part of the parents, of malign spirits or influences, while others were pedagogical in character, their aim being to orient the child along the path of traditional tribal deportment or to subject him indirectly to the authority of adults.

Frank Clarence Spencer, to whom we owe one of the most interest-

---

[184] A varicolored clay used in pottery-making. (Translator.)
[185] Tree of the *Leguminosæ* family (*Centrolobium tomentosum Benth.*). —Lima and Barroso, op. cit. (Translator.)

[186] The *tatajuba* (*tatajiba*) is a plant of the *Moraceæ* family (*Bagassa guianensis Aubl.*), also known as *jataíba*. —Lima and Barroso, op. cit. (Translator.)

ing studies of Amerindian pedagogy, "The Education of the Pueblo Child," lays emphasis on the fact that primitive life, not only in America but in general, is not the calm, idyllic existence that eighteenth-century Europeans supposed it to be, any more than it is "the dogged, sullen subjection described by later writers." But there is a middle term: "They are in constant subjection to their superstitious fears, and yet they are generally joyful and happy." [187]

The same investigator encountered among the Pueblos a dance designed especially to frighten children and inspire in them sentiments of obedience and respect toward their elders. The characters of the dance were something like hobgoblins, or the terrifying figures of another world who had come down to this one to devour or carry off bad children. Stevenson informs us of a similar dance among the Zuñi Indians, a macabre one, ending in the actual death of a child chosen from among the worst behaved of the tribe; but these dances were only staged at intervals, with long years between.[188] The moral and pedagogical purpose was to influence the child's conduct through fear and the example of a horrible punishment.

The work, today a classic one, of Alexander Francis Chamberlain, on childhood in primitive cultures and in the folklore of historic cultures [189] indicates that the hobgoblin was a generalized complex among those cultures, and almost always, so it would seem, with a moralistic or pedagogical end in view. Among the ancient Hebrews there was Lilith, a horrible hairy monster that roamed at night in search of children. Among the Greeks it was certain ugly old hags, the Strigalai, who carried away children. Among the Romans, Caprimulgus—possibly the remote ancestor of our cabra-cabriola [190]— would sally forth at night to suck the milk of the nanny-goat and eat the young child, while by day, in the forest, the evil spirit of the wood, Silvanus, held sway. Among the Russians it is a horrible goblin, terrifying as is everything that is Russian, that at midnight comes to snatch away children in their sleep. With the Germans it is Popanz; with the Scotch and the English the Boo Man, the Bogey Man. Champlain and the first chroniclers of Canada speak of a horrible monster, the terror of children among the natives. The Mayas believe

---

[187] Frank Clarence Spencer: "Education of the Pueblo Child," *Columbia University Contributions to Philosophy, Psychology and Education*, Vol. VII, No. 1 (New York, 1899).

[188] T. E. Stevenson: "The Religious Life of the Zuñi Child," *Bureau of Ethnology Report*, Vol. V (Washington).

[189] Alexander Francis Chamberlain: *The Child and Childhood in Folk-Thought* (New York, 1896).

[190] Literally, the "leaping nanny-goat," a mythical "*bicho.*" (Translator.)

in giants who come by night to kidnap children—the balams, the culcalkin. And among the Gaulala Indians of California, Powers found devil dances which he compares with the Haberfeldtreiber of Bavaria [191]—an institution for frightening women and children and keeping them in order. These were dances in which there appeared a horrendous figure, "an ugly apparition." On its head was a bear's skin, on its back a cloak of feathers, while its bosom was striped like a zebra. [192]

There were dances similar to the "devil dance"—or Juruparí's [193] dance—among the aborigines of Brazil, and with the same object in view, that of frightening the women and children and keeping them in line. Among the Indians in this part of America dance masks had an important function. Koch-Grünberg observes that they were guarded as something sacred and that their mysterious power was supposed to be transmitted to the dancer. These were masks imitating demoniac animals, into which the savage imagined that the dead had been transformed, and their magic efficacy was augmented by the fact that many of the materials in their composition were of human or animal origin: human hair, animal skin, feathers, etc. The dancer, for his part, must imitate the movements and voices of the demoniac animal, as in those dances described by the first chroniclers. And like the masks, the sacred instruments were similarly looked upon as being filled with a mysterious power.

The Jesuits preserved the dances of the native children and, in doing so, made of the devil a comic figure, clearly with the object of depriving the Juruparí complex of its prestige, through ridicule. Cardim [194] alludes to one of these dances. With the disparagement of Juruparí and of the sacred masks and cymbals, there was destroyed among the Indians one of their most powerful means of social control. This, up to a certain point, represented a victory on the part of Christianity. But there remained, meanwhile, in the descendants of the aborigines a residuum of all this animism and totemism. Under Catholic forms, superficially adopted, these totemistic elements in Brazilian culture have been prolonged to this day. There are survivals easy to identify, once the varnish of European dissimulation or simulation has been scraped away. Many of them are to be found in the

---

[191] "*Haberfeldtreiben*: kind of popular lynch justice practiced at night by Bavarian peasants. *Haberfeldtreiber*: one taking part in this popular justice."—Karl Breul: *A New German and English Dictionary* (New York and London: Funk & Wagnalls Company [*Cassell's New German-English Dictionary*]). (Translator.)

[192] Powers, in Chamberlain, op. cit.

[193] Juruparí was the demon of the Tupís. (Translator.)

[194] The sixteenth-century missionary and chronicler. (Translator.)

play and the games of children in which there is an imitation of animals, either real ones or vague, imaginary, demoniac creations of the childish fancy. They are to be found also in the tales of serpents, which have a special fascination for the Brazilian young. As a sort of social memorial, inherited as it were, the Brazilian, above all in his childhood, when he is more instinctive and less intellectualized by European education, feels strangely close to the living forest, filled with animals and monsters known to him by their indigenous names [195] and, in good part, through the experiences and superstitions of the Indians.[196] It is a quasi-instinctive interest that the Brazilian child of today has for the fear-inspiring *"bichos."* [197] It is similar to the feeling that the European child has for stories of the wolf and the bear, but much more lively and strong, much more powerful and overwhelming in its mixture of fear and fascination, even though more vague in essence. The Brazilian child is not afraid of any particular *bicho,* but of the *bicho* in general, a *bicho* that he cannot very well describe, but which represents a kind of synthesis of the Brazilian's ignorance of the fauna as well as the flora of his country. A mythical *bicho,* horrible, indefinable; possibly the carrapatú.[198] To this day, little children in northern Brazil are lulled by the following cradle-song:

> *Sleep, sleep, my little one.*
> *There in the jungle is a bicho*
> *Called the carrapatú.*[199]

---

[195] For a vivid picture of all this by a contemporary Brazilian novelist, see the *Terras do sem fim* of Jorge Amado, translated by Samuel Putnam and published in English under the title of *The Violent Land* (New York: Alfred A. Knopf; 1945). See Chapter ii, "The Forest." (Translator.)

[196] In Brazil of the early days, as among the savages, one was exposed to the stings and bites of venomous or harmful insects and other animals: serpents, the big hairy spider, scorpions, centipedes, mosquitoes, gadflies, chicken-lice, hornets, fleas, jaguars, the piranha fish, beetles, etc. Forest, beach, and the water of the rivers, all were inhabited by worms and insects, reptiles and fish that were ravenous for human blood. In this connection Sigaud (op. cit.), referring particularly to the Indians, writes: *"Les piqûres, les morsures des animaux ou insectes venimeux les expose au tétanos. . . ."*

[197] The term *bicho* is an extremely vague one. As the traveler cited by Roquette Pinto, a little later on, remarks: "in Brazil, every animal is, simply, a *bicho.*" The word commonly refers to a worm or insect, but takes in other wild animals, and imaginary ones, as well. (Translator.)

[198] The *"bichos"* listed here are mythical in character. On the *hupupiara*, see below and note 257. (Translator.)

[199] *Durma, durma, meu filhinho.*
Lá no mato tem um bicho
Chamado carrapatú.

It may possibly be the *hupupiara;* or the *macobeba,* a name and conception with which a friend of mine recently became acquainted through a child of six, in Barreiros, in the state of Pernambuco. Practically every Brazilian child who is a little more inventive or imaginative than other children creates his own *macobeba,* based upon that fear, a vague but enormous one, not, as I have said, of any *bicho* in particular—not of the serpent, the jaguar, the water-hog[200]—but simply of the *bicho*: of the *bicho* known as *tutú,*[201] of the *carrapatú,* of the *zumbí*[202]—in the last analysis, of Juruparí. A fear that makes us aware of how close we still are to the living and virgin forest, and to what an extent an aboriginal animism still survives in us, diminishing but not as yet destroyed.

The Brazilian *bicho* complex is deserving of a separate study; it is one of the most interesting that there are for the one who is concerned with problems having to do with the relations and contact between unequal cultures. The vague character of our fear of the *bicho* shows us that we are still in large part a people incompletely integrated in the tropical or American habitat; but the fascination that we feel for anything in the nature of animal lore, even though the animals are but vaguely known to us, and the large number of superstitions that are bound up with animals,[203] point to a process,

---

[200] *Capivara:* Species of rodent (*Hydrochoerus capybara*).—Lima and Barroso, op. cit. (Translator.)

[201] Goblin with which children are frightened. (Translator.)

[202] "Ghostly being which, according to popular Afro-Brazilian belief, wanders about in the late hours of the night."—Lima and Barroso, op. cit. (Translator.)

[203] Many of these were inherited from the aborigines. The author of the *Dialogues on the Grandeurs of Brasil* (op. cit.), p. 275, tells us of the Indians that, however stout-hearted they might be, if upon setting out on some undertaking "they were to hear the song of a bird [the peitica], of which mention has been made, swayed by this augury they would abandon the journey and turn back." The superstition attached to the peitica is one that remains with the Brazilian of the north: "In the states of the north they still look upon it as

an ill omen and cannot abide its presence in the neighborhood of their dwellings." So writes Rodolfo Garcia, in commenting on the sixth dialogue of the sixteenth-century chronicler. And in some of the obviously totemistic beliefs and superstitions mentioned by Father João Daniel it is easy to recognize the origin of many of those that today are current in the north, when they are not prevalent throughout the whole of Brazil, among the common people: "From the time they are small they believe in certain omens connected with birds, beasts of the jungle, and many other such things; and for this reason there are birds that they do not kill or even harm. And when they encounter certain beasts at such and such a time or on such and such an occasion, they learn that this or that misfortune is coming to them, or that they are going to die; and they cling so tenaciously to these dogmas, in which the

even though a slow one, of complete integration with our environment and at the same time indicate the survival of totemistic and animistic tendencies among us. Ruediger Bilden, a German, upon his visit to Brazil, was astonished at our ignorance of the precise, exact names for designating plants and animals; and another traveler, cited by Professor Roquette Pinto, noted that in Brazil every animal is, simply, a *bicho*.[204] Roquette Pinto's comment is: "Even in the rural districts, every June bug is a beetle and nothing more."[205] . . . With

---

elders believe, that even when they see the contrary happening, there is no getting it out of their heads. One of these means of divination is the tapir, of which I have spoken above; and the same is true of the hedgehog, which they call the *gandú-acú*, and which is the harbinger of death when they behold it in this or that manner; and so with many other animals." —*Thesouro Descoberto no Maximo Rio Amazonas* (*Treasure Discovered in the Great Amazon River*), beginning of Part II, which treats of the Indians of the Amazon region, of their faith, life, customs, etc., copied from a manuscript in the Public Library of Rio de Janeiro: *Revista do Instituto Histórico e Geográphico Brasileiro*, Vol. II, No. 7 (Rio de Janeiro, 1858).—Montoya ("Guaraní Manuscript of the National Library of Rio de Janeiro on the Primitive Catechism of the Indians of the Missions," *Anais da Biblioteca Nacional* [*Annals of the National Library*], Vol. VI) informs us that among the Indians observed by him, when a stag or a toad would put in an appearance, this was looked upon as a sign that one of those present would die soon. From the list of superstitions prepared by Professor Ulysses Pernambucano de Mello and his colleagues of Recife, it may be seen that a large number of popular superstitions in the north, as with the Indians, have to do with animals and vegetables that are ill-omened or that bring happiness. When the mangangá beetle enters the house, it is a very bad omen,

and the same is true of the black butterfly or the toad; but the spider, on the other hand, is "hope," come to announce happiness. On this subject, see the interesting essays of João Alfredo de Freitas: "*Algumas Palavras Sobre O Fetichismo Religioso e Político Entre Nos*" ("A Few Words on the Religious and Political Fetishism among Us") (Pernambuco, 1883); and "*Lendas e Superstições do Norte do Brasil*" ("Legends and Superstitions of Northern Brazil") (Recife, 1884). See also the *Folk-lore Brésilien* of the Baron de Sant' Anna Nery (Paris, 1889). The work of Basilio de Magalhães, *O Folclore no Brasil* (op. cit.), has an excellent bibliography, listing the most important works that have appeared on the Brazilian's beliefs and superstitions.

[The bird known as the *peitica*, mentioned in the author's note above, is the *Tapera nævia nævia*, and is described by Lima and Barroso (op. cit.) as having a "monotonous and annoying song."—The term *mangangá* in northeastern Brazil is applied to a species of large wood-gnawing beetles.—Lima and Barroso, ibid. (Translator.)]

[204] Mansfield had observed, in 1852: "I find the people here (at least the English people to whom I have spoken) know very little about the natural productions."—Charles B. Mansfield: *Paraguay, Brazil and the Plate* (Cambridge, 1856).

[205] Freely translated: "*todo besouro é um cascudo e nada mais.*"

plants, it is a little better; our people are able to distinguish and christen various natural groups: there is the gravatá; [206] there is the angico; [207] there is the coqueiro.[208] As a result of cultural antagonisms, the names of animals and plants have been preserved in the native tongue, to be handed down to the largely illiterate descendants of the backland Indians in place of being transmitted to the accentuatedly European or African culture of the seaboard and the agricultural zone. However abundant the means of communication between the two subcultures may have been, it was from the more instinctive, less intellectualized element, which in its illiteracy preserved a greater knowledge of the indigenous flora and fauna, that the other element, more European in its culture, was to receive an extremely rich contingent or layer of native values, which still are without a vital, creative function in the social system of Brazil.

Let us now turn to the childhood of the savage, stressing the point that from the cradle—that is to say, from the hammock or *tipóia*—it was surrounded by superstitions and fears having to do with monstrous animals. The *tipóia*—the infant carried on its mother's back, held there by a band of cloth—is a trait that has been lost among our Brazilian customs, a fact that is only to be explained by the extradomestic activity of the Indian woman. Along with the hammock complex, the custom of the hammock-cradle won out and is only now beginning to disappear from the traditions of the north. Many an illustrious personage from the northeast, today a made man, must have been reared in a hammock, rocked by his Negro nurse.[209] Many

[206] The same as *caraguatá*, mentioned above: name applied to a number of plants of the *Bromeliaceæ* family.—Lima and Barroso, op. cit. (Translator.)

[207] Name common to various trees of the *Leguminosæ* family, *Mimosaceæ* division, genus *Piptadenia.*—Lima and Barroso, op. cit. (Translator.)

[208] Commonly, the coco tree. — "Vulgar name given to all the palms that produce edible fruit or are in wide use industrially."—Lima and Barroso, op. cit. (Translator.)

[209] The hammock figures in the social history of Brazil as a bed, as a means of conveyance or travel, and as a means of transport for the sick and the dead. There exists a convention in accordance with which the white hammock is used for carrying cadavers and a red one for the wounded or injured. "The transport of corpses in the rural regions, throughout the whole of Brazil, was effected in the past, and still is today, by means of hammocks. These hammocks, slung over the sturdy shoulders of *sertanejos* and backwoodsmen, eat up the miles until the corpse is deposited in the parish cemetery." —Francisco Luiz da Gama Rosa: *"Costumes do Povo nos Nascimentos, Batizados, Casamentos e Enterros"* ("Customs of the People with Regard to Births, Christenings, Marriages, and Interments"), *Revista do Instituto Histórico e Geográphico Brasileiro*, special volume, First Congress of National History, Part V (Rio de Janeiro, 1917).

times, as an infant, he must have dropped off to sleep listening to the mournful creaking of the hammock-hook. Cardim notes that with this hammock-hook the Indians associated the first ceremonies attendant upon the birth of the child; upon it they hung, in case the newborn was a male, a bow with flowers and "bundles of grass." All of which was symbolic, or possibly prophylactic. Throughout infancy the prophylactic measures for guarding the child against malign influences were kept up: "they have many modes of augury, for they place cotton upon the child's head and rub the palms of its hands with bird-feathers and sticks of wood in order that it may grow." [210]

There was also the painting of the body with urucú or genipap; there was the perforation of the lips, the nasal septum, and the ears; there was the insertion of plugs, spindles, stalks into the orifices of the body; there was the stringing of animal teeth about the neck. All this by way of disfiguring, mutilating the child with the object of rendering it repulsive to evil spirits, preserving it from the evil eye and other malign influences.

Some of these prophylactic preoccupations, disguised at times or confused with devout and decorative motives, continue to surround the Brazilian child. In the north it is still common to see children laden down with trinkets about their necks: animal teeth, gold or wooden amulets,[211] Catholic holy medals and other symbols, locks of hair, and the like. It is the custom among the most devout Catholic families of northern and central Brazil to offer the child's hair or ringlets, when it has reached the age to have its locks shorn, to the image of Our Lord on the Cross, the dead Saviour; and in this, perhaps, we have a survival of the Amerindian fear that the hair, teeth, or nails of an individual, and especially of a child, might serve as an object for practices of witchcraft or magic. What better way of avoiding such a risk than by offering the child's hair to Jesus Himself?

That idealization of which Indian children were the object in the early days of the catechism and of colonization—the era, precisely, of a high death-rate among the young, as is to be gathered from the chronicles of the Jesuits themselves[212]—frequently took on a semi-

[210] Fernão Cardim: *Tratados da Terra e Gente do Brasil* (op. cit.), p. 170.

[211] The word here is *figa*. The *figa* was a "little object in the form of a closed fist, with the thumb between the index and the middle finger" and "is used superstitiously to ward off evil spells, disease, etc."—Lima and Barroso, op. cit. (Translator.)

[212] Montoya (op. cit., p. 296) speaks of the settlements of Itapuã, where "the life of children was not of long duration and they died very readily; some of them even died in their mothers' wombs, others shortly after they were born, without being baptized." On this subject, read also

morbid character, the result, perhaps, of an identification of the child with the angel of the Catholics. The death of the child came to be accepted almost joyfully, at any rate without horror. The influence of such an attitude is to be seen in our own customs; to this day, among the backwoodsmen and *sertanejos,* and even among the poor of the cities in the north, the burial of the infant, or "angel" as they generally say,[213] contrasts with the somber mournfulness of adult funerals. In the days of the catechism, the Jesuits, possibly by way of attenuating among the Indians the bad effect of an increased infantile death-rate, which was a consequence of contact or intercourse between the two races under unhygienic conditions, did everything in their power to adorn and embellish the fact of death in the case of a child. This was no sinner who was dying, but an innocent angel whom Our Lord was calling to Himself. The story that Montoya has to tell us is typical of this morbid atmosphere created by the excessive idealization of the infant. A child, the son of a Brother of the Rosary, was envious when it witnessed the burial of one of its playmates. "The body, according to established custom, was all decked out with flowers and on the dead child's head was one of the prettiest of floral wreaths. This led the other young one to beg his father that he too

---

Affonso de E. Taunay: *S. Paulo nõs Primeiros Anos* (op. cit.) (1920). Sergio Milliet makes the intelligent suggestion that the importance attributed to angels and children in our colonial society (in accordance with the evidence presented in this essay) is possibly related to the "development of the baroque" in Brazil, as brought out by Professor Roger Bastide in his paper *"Psicologia do Cafuné"* ("Psychology of the Cafuné"), *Planalto* (São Paulo), September 1, 1941.

[With reference to the baroque, Lima and Barroso (op. cit.) observe that the "architecture of colonial churches in Brazil" was "marked by its influence."—Sergio Milliet is one of the present editors of the *Revista do Arquivo Municipal* of São Paulo and is a distinguished essayist and novelist as well.—*Cafuné* is the name applied to the custom of snapping with the fingernails on the head of another person. (Translator.)]

[213] See Jorge Amado's *The Violent Land* (op. cit.), p. 75: "And Damião would come and lift the little sky-blue casket of the child, dressed like an angel. It was almost always he who bore the caskets of the 'little angels' when a child died on the plantation. Damião would arrange the wildflowers, strew them over the casket. . . ."—See Euclides da Cunha's vivid description of the death of a *sertanejo's* child, *Os Sertões,* 16th edition, p. 143, and, in translation, *Rebellion in the Backlands* (op. cit.), p. 113: "The death of a child is a holiday. In the hut of the poor parents guitars twang joyfully amid the tears; the noisy, passionate samba is danced again and the quatrains of the poetic challengers loudly resound; while at one side, between two tallow candles, wreathed in flowers, the dead infant is laid out, reflecting in its last smile, fixed in death, the supreme contentment of one who is going back to heaven and eternal bliss—which is the dominant preoccupation of these simple, primitive souls." (Translator.)

might die. '*Let me die, father*,' he would say; and he then would stretch himself out on the ground like the body of his playmate as he had seen it. Having heard his son say this many times, the father one day replied: '*My son, if God wills that you should die, may His will be done.*' Upon hearing these words, the child said: '*Very well, Father, I am going to die now.*' And throwing himself down upon the bed, with no sickness whatsoever, he passed away." [214]

The Indian mother, as she cradled her child in the hammock, would lull it to sleep with tender expressions for the little one that, under the influence of Catholicism, was to be idealized into an angel. Roquette Pinto has preserved for us a song of the Parecí Indians, beginning:

> *Essá-mokocê cê-maká*
> (*Sleep, little one, in your hammock.* . . .) [215]

And in the *ocas*, or collective dwellings of the Indians—large houses that, by reason of their communistic character and the vegetable material employed in their construction, were quite different from the strong, solid structures of clay or of stone and mortar that the imperialist colonizers from Europe erected in the neighborhood of the sugar plantations—in the *ocas* the mingled songs of the mothers lulling their young to sleep must have been heard many times. For these enormous sheds (consisting of rafters covered with pindoba fronds) were inhabited by eighty or a hundred persons, and there were many children among them.[216]

In some of the tribes the mothers fashioned for their young ones playthings made of unbaked clay, representing the figures of animals and people, the latter being "predominantly of the feminine sex," notes the ethnologist Erland Nordenskiöld in his recent studies of the tribes of northern Brazil.[217] These figures were "greatly simplified in form . . . being generally deprived of extremities, including even the head, but with the indication of tattooing on the upper part of the body." Nordenskiöld attributes the extreme simplification of the clay dolls of the natives of the Pilcomayo region to "their concern with rendering them unbreakable in the hands of children." It would seem, however, that these figures of people and of animals had an occult significance, that they were not mere playthings; or rather that ani-

---

[214] Montoya, op. cit., p. 308.
[215] Roquette Pinto: *Rondônia* (op. cit.).
[216] Léry, op. cit., Vol. II, p. 95.
[217] Erland Nordenskiöld, cited in the bibliographical analysis of the *Bulletin* of the Goeldi Museum (Museum of Pará) of Natural History and Ethnography, Vol. VII (Pará, 1913).

mism, totemism, and sexual magic were unctuously extended to these children's toys. In the clay dolls of the Carajá Indians,[218] in the Araguaia River region, Emilio Goeldi encountered a reminiscence of "the phallomorphic idols of baked clay such as are to be found in the burying-ground of the Indians that formerly dwelt at the mouth of the Amazon."[219] The native tradition of clay dolls was not communicated to Brazilian culture; the prevailing doll with us came to be the rag doll, possibly of African origin. But the fondness our children have for playing with animal figures is still a characteristic trait, although it is disappearing with the standardization of industry according to American and German patterns and the introduction of mechanical toys. Meanwhile at our backland fairs one may still come upon these interesting figurines, notably those of monkeys, beetles, turtles, newts, and toads. Nor should we overlook the native custom of employing domesticated birds to amuse the young;[220] even today the catching of birds with clay pellets[221] or with banana-stalk traps is a very characteristic habit with the Brazilian child.

In his "Report on the Mission of Father Christovão de Gouvêa to the Regions of Brazil in the Year '83," Father Cardim tells us that the Indian children had "many games of their own sort," but he does not describe any of them in precise detail. He notes that the young *caboclos* disported themselves "with much greater merriment and joy than Portuguese children." And he does give us a general idea of the nature of their play: "in these games they imitate various birds, serpents, and other animals; they are quite charming and carefree, nor is there any quarreling, wailing, or fighting among them, and one does not hear any obscenity or calling of bad names." Possibly out of modesty as a missionary, he does not speak of erotic games; for there may have been such games among the young children and adolescents of Brazil, of the kind that Professor Malinowski observed in Melanesia.[222] To judge by the "lascivious songs" to which a number of the early missionaries allude, songs for which Father Anchieta undertook to substitute hymns to the Virgin and devout canticles, it is to be presumed that such erotic games did exist among the Brazilian aborigines. In

---

[218] Indians of the state of Goiás. (Translator.)

[219] *Bulletin* of the Goeldi Museum. —J. W. Fewkes arrives at the conclusion that dolls among civilized peoples are a survival of primitive idols (in A. F. Chamberlain: *The Child*, 3rd edition, London, 1926).

[220] Roquette Pinto: *Rondônia* (op. cit.).

[221] That is, clay pellets hardened in the fire and shot from the *bodoque*, or double-stringed bow.—Lima and Barroso, op. cit. (Translator.)

[222] Bronislaw Malinowski: *The Sexual Life of Savages in Northwestern Melanesia* (New York and London, 1929).

Cardim we find a reference to the river sports of the young Indians: "the lads of the village, swimming in the river, would lie in ambush for one another and then would burst forth with a great shouting and bellowing; and they had other games and water sports of their own kind that were very charming, some of the lads being in canoes while others would dive to the bottom and then rise to the surface and leap ashore with their hands raised, crying: 'Praised be Jesus Christ!'—and then they would come to receive the padre's benediction. . . ."

In connection with the childish pastimes of which Father Cardim speaks, as in the magic dances, the war dances, and the love dances of adults, there is to be noted the tendency of the American savage to mingle his own life with that of animals. His devils have animal heads and are thus represented in his dance masks. His songs imitate the voices of animals as his dances do their movements; his drinking-cups and earthenware jars are a repetition of animal forms.

Out of this aboriginal tradition there remains with the Brazilian a fondness for infantile games and sports that involve the imitation of animals. The basis of the great popularity of the game of chance known as *bicho* lies in the animistic and totemistic residuum of Amerindian culture, later reinforced by the African.[223] There is, meanwhile, a more positive contribution that the American Indian child has made to the play-life of European children. This is a game that consists in batting about a rubber ball. It was played by the Indians with a ball that probably had a rubber covering, but which to the first Europeans appeared to be made of very light wood. The batting was done with the backs of the players, who at times had to throw themselves flat on the ground in order to accomplish this. It was obviously a game of the same sort as the one called *mata-naariti*, which General Cândido Rondon encountered among the Parecís, the ball in the latter instance—according to Roquette Pinto, in his *Rondônia*—being made of the rubber of the mangaba tree [224] and batted about in

---

[223] A. F. Chamberlain brings out a fact that, it seems to me, may legitimately be associated with the Brazilian complex represented by the game of *bicho*: namely, the seclusion or enforced fasting of novices and neophytes in various primitive societies to the point where, in their dreams or a state of hallucination, they behold the animal that is destined to be their tutelary genius and whose form, very often, is tattooed on their bodies. (*The Child and Childhood in Folk-* *Thought*, London, 1896.) Many a *bicho*-player has his favorite animal, which appears to him in a dream to "bring him luck."

[224] The tree known as *mangabeira* (*Hancornia speciosa Gomez*). The mangaba is a round orange-colored fruit that is eaten when over-ripe. The *mangabeira* yields a milky juice from which the so called "Pernambuco rubber" is produced (Translator.)

the same manner. Following the discovery of America, the Ambassador of Venice to the court of Charles V of Spain saw this game played by young savages in Seville, which was the point of confluence for American novelties in the sixteenth and seventeenth centuries, by virtue of its *Casa de Contratación*.[225] The Ambassador tells us that the ball was "as big as a peach or bigger, and they did not bat it with their hands or with their feet, but with their backs, and this they did with such dexterity that it was a marvel to behold. At times they practically threw themselves on the ground in order to repel the ball, and it was all done with great cleverness."[226]

A number of the games and dances of the Brazilian savages had an evident pedagogical intention. We may note the "*quietação e amizade*," the "orderliness and friendship"–in other words, the "fair play"[227]–that Father Cardim so greatly admired in the Brazilian *caboclos* of the sixteenth century. No "bad names or obscenity" from one player to another, no "calling the father and mother names." It is possible that, by way of emphasizing the contrast with European children, the padre is exaggerating when he says: "rarely in their play do they lose their tempers or quarrel for any reason whatever, and rarely do the fight with one another."[228]

At an early age the Indian lads learned to dance and sing. The same Father Cardim describes a number of the children's dances. Some of these were adopted by the Society of Jesus in its system of education and catechism. The most common, perhaps, was the *Sairé*, described by Father João Daniel.[229]

As a generalization, it may be stated that the Indian child grew up free of corporal punishment and of paternal or maternal discipline. But childhood for him none the less followed a species of liturgy or ritual, as did the whole of primitive life.

Upon attaining the age of puberty the boy had his head shorn in the manner which Brother Vicente do Salvador[230] describes as the friar's haircut, and the girl likewise had her locks trimmed in mascu-

---

[225] Clearing house. (Translator.)

[226] J. García Mercadal: *España Vista por Los Estranjeros, Relaciones de Viajeros y Embajadores (Siglo XVI)* (Madrid, n. d.).

[227] The words are in English in the text. (Translator.)

[228] Cardim, op. cit., pp. 175 and 310. In an article in the newspaper *A Manhã*, April 12, 1942, under the heading "Imaginary World," Senhor

Affonso Arinos de Mello Franco laments that he is unable to recall any Brazilian work on traditional sports and games. The pages devoted to the subject in the present essay date from 1933.

[229] João Daniel, op. cit., p. 112.

[230] Early and notable Brazilian historian, born at Bahia in 1564. (Translator.)

line fashion. The segregation of the lads upon reaching puberty, in clubs or houses accessible only to men—houses known by the name of *baito* in central Brazil—appears to have been designed to assure the domination of the masculine over the feminine sex, by educating the adolescent male to exert such a dominion. These houses were forbidden to women (unless they happened to be old women, rendered masculine or sexless by age) and to other children who had not as yet been initiated. Here were preserved the flutes and cymbals, which no woman could recall ever having glimpsed, nor did she care to glimpse them, even from afar, for such a sight meant certain death. During the period of segregation the lad learned how to treat the woman, to feel always superior to her and never to unbosom himself in confidences to his mother or any female whatsoever, but only to his father and his men friends. The affinities that were exalted were fraternal ones, those of man for man, virile in character. The result of all this was an environment that was propitious to homosexuality.

The tests that were given the youth upon his initiation were rude ones. Some of them were so brutal that the neophyte could not endure them and died as a consequence of the excessive rigor of the ceremony. I have already spoken of flagellation, tattooing, the perforation of the septum, the lips, and the ears. Other tests that were in use consisted in the pulling and filing of teeth; reminiscences of this and of African tattooing are still to be found among the backlanders of the northeast and among fishermen. According to Webster, in his classic work, *Primitive Secret Societies*,[231] a true process of moral and technical education took place within these organizations, the object being the preparation of the youth for the responsibilities and privileges of manhood. The adolescent was here initiated into the most useful mysteries having to do with the technique of building houses, hunting, fishing, making war, singing and music, and everything that the neophyte ought to know concerning magic and religion. Here, in contact with the elders, he was impregnated with the traditions of the tribe. It was a rapid but intense educational process, the indoctrination and instruction being brought to bear upon green novices in a state of extreme sensitivity as a result of their fastings, vigils, and privations. If corporal punishment and the discipline of father and mother were lacking among the natives of Brazil—a fact that so astonished the first chroniclers—there was, on the other hand, this severe discipline which has just been described and which was imposed chiefly by the elders. Father João Daniel tells us of another

---

[231] Hutton Webster: *Primitive Secret Societies, A Study in Early Politics and Religion* (New York, 1908).

missionary, an acquaintance of his, who, having heard the cries of a child during the night, at dawn next day sent to inquire what the trouble was, only to learn that it was "F., who all night long had been beating his nephew to make him strong, brave, and stout-hearted." [232] One thing of which childhood among the savages was free was disciplinary ear-pullings, pinchings, and the like. Even "misdeeds and crimes," as Friar Vicente observes, went unpunished among the Brazilian aborigines.[233] And Gabriel Soares, writing in his *Log Book* of the Tupinambás,[234] has this to say: "The Tupinambás do not inflict any punishment upon their children, nor do they preach them sermons or reprimand them for anything they do." But at times the young ones were flogged—and adults would even flog one another—with a pedagogical end in view or as a means of prophylaxis against evil spirits, as I have mentioned above. Possessing, thus, the flagellation complex, it was easy for them to adapt themselves to the concept of penance introduced by the missionaries, and from the earliest times they were notable for the practice of such rites. Cardim records the fervor with which the natives fulfilled the penances imposed upon them by the Catholic Church.

The maltreatment of the person, even to the point of pulling out the tongue or scarifying it with a sharp animal's tooth, was for the primitive a process of purification and of conjuration, applied with especial rigor to the boy or girl upon initiation into puberty. The same thing, according to Rafael Karsten, may be said of the violent physical exercises of the Indians—their dances, wrestling matches, races, the arm-breaking game [235]—calculated, all of them, to produce abundant perspiration. For the primitive supposed that, by means of sweat as well as blood, he would be able to cast out the demon from the individual's body. It was for this reason that certain savages subjected the sick—always looked upon as demon-possessed and shameful beings—to strenuous choreographic exercises of a strictly ceremonial and magic character, by no means intended as a diversion or as an expression of sociability. It is not lubricious but mystical sweat that is sought in these dances, in the course of which it is common for individuals to flog one another. A number of Brazilian children's

---

[232] João Daniel, op. cit., p. 291.
[233] Frei Vicente do Salvador: *História do Brasil* (op. cit.), p. 59.
[234] "Generic designation of various Tupí tribes that, in the sixteenth century, inhabited the seacoast of Brazil." —Lima and Barroso, op. cit.

[235] This is the *queda de braço*, or *quebra de braço*: "a game in which the contestants endeavor to bend each other's forearm over the horizontal support on which their elbows rest." —Lima and Barroso, op. cit.

games—among them, "hot-strap" (*peia queimada*) and "*manja*" [236]—are a reflection of the flagellation complex.

The native child did not lack a mother's care so far as its health was concerned; this is indicated by the many prophylactic measures that were taken; it is shown by the state of cleanliness in which the young one was kept. It is shown, above all, by the child's joyfulness and sense of well-being.

Among the best memories of his contact with Brazilian Indians that Léry took back to Europe with him was that of the "*conomis-miri*," [237] playing or dancing on the village green of the *tabas*, or native settlements. The only one who was even more charmed than he was Father Cardim. The young lads described by the padre had already been instructed by the missionaries; but it is evident that they had not lost, in the shadow of the Jesuit cassocks, the light-heartedness of savages. Léry found them enjoying perfect freedom: "*fessus, grassets & refais qu'ils sont, beaucoup plus que ceux de par deçà, avec leurs poinçons d'os blancs dans leurs lèvres fendues, les cheveux tondus à leur mode & quelquefois le corps peinturé, ne failloyent iamais de venir en troupe dansans au devant de nous quand ils nous croyoyent arriver en leurs villages.*" In their faulty speech, the youthful *caboclos* would ask the visitors to toss them fishhooks: "*Couto-affat, amabé pinda.*" When Léry acceded to their request, there was great merriment: "*. . . c'estoit un passe temps de voir ceste petite marmaille toute nue laquelle pour trouver & masser ces hame-çons trepilloit & gargoit la terre comme connils de garenne.*" [238]

These young ones whom the Frenchman found to be so sturdy had come into the world like animals. Hearing a woman's cries, once upon a time, Léry, like every good Franchman something of an alarmist, immediately thought of the *ian-ou-are*, a *bicho* that from time to time devoured savages. But when, accompanied by another Frenchman, he went to see what was happening, the pair discovered that the cries were those of a woman giving birth. The husband was acting as midwife; and it was he whom Léry saw cutting the umbilical cord with his teeth; it was he who flattened the baby's nose in place of straightening it according to the European custom, after which he bathed the newborn infant and proceeded to paint its body red

---

[236] On "hot-strap," see what the author has to say in Chapter iv, p. 349–350. *Manja* is a game something like our hide-and-seek, with occasional sadistic variations, in the form of spank-ings administered by the winners at the end. (Translator.)

[237] That is, the young Indian chil-dren; a native term.

[238] Léry, op. cit., Vol. I, pp. 137–8.

and black.[239] The child was then laid in a small cotton hammock or was placed in "shreds of hammocks, called a *tipóia*," [240] and was fastened to its mother's back or to her hips.

Léry was delighted with the infantile and domestic hygiene of the natives, contrasting it with that of Europeans and concluding that the American process was the superior one. The child grew up free of skirts, swaddling-clothes, and diapers that would have rendered its movements difficult. But this did not imply any lack of care on the part of the mothers. While they may not have had skirts and diapers, the Tupí babies did not for this reason grow up dirty and unkempt. On the contrary, the French observer was impressed by their cleanliness and neatness. In the frank words of Léry: "*qu'en-cores que les femmes de ce pays là n'ayent aucuns linges pour toucher le derrière de leurs enfants, mesmes qu'elles ne se servent non plus à cela feuilles d'arbres & d'herbes, dont toutesfois elles ont grande abondance: neantmoins elles en sont si soigneuses, que seulement avec de petits bois que elles rompent, comme petites chevilles, elles les nettoyent si bien que vous ne les verriez iamais breneux.*" [241] Leaves and bits of wood served the natives of Brazil, not only as dishes, towels, and napkins, but also as toilet-paper and infants' diapers.

Gabriel Soares records the custom that the Indians had of giving to their offspring the names of animals, fishes, trees, etc.,[242] names that Karsten shows to have been, generally, those of the same animals represented by their sacred dance masks.[243] This was, therefore, an expression of that animism and magic with which the whole of primitive life is found to be suffused. Whiffen stresses the fact that the names of persons among the Brazilian tribes of the northeast are only pronounced in a low voice, religiously.[244] These names,[245] in certain tribes, were displaced by something in the nature of so-briquets, belonging apparently to that category of "non-poetic" names as collected by Theodoro Sampaio: Guarquinguara (bird's behind); Miguiguacú (big buttocks); Cururupeba (little toad); Man-diopuba (rotten manihot); etc. It would seem that the object of these names was to render the persons bearing them repugnant to the demons.

One thing of which child-life among the savages was not free was

---

239 Ibid., Vol. II, p. 88.
240 Cardim, op. cit., p. 170.
241 Léry, op. cit., Vol. II, p. 91.
242 Soares, op. cit., p. 314.
243 Karsten, op. cit.
244 Whiffen, op. cit.

245 That is to say, the true names, received in infancy; these were sup-posed to be magically bound up with the soul of the individual.—Karsten, op. cit.

horrible fears. The fear of the young ones that the sky would fall upon their heads. The fear that the earth would flee from under their feet.[246] All this in addition to the great dread they had of Jurupari.

Even in broad daylight, with the sun shining brightly on the green, the children in the midst of their play would be seeing ghostly forms, including that of the devil himself, and would come running to the house screaming with terror. The demons generally appeared with terrifying animal-heads. Some of them Father Antônio Ruiz Montoya describes with a certain luxury of detail as having appeared to none other than a steward of the Jesuits—this, to be sure, was in the days of the catechism. The padre tells us that they had "feet like animals, long nails, slender legs, and hot-glowing eyes." [247] Here, perhaps, is the influence of the Christian devil; for the devil of Catholic theology was to be added to the Jurupari complex and was even to absorb the latter.

But it was not merely a matter of ghosts, nor was it the devil in the form of animals that alone made life miserable for the savage. There were monsters that today we do not know how to describe: the guaiazis; the coruqueamos; the maiturús (men with feet turned backward); the jiboiucús; the horrible simiavulpina; [248] and, more damnable than any of the others, the hipupiaras, or hupupiaras. These last were certain men of the sea who spread terror along the beaches.[249]

---

[246] ". . . some of them in the morning, upon awakening, rise and, planting their feet on the ground, raise their arms heavenward as if to uphold the sky and keep it from falling; and in so doing they believe that all will be well with them for the whole of that day." Father Luis Figueira: *Relação do Maranhão, Documentos para a História do Brasil e especialmente do Ceará, 1608–1625* (*Account of Maranhão, Documents for the History of Brazil and Especially of Ceará,* etc.) (Fortaleza, 1904).

[247] Montoya, op. cit., pp. 164–5.

[248] Simão de Vasconcellos: *Vida do Veneravel Padre Joseph de Anchieta da Companhia de Jesu, Taumaturgo do Novo Mundo na Provincia do Brasil . . .* (*Life of the Venerable Father Joseph de Anchieta of the Society of Jesus, Miracle-Worker of the New World in the Province of Brazil*) (Lisbon, 1672), p. 102.

[249] Cardim, Gabriel Soares, and Gandavo all allude with horror to this marine monster. In his *História da Provincia de Santa Cruz* (*History of the Province of Santa Cruz*), edition of 1858, Gandavo gives us a picture of the hipupiara, and a terrifying one it is. Of this monster Father Cardim (*op. cit.*) tells us that the natives had so great a fear that, "merely upon hearing tell of it, many of them die, and none who sees it escapes." He then goes into detail: "they have the appearance of men of good stature, but their eyes are deeply sunken." There were females of the species, too: "the females appear to be women, they have long hair, and are shapely creatures; and these monsters are to be met with along the banks of the fresh-water streams. In Jagoaripe, seven or eight leagues from Bahia, many of them have been found. . . ." Arthur Neiva believes that the hipu-

Gourmets after their fashion, the hipupiaras did not devour the entire flesh of a person, but took only a bite here and there. It was sufficient, however, to leave the individual a wreck. They ate his "eyes, nose, the tips of his toes and fingers, and his genitals." The rest they left to rot on the beach.

The truth of the matter is that savage life in its various phases is found to be imbued with an animism, a totemism, a sexual magic that was, perforce, communicated to the culture of the invader, which did no more than deform these elements—it did not destroy them.

Of the totemistic and animistic culture of the aborigine, there remains with the Brazilian, especially as a child, an attitude that insensibly embodies this animism and totemism with regard to plants and animals (still so numerous in our country), some of which are endowed by the popular imagination, as well as by the childish fancy, with a truly human malice, with other semi-human qualities, and with an intelligence and a power superior to those of men. This is shown by our folklore and popular tales, by our superstitions and traditions. It is shown by the many stories, so Brazilian in flavor, of the marriage of human beings with animals, of friendship or love between men and beasts of the sort that Hartland associates with totemistic cultures.[250] Stories that correspond to an attitude of tolerance, when not an utter lack of repugnance, in real life, toward a sexual union of man and beast, an attitude that is very common among Brazilian children of the interior.[251] It is to be found in the *sertanejo's* offspring more than in the plantation child; in the latter, nevertheless, it is sufficiently common to be recognized as a complex—in this case sociological as well as Freudian—of our Brazilian culture. In both cases—that of the plantation child and that of the young *sertanejo*—

piara was some "stray example of the *Otaria Jubata* Forster, 1755."—*Esboço Histórico sobre a Botânica e Zoologia no Brasil (Historical Sketch of the Botany and Zoology of Brazil)* (São Paulo, 1929).

[250] "It follows," says Hartland, "that peoples in that stage of thought cannot have, in theory at all events, a repugnance to a sexual union between man and the lower animals with which religious training and the growth of civilization have impressed all the higher races. Such peoples admit the possibility of a marriage wherein one party may be human and the other an animal of a different species, or even a tree or a plant." —Edwin Sidney Hartland: *The Science of Fairy Tales* (2nd edition, London, 1925).

[251] Gilberto Freyre: *Vida Social no Nordeste"* ("Social Life in the Northeast"), in the *Livro do Nordeste (Book of the Northeast)*, commemorative of the centenary of the *Diário de Pernambuco* (Recife, 1925); and more recently José Lins do Rego: *Menino do Engenho (Plantation Lad)*, a novel (Rio de Janeiro, 1932). Cicero Dias also deals with this subject in his unpublished autobiographical novel, *Jundiá*.

the physical experience of love is anticipated by the abuse of animals and even of plants; in an effort to satisfy that fury with which the sexual instinct dawns in them, the lads make use of cows, nanny-goats, ewes, hens, and other domestic animals, or of plants and fruits: of the banana tree, the watermelon, or the fruit of the mandacarú. These are practices which, with the *sertanejo*, up to the period of his adolescence and sometimes until he is married, make up for the lack or scarcity of domestic or public prostitution: nurses, mulatto girls, Negro houseboys, public women, through whom the plantation lads and those in the cities of the seaboard so soon become contaminated.

Other traces of elementary, primitive life persist in Brazilian culture. In addition to the fear of the *bicho* and the monster, already mentioned, there are others, equally elementary, that are common to Brazilians, especially in their childhood, and which go to show that we are perhaps nearer to the tropical forest than any other civilized people of modern times. So far as that is concerned, the most civilized man has within himself many of these great primitive fears; with us Brazilians, they merely make their appearance more forcefully, for the reason that we still dwell in the shadow of the jungle, the virgin forest. In the shadow, likewise, of that *culture of the tropical forest—* of America and of Africa—which the Portuguese incorporated and assimilated with his own as no other colonizer of modern times has done; and it is for this reason that we are subjected to frequent relapses into the primitive mentality, with its instincts and its fears. Hall states that every civilized man has preserved out of his savage ancestry a tendency to believe in phantasmal beings, souls from another world, goblins, and the like: "a prepotent bias, that haunts the very nerves and pulses of the most cultured, to believe in ghosts," [252] Brazilians are, *par excellence*, the people with a belief in the supernatural; in all that surrounds us we feel the touch of strange influences, and every so often our newspapers reveal cases of apparitions, ghosts, enchantments. Whence the success among us of spiritualism in both its higher and its lower forms.[253]

---

[252] G. S. Hall: "A Study of Fears," in Alexander Francis Chamberlain's *The Child, a Study in the Evolution of Man* (3rd edition, London, 1926).

[253] Those fears which Hall terms fears of "gravity,"—that is to say, the fear of falling, of losing one's direction or senses, of the earth's fleeing from under one's feet, etc., common among primitive peoples—find expression in various superstitions and legends current in Brazil from the earliest times and still to be met with in the interior of the country and in the *sertões*. "Of the waters of the Grão-Paraguai," writes Theodoro Sampaio (he is speaking of the sixteenth century), "there in the heart of

Also frequent among us are relapses into a savage, or primitive, fury of destruction, manifested in assassinations, pillagings, the invasion of plantations by *cangaceiros*, or bandits. Rarely is there a political or civic movement in which explosions of this fury, in normal times repressed or held within bounds, do not occur. Silvio Romero even goes so far as to criticize us for the ingenuousness with which we "give the pompous name of *liberal revolutions*" to "disorderly outbursts of wrath." The true character of these movements, as being representative of the clash of dissimilar or antagonistic cultures, rather than civic or political, appears not to have escaped this astute observer: "the savage or barbaric elements that lie on the ethnic bottom of our nationality freely come to the surface, lift their heads, and prolong the anarchy, the spontaneous disorder." So writes Romero,[254] apropos of the revolts known by the names of Balaiada, Sabinada, Cabanada,[255] and so on, which have agitated Brazil in the past. And might not the same characterization be extended to apply to such other uprisings as those of the *mata-mata-marinheiros*, the *quebra-quilos*, the *farrapos?* [256] Who can say if, bringing it down to the

the backlands, the report was current that, rushing over a formidable cataract with a frightful thunder of sound, they caused the earth to tremble and the living being who heard them to lose his senses."—Cited by Taunay: *São Paulo nos Primeiros Tempos* (op. cit.). For other legends and superstitions of Amerindian origin, bound up with the great rivers and the jungle, see the posthumous work by Affonso Arinos: *Lendas e Tradiçoes Brasileiras (Brazilian Legends and Traditions)* (São Paulo, 1917).
[On spiritualism in Brazil as reflected in literature, in the year 1942, see my observations in *Handbook of Latin American Studies*, No. 8, p. 380. (Translator.)]
[254] Silvio Romero: *Provocações e Debates* (op. cit.).
[255] Names given to various revolts in Brazil. *Balaiada* is applied to the uprising of the *Balaios*, which resulted in civil war in Maranhão from 1838 to 1840. *Balaio* (literally, straw basket) was the name given to one of the leaders, Manuel dos Anjos Fer-

reira. The *Sabinada* was the separatist revolution of Bahia, in the time of the Regency (it lasted from 1835 to 1837), and was so named from one of its leaders, a Dr. Sabino. The *Cabanada* (1832–5) was a revolt in Pernambuco that had for object the restoration of Pedro I to the throne. (Translator.)
[256] *Mata-mata-marinheiros* was the name given to the participants in an anti-Portuguese revolt of the eighteenth century. The *Quebra-quilos* were those who participated in a seditious movement in Paraiba, in 1875, provoked by the imposition of new provincial taxes and the law establishing the metric system in Brazil (*quilo*: kilogram; *quebrar*, to break or shatter). The term *Farrapos*, a famous one in Brazilian history, literally means "the ragged ones" and was first applied by the legalists, as a derogatory epithet, to the insurrectionary republicans, or "crackbrain liberals (*liberais exaltados*)," of Rio Grande do Sul, in 1835. (Translator.)

present time, we might not apply it to more recent movements, even though these latter are animated by a more intense ideological fervor than the former ones. The Pernambuco revolution of 1817 impresses me as being, in the words of Oliveira Lima,[257] "the only one worthy of the name" in our political history. It is, without a doubt, the one that less than any other has the character of a mere riot, propitious to pillaging, the one that suffers least from a deformation of political or ideological objectives. Not that I regard it as being exclusively political, without economic roots; what I wish to stress is that it was carried out in a manner different from such revolts as the Abrilada,[258] with a definite program and political style. Of the Vinagrada uprising of 1836, in Pará, Silvio Romero writes: "the Tapuia element reared its head, tripping merrily over the lives and property of others."

This is not to speak of those movements that were plainly slave revolts, explosions of race hatred or of rebelliousness on the part of a socially and economically oppressed class—the insurrection of the Negroes in Minas, for example. Nor are we concerned here with those cultural earthquakes, for they were something very like that, on the part of oppressed cultures bursting forth in order not to die of suffocation and breaking through the incrustations of the dominant culture that they might be able to breathe, as would appear to have been the case with the Negro movement of Bahia in 1835. This last was the case of a Mohammedan Negro culture against a Portuguese Catholic one.[259] These are movements apart, with a profound social direction and significance, just as was that of Canudos,[260] which was a result of the differentiation between the culture of the seaboard and that of the *sertão*. The relapses into the fury of the savage are rather to be observed in movements with objectives that are apparently political or civic in character, but which in truth are only a pretext for a retrogression to a primitive culture that has been trampled underfoot but not destroyed.

---

[257] Prominent diplomat, statesman, and historical essayist of the turn-of-the-century era. (Translator.)

[258] *Abrilada*: literally, April Revolution, referring to the restorationist revolt in Pernambuco in 1832. (Cf. *Cabanada*, note 255 above.) *Vinagrada* was the name given to the uprisings in the state of Pará during the period of the Regency (in 1835–7), so called because they were headed by Francisco Vinagre. (Translator.)

[259] Abbé Étienne: "*La Secte Mus-salmane des Malés du Brésil et leur Révolte en 1835,*" *Anthropos*, January-March, 1909.

[260] The backlands village that served the fanatic, Antonio Conselheiro, as his fortified stronghold against the armies of the Brazilian government, as described in Euclides da Cunha's *Os Sertões* (*Rebellion in the Backlands*). Da Cunha's underlying thesis is this cultural conflict. (Translator.)

It is natural that, with regard to the notion of property as with that of other moral and material values, including human life, Brazil should still be a field of conflict between the most violent antagonisms. With respect to property, it is a struggle with us to find a point of fixation between Amerindian communism and the European notion of private property. A struggle between the descendant of the communistic Indian, with practically no notion of individual ownership, and the descendant of the Portuguese individualist, whose life, down to the beginning of the nineteenth century, was spent amid the alarms of corsairs and highwaymen, who was in the habit of burying his money in an earthen jar and hiding his valuables in cellars, while the stone walls with which he surrounded himself bristled with shards of broken glass as a protection against robbers. Saint-Hilaire, on his journey into the interior of São Paulo in the early 1800's, found what he believed to be a reminiscence of the days of the discovery, in reality an expression of the conflict mentioned above between the two notions of property: the fact that merchandise in wayside inns, instead of being exposed to the public view, was kept on the inside of the house, the merchant supplying the customer by putting his hands out through a wicket. The French scientist interprets it thus: "The tavern-keepers naturally have to take precautions against the covetousness of the Indians and the rapacity of the mamelucos, who, when it comes to discriminating between what is mine and thine, have, surely, ideas that are not much more exact than those of the Indians themselves." [261]

Gabriel Soares, with his practical man's sagacity, pictures the sixteenth-century *caboclos* that he encountered here as being "ingenious in learning as much as the whites will teach them." He makes an exception, however, of those exercises in mnemonics, ratiocination, and abstraction which the fathers of the Society of Jesus from the start insisted upon giving to the Indians in their schools: "matters of reckoning" and of "understanding," in the chronicler's words.[262] To read, do sums, write, spell, and pray in Latin—that was what they taught them. For such exercises the natives displayed no inclination, and it is easy to imagine how dull it must have been for them in these institutions kept by the padres, a boredom that was only relieved by lessons in singing and music, by the dramatic representation of

---

[261] Auguste de Saint-Hilaire: *Voyages dans l'intérieur du Brésil* (1852).

[262] Soares, op. cit., p. 321.

miracles and religious *autos*,[263] and by instruction in some manual trade or other. This led to Anchieta's conclusion, of a "lack of ability" on the part of the aborigines, while Gabriel Soares himself describes the Tupinambás as "very barbarous" in understanding.

The latter chronicler encountered among the Tupinambás "a condition very good for Franciscan friars": they possessed everything in common. He might have mentioned another: their inclination toward manual tasks, their repugnance for any considerable amount of book-learning. The Brazilian aborigine was precisely the type of neophyte or catechumen who, once the light of the catechism had dawned upon him, was not a good prospect for Jesuit ideology. An enthusiast of the Seraphic Order well might sustain the thesis that the ideal missionary for a people communistic in tendency and rebellious to intellectual discipline, as was the American native, would be the Franciscan. The theoretical Franciscan, at any rate: an enemy of intellectualism; an enemy of mercantilism; lyric in his simplicity; a friend of the manual arts and of small industry; and almost animistic and totemistic in his relation to nature, to animal and vegetable life.

For St. Francis the two great evils afflicting the Christian world of his time were: the arrogance of the rich, and the arrogance of the erudite. It is said that, upon being informed that a certain Parisian doctor, of the fine and subtle kind, had entered a Franciscan monastery as a friar, he exclaimed: "These doctors, my sons, will be the destruction of my vineyard!" And it was precisely the Jesuits who became the doctors of the Church, its great men of science, noted for their grammars, their compendiums of rhetoric, their clocks, maps, and terrestrial globes. But meanwhile, as Freer observes, "with all their self-confidence they failed; for unlike the Franciscans, their spirit was not the spirit of the coming ages." [264]

The great failure of the Jesuits may be said to have been in America. In Paraguay. In Brazil. The Brazilian Indians appear to have benefited more from the teachings of the Franciscans missionaries and the orientation thus acquired. The Franciscans, as Fray Zephyrin Engelhardt brings out, where they were in charge gave a technical or practical direction to the work of the Indian missions, one that was lacking with the Jesuits.

The Franciscans were, above all, concerned with turning the na-

---

[263] In Portuguese, *auto* is the ancient term for a dramatic piece; it was applied to the old farces. It comes to mean, in general, a solemnity. (Translator.)

[264] Arthur S. B. Freer: *The Early Franciscans and Jesuits* (New York and London, 1922).

tives into artisans and technicians; they avoided overburdening them with that "mental exertion which the Indians hated more than manual labor." [265] With regard to the Franciscan method of Christianizing the aborigines, Brother Engelhardt adds this comment: "we do not find that Christ directed His Apostles to teach reading, writing, and arithmetic." A bit of irony that is obviously directed at those with the initials S. J. after their names. And in answering the charge that the Franciscans in their missions were interested chiefly in training apprentices or technicians: "they gave the Indians the education which was adapted to their present needs and probable future condition in society.'" Whereas the first Jesuits in Brazil, as may be seen from their chronicles, were almost ashamed of the fact that it was necessary for them to perform mechanical tasks; they would have preferred to devote themselves to making scholars and young bachelors of arts out of the Indians. From what Father Simão de Vasconcellos tells us, in his *Chronicle of the Society of Jesus in the State of Brazil and the Work of Its Sons in These Parts of Brazil*,[266] it may be seen that the fathers of the Society came here without any purpose of developing technical or artistic activities among the savages, but rather those of a literary and academic nature. The Jesuits were under the necessity of becoming artisans on the spur of the moment, of Franciscanizing themselves, and this is justified by Father Simão as something very like a weakness: "and from this time forth there was introduced the labor of the brothers at mechanical tasks and those works useful to the community, by reason of the great poverty in which they then lived. Nor should it be looked upon as a strange thing, and one that is very unbecoming, for the religious to occupy themselves with such employment; seeing that St. Joseph did not deem it unbefitting in the father of Christ (which he is, in the common estimation of mankind), nor did St. Paul find it unseemly in an Apostle of the College of Jesus to earn his bread by the labor of his

---

[265] Brother Zephyrin Engelhardt: *The Missions and Missionaries of California* (Santa Barbara, 1929).— See also Brother Basílio Rower: *Páginas da História Franciscana no Brasil* (*Pages of Franciscan History in Brazil*) (Rio de Janeiro, 1941), with extensive bibliography, including manuscripts, and various interesting notes on the conflicts between the activities of the Franciscans and those of the Jesuits in Brazil. The activity of the Jesuits has been abundantly described by Father Serafim Leite in his *História da Companhia de Jesús no Brasil* (*History of the Society of Jesus in Brazil*) (Lisbon, 1938), a work notable for its selection, order, method, and documentation. The selection, it goes without saying, has been made from the Jesuit point of view.

[266] *Chrônica da Companhia de Jesús do Estado do Brasil e do que Obraram Seus Filhos neste Parte do Brasil* (op. cit.).

hands and the sweat of his body: such were the examples that were followed by the most perfected among the religious of old, who thus accustomed their bodies to labor and their souls to humility, until it came to be the rule of heaven, which the angels dictated to the holy abbot Pacomio." [267] Among the early Jesuits in Brazil it would seem that Father Leonardo alone had brought with him out of secular life an artisan's trade, that of a blacksmith; practically all the others had a purely academic background or were doctors of the sort that St. Francis of Assisi so greatly feared, and these it was who of a sudden had to become carpenters and molders. They had no enthusiasm, however, for manual toil or artistic labor, but rather felt the necessity of apologizing for it by the allegation that it was unavoidable under the rude circumstances in which they had to carry on their gospel teaching.

That the Franciscan system would have been better for the natives than that of the Jesuits appears to me to be obvious. Gabriel Soares describes the Tupinambás as possessing a "great inclination for learning these trades"; that is to say, an inclination to become "carpenters, hewers and sawers of wood, pottery-makers." They were likewise inclined "to all the tasks of the sugar plantations," including even the "raising of cows," while the women were adapted to "raising hens," "sewing and washing," doing "needlework," etc.[268]

Coming into the life of the colonizers as legitimate wives, concubines, mothers of families, wet-nurses, and cooks, the native women might find self-expression in activities suited to their sex and their tendency toward stability. The Indian male, on the other hand, almost always encountered, in his intercourse with the foreign-comers, one of two conditions: either he had to labor in the fields of sugar-cane for the plantation-owners; or else he was obliged by the padres to learn to read, write, and do sums. Later he was to have to drudge on the cacao and mate[269] farms. Some of these activities, imposed upon the captive Indians or the catechumens, had the effect of diverting their energies into channels that were the most repugnant to their primitive mentality.[270] The padres, for example, kept them from contact with those European tools which were the very thing that so

---

[267] Vasconcellos: *Chrônica* (op. cit.), p. 43.

[268] Soares, op. cit., p. 321.

[269] *Mate* is the name both of a tree (the *erva-mate*) and of a drink that is made from it. The latter is variously known, in English, as mate, Paraguayan tea, South Sea tea, and

yerba. The tree belongs to the *Aquifoliaceæ* family (*Ilex paraguariensis* Hil.). (Translator.)

[270] On the characteristics and tendencies of the so-called "primitive mentality," read the work by Lévy-Brühl: *Mentalité primitive* (Paris, 1922).

greatly attracted them to the strangers from overseas; instead they bored them with copybooks and grammatical exercises,[271] Other practices offended an instinct in them that is so deeply rooted in the savage, just as it is in civilized beings: one toward the sexual division of labor. This obliged them to a sedentary mode of life, which, for men of so stout and roving a disposition, was lethal in effect. They were segregated,[272] concentrated on plantations and in large villages, in accordance with a criterion that was wholly foreign to tribes accustomed to a communal way of life, but who lived in small groups that were, moreover, exogamous and totemistic in character. What would have best suited these savages, thus snatched out of the jungle in their primitive state and subjected to the deleterious conditions of a sedentary life, was to let them wrestle with European tools; this would have been a mild form of manual labor that would not have been so exhausting as the other form they knew: work with a hoe; it would have prepared them for the transition from a savage to a civilized mode of existence.

The realization of such a transition should have been the great, the principal mission of the catechists. Through such a process much of the manual dexterity, artistic aptitude, and decorative talent of the Brazilian natives, which has been almost wholly lost, might have been preserved under new forms through the ample plastic resources of European technique. The truth of the matter is, however, that the Jesuits were dominated at times by a criterion that was exclusively religious, with the padres endeavoring to make of the *caboclos* docile and mellifluous seminarists; and at other times by one that was largely economic, with the missionaries making use of their Indian parishioners for mercantile ends, that they might enrich themselves as well as the colonists industrially and through the trade in mate, cacao, sugar, and drugs.

Champions of the Indians' cause, the Jesuits were in good part responsible for the fact that the treatment of American natives by the

---

[271] Copybooks written by hand, by Anchieta: "at that time still there were in these parts no copies of books by means of which the pupils might learn the precepts of grammar. This great need was charitably supplied by José [Anchieta], at the cost of his sweat and labor as he copied out by his own hand as many notebooks containing the said precepts as there were pupils to be taught. . . ." Vascon-

cellos: *Chrônica* (op. cit.), p. 118.

[272] Studies of the so-called "primitive mentality" show how painful it is for such individuals to be decisively separated from the physical environment of the region in which they live and to which they are bound by a set of mystic relations: totemistic and animistic. This equilibrium of mystical relations was broken by the segregation imposed by the Jesuits.

Portuguese was never so harsh and pernicious as that which the red man received from the English Protestants. But even so, the natives in this part of the continent were not treated fraternally or idyllically by the invaders, and even the Jesuits in their catechizing had resort to extreme and exceedingly cruel methods. It is from the mouth of one of them—and one of the most pious and saintly of them all, José de Anchieta—that I take these stern words: "the sword and the iron rod are the best kind of preaching." [273]

The attentions of the Brazilian Jesuit were most advantageously directed to the native child. Advantageously from the point of view by which the padre of the Society of Jesus was governed: that of dissolving in the savage, in as short a time as possible, any native value that was in serious conflict with the theology and morality of the Church. The eternal oversimplified criterion of the missionary, who never perceives the enormous risk involved, seeing that he will be incapable of repairing or finding a substitute for all that he destroys. Even today, the same oversimplification is to be seen in the English missionaries in Africa and in the Fiji Islands.[274]

The untutored Indian lad was taken out of savage life by the padre when he had no more than his milk-teeth with which to bite the intruding hand of this bringer of civilization, when he had as yet no definite code of morality and his tendencies were vague in character. He, it might be said, was the axis of missionary activity; it was out of this lad that the Jesuit was to fashion the artificial being so dear to his

---

[273] Cited by João Lúcio de Azevedo: *Os Jesuítas no Grão-Pará* (*The Jesuits in the Grão-Pará Region*) (2nd edition, Coimbra, 1930). [F. A. Kirkpatrick, in his *Latin America, A Brief History* (New York and Cambridge, England, 1939), p. 36, quotes Anchieta as saying: "Conversion must be the work of fear rather than love." This would seem to point to that "religious imperialism" of which Freyre speaks. (Translator.)]

[274] An oversimplification looked upon by Sir J. G. Frazer as "always dangerous and not seldom disastrous" is that which consists in abolishing ancient moral codes without assuring a real and not an artificial substitution.—Introduction to C. W. Hobey's *Bantu Beliefs and Magic* (London, 1922).—Wissler, also (*Man and Cul-*

ture, op. cit.), points out the disadvantages that result for savage populations from the good, moralizing, and civilizing intentions of missionaries, even when the latter are not anticipating the economic imperialism of the great capitalist countries.—And Pitt Rivers (op. cit.) writes: "the inevitable result of destroying all the old culture-forms and environmental conditions in the endeavor to impose too dissimilar a culture upon a people specialized by a long process of adaptation to particular conditions is actually to exterminate them." He adds: "It follows from this that all missionary endeavor among heathen and savage peoples . . . is incapable of achieving any result in the end except to assist in the extermination of the people it professes to assist."

heart. The civilizing process of the Society was largely an inverted one: that of having the son educate the father, of having the child serve as example to the man, of having the young ones lead their elders along the path of Our Lord—the path that was trod by Europeans.[275]

The *culumim*,[276] or Indian lad, became the accomplice of the invader in drawing the bones, one after another, from the native culture, in order that the soft portion might be the more readily assimilated to the patterns of Catholic morality and European life. He became the enemy of his elders, of the *pajés*, of the sacred cymbals and secret societies, of whatever was hard and virile in that culture and capable of offering a resistance, even if but a feeble one, to European compression. It was far from the padres to wish the destruction of the native race; what they desired was to see it at the feet of Our Lord, domesticated by Jesus. This, however, was not possible without breaking the backbone of that culture and morality which was the savage's own, of everything that was imbued with beliefs and superstitions difficult of assimilation to the Catholic system.

---

[275] "The first stratagem that they employed," writes Father Simão in speaking of the Jesuits, "even though it had to be accomplished through gifts and much petting, was to make of the Indian children household companions; for these latter, being less inattentive and more clever than the adults, in all the nations of Brazil, are more readily indoctrinated, and once the children have been indoctrinated, they in turn indoctrinate their parents. This was a stratagem which experience has shown to have been heaven-sent. . . ." Once they had been gathered in, the Indian young ones were taught by the Jesuits to "read, write, do sums, and aid in serving Mass, and were instructed in Christian doctrine as well; and those who were the most advanced would go through the streets intoning hymns, prayers, and the mysteries of the faith, composed in befitting style, with all of which the fathers were enormously delighted. . . . The Indians came to have an exaggerated opinion of these young ones, for they re-spected them as something sacred; no one dared do anything against their will, for the others believed what they said, and were convinced that some divinity had been lodged in them; and they even strewed with boughs the roads along which they passed."—Vasconcellos: *Chrônica* (op. cit.), p. 125.—On this subject Couto de Magalhães writes: "These children, when they grew up, were living schools, and inasmuch as they possessed an equal command of the two languages, they were the indispensable link in bringing the two races together."—*O Selvagem* (op. cit.).—On the catechistic and pedagogical methods of the first Jesuits, read also Pires de Almeida: *L'Instruction publique en Brésil* (Rio de Janeiro, 1889).

[276] This word, which still exists in modern Brazilian speech, has a number of forms: *culumin; culumi; curumí; curumim; curumbim*. Lima and Barroso (op. cit.) give *curumi* as the preferred form. The word now means, in general, a small boy, a lad, a servant. (Translator.)

The fathers of the Society strove, at times successfully, to turn the young ones away from this culture by rendering it ridiculous in the eyes of the catechumens. They did this in the case of the witch-doctor of whom Montoya tells us. The missionaries had persuaded the old fellow, a grotesque and twisted figure, to dance in the presence of the assembled young. It was a success. The Indian youths thought him absurd and lost the respect they formerly had held for the sorcerer, who from that time forth had to be satisfied with serving the padres as their cook.[277]

Possession of the *culumim* signified the preservation, in so far as possible, of the native race without the preservation of its culture. Meanwhile the Jesuits wished to go further and, in the hothouse atmosphere of the sixteenth-century schools or the Guaraní missions, to make unnatural individuals out of the aborigines, individuals who not only had no bond with the moral traditions of their own culture, but who were, in addition, cut off even from the colonial environment and the social and economic realities and possibilities of that environment. For this reason the educational and civilizing efforts of the Jesuits took on an artificial character, and later their system of organizing the Indians into missionary villages ("*aldeias*") or "missions" was unable to hold out against the powerful blows that were dealt it by the anti-Jesuit policy of the Marquis of Pombal.[278]

Even though artificially achieved, the civilizing of the aborigines of Brazil was almost exclusively the work of the Jesuit fathers; and the result of their labors was the Christianization, if superficial and on the crust alone, of a large number of caboclos.

This process of Christianization, I repeat, was accomplished through the Indian youth, the *culumim*, who played an extremely important part in the formation of Brazilian society, in the making of a Brazil that should be different from the Portuguese colonies in Africa, with an entirely different orientation from that of the African colonial administrations. Joaquim Nabuco, like Eduardo Prado an apologist for the Jesuit or, better, the Catholic missionary effort in Brazil, exaggerates little when he states: "Without the Jesuits, our

---

[277] He was an old witch-doctor named Ieguacarí. The padres had him dance in the presence of the children, who at first were frightened; but "little by little their fear passed, and finally they all came over to him, fell upon him, threw him to the ground, and mistreated him in every fashion." —Montoya, op. cit., p. 250.

[278] Pombal, iron-handed Portuguese Minister (1750–77), was the author of sweeping reforms. He decreed the Indians free men and provided for grants of land to them. The Indian villages in 1758 were wrested from the power of the Jesuits. (Translator.)

colonial history would be nothing other than a chain of nameless atrocities, of massacres like those of the Reservations (*Reduções*);[279] there would be roads throughout the country such as those that run from the heart of Africa down to the markets of the coast, and over these roads would pass long rows of slaves."[280]

In Brazil the missionary priest made use, chiefly, of the Indian lad in gathering from the latter's mouth the material out of which he formed the Tupí-Guaraní tongue, the most potent instrument of intercommunication between the two cultures, that of the invader and that of the conquered race. Not only moral intercommunication, but commercial and material as well. A tongue which, with all its artificiality, was to become one of the most solid bases of Brazilian unity. From now on, owing to the formidable pressure of the Jesuit missionary's religious imperialism and his tendency to standardize and render uniform moral and material values,[281] Tupí-Guaraní was to bring closer together native tribes and peoples, diverse and distant from one another in point of culture and even enemies in time of war; and later it was to bring them all nearer to the European colonizer. This language, formed by the collaboration of the *culumim* and the padre, was the one employed in the first social and commercial relations between the two races. It may be stated that the invaders made current use of the language of the conquered people, reserving their own tongue for restricted usage and state occasions. When later the Portuguese language—always the official one—came to predominate over the Tupí, becoming, alongside the latter, the idiom of the people, the colonizer by that time had become thoroughly imbued with the native jungle influence, his Portuguese had already lost the bite and hardness of that spoken in the Kingdom; it had been softened

---

[279] *Redução* (plural, *Reduções*) was the term applied to those places where the Indian converts were gathered, more or less forcibly ("reduced"), by the Jesuit missionaries. The "massacres" appears to be an allusion to assaults or aggressions upon these reservations by the *bandeirantes* or Paulistas. (Translator.)

[280] *III Centenário do Veneravel Joseph de Anchieta* (*Third Centenary of the Venerable Joseph de Anchieta*) (Paris and Lisbon, 1900).

[281] Ethnologists lament the fact that in Brazil "the Church exerted too great a leveling influence, blotting out the characteristic ethnic traits, traits peculiar to so many of the indigenous tribes and now extinct or on the verge of being extinguished. A mighty current swept away everything that it encountered in its path, spreading uniformity everywhere."— Emílio Goeldi: *O Estado Atual dos Conhecimentos sobre os Indios do Brasil*" ("The Present State of Knowledge Regarding the Indians of Brazil"), in the *Boletim do Museu Paraense de História Natural e Etnografia* (*Bulletin of the Natural History and Ethnographical Museum of Pará*), Vol. II, No. 4.

into a Portuguese without double *r*'s or double *s*'s—it had become infantile almost, the speech of a child, under the influence of the Jesuit's collaboration with the Indian lad.

The result was an initial duality of languages: the speech of the gentry and that of the natives, one the official, upper-class tongue, the other popular, for daily use. This was a duality that was to endure steadily for a century and a half and afterwards was to be prolonged under another guise: in the antagonism between the speech of the whites who lived in the Big Houses and that of the Negroes in the slave huts. Out of it all, meanwhile, there was to be left with us a linguistic vice which only today is being corrected or attenuated by our latest novelists and poets, and which is represented by the enormous void that exists between the written and the spoken language, between the Portuguese of university graduates, priests, those holding a doctor's degree, who are almost always prone to be purists, inclined to preciosity and classicism, and the Portuguese that is spoken by the people, by the former slave, by children, by the illiterate, the backwoodsman, and the *sertanejo*. The latter is still full of native expressions, while the speech of the ex-slave still glows with an African warmth.

This may be explained by the fact that the conquest of the backlands was achieved in the period when Tupí was the influential or predominant tongue. "The contingents that set out from the seaboard to make discoveries," writes Theodoro Sampaio, "generally spoke Tupí, and it was with Tupí names that they designated their fresh discoveries: rivers, mountains, and the very villages that they founded, which were merely so many new colonies scattered through the backlands, colonies whose inhabitants likewise spoke Tupí and who naturally took it upon themselves to spread the language."[282]

Almost all the animals and birds in Brazil, nearly all the rivers, many of the mountains, and a number of domestic utensils have retained their Tupí names. Father Antônio Vieira (who was so greatly concerned with problems having to do with the relations between the colonists and the natives), had this to say, in the sixteenth century: "In the first place, it is certain that the Portuguese and Indian families in São Paulo are today so bound to one another that the women and children mingle freely in the home; and the language that is spoken in the said families is that of the Indians, while the children go to school to learn Portuguese; and to destroy a unity that is so natural, or which has become so naturalized, would be a species of cruelty

---

[282] Theodoro Sampaio: *O Tupí* (op. cit.).

toward those who have lived together after this manner for so many years. I say, therefore, that all these Indians, and Indian women, who have so great a love for their so-called masters that they remain with them of their own free will—I say that they may do so without any obligation other than that of the said love, which is the gentlest of captors and the freedom that is most free." [283]

While in the homes Portuguese and Indians were "mingling freely," with the language of the slaves or semi-slaves predominant in domestic relations, in the missionary schools the language of the natives was being taught and cultivated alongside that of the whites and the churchly Latin, and in the pulpits preachers and evangelists were making use of the Tupí tongue. "The fathers spoke the language of the aborigines," Theodoro Sampaio tells us; "they wrote for it a grammar, compiled a vocabulary, and taught and preached in that idiom. In the schools for young boys and girls (the *curumins* and *cunhatains*,[284] offspring of Indians, mestizos, or whites) both Portuguese and Tupí were ordinarily taught, and in this manner the first catechumens, the most suitable ones, were prepared for bringing conversion to the paternal hearth." [285]

It was from the native child, as I have already said, that the padres gathered the material for the organization of the "Tupí language," result of the intellectual intercourse between catechist and catechumen. Through the Indian woman there was transmitted to Brazilian culture from that of the aborigines the better part of what remains to us of Amerindian values, while from the child there came to us the major portion of those moral elements which have been thus culturally incorporated: a knowledge of the tribal speech, of the various fears and superstitions with which the life of the red man was beset, and an acquaintance with his sports, games, and recreative dances.

Father Simão de Vasconcellos enlightens us in regard to the mode of intellectual intercourse adopted by the Jesuits in relation to the *culumim*. Thus, in speaking of Anchieta, he informs us that the latter was "at one and the same time Master and disciple"; and with reference to the Indian lads: "they served him as disciples and Masters"; for it happened that the padre, "while speaking Latin, in the same class was taking from the speech of his listeners the major part of the language of Brazil." [286]

[283] Cited by Taunay: *História Geral das Bandeiras* (op. cit.).

[284] The Indian girl, corresponding to the *culumim* (*curumí;* plural, *curumins*). Cf. the term for Indian woman: *cunhã*. (Translator.)

[285] Theodoro Sampaio: *O Tupí* (op. cit.).

[286] *Vida do Veneravel Padre Joseph de Anchieta da Companhia de Iesu*

In another sphere, also, the *culumims* were masters: the masters, the teachers, of their own parents, of their elders, of their people. They were the allies of the missionaries against the medicine-men in the work of Christianizing the heathen. Of the first of them to be brought by the Jesuits into their schools, the same Father Simão says: "At night they would scatter out to the houses of their parents, there to sing the pious canticles of Joseph [Anchieta] in his own tongue, in place of those vain and pagan songs that they had been accustomed to sing; and so· it was that they who were still disciples became Masters. . . ." [287]

E. Varnhagen comments on the emulation provoked among the heathen by the Jesuits with their processions of Christianized young Indians: "The first of these tamed *piás* [288] having been made acolytes, all the other young *caboclos* were envious of them, and the Jesuits made the most of this as their processions filed through the villages with upraised cross, intoning the litany, chanting prayers, and gathering many sheep for the fold; by all of which the parents at times felt greatly honored." [289] Father Américo Novaes has given us an account of one of these processions, based upon Southey, in which he pictures the scene for us in the liveliest of colors: white-clad children and adolescents, some bearing baskets of flowers, others vases of perfume, while still others carried censers, and all of them praised Jesus triumphant amid the chiming of the bell and the rumble of artillery.[290] Here were the future feasts of the Church, so Brazilian in character, with incense, cinnamon leaves, flowers, sacred songs, bands of music, fireworks, chiming bells, and *vivas* to Our Lord Jesus Christ—it was all here in embryo in these processions of *culumims*. This was a Christianity that, coming from Portugal and full of pagan survivals, was here being enriched with vociferous and sensual notes by way of seducing the Indian. Nobrega came to the conclusion that it was through music that the naked savage of the American jungle was to be drawn into the bosom of the Catholic Church; and through the impulse that he gave to music the venerable padre became, says Varnhagen, "something like a second Orpheus." [291]

The life of the catechumen was flooded with music. The Indian youths began singing early in the morning, blessing the names of

---

. . . *Composta Pello P. Siman de Vasconcellos* . . . (*Life of the Venerable Father Joseph de Anchieta of the Society of Jesus* . . . Composed by Father Simão de Vasconcellos) (Lisbon, 1672), p. 126.

[287] Ibid., p. 130.

[288] Endearing term for a young Indian or *caboclo*. (Translator.)

[289] F. A. Varnhagen: *História Geral do Brasil* (op. cit.).

[290] *III Centenário do Veneravel Joseph de Anchieta*, etc. (op. cit.).

[291] Varnhagen, op. cit.

Jesus and the Virgin Mary: "chanting in chorus: 'Blessed and praised be the most holy name of Jesus,' while the others would respond: 'and that of the blessed Virgin Mary, forever, amen.' And then all of them together, in the stately Latin of the Church: '*Gloria Patri & Filio & Spiritui Sancto, amen.*' " [292]

But these praisers of Jesus and the Virgin did not limit themselves to Portuguese or Latin, but lapsed into Tupí as well. At the sound of the Ave Maria, practically all the people would say in a loud voice, as they made the sign of the cross: *Santa Caruçá rangana recê*, and then each would repeat in his own tongue the evening prayer. It was in Tupí, also, that individuals greeted one another: *Enecoêma*, which means "good day." [293]

Out of this collaboration of the Jesuit fathers and the Indian youths Brazilian music and poetry were to spring. When later the "*modinha*" [294] made its appearance, it still preserved a certain gravity from the Latin of the Church, a certain pious and sentimental sweetness of the sacristy, by way of sugaring the eroticism, a certain mysticism of the padre's school, by way of cloaking a lasciviousness that was more African than Amerindian. From the first century, however, the astute compromise that was effected between the religious or Catholic-liturgical style and the native forms of song was clearly to be perceived. "In Brazilian lyric poetry of the era of colonization," notes José Antônio de Freitas, "the Jesuits . . . taught those forms that most resembled the songs of the Tupinambás, with refrains and the like, seeking in this manner to attract and convert the natives to the Catholic faith." And he adds: "In an age in which popular songs were forbidden by the Church, in an age in which the poetic feeling of the multitudes was completely suffocated and atrophied, the colonist by way of giving expression to the longing in his soul never tired of repeating those sacred compositions that the Jesuits authorized." [295] Thanks to the Emperor, Dom Pedro II, who obtained in Rome a copy of the quatrains written by the Jesuits for the young of their schools and missions in Brazil, we are familiar today with the following one, published by Taunay:

---

[292] Vasconcellos, op. cit., p. 130.

[293] Theodoro Sampaio: *O Tupí* (op. cit.).

[294] *Modinha*: "formerly, a variety of drawing-room ballad, in the vernacular; today, a variety of urban popular song" (Lima and Barroso, op. cit.). *Modinha* is a diminutive of *moda*: a "new song," one in the mode. (Translator.)

[295] José Antonio de Freitas: *O Lirismo Brasileiro* (*Brazilian Lyricism*) (Lisbon, 1873).

O Virgem Maria
Tupan ey êté
Aba pe ara pora
Oicó endê yabê.

Which translated means, according to Taunay: "O Virgin Mary, true Mother of God, the men of this world are indeed with thee." [296]

"The Jesuits," writes Couto de Magalhães, "did not collect the literature of the aborigines, but they did make use of their music and their religious dances by way of attracting them to Christianity. . . . The profoundly melancholy musical airs and the dance were taken over by the Jesuits and, with that deep knowledge of the human heart which is theirs, were adapted to the feasts of the Holy Spirit, St. Gonçalo, Holy Cross, St. John, and Our Lady of the Conception." [297]

There is another trait that characterized the first relations of the Jesuits with the young Indians, a trait that will appeal to one who estimates the missionary effort, not with the eyes of an apologist or sectarian of the Society, but from a Brazilian point of view, that of the fraternization of races: namely, the equal treatment that the padres would appear to have accorded, in their sixteenth- and seventeenth-century schools, to Indian and Portuguese children alike, Europeans and mestizos, *caboclos* snatched from their native villages, and young orphans who had come over from Lisbon. The chronicles do not show any discrimination or segregation due to race or color prejudice against the Indians; the regime adopted by the Jesuits seems to have been one marked by a fraternal mingling of their pupils. Thus the school established by Nobrega at Baía da Varnhagen was attended by children of the colonists, young Lisbon orphans, and the *piás* of the land.[298] Life in these schools must, then, have been a process of coeducation of the two races, the conqueror and the conquered, a process of cultural reciprocity between the sons of the soil and the young ones of Portugal. The patios of such establishments must have been a place where indigenous traditions met and mingled with the European, where there took place an interchange of games and playthings, of words in process of formation, and mestizo superstitions. The young Indian's *bodoque,* or double-stringed bow for hunting birds, the paper kite of the Portuguese children, the rubber ball, the dances, etc., here encountered one another. The *"carrapeta,"* or Bra-

---

[296] Affonso d'Escragnolle Taunay: *S. Paulo no Seculo XVI (São Paulo in the Sixteenth Century)* (Tours, 1921).

[297] *III Centenirio do Veneravel Joseph de Anchieta* (op. cit.).
[298] Varnhagen, op. cit.

zilian form of top, must have been the result of this childish interchange, as well as the papaya-reed flute and perhaps certain games
played with coconut shells and cashew nuts.

It is to be regretted that later, either as the result of a deliberate
orientation on the part of the missionaries or under the irresistible
pressure of circumstances, the padres had come to adopt the method
of rigorous segregation of the natives in *"aldeias"* (missionary villages) or missions. Apologists justify this by asserting that the sole
object of this segregation was to remove the Indians "from the de-
moralizing influence of lax Christians." [299] But the truth is that, as a

---

[299] J. M. de Madureira, S.J.: *A
Libertade dos Indios e a Companhia
de Jesús, sua Pedagogia e seus Re-
sultados (The Freedom of the Indi-
ans and the Society of Jesus, Its
Pedagogy and Its Results)* (Rio de
Janeiro, 1927), special volume of the
International Congress of American
History, Vol. IV.

"As for us," writes Canon Fernandes Pinheiro regarding the system
of the Jesuits, "the great mistake lay
in wholly annihilating the will of the
catechumens and neophytes and reducing them to the paltry role of
perambulating machines. Looking
upon the Indians as children who
stood in need of guidance if they
were not to fall headlong into abys-
mal vice, who had need of tutors if
they were not to dissipate their own
substance, the apostolic worthies who
first called them to the bosom of the
Church and civilization felt that they
themselves were the ones who should
be the guides, and in this they were
not wrong. However, carrying further the zeal that they had for the
spiritual family, they proceeded to
transmit so great a power as this intact to their successors, forgetting
that it was by its very nature a
precarious one and suited only to the
first phase of transition from a savage
to a civilized way of life. Hence
arose the abuse that we have mentioned; hence it was that the Indian
never possessed autonomy, never
thought of shaping his conduct in ac-

cordance with his own inspirations or
of assuming the responsibility for his
actions; and hence, finally, came the
total destruction of the work of the
catechism, which had appeared to be
prospering in so lively a fashion, the
moment the supporting arm of the
Jesuit was withdrawn."—Introduction to *Chrônica da Companhia de
Jesús do Estado do Brasil*, etc., by
Father Simão de Vasconcellos (2nd
edition, Rio de Janeiro, 1864). Read
the same author's "Essay on the Jesuits" in the *Revista do Instituto Histórico e Geográphico Brasileiro*, Vol.
XVIII.—To be read alongside those
essays on the Jesuits that are more or
less impregnated with apologetic fer-
vor are the ones by Joaquim Nabuco,
Eduardo Prado, and Theodoro
Sampaio; see also: Brazilio Machado:
*III Centeonário do Veneravel Joseph
de Anchieta* (Paris and Lisbon, 1900);
J. P. Calogeras: *Os Jesuitas e o Ensino
(The Jesuits and Education)* (Rio de
Janeiro, 1911); Eugénio Vilhena de
Moraes: *"Qual a Influência dos Jes-
uitas em nossas Letras?"* ("What has
Been the Influence of the Jesuits in
Our Literature?"), *Revista do Instituto
Histórico e Geográphico Brasileiro*,
special volume, Congress of National
History, Part V (Rio de Janeiro,
1917). For one of the few attempts at
historical criticism, see the *"Apunta-
mentos para a História dos Jesuitas,
Extrahidos dos Chronistas da Com-
panhia de Jesús"* ("Notes for the History of the Jesuits, Extracted from

consequence of the separation of the catechumens from social life, they became an artificial population, living apart from the colonial one, a stranger to the latter's necessities, its interests, and its aspirations; it was a population of grown-up children in a state of paralysis, men and women incapable of autonomous life and normal development. Nor did the fathers of the Society, once they had been transformed into masters of men, always remain faithful to the ideals of the first missionaries; many of them, on the contrary, lapsed into that mercantilism in which the violent Marquis de Pombal was to discover them.

When the period that Pires de Almeida regards as the heroic age of Jesuit activity in Brazil had passed, a number of the missions became little more than export warehouses, dealing in sugar and drugs, but chiefly in mate in the south and cacao in the north. This to the prejudice of the moral and even the religious culture of the natives, who were now reduced to a mere instrument for commercial exploitation. General Arouche, who in 1798 was named Director General of Indian Villages in Brazil, was to accuse the missionaries—the Jesuits as well as the Franciscans—"of promoting the marriage of Indians with black women and men, baptizing the offspring as slaves." [300] The feet of the good fathers must have slipped again: they must have yielded to the delights of the slave traffic just as they had to the pleasures of commerce. Had they not done so, they would not have been good Portuguese, possibly even good Semites, whose traditional tendency to trade and barter was not modified beneath the Jesuit's cassock nor by the vows of a seraphic poverty.

It may be added that, fleeing not only segregation and a sedentary

the Chroniclers of the Society of Jesus"), *Revista do Instituto Histórico e Geográphico Brasileiro*, Vol. XXXIV (Rio de Janeiro, 1871), by Antonio Henriques Leal. This author, incidentally, was the first to recognize the difficulty of "critically reflecting" upon the work of the Jesuits, inasmuch as "they themselves are the writers in the case and, as a consequence, there is a large amount of partiality and lack of verisimilitude."—On the organization of labor in the Jesuit missions in Brazil, see L. Captain and Henri Lorin: *Le Travail en Amérique avant et après Colomb* (Paris, 1930), Book IV, Chapter i. The recent works of Father Serafim Leite on the history of the Society of Jesus in Brazil are rich in valuable data; it is to be noted, however, that the material is presented from the point of view of an apologist for the Jesuits.

[300] Jose Arouche de Toledo Rendon: "*Memória sobre as Aldeias de Indios da Provincia de São Paulo*" ("Memoir on the Indian Villages of the Province of São Paulo"), *Revista do Instituto Histórico e Geográphico Brasileiro*, VI.—João Mendes, Jr.: *Os Indigenas no Brasil—Seus Direitos Individuais e Políticos (The Natives of Brazil—Their Individual and Political Rights)* (São Paulo, 1912).

mode of life, but the violence of the civilizers as well, practiced upon them even in the missionary villages,[301] many of the Christianized natives made for the jungle, "without a thought," says Arouche, "of the women and children they were leaving behind. . . ."[302] This was a situation that was to grow more acute when, once the powerful civilizing mechanism of the Jesuits had been dismounted, the Indians found themselves, on the one hand, in the light of the morality that had been imposed upon them, under the obligation of supporting their wives and children, and, on the other hand, faced by economic conditions that made it impossible for them even to support themselves. The exploitation of the native worker had been so systematized, to the benefit of the whites and the Church, that out of a daily wage of 100 reis the Indian of the missions received but the miserable sum of 33 reis a day.[303] What happened then was that many a Christianized *caboclo* family was broken up from lack of an economic base of support. Under such circumstances (bearing in mind the misery to which many of the artificially organized Christian homes had been reduced), the infantile death-rate increased and the birth-rate at the same time decreased, not alone from "lack of propagation," but as the result of the abortions that, in the absence of husbands and fathers, were practiced by women in whom the Christian scruples having to do with adultery and virginity had become decayed.[304] Whence it may be seen that the Jesuit system of catechizing and bringing civilization, by imposing upon the natives a new family morality without first setting up a permanent economic base, led to an artificial form of labor incapable of surviving the hothouse atmosphere of the missions and thereby contributed greatly to the degradation of the race it was supposed to save. It led to Brazil's being depopulated of its own autochthonous folk.

The methods connected with the mere capture of the native, not to speak of his later segregation and the forced or excessive labor at which he was put, on the plantations or in the missions, hastened this

[301] "The tyranny of the religious in the mission," writes Jõao Lúcio de Azevedo, "was perhaps not less than that of the master on the plantation." And he goes on to say: "there is no doubt that certain of the fathers were not as charitable as they should have been toward the neophytes. For slight offenses they would have them flogged or imprisoned; nor were even the *chiefs*, whom the prestige of their authority should have saved, exempt from humiliating punishments.—*Os Jesuítas no Grão-Para, suas Missões e a Colonização* (*The Jesuits in Grão-Para, Their Missions and* [*the Process of*] *Colonization*) (2nd edition, Coimbra, 1930).

[302] Arouche: Memoria (op. cit.).

[303] Ibid.

[304] João Lúcio de Azevedo, op. cit.

depopulation in an infernal manner. They were methods accompanied by a great loss of life, possibly greater than in the capture and transport of Africans. Speaking of the expeditions carried out in the Amazon region by way of supplying slaves or "help" (*administrados*) for the plantations of Maranhão and Pará, João Lúcio de Azevedo tells us that when these undertakings were successful, "only half arrived at their destination; one can imagine what happened in the case of the others." [305] And the historian reminds us of these words of Vieira: "However many they enslaved, there were always more who died. . . . A contributing factor here," he goes on to explain, "was the labor that the slaves had to perform on the plantations, especially the sugar plantations, which was too heavy for Indians unaccustomed to such continuous and back-breaking toil. In addition to the diseases that these inferior races always acquire upon contact with the whites, the ill treatment they received was a cause of illness and death, notwithstanding the laws against it that were repeatedly promulgated. With regard to the torture to which they were subjected, we have but to remember that it was the common practice to brand the captives with a hot iron in order to distinguish them from the freedmen, and also to enable their masters to recognize them." [306]

The wars waged by the Portuguese, with an obvious technical superiority on their side, by way of repressing or punishing the Indians likewise had much to do with the depopulation of the native stock.[307] The victors not infrequently displayed their superiority over the vanquished by tying the latter to the cannon's mouth and "scattering to great distances their dilacerated members." [308] Or else they would inflict upon them tortures taken from classical antiquity and adapted to conditions in the wilds of America. One of these methods, which had been employed by Tullus Hostilius, consisted in tying the victim to two fiery horses, then releasing the animals in opposite directions. In the far north of Brazil this horrible "punishment" was modified by substituting for the horses a couple of canoes to which the Indian was bound; the canoes being paddled away from each other, the unfortunate one's body was torn in two.[309] In Maranhão and in

---

[305] Ibid.

[306] Ibid.

[307] The depopulation would appear to have been enormous. It is difficult to state exactly what the aboriginal population of Brazil was at the time of the discovery, but there is evidence to the effect that it was relatively dense, "at least," as Azevedo says, "on the seaboard and along the banks of the rivers." The same point is made by M. Bomfim: *O Brasil na América* (op. cit.).

[308] Azevedo, op. cit.

[309] *Chrônica da Companhia de Jesús pelo Padre Jacinto de Carvalho*, manuscript in the Evora Library, in Azevedo, op. cit.

Pará[310] the cruelties practiced upon the natives were no less than those inflicted upon them by the Paulistas in the south. These latter had come to take upon themselves the "wars against the Indians" as a sort of macabre specialty.[311] The very government itself, as a means of raising funds for the building of churches,[312] would engage in the ransoming, or it might be the sale, of Indians who had been captured and brought from the backlands to the plantations under such conditions that only a half or a third of them arrived at the end of the journey.

Speaking of the effects of Indian slavery in Maranhão, João Lúcio de Azevedo informs us that the colonists, "absolutely given over to the exploitation of the Indian, were unable to do anything without him."[313] This in the second century of colonization. The same was true in the first century. The plantation-owner was a parasite on the Indian, and was in turn preyed upon by the royal functionary. The two of them were equally adept at the "conjugation of the verb *rapio*," to quote the words of the preacher in his celebrated sermon on Mercy.[314]

Everything depended upon the slave or the "help,"[315] whose good right arm was "the only wealth, the sole objective toward which the ambitions of the colonizers were directed."[316] And even this was a wealth that was readily corruptible owing to the unhygienic effects upon the slave of the new mode of life. The stationary and continuous labor and the diseases acquired through contact with the whites or through the forced or spontaneous adoption of their customs—diseases such as syphilis, smallpox, dysentery, and catarrhs—were working havoc with the Indians, impairing their blood-stream, their vitality, and their energy.

---

[310] *Memórias sobre o Maranhão* (*Memoirs on Maranhão*), by Father José de Moraes, in A. J. de Mello Moraes: *Chorographia* (*Chorography*) (Rio de Janeiro, 1859); João Francisco Lisboa: *Timon* (op cit.); Arouche: *Memória* (op. cit.); Father Antônio Vieira: *Obras Várias* (*Miscellaneous Works*) (Lisbon, 1856-7); Agostinho Marques Perdigão Malheiro: *A Escrividão no Brasil* (*Slavery in Brazil*) (Rio de Janeiro, 1866); J. J. Machado de Oliveira: "*Noticia Raciocinada sobre as Aldeias de Indios da Provincia de São Paulo* ("Rationalized Account of the Indian Villages in the Province of São Paulo"), in the *Revista do Instituto Histórico e Geográphico Brasileiro*, VIII.

[311] Perdigão Malheiro, op. cit.

[312] J. F. Lisboa: *Timon* (op. cit.).

[313] Azevedo, op. cit.

[314] The preacher in question was Father Antonio Vieira; see the edition of his sermons by J. M. C. Seabra and Q. Antunes: *Sermões*, (Lisbon, 1854-6). (Translator.)

[315] The word in the original is *administrado;* literally, one who is "administered" or governed. (Translator.)

[316] Antônio Vieira, cited by Azevedo, op. cit.

From São Paulo we have a document of 1585: "This land is in such straits that there is not to be found food to buy, an unheard-of thing up to now, and all this by reason of the fact that the inhabitants do not have the slaves to plant and harvest their crops." And we further learn that "in the 1580's a terrible epidemic of dysentery killed off thousands of captive Indians . . . more than two thousand head of slaves. . . ."[317]

These new diseases the Indians were inclined to attribute, and not without some reason, to the Jesuits. In certain places the natives would burn pepper and salt as an exorcism when the padres drew near.[318] It was all in vain, however. The slave-holding system on the one hand and the missionary on the other continued their work of racial devastation, even though it proceeded more slowly and was less cruel in character than in Spanish America or among the English in North America. And there were creative aspects to be set over against the destructive ones.

The tendency, representing a quasi-biological differentiation, of the Portuguese toward slavery—a differentiation that Keller compares to that of certain ants studied by Darwin[319]—found in the American Indian an easy prey. The number of Indians possessed by a colonist, whether under the name of "pieces" or disguised as "*administrados*," came to be an index of his power and social standing; these slaves became the capital with which he installed himself on the land (the value of the land itself being secondary). At the same time, each "piece" took the place of commodities or money; for debts were paid and provisions acquired with slaves or by "ransoming."[320] Copper-colored coins were later to be substituted for these "pieces of Guinea" —in reality, fleshly coins, all of them, coins that, being readily corruptible and subject to decay, constituted an uncertain, an unstable variety of capital. It was, accordingly, natural that the economic policy should be one marked by a greed for slaves, for Indians, for human beings that could be exchanged like coins; and it was likewise natural that this capital should have to be renewed, as old age, sick-

---

[317] Taunay: *São Paulo no Século XVI* (op. cit.)

["Two thousand head": the original has "*duas mil peças*," two thousand "pieces" (see below). (Translator.)]

[318] Vasconcellos: *Chrônica* (op. cit.), p. 65.

[319] Keller writes, of the Portuguese: "They were so given to the slave-

system that they could no longer provide for themselves. A biological differentiation of functions, as it were, had left them, like Darwin's slave-making ants, in a sort of parasitic relation to a subject race."—A. G. Keller: *Colonization* (New York, 1908).

[320] See the Acts of the Chamber of São Paulo.

ness, and failing strength produced their devastating effects upon the frailty of human flesh that at times had to take the place of the strongest metals. "The expenditure of human life here in Bahia these past twenty years (1583)," says one Jesuit cited by Taunay,[321] "is a thing that is hard to believe; for no one would believe that so great a supply could ever be exhausted, much less in so short a time." It was expended in labor, through abuses, in transport; it was expended in passing from one master's hand to another, like an inanimate object or a beast of burden. Alluding to the transition from the native slave to the one from Guinea (who, as we shall see further on, was to end by bearing almost alone, without the Indian's aid, the burden of labor on the plantations and in the mines), Father Cardim tells us that the plantation-owners were constantly in debt for the reason that "many slaves" died on their hands.[322] And the most killing labor of all, perhaps, was that connected with the raising of sugar-cane.

That the Indian slaves, as later the Africans, from the earliest times in Brazil, were the capital with which the whites set themselves up, many of the latter having come here without any resources whatsoever, is indicated by the following passage from Gandavo: "If a person comes to this land and contrives to get hold of a couple of them (even though he has nothing else that he can call his own), he then has a means of honorably supporting his family; for one of them will fish for him, another will hunt for him, and the others will cultivate and harvest his plantings; and in this way he is at no expense for food, either for them or for his family and himself." [323] And Father Nobrega makes it still more clear: "Those who come here find no other means of livelihood except through the labor of slaves, who fish for them and go in search of food; and so greatly are they ruled by sloth and so given are they to sensual things and vices of various kinds that they have no fear of being excommunicated for possessing the said slaves." [324]

The work demanded by the colonist of the Indian slave consisted in felling trees, transporting the timber to the ships, harvesting crops, hunting, fishing, defending his masters against enemy tribes and foreign corsairs, and guiding explorers through the virgin jungle. The aborigine was now finding what servile labor meant. He was no longer the free savage that he had been in the days before the Portuguese colonizers came; but still he had not as yet been uprooted from his

---

[321] História Geral das Bandeiras Paulistas (op. cit.).
[322] Cardim, op. cit., p. 320.
[323] Gandavo, op. cit. p. 119.
[324] Nobrega: Cartas, op. cit., p. 110.

physical and moral environment, from his primary, his elementary hedonistic interests: from hunting, fishing, making war, and from a mystic, one might say a sportive, contact with waters, wood, and animals. This uprooting was to come with an agrarian—that is to say, a latifundiary—form of colonization; it was to come with monoculture, represented chiefly by sugar. It was sugar that killed the Indian. It was to free him from the tyranny of the plantation that the missionary segregated him in villages, another method, if a less violent and more subtle one, of exterminating the Brazilian native: by preserving him in brine, but not allowing him to preserve his own proper and autonomous life.

The Indian, ill adapted to the needs of the new form of agrarian labor, became enveloped in the sadness of the introvert, and it was necessary that his place be taken by the Negro, who, with his youthful, tense, vigorous energy, his extroversion and vivacity, stood in marked contrast to the American savage. Not that the Portuguese of the sixteenth century encountered here a race that was weak and soft, incapable of any greater exertion than that of hunting birds with a bow and arrow and swimming lakes and deep rivers; the statements of the first chroniclers are all to the contrary. Léry emphasizes the great physical vigor of the aborigines, in felling enormous trees and carrying them to the ships on their bare backs.[325] Gabriel Soares describes them as individuals "well made and well set up"; [326] Cardim stresses their swiftness and endurance on long journeys by foot; [327] and the Portuguese who first surprised them, naked and naïve, on the shores discovered by Pedro Alvares speaks with enthusiasm of their robustness, their health and comeliness: "like birds or wild animals . . . their bodies could not be any cleaner, plumper, more vibrant than they are. . . ." This robustness and health he does not forget to associate with the mode of life and the diet followed by the savages, with the "air"—that is to say, the open air—"in which they grow up," and with "the yams, of which there are many here. . . . They do not till the earth nor breed cattle, nor are there here any oxen, any cows, any goats, any sheep, any hens, or other animals of any kind of the sort that one is accustomed to find about the habitations of men; nor do they eat anything but yams, of which there are many, and the seeds and fruits of the earth and of the trees that grow here; and with

---

[325] Léry, op. cit., pp. 122–3.
[326] Soares, op. cit., p. 306. He adds: ". . . good teeth, small and white, none of them ever decayed . . .

shapely legs, small feet . . . individuals of great strength."
[327] Cardim, op. cit.

all this, they are far more sleek and sturdy than are we for all the wheat and vegetables that we consume." [328]

If the Indians with such an appearance of good health broke down once they had been incorporated into the economic system of the colonizer, this was for the reason that the passage from a nomadic to a sedentary way of life, from sporadic to continuous activity, had been too abrupt for them; it was due to the fact that their metabolism had been disastrously modified by the new rhythm of economic life and physical exertion. Nor did the *cará* and the fruits of the earth any longer suffice for the diet of the savage subjected to slave labor on the sugar plantations. As a result, the Indian was to prove to be a sorry worker and an indolent one, and the Negro had to be substituted for him. The latter, coming out of a state of culture superior to that of the American native, was to show himself better adapted to Brazilian needs, to the necessity of intense and sustained physical exertion, as a stationary agricultural worker. He was a being of a different kind, adapted to agriculture. Moreover, his diet was to undergo little change in Brazil, many of the edible plants of Africa having been transplanted here, such as the kidney bean, the banana, and the okra; just as, from the Portuguese islands in the Atlantic, oxen, sheep, goats, and sugar-cane were brought to America.

So far as the aborigine's culture was concerned, it was, so to speak, the feminine part that was to be saved. As a matter of fact, in its more complex technical organization that culture was almost wholly feminine, the man confining himself to hunting, fishing, rowing, and making war. Activities of value, but of secondary worth for the new economic organization, an agrarian one, set up by the Portuguese in these American lands. What the Portuguese system basically needed was the worker with a hoe for the sugar plantations. A worker firmly attached to the soil and settled in his mode of life.

In the case of cultures with interests and tendencies that were so antagonistic, it was natural that contact between them should result to the disadvantage of each. Only a special combination of circumstances in the case of Brazil prevented the Europeans and the natives from becoming deadly enemies, before they had come together as man and wife, as master and disciple, a form of contact that was to lead to a cultural degradation through processes that were more subtle, marked by a slower rhythm, than in other parts of the continent.

Goldenweiser calls attention to the fate of the Mongols subjected

---

[328] Pero Vaz de Caminha: Letter published by Manuel Ayres de Cazal: *Chorographia Brasílica* (op. cit.).

to Russian rule; and the same goes for the Amerindians, the natives of Australia, Melanesia, Polynesia, Africa—always the same drama: the backward cultures disintegrating beneath the yoke or pressure of the more advanced ones. What kills off primitive peoples is the loss, as it were, of their will to live, the loss of an "interest . . . in their own values," as Goldenweiser puts it,[329] once their environment has been altered and the equilibrium of their lives has been broken by civilized man. Of the primitives of Melanesia, W. H. R. Rivers had previously written that they were "dying from lack of interest."[330] Dying of "*banzo*,"[331] of melancholy. Or sometimes they even kill themselves, like those Indians whom Gabriel Soares observed going about with emaciated and swollen bodies: the devil had appeared to them and set them to eating earth until they died.

Even so, of all the American countries Brazil is the one where native culture values have been saved to the largest extent. Portuguese imperialism—the religious imperialism of the padres, the economic imperialism of the planters—from the time of its first contact with the indigenous culture, struck the latter a death-blow. It did not strike it down suddenly, however, with the fury displayed by the English in North America, but gave it time to perpetuate itself in the form of a number of useful survivals. Although a perfect intercommunication between its cultural extremes has not been achieved in Brazil—extremes that are still antagonistic and at times explosively so, clashing with one another in such intensely dramatic conflicts as that of Canudos—none the less, we may congratulate ourselves upon an adjustment of traditions and tendencies that is rare among peoples whose social formation has taken place under the same circumstances of modern imperialist colonization in the tropics.

The truth is that in Brazil, contrary to what is to be observed in other American countries and in those parts of Africa that have been recently colonized by Europeans, the primitive culture—the Amerindian as well as the African—has not been isolated into hard, dry, indigestible lumps incapable of being assimilated by the European social system. Much less has it been stratified in the form of archaisms and ethnographic curiosities, but rather makes itself felt in the living, useful, active, and not merely picturesque presence of elements that have a creative effect upon the national development. Neither did the social relations between the two races, the conquering and the in-

---

[329] Alexander Goldenweiser: "Race and Culture in the Modern World," *Journal of Social Forces*, Vol. III, No. 1 (November 1924), pp. 127–36.

[330] Rivers, in Goldenweiser, loc. cit.
[331] Term applied to "the mortal nostalgia of African Negroes."—Lima and Barroso, op. cit. (Translator.)

digenous one, ever reach that point of sharp antipathy or hatred the grating sound of which reaches our ears from all the countries that have been colonized by Anglo-Saxon Protestants. The friction here was smoothed by the lubricating oil of a deep-going miscegenation, whether in the form of a free union damned by the clergy or that of regular Christian marriage with the blessing of the padres and at the instigation of Church and State.

Our social institutions as well as our material culture were suffused with Amerindian influence, as later with that coming from Africa. Even our laws were contaminated by it, not directly, to be sure, but subtly and indirectly. Our "juridical benignity" has been interpreted by Clovis Bevilaqua as a reflex of the African influence.[332] A certain characteristically Brazilian mildness in the punishment of the crime of theft possibly reflects the special compromise that the European had to make with the Amerindian, the latter being almost wholly insensitive to the notion of this crime by reason of his communistic mode of life and economy.[333]

There are a number of characteristic complexes in our modern Brazilian culture that are purely, sometimes strikingly, of Amerindian origin: the hammock; manihot; the river bath; the cashew nut; the *"bicho"; "coivara,"* or the burning over of the land; the *"igara"* (small boat or canoe); *"moquem,"* or the roasting of fish over the coals; the turtle; the *bodoque,* or double-stringed bow for shooting clay pellets at birds; wild-coconut oil; the *"caboclo's* hut"; Indian corn; the habit of resting or defecating while squatting on one's heels; [334] the gourd used as a container for flour; the porringer-bowl; the coconut drinking-cup; etc. There are others that are chiefly of native origin: the

---

[332] Cited by J. Izidoro Martins, Jr.: *História do Direito Nacional (History of National Law)* (Rio de Janeiro, 1895).

[333] In what he terms "internal public law" among the aborigines, Bevilaqua finds "almost no repression of theft . . . a tribal communism with an absolute absence of territorial jurisdiction," penalties inflicted upon women for adultery, as a matter of reprisal, family vengeance, etc. "*Instituições e Costumes Jurídicos dos Indígenas Brasileiros no Tempo da Conquista*" ("Juridical Institutions and Customs among the Brazilian Aborigines at the Time of the Conquest"), in Martins, op. cit.

[334] Euclides da Cunha mentions the *sertanejo's* constant habit of squatting down on his heels to rest a moment, to converse with someone, or to light his cigarette: "And if in the course of his walk he pauses for the most commonplace of reasons, to roll a *cigarro,* strike a light, or chat with a friend, he falls—'falls' is the word—into a squatting position and will remain for a long time in this unstable state of equilibrium, with the entire weight of his body suspended on his great toes, as he sits there on his heels with a simplicity that is at once ridiculous and delightful."—*Os Sertões,* 16th edition, pp. 114–15; *Rebellion in the Backlands,* p. 89.

habit of going barefoot;[335] *"moqueca,"* or fish stew; the use of red paint; pepper; etc. This is not to speak of tobacco or of the rubber ball, which is in universal use and which is of Indian, probably Brazilian Indian derivation.

The influence of Amerindian culture is also to be seen in the custom, which is very Brazilian, especially in the interior of the country and in the *sertão,* of keeping the women and children out of the sight of strangers. This, as pointed out by Karsten,[336] is due to the belief that they are more exposed than men to evil spirits. Among the *caboclos* of the Amazon region, Gastão Cruls recently noted that the women and children are always "sheltered from the gaze of strangers."[337]

---

[335] This native custom was adopted by the first colonists. Referring to the colonists and to the padres, Anchieta writes: "It is the custom of the country to go barefoot, and they do not find labor so grievous as in Europe, and this is true of the richest and most honored of the land."—*Informações e Fragmentos do Padre Joseph de Anchieta, S.J., 1584–1586* (op. cit.).

[336] Op. cit.

[337] Gastão Cruls, op. cit.—Silvio Romero and João Ribeiro thus sum up the Amerindian contribution to Brazilian culture: To the Indians our people of today owe—especially in those regions where the greatest amount of racial crossing took place, as is the case in the center, the north, the east, the west, and even in the south of the country—much of their knowledge and many of the implements having to do with hunting and fishing; various edible and medicinal plants; many of the words current in our language; many local customs; a few phenomena of popular mythology; a number of plebeian dances; and a certain influence upon anonymous poetry, particularly in connection with the cycle of cowboy ballads (*romances de vaqueiros*) quite common in the backlands region of the north, in the famous drought zone, between Paraguaçú and Parnaíba, the ancient fatherland of the Cariris."—

Compêndio da História da Literatura (Compendium of Literary History) (2nd edition, revised, Rio de Janeiro, 1909).

Affonso Claudio, in his paper on "The Three Races in Colonial Society—the Social Contribution of Each One," states that in the formation of Brazilian society the aborigine contributed: (1) his arm, which was one of the implements of colonial labor; (2) an acquaintance with the streams in the interior of the country, streams that he navigated, and with the forests that bordered them, where he was always the guide on industrial and scientific expeditions and religious missions; (3) the divulgation of those vegetables and their products suited to alimentary purposes, such as manihot flour, the drink known as *cauim* and the vessel that contained it (*cauaba*), nuts and wild chestnuts; (4) the process of extracting from roots, fruits, oils and leaves, lianas, and flowers therapeutic properties unknown to Europeans; (5) instruction in the handling of the bow and arrow, the lasso, and traps for fishing and hunting, such as the *mundéu,* the *fojo,* the *jequiá,* along with the process of catching fish with poison (*tingui*); (6) words from his dialectical vocabulary to designate things for which there are no corresponding expressions in the Portuguese and African languages; (7) instruction in the preparation of the *coivara*, the steering of canoes on rivers and lakes, the manner of carrying them over rapids and waterfalls; (8) the application to domestic use and for purposes of clothing of textile fibers, lianas, and taquara cane; (9) the weaving of hammocks for sleeping and of fishing-nets, the mode of fashioning the tu-cum-palm net, and the use of the fish-spear or harpoon; (10) the method of preparing ticuna (curare) or curape." —*Revista do Instituto Histórico e Geográphico Brasileiro*, Special volume, Vol. III (1927).

Among other Tupí words that have been preserved in our language, Theodoro Sampaio mentions the following: *arapuca* (bird-trap), *pereba* (abscess or ulcer), *sapeca* (a drubbing), *embatucar* (to nonplus someone or to be nonplused), *tabaréu* (back-countryman), *pipoca* (grain of corn roasted in the fire), *tetéia* (a "nice" person or thing), and *caipira* (inhabitant of the open country, rustic), all in current use in Brazil.— "S. Paulo de Piratininga no Fim do Século XVI" ("São Paulo de Piratininga at the End of the Sixteenth Century"), *Revista do Instituto Histórico e Geográphico Brasileiro*, Vol. IV.

III

THE PORTUGUESE COLONIZER:
ANTECEDENTS AND PREDISPOSITIONS

VARIOUS points that I touched upon lightly in the first chapter of this book I shall here treat with greater emphasis, by way of portraying the figure of the Portuguese colonizer of Brazil. A vague figure, lacking in the contours and the color that would individualize him among modern imperialists. In certain respects he resembles the Englishman, in others the Spaniard. A Spaniard without the warlike flame or the dramatic orthodoxy of the conquistador of Mexico and Peru; an Englishman without the harsh lineaments of the Puritan. The compromiser type. With no absolute ideals, with no unyielding prejudices.

The terrible slave-driver, who came near transporting from Africa to America, in filthy vessels that could be recognized from afar by their stench, an entire population of Negroes, was, on the other hand, the European colonizer who best succeeded in fraternizing with the so-called inferior races. He was the least cruel in his relations with his slaves. This, it is true, was in good part owing to the impossibility of setting up a European aristocracy in the tropics; the human capital was insufficient; if there was no shortage of men, white women were few in number. But independently of the lack or scarcity of women of the white race, the Portuguese always was inclined to a voluptuous contact with the exotic woman. For purposes of racial crossing, miscegenation. A tendency that appears to have been due to the greater social plasticity of the Portuguese as compared with any other European colonizer.

No one was less rigid in contour, less harsh in the lineaments of his character. Which accounts for the fact that he lent himself to so many and such profound deformations. It is not any "black legend" such as that huge, sinister one that confers prestige upon, even as it blackens, the figure of the Spanish conquistador—it is not any legend of this sort that envelopes the Portuguese colonial, but rather a clinging tradition of ineptitude, stupidity, and salaciousness.

Deformation of the naturally Gothic, vertical countenance of the

185

Castilian resulted in the El Greco-ish type.[1] A morbid elongation. An "ironlike austerity" exaggerated to the point of cruelty. Pride that has become quixotic rodomontade. Bravery become bravado. But with the angular nobility of the whole preserved. Deformation in the case of the Portuguese, on the other hand, was always in a horizontal direction. A flattening out. A rounding out. Flesh exaggerated into fat. His economic realism rounded out into mercantilism, avarice, a crude materialization of all of life's values. His cult of the dark Venus, as romantic in origin as that of his blonde virgins,[2] disfigured into a vulgar eroticism: the fury of a Don Juan of the slave huts become a reprobate chaser of Negro women and girls.

It is not through a study of the modern Portuguese, so spotted with decay, that one may succeed in forming an exact and balanced idea of the colonizer of Brazil—the Portuguese of the fifteenth and sixteenth centuries, his energies still verdant, his character debased by no more than a century of corruption and decadence. This it was that led Keyserling to conclude that he was essentially a plebeian and to deny him, almost, the quality of an imperial people. But even if this plebeianism were characteristic of the Portuguese of today, it certainly was not true of the Portuguese of the fifteenth and sixteenth centuries. Without ever achieving the aristocratic refinement of the Castilian, he anticipated the European bourgeois. But his precociously bourgeois character was to suffer in Brazil a serious set-back in view of the physical conditions of the country and the state of native culture; and the people that, according to Herculano, had hardly known feudalism [3] was to retrogress, in the sixteenth century, to the feudal era, by reviving aristocratic methods in the colonizing of America. Something like a compensation or rectification of its own history.

The colonization of Brazil proceeded aristocratically—more than in any other part of the Americas. In Peru there must have been a greater scenographic brilliance, more of formal ostentation and of the accessories of European aristocracy. Lima came to have four thousand carriages rolling through its streets, and within them, magnificent and useless, hundreds of Spanish grandees. Forty-five families of marquises and counts alone. But where the European colonizing process asserted itself as essentially aristocratic was in the north of Brazil. Aristocratic, patriarchal, slave-holding. The Portuguese here made himself master of lands more vast and men more numerous than any other American

---

[1] *Grecóide:* literally, "El Greco-ish." (Translator.)
[2] See Chapter i, p. 12.
[3] Alexandre Herculano: *História de Portugal*, op. cit.; *Controvérsias e Estudos históricos* (*Controversies and Historical Studies*) in the series *Opúsculos* (Lisbon, 1887).

colonizer. Had he been essentially plebeian, he would have failed in that aristocratic sphere in which his colonial dominion in Brazil was to develop. He did not fail, but instead founded the most modern civilization in the tropics.

There is much to be discounted in the pretensions to greatness on the part of the Portuguese. Since the end of the sixteenth century he has lived parasitically on a past whose splendor he exaggerates. Imagining that his stature is diminished or negated by foreign criticism, he has artificialized himself into a Portuguese-for-English-eyes,[4] but the English have been the most perspicacious of all in portraying him from the life, restoring to him his precise contour and coloring. Some of them have done so in admirable books, such as those of Beckford and Bell, others in stupidly realistic drawings or watercolors like those of Kinsey, Bradford, and Murphy. Already in the sixteenth century Buchanan was satirizing him in Latin verses. Satirizing the mercantile, rather than imperial, grandeur of his King:

> Thou art the incomparable Lusitanian,
> The Algarvio [5] of here and beyond the sea,
> Arab, Indian, Persian, and man of Guinea;
> Great lord of African lands,
> Of Congo, Manicongo, and Zalofo.

And then, prophetically anticipating the disastrous effects of official mercantilism, the British man of letters continues:

> But if, some day, before the king of names
> War or the sea, inflamed with fury, should arise
> And shut his pepper shop,
> Well may he feed himself upon that fame
> Won by his traffickings in lands across the deep! . . .
> He will be weighted down with debts,
> Or die of hunger.[6]

And this was what happened, once the Asiatic sources of opulence had been shut off. Far from resigning itself to the honest poverty of a nation fallen into decay—as later Holland was to do when, after being mistress of a vast empire, she devoted herself to the making of cheese and butter—Portugal, after Alcacer Quibir, went on imagining

---

[4] Português-para-inglês-ver.
[5] Inhabitant of the province of Algarve; comes to mean a boaster.
[6] The Portuguese version given by Freyre is from the translation by M. Gonçalves Cerejeira, "today Cardinal Patriarch of Lisbon, published in his excellent study, O Humanismo em Portugal—Clenardo (Humanism in Portugal—Clenardus) (Coimbra, 1926)." (Translator.)

itself to be the opulent land of Dom Sebastiano's lifetime. It went on feeding upon the fame acquired by its overseas conquests. Went on deluding itself with an imperial mysticism that no longer had any base. Went on poisoning itself with delusions of grandeur. "They sing the praises of Lisbon with such an abundance of words as to make it appear equal to the principal cities of the world, and for this reason they are accustomed to say: 'He who hasn't seen Lisbon hasn't seen anything worth seeing.'" So wrote Trom and Lippomani, the Venetian ambassadors, at the end of the sixteenth century. And they add: "The lower classes love to be addressed as 'Senhor,' a custom that is common throughout Spain." [7]

From the sixteenth century down to the present time the Portuguese has more and more tended to simulate those European and imperial qualities which he possessed or incarnated for so brief a period. The Portuguese people live by making themselves believe that they are powerful and important. That they are supercivilized in the European manner. That they are a great colonial power. Bell observes of the Portuguese at the beginning of the twentieth century that their ideals of national aggrandizement continue to vary between "the construction of a fleet" and "the conquest of Spain." [8] Switzerland might go on condensing its milk and Holland making its cheeses, but Portugal continued to stand on tiptoe in an effort to appear to be one of the great European powers.

For such exaggerations as these Keyserling, with his impressionistic method, is unable to make sufficient allowances; instead he reduces the Portuguese to a people without any greatness whatsoever: a nation something like an Andorra or a San Marino. An operatic republic where all the men go about addressing one another as "Doctor" and "Your Excellency." He diminishes the importance of the creative role they played in the fifteenth and sixteenth centuries, as manifested not alone in the technique of navigation and shipbuilding, but in the boldness of their discoveries and conquests, in the wars that they waged in Africa and India, in their rich travel literature, and in their efficiency as imperial colonizers. The only thing that he leaves them in the way of originality is their popular or plebeian music and the great hatred that they have for the Spaniard. A hatred that is likewise plebeian.

It was this hatred or antagonism toward the Spaniard that made and kept the Portuguese an autonomous being. An independent one. But rather than this hatred for the Spaniard which Keyserling

---

[7] Alexandre Herculano: *Opúsculos* (op. cit.).   [8] Aubrey F. G. Bell: *Portugal of the Portuguese* (op. cit.).

stresses, there was another, perhaps deeper and more creative, that had its effect upon the character of the Portuguese, predisposing him to nationalism and even to imperialism. This was his hatred for the Moor. Practically the same hatred that was later to be manifested in Brazil, in the wars against the buggers [9] and the heretics. Chiefly the heretics—the common enemy against whom dispersed and even antagonistic energies were united. Jesuits and planters. Paulistas and Bahians. Without this huge common scarecrow, a "consciousness of the species" [10] would possibly never have been evolved among groups so distant from one another, so lacking in political ties, as were the first foci of Lusitanian colonization in this country. Moral and political unification was in good part achieved through the solidarity of the different groups against heresy, a heresy now incarnated by the Frenchman, now by the Englishman, and now by the Dutch; at times simply by the bugger.

There was repeated in America, among the Portuguese scattered over so vast a territory, the same process of unification that had occurred in the peninsula: Christians against Moors. Our Indian wars were never wars of whites against redskins, but of Christians against buggers. Our hostility to the English, French, and Dutch always had the same character of a religious prophylactic: Catholics against heretics. The padres of Santos who in 1580 treated with the English corsairs of the *Minion* did not manifest against the latter any harsh rancor, but were mild-mannered toward them. Their hatred, to repeat, was prophylactic. It was a hatred of sin and not of the sinner, as a theologian would say. The sin, the heresy, the infidelity that could not be permitted to come into the colony. It was not a hatred of the foreigner as such. It was the infidel whom they were treating as an enemy in the person of the aborigine, and not the individual of a different race or color.

Bryce touches upon this religious direction in the social formation of Hispanic America. "Religion has been in the past almost as powerful a dissevering force as has racial antagonism," he writes, adding: "In the case of the Spaniard and the Portuguese, religion, as soon as the Indians had been baptized, made race differences seem insignificant." [11] Especially—he might have said—in the case of the Portuguese, who were still less conscious of race than were the Spaniards. The

---

[9] See p. 124. (Translator.)

[10] I make use here of the well-known sociological expression created by my former teacher at Columbia University, Professor Franklin Giddings.

[11] James Bryce: *South America— Observations and Impressions* (London, 1911).

latter had a greater sense of Catholic orthodoxy than the Portuguese, a sterner feeling with regard to punishment; but in either case there remained from the struggle against the Moors a prophylactic hatred of the heretic.

At bottom this religious purism, like the most modern and characteristically Anglo-Saxon or Teutonic purism of race, almost always originates in and feeds upon economic antagonisms. Nothing other than economic in essence were those wars between the Christians and the Moors out of which was to come the ardent nationalism of the Portuguese. If I consider the matter from the religious aspect, it is that we are here less concerned with essential motives than with mystical form. João Lúcio de Azevedo has observed: "In the reconquest the principal basis was not religion, nor was it race." [12] And in his study of "Economic Organization" he strikes the same note: in the wars of reconquest Moors and Christians were indiscriminately dispossessed and enslaved. As a consequence: "Christians at times fought against those of their own faith, alongside the Saracens, thus defending the possession of their property and their freedom." It may be stated that in these cases dispossession and enslavement resulted to the advantage not so much of the old Hispano-Romans as to that of certain elements that were "in origin foreign to the soil, as much as the Saracens could possibly have been." [13]

A large majority of these elements were new to the peninsula; they were foreign-comers. Blond adventurers out of the north who took advantage of the wars or crusades against the infidels to set themselves up as a propertied class, thanks to the pleasing legend of Christian reconquest. The truth is that this adventurous element very often found its initial capital in the Mozarabic war-captive, who was, of course, a Christian; and it was the cattle, land, and other possessions of these coreligionists, as well as those of the infidels, that they appropriated.

It is on the mystic-religious side, however, that the reconquest movement takes on definite form. As a movement of Christians against unbelievers. "When it came to applying a designation to the inhabitant of the peninsula who was free of the yoke of Islam, there was but one, that of *Christians*," Alexandre Herculano tells us [14] in speaking

---

[12] João Lúcio de Azevedo: "*Algumas Notas Relativas a Pontos de História Social*" ("Some Notes Relative to Points of Social History"), in *Miscelânea de Estudos em Homenagem de D. Carolina Michaëlis de Vasconcellos (Miscellaneous Studies in Homage to . . .*) (Coimbra, 1930).

[13] Azevedo: "*Organização Econômcia*," in *História de Portugal*, ed. monumental, Vol. III (Barcelos, 1931).

[14] Introduction to *O Bobo* (*The Buffoon*), era of Dona Thereza, 1128 (Lisbon, 1897).

of the warring epoch that preceded the organization of the Portuguese and Spaniards into nations. "The epithet that indicated the form of belief was representative of nationality." This was true only after the people had become politically defined; but meanwhile the religious bond or imprint was not wholly lost, at least not for long centuries after the reconquest.

The popular expression, today an ironic one: "*Vá queixar-se ao Bispo*" ("Go tell it to the Bishop")—an expression employed after appeals to the police, the government, and courts of justice have been exhausted—is a survival of the old idea, historically imbedded in the peninsular mind, that ecclesiastical prestige was greater than that of the civil authorities. Especially in Spain. In Brazil this prestige was not to be so great. The conditions attendant upon colonization, created by the political system of hereditary *capitânias* and maintained by the economic regime of allotments and large-scale agriculture, were decidely feudal in character; and if there was an attitude of superiority to governments and the King's justice, it was shown in the abuse of the right of asylum on the part of the big plantation-owners; the blame did not lie with the cathedrals and monasteries. The criminal or fugitive slave who sought the aid of a planter was certain of being freed from the wrath of courts and the police. Even if, in captivity, he was merely passing in front of the Big House, he had but to cry out: "Help me, Colonel[15] So-and-So," and cling to the gate or one of the near-by posts; just as in Portugal, in the old days, the criminal who took refuge in the shadow of the churches escaped the rigor of royal justice.

The Portuguese churches went so far as to become a scandal in the matter of the protection they accorded to criminals, thereby anticipating the abuses of the patriarchal plantations of Brazil. The plantation owned by Dona Francisca do Rio Formoso in Pernambuco, for example, and that of Machado da Boa Vista in Bahia.[16]

In the sixteenth century, canonical discipline combined with the royal authority (Affonso V) in restricting the conditions of asylum in the Portuguese churches; just as later in Brazil, the Emperor, Dom

---

[15] "Colonel" (*coronel*): title applied to plantation-owners; cf. our "Kentucky colonel." On the "colonels" in the land of cacao, in southern Bahia, during the turn-of-the-century cacao-rush, see Jorge Amado: *Terras do sem fim* (*The Violent Land*), *passim*. (Translator.)

[16] Dona Joaquina de Pompeu, of Paracatú (Minas Geraes), would appear to have been of the same matriarchal mold, so to speak, as Dona Francisca do Rio Formoso (who was one of the Wanderley family). Dona Joaquina was the mistress of great estates and, when her husband fell ill, became the "man of the house."

Pedro II, was to attempt to limit the omnipotence of the planters, who very often sheltered assassins. Through the limits imposed on the churches in seventeenth-century Portugal,[17] we are afforded a glimpse of the disorderly conduct that went on inside them, on the part of those who had sought shelter there. These refugees would stage feasts, would stand in the doorway or in the churchyard strumming their guitars, would gamble and indulge in obscene talk, and would make contacts with women of shady character. The boldest of them would eat, drink, and sleep on the high altar itself.

In Brazil the place of the cathedral or church, more powerful than the King, was taken by the plantation Big House. Our society, like that of Portugal, was shaped by a solidarity of ideals or religious faith, which with us made up for the laxness of political or mystic ties and the absence of race consciousness. But the church that affected our social development, serving to articulate our society, was not the cathedral with its bishop, to whom those disabused of secular justice might have resort, nor was it the isolated church, standing alone, nor the monastery or abbey to which criminals might flee and where the destitute might go for a few crumbs of bread. It was the plantation chapel. We did not have a clericalism in Brazil. The fathers of the Society of Jesus made a start in this direction, but their efforts went up in smoke when the padres were overcome by the oligarchic nepotism of the big landowners and masters of slaves.

The Jesuits felt from the beginning that the planters were their great and terrible rivals. But the other clergy, including the friars, grew big-bellied and soft in fulfilling the functions of chaplains, ecclesiastical tutors, priestly uncles, and godfathers to the young ones, and they proceeded to accommodate themselves to the comfortable situation of members of the family or household, becoming allies and adherents of the patriarchal system. In the eighteenth century many of them even lived in the Big Houses. This, indeed, was contrary to the counsels of the Jesuit Andreoni, who perceived in this intimacy a danger that the padres would become subservient to the lords of the manor, and the peril, also, of too much contact—he does not state this clearly, but hints at it—with Negro women and mulatto girls. As he saw it, the chaplain ought to conduct himself as a "member of God's

---

[17] These limits were imposed by Affonso V, in accordance with canonical law. From the Constitutions of the Bishopric of Porto, laying down conditions of churchly asylum that were not so mild, we may form an idea of the abuses in question. See the excerpt from the *Constituições* quoted by A. A. Mendes Corrêa: *A Nova Antropologia Criminal* (*The New Criminal Anthropology*) (Porto, 1931).

household, not that of another man"; he ought to dwell alone, out-side the Big House; and he should have as his servant some old Negro woman.[18] This was a norm that would appear to have been but rarely followed by the vicars and chaplains in colonial times.

In certain interior regions of Pernambuco there are malice-inspired traditions that would attribute to the plantation chaplains of old the useful, if not at all seraphic, function of procreators. Over this point we shall have to tarry later on, and, I trust, without malice or in-justice toward the Brazilian cleric of the days of slavery. If, when not wearing a Jesuit's cassock, he was never noted for his asceticism or his orthodoxy, he always distinguished himself by his Brazilianism. Throughout a certain epoch the torch of culture and of civic con-sciousness was in his hands, until the bachelors of arts and doctors of the law came to take the lead, under the protection of Pedro II. The latter, everything goes to show, would have preferred the title of doctor to that of emperor; he would have preferred the scholar's gown to the cloak with the toucan's maw.[19]

In the absence of a feeling or consciousness of racial superiority such as is so prominent in the English colonizers, the Brazilian fell back upon the criterion of faith. In place of his blood-stream, it was his faith that was to protect him against any taint of infection or con-tamination with heresy. He made of his orthodoxy a condition of political unity. But this criterion of prophylaxis and selection, so legitimate in the light of the ideas of the time, is not to be confused with the eugenic standard of modern peoples; it is not to be confused with pure xenophobia.

Handelmann makes of the Portuguese colonizer of Brazil almost a xenophobe by nature.[20] But the colonizer's antecedents contradict this, and the history of Lusitanian law—in this respect the most liberal of European codes—constitutes a denial of it. That body of law was so liberal that there never figured in it a provision whereby the State might seize the property of foreigners who had died within its bounds, to the exclusion of heirs and legatees (the law of *albinagio*); nor one by which the State might deduct a quarter part of the possessions of dead foreigners when the property in question was sent out of the country (the law of *detração*); nor one by which the kings and lords of the land might take possession of the persons and cargo of vessels shipwrecked on the high-seas or on rivers (law of *naufragio*, or ship-

---

[18] André João Antonil (João Antônio Andreoni, S.J.): *Cultura e Opulência do Brasil*, etc., edited by Affonso de E. Taunay (op. cit.), p. 80.

[19] The Imperial cloak. (Translator.)
[20] *História do Brasil* (op. cit.).

wreck).[21] Portuguese law began, not by stifling and treading underfoot the ethnic minorities within the realm—the Moors and the Jews
—along with their traditions and customs, but by recognizing the
right of these minorities to rule themselves by their own laws; it even
permitted them magistrates of their own, as later was done in colonial
Brazil in the case of the English Protestants.

In the Ordinances of Affonso (*Ordenações Afonsinas*), which
Coelho da Rocha in his *Ensaio sobre a História da Legislação de Portugal* (*Essay on the History of Legislation in Portugal*) and Cândido
Mendes in his Introduction to the *Code of Philip* (*Código Filipino*)
stress as having been the first complete compilation of its kind
throughout all Europe since the Middle Ages—in these Ordinances,
based upon letters royal and the customs of the country, we may
discern the tendency to concede privileges to the Moors and the
Jews. A tendency that in the Ordinances of Emanuel (*Ordenações
Manuelinas*) yields to the pressure of religious prejudice, by that time
inflamed, but never gives way to pure xenophobia. So true was this
that the advantages there granted to foreign Catholics were afterwards
pleaded in court by the nationals of the country themselves. The
explanation lies in the fact that the struggle against the Moors, as
later the separatist movement that resulted in independence, was
favorable to that cosmopolitanism which was developing in the Portuguese character, alongside of and in harmony with a precocious
nationalism. Consequently neither of the two hatreds or antagonisms
—directed at the Moor in one case, at the Spaniard in the other—can
be blamed for having led the Portuguese along the inferior path of a
restricted nationalism, by shrinking and confining his national spirit
and causing his character to bristle with shards of glass against each
and every comer.[22]

In the absence of great natural or physical frontiers to protect them

---

[21] Rodrigo Octávio says: "It must
be set down to the liberal legislative
spirit of the little Kingdom that
the rights of *albinagio* and *detração* [property-seizure] never existed
there."—*Direito do Estrangeiro no
Brasil* (*Laws Affecting the Foreigner
in Brazil*) (Rio de Janeiro, 1909).
And Pontes de Miranda: "In Portuguese law we never meet with the
right of *albinagio* . . . nor that of
naufragio, authorizing kings and lords
to take possession of persons and
cargo in vessels wrecked at sea or on
the rivers; nor do we find a law of
reprisals."—*Fontes e Evolução do
Direito Civil Brasileiro* (*Sources and
Evolution of Brazilian Civil Law*)
(Rio de Janeiro, 1928).

[22] The allusion here is to Brazilian
owners of semi-urban estates, who
were in the habit of putting shards of
glass on top of the walls surrounding
their property. (Translator.)

against aggression or absorption, the Portuguese were under the necessity of defending themselves by walls of living flesh against Mussulman imperialism and, later, that of Castile; but in this very effort to make pure human resistance or tension supply the lack of almost any kind of geographic defense—any great river or mountain range—they availed themselves of the aid of foreigners. In the Crusades, as in the wars of independence, this was very evident, and this it is that explains not only Portuguese nationalism, which is practically without a geographic base, but Portuguese cosmopolitanism as well. A cosmopolitanism largely favored, it is true, by the geographic situation of the Kingdom: that of a prevailingly maritime country which from remote times has had a great variety of human contacts. On the one hand, it has received upon its shores successive waves, or, more frequently, driblets, of maritime peoples. On the other hand, its navigators, fishermen, and merchants have gone to foreign shores and foreign waters to do their fishing and their scenting-out of new markets.

It was not long after 1184, João Lúcio de Azevedo believes, that commercial relations between Portugal and Flanders must have begun, while those with England date from the opening years of the thirteenth century. And there were also "merchants who went to Levantine ports, designated in the language of the epoch as overseas ports." [23] In the time of Dom Diniz, Portuguese vessels, some of them enormous for the period, of more than a hundred tons, were frequenting the northern ports and those of the Mediterranean. Porto intensified its maritime and mercantile activity, and in 1230 its burghers succeeded in getting themselves exempt from military service in connection with the conquest of Algarve by "contributing money for the purpose." [24] From this it may be seen how precocious was the effect that a commercial cosmopolitanism was having upon the formation of Portuguese society. Cosmopolitanism and finance, a bourgeois mercantilism.

It is, thus, to the "non-Hispanic" elements, as Antônio Sérgio puts it, foreign elements of diverse origin, that we must attribute the failure of Castile to incorporate the western portion of the peninsula, "where the commerce of northern Europe met that of the Mediterranean." [25] It was the foreign elements of the population at this dubious and impressionable point of confluence between northern and southern Europe and the Levant that were responsible for the dissemination of

---

[23] João Lúcio de Azevedo: *Organização Econômica*" (loc. cit.).
[24] Azevedo, loc. cit.

[25] Antônio Sergio: *A Sketch of the History of Portugal* (op. cit.)

cosmopolitan and separatist, maritime and commercial tendencies, tendencies that soon were to evolve into impetuous forces making for differentiation and autonomy.

The precocious ascendancy of the martime and commercial classes in Portuguese economy and politics was a result, likewise, of the extraordinary variety of seafaring and mercantile stimuli. In the beginning the great agents of differentiation and autonomy were the Crusaders, northern adventurers who, in the earldom of Portucale, set themselves up as a military and territorial aristocracy. One of them even became a founder of the monarchy. But this element was afterwards to form a conservative stratum, inclined out of economic class interest to a reunion with Castile. It was then that the differentiating and autonomist activity, and native or patriotic sentiment as well, came to be concentrated in the maritime and mercantile cities. In Lisbon. In Porto. Among the bourgeoisie and the popular classes. According to Alberto Sampaio and Antônio Sérgio, it is from the beginning of Portuguese national life that the antagonism between the commercial class of the maritime cities and the landed aristocracy of the center of the country really dates.[26] As this economic class antagonism grew sharper, accentuating the divergence between rural and seafaring interests, the kings, in a desire to free themselves of any kind of aristocratic pressure upon their royal power, were inclined to adopt a policy that favored the commercial bourgeoisie and the people of the cities. The laws promulgated by Dom Fernando in the way of protecting maritime commerce and encouraging naval construction; the support given to the Master of Avis against the territorial aristocracy; the conquest of Ceuta—all these are initiatives and movements that reflect the precocious ascendancy of the bourgeoisie in Portugal.

The discovery of Brazil is to be placed within the framework of the great maritime and commercial program inaugurated by Vasco da Gama's voyage. The colonization of the vast American land, however, represented a departure from the mercantile-bourgeois norms of the first century of Portuguese imperialism; it represented a revival of methods of aristocratic and agrarian autocolonization such as had been applied in Portugal itself to the territory reconquered from the Moors. Brazil was like a club [27] that is played in a game where diamonds are

---

[26] Alberto Sampaio: *Estudos Históricos e Econômicos* (*Historical and Economic Studies*) (Lisbon, 1923); Antonio Sergio, op. cit.

[27] The Portuguese word for the card known as a club is *pau*, which also means "wood." Early Brazil was looked upon as the land of brazilwood, dyewood, etc. (Translator.)

trumps. It was a disappointment for an imperialism that had begun with Vasco da Gama. Hence the flabby, disinterested, spineless manner in which the crown received into its dominions the lands of dyewood discovered by Pedro Alvares Cabral. It was only in the new phase of Portuguese activity—the colonizing phase, properly speaking, at the end of the sixteenth and covering a part of the seventeenth century—that Brazil was to have the strength of a trump card in the game of imperialist competition between the European nations. This transformation was due to the value that sugar suddenly took on in the aristocratic and bourgeois markets of Europe. Sugar became an object of luxury, sold at the highest of prices, affording an enormous profit for producers and middlemen. Even unrefined brown sugar, notes Dampier, when he was in Bahia at the end of the seventeenth century, upon being exported to Europe was worth around twenty shillings the hundredweight.[28]

We are not interested in this essay, however, save indirectly, in the economic or political aspect of the colonization of Brazil. Directly, it is the social alone that holds an interest for us. And there is no social antecedent that it is more important to consider in the case of the Portuguese colonizer than his extraordinary wealth and variety of ethnic and cultural antagonisms and his cosmopolitanism.

Brazil did not inherit from Portugal the supposed lack of freedom for the foreigner that some have discerned in the Lusitanian colonization of America. The policy of segregation in Brazil was only inspired, in the seventeenth and above all in the eighteenth century, by the envious greed for gold; what previously had appeared to be xenophobia was merely a policy of sanitary defense, as it were, on the part of the colony against heretical infections.

Once the colonization of Brazil had been begun through the efforts of the Portuguese, the blood of many European peoples—Englishmen, Frenchmen, Florentines, Genoans, Germans, Flemings, Spaniards—was freely mingled with that of the official colonizer. I have given the English first mention for the reason that they stand out in greater relief as representative of that Protestant heresy which was as odious in the eyes of sixteenth-century Portuguese and Spaniards as are trachoma, Negro blood, and Bolshevism in those of the North American bourgeoisie of today. The presence of Englishmen among the first colonists at São Vicente shows that, when free of the suspicion of heresy, they were fraternally received. Coreal tells us that, in

---

[28] William Dampier: *Voyages . . . aux Terres Australes, à la Nouvelle*   *Hollande, &C, fait in 1699* (translation) (Amsterdam, 1705).

speaking one day with a native of Santos,[29] he mentioned the fact that he had served with the English filibusters, whereupon a shudder immediately ran over the man, who inquired more than thirty times if Coreal were not, certainly, a heretic; and despite all assurances to the contrary, the Santista could not resist the impulse to sprinkle with holy water the room in which they were.[30] On the other hand, we meet with the Englishman, John Whithall, who was perfectly at home among the first Brazilian colonists. We find him writing from Santos a letter to his fellow countryman Richard Stapes, in England, that shows us clearly the liberality with which foreigners in the Portuguese colony in America were treated. Whithall thanks God for having given him so large a portion of honor and abundance of all things. And, content with having become a subject of Portugal in Brazil, he adds: "now I am a free denizen of this country." He married the daughter of "Signor Ioffo Dore," a native of the city of Genoa, who for his part had set himself up in princely fashion in Brazil, being in a position to present his son-in-law with a plantation, along with sixty or seventy slaves. And just as later the name of Henry Koster[31] was to become in Portuguese Henrique da Costa, so John Whithall's became Leitão:[32] "Here in this countrey they have called me John Leitoan: so that they have used this name so long time that at this present there is no remedie but it must remaine so."[33]

Before Whithall, other Englishmen had been in Brazil, engaged in trade or in quest of novelties: Robert Renigar and Thomas Borey in 1540; a certain Pudsey in 1542; Martin Cockeran and William Hankins in 1530 and 1532. Hankins, according to the chroniclers of the period, took back to England with him an Indian chief from Brazil and created a great sensation by presenting him to the King and court.[34] The poor *murubixba*, however, was not able to hold out and succumbed—whether to the cold or the horrible English cooking, we do not know.

The fact of nationality or race in itself did not prevent any Englishman or Fleming from being admitted to Portuguese colonial society in sixteenth-century America. All that was necessary was that he be

---

[29] In the state of São Paulo; the inhabitants of this town were known as *santistas*. (Translator.)

[30] Coreal, cited by Affonso de E. Taunay: *Non Ducor, Duco* (op. cit.).

[31] The author of *Travels in Brazil* (op. cit.). (Translator.)

[32] The name corresponds to the English *Suckling*. (Translator.)

[33] *The Principal Navigations Voyages Traffiques and Discoveries of the English Nation . . .* by Richard Hakluyt (op. cit.), Vol. VIII, p. 16.

[34] *The Principal Navigations*, etc., Vol. VIII, p. 19.

a Roman Catholic or that he be disinfected of his pestiferous heresy by holy water, that he be baptized and profess the Roman, Catholic, and Apostolic faith. This is what we find Thomas Avilkinson doing, aged twenty-six; Thomas Pratt, aged thirty-two; Patricio Guatusmus, aged twenty-seven; Thomas Perking, aged forty-eight; all of them "Englishmen of the nation," who had appeared before the father of the Society of Jesus charged by the Bishop of Pernambuco, Frei Luis de Santa Thereza, with the task of absolving the excommunicated of heresy.[35] The Church was a species of disinfectant chamber at the service of the colony's moral health, a hospital where souls remained in quarantine.

Handelmann stresses the point that the chief thing necessary in order to acquire a land grant in Brazil was to profess the Catholic religion.[36] Whithall must either have been a Catholic or else have joined the Church before marrying Adorno's daughter; just as Gaspar van der Lei, before marrying into the Mello family, in Pernambuco, had to embrace the religion of his bride, the daughter of a rich planter. In the case of the Dutch gentleman, it is true, his compatriots went on muttering that he was a doubtful and uncertain fellow; for they could never forgive the illustrious founder of the Wanderley family in Brazil for having gone over to the side of the Portuguese and popery.

The liberality with which the foreigner in Portuguese America was treated in the sixteenth century is evident to us. This is a liberality that goes far back, to the very roots of the Portuguese nation. It is not a matter of any virtue that has descended from the heavens upon the Portuguese; it is the quasi-chemical result of the cosmopolitan and heterogeneous background of this maritime people.

Those who would divide Portugal into two countries, one blond and aristocratic, the other brown-skinned or Negroid, which would be the plebeian one, are ignorant of the true meaning of Portuguese history, where we find a constant alternation of hegemonies, not only of races, but of cultures and classes as well, with now one and now another predominating. The near-permanent state of war in which the nation lived for long years, situated as it has been between Africa and Europe, gave it a volcanic social constitution that is reflected in the warmth and plasticity of the national character, of its classes and institutions, which are never indurated or definitely stratified. The state of conquest and reconquest, of flux and reflux, never permitted the establishment in Portugal of any hegemony, unless it was one of

---

[35] Manuscript in the Archives of the Archeological Institute of Pernambuco.
[36] Handelmann, op. cit.

the moment. No exclusivism—unless official or superficial—of race or of culture.

Predisposed by its geographic situation to be the point of contact, of transit, intercommunication, and conflict between diverse elements, whether ethnic or social, Portugal in its anthropology as in its culture displays a great variety of antagonisms, some of them in a state of equilibrium, others in conflict. These latter are merely the undigested portion of its history; the major part is seen to be harmonious in its contrasts, forming a social whole that, in its plastic qualities, is characteristically Portuguese.

We shall discover this ethnic and cultural heterogeneity in the remote origins of the Portuguese people. As to paleolithic man in Portugal, we do not possess enough knowledge regarding him to enable us to state definitely what his origin was: European according to some, African according to others. Mendes Corrêa admits the first hypothesis in the case of the Chellean-Acheulean but considers it doubtful in the case of the Mousterian.[37] Here we are afforded a glimpse of that indecisive position between Europe and Africa which the peninsula has occupied from the earliest times. This is an indecisiveness that is accentuated with respect to the upper paleolithic era, a period during which, probably, there were in Europe considerable ethnic and cultural infiltrations of African (Capsian)[38] origin, infiltrations that left deeper traces, more dense localizations, in the far southern zones. Among the other indications of African penetration in this period may be noted examples of sculpture in the Capsian art of the peninsula showing women with protruding buttocks that are reminiscent of the disease known as steatopygia[39] among the Bushman and Hottentot women.[40] Practically the same may be said

---

[37] Mendes Corrêa: *Os Povos Primitivos da Lusitânia* (*The Primitive Peoples of Lusitania*) (Porto, 1924); *Raça e Nacionalidade* (op. cit.).

[38] Natives of Capsa, a town in that part of northwestern Africa (the ancient Gætulia) now known as Morocco; they were known to the Romans as *Capsenses* or *Capsitani*. (Translator.)

[39] "An excessive accumulation of fat in the buttocks, especially in women, frequently found among the Hottentots, the Bushmen, and the Pygmies."—Lima and Barroso, op. cit. (Translator.)

[40] Boule: *Les Hommes fossiles*, in Mendes Corrêa: *Os Povos Primitivos da Lusitânia* (op. cit.).

[Chellean (chellian): referring to the first paleolithic period, characterized by crudely chipped and pointed flints, discovered at Chelles, France. Acheulean (acheulian): referring to the third paleolithic period, so called from the type station at Saint-Acheul, near Amiens, France. Mousterian (moustierian): referring to a paleolithic period named after the type station of the Moustier cave, on the bank of the Vézère, in France. (Translator.)]

of the post-paleolithic ethnology of that Portuguese territory where the *Capsenses H. Taganus*, a brachycephalic folk (Mugem), and the new Capsians of the east were united with a dolichocephalic people, "descendants, perhaps, of the European dolichocephalic type" and the possible bearers of the "essential elements of neolithic culture," not to speak of fresh penetrations—a matter of doubt, so far as that goes—of African origin.[41]

In the neolithic and neo-neolithic period an intimate contact between Europe and Africa continued in the peninsula. This was followed by a period—the bronze age—looked upon by some as one of stabilization. The man of the peninsula, having gone through the first seething phase of miscegenation, was left to cool for a number of centuries, without invasions either from Africa or from the north to disturb the process of what may be termed cultural induration, marked by a definition of the physical type. But the final African invasion—that of Almería—left much for Europe to digest during this long period of assimilation. As we shall see later, contact with the Greeks and Carthaginians was to give fresh colors to peninsular culture in the south and east, while at the same time, in the center and in the west, post-Hallstattian cultural forms were springing up, the work, possibly, of the Celts,[42] who had staged an invasion first by way of the northeast and later by way of the western Pyrenees. Two cultural areas were thus outlined: one representing the northern or Celtic influence, the other the Mediterranean influence. But this without losing indigenous traits held in common, which, even in the zone looked upon by some as being predominantly under the influence of the Celts, survived in the badly baked ceramics to be found there.

The peninsula in general and that territory which today is Portuguese in particular were marked by this duality of cultural forms at the time the Roman invasion took place. It is likely, meanwhile, that the brown-skin, curly-haired type was the more characteristic, embodying cultural forms that were, it may be, more Mediterranean than Nordic, more African than European. Martial's famous self-portrait is highly expressive: *"hispanus ego contumax capillis."* This brown-skin, possibly Negroid type was the nearest to the aborigine and was the most common. It was not, however, the exclusive type. The point to keep in mind is precisely this: that there is no exclusive type to be found in the ethnic past of the Portuguese people, whose anthropology from remote pre- and proto-historic times has been a

---

41 Mendes Corrêa, op. cit.
42 Opinion of Bosch, cited by Mendes Corrêa, op. cit.

mixed one; we are to remember the extreme mobility that has characterized the social formation of this folk.

The data furnished Ripley by Ferraz de Macedo permitted that anthropologist to reach the conclusion that a dolichocephalic type, low in stature, had been the persistent one in Portugal,[43] though without the predominance of any one pure stock.[44] This is the conclusion, likewise, of Fonseca Cardoso.[45] The latter gives as the basic characteristics of the Portuguese population, amid all the extraordinary variety of types, the following features: stature below the average; dolichocephalic skulls; dark hair and eyes; long, leptorrhine nose, somewhat elongated at the bottom. These are characteristics that point to the persistence of a small, dolichocephalic, brown-skin race that is supposed to have constituted the autochthonous base of the population—the descendants of Beaumes-Chaudes-Mugem, whose purest representatives are to be met with today in the mountainous regions of upper Minho province (Castro Laboreiro). In the Cantabrian region of Oviedo, on the right bank of the lower Guadalquivir, and elsewhere in the north, the Portuguese anthropologist came upon purer specimens of the brachycephalic, low-statured, mesorrhine race, with globular head and vertical occiput, a race that must have been the first among the immigrants; while at various points in Minho, Gaia, and Povoa de Varzim, localizations of tall-statured, dolichocephalic or mesodolichoid Nordics, with long, finely modeled, leptorrhine noses, pinkish skins, blond or reddish hair, and light-colored eyes were to be found. These latter are the purest representatives of the blond northern race which a number of times invaded the territory that today is Portuguese. To the influence of this race upon the population of Portugal Fonseca Cardoso attributes the mestizo visage that is everywhere to be noted among the Portuguese.

To these elements are to be added the Semito-Phœnicians, of whom the Portuguese anthropologist finds the purest representatives among the fishing population of that portion of the seaboard which lies between the two rivers, and among the more recent invaders: the Jews, Berbers, Moors, Germans, Negroes, Flemings, and English.

If, as Haddon assumes,[46] the invasions from the south accentuated the basic characteristics of the indigenous population, those from the

---

[43] W. Z. Ripley: *The Races of Europe*, London. s.d.

[44] The word *stock* is in English in the text. (Translator.)

[45] Fonseca Cardoso: "*Antropologia Portuguesa*," in *Notas sobre Portugal* (Lisbon, 1908).

[46] A. G. Haddon: *The Races of Man and Their Distribution* (Cambridge, 1929).

north brought to Portuguese anthropology new and even antagonistic elements. These elements engaged in conflict with the natives and at times came near to conquering them, but always ended by making peace with them. The result was a compromise that led to bizarre dualities of interbreeding such as are so typical of that population which is properly termed Portuguese.

Portugal is, *par excellence*, the land of the transitory blond or demi-blond. In those regions most deeply penetrated by Nordic blood, many a child grows up as blond and pink as a Flemish Christ Child, only later, upon reaching maturity, to turn out to be brown-skinned and dark-haired. Or—and this is more typical—it then reveals that duality, that balance of antagonisms, to be seen in the natives of Minho whom Alberto Sampaio describes for us: men with blond beards and dark hair.[47] Dark-skinned men with blond hair. It was, as I see it, these two-colored mestizos who constituted the majority of the Portuguese colonizers of Brazil in the sixteenth and seventeenth centuries; these and not any blond or Nordic, pure white élite; nor, on the other hand, were they all brown-skinned and black-haired. They were neither Oliveira Vianna's dolicho-blonds [48] nor Sombart's Jews, nor Debbané's [49] Mozarabs, but typical Portuguese. Anthropologically and culturally a mixed people. The frequency with which a transitory blond pigmentation occurs, not only in Portuguese children but in those of the Mediterranean type generally, is seen by Mendes Corrêa as suggesting a possible "vestigial filiation of the Mediterranean type to an old racial crossing into which the Nordic race and a proto-Ethiopian type might have entered." [50] A supposition that is also entertained by Italian anthropologists.

In Brazil the transitional blond, demi-blond, and false blond are still more frequent than in Portugal. But before Brazil became the land of the reddish-haired Sarará, as described by Gabriel Soares in

[47] Alberto Sampaio: *Estudos Históricos e Econômicos* (op. cit.).

[48] F. J. Oliveira Vianna, is the author of: *Evolção do Povo Brasileiro* (*Evolution of the Brazilian People*) (2nd edition, São Paulo, 1933); *Populações Meridonais do Brasil* (*Southern Populations of Brazil*) (3rd edition, São Paulo, 1933); and *Raça e Assimilação* (*Race and Assimilation*) (2nd edition, São Paulo, 1934). He is known in contemporary Brazil as the leading exponent of the thesis that the Negro is an inferior race and can only become a valuable factor in society through "Aryanization"—i.e., when he loses his racial purity and interbreeds with the white. (*Evolução do Povo Brasileiro*, p. 161.) (Translator.)

[49] Nicolas J. Debbané: *L'Influence arabe dans la formation historique, la littérature et la civilization du peuple brésilien* (Cairo, 1911). (Translator.)

[50] Mendes Corrêa, op. cit.

a sixteenth-century chronicle [51]—and, more characteristically, of the "pink-skinned mulatto," as Eça de Queiroz [52] once put it in an intimate conversation with an eminent Brazilian diplomat—Portugal had already anticipated the production of curious types, with light pigmentation or reddish hair but with the lips or nostrils of the Negro or the Jew. Let us not forget, however, in speaking of blonds in Portugal, that ancient localizations of blonds have also been identified in North Africa; [53] and that among the brown-skinned mass of Mussulmans who invaded the country there were also individuals with light hair. Or that many a Moorish charmer [54] was glimpsed by night combing locks which were as golden as the sun. Portugal also got its blonds from the southern side. From Africa—sandwiched in between heavy layers of dark men, many of them Negroid.

Throughout the historical era racial and cultural contacts in Portugal, merely rendered difficult but never impeded by religious antagonisms, were the freest to be found anywhere, between the most diverse elements. When the peninsula was invaded by the Romans, the natives put up at first a tremendous and heroic resistance, but they ended by yielding to Imperial pressure. There then began the period of the Romanization or Latinization of Iberia. Roman rule was chiefly economic and political in character, and it brought to the subjected populations—subjected but not crushed—the advantages of Imperial technique: roads, baths, aqueducts, arches, pottery-fac-

---

[51] Alluding to the descendants of the French who, at the beginning of the sixteenth century, lived in a state of concubinage, a mild form of polygamy, with the Tupinambá women, "with no desire to return to France," Gabriel Soares has this to say: "There is nothing astonishing in the fact that these descendants of the French are white-skinned and fair-haired, since they are merely reverting to their forebears."—"Fair-haired, white-skinned, and freckled," he says in another place. The chronicler's observation leads to the belief that pure blonds were not common among the sixteenth-century Portuguese colonizers, and that the latter identified the striking blond with the French. In this connection it is well to keep in mind also the words of another chronicle-writer of the same century, Hans Staden, cited

by Pedro Calmon in his recent and provocative *História da Civilização Brasileira* (*History of Brazilian Civilization*) (Rio de Janeiro, 1933): "They told me that if I had a red beard like the Frenchmen, they had also seen Portuguese with the same kind of beard, but that the latter generally had black beards." The Indians—Calmon, basing his statement upon Gonçalo Coelho's account, reminds us—were in the habit of distinguishing the French from the Portuguese by the color of their beards.

[52] Portugal's famous nineteenth-century novelist. (Translator.)

[53] Haddon: *The Races of Man and Their Distribution* (op. cit.).

[54] On the "enchanted Moorish woman" (*moura encantada*), see Chapter p. 12. (Translator.)

tories; it went down into the bowels of the earth to exploit the mines; and it exerted a palpable influence upon the moral culture and, to a lesser degree, the anthropology of the land. In the shadow of Imperial Rome temples to the Latin gods were erected in what is now Portugal, gods that were to win for themselves so deep a feeling of popular devotion that the Catholic saints were later to have to take on a likeness to them, along with many of their attributes, in order to gain the affections of the people. The peninsular speech was Latinized and the ancient type of habitation was Romanized. Romanized, also, were the various institutions. Annato Lusitano has even noted resemblances in physiognomy between the natives of Lisbon and those of Rome.[55]

The Roman conquest was followed by the invasions of the Alani,[56] the Vandals, and the Suevi.[57] The Roman hold having been broken by the first wave of reddish-haired barbarians, a large portion of the peninsula was overrun with northern-comers, who later with no great effort set up the Visigoth rule. This rule, lasting three centuries, did not destroy the influence of the Roman colonists, but rather accommodated itself to the general lines of the Latin and Imperial structure. In the matter of religion it was the invaders who abandoned their Aryan doctrines to adopt the Catholic creed of the Hispano-Romans. In law they underwent the influence of the Roman code, while maintaining their own customs, which were to leave definite roots in the former Roman province.

It was between these two influences—that of the written law of the Romans and that of the unwritten body of customs of the invaders from the north—between them and smoothing out the antagonisms—that a third one was subtly to intervene, giving to peninsular institutions a new juridical flavor in the form of the canon law. There was then set up an episcopal nobility, with the appearance of blessing and pacifying, but in reality commanding and dominating. And an effective domination it was, owing to the authority, conferred upon the bishops, of rendering judgment in civil cases.

With the conversion of the Aryan Goths to Catholic orthodoxy, the Church through its bishops acquired in Spain a prestige superior to that of kings, judges, and barons. In Toledo, at the council held in 633, the bishops had the pleasure of seeing the King prostrate at

---

[55] Alberto Sampaio: *Estudos* (op. cit.); Mendes Corrêa, op. cit.

[56] A warlike Scythian tribe living along the banks of what is now the River Don; they are referred to by Martial, Pliny, Suetonius, and other Latin writers. (Translator.)

[57] A powerful Germanic people in the northeastern part of Germany; referred to by Tacitus, Cæsar, and others. (Translator.)

their feet.[58] In the new peninsular laws, or better the code to which the fusion of Roman law with that of the barbarian had given rise—the so-called *Fuero Juego*—canonical prestige had led to the insertion of provisions authorizing the jurisdiction of the bishop in civil cases whenever plaintiff or defendant expressed a preference for an episcopal verdict, whenever either of them chose to "tell it to the Bishop." For in the words of the Spanish jurisconsult Sempere y Guarinos, who lived in the time of Buckle: *"los querellantes lesionados por la sentencia de un juez, podiam quejarse a los bispos, y estos avocar a si las pendencias, reformarlas y castigar a los magistrados."* [59] In other words, the bishops might intervene in a case that had been begun before a civil tribunal and reverse the finding. Durham stresses the constant vigilance exercised by the bishops over the administration of justice and over the judges.[60] Over kings themselves, he might have added. One monarch in Portugal—Sancho II—who attempted to govern without the bishops had his Kingdom cut in half and barely escaped with his head. It was with the aid of Sancho's own brother, later consecrated King under the name of Affonso III, that the clergy put down this bold rebellion.

In Spain and in Portugal the higher clergy came to enjoy an extraordinary prestige, mystic, moral, and juridical as well, over peoples that, by reason of the physical and social circumstances of their lives—earthquakes, droughts, famines, plagues, wars, and all the upsetting conditions peculiar to regions of transit and of conflict—had come to be endowed with an extreme religious sensitivity, a sensitivity that, in the case of both the Spaniards and the Portuguese, Buckle regards as constituting a great intellectual and political force. A reflection of that force irradiated from papal Rome over the new Europe, converted to Christianity. In Portugal there were religious orders that were at the same time military, thus adding the warrior's prestige to that of the ecclesiastic. Through its military orders the Church took advantage of the wars of reconquest in the peninsula chiefly to make itself the proprietor of large landed estates; for it did not leave exclusively to the Crusaders themselves the matter of dividing the lands reclaimed from the infidels. A fat portion fell to the Templars, who from the time of Dona Thereza were the lords of Soure and of all the pleasant region between Coimbra and Leiria, and later of Tomar, Almoral, and Pombal also. Other orders followed their example and became landed proprietors of Aviz and Santiago,

[58] Fleury: *Historia Ecclesiastica*, in Buckle: *Bosquejo de Una Historia del Intelecto Español* (translation) (Madrid, n.d.).

[59] Buckle, op. cit.
[60] Durham, cited by Buckle, op. cit.

while others still acquired lands that were not so rich.[61] The latifundi-ary and semi-feudal method of colonization later applied in Brazil had its beginnings in Portugal in this semi-ecclesiastic effort. The only thing is that with us the ecclesiastics were eclipsed by the individual initiative of our Duarte Coelhos, our Garcia d'Avilas, our Paes Ba-rretos, by *sertanistas* [62] of the stamp of Domingos Affonso Mafrense, nicknamed "the Sertão," who upon his death left thirty cattle-ranches in Piauí.

In Portugal the religious orders fulfilled an important creative function, not only in the economic reorganization of the territory reconquered from the Moors, but also in the political organization of the heterogeneous populations. With their canonical discipline they provided a political bond. The nation was thus put upon a religious basis, without prejudice to the two great dissident bodies, the Jews and the Moors, who, thanks to the political tolerance of the majority, were safe in the very shadow of the Moor-slaying warriors. This tolerance was to continue until the segregated ones—owing either to their superior industrial and mercantile genius or to the fact that, be-ing somewhat strange to their milieu, they were more unscrupulous than the others—had become the holders of large peninsular fortunes. It was then that the majority came to feel that their tolerance was being abused. At least by the Jews.

It was by way of containing within bounds the burning, seething hatreds that had arisen against the Israelite majority that the Tribunal of the Holy Office was set up, combining with the function of ex-amining consciences the power of examining, coldly and methodi-cally, the worldly possessions that the heretic had accumulated. The Jews had rendered themselves antipathetic less by reason of their religion, looked upon as an abomination, than by what was regarded as an utter lack of any delicacy of feeling in their dealings with Christians where money matters were concerned. Their fortunes had been accumulated chiefly through usury, which was forbidden by the Church to Christians, or through the holding of those public ad-ministrative posts, or positions in the manor houses of the gentry and even within the Catholic corporations, which it was to the interest of the big landowners among the Christians to have filled by indi-viduals supposed to be free of all scruples and outside the laws of the Church.

---

[61] Antônio Sergio: *A Sketch of the History of Portugal* (op. cit.).

[62] *Sertanista* (not to be confused with *sertanejo*, a native of the back-lands) sometimes, as here, means a pioneer or explorer of the *sertão*, and at other times, a student of or author-ity on the subject. (Translator.)

The duality of Portuguese culture and the Portuguese character was accentuated under Moorish rule; and even after it had been conquered, this people from Africa continued to exert its influence through a series of effects produced upon the masters by slaves and slave labor. That form of slavery to which the Moors and even the Mozarabs were subjected following the Christian victory was the medium through which there was brought to bear upon the Portuguese, not the influence of the Moor, the Mohammedan, or the African in particular, but that of the slave in general. An influence that predisposed him as none other could to the agrarian, slave-holding, and polygamous colonization—the patriarchal colonization, in short—of tropical America. The physical conditions in that part of America which fell to the Portuguese called for a colonization of this type; and without the Moorish experience he would in all probability have failed at this formidable task. He would have failed for the reason that he would have been powerless to meet conditions so beyond the range of his own European experience.

There is not the space here to go into detail regarding the racial and cultural relations between Mussulmans and Christians in the Iberian Peninsula, especially those between Moors and Christians. Accordingly, I shall merely point out certain traces of the Moorish influence in the character and culture of the Portuguese people that appear to me to have been the most profoundly effective in fitting them for the victorious colonization of the tropics.

I have already indicated that the Moorish and Berber invasion was not the first to inundate with Negro and Mulatto strains the extreme southern tip of Europe, and particularly Portugal, a region of easy transit by way of which the first and most vigorous waves of African exuberance might overflow the continent. I have also indicated the possibility that the basic racial stratum in the peninsula, looked upon as indigenous, might be of African origin. Looked at it in this way, the Arabs, Moors, Berbers, and Mussulmans, in the course of their invasion, would simply have been taking possession of a region where the way had been prepared for them by an infusion of their own blood and culture—theirs, it may be, rather than Europe's. A region that was theirs by reason of its human past and, over large stretches, by reason of its climate and its vegetation as well.

In their invasion of the peninsula the Mohammedans from Africa must have had the aid of those Hispanic elements opposed to the Visigoths—a circumstance I mention here by way of stressing the fact that, from the first, European and African interests were deeply intermingled. With the exception of a small number of intransigents concentrated in Asturias, the center of Christian independence, a large part of the populations submitted to the political rule of the Moors and proceeded to develop intimate relations with them, preserving all the while a comparative purity of faith.

It was these populations—Mozarabic ones—a people imbued with the invader's culture and with the invader's blood in its veins—that were to constitute the base and sinews of Portuguese nationality. A nationality that, at first differentiated from Castile by the separatist interests of the ruddy adventurers from the north, who had come there to take part in the struggle against the Moors, later was to assert itself not so much through the ardor of its nobility, who, out of economic class interest, were ready to fraternize with their neighbors, as through the uncompromising attitude of the Mozarabic masses. João Lúcio de Azevedo looks upon this intransigence of national sentiment in the people and the weakness of the same sentiment in the nobility as being a mark of racial psychology in Portugal. These were tendencies that were to reveal themselves in the great crises of 1383, 1580, and 1808. "When," writes Azevedo, "the concept of the fatherland, which had been lost in Roman unity, was once more awakened in the peninsula, it was the people who proved to be the depository of that national feeling which was lacking in the ruling class." [63] To the popular element the Portuguese historian further attributes, in addition to patriotic ardor, a peaceful and negligent disposition and a touch of Semitic fatalism, while the nobles were characterized by warlike proclivities and predatory habits.

I am able, however, to accept only in part this ethnocentric interpretation suggested by João Lúcio de Azevedo, with respect to the part that was played in Portuguese development by the aristocracy of Nordic background on the one hand and, on the other, by the native masses, deeply penetrated with Moorish and Berber blood; for in no modern country has there been so great a mobility from one class to another, and, if I may so put it, from one race to another, as in Portugal. The fact as I see it is that in the history of the Portuguese people major consideration must be given to the social and economic aspect, represented by the precocious ascendancy of the bourgeoisie, which soon was to ally itself with the kings against the nobles, whose prestige was speedily to pale before that of the burghers. Moreover, practically all the sap of the landed aristocracy was to be absorbed by the omnipotence of the religious orders, with their

---

[63] João Lúcio de Azevedo: *"Algumas Notas Relativas a Pontos de História Social"* (loc. cit.).

large holdings, or by the astuteness of Jewish capitalists. This goes to explain why it is that the landed aristocracy in Portugal is not endowed with the same stern and bristling prejudices as in countries with a feudal background, either against the burghers in general or against the Jews and Moors in particular. Weakened by the pressure of the big landowning ecclesiastics, not a few aristocrats of Nordic origin went to the middle class, which was impregnated with Moorish and Hebrew blood, in search of rich young women whom they might marry. From this there resulted in Portugal a nobility that showed as great a racial admixture, almost, as the bourgeoisie or the masses. For the mobility of families and individuals from one class to another was formidable; and it is, accordingly, impossible to draw conclusions from the ethno-social stratifications in a people that has been so restless and so plastic in its movements.

During the Moorish rule the aboriginal culture took from that of the invader a long series of values, as the two blood-streams mingled intensely. To state, as Pontes de Miranda does in a recent learned work, that "the Arabs floated like oil on the surface of the peoples that they invaded or ruled, and never displayed a sufficient degree of miscibility with them" [64] is to give to the word *miscibility* an extraordinary meaning which we are at a loss to explain For if the Arabs—Moors, the young master of the law, who is so rigorous in matters of terminology, might better have said—if the Moors did not mingle freely with the Lusitanian populations, then I do not know what miscegenation is. What is more, this same Pontes de Miranda, thirty pages beyond the one where he makes this curious statement, corrects himself by saying: "Only the best-established and most stabilizing of religions prevented the complete fusion of the races." And in this connection he cites the passage from Alexandre Herculano in which the social fusion of vanquished Christians with the victorious Moors is masterfully portrayed.

Those elements which the peninsular culture preserved from that of the invaders throughout the broad territory where Arabic or Moorish rule prevailed—or where the enslavement of African captives took place, once the roles of master and slave had been reversed—are today those which tend most to differentiate and individualize this part of Europe. While the religion and civil law of the conquerors was in large part preserved by the conquered, in other spheres of economic and social life the Arabic influence in certain regions and the Moorish in others was profound and intense. The masses of the

---

[64] Pontes de Miranda: *Fontes e Evolução do Direito Civil Brasileiro* (op. cit.).

Hispano-Roman-Gothic population, excluding only the obstinate minority that had taken refuge in Asturias, had permitted their most intimate tastes to be influenced by the Arab and the Moor; and when, in the form of the Mozarabs, this pliable majority flowed back over Christian Europe, it was to constitute the very substratum of nationality. A military and political nationalism was to be founded by others; the economic and social phase was the task of the Mozarabs, and down to the glorious era of voyages and conquests they were to give to it their blood and sweat. When this socially mobile population —extremely mobile, in fact—returned to Christian Europe, it was to bring with it a dense layer of culture and an energetic infusion of Moorish and Negro blood, the effects of which persist to this day in the Portuguese people and the Portuguese character. These were a blood and a culture that were to be brought to Brazil; which explains much in the Brazilian that is neither European, nor native, nor the result of direct contact with Africa through the Negro slaves. It explains much that is Moorish in the private life of the Brazilian in colonial times and that still persists today, even so far as the physical type is concerned.

In the course of the journey which, as Director General of Mines and Forests, he made through the interior of the capitânia of São Paulo, at the beginning of the nineteenth century, Martim Francisco de Andrade observed that, throughout an extensive tract, individuals with pronounced Moorish physiognomies were to be encountered. If Portuguese of this racial origin were extinct in the metropolis, it is apparent from what Martim Francisco tells us that there were still in our country many who preserved the splendid purity of the primitive race, so numerous did the paulistas of Moorish origin and characteristics appear to him to be.[65]

Great as was the influence of the Moorish ruler, that of the Moorish war-captive fully equaled it. It was the vigor of the latter's arm that was to render possible in Portugal the regime of agrarian autocolonization through large-scale property and slave labor, one that was afterwards advantageously employed in Brazil. It was thanks to the Moors and the religious, J. M. Esteves Pereiro tells us, that from the earliest times in Portugal "agriculture, its principal industry, was better developed than in other countries farther to the north."

---

[65] Martim Francisco: *"Jornal de Viagens por Diferentes Vilas da Capitânia de São Paulo"* ("Journal of Travels through Different Towns of the Capitânia of São Paulo"), *Revista do Instituto Histórico e Geográphico Brasileiro*, No. 45.

Thanks chiefly to the Moors. "The *picata* or *cegonha*, that simple and primitive mechanism for drawing water from the bottom of wells, was their work. The *nora*, that other device for raising water, associated with the pleasing poetry of the countryside, with its rope and pulley and its buckets, is an invention of the Arabs, or at least one of the mechanisms that they brought with them to the peninsula." [66] If it was the Crusaders who brought to the two Spains the windmill, applied in certain parts of America—the West Indies, for example— to the manufacture of sugar, it was the Moors who introduced into Portugal the water-mill, or *azenha*, ancestor of the colonial device for grinding cane through the power of water falling over a large wooden wheel. João Lúcio de Azevedo brings out the point that the olive tree itself would appear to have been better utilized in Portugal after the coming of the Moors. He goes on to explain: "the nomenclature for the trees comes from the Latin: *oliveira* (olive tree), *olival, olivedo* (terrain planted in olives); whereas the names of the products are of Arabic derivation: *azeitona* (an olive), *azeite* (olive oil); all of which leads us to think that a better use was made of this vegetable species during the Mussulman period." [67] This is significant. Significant likewise is the fact that the verb *mourejar* [from *mouro*, a Moor] has become synonymous with "to work" or "to labor" in the Portuguese language; and there is also the phrase, as common in Portugal as in Brazil: "to work like a Moor." The explanation is that the Moor was the great labor force in Portugal. The technician. The agriculturist. It was he who was responsible for a greater and better utilization of resources, who got value out of the land, who saved it from droughts through intelligent irrigation. It was not only the olive tree that was increased in value and utility through Moorish science, but the vineyards also. Not to speak of the orange tree, cotton, and the silkworm, all of which the Moors brought to the peninsula. They fulfilled the function of technicians; nor was their energy chiefly of the animal variety (as was later that of the slaves from Guinea); nor

---

[66] J. M. Esteves Pereira: *A Indústria Portuguesa (Séculos XII a XIX), com uma introdução sobre as corporações operárias em Portugal (Portuguese Industry from the Twelfth to the Nineteenth Centuries, with an Introduction on the Trade Guilds in Portugal)* (Lisbon, 1900).

[67] João Lúcio de Azevedo: *"Organização Econômica"* (loc. cit.).—In his study of the towns of northern Portugal, Alberto Sampaio writes: "Most interesting is the agro-industrial terminology of the olive tree, which has the singularity of being part Latin and part Arabic—*oliveira, olival, olivedo* come under the first head, *azeite* and *azeitona* under the second." *Estudos Históricos e Econômicos* (op. cit.).

was it a case of simple mercantilism on their part as with the Jews.

It was not only cotton, the silkworm, and the orange tree that the Arabs and Moors introduced; they also developed the cultivation of sugar-cane, which, transported from the Madeira Islands to Brazil, was to condition the economic and social evolution of the Portuguese colony in America, giving it an agrarian organization and the possibilities of permanence. It was the Moor who furnished the Brazilian colonizer with the technical elements for the production and economic utilization of the cane.

The Portuguese who on this side the Atlantic, somewhat in the manner of the Templars in Portugal, became large estate-owners were on the one hand following the example of the Crusaders, and especially that of the friars—capitalists and landed proprietors whose sole initial capital, not infrequently, was the goods, cattle, and men of the lands reclaimed from the infidel—and on the other hand were repeating the technique of the African invaders, if not with regard to the processes of laying waste the land (in which they preferred to be guided by native suggestions), at least with respect to the industrial utilization of products. As a result, the shadow of the Moor, no mere exploiter of values but a great creative figure, was beneficently projected over the beginnings of Brazilian agrarian economy. The economic system adopted in Brazil was the same as that inaugurated by the Nordic adventurers in Portugal following the Christian reconquest, the only difference being that ecclesiastical prestige did not here absorb that of the individual, the family, and the feudal lord. But the industrial technique was that of the Moors. Above all, the device of the water-wheel.

To what extent the Portuguese blood-stream, with already a large strain of the Semitic as a result of remote Phœnician and Jewish infiltrations, was still further infiltrated by the Moor during the flux and reflux of the Mohammedan invasion, it is practically impossible to determine. But the infiltration of infidel blood must have been profound, when one considers not only the intimate relations that existed between conquerors and conquered during the African invasion, but those between Christians and captive Moors and between Hispano-Romans and Mozarabs in the period that followed. The last mentioned, by reason of their technical superiority, were to work their way toward the top of the economic and social ladder, their ascent being favored by the precocious development of the Portuguese bourgeoisie and the consequent exodus of workers from the land to the cities. In the course of this development, the industrial arts and those crafts that were of urban rather than rural utility played an extraordinarily important role, and these were arts and crafts that were dominated by Moorish intelligence.

There was another circumstance that was favorable to their ascendancy: the state of wars, droughts, plagues, and famines that for long afflicted the Portuguese population, which by reason of the situation of its ports—a point of contact between the north and the Mediterranean—was subject to all sorts of unhygienic contacts. Two great plagues darkened the reign of Sancho I, one of them (that of 1348) being of pandemic proportions and Oriental origin. In 1356, we learn from a monastic chronicle cited by Azevedo, two thirds of the population of the Kingdom died as the result of famine.[68] Disturbances of climate and physical milieu combined in Portugal with the evils of the latifundiary regime—including the laying waste of forests—to produce frequent social crises as a consequence of the scarcity of food.

The law of allotments of Dom Fernando, promulgated in 1375, endeavored to face two problems: that of large-scale property, and that of the exodus of agricultural laborers to the city. In the former case it provided for the dispossessing of the estate-owner who, out of negligence or from lack of means, should leave his arable lands untilled. But even in the provisions of such laws as these, if the door was not left wide open, it was at least left ajar for the Moors and Mozarabs to migrate from the countryside to the town, to those ports so full of life and movement whose progress the sovereign took the lead in stimulating. Certain obligations of permanence were imposed upon the sons and grandsons of cultivators of the land, and upon rural laborers as well; but it would have been comparatively easy for those endowed with a superior and valuable aptitude as technicians to evade the provisions of the statute and make their way to the maritime and commercial cities. At this point the fact should be noted that the medieval cities had need of including in their population workers capable of cultivating gardens and the so-called "bread lands," destined to provide sustenance for the urban dwellers;[69] so that even where rural labor was concerned, the skilled arms of the Moors and Mozarabs, who had fled a humiliating state of servitude to take shelter under the protecting wing of the burghers and their laws, could still be employed to advantage. Everything goes to indicate that in Portuguese society at this time the vertical as well as the

---

[68] Azevedo: *"Organização Econômica"* (loc. cit.).
[69] Ibid.

horizontal movement of the Moorish and Mozarabic element, left bound to the soil by the reconquest, was tremendous in scope: from one sphere of life to another, from one to another economic zone. It was certainly this element that, by reason of its greater wealth of industrial aptitudes, availed itself most effectively of the opportunities afforded the downtrodden to leave the land, to which they were bound by the obligations of a captive or a slave, for other employment that was likewise agricultural or semi-urban in character, but where their situation would be quite different from what it had been in the past. They would now be free tillers of the soil, and economic success would be easy for them under these new circumstances.

This explains why it was that the indigenous Hispanic element, whose blood had recently received a lively coloring from Moor and Berber, now ceased circulating on a lower level only, beneath that of the victorious Hispano-Gothic stratum, and ceased to be localized in any one region, but instead spread out advantageously over the entire country, rising at times to the most elevated stations in society. It is well, moreover, not to forget that this Hispanic element, which after contact with the Moors was known as Mozarabic, during the period of Mussulman rule had suffered an economic and social diminution, and that for a great many this diminution was accentuated during the reconquest, which was almost wholly directed by foreign-comers from the north—a species of new-rich and new-power-endowed beings. What happened afterwards, therefore, was not so much an ascension as a readjustment of position, due in part to the fact that during the period of Mohammedan rule the technical and industrial capacities of the Hispanic folk, who had compromised with the invader, had been enriched and refined by contact with the superior North African culture.

But before this process of social readjustment had taken place, at the time of the first contact of the Mohammedan invaders with the Christian populations, both the popular and the upper classes among the latter had undergone a penetration by the victors. This penetration was facilitated not alone by the dominant position of the African race, but also by its tendency to polygamy. Abdul-Aziz ibn-Muza not only wed the widow of Roderico, but took may Christian virgins for his concubines. On the other hand, Ramiro II, of León, fascinated by the beauty of a Saracen maid of noble lineage—undoubtedly one of those who later became "enchanted Moorish damsels"—slew his legitimate wife and married the exotic creature, by whom he had a numerous progeny. The two cases are typical: on the one hand, a violent penetration of the conquered people by the polygamous in-

vader, through their womenfolk; and on the other, the attraction
exerted by the Saracen woman, especially when of noble birth, upon
men of the defeated race.

The noble families in Portugal as in Spain that absorbed the blood
of the Arab or the Moor were innumerable. Some of the knights who,
in the wars of reconquest, most distinguished themselves by the
Moor-killing ardor of their Christianity had such blood, the blood
of the infidel, in their veins. On the other hand, there must have been
much Spanish or Portuguese orthodox Christian blood in the Mohammedans who emigrated to Africa. It is known that the African reflux
carried with it even Franciscan friars, polygamous ones, with an
overfondness for women. There was many a Mem or Mendo, many
a Pelagio, many a Soeiro, many an Egas, many a Goncalo—many
who, one would have said, to judge from their Christian fervor, were
Hispano-Goths without the slightest trace of Islamism in their ancestry, but who in reality were Portuguese with a Moorish or Arabian
grandfather or grandmother. Of the Count of Coimbra, Dom Ses-
nando, the chronicles tell us that he was a mixed-blood, of Christian
and Moor, and that he was even a vizier among the Saracens. And
we know that another mixed-blood, Dom Fifes Serrasim, became a
member of the Christian nobility by marrying a Mendes de Bragança.

No means of identifying Hispanos and Moors, Christians and infidels, conquered and conqueror, nobles and plebeians in Portuguese
society is more uncertain than individual and family names. Races,
cultures, and social classes were so jumbled in the peninsula that the
weight attached to the feet of some through slavery or the spoils of
war never succeeded in preventing them from fluctuating anew.
Alexandre Herculano observes that, following the intense miscibility
that accompanied the invasion, names of mixed lineage became common: Pelagio Iban Alafe, Egas Abdallah Argeriquiz, etc.[70] This gives
a good idea of the degree of social compromise between the conquered and their conquerors. It conveys a precise idea of how plastic,
filled with movement, and fluctuating Mozarabic society in Portugal
really was. What happened in the case of the Moors happened also,
to a certain extent, with the Jews. Both allowed themselves to be
penetrated in their various strata. And never—we may stress it: never
once—did classes in Portugal become stratified to that point where
an individual or a family might be identified simply by the noble or
plebeian, Jewish or Christian, Hispanic or Moorish character of a
name.

---

[70] Alexandre Herculano: *História de Portugal* (op. cit.).

In the wars against the Moors and Castilians there were many Portuguese who became ennobled, winning for themselves the right to lands and titles. Few of them, however, remained in possession of estates which were difficult to exploit in competition with those great capitalistic enterprises represented by the religious and military orders. When the attention of the Portuguese came to be directed chiefly toward the sea, many individuals who had been born in rural servitude now found themselves promoted to the position of free laborers in the city. At the same time, while they were going up the ladder, others were coming down, among them the small rural proprietors, the owners of estates that had been granted them for their services in time of war; these were individuals incapable of competing with the latifundiary enterprises, and were, accordingly, absorbed by the latter. The very laws of Dom Fernando designed to curb the latifundia almost never had any other effect than that of taking away the holdings of the lesser gentry, who through penury or lack of labor were incapable of exploiting them, to incorporate them with the domains of the all-powerful monopolists. Whence a numerous nobility of "landless Johnnies" ("*joões-sem-terra*") in Portugal, a nobility that began drifting to the cities, principally to the court, to seek out public employment in the vicinity of the King and, later, in the overseas possessions.

Alberto Sampaio provides us with valuable data regarding the utter lack of rigidity or aristocratic exclusiveness in the concept of lineage among the early Portuguese. The names of individuals were then, as they still are to a certain extent today, in Portugal and in Brazil, the same for the humble as for the great. These names were generally Germanic; "for following the coming of the Suevi and the Visigoths, the Hispanos adopted their names in place of those of the Romans." And Sampaio adds: "In documents of the late Middle Ages personal names are held in common by all and are so uniform that in the writs of assignation no legal differentiation is made between knights and others; this is especially noticeable in the judicial inquiries, where, alongside patronymics in general use, there begin to appear present-day surnames designating now nobles and now commoners. . . . A dominant race with a blood-stream different from that of the inhabitants," the writer goes on to say, "is inadmissible without personal names that are its exclusive property; and the counter-proof is patent in the extreme admixture of names and physical types throughout the whole of the population." [71] In this regard,

---

[71] Alberto Sampaio: *Estudos* (op. cit.).

the Portuguese historian cites a statement of major interest from the *Old Book*, or *Livro Velho*, itself, a work of ancient lineage, where we read: "There be many who come of good stock and they know it not . . . and many there be who by natural right may claim a share in many monasteries and many churches, many cities of refuge, and many honors, but who lose all from want of knowing of what stock it is that they come." [72]

It was, moreover, in the interest of the kings, who in Portugal so quickly asserted themselves against the vague outlines of feudalism, to level off social classes in so far as possible, permitting no one class to predominate. They achieved this in part by showing more favors to the bourgeoisie than to the aristocracy, by granting special rights to artisans, and, so far as lay within their power, by depriving the landed gentry of their prestige. The only exception was the ecclesiastical nobility, which in time and with the protection of the Pope was able to restrain the impulsiveness of the two Sanchos and to preserve for itself enormous economic privileges.

To be the "son of a somebody" (*"filho d'algo"*) in Portugal did not mean so much as to be a friar—that is to say, one who combined the knight's sword with the religious habit of one of the powerful military orders. The impoverished gentry had their answer from Dom Diniz at the end of the Middle Ages, when he deprived the nobles of their honors so long as they lived by industrial crafts or agricultural labor for others: "following the trade of blacksmith, or shoemaker, or tailor, or waxchandler, or any trade similar to these because they are in want of funds, or who labor for a price on the lands of another." [73] What is more, this state of things was prolonged in Brazil. Colonists of elevated birth were here shorn of their prestige when vanquished in the competition for the best lands and the largest number of agrarian slaves. At the beginning of the nineteenth century, Martim Francisco, in the interior of the *capitânia* of São Paulo, met with individuals of noble origin who were performing mechanical tasks as though they were plebeians, [74] to the detriment of their ancestral status, inasmuch as the laws of the Kingdom in such cases annulled their rights of nobility.

After five centuries there still were in Portugal no stratified and exclusive social classes with insurmountable barriers. "However preponderant it may have been once upon a time," writes Alberto Sampaio, "the nobility never succeeded in forming a closed aristocracy; the widespread use of the same names by persons of the most diverse

---

[72] Ibid.
[73] Ibid.

[74] Martim Francisco: *"Jornal de Viagens"* (loc. cit.).

conditions in life, as happens with present-day surnames, is not something new in our society; it is sufficiently explained by the constant shifting of individuals, some becoming distinguished while others returned to the masses from which they had sprung. In this respect the law of Dom Diniz is like a milestone between two eras, lending us historical confirmation." [75]

All of which reinforces my own conviction to the effect that Portuguese society was more mobile and fluctuating than any other, setting itself up and evolving, as it did, through an intense vertical as well as horizontal circulation of the most diverse elements so far as origin was concerned. Sorokin could find no better laboratory for the study and verification of his theory of mobility than among this people whose ethnic and social past shows the exclusive or absolute predominance of no one element, but a succession of compromises and interpenetrations.

One more observation regarding the Moors and the Mozarabs, regarding the process by which these two elements asserted their worth. The Portuguese commercial era, with a commerce that at first was limited to Europe, being extended at most only to the Levant, but which from the fifteenth century on was marked by bold overseas expeditions—this era, as I have said, was especially favorable to the ex-slaves, permitting them, as free men now, to embark upon adventures filled with possibilities of economic and social aggrandizement. With respect to Brazil, it is likely that among the first settlers were numerous individuals of Moorish and Mozarabic origin, along with new-Christians and old Portuguese. Debbané supposes that they were the principal colonizers of our country: *"de l'an 1550 à l'an 1600, les premiers colons de l'Amérique du Sud appartiennent à l'Espagne et au Portugal méridional, c'est à dire à la partie fortement orientalisée et arabisée de l'Espagne et du Portugal."* And again: *"Ce n'etaient pas en effet les Espagnols ni les Portugais du Nord descendants des Visigothes qui émigraient en Amérique; ceux-ci étaient les triomphateurs, les vainqueurs des guerres livrées contre des populations arabisées du Sud de la péninsule Ibérique."* [76] It may be said that Debbané's supposition, the opposite of Oliveira Vianna's, is too extreme. Vianna conceives a Brazil colonized in large part and chiefly organized by dolicho-blonds; [77] but the most minute researches in this

---

[75] Sampaio, op. cit.

[76] Nicolas J. Debbané, op. cit.—It is timely to recall the localizations of individuals of Moorish origin observed in São Paulo by Martim Francisco.

[77] In the second edition of his *Evolução do Povo Brasileiro* the distinguished sociologist stresses the fact that he presents this thesis "as a pure hypothesis, a purely conjectural sup-

field, such as the study of sixteenth-century inventories and wills to be found in São Paulo, tend to show that Brazilian colonization was effected very much in the Portuguese manner; that is to say, heterogeneously so far as racial and social origins are concerned, with neither brown skins nor blonds predominating; neither Mozarabs, as Debbané assumes, nor aristocrats, as Oliveira Vianna with his quasimystical Aryanism imagines; neither the gilded fidalgos of Frei Gaspar nor those dregs of the Kingdom—criminals and prostitutes— with which Portugal is so commonly accused of having filled Brazil during the first centuries of colonization.

Those descendants of the Mozarabs and Christianized Moors who made their way to Brazil—and among them, Debbané finds, were even prisoners of war from the Moroccan campaigns and Moors who had been expelled in 1610—did not come directly out of a state of rural servitude, but had been in the service of the powerful of the realm, engaged in urban occupations which many of them had taken up by way of evading the laws of Dom Fernando. Others had come from free labor on lands held in fief. Still others had the useful trades of shoemaker and tailor. Among the newcomers in the cities and towns of the sixteenth century there must have been many who had already improved their condition, economically and socially, by dealing in hides and by practicing the trades not only of shoemaker and tailor, but of blacksmith and furrier as well. But there were some who still had to struggle against difficulties and were anxious for an opportunity to better their way of life, and their technical aptitudes were undoubtedly of great value in the colonizing epeditions of ruined fidalgos and military adventurers, who possessed no other knowledge than that of how to handle a sword, a knowledge that was all but useless to them now.

"It is this scarcity of manual labor," writes João Lúcio de Azevedo, with reference to Portugal, "that accounts for the importance that master craftsmen and artisans came to have in our towns and for their influence in our deliberative assemblies." [78] Blacksmiths, shoemakers, furriers, stonemasons, gold- and silver-smiths, minters, coopers—these formed a true aristocracy of technicians, commanding the respect of

position," never as a "definite assertion." He adds: "I must confess, meanwhile, that a more profound study of the problems of Race and an increasing contact with the great sources of scientific elaboration in this field have led to a deep-going revision of my ideas on this and other problems of ethnology and anthroposociology."—Op. cit., Preface to 2nd edition (São Paulo, 1933).

[78] João Lúcio de Azevedo: *"Organização Econômica"* (loc. cit.).

a society that all of a sudden, as it were, had emerged from the monotonous simplicity of rural and agricultural life, one that had suddenly emerged from a regime in which its limited industrial needs had been supplied by its own servants or by the household arts of its womenfolk, and which now was called upon to give its attention to the diversifications and refinements of a free industrial activity in the new urban centers. Hence the social force into which, along with the merchants of the maritime cities, the technicians, workers, and artists were transformed. Street names in Lisbon to this day recall that dominance over the life of the city which, under a mildly religious form, was exercised by them, concentrated as they were in certain, one might say strategic, quarters or squares that were like so many fiefs. Shoemakers, linen merchants, blacksmiths, fishermen, gilders. All trades, all activities—each with its own saint, its own banner, its own privileges. And through the *casa-dos-vinte-e-quatro* (chamber of aldermen) these technicians and artists exerted a palpable influence over the city administrations. Various privileges were granted them by the kings,[79] privileges carrying with them an elevation in the social and political scale. It was from the syndicates of master workmen that the religious brotherhoods and confraternities were derived, which later were to flourish also in Brazil, being there extended to take in even slaves, but without any slightest trace of the prestige that they had enjoyed in Portugal as an expression of class rights.

Analyzing the first strata of São Vicente settlers, through inventories and wills of the sixteenth and seventeenth centuries, Alfredo Ellis, Jr., makes the point that the "southern region of Portugal, taking in Alentejo, Portuguese Estremadura, and the Algarves"—the zone, be it noted, that was most deeply penetrated with Moorish blood—"was the one that sent us around twenty-eight per cent of our settlers of known origin, a percentage equal to that of the Lusitanian north." [80] And contrary to the theory of Lapouge, represented among us by

---

[79] In his study of "The Evolution of Portuguese Industry," J. de Oliveira Simões has this to say: "The *Casa dos 24*, with its people's judge, clerk, and bailiff, a junta formed by delegates from the mechanical trades which functioned in the principal cities, shows the social importance that the labor of the people had attained in the life of the nation."— *Notas sobre Portugal* (op. cit.).—See

also on this subject the studies by João Lúcio de Azevedo: "*Organização Econômica*" (loc. cit.); J. M. Esteves Pereira: *A Indústria Portuguesa* (op. cit.); and Paulo Merêa: "*Organização social e administração pública*" ("Social Organization and Public Administration"), in *História de Portugal*.

[80] Alfredo Ellis, Jr.: *Raça de Gigantes, a civilização no planalto paulista* (op. cit.).

Oliveira Vianna,[81] to the effect that the Nordics are the race that is most highly endowed with the qualities of initiative and daring, the researches of the writer just quoted show the twenty-eight per cent from the south and their descendants to be eugenically superior to the twenty-eight per cent from the north. This, whether we have in mind the deeds of the *sertanistas*, the backland explorers, or the fecundity, longevity, and virility that the latter display.

Many of the carpenters, blacksmiths, tailors, shoemakers, butchers, who to a large extent made up São Paulo society, must have come originally from the Mozarabic masses, who for two centuries had established their worth and had risen in the social scale. We have seen, however, that throughout the first centuries of Portuguese national life the classes were never stratified or isolated behind frontiers that were not to be crossed. The King, Dom Diniz, recognized the value of the shoemakers and tailors, and it was only their lack of resources that prevented their being granted the prerogatives of nobility. For them emigration to American and the colonization of its virgin lands must have offered splendid opportunities of social ascent or readjustment. The master-builder who accompanied Thomé de Souza [82] to Brazil was liberally recompensed by His Majesty for technical services rendered, and the carpenters, plasterers, and stonemasons must have been similarly rewarded.

To the representatives of the Mozarabic masses among the first colonists of Brazil should be added those who represented the small but substantial agrarian nobility, who in Pernambuco were gathered around the patriarchal figure of Duarte Coelho. There was also a lesser number of representatives of the military and foot-loose aristocracy who had been drawn to Brazil through a spirit of adventure or who had come to serve a term of exile in the tropical wilderness. But the point to be stressed is the presence of the Mozarab descendants—not scattered here and there, but in large numbers—among the early settlers, for they were the representatives of the energetic and creative plebeian strata. It was through this element that so many traces of Moorish culture were transmitted to Brazil. Traces of moral and material culture. Debbané mentions one: the mild treatment accorded to slaves,[83] who, to tell the truth, among the Brazilians as among the Moors, were members of the household rather than beasts

---

[81] See his *Populações Meridionais do Brasil;* also *Evolução do Povo Brasileiro.*

[82] Thomé (or Tomás) de Souza was the Portuguese soldier appointed Governor of Brazil by King John III in 1549. He ruled the country from the then capital of Bahia. (Translator.)

[83] Debbané, loc. cit.

of burden. Another trace of Moorish influence to be identified in Brazil is the idealization of the fat woman as a type of beauty, an ideal that was so firmly fixed in the minds of the colonial generations and those under the Empire.[84] And still another: the fondness for voluptuous tub or "canoe" baths,[85] as well as for the sound of running water in the gardens of the Big Houses. Burton came upon various reminiscences of Moorish customs in nineteenth-century Brazil. That of having the children recite in concert the multiplication table and their spelling lesson reminded him of Mohammedan schools.[86] And having traveled into the interior of Minas and São Paulo, he there found the women going to Mass clad in the mantilla, their faces almost wholly covered in the manner of the Arab women. In the sixteenth, seventeenth, and eighteenth centuries veils and mantillas were to be seen all over Brazil, giving to feminine fashions an air that was more Oriental than European. The veils were a sort of "black domino," funereal cloaks in which many of the Portuguese beauties went shrouded, as they are described by Sebastião José Pedroso in his *Itinerary*, in speaking of the women of the Kingdom.[87]

And let us not forget that our colonial grandmothers always preferred rugs and mats to armchairs and stuffed sofas, thus leaning to Oriental custom rather than to the refinements of European taste. In the house and even in church it was upon cool pipiri [88] mats that they seated themselves, legs crossed in Moorish fashion, their tiny feet covered by their skirts. "When they go visiting," we learn from a seventeenth-century Dutch manuscript, with reference to the Luso-Brazilian women, "they first of all send ahead to announce their coming; the mistress of the house then seats herself upon a beautiful Turkish carpet, made of silk and spread out on the floor, and waits for her women friends, who take their places on the rug beside her, sitting like tailors, but with their feet covered, for it would be a great shame for them to permit anyone to see their feet." [89]

---

[84] "One of the greatest compliments that can be paid a lady is to tell her that she is becoming fatter and more beautiful," notes George Gardner in *Travels in the Interior of Brazil, Principally through the Northern Provinces* (London, 1886).

[85] So called because the bath had the shape of a canoe. (Translator.)

[86] Richard F. Burton: *Explorations of the Highlands of the Brazil* (London, 1869).

[87] *Itinerario de Lisboa e Viana do Minho*, etc. (*Itinerary of Lisbon and Viana do Minho*), in Leite de Vasconcellos: *Ensaios Etnográficos* (*Ethnographic Essays*) (Lisbon, 1910).

[88] The pipiri is a herbaceous plant of the *Ciperaceæ* family (*Rhynchospora storea*). (Translator.)

[89] The account tells us that when the seventeenth-century senhoras went out, it was in hammocks with rugs thrown over them, or else they went cloistered in palanquins. They were clad in costly apparel, with

There were various other material values that were absorbed by the Portuguese from Moorish or Arabian culture and that they transmitted to Brazil: the art of glazed tiling, of which so prominent a use is made in our churches, convents, residences, bathhouses, waterspouts, and fountains; Moorish tiles; windows with quartered or checkered panes; latticework (Venetian) shades; the *abalcoado*;[90] the thick walls of houses.[91] To this influence likewise we owe our acquaintance with a number of delicacies and culinary processes, along with a certain taste that we have for fat and oily foods, rich in sugar. The couscous, today so very Brazilian, is of North African origin.

The chronicle-writer who accompanied Cardinal Alexandrino to Lisbon in 1571 noted the abuse of sugar, cinnamon, spices, and eggyolks in Portuguese cooking. He was told that the greater part of the dishes in question were Moorish. He also observed the fact that napkins were changed in the middle of the meal, a refinement of cleanliness that was perhaps unknown to the Italians. The old Portuguese cook-books, such as the *Arte de Cozinha* of Domingos Rodrigues, master cook to His Majesty (Lisbon, 1692) is filled with Moorish recipes: "Moorish lamb," "Moorish sausage," "Moorish hen," "Moorish fish," "Moorish broth."

As to the general influence of the Mohammedans upon the Hispanic peninsula—on its medicine, hygiene, mathematics, architecture, and decorative arts—I shall confine myself to the observation that,

---

many jewels, even though some of them were imitation ones.—"Brief Discourse on the State of the Four Conquered Capitânias, of Pernambuco, Itamaracá, Paráhybá, and Rio Grande, Situated in the Northern Part of Brazil," translated from the Dutch of a manuscript in the Archives of The Hague and published in the *Revista do Instituto Arqueológico, Histórico e Geográfico de Pernambuco*, No. 34.

[90] A kind of Moorish balcony. (Translator.)

[91] Araujo Vianna, in a paper on "The Plastic Arts in Brazil in General and the City of Rio de Janeiro in Particular," in the *Revista do Instituto Histórico e Geográphico Brasileiro*, notes among the Moorish reminiscences in our Big Houses the "*rótulas*" (latticed shades) and the "strips of glazed tiling in the patios and dining-rooms."—José Marianno, in writing on "The Reasons for Brazilian Architecture," in the Rio newspaper *O Jornal*, says: "The excess of luminosity in the environment was intelligently corrected by thick layers of wall; by broad verandas (the entry-ways of Pernambucan houses), especially designed to protect the living-rooms against the rigors of the sun's direct rays; by Venetian or latticed blinds (*rótulas*); and by Moorish porches and balconies."—Another trace of Moorish culture should be mentioned: the good sense displayed by the Portuguese colonizer of Brazil in the narrow streets of his time; today, unfortunately, they are wholly disappearing and their place is being taken by broad streets and avenues."

put down by repressive measures or Catholic reaction, this influence still survived the Christian reconquest. The Moorish art of decoration as applied to palaces and dwellings came down intact through the centuries of greatest Christian splendor, to vie favorably with the eighteenth-century rococo style. Dominant in Portugal, it flowered anew in the decoration of the Big Houses in nineteenth-century Brazil.

The colonial craftsmen to whom Brazil owes the designing of its first habitations, churches, fountains, and portals of artistic interest were men who had been brought up in the Moorish tradition. From their hands it was that we received the precious heritage of glazed tile. If I insist upon this cultural trait, it is for the reason that it is so intimately bound up with hygiene and family life, in Portugal and in Brazil. More than a mere mural decoration rivalling Arras-cloth, the Moorish tile represents, in the domestic life of the Portuguese and his Brazilian descendant in colonial days, a survival of that taste for cleanliness and neatness, for brightness, and for water, that almost instinctive sense of tropical hygiene, which is so keen in the Moor. This was a sense or an instinct that the Portuguese, re-Europeanized in the shadow of the Christian reconquest, had in large part lost. With the Christians the glazed tile was practically transformed into a decorative carpet, of which the hagiologist made the most advantageous use in the pious decoration of chapels, cloisters, and residences. It retains, however, by reason of the very nature of the material, those hygienic qualities which are characteristically Arabian and Moorish: it is cool, clean, and easily polished.

The contrast afforded by the truly feline hygienic habits of the Mohammedans and the uncleanliness of their Christian conquerors is one that should be noted. Condé, in his history of the Arabic rule in Spain, a work so often cited by Buckle, portrays the peninsular Christians—that is, the intransigents of the seventh and ninth centuries—as being individuals who never took a bath, never washed their linen, and never removed their clothes until they were falling off them in shreds. This horror of water, this neglect of bodily hygiene and care of the clothing, remains with the Portuguese of today, and I believe it may be stated that this is especially the case in those regions that have benefited least from the Moorish influence. Alberto Sampaio dwells upon the unclean habits of the native of Minho province, who represents the blondest, most European and Christian type to be found in Portugal.[92] It is true that Estanco Louro,

---

[92] Alberto Sampaio: *Estudos* (op. cit.).

in a recent monograph on Alportel, a rural parish in southern Portugal, reports a "flagrant neglect of bodily cleanliness" on the part of the natives of the place, "a lack of bodily hygiene, bathing in the majority of cases being limited to washing the face on Sunday in very cursory fashion"; "a lack of public toilets and urinals in the towns; in the country, privies adjoining the houses . . . pigsties and dung-heaps kept near the dwellings and stables communicating with the latter." [93] But on the other hand, this writer mentions certain notions of cleanliness on the part of the inhabitants that are carried to the point of an obsession, and that possibly have been preserved from the time of the Moors. "This may be seen in the frequent scrubbing of the house floor, in the constant whitewashing of houses and walls, in their unfailing habit of changing into very clean linen every week. . . ." [94] Moreover, in connection with the south of Portugal, one should take into account the scarcity of water, which places the inhabitant of town or countryside under conditions that are identical with those that confront the Brazilian backlander—another one who rarely takes a bath, although he piques himself upon his scrupulously clean linen and the neatness he displays in his person and in his home.

The Franciscan brightness of the house in southern Portugal, always freshly whitewashed, forms a striking contrast with the dwellings to be found in the northern and central portions of the country, which are grimy, ugly, filthy abodes. In the former the influence of the Moor in the direction of brightness and a pleasing coolness is evident. The inside affords the same contrast. It is a pleasure to enter a southern house, with the kitchenware gleaming like mirrors along the walls, conveying a charming impression of clean dishes and laundered towels.

There is another influence exerted by the Moor upon Portuguese character of which we should take note: the influence of Mohammedan upon Christian morality. No form of Christianity is more human or more lyric than that of the Portuguese. From the pagan religions, but from that of Mohammed as well, it has preserved as none other in Europe a taste for the fleshly things of life. It is a Christianity in which the Infant Jesus is identified with Cupid, and the Virgin Mary and the saints with the concerns of procreation and love rather than with chastity and asceticism.[95] In this respect Portu-

---

[93] Estanco Louro: *O Livro de Alportel—Monografia de uma freguesia rural (The Book of Alportel—Monograph on a Rural Parish)* (Lisbon, 1929).

[94] Ibid.

[95] For an expression in modern short-story form of this spirit of

guese Christianity may be said to go further than Mohammedanism itself. Tiles with a-sexual designs among the followers of the Prophet take on near-aphrodisiac forms in the cloisters of convents and along the baseboards of sacristies. Nude figures. Divine infants in whom the nuns very often adore the pagan god of love in preference to the Nazarene, gloomy and full of wounds, who died on the Cross. One of these nuns it was, Sister Violante do Céu, who compared the Christ child to Cupid:

> *Divine little Shepherd,*
> *Who slayest with love,*
> *Withhold not thine arrows*
> *From falling in my heart!*
> *But draw thy bow and strike me,*
> *Slay me with love,*
> *That I may no longer wish for life,*
> *Save but to die for thee!* [96]

In connection with the worship accorded the Infant Jesus, the Virgin, and the saints there is always an idyllic, even a sensual note. One of love or human desire. The influence of Mohammedanism would appear to have been favored by the mild, one might say the aphrodisiac climate of Portugal. Our Lady of Expectation in the image of a pregnant woman.[97] São Gonçalo do Amarante comes near turning human in order to take the women who beset him with promises and frictions.[98] And St. John the Baptist is feasted on St. John's Day as if he were a handsome young lad and lover let loose among the marriageable maidens, who address to him such nonsense as this:

> *Whence comest thou, St. John,*

---

paganism in Portuguese Catholicism, see Aquilino Ribeiro's "The Last Faun," published in my translation in *Heart of Europe*, the anthology edited by Klaus Mann and Hermann Kesten (New York: L. B. Fischer; 1943), pp. 193–204. (Translator.)

[96] Soror Violante do Céu: *Parnaso de Divinos e Humanos Versos*, in Leite de Vasconcellos: *Ensaios Etnográficos* (op. cit.).

[The translation given is a free one. The original lines are:

Pastorzillo divino
Que matas de amor

Ay, tened no flecheis,
No tereis, nó,
Que no cabem más flechas
En mi coraçon!
Mas tirad, y flechadme
Matadme d'amor,
Que nó quiro más vida
Que morrir por vós!
(Translator.)]

[97] "*Nossa Senhora do O*." See p. 30, note 78. (Translator.)

[98] The women would rub themselves against the saint's legs. (Translator.)

> *that thou comest so all bedewed?* [99]

Or:

> *Whence comest thou, O Baptist,*
> *that thou smellest thus of rosemary?* [100]

And the young fellows threaten the saintly protector of lovers and love's idylls in this manner:

> *If the lasses do not care for me,*
> *I will beat the little saint.*[101]

It is impossible to conceive of a Portuguese or Luso-Brazilian Christianity without this intimacy between the worshipper and the saint. Semi-obscene ceremonies came to be associated with St. Anthony, while on feast-days in colonial times São Gonçalo's image was batted around like a ball.[102] In Portugal as in Brazil the favorite images of the Virgin and the Infant Jesus were decked out with trinkets, jewels, bracelets, earrings, and gold and diamond crowns, as if they had been members of the family, and the human attributes of king, queen, father, mother, son, and sweetheart were attributed to them. Each of them was closely associated with some phase of domestic and private life. There is no more interesting result of the many centuries of contact between Christianity and the religion of the Prophet—a contact sharpened at times into the asperities of rivalry—than the military character that certain saints came to take on in Portugal and later in Brazil. Miracle-working saints such as St. Anthony, St. George, and St. Sebastian with us became captains or military leaders, like some powerful lord of the plantation. In the processions of old the heavily laden litters of the saints resembled those of great chieftains who had triumphed in war. Some of the holy ones were even placed on horseback and clad as generals. And

---

99 "All bedewed": as a child that has wet itself. The original of these verses is:

> *Donde vindes, S. João,*
> *que vindes tão molhadinho?*
>   (Translator.)
> 100 *Donde vindes, ó Batista,*
> *que cheirais a alecrim?*
> 101 *As moças não me querendo*
> *dou pancadas no santinho.*

From Portuguese folklore.—In Brazil, when it rains on St. John's Night, it is said, without the least respect for the infant saint, that he is *mijão* (that is, has wet himself). They even say the same thing of the venerated St. Peter in case of rain on his night.

102 Literally, "played peteca with." The *peteca* is "a certain plaything, made of hide and feathers that is batted in the air with the palms of the hands; in Alagoas they play it with a cornstalk and a head of Indian corn and call it corn-ball (*bola de milho*)." —Lima and Barroso, op. cit. (Translator.)

accompanying these processions there was always a feast-day multitude, a fraternal and democratic jumble of humanity. Great ladies in church-bonnets and prostitutes with ulcerous sores on their legs. Fidalgos and slave boys.

The feast of the Church, in Brazil as in Portugal, is an institution that has in it as little as could be of the Nazarene, that side of him which was so detested by Nietzsche. The stern and gloomy side. With regard to Hispanic Christianity, it may be said in a general way that the whole of it was dramatized in this festive cult of saints with the arms and trappings of generals—São Tiago, St. Isidore, St. George, St. Emiliano, St. Sebastian—in this homage paid to saints who were, at the same time, Moor-slayers, champions of the cause of independence. In Brazil the rites of St. George, on horseback and sword in hand, armed for combat against heretics, and those of St. Anthony, who, we do not know exactly how it came about, has been militarized into a lieutenant-colonel, have prolonged through the colonial era and the Empire this nationalistic and militaristic, civic and patriotic aspect of peninsular Christianity, a Christianity that had been obliged, through clashes with Moor and Jew, thus to clothe itself in armor and don the warrior's feathered bonnet. Certain "Praised be the Most Blessed Sacrament" inscriptions, such as one that is to be seen today at the entrance of an old street in Salvador da Bahia, are but the remnants of war-cries from an age when Portuguese Christians felt themselves to be surrounded by enemies of the faith.

Just as with regard to the Moors, social contact with the Jews left its unmistakable traces upon the Portuguese colonizers of Brazil, exerting an influence over their economic, social, and political life and their character. This influence, like that of the Moor, was in the direction of de-Europeanization. In either case, when the relations between the two peoples came to the point of bloody conflict, the cloak of mysticism which the struggle took on was not one that had to do with racial purity, but was concerned with purity of faith. Publicists who today presume to interpret the ethnic and political history of Portugal after the European pattern, by explaining the conflicts with the Jews on the basis of racial hatred, end by contradicting themselves. Thus, Mário Sáa, after advocating this thesis and defending it with all the ardor and verve of a pamphleteer, in the end has to confess that "everywhere the Jews have the consciousness of being Jews save in Portugal; there they do not have it. They came down through the ages under the designation of new-Christians, and it was only a little more than a hundred years ago that this ill-famed

designation was abolished by the decree of Pombal.[103] The consequence was that, with the loss of religious uniformity, they became
forgetful of themselves." [104] In essence the Jewish problem in Portugal was always an economic one, created by the irritating presence
of a powerful suction-mechanism operating upon the majority of the
people, not only to the benefit of the Israelite minority, but to that of
the great plutocratic interests in general.[105] The interests of the kings,
the great lords, and the religious orders.

Thus have historical circumstances shaped the Jews. Max Weber
attributes their development into a commerical people to a ritualistic
determinism, which after their exile forbade their settling in any land
and becoming tillers of the soil. Weber stresses what he sees as the
dualism of their commercial ethics, permitting them two attitudes,
one for their coreligionists and one for strangers.[106] It was natural that
such exclusiveness should give rise to economic hatreds. This goes
to explain the protection that was accorded them by the kings and big
landed proprietors, and in the shadow of this protection they prospered into large-scale plutocrats and capitalists. Concentrating in the
cities and maritime ports, they contributed to the victory of the
bourgeoisie over the great agricultural landowners, who were allied
with the Church rather than with the crown. But it is interesting to
observe that even the landed gentry, when weakened by the maritime, anti-feudal policy of the sovereigns, did not hesitate to seek a
revivifying strength in the Israelite plutocracy, through the dowries
brought them by wealthy Jewish brides. The blood of the best of
Portugal's nobility thus mingled with that of the Hebraic plutocracy

[103] Pombal, Portuguese Minister
(1750–77), not only declared the Indians in Brazil to be free men, but at
home banished the Jesuits, abolished
the Inquisition, and introduced other
sweeping reforms. (Translator.)

[104] Mário Sáa: *A Invasão dos Judeus*
(*The Invasion of the Jews*) (Lisbon,
1924).

[105] In connection with Freyre's discussion of the Jews in Portugal, the
reader should bear in mind that what
he is striving for, here as elsewhere
throughout his work, is the rigorous
objectivity of the social scientist. One
may recall, for example, the harsh
things he has already had to say about
the Portuguese (see p. 185 f.) and the
Jesuit (see p. 173). Historical circum-

stance happened to identify the Portuguese Jew with mercantilism and
"plutocracy" in this era, and at times
cast him in the role of oppressor, or
seeming oppressor, the ally of the
powerful against the "little people";
but to assume from this that the
author regards such attributes as permanent racial ones is to contradict the
very method of historical determinism that he professes and so con-
sistently endeavors to practice. It may
also be recalled that Karl Marx, himself a Jew, had equally harsh, if not
harsher, things to say on this subject.
(Translator.)

[106] Max Weber: *General Economic
History* (translation) (New York,
1927).

when fidalgos threatened with ruin took to wife the daughters of rich stockjobbers. Hence it was that distinguished Jews, already of the aristocracy through their bonds with the nobility, came to take the essentially aristocratic position of supporting the Queen, Dona Leonor, against the people and the bourgeoisie in connection with the succession of His Majesty Dom Fernando.

Varnhagen [107] tells us that, in Spain and Portugal, stockjobbing had come to monopolize the "sweat and labor of the entire industry of the tiller of the soil and the shipbuilder, and even the revenues of State." And he adds: "The rapid circulation of funds made possible by bills of exchange, the speed with which large credits could be extended from Lisbon to Seville, to the fair of Medina, to Genoa, to Flanders, gave to this class—aided by the establishment of couriers, of whom they knew how to make good use—so great a superiority in business matters that no one else could compete with them. They even came to the aid of the State when it was hard pressed, and their assistance was reputed a great service and they were recompensed accordingly. Other times it was the heir to a great name and the representative of many heroes who, by the way of accommodating himself to the fashion of the age, did not disdain to ally himself with the granddaughter of a converted hangman whose descendant had become a rich *tratante*, or dealer, as the saying then was, without the word's taking on the evil sense that was to be associated with the actions of those same dealers." It may be seen that, in the case of the Jews as in that of the Moors, there was a great vertical mobility that ended in a mingling of strains in the marriage between those of diverse ethnic stocks.

The Jews in Portugal constituted a great and subtle influence through commerce, through stockjobbing, through the high technical posts that they occupied in the administration, through their blood-bonds with the old military and landowning nobility, and, finally, through the superiority of their intellectual and scientific culture. This was especially true in the case of the physicians, who were powerful rivals of the priests in the influence they exerted over families and over the sovereigns. The bourgeois and cosmopolitan direction so precociously taken by the Portuguese monarchy, contrary to its first agrarian and military tendencies, was due above all to the economic interests represented by the Jews, who, strategically and out of the horror of "men of the nation" for agriculture, were concentrated in the maritime cities, where they had an easy and

---

[107] Varnhagen: *História Geral do Brasil* (op. cit.).

permanent contact with the international centers of Jewish finance.

It is obvious that the kings of Portugal did not protect the Jews out of love for the latter's beautiful Oriental eyes; they did it out of self-interest, forcing the Jew to contribute, through heavy taxes and duties, to the wealth of the crown and the State. It is worthy of note that the Portuguese merchant marine was in large part developed through the special taxes paid by the Hebrews for every ship that was built and launched. In this manner the crown and State took advantage of Israelite property for their own enrichment. Portuguese imperialism and imperialist expansion were based upon Jewish prosperity.

Chamberlain brings out the point that the Jews, from the beginning of the Visigoth period, were able to impose themselves upon the peninsular peoples as slave-traders and money-lenders; so that the inclination of the Portuguese to live off slaves would appear to have been abetted by this Sephardic impulse. An enemy of manual toil, the Jew from remote times had a bent toward slavery. Chamberlain tells us that it was Isaiah who was responsible for the idea that aliens ought to be tillers of the soil and workers in the vineyard for the Hebrews.[108] And certain it is that many Jews in the peninsula, from a time beyond that of which we have any record, were the owners of Christian slaves and possessed Christian concubines.[109]

As for their economic specialization, it would seem that it was later extended to the commerce in foodstuffs: "dried fish and many things," says a petition of 1602, accusing them of being exploiters "of the little people, who live on dried fish." [110]

It was in 1589 that the Table of Conscience and Order in consultation with His Majesty took up the problem raised by the fact that the new-Christians, in addition to their other activities, were monopolizing the professions of physician and apothecary, and the further fact that the realm was filling up with bachelors of the arts.[111] In either case the excess appears to us to have been due to the endeavor on the part of the new-Christians to rise in the social scale by making use of their Sephardic traditions of intellectuality, the superiority in intellectual pursuits that they possessed over the rude sons of the soil. To the Israelite influence may be attributed much of the mercantilism in the character and tendencies of the Portuguese; but it is also fitting

---

[108] Houston Stewart Chamberlain: *The Foundations of the Nineteenth Century* (London, 1911).

[109] João Lúcio de Azevedo: *História dos Cristãos-Novos Portugueses* (*History of the Portuguese New-Christians*) (Lisbon, 1922).

[110] Ibid.

[111] Ibid., cited by Mário Sáa, op. cit.

that we attribute to it the opposite excesses of a fondness for learned trappings,[112] legalism, juridical mysticism. The very ring on the finger of the Brazilian bachelor of arts or one holding a doctor's degree, a ring set with an emerald or a ruby, impresses us as being reminiscent of the Orient and the Israelites. Another Sephardic trait may be seen in the mania for eyeglasses and pince-nez—employed as an outward mark of learning or of intellectual and scientific attainment. The Abbot of La Caille, who was in Rio de Janeiro in 1751, tells us that everyone he saw who was a doctor or bachelor in theology, law, or medicine had a pair of glasses on his nose *"pour se faire respecter des passans."* [113] And that very mania itself that we all have for being doctors, in Portugal and above all in Brazil—even our bookkeepers who are bachelors of commerce, our agronomists, our engineers, our veterinarians—what is all this if not another Sephardic reminiscence?

Varnhagen reminds us that it was by making use of the middle class and the educated laity that the monarchy in Portugal was able to free itself of the pressure of the clergy and the former landed gentry. He says: "This educated magistracy, by its learning, its plottings, its activity, its loquaciousness, and the protection afforded it by the Ordinances, drawn up by members of its own class, was to come to assume a dominant position in the country as time went on, and was even to win for itself a place among the topmost aristocracy, after having, in general, displayed a hostility to that class before attaining it." [114] This was a case of rapid social promotion. For this

---

112 The author's word is *bacharelismo*, from *bacharel*, one who has finished the secondary course, corresponding to the *lycée* or *Gymnasium*. (Translator.)

113 *Journal historique du voyage fait au Cap de Bonne Esperance* (Paris, 1763), p. 211.—On the mania for spectacles, or *quevedos*, in Portugal in the sixteenth, seventeenth, and eighteenth centuries, see Júlio Dantas: *Figuras de Ontem e de Hoje* (*Figures of Yesterday and Today*) (Lisbon, 1914). The writer reminds us that the two traits that Montesquieu particularly noticed in the Portuguese were their eyeglasses and their mustaches (*les lunettes et . . . la moustache*). Montesquieu interpreted the abuse of spectacles in Portugal in the same fashion that the Abbot of La Caille did in Brazil. Let us not forget that, as it would appear, at least nearly all the doctors of medicine were Jews. The author of the *Voyage de Marseille à Lima et dans les autres Indes Occidentales* (Paris, 1720), p. 132, states that the city of Salvador was filled with Jews. Frezier makes a similar observation. He tells the story of a vicar who fled from Bahia to Holland, after long years of false Catholic devotion, when it became known that he was a Jew.— *Relation du voyage de la Mer du Sud aux côtes du Chily et du Pérou* (Paris, 1716), p. 276.

114 There must have been also many concealed Jews or individuals of Hebraic origin among the advocates who, from the sixteenth century on, emigrated from the Kingdom to the

educated bourgeoisie that so rapidly became aristocratic, through its university culture and its intellectual and juridical services rendered to the monarchy, was largely made up of new-Christians or "men of the nation," the remnants of another bourgeoisie: one of merchants, traders, stockjobbers, middlemen. So eager were the new-Christians to elevate their sons who had become doctors and bachelors to university chairs and the magistracy that the Table of Conscience and Order at the end of the seventeenth century made up its mind to limit the bestowing of the bachelor's degree in Portugal and suggested to the King that the number of sons whom a person of noble birth might send to the university be limited to two, and that the father who was an artisan be allowed to send but one, while the matriculation of new-Christians should depend upon His Majesty's licensing power; for "even with this, there will be a surplus of lettered ones in the realm." The new-Christians constituted the majority of lecturers in the higher schools—one of them being the famous doctor Antônio Homem; they were prominent among the lawyers, magistrates, and physicians; and Coimbra, in the phrase of João Lúcio de Azevedo, came to be a "den of heretics," so large was the number of Jews in students' cassocks and professors' gowns.[115]

It is understandable that the new-Christians, with their background of usury, the slave trade, and stockjobbing, should have found in the university degrees of bachelor, master, and doctor a token of social prestige in keeping with their Sephardic tendencies and ideals; it is natural that they should have found in the law, medicine, and higher education an ideal way to enter the aristocracy. It is interesting to observe how their surnames were dissolved into the Germanic and Latin names of the old-Christians. Dom Manuel I, moreover, made it easy for the new-Christians to become naturalized and at the same time to change their family names to more aristocratic-sounding ones, by permitting them to make use of the noblest names in Portugal. Other persons were prohibited from taking "the surnames of fidalgos of known estate who have lands within the jurisdiction of our realm," but this privilege was freely granted to the new-Christians: "How-

colonies, with their eyeglasses, their chicaneries, and their parasitism. Of the city of Goa, which in the sixteenth century was invaded by usurers and shysters, a contemporary writes: "The city of Goa has the appearance of an academy of litigants, rather than that of a school of arms." —Ferdinand Denis: *Portugal* (Paris, 1746). Of the Realm, an eighteenth-century observer has this to say: "The multitude of lawyers is notorious and their utility very doubtful." —*Os Frades Julgados no Tribunal da Razão* (*The Friars Judged at the Bar of Reason*) (Lisbon, 1814).

[115] João Lúcio de Azevedo: *História dos Cristãos-Novos* (op. cit.).

ever, those who have recently turned to our holy faith may take and hold during their lifetime, and may pass on to their sons alone, names of whatsoever lineage they desire, without any penalty." All this shows us how intense was the mobility and how free the circulation, so to speak, from one race to another, and, literally, from one class to another, from one to another social sphere, even in the case of the Jew.

The Jews in Portugal and in parts of Spain contributed to that horror of manual toil and the bent toward a system of slave labor that is so characteristic of both countries. They contributed to that state of artificial wealth which was observed by Francesco Guicciardini, the Italian historian, who early in the sixteenth century came to the Hispanic peninsula as Florentine Ambassador to the King of Aragon: "The poverty is great, and, as I see it, is due not so much to the nature of the country as to the temperament of its inhabitants, who are opposed to toil; they prefer to send to other nations those raw materials that their Kingdom produces and to buy them back in another form, as happens in the case of wool and silk, which they sell to foreigners and then buy back in the form of cloth and woven goods." [116] To be excepted from Guicciardini's generalization are those agricultural zones which for long had enjoyed the benefits of Moorish science and technique, among others the regions round about Granada. These were privileged zones. Another traveler, Navajero, describes them in truly lyrical fashion: a land thickly planted with trees, with much ripe fruit hanging from the boughs, a large variety of grapes, and dense groves of olive trees. And in the midst of all this luxuriant verdure, the houses of the Moorish descendants: small ones, it is true, but all of them with water and rosebushes, "showing that the land was even fairer when under Moorish dominion." [117] With the activity of this Moorish folk Navajero contrasts the negligence and sloth of the Hispanic population, which was not at all industrious and had no love whatever for the soil, its major enthusiasms being reserved for warlike undertakings and commercial adventures in the Indies. What was true of the Andalusian region was also to be observed in southern Portugal and in Algarve; here, too, were lands that had been benefited by the Moors, and the Polish traveler Nicolas de Popielovo at the end of the fifteenth century found almost no difference between this region and Andalusia: "In all the lands of Andalusia, Portugal, and Algarve . . . the dwellings and the inhabitants are alike, and the difference in education and customs be-

---

[116] J. García Mercadel: *España vista por los Estranjeros* (op. cit.).   [117] Ibid.

tween Saracens and Christians is only to be perceived in the matter of religion. . . ." [118] It should be noted, in passing, that the Christians were not remarkable for their devoutness; they only confessed themselves in the hour of death and fasted but rarely. It was not easy to practice fasting in a land that, in place of being poor in foodstuffs as was the greater part of the peninsula, had for long, thanks to the Moorish inheritance, been rich in grain, meat, and wine.

With regard to Portugal, the point should be stressed that its beginnings were wholly agrarian; agrarian likewise was its early history, later perverted by the commercial activity of the Jews and the imperialist policy of the monarchs. Its first exports were also agrarian: products of the land such as olive oil, honey, wine, and wheat. For the Moors, as we have seen, got the most out of the soil, especially in the south, where irrigation was called for and where the region was rendered productive through the science of the invaders.

The reconquest, although followed by the granting of large tracts of land to the great warriors, did not have the effect in Portugal of accentuating feudal traits and characteristics. In connection with the land grants to individuals, the domains of the crown were always set apart, to be cultivated by tenants or share-croppers, from whom the monarch through his overseers received a rent or share of the produce that was at times excessive, amounting to a half of the vintage, a third of the wheat crop. On the lands of the great lords it was incumbent upon the tenants to erect and keep in repair the castles, mills, ovens, and granaries. Behind the *solar*, or seignorial mansion, built of earth or packed clay—ancestor of the Big House of the Brazilian plantation—there was an economic unity. It cannot be said that the economic regime was from the first one of large-scale landownership—the King, the ecclesiastical foundations, and all those who shared in the spoils of the conquest being looked upon as big proprietors; it was, rather, a system of large holdings combined with smaller ones that had been parceled out for cultivation: "the soil of each lordly estate being divided into sub-units which in the beginning were in the charge of serfs, but which later were entrusted to tenants and share-croppers. [119] Thus, in the first phase of its agrarian development, Portugal enjoyed a balance and a stability that neither of the two systems in itself would have been able to maintain. Small property, on the one hand, would not have been capable of the military tension necessary in the case of farming lands surrounded by powerful enemies; and on the other

[118] Ibid.

[119] João Lúcio de Azevedo: "Organização Econômica" (loc. cit.). See also *Épocas de Portugal Econômico* (*Economic Epochs in Portugal*) (Lisbon, 1929), by the same author.

hand, large-scale ownership, without the parceling-out of land, would not have given to the beginnings of Portuguese agriculture so great a glow of health. An additional advantage lay in the fact that the ownership of large estates in Portugal never meant an unbridled individualism, inasmuch as the power of the crown, as well as that of the great religious corporations, which controlled some of the best land that there was for agricultural purposes, was very frequently asserted against the interests of individuals. The right of the Church to its lands had been won through the military exertions of the friars in the wars of reconquest, and had afterwards been increased by donations and legacies on the part of monarchs and those persons who were not fitted for an agricultural mode of life. "In populating and putting under cultivation a country devastated by wars, a notable part was played by the Church," writes João Lúcio de Azevedo. "Around the monasteries," he goes on to say, "agricultural labor was developed. A considerable part of Estremadura was tilled and populated by the monks of Alcobaça, and as much may be said of other places and regions. Bishops, monks, and ordinary parish priests were great builders and repairers and busied themselves with works of the most meritorious sort in those rude times." [120]

During the indecisive period of the struggle with the Moors it was chiefly in the shadow of the abbeys and the great monasteries that agriculture found a refuge, under the care of the monks, while industry and the arts took shelter inside the cloisters. Esteves Pereira observes that the Portuguese monasteries, "as well as being houses of prayer and studies, were turned into centers and schools of industrial activity, into laborious agricultural colonies that plowed up the backlands, tilled uncultivated fields, and rendered fertile various tracts of territory that until then had been a desert or had lain fallow." [121] The same writer further informs us that individuals were in the habit of donating lands to the monasteries and monastic and religious corporations, "since they themselves lacked the means of cultivating them." From this it is to be seen that the colonizing and civilizing capabilities of large-scale property were such as the small proprietors and absentee landlords did not possess. These latter were absorbed by the big estates, not only through donations made when they came to realize their own incapacity, but as a result of obligations incurred through loans which the wealthy religious corporations had readily made them, in fulfillment of their function as rural bankers, one that they exercised

---

[120] Azevedo: *Épocas de Portugal Econômico* (op. cit.).

[121] J. M. Esteves Pereira: *A Indústria Portuguesa* (op. cit.).

for a long time in the economic life of Portugal. This was advantageous to the agrarian interests, in that it did not permit lands and goods to pass into the possession of Jewish capitalists or the rich burghers of the town.

One point emerges as clear and evident to us, and that is, the creative and by no means parasitic role that was played by the big religious bodies—the Carthusians, the monks of Alcobaça, the Cistercians of St. Bernard, and other friars—in the economic development of Portugal. They were by way of being the true forebears of the great Brazilian proprietors, whose plantation Big Houses were likewise centers of industrial and charitable activity, being workshops, orphan asylums, hospitals, and hostelries all in one. As for the Portuguese friars, they were not the mere mountains of sterile flesh, choking in their own fat, that they are sometimes caricatured as being; in agrarian history of the time of the Affonsos they were the most creative and most active element. They and the sovereigns. Along with the Moorish tradition, those large-scale agriculturists, the friars, were the force that in Portugal did most to offset the Jewish influence. If parasitism was later to invade the convents, it was for the reason that not even the formidable energy of the monks was able to row against the tide. Against the Atlantic Ocean, it might be said, in all literalness. Especially when the powerful Israelite interests, traditionally maritime and anti-agrarian in character, were rowing in the direction of the great ocean, in the direction of overseas adventures in imperialism and commerce.

Portugal even exported wheat in its first, agrarian phase of economic health, the period during which the monasteries were most active. "We sent bread to the English from the reign of Senhor Dom Diniz down to that of Senhor Dom Fernando," is the reminder given us by the enlightened author of a certain brochure written at the end of the eighteenth century in defense of the Portuguese friars.[122] As this publicist saw it, the decline of agriculture was to be attributed to the inertia of the absentee landlords, given over to the luxurious life of the capitals; whereas in the case of the ecclesiastical holdings it was not so easy to be guilty of neglect and absenteeism: the estates in the hands of the friars "are ordinarily better cultivated, for the reason that if a prelate in charge is neglectful, his superior upon his visitations will admonish him, and his companions will accuse him of his ignorance or negligence; thus it is that these properties always have eyes and

---

[122] *Os Frades Julgados no Tribunal da Razão* (*The Friars Judged at the Bar of Reason*), posthumous work by Friar — —? — —, Doctor of Coimbra (Lisbon, 1814).

arms to aid them, and hence their yield is constantly being improved." [123] The agricultural wealth of Portugal was, accordingly, better conserved in the convents than in the hands of private individuals; it was well administered by the friars and very badly by the lords of large and sterile estates. Beckford, visiting Portugal in the eighteenth century—already a country of ruined fidalgos—still received an impression of great abundance from the monasteries. The kitchen of Alcobaça, for example, was an object of wonderment to him. He confesses that in no convent in Italy, France, or Germany had he beheld so large a space devoted to culinary rites. There were many fresh fish from the monastery's own waters, an abundance of game from the neighboring forests, and greens and ripe fruit of every sort from the gardens tended by the monks. Mountains of flour and sugar. Huge jars of olive oil. And laboring amid this tremendous abundance of pastry, fruits, and green vegetables was a numerous tribe of servants and laymen, all of them happy and singing as they prepared the tarts and cakes for the hospitable Alcobaça table. And when his foreign guest marveled at all this, the Abbot remarked to him: "In Alcobaça, no one is going to die of hunger." [124]

There is nothing to indicate that the country houses of Portugal —unless it was that of Marialva—had anything like this abundance and variety of victuals, all of them fresh and of the best quality, with which to regale the visitor. Victuals intended for the sustenance of hundreds of ecclesiastics, which also were offered to numerous travelers and needy ones. Yet this same Portugal, which had reached the point where it could export wheat to England, in its later mercantile phase was to have to import everything it needed for its table, with the exception of salt, wine, and olive oil. From abroad came wheat, rye, cheese, butter, eggs, and poultry. And the last strongholds of agricultural production, and hence of fresh and wholesome food, were the convents.

From this it may be seen that Ramalho Ortigão [125] was not without a basis in fact in evolving his curious theory with regard to the Por-

---

[123] Ibid.

[124] William Beckford: *Excursion to the Monasteries of Alcobaça and Batalha* (London, 1835). See also the same author's *Italy, with Sketches from Spain and Portugal* (London, 1834).

[125] Ramalho Ortigão (1836–1915) was one of Portugal's leading writers of the nineteenth century. Progres- sive in outlook and in all domains, with a remarkably balanced and virile personality, he was an exponent of social criticism in literature and edited a publication called *As Farpas* (*The Banderillas*) that was something of a cross between a pamphlet and a magazine and that made literary history. (Translator.)

tuguese friars and the profound influence the convents exerted upon the progress of the country. The monks, he argued, had constituted for a number of centuries the thinking class of the nation; and once the religious orders had been suppressed, Portuguese civilization remained acephalous, there being no other class to inherit their intellectual authority. All this, Ortigão concluded, was due to the regular and perfect diet of the friars, whereas the other classes, with an irregular and imperfect one, were handicapped in their capacity for labor and study by an alimentary insufficiency.

Brazil was colonized by a nation of the undernourished. The prevalent conception of the Portuguese as an overnourished individual is a false one. Ortigão comes to grips with this error, even though it is by an uncertain route: the reduced consumption of meat in Portugal. It would be unhygienic if in a country with an African climate the same amount of meat were consumed as in northern lands. The great publicist was building up an ideal of a Portuguese nourished on the same abundance of beef as the Englishman, which would be an absurdity. But the reduced consumption of meat that in the course of his researches he discovered in Lisbon is frightening by reason of the poverty to which it points: a kilogram and a half [3.3 pounds] per month for each inhabitant.[126]

The deficiency, however, was not limited to beef, but applied to milk and vegetables also. The preponderance of dried fish and preserved food in their diet appears to have had a speedy and unfavorable effect upon the health of the Portuguese people. "The lower classes live poorly, their daily food consisting of cooked sardines," we learn from Trom and Pippomani,[127] who were in Portugal in the year 1520. "Rarely do they buy meat, for the cheapest food is this variety of fish. . . ." And the bread was "not at all good . . . all full of

[126] Ramalho Ortigão: *As Farpas* (Lisbon).—There are a number of modern physiologists, like McCollum, Simmonds, Benedict, McCarrisson, McCay, Nitti, and Crichton Browne, who associate the amount of proteins consumed with the prosperity and efficiency of peoples. Especially meat and milk. The statistics furnished by Roberts for the Department of Agriculture of the United States appear to indicate this relation. The consumption of meat is greater in countries with a more efficient and prosperous population: Australia, 262 pounds; United States, 150; England and Ireland, 122; Germany, 99; France, 80; Sweden and Norway, 62. —"Annual Production of Animals for Food and Per Capita Consumption of Meat in the United States" (U. S. Department of Agriculture, 1905), cited by Ruy Coutinho: *Valor Social da Alimentação* (*Social Value of Diet*) (São Paulo, 1935).

[127] The Venetian ambassadors previously mentioned a number of times. (Translator.)

earth." Veal was scarce, and wheat came from abroad, from France, Flanders, and Germany.[128]

Estrabão states that in the peninsula, prior to the Roman occupation, the inhabitants for three-quarters of the year lived on acorn bread—that is, on a dough made of mashed acorns pounded after they are dried. Wine only on feast-days, at banquets, or on similar festive occasions, when the menu would obviously be a more plentiful and varied one.[129]

This distinction, indeed, between feasts and banquets and the diet of every day is one that dates from remote times. A distinction also is to be made between the diet of a small number of the rich and the vast majority of the population—the masses of the cities and the countryside. Generalizations on the subject are commonly based upon exceptional instances, which are practically the only ones reported by the chroniclers; whence the belief in a Portuguese who is traditionally a merrymaker, always surrounded by a host of good things to eat. Whole oxen roasted on the spit. Poultry, pork, lamb. All of which results from a failure to make allowance for the fact that the chronicles record only the exceptional, the extraordinary.

Alberto Sampaio tells us that in the peninsula, at the time of the Roman rule and thereabouts, rye, barley, oats, bran, and wheat were cultivated—the wheat, owing to the small amount of it that was produced, being reserved for the rich, "while the most common practice was to mix rye and white corn." Of the leguminous vegetables, the historian assures us that the following were to be found: beans, peas, lentils, and chick-peas. The Romans introduced various species of fruits into the provinces and developed the culture of other, indigenous varieties; but it was the Arabs who brought oranges, lemons, and tangerines, together with advanced processes of preserving and of putting up "dried fruits," processes that were later to be advantageously brought to Brazil by those Portuguese matrons of the sixteenth century who so quickly became skilled in the making of sweets from tropical fruits.

A circumstance not to be lost sight of and one that was particularly unfavorable to agriculture, and hence to the supply of fresh food in Portugal, even in the days when the country was enjoying its greatest degree of economic health, was the crises that the land had to undergo: climatic crises on the one hand; and on the other, social crises

---

[128] Alexandre Herculano: *Opusculos* (op. cit.).

[129] Estrabão, in Alberto Sampaio: *Estudos* (op. cit.).

or disturbances—wars, epidemics, invasions, and the like. But with all this it is still safe to conclude that in the beginning, before being transformed into a martime power, the Portuguese people went through a period of balanced diet, which, it may be, goes to explain much of its efficiency and superior qualities of boldness and initiative down to the sixteenth century. This is indicated by old documents that have been deciphered by Alberto Sampaio. For example, the menus of the meals furnished the royal major-domos when they came to receive the rent. The menus consisted sometimes of bread, meat, and wine, and at other times of bread, wine, boiled milk, young cocks, pancakes, pork, cheese, butter, eggs, etc. Sampaio is the first to note how much more common milk-products were then than now in the Portuguese diet, which has since become impoverished in this respect and in fresh meat. This latter fact the distinguished historian, with obvious partiality, attributes to "the cultural revolution brought about by the introduction of Indian corn." [130]

The causes of the impoverishment, as I see it, are more deep-going and complex. It is a reflection of the state of widespread poverty that was created in Spain by the abandonment of agriculture, sacrificed to maritime and commercial adventures, and that was later heightened by monoculture, stimulated in Portugal by England through the Treaty of Methuen. The accounts of banquets given us in the chronicles, the feast-day traditions, and the laws against gluttony should not leave us with the illusion of an overnourished people. Sampaio himself, apropos of the populations of Minho, enables us to glimpse the contrast between the weak and insufficient diet of every day and the enormous banquets on festive occasions. "On feast-days," says Sampaio, "the victuals are piled high: great tureens and bowls filled with food; and big platters with tremendous portions follow one another in endless succession, interspersed with pitchers and bumpers of young wine that, however it may grate upon the palate, has the effect of stimulating the appetite, which for the matter of that needs no stimulation." [131] All this points to a normally poor diet; for let us never lose sight of the exceptional character of these feasts, their very intemperance leading us to think of badly nourished stomachs that, so many times a year, are permitted this expansiveness and excess, as if in compensation for the parsimonious diet of ordinary days.

Fastings, also, have to be taken into account by anyone who makes a study of the diet of the Portuguese people, above all during those centuries when domestic life was being watched over by the stern

---

[130] Alberto Sampaio: *Estudos* (op. cit.). [131] Ibid.

eye of the Inquisition. By the Inquisition and the Jesuit. Two tyrannical sets of eyes, taking the place of God's at times. Watching over everything.

It is possible that the fasts and those frequent days when only fish was permitted are to be explained by weighty reasons of State. The fastings would have contributed toward establishing a balance between the limited supply of fresh food and the needs of the population, by encouraging the people to follow the regime of dried fish and preserves, imported from abroad in good part. The registry-book of Gaia, containing a letter-royal of Affonso III, in 1255, shows us that even in those days of comparative economic health, dried or salt fish loomed large in the diet of the Portuguese. The fishermen would cast their nets not only along the coast of their own country, but along the shores of Galicia as well, salting down their haul and sending it home for popular consumption. As far back as the thirteenth century, fresh meat had begun to be a luxury or a sin, with salt fish reigning triumphant and virtuous. Léon Poinsard, in his study *The Unknown Portugal*, reminds us that in the Middle Ages the Portuguese exported salt fish to Riga, and that in 1353 Edward III of England granted them the right to fish off the English coasts.[132] But this excessive consumption of dried fish, along with a deficiency of fresh meat and milk, became still more marked with the decline of agriculture in Portugal and must have had a good deal to do with the reduced economic capacity of the Portuguese people from the fifteenth century on, a circumstance that is vaguely attributed by some to racial decadence and by others to the Inquisition.

Pompeyo Gener assumes that "with the fasts preached by the clergy . . . eating little and badly" had degenerated "into a custom." He is referring to Spain, but what he says might be applied to Portugal: his curious manner of explaining how it came about that "the strong and intelligent races that previously had populated the peninsula had become weak and puny, physically and morally debilitated, unproductive and visionary."[133] Judging from the words just quoted, the Spanish critic appears to me to be inclined to place too great a burden of responsibility upon the Church for the deficiencies in Spanish diet, an exaggeration with which I by no means agree. It seems to me to be beyond a doubt that the religious appeal to the virtues of temperance, frugality, and abstinence, together with an ecclesiastical discipline that restrained in the people the appetite for a heavily laden

[132] Léon Poinsard: *Le Portugal inconnu* (Paris, 1910).

[133] Pompeyo Gener: *Herejias* (Barcelona, 1888), quoted in Fidelino de Figueiredo: *Crítica do Exílio* (*Criticism from Exile*) (Lisbon, 1930).

table—reducing that appetite to a minimum, giving it free rein only on feast-days and stifling it on other prescribed days—there would seem to be no doubt that all this, consciously or unconsciously, was in the interest of that desirable balance between the limited means of subsistence and the appetites and needs of the population. It is not, therefore, the clergy or the Church that is deserving of criticism. The evil is deeper-rooted than that. It dates from the decline of agriculture due to the highly abnormal development of maritime commerce. It comes from the impoverishment of the land following its abandonment by the Moors. Observers of peninsular life in modern times, following the era of discovery and conquest and the expulsion of the Moors, are the most insistent upon stressing the extreme parsimony of the Portuguese or Spanish diet. "Temperance or, better, abstinence is carried to unbelievable limits," writes one of them. Another emphasizes the utter simplicity of the meal that was eaten by the poor: a slice of bread and an onion. In the seventeenth century hunger reached even the palaces: the wife of the French Ambassador in Madrid at that time tells of having been with eight or ten ladies-in-waiting who for some while had not known what it was like to eat meat. People were dying of hunger in the streets.[134]

Already in the preceding century—the century in which Brazil was discovered—Clenardus[135] noted that even the gentry among the Lusitanians were *radish-eaters*, that they had little to eat and what they had was not of good quality. These letters of Clenardus, we may observe in passing, are admirable for their realism and exactitude. They are better than those of Sassetti,[136] who has a tendency to caricature that always results in distorting the subject—his abuse of the picturesque leads to a loss of clarity in the data he brings us. Clenardus, on the contrary, is restrained in his witticisms and presents us with an honest and faithful portrait of Lusitanian life in his time. Before Alexandre de Gusmão[137] had raised his cry of alarm against the regime of slave labor in Portugal, blaming this institution for the

[134] Buckle, op. cit.; Mercadel: *España vista por los Estranjeros* (op. cit.).

[135] Nicolaus Clenardus (Nicholas Cleynarts), Renaissance humanist (1493 or 1494–1542), professor of Greek and Hebrew at Louvain, came to Portugal from Salamanca as tutor to the Infante Henrique in 1533. He was noted for his witty letters, many of which were addressed from Portugal. (Translator.)

[136] Filippo Sassetti (1540–88) was a Florentine writer of the Renaissance era who traveled widely and whose impressions are given in his *Letters*, a modern edition of which was published at Florence in 1932. (Translator.)

[137] Alexandre de Gusmão, a Jesuit writer (1629–1724), born at Lisbon, spent eighty-five of his ninety-five years in Brazil. (Translator.)

indolence of the Portuguese native, his slowness of movement, and his sterility, Clenardus had noted the pernicious effects of the enslavement of war-captives upon Lusitanian character and economy. The difference being that where Alexandre de Gusmão was basing his diagnosis upon an empire that was already beginning to decay, Clenardus was prescribing for the first signs of hemorrhage. "If there is any people more given to laziness than the Portuguese, I do not know where it exists. . . . This people prefers to put up with anything rather than learn any kind of profession." And an indolence so great could only be due to slavery: "All services are performed by Negro and Moorish captives. Portugal is being overrun with this race of people. One could almost believe that in Lisbon there are more slaves, male and female, than there are Portuguese of free condition. . . . The richest have slaves of both sexes, and there are individuals who make a good profit from the sale of young slaves, born in the house. I even come to think that they breed them as they do pigeons, for purposes of sale, without being in the least offended by the ribaldries of the slave girls." [138] With the excessive number of slaves Clenardus associates the horrible dearth of the things of life in Portugal. The care of his beard alone cost him a fortune every week, and the barber, like a lord, kept him cooling his heels. Services and foodstuffs alike—all had to be snatched from the hands of dealers and artisans; and one had to wait on the butcher, also, as much as two or three hours.

Meanwhile, if the Portuguese had to suffer want, they preferred to do it in the privacy of their homes. When they went out, they imitated the airs and pomp of the gentry. At home they might fast and do without things, but in the street they paraded their grandeur. The case of the saying: "*Por fora muita farofa, por dentro mulambo só*" ("Outside he's a swell; inside, a ragamuffin").

Clenardus in his letters portrays for us the "pompous radish-eaters who go through the streets followed by their servants, the number of whom is greater than that of the reis that they spend on the upkeep of their houses." So great was this display in the matter of slaves that some gentlemen were accompanied by one to remove their hats, another to take their capes, a third with a brush to dust their clothing, and a fourth with a comb for their hair. But all this opulence in the street, in the matter of servants and apparel, was at the expense of a true asceticism at home. Those brilliant garments meant a real indi-

---

[138] The letters of Clenardus have been admirably translated by Cardinal Gonçalves Cerejeira and published in his book *O Humanismo em Portugal* (op. cit.).

gence at the table, an absolute lack of domestic comfort. Or else it meant running into debt, a situation that was common in the two Spains, as later in Hispanic America, among the Brazilian plantation-owners, for instance. In speaking of the Hispanic folk at the beginning of the sixteenth century the historian Guicciardini had made this generalization: "If they have anything to spend, they put it upon their backs, or their horses' backs, making a display of more than they possess at home, where they subsist with an extreme niggardliness and so economically that it is a marvel to behold." [139] From another Italian humanist, Lucio Marineo, we have precisely the same observation: "One thing I must not fail to state: that the majority of Spaniards take great care with their clothing and attire themselves very well, being folk who spend more on their garments and bodily trappings than they do on food and other things, however, necessary these other things may be." [140] The same report was made by English and French travelers in seventeenth- and eighteenth-century Brazil, where the splendor of silks and the excessive number of slaves seldom reflected a degree of domestic comfort equal to that of the nations of northern Europe. In Bahia, at the end of the eighteenth century, Dampier [141] found enormous but poorly furnished mansions, which, he notes, was a state of affairs that meant little to the Portuguese and Spaniards. Hence the Big Houses of plantation-owners that were to be seen, all of them with scanty furnishings and with few pictures on the walls— only here and there, in certain houses with greater pretensions to refinement.

It is, as I see it, a mistake to suppose that the Portuguese was corrupted by his colonization of Africa, India, and Brazil. By the time he had come to project his shadow, as that of a great owner of slaves, over two-thirds of the world, the sources of his economic life and health had already been imperiled. He was the corrupter, not the victim. The peril came, not so much from the effort—truly an exhausting one for so small a people—expended in colonizing the tropics as from the victory, within the Kingdom, of commercial over agricultural interests. Maritime commerce led to colonial imperialism, and it is probable that, independently of the latter, by reason of the excesses of the former alone, Portugal would have been ruined as an agricultural and economically autonomous country. The slavery that corrupted was not colonial but domestic, not that of Guinea Negroes so much as that of captive Moors. One can understand why those

[139] Mercadal, op. cit.
[140] Ibid.

[141] William Dampier: *Voyages . . . aux Terres Australes*, etc. (op. cit.).

who founded the culture of the sugar-cane in the American tropics, under physical conditions so adverse, should have become inbued with the belief that "work is for the black man." But some time before that their forebears, living in a mild climate, had transformed the verb *trabalhar* (to work) into *mourejar* (to work like a Moor).

As to just when Portuguese economy became possessed of the furious and parasitic passion for exploiting and transporting in place of producing wealth, it is not easy to state precisely. Two antagonistic Portugals had coexisted for some time, being mingled and confounded in the seething caldron of wars and revolutions, before bourgeois and commercial Portugal had emerged as the victor. Poinsard notes the coexistence of two types of family and of social background among the Portuguese: the feudal family and that of the commoner.[142] But the two great antagonistic forces that confronted each other were economic in character: agrarian versus commercial interests.

The decline of an agrarian economy in Portugal and the manner in which the nation was commercialized, to the point where it became one big business house with the King himself and the leading nobles transformed into business men—all this has been splendidly described by Costa Lobo, Alberto Sampaio, Oliveira Martins, and João Lúcio de Azevedo.[143] Before them, however, the old economists of the fifteenth and sixteenth centuries had hit upon the inconveniences of large-scale property on the one hand and of mercantilism on the other. The latter robbed agriculture of its human arms and best energies. The former made it difficult to take advantage of vast regions that lay uncultivated and sterile. "For being the heritage of many sons," writes Severim de Faria in his *Notícias de Portugal* (*Tidings of Portugal*) (Lisbon, 1655), "three quarters of it remain to be sown, and for this reason many of its fruits are lacking which might be gleaned from it, along with the benefits that might accrue to many who have no place where such a harvest is to be had." There was another economist among those of the sixteenth century who is to be admired for his intuition and good sense. He displays an understanding of how it was that Portugal, even though master of the Indies and of Brazil, through its lack of productivity and its satisfaction with its position as a purely commercial nation, could turn into a mere exploiter or transmitter of wealth: "Foreigners shall have the use of what our industry discovers in them [the colonies] and what our labor produces, and we shall

---

[142] Léon Poinsard, op. cit.
[143] A. Costa Lobo: *A História da Sociedade em Portugal no século XV* (op. cit.); Alberto Sampaio: *Estudos* (op. cit.); Oliveira Martins: *História de Portugal* (op. cit.); João Lúcio de Azevedo: *Épocas de Portugal Econômico* (op. cit.)

come to be in Brazil so many administrators for Europe, such as the Castilians are, and it will be for Europe that the gold and silver will be taken from the bowels of the earth." This prophetic voice, fore-telling so clearly the exploitation of Portugal by England, was that of Ribeiro de Macedo, who in 1675 wrote his essay *On the Introduction of the Arts*.[144]

Much has been made of the oceanic character of the Portuguese domain, as being the irresistible motive that led the Lusitanian people to abandon an agricultural way of life for one of commerce and overseas conquests. In accordance with this theory, Portuguese mer-cantilism, like the independence of the realm in itself, would have been the inevitable consequence of geographic conditions. All this is de-termined with a Moslem-like fatalism; and the old man of Restelo into whose mouth Camões puts the words that dramatize the conflict between the agricultural and oceanic interests was merely repeating the naïve gesture of King Canute in trying to halt the waves.

But geographical conditions do not determine in an absolute man-ner the development of a people; nor today are we to put our faith in the geographic and ethnic peculiarities of Portugal in relation to the peninsula as a whole. The oceanic character of Portugal as op-posed to the continental character of Spain constitutes but an in-significant factor of differentiation: "for the Spanish domain has its oceanic qualities, just as the Portuguese has continental ones," observes Fidelino de Figueiredo; and the erudite historian goes on to remind us that "there have been maritime peoples, such as the English and the French, who for centuries were uninterested in the sea."[145] The sea alone would not have determined either Portuguese independence or Portuguese commercialism. It may be pointed out that, on the contrary, Portugal broke the peninsular solidarity by making of ag-riculture and not of maritime commerce the principal basis of its political autonomy; that it was economic likenesses and not differences that separated Portugal from Spain. An excess of similarities, and not of differences. It is true that both the similarities and the differences were to be exploited by an exotic element, the newcomers from the north, who, in treason to Castile, founded the Portuguese monarchy.

---

[144] See Antônio Sérgio: *Antologia dos Economistas Portugueses* (*Anthology of Portuguese Economists*) (Lisbon, 1924). [The title of Ribeiro de Macedo's work in the original is *Sobre a Introdução das Artes*. (Trans-lator.)]

[145] Fidelino de Figueiredo: *Crítica do Exílio* (op. cit.).
[Fidelino de Figueiredo is con-temporary Portugal's outstanding lit-erary scholar and critic. For a number of years now (1945) he has resided in Brazil, where he occupies a uni-versity chair. (Translator.)]

This interpretation is an extravagant one only in appearance; Ganivet comes close to it, when, in his *Idearium Español*,[146] he alludes to "the historic antipathy between Castile and Portugal, born, it may be, of a close resemblance in character." Hatred of the Spaniard has already been mentioned as a psychologic factor in the political differentiation of Portugal; but it was neither this hatred nor the more basic hatred of the Moor that separated the Portuguese from the two great cultures he could claim, the one a maternal and the other a paternal culture, so to speak: the Hispanic and the Berber. It was as a reaction against these that Portugal's political formation took place, but it was under their influence that the Portuguese character was shaped. In that character the intense Romanization did not extinguish the essential Hispanic traits, nor did the Christian reconquest obliterate the profound traces of Berber and Moor. This is a point that I feel it necessary to stress, for the reason that it explains my insistence upon regarding as Hispanic the social and cultural background of that portion of the Americas which was colonized by Spaniards and Portuguese. Hispanic and not Latin. Catholic, tinged with mysticism and Mohammedan culture, and not the result of the French Revolution or the Italian Renaissance. Upon this point I am in agreement with Antônio Sardinha and against F. García Calderón.[147] It is impossible to deny that the economic imperialism of Spain and Portugal was bound up in the most intimate fashion with the Church and the religious. The conquest of markets, lands, and slaves—the conquest of souls. It may be stated that religious enthusiasts in Brazil were the first to become excited over possibilities that only later were sighted by the economic interests. Founded almost without volition, with leftovers of men, chips off the block of a nobility that had come near emigrating in its entirety from the realm to the Indies, Brazil was for some time the Nazareth of Portuguese colonies. Without gold or silver. With nothing but dyewood and souls for Jesus Christ.

The Portuguese, I may say once more, stood in no need of a stimulus to incline him toward a slave-holding regime. No European was more predisposed than he to a system of slave labor. In the case

[146] Angel Ganivet: *Idearium Español* (Madrid, 1897). Ganivet (1865–98) was one of the leading Spanish writers of the late nineteenth century. (Translator.)

[147] Francisco García Calderón (1883–   ), the well-known Peruvian writer, is the author of *La Creación de un continente* (Paris, 1909) and other works. His *Latin America, Its Rise and Progress* (in translation) was published in London in 1913. Antônio Sardinha (1887–1925) was the leader of the pro-monarchist literary school (*"integralismo"*) in Portugal, corresponding to the Action Française in France. (Translator.)

of Brazil, however, it appears to me unjust to find fault with him for having marred his formidable accomplishment in the way of tropical colonization with the blot of an institution that today is so repugnant to us. The milieu and the circumstances called for the slave. In the beginning it was the Indian. When the native, by his lack of ability and his slothfulness, proved unequal to the needs of colonial agriculture, it was—the Negro. With the great colonizing sense that was his, the Portuguese realized that only the Negro would serve for completing the task of founding an agricultural regime in the tropics. The African worker. But the African worker whose intermittent energies had been disciplined by the rigors of slavery.

Let us leave off our lyricism with regard to the Indian. Let us have done with setting him over against the Portuguese as the latter's equal. If his place was taken by the Negro—and once again I stress the point—this was not due to those moral motives which his enthusiastic admirers take so much pleasure in discovering: his proud and haughty attitude toward the Lusitanian colonizer in contrast to the Negro's passivity. It was due, precisely, to the inferior culture of the Indian, a nomadic culture, barely touched by the first vague tendencies toward agricultural stabilization. It was due to the fact that he was found wanting when it came to sedentary labor. The African's decided advantage over the Indian lay chiefly in the fact that he came out of cultural conditions of a superior sort, a mode of life that was definitely agricultural in character. It was not a question of pride on the one hand or of moral passivity on the other.[148]

Was it, indeed, "a crime to enslave the Negro and bring him to America"? asks Oliveira Martins. According to certain publicists, it was a tremendous mistake. But no one to this day has told us what other method of supplying his labor needs might have been adopted by the Portuguese colonizer of Brazil. Varnhagen, in criticizing the latifundiary and slave-holding character of our colonization, laments

---

[148] For that matter, the Negroes in Brazil were not so passive. On the contrary, by reason of their more advanced stage of culture they were able to put up a more effective resistance to exploitation by their white masters than were the Indians. "The Negroes struggled," writes Astrojildo Pereira, apropos of Oliveira Vianna's thesis that there has never been a class struggle in Brazil. According to A. Pereira, we did have "an authentic class struggle that filled centuries of our history and that had its culminating episode of heroism and greatness in the organization of the Republic of Palmares, headed by the epic figure of Zumbi, our Negro Spartacus."— Astrojildo Pereira: "*Sociologia ou apologética?*" ("Sociology or Apologetics?"), in *A Classe Operária* (*The Working Class*), Rio de Janeiro, May 1, 1929.

that we did not follow the system of small land grants. "Through small grants colonization would have been accomplished with more people, and Brazil would naturally be better populated today—possibly better even than the United States; its population would perhaps be more homogeneous, and there would not be among us those provincial rivalries which, if they still exist today, are in good part due to such *capitânias*." [149] He goes on to cite the example of Madeira and the Azores. But would these small grants have produced results in a country like Brazil, with a climate that is so harsh for the European and covering so vast an extent of territory? And from where would all the people come whom Varnhagen supposes capable of founding a system of agriculture in an environment so different from that of Europe? The saúba, or leaf-cutting ant,[150] alone, without any other affliction or misfortune, would have conquered the agricultural colonist by devouring his small property overnight, by consuming in a few hours the capital he had scraped together with such pains in order to set himself up, representing the labor of many months. Let us have the honesty to recognize the fact that only a method of colonization based upon large-scale property and upon slavery would have been capable of surmounting the enormous obstacles in the way of the European civilization of Brazil. Only the Big House and the slave hut. The rich plantation-owner and the Negro capable of agricultural exertion and compelled to it by a system of slave labor.

The best-advised individuals in Portugal, following the first explorations and the first word that was brought back from Brazil, realized that the colonization of this portion of America would have to be effected through agrarian effort. One of them, Diogo de Gouveia, wrote a letter along these lines to John III; and upon making up his mind to settle the American wilderness, His Majesty did indeed follow the agrarian method, based upon slavery, which had already been tried out in the islands of the Atlantic.

Everything, however, was left to individual initiative. The expenses of installation. The task of military defense of the colony. But with it all went the privileges of command and jurisdiction over a vast

---

[149] Varnhagen: *História Geral do Brasil* (op. cit.). Varnhagen always falls into a childish oversimplification when he leaves the field of pure historical research for that of the philosophy of history.

[150] The *saúba* (*saúva*) is "a species of leaf-cutting ant (*Œcodoma cephalotes*) that invades gardens and plan-

tations, cutting up the leaves of plants to carry them to underground nests; plunders stores or provisions; though painful, their bite or sting is not harmful to man."—*Glossary of Brazilian-Amazonian Terms Compiled from The Strategic Index of the Americas.* (Translator.)

extent of territory, one that by its very vastness became a lure, beckoning to men who had little capital but who did have courage and the instinct of possessiveness; and added to the rights of owner-ship were those of feudal lords over the ones who came there to work —like Moors (*mourejar*). It may clearly be seen what the attitude of the crown was: to populate the wilds of America without burden to itself, to clear the land of the jungle, to defend it against corsairs and the savage, and to transform it into a productive region, all at the ex-pense of those persons who were daring enough to undertake to de-flower so rude a portion of the earth. And it is, in truth, these latter who are to be credited with the courage and initiative, the firmness of mind, and the organizational capacity that were responsible for the establishment in Brazil of a great plantation-colony.

Viewing the success attained by the first planters, the crown be-gan to grasp the possibilities of colonial wealth that lay in the produc-tion of sugar. As João Lúcio de Azevedo observes, "the privilege accorded to the donee of being the only one permitted to manufac-ture or possess sugar-mills and the water-mill device shows that the introduction of sugar-cane culture was the chief object in view." [151] And all these grants, and, later, the *Regulations* (*Regimento*) of Thomé de Souza, were an affirmation of the same policy of conferring prestige upon the owner of the sugar plantation.[152] It is obvious that the result of it all could have been no other than what it was: on the advantageous side, the development of individual initiative, stimulated through the instincts of possession and command; and on the harmful side, an uncontrolled one-crop system. The domineering tendency of the great landowners and slave-holders. Abuses and acts of violence on the part of the autocrats of the Big Houses. The exaggerated sense

---

[151] João Lúcio de Azevedo: *Épocas de Portugal Econômico* (op. cit.).

[152] A policy that is also revealed in the jurisprudence forbidding the ex-ecution of judgment on the planta-tion-owners, whose situation as debt-ors thus came to be an exceptional one.—Gilberto Freyre: "*A Agricul-tura da Cana e a Industria do Açucar*" ("The Culture of the Sugar-Cane and the Sugar Industry"), in the *Livro do Nordeste* (op. cit.).—Among other documents, some of them already published, that indicate the privileged situation of the plantation-owner is the "provision of His Excellency Sr. Marquez de Ang.ª Viceroy and cap-tain-general of the sea and land of this state of Brazil, in favor of the inhabitants of this capitânia of Per-nambuco that they are not to be served with writs in their [sugar-] factories" etc., and the "provision of S. Magde, by the grace of God, in favor of the Lords of the Plantation and the tillers of the soil."—Letters-Royal, Decrees, and Provisions, 1711–1824, from a manuscript in the Li-brary of the state of Pernambuco.

of private property or individualism that went with these royal land grants.

Nevertheless, colonial economy as practiced in Brazil during the first two centuries restored to Portugal the glow of health that had some while since disappeared as a result of the morbid passion for the exploitation of riches, for robbery and plunder. As early as the end of the sixteenth century there were those who sensed the superiority of the method of colonization adopted in Brazil to the one followed in India and in Minas and who wished to see it put into general practice in the other lands belonging to the crown. "It is the judgment of God," argues the author of the "Discourse on the Affairs of India and and of Minas" (1573), "it is the judgment of God that, as a result of the money gained in Brazil through sugar and cotton, wood and parrots, Your Majesty's treasury should be enriched with much fine gold." [153] Words to which the sovereign turned—literally—a "tradesman's ear." [154] His passionate concern continued to be with those lands that were rich in precious metals.

The truth of the matter is that for Portugal the social policy demanded by an agrarian form of colonization represented an effort beyond its possibilities. However great may have been the elasticity of the Portuguese, these exigencies exceeded his resources in the way of people. In a factory, the human capital is a single whole; in an agricultural colony, it has to be much greater, even when relying upon the multiplying effect of polygamy and miscegenation. And Portugal, from the earliest historical times, had been a country in the grip of a populational crisis. The unhygienic conditions of a region of transit, with its plagues, epidemics, wars, and added to these the physical conditions of an environment that, over broad regions, was unfavorable to human life and economic stability—such conditions tended to keep the population on a bare level with the needs of the nation, by getting rid of the excessive number of individuals that might otherwise have resulted from the polygamy of the African conquerors and the patriarchal fecundity of the farmers and cattle-breeders in those parts of the land that enjoyed a milder climate and a soil of greater fertility.

The scarcity of the human element was reflected in Portuguese legislation, and it would appear that Catholic orthodoxy itself was sometimes sacrificed in order to fill the want. We even see the Church

---

[153] João Lúcio de Azevedo: *Épocas de Portugal Econômico* (op. cit.).

[154] *"Ouvidos de mercador,"* a pro-verbial expression meaning "to turn a deaf ear." (Translator.)

in Portugal consenting to *"de juras,"* or secret, marriages, consummated by coitus; and the Ordinances of Emanuel, and later those of Philip, permit couples to be looked upon as legally wed who live together in public and are reputed to be man and wife. There is, in short, a great tolerance for any sort of union that results in an increase of the population, a great indulgence toward natural offspring. In Spain travelers in the sixteenth and seventeenth centuries noted the heartiest contempt for the laws against concubinage, legitimate and bastard children being brought up together in many homes.[155] Nor can the asceticism of the friars and priests be said to have been an obstacle to the national and Imperial interests in the matter of population and generation. A good part if not a majority of them assisted in the work of procreation, and their co-operation was so gratefully accepted that the courts did not arrest or issue warrants for any cleric or friar on the charge of keeping a concubine.

The interests of procreation, it may be repeated, had the effect of breaking down not only moral prejudices but the scruples of Catholic orthodoxy as well, and in this respect they found an ally in Christianity itself, a Christianity that in Portugal has so frequently taken on the quasi-pagan characteristics of a phallic cult. The great national saints are those to whom the imagination of the people has come to attribute a miraculous intervention in bringing the sexes together, in impregnating women, and in protecting motherhood: St. Anthony, St. John, São Goncalo do Amarante, St. Peter, the Infant Jesus, Our Lady of Expectation, Our Lady of the Conception, Our Lady of the Blessed Event, of the Good Birth. Neither warrior saints like St. George nor the protectors of populations against the plague, like St. Sebastian, or against hunger, like St. Onofre—saints whose popularity reflects the grievous experiences of the Portuguese people—ever attain the importance and prestige of these others, the patrons of human love and agricultural fecundity. This importance and prestige were carried over to Brazil, where the problems of population, which had reached so anguished a pitch in Portugal, were prolonged through the difficulties attendant upon colonizing the new land with human resources that were so slight. One of the first semi-popular feasts of the Church of which the colonial chronicles tell us is that of St. John, and we find it already accompanied by bonfires and dances.[156] For the functions of this highly popular saint are essentially aphrodisiac, and sexual songs and practices are bound up with his rites. He is the marrying saint, *par excellence*:

---

[155] Mercadal: *España vista por los Estranjeros* (op. cit.).

[156] Fernão Cardim: *Tratados da Terra e Gente do Brasil* (op. cit.), p. 316.

Give me a bridgegroom, St. John, give me a bridgegroom,
Give me a bridgegroom, I pray, for I fain would be wed.[157]

The fortunes that are told on St. John's Eve or in the early dawn of his day, a day that is celebrated with rockets, firecrackers, and *vivas*, in Brazil as in Portugal, point to a union of the sexes, marriage, and the longing for a love that has not yet been found. In our country, fortunes are told with the white of an egg in a cup of water; with an ear of corn that is placed beneath the pillow so that the sleeper may behold in a dream the one who comes to eat it; with a knife that, in the dark, is plunged to the hilt in a banana tree, the spots or stains on the blade being eagerly deciphered early the next morning; with a basin of water; with needles; with a mouthful of liquid; etc. Other heart interests find a protector in St. Anthony. For example, lost love. Sweethearts, husbands, or lovers who have disappeared. Love that has grown cold or has died. He is one of the saints that we meet with most often in connection with the practices of aphrodisiac sorcery in Brazil. It is the image of this saint that is frequently hung head downward in a cistern or a well in order that he may fulfill his promises as speedily as possible. The more impatient ones place him in old privies. And São Gonçalo do Amarante lends himself to still more disrespectful treatment, the freest and most sensual practices being linked with his cult. These at times are downright obscene and filthy. To him is assigned the specialty of providing husbands or lovers for old women, just as St. Peter's function is to marry off widows. It is to São Gonçalo, however, that nearly all the amorous swains turn for comfort:

Get me a bride, get me a bride;
Little Gonçalo, hear my plaint;
That is why I pray to thee,
Friendly little saint.[158]

The young girls address him as follows:

São Gonçalo of Amarante,
Thou hearest the old ones' plea;
Why dost not marry the lasses, too?
What harm have they done to thee? [159]

It was to São Gonçalo that the sterile, the barren, the impotent clung as to their last hope. Formerly on the day of his feast there was

---

[157] *Dai-me noivo, S. Jôao, dai-me noivo,*
dai-me noivo, que me quero casar.
[158] *Casai-me, casai-me,*
Sao Gonçalinho,
Que hei de rezar-vos,
Amigo santinho.

[159] *São Gonçalo do Amarante,*
Casamenteiro das velhas,
Por que não casais as moças?
Que mal voz fizeram elas?

dancing in the churches—a custom that was imported from Portugal to Brazil. There was, indeed, much dancing and courting in the colonial churches. They also performed love comedies there. In one of his pastorals, of the year 1726, Dom Frei José Fialho, by the grace of God and of the holy apostolic faith Bishop of Olinda, recommended to the priests of Pernambuco "not to consent that there be performed comedies, colloquies, representations, or balls within any church, chapel, or churchyard." [160] This at the beginning of the eighteenth century. We thus see that Le Gentil de la Barbinais was not exaggerating in his description of the Christmas festivities of 1717 which he had witnessed in the convent of the nuns of Santa Clara in Bahia. The sisters sang and danced and created such a hubbub as to lead the traveler to believe that they were possessed of scoffing demons. After which they performed a comedy of love.[161]

In Pernambuco it would seem that Dom Frei José Fialho had raised his voice in vain, for at the beginning of the nineteenth century Tollenare found that in Recife they were still dancing in the Church of São Gonçalo of Olinda. Only in 1817 did the canons prohibit such dances, "for Europeans censure them as an indecency unworthy of the temple of God." [162] In Bahia they danced on São Gonçalo's Day, not only in the Desterro Convent, but in Nazaré Hermitage, in the São Domingos and Amparo churches, and various others.[163] And after dancing had been prohibited, love-making in the churches went on. Even at court. Max Radiguet still found young ladies of the best families of Rio de Janeiro flirting with lads in the Imperial Chapel: *"accroupies sur leur chaise de tapisserie prenaient sans scruple des sorbets et des glaces avec les jeunes gens qui venaient converser avec elles dans le lieu Saint."* [164] Flirting and taking sherbets in the churches

---

[160] Pastoral letter of Dom Frei José Fialho, "given in Olinda, under our hand and seal, this nineteenth day of the month of February of the year one thousand seven hundred and twenty-six." Manuscript in the Archives of the Cathedral of Olinda, kindly placed at my disposition by the Right Reverend José do Carmo Baratta.

[161] Le Gentil de la Barbinais: *Nouveau Voyage autour du monde* (op. cit.), p. 112.

[162] Tollenare: *Notas Dominicais tomadas durante uma viagem em Portugal e no Brasil em 1816, 1817 e 1818 (Dominical Notes Made on a Journey to Portugal and to Brazil,* etc.), the French portion, relative to Pernambuco, translated from the unpublished French manuscript by Alfredo de Carvalho, *Revista do Instituto Arqueólogico, Histórico e Geográfico de Pernambuco,* Vol. XI, No. 61, p. 448.

[163] J. da Silva Campos: *"Tradições Baianas"* ("Bahian Traditions"), *Revista do Instituto Geográphico e Histórico* (Bahia), 56.

[164] Max Radiguet: *Souvenirs de l'Amérique espagnolle* (Paris, 1848), p. 265.

exactly as ninety years later they were to be doing in the confectionery shops and on the beaches.

Other pagan characteristics of the cult of São Gonçalo are preserved in Portugal. Among them is the custom of manufacturing and selling phallic rosaries made out of pastry, these wares being "cried in an obscene jargon," as Luiz Chaves informs us, by the sweetmeat venders at the church doors. And I have already alluded to the sterile women who rub themselves, "all naked, against the legs of the prostrate image of the Blessed One, while the believers pray in a low voice and keep their eyes lowered that they may not see that which they should not behold."[165] This is the sexual friction of pagan times adapted to Catholic forms.

As was natural, these saints, protectors of love and fecundity in human beings, became also the protectors of agriculture. St. John and Our Lady of Expectation—the latter at times worshipped in the image of a pregnant woman—are saints who are friendly to farmers as well as to the lovelorn. In Brazil as in Portugal the people in the interior of the country, when they want rain, are accustomed to dip St. Anthony into the water. In certain regions of the north, when there is a fire in the cane fields, they place the image of the saint in one of the windows of the Big House to appease the flames. When the rivers overflow and there is a flood, it is again his image that is employed to offset the peril and stop the waters from washing away the crops. In addition to being an aphrodisiac festival, St. John's Day in Brazil is also an agricultural one. It is the feast of the maize, whose culinary products—*canjica, pamonha*, the corn-cake—filled the patriarchal tables for the great midnight feasts.

In the north, when the caterpillar is in the cotton, it is the custom to this day for the farmers to pray in each corner of the field: "Virgin in childbirth, Virgin before childbirth, Virgin after childbirth." And at the end they say three Hail Mary's.[166] It is the same association of the idea of human fecundity with that of the fertility of the earth.

The feast of São Gonçalo do Amarante that La Barbinais witnessed in eighteenth-century Bahia emerges from the French traveler's pages with all the traits of the ancient pagan festivals. Festivals not only of love, but of fecundity as well. Licentious dances around the image of the saint. Dances in which the visitor beheld the elderly Viceroy himself taking part, surrounded by friars, gentlemen, and Negroes. And by all the prostitutes of Bahia. A promiscuity that still charac-

---

[165] Luiz Chaves: *O amor Portugues —O namoro, o casamento, a família (Love among the Portuguese—Court-* *ship, Marriage, the Family)* (Lisbon).
[166] Alberto Deodato: *Senzalas* (1919).

terizes our church festivals of today. Guitars strumming. People singing. Fair-booths. Much to eat. Sexual exaltation. And all this for three days and in the midst of the jungle. From time to time, sacred hymns. An image of the saint taken from the altar passes from hand to hand and is batted about like a *peteca*. And this, notes La Barbinais, is exactly "what the pagans did in their annual sacrifice to Hercules, a ceremony in which they drubbed the demigod's image and heaped insults on it." [167]

This feast of São Gonçalo at Bahia had obviously been influenced already by African orgiastic elements absorbed in Brazil. [168] But the characteristic pagan residuum was brought from Portugal by the white colonizer, who had found it in his native, lyric, and festive Christianity with its merry processions graced by the figures of Bacchus, Our Lady Fleeing to Egypt, Mercury, Apollo, the Christ Child, the Twelve Apostles, satyrs, nymphs, angels, patriarchs, kings, and emperors, with the Blessed Sacrament bringing up the rear. [169] And

[167] La Barbinais: *Nouveau Voyage,* etc. (op. cit.), p. 114.

[168] It is hard to conceive of what the Corpus Christi processions were like in sixteenth- and seventeenth-century Portugal. One of the fifteenth century, described in *O Panorama* of Lisbon, Vol. II, (1838), may serve as an example. First, we see the procession being organized inside the church: guild banners and ensigns, dancers, apostles, emperors, devils, saints, rabbis, jostling one another and falling into line, soldiers with the flat of their swords being there to take care of the stragglers. Up in front a group is performing the *"judinga,"* a Jewish dance, as a rabbi raises the Pentateuch. Then, after all these, a clown making faces. An enormous serpent of painted cloth upon a wooden framework, with a number of men underneath. Blacksmiths. Carpenters. A gypsy dance. A Moorish dance. St. Peter. Stonemasons carrying little toylike castles in their hands. Fishwomen dancing and singing. Ferrymen with the image of St. Christopher. Shepherds. Soldiers. St. John surrounded by shoemakers. The Temptation, depicted by a dancing woman with lewd movements of her hips. St. George, protector of the army, on horseback and acclaimed in opposition to St. Iago, protector of the Spaniards. Abraham, Judith, and David. Bacchus seated on a hogshead. A semi-nude Venus. Our Lady on a donkey. The Christ Child. St. George, St. Sebastian naked and surrounded by ruffians who are threatening to fire upon him. Monks. Nuns. Upraised crosses. Sacred hymns. His Majesty. Gentry. The whole of Portuguese life, in short.

After the conquests Indian and Negro dances were added to the figures in the procession.

[169] The great importance of certain deities called Orixás among the Yorubas, looked upon as gods of agricultural fecundity, is well known. (See, on this subject, Wilson D. Wallis: *An Introduction to Anthropology,* London.) Even today, in the festivals of the African cults in Brazil, there are to be perceived reminiscences of earth-worship, the joy over a plentiful harvest associated with the sentiment of love and human fecundity. There are also reminiscences of the African phallic cult (the *Elegba* of the Yorubas).

the great processions in colonial Brazil were no less pompous and pagan in character. Froger noted, at the feast of Corpus Christi at Bahia, musicians, dancers, and maskers wiggling their buttocks in lubricious fashion. Another feast that was celebrated in Minas in 1733 was a veritable parade of paganism alongside Christian symbols. Turks and Christians. The Serpent in the garden of Eden. The four points of the compass. The Moon surrounded by nymphs. And bringing up the rear, as if in true consecration of the colored races, were Caiapó Indians [170] and Congo Negroes, performing with abandon their heathen and orgiastic dances in honor of the saints and the Sacrament.[171]

An ascetic, orthodox Catholicism, by hampering the freedom of the senses and the instincts of generation would have prevented Portugal from straddling half a world. The pagan survivals in Portuguese Christianity thus played an important role in connection with Imperial policy—pagan survivals and the tendencies toward polygamy that had been evolved in warming and voluptuous contact with the Moors.

Portugal's cuisine, as well as its hagiology, in the old names that are given to certain confections, in the semi-phallic forms and trimmings of certain sweetmeats, and in the piquant, not to say aphrodisiac seasoning of garnishings, dressings, and gravies, has preserved for us the erotic vibrancy, the procreative tension, which the country of necessity sought to maintain in the fervent era of Imperial colonization. The same is true of the Brazilian colonial kitchen, where we find similar stimuli to love and fecundity. Even in the names of convent sweets and cakes, made by the seraphic hands of nuns, there is to be perceived at times an aphrodisiac intention, an obscene touch, confounded with the mystic—such names as nuns' sighs, heavenly salt pork, nun's belly, heavenly manna, angel's titbits. These were the cakes and sweets for which the sisters' male friends sighed at the convent doors. Not being able to give themselves in the flesh to all their admirers, the nuns made use of the cakes and caramels as a substitute, and these came to take on a sort of sexual symbolism. Speak-

---

[170] "Indians of the linguistic family Gê. The Caiapós of the south ruled over the backlands situated between the headwaters of the Araguia and the upper basin of the Paraná. The Caiapós of the north lived in the region situated between the Araguaia and the Xingu, to the north of the river Tapirapé."—Lima and Barroso, op. cit. (Translator.)

[171] Affonso d'E. Taunay: *Sob El-Rey Nosso Senhor—Aspecto da vida setecentista brasileira, sobretudo em S. Paulo* (*Under His Majesty Our Lord—Aspect of Eighteenth-Century Life, above all in São Paulo*) (São Paulo, 1923).

ing of the patriarchal desserts, Afrânio Peixoto, in one of his Brazilian *romans de mœurs*, observes that "it was not we who enjoy
them who gave them such names, but their feminine creators, the
respective abbesses and nuns of Portuguese convents, who were more
occupied with the making of such dishes than they were with divine
service."[172] This after recalling some of the quite suggestive names of
Luso-Brazilian delicacies: little kisses, weaned sucklings, raise-the-old-
man, maiden's tongue, married couples, love's caresses. This list might
be still further extended by anyone. It is curious to note that certain
Brazilian fathers, when their sons, as they say, are of an age to "know
a woman," are in the habit of giving them "money to buy a cake"—
that is to say, the means of becoming acquainted with some other kind
of cake than one made of corn or starch. So far as all this is concerned, the intimate relation that exists between the libido and the
pleasures of the palate is a matter of common knowledge.[173]

Another aspect of the obsession that the problem of physical love
became in Portugal is to be found in the fact that there is, perhaps, no
country where the smutty or obscene anecdote has a more appreciative audience. Nor is there any other language that is so rich as the
Portuguese in coarse expressions, filthy words. Words and gestures.[174]

---

[172] Afrânio Peixoto: *Uma Mulher como as Outras* (*A Woman like the Others*) (Rio de Janeiro, 1927).— Sousa Viterbo, in *Artes e Artistas em Portugal, contribuição para a história das artes e indústrias portuguesas* (*Arts and Artists in Portugal, Contribution to the History of the Portugues Arts and Industries*) (Lisbon, 1892), had previously brought out the fact that the Portuguese nuns—not all of them the mistresses of kings, nobles, or ecclesiastics, but some of them merely enamored of their hangers-on (*freiráticos*), while many were true brides of Our Lord—"were in the habit of satisfying their domestic inclinations by devoting them-selves to the culinary arts, giving their best efforts to the 'breasts of Venus' and the 'angel's titbits.'"

[173] A reference to Freud is in-evitable here, and should have been made before this. Freud would de-rive from the primitive expression of the libido—the transmission of semen by the mouth, as in the case of the paramecium and other backward forms of life—the fact that even to-day there are to be observed in human love reminiscences of the an-cient process, as one of assimilation.— Sigmund Freud: *Psychologie collec-tive et analyse du moi* (translation) (Paris, 1924). In Brazil the use of the verb *comer* (to eat) is quite charac-teristic from this point of view. Like-wise the use that is made of the ex-pressions: *comida* (a meal), *pitéu* (a dainty dish), *suco* (juice), *pirão* (manihot broth), *uva* (grape), etc. The same criterion, I believe, may be employed in explaining the sexual symbolism of the names of Portu-guese and Brazilian cakes and sweet-meats and the phallic forms that are given to some of them.

[174] Gesture with the Brazilian is a language in itself. On this see Mont-gomery Merryman: *Portuguese, A Portrait of the Language of Brazil* (Rio de Janeiro; Irmãos Pongetti;

During his brief stay in Lisbon, Byron picked up a number of these expressions, which he used in the letters that he wrote to his friend the Reverend Francis Hogson; but fortunately he did not know how to transcribe them correctly: *carracho, ambra di merdo*, etc. *Carracho*, according to D. G. Dalgado, in his commentaries on Byron's letters, must be *caramba*,[175] an identification that does not appear to me to be correct. It is our opinion that the English poet meant to set down a word not so innocent and more Portuguese than *caramba*. This gross, plebeian eroticism was prevalent among all classes in Portugal, the man who did not make use of obscene words and gestures being looked upon as effeminate. The same thing was true in Brazil, where the Lusitanian fondness for the erotic found a propitious milieu in the lubricious circumstances attendant upon colonization. The Brazilian's greatest delight is to tell dirty stories. Stories of friars and nuns. Of Portuguese men and Negro women. Of impotent Englishmen. I believe, however, that only in Portugal could such drawing-room foolery take place as that which a distinguished friend described for me. At the supper hour it was announced that there was a surprise in store for the guests. This surprise was nothing other than the substitution of toilet paper for plates at table, and upon each bit of paper there lay a slender dark-brown sweet, cut up into small portions. Imagine such a thing among English or North American guests! They would have died of shame. But in Portugal and in Brazil it is common to jest about this and similar subjects, for we are endowed with a crude naturalness that contrasts with the excessive reticence characteristic of Anglo-Saxons.

In any event, the Reverend Mr. Creary, who came to Brazil in the days of slavery, and whose diary is preserved in the manuscript section of the Library of Congress in Washington, has some terrible things to say about the shamelessness of Brazilians. He cites the example of a girl eleven or twelve years old whom he, to his amazement, heard speaking of a younger brother, still small enough to be held in the lap, and remarking that the infant had "made pipi" in his clothes. Another thing that horrified him was the advertisements in the Rio newspapers, inserted by indecorous bachelors, stating that they had need of a housekeeper, but letting it be understood that they wanted

---

1945); see the chapter on "The Eloquence of Brazilian Hands." It would be interesting to know how many of these everyday gestures have an erotic base. (Translator.)

[175] D. G. Dalgado: *Lord Byron's*

Childe Harold's Pilgrimage to Portugal (Lisbon, 1919).

[*Caramba*, as in Spanish, is an untranslatable exclamation of astonishment. (Translator.)]

her for other functions than those of caring for the kitchen or the house.[176] Now, I do not imagine the Reverend Mr. Creary to have been any monster of Puritanism; he was living in the Victorian era, that is all, in an age when English books of etiquette advised young ladies of social standing not to mix books by masculine and feminine writers on the same shelf. Each sex must have a shelf of its own. In good society one did not speak, either in England or in the United States, of the leg of a table or a chair, but avoided the sensual suggestion of a woman's leg. In replying to an Englishman of practically the same stamp as Creary—the chemist Charles B. Mansfield—a fellow countryman of ours, A. D. de Pascual, wrote: "our Brazilian women are not dismayed if words like *leg, lap,* and so forth are uttered in their presence, although in the street and in their carriages and drawing-rooms they do not make a display of the realities behind the words." After having thus triumphantly set one social convention over against another, Pascual admits that "the presence of slaves in our dwellings" may be "a great inconvenience in the education of our daughters and our families. . . ."[177]

It is, indeed, in this social institution, that of slavery, that we encounter the great excitant to sensuality among the Portuguese, as later among the Brazilians. In the mother country, slavery was second in this respect only to the need of human beings for the task of colonization, a task disproportionate to the normal resources of the population, thereby obliging the people to maintain themselves in a constant state of superexcitation, in the interests of large-scale procreation.

Slavery, of which Portuguese economy had always made use, even in the days of its robust health, took on a pronouncedly morbid aspect as the monarchy became mercantile and imperialist. "The life of the slave," writes Alexandre Herculano, with reference to the sixteenth century, "was in this era a truly horrible one in Portugal." [178] This was due to the necessity of correcting at all costs the demographic and economic unbalance caused by the conquests and adventures overseas. This it was that corrupted the system of labor,

---

[176] R. Creary: "Brazil under the Monarchy—A Record of Facts and Observations" and "*Chrônicas Lageanas*"; manuscripts in the Library of Congress at Washington.

[177] A. D. de Pascual: *Ensaio Crítico sobre a Viagem ao Brasil em 1852 de Carlos B. Mansfield (Critical Essay on the Voyage to Brazil, in 1852, of* Charles B. Mansfield) (Rio de Janeiro, 1861). Mansfield's observations may be found in his book: *Paraguay, Brazil and the Plate* (Cambridge, 1856).

[178] Alexandre Herculano: *História da Origem e Estabelecimento da Inquisição em Portugal (History of the Origin and Establishment of the Inquisition in Portugal)* (Lisbon, 1779).

rendering more bitter the relations between masters and slaves, relations that, if not wholesome ones, had previously been confined within milder limits. Under the new stimuli the masters were the first to favor dissoluteness: "to increase the number of black offspring as one would enlarge a herd." "Concubinage was permitted among them [the slaves], the baptized and unbaptized mingling together, and illicit relations even with persons of free birth were tolerated." [179] This is precisely the impression that we get from the Italian, Gianbattista Venturino, who in 1571 accompanied the papal legate, Cardinal Alexandrino, to Portugal. The Portuguese of that day looked upon slaves as the Italians did race-horses, and they treated them in the same manner. "What they sought," the Italian tells us, "was to have many colts [180] to sell at thirty or forty crowns each." [181] The need of brawn, in the Realm itself now that immigration had fallen off, as well as in the agricultural colonies, made the commerce in human beings a profitable one.

One cannot attribute to the regime of slave labor in itself all that moral dissoluteness of Portuguese society that has been stressed by foreign travelers since the fifteenth century. The licentiousness they found was not merely Portuguese, but Iberian, although its grosser traits were to be met with among the Portuguese, where it took on an accentuated form. It is from Spain and not from Portugal that Mme d'Aulnoy writes, in the eighteenth century. Relying upon trustworthy informants, she gives us the following facts: that young aristocrats at the age of twelve or fourteen years began to take concubines, and that there were few of that age who were not suffering from venereal disease; that the concubines made a show of themselves in public, legitimate and bastard children being often brought up together, promiscuously; that in the noblest houses there was open talk of worldly diseases, which were borne by all with patience, no one being ashamed of such a misfortune. [182]

The colonists in general, and not alone the American ones, as a result of their contacts with exotic peoples and backward races, their conquests and overseas relations, underwent a decided influence in the direction of moral dissoluteness. Such was the moral onus of imperialism.

Recognizing this general influence of imperialism upon the lives

---

[179] Ibid.
[180] The word is *crias. Cria* is a colt or filly, and, in Brazil, a black slave born and reared in the master's house or on his plantation. (Translator.)

[181] *"Viagem do Cardeal Alexandrino"* ("Journey of Cardinal Alexandrino"), in Herculano, op. cit.
[182] Mercadal: *España vista por los Estranjeros* (op. cit.).

and sexual morality of the Hispanic folk, we should, meanwhile, keep in mind that they were affected by conditions of physical environment, geographic situation, and historical development that were particularly disturbing to Christian morality: the constant state of war, causing in the peninsula a flux and reflux of populations; the alternating hegemonies; the extreme social mobility; the economic instability; the cosmopolitan contacts by the maritime route; and the fact of living alongside polygamous Mohammedans. Add to these circumstances a certain disparity in the matter of clothing and practices of domestic hygiene between the demands or norms of Christian sexual morality in northern Europe and the African climate of Portugal and a large part of Spain. All these influences could not but concur in exciting a sexual hunger in Spanish and Portuguese adolescents at an earlier age than in the north.

As for the Brazilian, so fond of women from his infancy, there were influences of a social nature that acted upon him with greater force and that ran counter to continence, asceticism, and monogamy. With us the tropical climate could not but contribute to the sexual superexcitation of children and adolescents, leading at times to a morbid anticipation of the sexual and conjugal functions. This influence, however, was not so powerful as the purely social ones. I shall endeavor to show, in the following chapter, how tremendous a force these latter were.

Montesquieu and more recently Treitschke [183] have attributed to the tropical climate the existence of sensuality, polygamy, and slavery among us, the sensuality being due to the fact that young girls appear to become women at an earlier age in the tropics than in cold or temperate climates, while slavery itself, in Treitschke's opinion, is "the complement of the harem," and, consequently, of a precocious sensualism.

This question whether a tropical climate exerts a direct influence upon the sexual life is not one to be answered offhand. There are those who would substitute for it the question of race, or of class and social environment. That the sexual organs of those who have just come to such a climate are superexcited, with menstruation in women being hastened, would appear to be beyond a doubt.[184] That such excitation continues in individuals who have become acclimatized is open to question. As to the earlier occurrence of menstruation in the

---

[183] Heinrich von Treitschke (1834–96), author of *Deutsche Geschichte in neunzehnten Zahrhundert* (1879–94) and *Zwei Kaiser* (1888). (Translator.)

[184] A. Jousset, in William Z. Ripley: *The Races of Europe, a Sociological Study* (op. cit.).

tropics, statistics surprise us with the fact that among the Eskimos puberty is reached at a precociously early age.[185] Hence the preference of some for the criterion of race rather than that of climate. But despite so important an exception, the general tendency as shown by statistics is in the direction of an earlier menstruation in the tropics than in cold countries or temperate ones.

In dealing with the influence of the African climate upon the sexual life of the Hispanic peoples, let us consider less the direct than the indirect influence, as provocative of important reactions—those North African social institutions that answer to the necessities of milieu, physical environment, and climate. Polygamy and slavery, among others. The fact is that these institutions, with their series of sexual irregularities, are especially bound up with the Mussulman climate, if we may so term it, of North Africa, a climate that acted upon the Hispanic populations in favor of Moorish Africa and against

---

[185] The subject has been studied by Ribbing (*L'Hygiène sexuelle et ses conséquences morales*), who brings together the following statistical data regarding the age of beginning menstruation: Lapland and Sweden, 18 years; Christiania, 16 years, 9 months, and 25 days; Berlin, 15 years, 7 months, and 6 days; Paris, 15 years, 7 months, 18 days; Madeira, 14 years and 3 months; Sierra Leone and Egypt, 10 years. In Eskimo women menstruation begins at 12 or 13 years. Moll records the information (from Jacobus X: *Lois génitales*, Paris, 1906) that among French women in the Antilles menstruation rarely occurs before the age of 14; whereas among African women in the same islands menstruation begins, as it does in Africa, at 10 or 11 years. Moll emphasizes the possibility that climate may exert a cumulative influence upon successive generations, not producing its full effect until after a number of them.—Albert Moll: *The Sexual Life of the Child* (translation) (New York, 1924). In Brazil the age at which puberty appears varies from the Amazon region to the Rio Grande. See Joaquim Moreira da Fonseca: "*Casamento e Eugênia*" ("Marriage and Eugenics"), *Atas*, First Brazilian Eugenics Congress (Rio de Janeiro, 1929). In Portugal the age at which young girls attain puberty is fixed by Dalgado at 14.— D. G. Dalgado: *The Climate of Portugal* (op. cit.). According to the studies by G. J. Engelman, more recent than those of Ribbing, the age of menstruation varies with the climate from 12.9 years in hot countries to 16.5 years in cold countries.—G. J. Engelman: "First Age of Menstruation in the North American Continent," *Transactions of the American Gynecological Society*, 1901.—It should be noted that, in general, girls of the lower classes attain puberty sooner than do those of the upper classes.—Pitirim Sorokin: *Contemporary Social Theories* (New York and London, 1928).—Interesting researches in this field are being conducted by the Brazilian physician Nelson Chaves. See his paper on "*Aspecto da fisiologia hipotalamo-hipofisiario—Interpretação da precocidade sexual no Nordeste*" ("Aspect of Hypothalamic-Hypophisiary Physiology—Interpretation of Sexual Precocity in the Northeast"), *Neurobiologia* (*Neurobiology*), Vol. III, No. 4 (Recife, 1940).

Christian Europe, singularly predisposing the Portuguese and the Spaniards to the polygamous and slave-holding colonization of the American tropics.

The Portuguese colonizer in Brazil made many compromises with native hygiene, whether in the matter of habitation or bodily care. In the latter respect, he adopted the daily bath and freed his young ones of their cumbersome diapers and swaddling-clothes. With regard to his house, he adopted from the Indians the straw-thatched roof, just as he had taken from the Asiatics the thick walls and porches of his home. He also had the good sense not wholly to slight the native healers by having recourse always to officially approved medicine as practiced in Portugal. This despite the fact that the Jesuits had declared a war to the death upon the *"curandeiros,"* or tribal doctors. The priests themselves, however, even as they combated the mystic pharmacopœia of the medicine-men, absorbed from the latter a knowledge of a number of plants and herbs. It is, indeed, altogether probable that the life of a patient in colonial Brazil was safer in the hands of the native practitioner than in those of some physician from overseas who was a stranger to the milieu and its pathology. Frei Caetano Brandão, Bishop of Grão-Pará, and a man of profound good sense, remarked that it was "better to have a person treated by a Tapuia from the backlands, whose powers of observation were keener and whose instincts were more unhampered, than by some doctor come from Lisbon." [186] And Joaquim Jerônymo Serpa, who had studied surgery in Lisbon hospitals, upon returning to the colony was inclined more to the healing art of the Tapuias than to the science of physicians in the metropolis, and never lost an opportunity to prescribe *pau cardoso* in place of *altéia* root, or *pau tacagé* [187] as an astringent, or cashew gum instead of gum arabic.[188] All of these are

[186] Frei Caetano Brandâo, in Luis Edmundo: *O Rio de Janeiro em Tempo dos Vice-reis* (*Rio de Janeiro in the Time of the Viceroys*), (Rio de Janeiro, 1932).

[187] *Pau cardoso* (*Polypodium pungens*) is a fern with a fibrous, porous stalk and a thorny exterior bark, growing from one to three feet in height and somewhat resembling a lopped-off palm; used by the *curandeiros* to treat asthma and convulsive coughs. The *altéia* is a plant of the *Malvaceæ* or mallow family (*Althæa*

officinalis L.). As for *pau tacagé*, a term which, it will be observed, the author takes from a late-nineteenth-century treatise published at Recife (see note following), Senhor Freyre himself has not been able to identify this, nor has a large number of authorities on Brazilian botany whom I have consulted been able to throw any light on the matter. (Translator.)

[188] Antônio Joaquim de Mello: *Biografias* (published by command of the Governor, Barbosa Lima) (Recife, 1895).—In a work in preparation,

traits that indicate the bent of the Portuguese toward adaptation.

As to acclimatization, it is difficult to determine to what degree it was advantageously achieved in Brazil, for the reason that it is hard to separate acclimatization from adaptation. It is hard to state precisely up to what point southern Europeans, and Portuguese in particular, succeeded in acclimatizing themselves better than did those from the north. Any such comparison is practically out of the question, for the families in tropical Brazil that have remained white or almost white are few in number. However, in the north, a region that is essentially tropical and more aristocratic than any other in its background, there is one case that might possibly be studied: that of the Wanderleys of Serinhaem and Rio Formoso. This family, founded early in the seventeenth century by Gaspar van der Lei, a gentleman-in-waiting on Maurice of Nassau, sunk its roots in the extreme south of the *capitânia* and there preserved, through inbreeding,[189] a relative Nordic purity. This is attested by the predominance among its members of a pink skin, very bright blue eyes, and blond or reddish hair. This inbreeding—note well—was due not so much to racial as to social prejudices such as are observed by families in the old rural regions, where the intermarriage of cousins and the marriage of uncles with nieces has gone on for generations. Maria Graham was surprised at the frequency of these consanguineous unions, in which, it seems, she discerned a certain evil odor of incest; and in the middle of the nineteenth century marriages of this sort came to be the subject of many an alarmist doctoral thesis in medical schools under the Empire.[190]

Professor Silva Mello expresses the opinion that the clinician should not wholly despise the so-called "popular lore" with respect to foods, ailments, and the like.

[189] Freyre employs the English word. (Translator.)

[190] If consanguineous marriages were common in Brazil, this was due not merely to economic motives, readily understandable under a system of individual enterprise, but to social motives as well, based upon aristocratic exclusiveness. Writing of the rural aristocrats of Bahia, Sá Oliveira states that, while retaining their haughtiness, they revealed in everything about them "something of phys-

ical degenerescence," and he attributes this to "conjugal unions within a very limited sphere, in order not to bring into the family blood that would reveal the condition of an ex-slave."— J., B. de Sá Oliveira: *Evolução Psíchica dos Baianos* (*Psychic Evolution of the Bahians*) (Bahia, 1894). But he does not indicate what the signs of this degenerescence were. Modern studies in eugenics, in place of confirming in absolute fashion Darwin's idea—"Nature abhors perpetual self-fertilization"—indicate that the results of inbreeding, when evil, depend rather upon the genetic composition of the individuals than upon the pernicious influence inherent in

So far as the Wanderleys are concerned, they gave to political life, to the magistracy, and to the priesthood some distinguished men, even though none with the earmarks of genius—with the possible exception of the Baron of Cotegipe, who was one of the Empire's major statesmen. But he, it would appear, had his spot of Negro blood. On the other hand, from among the authentic Wanderleys—the blondest and the pinkest of the lot—one might collect numerous examples of alcoholic degeneracy, an irregularity for which the family came to be celebrated in rural folklore; just as the Albuquerques were noted for their tendency to lie (mythomania), the Cavalcantis—a Pernambucan family stemming from the Florentine nobleman Filippo Cavalcanti—for their horror of paying their debts, and the Sousa Leão and Carneiro da Cunha families for erotomania. In the words of the people: "There is not a Wanderley who does not drink, an Albuquerque who does not lie, a Cavalcanti who does not owe. Nor a Sousa Leão or a Carneiro da Cunha who does not like a Negro woman." [191]

the process.—East and Jones: *Inbreeding and Outbreeding*, in Fox Pitt-Rivers and George Henry Lane: *The Clash of Cultures and the Contact of Races* (London, 1927).

[191] Júlio Bello wrote an interesting comedy in which a representative of each of the three old families appears in all the splendor of the vice that tradition attributes to him. It is a work of which there exists only one edition and that a private one, edited by José Maria Carneiro de Albuquerque e Mello, Recife, *Revista do Norte*. See also, by Júlio Bello, the *Memórias de um Senhor do Engenho* (*Memoirs of a Plantation-Owner*) (Rio de Janeiro, 1939).—As to Negro women, there was also many a Wanderley who was mad about them. To one member of this family, a planter of Serinhaem, is attributed the saying: "Black boot and black woman only." Other traditional families have their popular or folklore attributes that are not always merited. Of the Mendonça Furtados it is said in the north that "there is not a Mendonça who has not stolen (*furtado*)." On the island of Itamaracá, in Pernam-

buco, the malicious ones used to repeat the following couplet:

Ilha, quem te persegue?
Formigas, passagens e os Guedes!

"Island, who is it plagues you? Ants, tolls, and the Guedeses (the Guedes family)."

Some families, in the north and in Minas Geraes especially, are noted for their love of a fight, a taste that has been handed down for generations, from father to son, as a sort of sacred fire. These are families of "bad men" (*valentões*). Others—not always justly, it goes without saying—are accused of being weak-minded, as is the case with the Machados of Alagoas, and the Lins in Pernambuco. Others still are held to be traditional misers, or sharpers in business, or gluttons.

There are not a few illustrious families in Pernambuco, Maranhão, Pará, Minas, Rio Grande do Sul, Rio de Janeiro, and even São Paulo—where not every plutocrat whose Aryanism is less pure is the descendant of *caboclos* alone—who have preserved Negroid traces, which similarly have

But over against those generalizations that would interpret the alcoholism of the Wanderleys as being a case of Nordic degeneration due to the effects of a hot climate, there is the fact that we do not know how far such excesses may or may not have been due to difficulties of adaptation to the climate. Alcoholism may very well be the result of a family defect, favored by social conditions. But in our country genealogical studies are generally very superficial; being undertaken chiefly to satisfy the vanity of Imperial barons or Republican snobs,[192] they are lacking in the realism [193] and depth that are needed to make them, properly speaking, scientific. In the case of the Wanderleys, a detailed study should be made of Gaspar's forebears. Concerning him we know, from Wätjen,[194] that he was of the nobility, but a man of weak character. At least—in the opinion of the Dutch chroniclers. What weakness of character might this be? That of a dowry-hunter? That of a fugitive? That of a drunkard? What credence are we to give to the statements of the Dutch, who are suspect on this subject, seeing that Gaspar was a sort of Calabar [195] in reverse, who betrayed his own people to go over to the side of the Pernambucans and his bride? She was a rich bride, it is true, the daughter of a plantation-owner. There were others among the Dutch

---

been consecrated by popular malice. Flattened nostrils, thick lips. A certain member of one of these families, who had been granted a title of nobility by Pedro II, was commonly called "Baron Chocolate."

[192] English word in the text. (Translator.)

[193] An editor of *O Sete de Setembro* of Recife, Vol. I, No. 34 (1846), states that the manuscript copy of Borges da Fonseca's "*Nobiliarchia Pernambucana*" ("Pernambucan Peerage"), preserved in the Library of S. Bento de Olinda, was found "with leaves torn out and others substituted." The same editor was not satisfied with the evidence that had so far been presented as to the noble origin of the Cavalcantis of Pernambuco. Apropos of the claims to this effect of João Maurício Cavalcanti da Rocha Wanderley, he wrote: "Down to this day no one has seen any document disinterred from the Italian archives

that would furnish convincing proof." He likewise demanded that the Wanderleys show proof of their descent from a noble family of Holland. See, in this regard, Gilberto Freyre's introduction to the *Memórias de um Cavalcanti* (*Memoirs of a Cavalcanti*) (São Paulo, 1940).

[194] E. Hermann Wätjen: "*Das Judentum und die Anfänge der modernen Kolonization*," in *Das holländische Kolonialreich in Brasilien* (op. cit.).

[195] Allusion to a Brazilian mestizo, Domingos Calabar, who fought in Pernambuco (1632) under Mathias de Albuquerque and who later passed over to the side of the Dutch, being responsible for several Portuguese defeats. He was finally captured and hanged. In the case of Gaspar van der Lei, we have a Dutchman coming over to the Brazilian side. (Translator.)

who took Brazilian wives, so the Marquês de Basto [196] informs us, but they came from less important families.

The fact that Wanderleys are to be met with suffering from alcoholic degeneracy and shorn of their former aristocratic prestige is to be attributed to causes that are chiefly social and economic and that involved other distinguished families of the colonial era who today have fallen into decadence: the instability of rural wealth, due to the one-crop system based on slavery; the inheritance laws, which favored the dispersion of property; and, finally, the law abolishing slavery, with no indemnity for the slave-owners, a law that found São Paulo filled with European immigrants, but that took the north unawares, the planters in this region possessing no other wealth than their African blacks.

The Paes Barreto family, for instance, also of Pernambuco, like the Wanderleys in Serinhaem and Rio Formoso had for centuries been rooted in a single section of the state, the present municipality of Cabo. As was the case with no other family in Brazil, the succession of its property and the purity of its aristocratic lineage had been guaranteed by the right of primogeniture that had been accorded it. And yet, a family so privileged and so protected against the perils of dispersion is today one of the most widely scattered and most decadent of any in the land. Where now are those Paes Barretos whose descendants down to the beginning of the nineteenth century exerted so preponderant an influence over the destinies of Pernambuco? Many of them today, of the purest blood, are small office-holders or the owners of wretched little farms.[197]

This question of the degenerateness of those Europeans who had kept their stock comparatively pure in Brazil is a very hard one to deal with, in view of the conditions of social instability that marked our agrarian development, by reason of that dependence in which

---

[196] Duarte de Albuquerque Coello (or Coelho), Marquês de Basto, Conde de Pernambuco, descendant of the first feudal lord of Pernambuco and author of the *Memorias Diarias de la Guerra del Brasil* (Madrid, 1634). (Translator.)

[197] In 1846 Father Lopes Gama wrote: "Of how many mule-drivers have I not bought meal, rice, beans, and corn who, if the truth were known, are noblemen of the first rank! I behold them barefoot, in their shirts and drawers, their hair disheveled, their skin roughened and the color of an old guitar, and I am in the habit of treating them unceremoniously enough; yet there are those who tell me that they are noblemen, for they are Cavalcantis, and not those whose names end in -tes, who are upstart nobility, but the -tis, who are bright and shining as a clyster!"—*O Sete de Setembro*, Vol. I, No. 34 (1845).

we lived: first a dependence upon sugar, afterwards upon coffee, and always on the Negro slave.

In regions with a different climate from ours—what is known as a *good* and even the *best* climate, in the technical sense of those terms—similar phenomena of degenerateness and dispersion have been observed as a result of the same social influence: slavery and the one-crop system. In our country Joaquim Nabuco, who was concerned with the slave-holding society of his day, noted the tendency of great fortunes to pass from the hands of the ones who had founded them to those of creditors; and he adds: "Few are the grandsons of agriculturists who have preserved the estates that they inherited from their fathers; the adage 'Rich father, noble son, impoverished grandson' is an expression of the long experience our people have had with slavery, the effect of which is to dissipate wealth, which not infrequently falls into foreign hands." [198] An identical situation is to be observed in the Southern United States, under pressure of the same social forces of inconstancy and instability—and in the North, too, for that matter, under the influence of other factors tending to degradation of families. [199] In Brazil it is to be seen in São Paulo, a region with a climate more favorable to north Europeans than that of Pernambuco, Bahia, or Maranhão.

The Leme family may serve as an example here. Likewise of Nordic origin and once illustrious, it is today half-decadent, all that remains of its former brilliance being the eloquence of Cardinal Dom Sebastião Leme. "And what has become of this family? What happened to it, anyway?" was the question put years ago by Antônio A. de Fonseca [200] with reference to the patriarch Leme and his direct descendants, the bearers of his name. "What happened to them is what is going to happen to nearly all the families that today are important, but which in the second or third generation will become what we call *caipiras* [201] or *caboclos*, just as are the descendants of the

---

[198] Joaquim Nabuco: *O Abolicionismo* (op. cit.).

[199] Factors of a general character having to do with degradation and renovation that made themselves felt in European countries in the course of the nineteenth and at the beginning of the twentieth century, with the rise of the proletarian masses in the social scale. With regard to the United States, Professor Pitirim Sorokin writes: "Many families of the old Americans are already extinct; part

are sunk; part are surrounded by the newcomers in the highest social strata. The rapidity of the burning-out of the best material has been grasped already in a popular statement that prominent American families rise and sink back within three generations." —Pitirim Sorokin: *Social Mobility* (op. cit.).

[200] Brazilian publicist and historical essayist. (Translator.)

[201] The word primarily means an inhabitant of the *campo*, or open

powerful Lemes of the 1720's. . . . I knew, in the Cajurú quarter, a *caipira* or *caboclo* who earned his living with a hoe and who used to accompany my father on deer-hunting expeditions as master of the hounds, being paid a few pennies for his services. This *caipira* was Apolinário Leme, descendant of those potentates whom His Majesty the King of Portugal pardoned for their crimes. . . ." And it was not only an Apolinário Leme, reduced to a master of hounds, whom Fonseca knew; there were also descendants of captains-major [202] of the *capitânia* engaged in the humblest of employment, some of them overseers, others men of all work. "The son of one of the signers of the amended Constitution" was now a mere writ-server of Itú. The legitimate grandson of a baron of the Empire was the foreman of a coffee plantation. On the other hand, the descendants of European plantation workers were going up, becoming the great ones of the land and taking the place of Pedro II's one-time barons with their titles of count conferred by the Pope himself.

This debacle was due principally to the instability of agrarian wealth based upon a single product, and that, a product subject like sugar or coffee to great fluctuations upon the consumer markets, and, moreover, one exploited by slave labor. For the degenerate or decadent families include not only the rare ones of Nordic blood that, through the intermarriage of cousins, uncles, and nieces, remained comparatively pure throughout the colonial era; there are also many that are Portuguese on all four sides, or that here in this country were reinvigorated by more than one admixture with colored stock; families that once were prominent, but now do not stand for anything whatsoever.

There remains for me to stress the fact, of great significance in the social history of the Brazilian family, that Brazil was discovered and colonized—from the end of the sixteenth century on, autocolonized, being its own defender against foreign aggression—in an era in which the Portuguese, lords of numerous lands in Asia and in Africa, had come into possession of a rich variety of tropical products, some of them not adaptable to Europe, but all of them the product of fine, opulent, and ancient Asiatic and African civilizations. And of all the parts of the Lusitanian empire, it was perhaps Brazil that made the most extensive and advantageous use of these cultural contributions: the parasol or sunshade; the palanquin; the fan; the Bengal stick or

country; comes to mean a rustic of low degree or uncouth manners. (Translator.)

[202] *Capitães-mores* (singular, *capitão-mor*), commander-in-chief of a *capitânia* in colonial Brazil. (Translator.)

cane; the silk counterpane; the Sino-Japanese roof, projecting over the sides of the house and curved at the corners like the horns of the moon; [203] Chinese poreclain; plants; spices; animals; sweetmeats; the coco tree; the jaqueira; [204] the mango; cinnamon; the breadfruit tree; couscous; [205] Indian and Chinese furniture.

The Brazilian aristocrat of the Pernambucan littoral and of the Reconcavo immediately began enjoying such advantages as only the refined courts of Europe could offer in the sixteenth century. It was, indeed, the Portuguese who first brought to Europe from the Orient the fan, table porcelain, counterpanes from China and India, tea-sets, and, it would seem, the parasol as well.[206] It is likely that even the

---

[203] This trace of Asiatic architecture, acquired by the Portuguese in China and in Japan and adapted to Brazil, is one of the best proofs of the plastic genius of the colonizers and their talent for adaptation to the tropics. Morales de los Rios supposes that the Sino-Japanese tile shaped like the wing of a dove and other features of Oriental architecture were introduced among us "by Lusitanian master workmen who had practiced their trades in the Asiatic colonies of the realm."—A. Morales de los Rios: "*Resumo Monográphico da Evolução da Arquitetura do Brasil*" ("Monographic Résumé of the Architecture of Brazil"), *Livro de Ouro Comemorativo do Centenário da Independência e da Exposição do Rio de Janeiro* (*The Golden Book, Commemorative of the Centenary of Brazilian Independence and of the Exposition of Rio de Janeiro*) (Rio de Janeiro, 1934). Unfortunately, details are lacking concerning the Portuguese master workmen who built the first houses, fortresses, and churches in Brazil. It is merely known of one of them, who accompanied Thomé de Souza, that he made a fortune for himself.

[204] Tree of the breadfruit genus (*Artocarpus integrifolia*). (Translator.)

[205] Couscous is a dish that is generally supposed to be very much our own. It is, as a matter of fact, an old patriarchal one from North Africa.

In the words of Edmond Richardin: "*plat primitif et lointain, plat patriarcal dont la saveur nomade réjouit la fantaisie du voyageur qui se souvient!*"—Edmond Richardin: *La Cuisine française du XIVe au XVe siècle* (Paris, 1913). In Brazil it was a case of applying the old North African process to native products.—Another illusion to be shattered: regarding giblets. This is not a Portuguese dish, much less Brazilian. It is a French confection. Origin: Chateauroux.

[206] In his *Culto da Arte em Portugal* (*Cult of Art in Portugal*), (Lisbon, 1896), Ramalho Ortigão asserts that the Portuguese were the first to manufacture and introduce the parasol in Europe. This may not be exact as regards Italy.—As to the first porcelain and crystal tea-sets, lozenge- and beauty-boxes, and the like, we are reminded that they were brought back, along with the first fans, by the companions of Fernão Mendes Pinto, the Portuguese, thus endowing "Rome and Florence, Paris and London with all the principal attributes and basic motives of the household art and feminine elegance that are characteristic of our modern civilization." So far as the fan, porcelain, and the tea-set are concerned, there appears to be no doubt. Ortigão further stresses the fact that Lisbon in the sixteenth century became "the first *jardin d'acclimatation*, the first zoological garden, and the first market of Europe,"

habit of the daily bath was transmitted by him from the Far East to England,[207] a circumstance that, if true, holds its irony, reminding one of the missionary who saved the souls of others and lost his own. It may have been the Portuguese, also, who introduced or at any rate popularized those Chinese rockets and fireworks that are so characteristic of Portuguese and Brazilian church festivals, and also the fashion of wearing many jewels and trinkets.

The stories that are told of the opulence and luxury of the Bahian and Pernambucan plantation-owners in the sixteenth and seventeenth centuries impress us as being, at times, friars' tales—tales told by colonial monks of good education but hard put to it for a subject for their exercises in grammar and calligraphy. These stories are told, not of one, but of many of the gentry of that day, especially of those great ones who were accustomed to leave their plantations and go down to spend the feast-days at Olinda—the feast of the ancients, which coincided with the rainy season, from Carnival to St. John's Day. There must be an element of exaggeration in such accounts, which tell of meals eaten with a fork, a refinement that was then little in use even in European courts. They also tell of tables laden with silver and fine porcelain, of beds with the richest of silk counterpanes, of doors with gold locks, and of ladies covered with precious stones. But if we stop to think that many of these luxuries of the table, the house, and personal attire, adopted by Europe in that age, had been brought from the Orient, it will not be so hard to understand this display or wealth and the appearance in a new land of unlooked-for refinements. After all, what was so strange about it, seeing that Pernambuco and Bahia speedily became ports of call for ships returning from the East with heavy cargoes of valuable merchandise, vessels that made their way across the sea with the slow movements

---

through the introduction of "tea, sugar, cotton, pepper, ginger from Malabar, sandalwood from Timor, teakwood from Cochin, benzoin from Achin, wood of Solor, and indigo from Cambaia, along with such animals as the panther, the elephant, the rhinoceros, and the Arabian pony." On the general influence of the overseas conquests on European life, see James E. Gillespie: *The Influence of Oversea Expansion on England to 1700* (New York, 1920); and Jay Barrett Botsford: *English Society in the Eighteenth Century as Influenced from*

Oversea (New York, 1924). See also on this subject Sousa Viterbo: *Arte e Artistas em Portugal* (op. cit.).

[207] Whether or not it was through the agency of the Portuguese, the English habit of the daily bath comes from the Orient. It did not become general in England before the eighteenth century. The parasol and umbrella, likewise, were not in general use there before the end of the seventeenth century.—Botsford: *English Society in the Eighteenth Century* (op. cit.).

of a pregnant woman, being filled with fine objects which the Portuguese were introducing to aristocratic and bourgeois Europe? The mere presence of silver plate among the Olinda planters in the sixteenth century is none the less cause for astonishment; such luxury surprises us in men who had just completed the first clearings of the virgin forest and who had just set up the first sugar-mills.

It is not only the chaplain friars, however, who speak of all this in a tone that reminds one of the panegyrics addressed to saints; foreign travelers like Pyrard de Laval also dwell upon it. Pyrard was perhaps the first European to praise the Brazilian Big Houses—"fine and noble dwellings" (*"de belles maisons nobles"*). He is alluding to those of the Reconcavo. It was in one of these that the Frenchman stopped as a guest; but he gives us only the last name of the master of the house, and this, it would seem, he has garbled: Mangue la Bote. In any event, this Mangue la Bote lived upon his plantation, in the early years of the seventeenth century, in the manner of a fine gentleman. He even kept a band of musicians to enliven his meals. It was a band of thirty pieces, all Negro players, under the direction of a Marseillais. Mangue la Bote was credited with a fortune of more than three hundred thousand crowns (*"riche de plus de trois cent mille écus"*),[208] a fortune that consisted of sugar and Negroes. For it was upon these two commodities that the aristocratic society of colonial Brazil was based.[209]

Similarly, those "inhabitants rich in estates" of whom Gabriel Soares speaks must have made their fortunes in sugar and the black man; and the same is true of the more than one hundred residents of sixteenth-century Bahia, who each year had an income of from four to five thousand cruzados,[210] while their plantations were worth from twenty to fifty or sixty thousand. These planters—so the chronicler

---

[208] In an article on this book, Senhor Affonso Arinos de Mello Franco recalls the fact that "Rodolfo Garcia, in his notes on Frei Vicente do Salvador's *History of Brazil*, had already clearly indentified this Mangue la Bote as being the celebrated captain-major Balthazar de Aragão, who died bravely at sea."

[209] Regarding the feudal-aristocratic system of the plantation-owners in the Portuguese colony in America, Pyrard adds: "*Il y a des Seigneurs qui y ont un grand domaine, entr'autres force engins à sucre, que le Roy d'Espagne leur a donné en récompense de quelque service, et cela est érigé en titre de quelque dignité, comme Baraonie, Comte, etc. Et ces Seigneurs là donnent de terre à ceux qui y veulent aller demeurer et planter des cannes de sucre à la charge de les porter aux moulins aux engins de ces Seigneurs en leur payant le prix.*"—*Voyage de François Pyrard de Laval contenant sa navigation aux Indes Orientales, Maldives, Mologues et au Bresil*, etc. (Paris, 1679), p. 203.

[210] The cruzado was worth four hundred reis. (Translator.)

tell us—"were very fastidious about their persons, with many horses, servants, and slaves, and with a superfluity of garments, especially the women, who wear nothing but silk. . . ." On their tables was "silver service." Many of their plantations were sumptuous ones, with water-wheel mills, like that of Sebastião de Faria, on the banks of the Cotegipe: "great edifices for the refining of the sugar and great dwellings as well, and a Church of St. Jerome, all of stone and mortar, on which he spent more than twelve thousand cruzados"; or else there were mills worked by oxen, like that of Vasco Rodrigues Lobato: "all surrounded by fields of cane, of which they make many arrobas [211] of sugar." [212]

From this it may be seen that Father Fernão Cardim was perhaps not exaggerating when he described the plantation-owners whom he knew in Pernambuco in 1583 as being "very wealthy men, worth forty, fifty, and eighty thousand cruzados," while their estates were "greater and richer than those of Bahia." The truth is, on the other hand, that even at this time, when the price of sugar was still high—460 reis the arroba for white sugar and 320 for brown—many of these planters were burdened with debt, precisely by reason of their "excesses and the great amount they spend on their personal upkeep." Horses costing two hundred and three hundred cruzados. Damask beds, fringed with gold. Counterpanes from India. Far more slaves than they needed. Banquets, marriage feasts, and christenings, with extraordinary dishes and much costly food and drink. [213]

An opulent life, astonishingly so, the one that was led by these Portuguese colonists who, investing their capital in the land, succeeded in prospering in those early days in Brazil by living off sugar and the Negro. Those of Pernambuco had twenty-three sugar-mills, worked by oxen or by water, producing, in 1576, from fifty to seventy thousand arrobas of sugar. Those of Bahia had eighteen such establishments. Each of these mills was built at a cost of ten thousand

---

[211] Portuguese measure of weight equivalent to thirty-two pounds; cf. the Spanish arroba (a little over twenty-five pounds). (Translator.)

[212] Gabriel Soares de Sousa: *Tratado Descriptivo do Brasil em 1587* (*Descriptive Treatise on Brazil in 1587*), edited by F. A. Varnhagen, *Revista do Instituto Histórico e Geográphico Brasileiro* (Rio de Janeiro, 1851), p. 133.

[213] Fernão Cardim: *Tratados da* *Terra e Gente do Brasil* (op. cit.), pp. 329 and 334–5.—In an interesting study, "The Rise of the Brazilian Aristocracy," *Hispanic American Historical Review*, Vol. XI, No. 2, Alan P. Manchester reminds us that while the Pernambucan was sleeping in a bed of crimson damask, the Paulista was sleeping in a hammock. This was a state of affairs that later was reversed, with the victory of coffee over sugar.

cruzados, more or less, and had fifty head of slaves and twenty yoke of oxen. Their annual production—that of the best ones, at any rate—was from six to ten thousand arrobas of unrefined sugar.[214]

Silveira Martins[215] in the last century observed that "Brazil is coffee, and coffee is the Negro." So, in this first century of slavery, it might have been said: "Brazil is sugar, and sugar is the Negro." For in Bahia and in Pernambuco, the two great centers of economic and social opulence, the two great international ports of sixteenth-century Brazil, the Indian was relegated to a secondary plane by reason of his cultural inferiority. Lacking in capabilities, he was useless in the system of colonization that was to lay the foundations of Brazilian economy. The "cultivation of foodstuffs" had likewise been stifled by the rows of sugar-cane. It was in those rows that the Portuguese, disillusioned with regard to the riches of India, beheld almost at once the *In hoc signo vinces* which was to inspire the agrarian colonization of Brazil with slavery as its base."[216]

---

[214] Pero de Magalhães Gandavo: *História da Província de Santa Cruz e que vulgarmente chamam Brasil* (*History of the Province of Santa Cruz, Vulgarly Known as Brazil*) (Rio de Janeiro, 1924). See the *Diálogos das Grandezas do Brasil* (op. cit.). See also Pereira da Costa: *Origens, Históricas da Indústria Açucareira de Pernambuco* (Recife, 1905). This author reminds us that there was a royal decree, dating from 1555, per-mitting each plantation-owner to import up to 120 slaves from the Congo, and that in 1584, according to the statement of Father Anchieta, there were some 10,000 sugar-mills in Pernambuco.

[215] A nineteenth-century Brazilian writer, known as a publicist for the abolitionist cause. (Translator.)

[216] End of Volume I in the Portuguese text. (Translator.)

IV

THE NEGRO SLAVE
IN THE SEXUAL AND FAMILY LIFE
OF THE BRAZILIAN

EVERY Brazilian, even the light-skinned fair-haired one, carries about with him on his soul, when not on soul and body alike—for there are many in Brazil with the mongrel mark of the *genipap* [1]— the shadow, or at least the birthmark, of the aborigine or the Negro. Along the seaboard, from Maranhão to Rio Grande do Sul, it is chiefly the Negro. The influence of the African, either direct or vague and remote.

In our affections, our excessive mimicry, our Catholicism, which so delights the senses, our music, our gait, our speech, our cradle songs— in everything that is a sincere expression of our lives, we almost all of us bear the mark of that influence. Of the female slave or "mammy" [2] who rocked us to sleep. Who suckled us. Who fed us, mashing our food with her own hands. The influence of the old woman who told us our first tales of ghost and *bicho*. Of the mulatto girl who relieved us of our first *bicho de pé*,[3] of a pruriency that was so enjoyable. Who initiated us into physical love and, to the creaking of a canvas cot, gave us our first complete sensation of being a man. Of the Negro lad who was our first playmate.

There have been others who have hinted at the possibility that the inclination to colored women to be observed in the son of the family in slave-holding countries is a development out of the intimate relations of the white child with its Negro wet-nurse. The psychic importance of the act of suckling and its effects upon the child is viewed as enormous by modern psychologists, and it may be that Calhoun is

---

[1] Lima and Barroso (op. cit.) define the *jenipapo* as a "dark stain on the body of children, in the inferior dorsal region, held to be a mark of mixed breeding." (Translator.)

[2] *Sinhama*, an affectionate term. Cf.

sinha, sinhazinha, etc. (Translator.)

[3] A *bicho de pé* is a type of flea that burrows beneath the skin of the foot and lays its eggs there. On the "*bicho* complex," see Chapter ii, p. 139 f. (Translator.)

right in supposing that these effects are of great significance in the case of white children brought up by Negro women.[4]

The truth is that the social conditions surrounding the development of the child on the old sugar plantations of Brazil, as on the ante-bellum plantations of Virginia and the Carolinas—where the young one is constantly surrounded by the Negro or mulatto girl who is easily to be had—are in themselves sufficient to explain the predilection mentioned. In Brazil, cases are known where white men not only prefer Negro women but are incapable of enjoying themselves with any other. Tradition has it that this was the case with the son of an important rural family of Pernambuco; his parents found it impossible to arrange a marriage for him with one of his cousins or any other white girl who belonged to a family that was equally prominent, for the reason that he only wanted Negroes. Raoul Dunlop tells us of another instance, involving the young man of a well-known slave-holding family in the south. It was necessary for this youth, in order to excite himself for his white bride, to take with him to the bedroom the sweaty nightgown, imbued with the *budum*,[5] or odor, of the Negro slave girl with whom he had been having an affair. These are cases of exclusive fixation. Morbid, of course; but they enable us to sense that shadow which the Negro slave cast over the Brazilian's sexual and family life.

In this essay we are not concerned, save indirectly, with the importance of the Negro in the æsthetic life, and still less in the economic progress, pure and simple, of Brazil. We must note in passing, however, that his role was a most impressive one. Along the agrarian seaboard it was, in my estimation, much greater than that of the aborigine. Greater in a certain sense than that of the Portuguese.

For the orthodox and official milieus of Brazil this idea of the Negro's being superior to the Indian and even to the Portuguese in various aspects of his material and moral culture is an extravagant one. Superior in his technical and artistic capacity. But an academician has already come forward to defend the first thesis—that of the superiority of the Negro to the Indian—in the pages of a didactic treatise. He gives the master his due by recognizing the fact that the African, who was brought here by the Portuguese colonist, did possess a higher culture than the native: "they [the Africans] were

---

[4] Arthur W. Calhoun: *A Social History of the American Family from Colonial Times to the Present* (Cleveland, 1918).

[5] ". . . the body odor, the so-called *catinga*, or *budum*, reputedly characteristic of the African."—Donald Pierson: *Negroes in Brazil* (op. cit.), p. 175.

in a more advanced stage of social evolution than our Indians." [6]
Such daring, it is true, on the part of Professor Afrânio Peixoto called
down upon him a severe reprimand from the *Revista do Instituto
Histórico e Geográfico Brasileiro*. "The fact of the matter is," says
the learned *Revista*, in commenting on Professor Peixoto's book, "that
our aborigines were already star-worshippers while the sons of the
black continent who were introduced here had not as yet progressed
beyond the stage of a pure fetishism, some of them being, simply,
tree-worshippers." The writer then goes on, with a sovereign disdain
for reality: "With respect to neither the arts and crafts, nor the
cultivation of vegetables, nor the domestication of zoological species,
nor family and tribal organization, nor astronomical knowledge, nor
the creation of language and legends, were the blacks superior to our
forest-dwellers"; and he concludes, with an air of triumph: "In so
far as the separation of temporal and spiritual powers and a rudimentary form of political organization are concerned, the authoch-
thonous peoples of Brazil are, once again, not to be placed on a lower
rung of the ladder than are the sons of the burning land of Kam." [7]

The studies that have been carried out among the primitive societies
of America with respect to the cultural values unevenly accumulated
in various parts of the continent—an accumulation that, rising to a
peak in the semi-civilizations of Central America, undergoes a de-
pression in the impoverished culture of the tropical jungle, to level
out again, more or less, with that of Patagonia—such studies show
that a large part of the indigenous population of Brazil lay in the two
less favored areas. Only on the margin, as in Marajó, are more striking
cultural expressions to be met with, the result, naturally, of a contagious contact with the Central American regions.

The map of the cultural areas of America drawn up by Kroeber [8]
affords us a precise idea of the greater or less quantity or the greater
or less degree of elaboration of values, of the higher and lower characteristics of our continental culture. It may be seen that the Pata-

---

[6] Afrânio Peixoto: *Minha Terra e
Minha Gente* (*My Land and My
People*) (Rio de Janeiro, 1916).—
This is the opinion likewise of a
couple of other distinguished pedagogues, who, however, are anything
but orthodox. I refer to Silvio Romero and João Ribeiro in their *Compêndio de História da Literatura Brasileira* (*Compendium of Brazilian*

Literary History) (2nd edition, Rio
de Janeiro, 1909).
[7] *Revista do Instituto Histórico e
Geográphico Brasileiro*, Vol. LXX-
VIII, Part II.
[8] A. L. Kroeber is the author of numerous works on the languages and
customs of Amerindian tribes. The
map in question is from his book,
*Cultural and Natural Areas of Native
North America*. (Translator.)

gonian area, more nearly on a level than that of the tropical jungle, still remains in notable contrast to the two or three American continental areas that stand out in boldest relief.

One may not speak of the native culture of the Americas without a high degree of rigorous discrimination, so great is the inequality in the cultural-relief map; nor in dealing with Africa should one leave out Egypt, with its unmistakably opulent civilization, and speak at will of African culture as if it were a lowly thing and all of one piece. For Africa likewise shows notable differences of relief, its values varying, as· is the case in the Americas, in quantity and degree of elaboration. A map of the different areas that have been identified, some by Leo Frobenius,[9] others in a general way by Melville J. Herskovits,[10] makes it easier for us to appreciate these at times profound variations of African continental culture than would be possible through the dry-as-dust words of anthropologists or ethnologists. Such a map, with its high points and its low points, should put us on our guard against the peril of generalizations where the African colonizers of Brazil are concerned.

For nothing could be more unscientific than to speak of the inferiority of the African Negro in relation to the American Indian without first making it plain what Amerindian, what Negro is meant. Whether Tapuia, Bantu, or Hottentot. Nothing is more absurd than to deny to the Sudanese Negro, for example, who was brought to Brazil in considerable numbers, a culture superior to that of the most advanced native. To state that "with respect to neither the arts and crafts, nor the cultivation of vegetables, nor the domestication of zoological species, nor family and tribal organization, nor astronomical knowledge, nor the creation of language and legends, were the blacks superior to our forest-dwellers" is to produce an affirmation that, if conversely stated, would be quite correct, since it was precisely by all these evidences of a material and moral culture that the Negro slaves show that they came from more advanced stocks,[11] and that they were in a better position than the Indians to contribute to the economic and social formation of Brazil. At times, in a better position than the Portuguese themselves.

---

[9] The well-known contemporary German anthropologist. See his *"Ursprung der afrikanischen Kulturen,"* cited in the paper by Herskovits (see the following note). (Translator.)

[10] Melville J. Herskovits: "A Preliminary Consideration of the Cultural Areas of Africa," *American Anthropologist*, Vol. XXVI, No. 1.— This first attempt at a delimitation of such areas has been further developed by Professor Herskovits in recent studies, with the addition of fresh characteristics.

[11] Word in English. (Translator.)

In addition to their technical and cultural superiority, the Negroes were possessed of something like a biologic and psychic predisposition to life in the tropics. There was their greater fertility in hot regions. Their taste for the sun. Their energy, always fresh and new when in contact with the tropical jungle. A taste and an energy that Bates was the first to contrast with the easy discouragement of the Indian and *caboclo* beneath the intense sun of northern Brazil. Bates noted in the Indians—whom he knew, not superficially, but intimately, having lived among them from 1848 to 1859—a "constitutional dislike to the heat." He adds that he always saw them most merry, well disposed, and lively on rainy days, their nude bodies dripping with water. A nostalgia, possibly, for an ancestral cold. "How different all this is with the Negro, the true child of tropical climes!" [12]

Waldo Frank recently, in an admirable essay on Brazil, practically repeats the high praise that Bates accords to the Negro as the true son of the tropics,[13] as the Lord's annointed for regions of intense heat, as the individual best integrated with the Brazilian climate and conditions of life. This is an adaptation that, it may be, is principally achieved through psychic and physiological factors. As McDougall asserts, a question of psychological constitution. Physiological, also, in view of the Negro's ability to perspire all over his body and not merely under his armpits. As if his entire body were shedding oil and not merely exuding isolated drops of sweat as the white man's does, a circumstance that is to be explained by the fact that there is a maximum surface of evaporation in the Negro, a minimum in the white.[14]

Somewhat in the manner of Bates, Wallace contrasts the taciturn

---

[12] H. W. Bates: *The Naturalist on the River Amazon* (London, 1864).

[13] Waldo Frank: "*La Selva*," *Sur*, No. 1 (Buenos Aires, 1931).

[14] In the words of Professor L. W. Lyde, "the black man is normally covered with a complete and continuous film, and this means a maximum surface for evaporation—in which quantities of heat are consumed—a maximum reflection of light, and maximum protection against nerve injury."—L. W. Lyde: "Skin Colour," the *Spectator*, London, May 16, 1931. —"Of all the human races," writes A. Ozório de Almeida, "the Negroes alone are perfectly adapted to life in the tropics; and they alone, wholly nude, are able to endure without suffering the ardent sun of these regions. This special resistance that they possess is due to their black skin, which protects them against the actinic rays, but which would present the serious inconvenience of being subject to overheating in the sun if it were not for the defense mechanism in question, supplemented by another one of a general nature—namely, their great capacity for sweating, which corrects the tendency to overheating of the cutaneous surface.—A. Ozório de Almeida: "*A Ação Protetora do Urucú*" (loc. cit.).

and morose Brazilian native with the merry, lively, and loquacious Negro.[15] In modern psychologic terms, this difference would be expressed by attributing to the Amerindian the quality of an introvert and to the Negro that of an extrovert. This is the theory outlined by McDougall in his studies *National Welfare and National Group* and *Group Mind*.[16] It is a daring theory, in that it implies the application of a criterion that up to now has been employed in individual cases, one practically limited to the psychiatric clinic, to the difficult problem of discriminating among and describing ethnic traits.[17] To this

---

[15] Alfred R. Wallace: *A Narrative of Travels on the Amazon and Rio Negro* (London, 1852).

[16] *National Welfare and National Group* (London, 1921); *The Group Mind* (Cambridge, 1920).

[17] Discussing the manner in which adaptability to new forms of culture differs among primitives—the Melanesian compared to the Polynesian, the Amerindian contrasted with the Negro—Pitt-Rivers (op. cit.) stresses the opinion of McDougall to the effect that these variations result from "differences of physiological constitution"; and he reminds us of Wallace's contrast between the American aborigine and the jovial and talkative Negro.

In their study *Da Esquizofrenia—Formas Clínicas—Ensiao de Revisão da Casuística Nacional* (*On Schizophrenia—Clinical Forms—Essay in Revision of the National Casuistry*) (Rio de Janeiro, 1931), Cunha Lopes and Heitor Péres undertake to distinguish "the contribution of the principal races to each clinical form." From their "distinguishing table of ethnic types," it may be seen that the most frequent clinical form among all ethnic types is the hebephrenic. Meanwhile, it is the Negro who is shown to be "above all, hebephrenic," and "the mestizo a paranoid." In a previous communication to the Brazilian Psychiatric Society, in 1927, Professor Cunha Lopes sustained the thesis that "the autochthonous savage, as may be seen through the literature and data of our chroniclers, is predominantly cyclothymic and only by exception schizothymic. . . ." In the course of his researches in Pernambuco regarding "the mental diseases of Negroes," Professor Ulysses Pernambucano found a "lesser frequency of schizophrenia and the so-called neuroses among Negroes," together with a higher percentage of "psychopaths with anatomical lesions, except as regards epilepsy and general paralysis," than in the other two races combined; "a greater frequency of alcoholism and infectious states of delirium among Negroes."—*Arquivos da Assistência a Pscicopatas de Pernambuco* (*Archives of the Psychopathic Clinic of Pernambuco*), No. 1 (April 1932). In a recent statistical study specially devoted to general paralysis, the same authority discovered, in one hundred cases of the disease, a "less number of whites" and a "greater number of Negroes."—*Arquivos*, etc. (op. cit.), No. 2 (1933).

Adauto Botelho, in a study made in Rio in 1917, concluded that dementia præcox was of infrequent occurrence among Negroes and mulattoes (*pardos*).—*Boletim de Eugênia* (*Eugenics Bulletin*), Rio de Janeiro, No. 38 (April–June 1932). On this subject see also the recent studies by W. Berardinelli, who admits that the Indian is not exclusively schizothymic nor the Negro exclusively cyclothymic. See, further, Isaac Brown: *O Normotypo Brasileiro* (*The Brazilian Normotype*) (Rio de Janeiro, 1934);

difference in psychic constitution McDougall attributes the fact that the Indian had a greater tendency than the Negro to withdraw from civilizing contact with the European and offered a greater resistance to the latter's rule, only to perish finally in an unequal struggle. The American native, characteristically an introvert, accordingly finds it difficult to adapt himself. The Negro, on the other hand, is the extrovert type, the easy-going, plastic, adaptable type of individual. But even if this criterion is accepted as absolute, the Indian enthusiasts will not cease to find reasons for believing in the moral superiority of the aborigines. Did not the latter refuse to labor with the hoe in the cane fields of the Portuguese, with the superior gesture of Spanish grandees? Why, they *are* Spanish grandees by temperament. Stern, unyielding, unadaptable.

The historico-cultural criterion, however, which so often has corrected the psycho-physiologic one in connection with the process of discriminating among ethnic traits, shows us that the incapacity of the Amerindians was social and technical rather than biologic or psychic. Although we should not overlook the psychic indispositions, the fact looms large that the nomadic character of their economic life reacted powerfully upon the Indians, rendering them incapable of sustained agricultural labor; whereas the various African societies out of which large masses of our slaves came to us were already used to such labor, as well as to the raising of cattle and the utilization of their flesh and milk.

One thing, none the less, should be made clear: I am not presuming to deny the possibility of an advantageous application of a criterion based upon psychologic types to the task of distinguishing ethnic traits. The introversion of the Indian, in contrast to the extroversion of the Negro may be verified at any moment in that ready-waiting laboratory which is Brazil, by reason of its experiences in this field. If one contrasts the deportment of Negroid populations such as that of Bahia—merry, expansive, sociable, loquacious—with that of others less influenced by Negro blood and more by that of the Indian—the natives of Piauí, Paraíba, or even Pernambuco—one has the impression of being among diverse peoples. These latter populations, which are chiefly to be found in the backlands of the northeast, are gloomy,

---

and the work by Alvaro Ferraz and Andrade Lima, Jr.: *A Morfologia do Homem do Nordeste* (*The Morphology of the Man of the Northeast*) (Rio de Janeiro, 1939). From the sociological point of view, Oliveira Vianna is concerned with the problem in a number of his provocative essays.

silent and reserved, sly, and even surly, without the infectious cheerfulness of the Bahians and without their at times irritating petulance, without their grace, their spontaneity, their courtesy, their hearty and contagious laughter. In Bahia one has the impression that every day is a feast-day. A feast of the Brazilian church, with cinnamon leaves, cakes, fireworks, and lovers courting.

Pitt-Rivers contrasts the Negro dances with those of the Indians, stressing in the former the spontaneity of emotion expressed through great mass effects, but without any rigidity of ritual or the restrained and measured movements of the Indian dances.[18] These latter are almost purely dramatic in character, Apollonian, as Ruth Benedict would say, to whom we owe such interesting studies[19] of the peoples that she terms Apollonian in opposition to the Dionysiac ones. This contrast is to be observed in connection with the Afro-Brazilian Xangô sects,[20] which are noisy and exuberant, with practically no repression of individual impulses, none of the impassivity of the native ceremonies.

Such contrasts, having to do with psychic disposition and a possibly biologic adaptation to a hot climate, explain in part the Negro's role in Portuguese America as the white man's greatest and most plastic collaborator in the task of agrarian colonization. It explains likewise how it was he came to perform a civilizing mission, in the sense of Europeanization, among the aborigines, a mission that we could wish were better known by our Indian lovers. Roquette Pinto found evidence among the populations of central Brazil of the Europeanizing effect of the Negro *quilombos*, or runaway-slave colonies. Runaway slaves had spread among the Indians a knowledge of the Portuguese language and the Catholic religion before any white missionary had done so. Having set up their *quilombos* on the highlands where the Parecí Indians dwelt, the fugitive Negroes had interbred with women whom they had taken from the Indians. A *bandeira* that was sent out to disperse them, in the eigthteenth century, found these former slaves ruling over *cafuso* populations in the *quilombos*. They found large plantations, poultry-raising, cotton under cultivation, the manufacture of heavy cloth. And the *bandeirantes* further discovered that all the Negro-Indian mestizos of mature age "knew something of

[18] Pitt-Rivers: *The Clash of Cultures and the Contact of Races* (op. cit.).

[19] See her *Patterns of Culture* (Boston and New York, 1934). (Translator.)

[20] Followers of Xangô, one of the most powerful of the Orixás, or African deities. (Translator.)

Christian doctrine, which they had learned from the Negroes . . . they all spoke Portuguese with the same skill as the blacks who had taught them." [21]

But granting that extroversion was predominant among the Negroes, we should not attribute to it an absolute influence. The cultural antecedents and predispositions of the African are to be given major consideration, and along with them, the diet or alimentary regime of the black man.

The height and weight of men vary considerably under the effect of diet, not only from region to region, but from class to class. Individuals of the upper classes are almost always taller and more corpulent than those of the lower strata, a superiority that modern research specialists would explain by the fact that these individuals consume a greater quantity of products rich in "vitamins of growth." [22] F. P. Armitage undertakes to prove that even color and the shape of the cranium are dependent upon the quality of nourishment. [23] In Russia, Sorokin tells us, as a result of the famine of 1921–2, it was found that stature had diminished, [24] while in Holland, according to Otto Ammon, [25] and in America, according to Ales Hrdlička, there is to be observed an increase in stature, due probably to modifications in social conditions and in diet. [26] In the case of the Negroes as compared

[21] Unpublished documents found by Professor Roquette Pinto in the archives of the Brazilian Historical Institute (archives of the Overseas Council, correspondence of the Governor of Mato Grosso, 1777–1805, codex 246); see Roquette Pinto: *Rondônia* (op. cit.).

[22] Eugene Apert: *La Croissance*, in Sorokin: *Social Mobility* (op. cit.).

[23] F. P. Armitage: *Diet and Race* (op. cit.).

[24] Sorokin: *Social Mobility* (op. cit.).

[25] German anthropologist (1842–1916), author of numerous works. (Translator.)

[26] Hrdlička: *The Old Americans* (op. cit.).—McKay, having made a study of the diet of the various peoples of India in order to verify its effect upon their physical development and capacity, found that the lower-caste Bengali made out with small quantities of protein, even smaller than the amount that, according to Chittenden, is the minimum compatible with physical well-being. The observations made by McKay upon students of the same school, under the same climatic conditions and doing exactly the same kind of work, but receiving different diets, show that the Anglo-Indians have a greater degree of physical development than the Bengali. The former received 94.97 gr. of protein, of which 38.32 gr. were of animal origin, while the Bengali received 64.11 gr., only 9.3 gr. being of animal origin. McCarrison, in turn, in the course of recent researches, has arrived at identical results, chiefly with respect to the greater resistance and physical beauty of the peoples of northern India in comparison with those of the south and east.—D. McKay: "The Relation of Food to Physical Development," Part II, *Scientific Memorial by Officers of the Medical and Sanitary De-*

with the natives of Brazil, their superior economic and eugenic efficiency is in part to be credited to their diet, which was richer and more varied than that of peoples still in the nomad stage, without any regular form of agriculture or cattle-raising. Moreover, a number of the most characteristic nutritive values that the Negroes possessed—at least so far as vegetables went—were brought with them to America, and this contributed to the process, which was by way of being one of Africanization, that the whites and the natives underwent, while at the same time it smoothed over for the Africans the disturbing effects of transplantation. Once in Brazil, the Negroes became, in a sense, the masters of the land: they dominated the kitchen, preserving in large part their own diet.

There was, it is true, a certain tendency on their part to conform to the usages of the native, but in lesser degree than was the case with the newcomers of European origin, for whom transplantation was a more radical experience and who encountered here a greater novelty in the matter of climate and of physical and biochemical environment.[27]

In 1909 Leonard Williams, in a work laden down with the orthodox ideas of the Weismann biology,[28] suggested the possibility that the influence of climate upon racial character might make itself felt through the endocrine glands. This appeared to him to explain the difference between Asiatics and Europeans, Latins and Anglo-Saxons. If in one of his examples—taken over, for that matter, by W. Langdon Brown without any correction whatsoever—Williams was altogether unfortunate: with respect to the Jews' having acquired in the cold climates of Europe a reddish hair and fine-textured skin, on other points his argument is one that commands the interest of modern anthropologists. The endocrinological basis of Leonard Williams's theory is that the skin may be compared to a sensitive plate that, when sensitized, produces reflex activities in distant organs.[29] In accordance with this theory, the cutaneous pigment would have evolved as a protection against an excess of such stimuli; and those distant organs in which the most important reflex activities are pro-

---

partment of the Government of India, 1910; N.S., No. 37, "The Relation of Food to Development," 1910, Vol. V; R. McCarrison: "Relative Value of the National Diets of India," *Transactions of the Seventh Congress of British India* (Tokyo, 1927), Vol. III, in Ruy Coutinho: *Valor Social da Alimentação* (op. cit.).

[27] On the biochemical environment, see pp. 292–293. (Translator.)

[28] *Business Geography,* by E. Huntington and Leonard Williams (New York, 1909). Cf. note 29, following. (Translator.)

[29] Leonard Williams, in W. Langdon Brown: *The Endocrines in General Medicine* (London, 1927).

duced are the endocrine glands. The Williams theory, to which in 1909 almost no attention was paid, is now being studied with interest. In one of the more provocative medical monographs published by Professor Maclean of the University of London, W. Langdon Brown considers the subject apropos of the relation of the endocrine glands to general metabolism.[30] It appears to him to be beyond a doubt that, in the production of pigment, the suprarenal and pituitary glands play a part; and that the pituitaries as well as the suprarenals have a great deal to do with the process of pigmentation, he believes is demonstrated by the manner in which tadpoles, after the extraction of these glands, turn into albinos. He is of the opinion that the intimate relation between the heat-producing glands and pigmentation has been established; which leads him to conclude that brown-skinned individuals are better adapted than blonds and albinos to hot climates. In this regard, Brown cites the action of the French government in refusing to employ white-skinned and blond individuals in the colonial service in the tropics, preferring Frenchmen from the south, "capable of developing a protective pigment." [31]

According to Leonard Williams, there are other alterations that occur in newcomers as a result of the climate and through the chemical process whose importance he stresses; and as we shall see farther on, the possibilities inherent in such alterations constitute one of the, so to speak, dramatic problems in modern anthropology and sociology. Thus, the descendants of Europeans in North America would appear to be conforming to aboriginal traits: "the stereotyping by the climate of the North American continent of the descendants of its widely dissemblant annual European recruits into the hatchet-shaped face and wiry frame of the red Indian aborigines." [32]

The subject is one that is still far from being cleared up. What we know for a certainty concerning it amounts to almost nothing—barely enough to warn us against preconceived systems and exaggerations of theory. The true relation of the pigment to the physical environment remains one of the most obscure problems in anthropology. The generalization to the effect that man is dark or black in hot regions and pink or white-skinned in the northern hemisphere is subject to important restrictions. Haddon brings out the fact that peoples of different color and different physical characteristics are to be met with whose environmental and climatic conditions are analogous; and he cites the example of the very black Negro of the

---

[30] Brown, op. cit., preceding note. (Translator.)
[31] Leonard Williams, in W. Langdon Brown, op. cit.
[32] Ibid.

Congo whose physical milieu differs little from conditions in the interior of Borneo and the Amazon region, where the natives are of a pale yellow or cinnamon hue. Nor does he see how climate can explain the fact that the natives of Australia have so dark a skin. The Australians and the Tasmanians. According to this anthropologist, we may conclude: (a) that pigmentation arises spontaneously, independently of the effect of environment, in a period of variability, and that individuals of dark pigment are more apt to hold out against tropical conditions and survive the others; (b) or, on the other hand, that pigmentation represents an adaptation to environment, resulting from the long influence of the latter upon man in an epoch when his tissues were more plastic and susceptible than they are today; the variation thus acquired would have become transmissible, although we are in ignorance as to the mechanism by which the germ-cells could have received the external influence.[33]

And here is where the problem is joined to another, possibly the most important one with which modern biology is concerned: that of the transmission of acquired characteristics. No one today any longer accepts so unquestioningly as ten or fifteen years ago the judgment of Weismann to the effect that such characteristics are not transmitted. On the contrary, a neo-Lamarckism is now springing up in the very laboratories where it was the custom to smile at Lamarck, laboratories where the atmosphere is coming to resemble somewhat that of Catholic cathedrals of the seventeenth century. If we are to believe Bertrand Russell, that scientific skepticism of which Eddington is perhaps the most distinguished representative may lead to the end of the scientific era, just as the theological skepticism of the Renaissance led to the end of the Catholic era. Not only does the man of scientific culture today smile at the orthodox Darwinism of his grandfathers; he is beginning to smile also at the enthusiasm for Weismann's theories that was manifested by his parents' generation. But this profound skepticism does not necessarily signify the end of the scientific era; it is possible that science will take advantage of it to reinvigorate itself, in place of being weakened. Not again, however, will it be so puffed up with those pretensions to omnipotence that characterized it during the second half of the nineteenth and the opening years of the twentieth century.

In the light of the new scientific skepticism, the problem of acquired characteristics is seen to be one of those that must take their place among the fluctuating questions still open to debate. Weismann's

---

[33] A. G. Haddon: *The Races of Man and Their Distribution* (op. cit.).

word, telling us that such characteristics are not transmitted, that somatogenic traits are not converted into blastogenic ones, is no longer as persuasive as it once was. There are the experiments of Pavlov in Russia and of McDougall in the United States, which are enriching neo-Lamarckism, or, at any rate, embellishing Weismannism. In a paper read before the Physiological Congress in Edinburgh the Russian professor discussed the problem of reflexes that is to say, of "automatic responses to stimuli of various kinds, effected through the agency of the nervous system." Pavlov distinguished conditioned reflexes—that is, those acquired individually—from non-conditioned ones, and presented the results of his researches regarding the stimuli provided by the sight and smell of food. Certain characteristic movements took place: saliva flowed, the mouth watered; a whole series of non-conditioned reflexes. But if each time that food was given to the animal an association was established between the sound of a bell and the alimentary reflex, after this coincidence had been repeated a sufficient number of times the alimentary reaction would occur merely at the sound of the bell. In Pavlov's own words: "We established the conditioned food reflex in white mice, using the sounds of an electric bell. With the first set of wild white mice it was necessary to repeat the combination of the ringing of the bell and feeding three hundred times in order to form a well-established reflex. The next generation (second) formed the reflex after one hundred repetitions. The third generation acquired this after thirty repetitions, the fourth after ten, and the fifth after five only. . . . On the basis of these results I anticipate that one of the next generations of our mice will show the food reaction on hearing the sound of the electric bell for the first time." [34]

---

[34] *British Medical Journal*, August 2, 1923, cited in Arthur Dendy: *The Biological Foundations of Society* (London, 1924).—According to Professor G. V. Anrep, the "positive conclusions" of Pavlov's experiments, which McDougall, a professor at Harvard University, suspected from the first were rendered faulty by an error in technique, were provisionally withdrawn by the Russian investigator himself. Anrep, a professor in Cambridge University, has published in English, under the title *Conditioned Reflexes*, Pavlov's work on the physiological activity of the cerebral cortex. In this work, published (in 1927) after Pavlov's Edinburgh Congress paper, the problem of the hereditary transmission of conditioned reflexes is considered an open question. McDougall, after 1920, carried out experiments from another point of view, with a different objective from that of Pavlov. In these experiments he was said to be obtaining results that would appear to indicate the validity of the Lamarckian principle. —J. T. Cunningham: *Modern Biology, a Review of the Principal Phenomena of Animal Life in Relation to Modern Concepts and Theories* (London, 1928).

While emphasizing the social importance of the Russian scientist's experiments, Professor Arthur Dendy calls attention to one of the most suggestive bits of indirect evidence in favor of the possible transmission of acquired characteristics: the hardening of the skin, or callosity, of the human heel. It is known, he points out, that callosities of this sort may be produced by friction or by pressure; consequently, the fact that the child is born with the sole of the foot already hardened, and that this hardening is to be seen even before the child is born, a long time before—so that it cannot be attributed to friction or pressure—leads us to conclude that a modification originally caused by the use of the foot has become, one may say, fixed by heredity.[35] In other words, this would be a case of a somatogenic characteristic which, in the course of many generations, has become blastogenic.

Impressive, likewise, are the experiments of Kammerer, having to do with changes of color and reproductive habits in amphibians and reptiles, in reaction to the stimulus of a new environment or atmosphere.[36] Among the most recent studies may be noted: those of Guyer and Smith regarding acquired defects of vision, which, it would seem, are transmitted by heredity and which behave like Mendelian recessives; [37] and those of Little, Bagg, Harrison, and Muller. These experi-

---

[35] Dendy, op. cit.

[36] P. Kammerer: *The Inheritance of Acquired Characteristics* (New York, 1924).

[37] M. F. Guyer and E. Smith, in *Our Present Knowledge of Heredity*, a series of lectures given at the Mayo Foundation, etc. (Philadelphia and London, 1923-4).—Neo-Lamarckism finds its most vigorous expression in Oskar Hertwig, who upholds the metabolic influence of the atmosphere upon hereditary dispositions, criticizing at the same time the *theory of selection.—Das Werden der Organismen* (1916), in Erik Nordenskiöld: *The History of Biology, a Survey* (translation) (New York and London, 1929). In connection with the experiments of Kammerer and Tower, cited by Hertwig, an atmosphere of doubt is forming on the part of some, while others differ in their interpretations of results; until it comes to the point where the suicide of the first of these two investigators, which occurred in 1926, is attributed to a lack of rigor or scrupulousness in his researches. Lentz, stressing the fact that Kammerer was a Jew, remarks that the latter had the fondness of the Jews for Lamarckism; and according to Lentz, many of the defenders of the "inheritance of acquired characteristics" are Jews, possibly out of a desire on the part of the Israelites—this is Lentz's opinion—to have no "inextinguishable race distinctions."— Erwin Bauer, Eugen Fischer, Fritz Lentz: *Human Heredity* (translation) (London, 1931).—The Swedish Nordenskiöld, however, op. cit., sees the theory of the possible transmission of inherited characteristics as having been enriched, subsequent to Kammerer's researches, by those of the Englishmen Little, Bagg, and Harrison, particularly by Harrison's studies of melanism in butterflies "due to mineral substances . . . taken in with

ments, doubtless, stand in need of confirmation, but they indicate the highly fluctuating character of the subject. Fluctuating and doubtful. Weismannians and neo-Lamarckians are today, in physiology and biology, like the advocates of predestination and freewill in theology.

In view of the possibility of the transmission of acquired characteristics, the environment, physical and biochemical, arises before us with an intensity capable of affecting the race and modifying mental traits that are supposed to be linked with bodily ones. The researches of Franz Boas [38] would appear to indicate that the *biochemical content,* as Wissler calls it,[39] is capable of altering the physical type of immigrant. Once this alteration is admitted, and along with it the

their food." There are also the studies by the American Muller. J. T. Cunningham, a professor of the University of London, in his work *Modern Biology* (op. cit.), presents us with an impartial description, accompanied by critical observations, not only of Kammerer's researches, but of more recent ones in this field. The problem is one of the greatest importance for studies in social anthropology.

[On the subject of melanism in butterflies, see Heslop Harrison and F. C. Garret: "Induction of Melanism in Lepidoptera," *Proceedings of the Royal Society,* B, Vol. XCIX (1926). (Translator.)]

[38] Franz Boas: *Changes in Bodily Form of Descendants of Immigrants* (Senate Documents, Washington, 1910–11).

On the problem of "race" as modern authorities see it, consult also Eugen Fischer: *Rasse und Rassenenstehung bein Menschen* (Berlin, 1927). And in opposition to the Boaz theory, on various essential points, see the work, by H. F. K. Gunther: *Rassenkunde des deutschen Volkes* (11th edition, Munich, 1927), and G. Sergei's *Europa* (Turin, 1908).

In addition, the following works may be looked upon as basic in connection with this subject: H. E. Ziegler: *Die Vererbungslehre in der Biologie und in der Soziologie* (Jena,

1918); Fischer, Mollison, Schwalbe, Hoernes, Graebner, and Ploetz: *Anthropologie* (Leipzig and Berlin, 1923); Baur, Fischer, and Lentz: *Human Heredity* (translation, with additions by the authors) (London, 1931); W. Scheidt: *Allgemeine Rassenkunde* (Berlin, 1926); Eugen Fischer: *Die Rehobother Bastards und das Bastardierungsproblem bein Menschen* (Jena, 1913); S. J. Holmes: *The Trend of the Race* (New York, 1923); M. Boldrini: *Biometrica, Problemi della vita della specie e degli individui* (Padua, 1928); Schmidt and Koppers: *Völker und Kulturen* (Regensburg, 1924); F. B. Davenport and Morris Steggerda: *Race Crossing in Jamaica* (Washington, 1929); Edmund V. Cowdry, Ales Hrdlička, and others: *Human Biology and Racial Welfare* (New York); Henri Neuville: *L'Espèce, la race et la métissage en anthropologie* (Paris, 1933); A. Keith: *Ethnos* (London, 1931); H. Muckermung, S.J.: *Rassenforschung und Volk der Zukunft* (Berlin, 1932); Rosseli y Vilar: *La Raza* (Barcelona, 1930); Eli Faure: *Trois Gouttes de sang* (Paris, 1929); R. Martin: *Lehrbuch der Anthropologie* (Berlin, 1914); R. R. Bean: *The Races of Man* (New York, 1932); and E. A. Hooton: *Up from the Ape* (New York, 1931).

[39] Cf. p. 287. (Translator.)

possibility, in the course of generations, of the newcomer's gradually conforming to the new physical type, the importance assigned to hereditary differences in the mental make-up of various races diminishes considerably. Differences that are commonly interpreted in terms of superiority and inferiority and linked to physical traits or characteristics.

With regard to this question of racial inferiority or superiority, the shape of the cranium is no longer accepted as an indication, and the discarding of this criterion takes away much of what appeared to be scientific in the pretensions to an innate and hereditary mental superiority on the part of whites over blacks. The theory of the superiority of dolicho-blonds has recently been dealt telling blows in its own strongholds. Basing his statements on the researches of Nystrom among five hundred Swedes, Hertz has recently shown that in this hive of dolicho-blonds the individuals of the upper classes were in the large majority brachycephalic, and this was similarly true of eminent men who had come from the lower classes. It is Hertz, too, who makes the point that neither Kant nor Goethe, nor Beethoven, nor Ibsen, nor Luther, nor Schopenhauer, nor Schubert, nor Schumann, nor Rembrandt was a pure Nordic.[40]

As to the significance of brain-weight and cranial capacity, that is an undecided point. The anthropometric researches carried out by Hunt in the American army during the Civil War and continued by Bean indicate that the Negro's brain is lighter and smaller in size than that of the white man, while those of Pearson tend to show that the Negro's cranial capacity is less than that of the European white; but there is a considerable body of facts opposed to any conclusions as to the inferiority of the black race based upon such results. If we accept the medium brain-weight of the Negro as 1.292 grams and that of the while male as 1.341, we still have to take into consideration the fact that the weight of the white woman's brain is 1.250 grams, while that of the Chinese is 1.428.[41] According to these figures, the

[40] F. Hertz: *Rasse und Kultur*, in Carl Kelsey: *The Physical Basis of Society* (op. cit.).—As for the words of Jean Rostand (*Hérédité et racisme*, Paris), George Lahkowsky (*La Civilisation et la folie raciste*), and Warner Siemen (*Theorie de l'hérédité*), they are interesting by reason of the at times daring manner in which they discuss the anthropological and sociological problem of races in relation to culture, and of heredity in relation to environment; but they add little that is scientifically or philosophically important to the above mentioned studies.

[41] R. R. Bean: "The Negro Brain," *Century Magazine*, 1906; Kelsey, op. cit.; Franc Boaz: *The Mind of Primitive Man* (New York, 1911); Alexander Goldenweiser: "Concerning Race Differences," *Menorah Journal,*

white woman's brain is notably inferior in size to that of the Negro male, and that of the yellow man (the Chinese) is superior to that of the white man.

What is known of the differences of cranial structure in whites and blacks does not permit of any generalizations. The fact has some while since been observed that certain famous men have been individuals of small cranial capacity, and that some idiots have enormous brains.

The superstition to the effect that the Negro, by reason of his bodily characteristics, is the type of race that is nearest to the ancestral form of man, whose anatomy is supposed to resemble that of the chimpanzee, does not merit refutation. Yet it is upon this superstition that many of the unfavorable judgments with regard to the Negro's mental capacity are based. But, Professor Boas reminds us, the lips in monkeys are thin, as in the white race, not thick as in the black race.[42] Among the races of mankind, it is the Europeans and Australians who have the most hair on their bodies, and not the Negroes. So that the comparison is reduced to the fact that the nostrils are flatter and more flaring in the Negro than in the white.

It is physical characteristics such as the ones mentioned above—but chiefly those having to do with the shape of the cranium—that have been brought forward as an indication of the Negro's inferiority in the matter of intellectual and technical initiative and achievements, an inferiority that is made out to be congenital; but investigators who have most painstakingly compared the intelligence of Negro and white have reached a different conclusion. Bryant and Seligman, for example, as the result of a comparative study of Bantu and European school children in South Africa, are of the opinion that the mental development of the Bantus up to the age of twelve is the more rapid, while that of the European, which is slower, more sluggish, until puberty is attained, is the greater from then on. These writers further conclude that while the European excels the African in qualities of reflection, judgment, and comprehension, the Negro is superior as regards memory, intuition, or the immediate perception of things and capacity for assimilation.[43] These, as Pitt-Rivers notes, are differences

---

Vol. VIII (1922). According to Pearson (cited by Kelsey), the cranial capacity in Negroes is 140 cc. in men and 100 cc. in women, less than in modern Europeans. On this subject, see also the book by Professor E. B. Reuter: *The American Race Prob-* *lem* (New York, 1927).

[42] Franz Boas: *Anthropology and Modern Life* (London, 1929).

[43] A. T. Bryant and C. G. Seligman: "Mental Development of the South African Native," *Eugenics Review*, Vol. IX.

hard to reduce to a factor indicative of general intelligence that might serve as a basis for conclusions as to the inferiority or superiority of one race compared with the other.[44]

The testimony of anthropologists reveals for us traits in the Negro showing a mental capacity that is in no wise inferior to that of other races: "considerable degree of personal initiative, a talent for organization, and . . . imagination, with technical skill and thrift," as Professor Boas puts it.[45] And there are other superior traits that might be mentioned. The difficult thing is, to compare the European with the Negro in equal terms and under similar conditions, in a purer sphere beyond the conventions, where values and qualities may really be contrasted. African sculpture, for instance, with its great beauty and strength, was for a long time looked upon by Europeans as a grotesquerie, simply because its lines, its form of expression, its artistic deformation of proportions and relationships, clashed with the conventional Greco-Roman sculpture of Europe. In Brazil this narrow standard of judgment threatened to stifle our first spontaneous and forcefully creative artistic expressions as revealed for the most part by our mixed-blood, whose mothers or grandmothers had been slaves. It is little short of a miracle that we possess today certain works of Aleijadinho.[46] Those with a taste for the refinements of European art, and who are inclined to be over-zealous in their Catholic orthodoxy, have a number of times demanded the destruction of these "figures that look more like fetishes." [47]

As to so-called intelligence tests, many of which have resulted unfavorably for the Negro,[48] their technique is subject to serious restric-

---

[44] George Henry Lane and Fox Pitt-Rivers: *The Clash of Cultures and the Contact of Races* (op. cit.).

[45] Franz Boas: *The Mind of Primitive Man* (op. cit.).

[46] Aleijadinho (the name means "little cripple") was a Brazilian sculptor of the later eighteenth century whose work may be viewed in the churches of Minas Geraes today and whose reputation is steadily growing. In his *Brazilian Literature: An Outline* (op. cit.), Érico Verissimo says: "It was there, too [in Minas Geraes] that a remarkable sculptor unassumingly made his appearance. He was a poor, crippled little man, Antônio Francisco Lisboa, nicknamed the Aleijadinho. Since he had no hands, he used to have the hammer and the chisel tied with ribbons to his wrists; and so he painfully carved the stone, giving it the shape of angels and saints and leaving on the face of those images the marks of his suffering soul. . . . The faces of his saints remind us—or rather *me*—of the tortured features of Van Gogh's figures." (Op. cit., pp. 30–1.) (Translator.)

[47] Padre Júlio Engrácia: *Relação Cronológica do Santuário e Irmandade do Senhor Bom Jesus de Congonhas no Estado de Minas Gerais* (*Chronological Account of the Sanctuary and Confraternity of Our Lord the Good Jesus of Congonhas in the State of Minas Geraes*) (São Paulo, 1908).

[48] Especially those carried out in

tions. Goldenweiser has ridiculed them as a method of measuring racial qualities; they leave the Negro a little above the monkey, he observes. "The statistical attitude, the desire of expressing things in numbers and in curves, is a very laudable attitude, the outgrowth of objective and critical method, but it has its dangers. When one is talking nonsense and puts it in plain words, why, there is no harm done, but if one talks nonsense and expresses it in mathematical formulæ, there is danger that the respectable mathematical garb will save the underlying nonsense from detection." [49] Kelsey also criticizes the tests and their pretensions, pointing out grave defects and irregularities of technique that work against the Negro.[50]

What is more, the results of such tests have been contradictory; they are far from unanimous in establishing the "mental inferiority" of the Negro, as Sorokin assumes. Investigations carried out with 408 Negro school children in Missouri point to the conclusion that the difference in mental capacity between them and white children diminishes with age, while those made in Atlanta show that the differences increase with age. Freeman's investigations lead him to conclude that white Americans are superior to Negroes in all age groups except the ten-year-olds; but it is also his opinion that American Negroes are superior to Italians, with the exception of two groups. Pintner and Keller found among the Negroes an I.Q. the same as among the Scotch and superior to that of Greeks, Italians, and Poles. And Hirsh encountered in the Negroes a higher I.Q. than among the Portuguese. In the American army tests, which are so often cited against the Negro, the results show greater differences between Northern and Southern Negroes in the United States than between Negroes and whites, while the Negroes of the state of Ohio are on a higher plane than the whites of all the Southern states with the exception of Florida.[51]

the United States. Basing his opinion upon these tests, Hankins regards as of great importance the hereditary differences in mental characteristics between the two races; and he goes on to warn us against the danger of replacing a racial mysticism by one based upon culture: the mysticism of a Lapouge and a Gobineau—who created the myth of Nordic superiority—by that of the anthropologists and sociologists, who insist upon attributing racial differences to the phenomenon of cultural diffusion alone, the simple question of a greater or less degree of social opportunity.— F. H. Hankins: "Individual Differences and Their Significance for Social Theory," *Publications of the American Sociological Society*, Vol. XVII (1922).

[49] Alexander Goldenweiser: "Race and Culture in the Modern World," *Journal of Social Forces*, November 1924, (Vol. III, No. 1) p. 135.

[50] Kelsey, op. cit.

[51] *Opportunity*, 1927, in Kelsey (op. cit.). See also Sorokin: *Contemporary*

That mental differences exist between whites and Negroes is not denied; but as to how far these differences represent innate aptitudes on the one hand or, on the other hand, specializations due to environment or to economic and cultural circumstances, it would be hard to determine. Sorokin is inclined to admit the superiority of the factor of *heredity* over that of *environment*, thus coming near to a biological position. No one inveighs with greater vigor against Huntington and geographic determinism.[52] He forgets, however, it seems to me, that the two factors overlap at many points, it being difficult to separate heredity from environment; especially if we admit the possibility that influences acquired in a new environment or as the result of biochemical action may be passed on.

It is Lowie, as I see it, who poses the question in its true terms. Like Franz Boas, he considers the phenomenon of mental differences between human groups rather from the point of view of the cultural history and environment of each group than from that of heredity or of pure geography. How explain, he asks, if not by history, the great oscillations in Britannic culture? "Did the Elizabethans carry in their sex cells an extra dose of animal spirits that was blighted by a charge of gloom under Puritanism but revived by the Restoration? And what of Japan? There was a sudden influx of a new stock in 1867; there was a sudden change in culture because new ideas were allowed to enter. . . ." The same question might be asked with regard to Athens and its rapid flowering of genius from 530 to 430 B.C. And again, what of Germany and its brilliant musical superiority? Is this a racial superiority? But basically the race is the same as the English—a people that is barely able to whistle in the bathtub and sing hymns in church. What ethnic difference there is ought to be on the side of the English, for they are nearer to the Greeks. . . . German society has been for some time systematically stimulating musical culture, while English society, on the contrary, has been neglecting it. In the former instance, a natural musical ability finds free scope for its development; in the latter case, it meets with little

Social Theories (New York and London, 1928).—In connection with these tests, Lentz endeavors to explain the results favorable to Negroes of the Northern United States in comparison with the whites of certain regions of the South by observing that in the Northern states of that country there is a large mixed-blood population that is indiscriminately called Negro. The pure Negroes, for the most part, would be those that have remained in the rural zones of the South.—Erwin Baur, Eugen Fischer, and Fritz Lentz: *Human Heredity* (op. cit.).

[52] Sorokin: *Contemporary Social Theories* (op. cit.). [See E. Huntington: *Civilization and Climate* (New Haven, 1915). (Translator.)]

sympathy: ". . . the pre-eminence of Germany is very recent. A few centuries ago she was rather backward—definitely behind Holland, Italy, and even England. Mozart, in the eighteenth century, was still under the sway of Italian traditions. . . . Admit frankly that musical ability, while inborn in individuals and hereditary in families, is not inborn in races. . . ."[53]

In the case of those Africans who were transported to Brazil from the beginning of the sixteenth to the middle of the nineteenth century, what we should endeavor to do is to discover, in the principal stocks[54] from which these immigrants came, not only the degree but the moment of culture that they brought with them. The moment, among the different tribes, varies considerably in the course of the three hundred-odd years of Mohammedan infiltration into black Africa. The degree, in turn, varies notably from the Sudanese to the Bantus. It is important, also, to determine the cultural area in which the slaves originated and to avoid the mistake of seeing in the African the single and indistinct figure of a "piece of Guinea" or the "black man of the coast."

The fact of the matter is that the Mohammedan Negroes brought to Brazil from that African area which had been most deeply penetrated by Islamism were culturally superior not only to the natives, but to the great majority of the white colonists—Portuguese and the sons of Portuguese, with almost no education, some of them illiterate, most of them semi-literate. These latter were individuals who could not write a letter or cast an account, unless it was by the hand of the padre schoolmaster or with the brain of some clerk. Almost none of them were able to sign their names, and when they did so, it was in a broken script, like that of a child learning to write.

The Abbé Étienne reveals to us some aspects of the Malê[55] uprising in Bahia in 1835 that identify this supposed slave revolt as an outbreak or eruption of a more advanced culture downtrodden by another, less noble one.[56] Let us not romanticize. This was purely a Malê or Mohammedan movement, or a combination of various groups under Mussulman leaders.[57] One thing is certain, it is to be distinguished from slave revolts in colonial times. It deserves a place, in-

---

[53] Robert H. Lowie: *Are We Civilized?* (New York and London, 1929), pp. 31, 191–2.

[54] Word in English. (Translator.)

[55] The Malês are Mohammedan Negroes of Bahia and Rio de Janeiro. (Translator.)

[56] For an account in English of this uprising, see Donald Pierson: *Negroes in Brazil* (op. cit.), pp. 43–5. See an article by Padre Etienne Ignace Brasil: *"Os Malês,"* *Revista do Instituto Histórico e Geográphico Brasileiro,* Vol. LXII, Part II (1909). (Translator.)

[57] Word in English. (Translator.)

deed, among the libertarian revolutions of a religious, social, or cultural nature. The report of Dr. Francisco Gonçalves Martins, Chief of Police of the province of Bahia, on the occasion of the uprising, lays emphasis on the fact that all the rebels were able to read and write in unknown characters. Characters that "were like the Arabic," adds the learned commentator, who is naturally astounded at such literary ability on the part of a slave. "It is not to be denied that there was a political end in view in connection with these uprisings, for they did not commit robberies nor slay their masters secretly." [58] The truth is: in the slave sheds of Bahia in 1835 there were perhaps more persons who knew how to read and write than up above, in the Big Houses. After ten years of independent life,[59] the nation had just begun to emerge from the state of profound ignorance in which the crown had kept it throughout the eighteenth century and during the first years of the nineteenth, an era when "the simplest rudiments were so little diffused that not infrequently wealthy ranchers of the interior would charge their friends of the seaboard to secure for them a son-in-law who, in place of any other dower, should be able to read and write." [60]

Nineteenth-century historians looked upon the slaves brought to Brazil as coming, all of them, of Bantu stock. This is a point that should be corrected. Slaves were brought in large numbers from other African cultural areas as well, and many of these areas were superior to that of the Bantus. Brazilian society in its formative stage benefited from the best that African Negro culture had to offer; it absorbed those élite elements, if one may put it that way, which were lacking in the same proportion in the Southern United States. "I have often thought that slaves of the United States are descended not from the noblest African stock," remarks Fletcher, in contrasting the slaves of the Brazilian *senzalas* with those of the U. S. A.[61]

Sá Oliveira is in error in stating that, in the social stratification of

---

[58] Abbé Étienne: *"Le Secte Mussulman des Malês du Bresil et leur révolte en 1835,"* in *Anthropos,* Janvier-Mars 1909.

[59] Brazilian independence was proclaimed in 1822 and secured by November 1823, under the form of a constitutional monarchy; it was recognized by the United States in 1824, followed by England in 1825. In 1825 Portugal itself granted recognition. (Translator.)

[60] Handelmann: *História do Brasil*

(op. cit.). See also Henry Koster: *Travels in Brazil* (op. cit.), which probably afforded Handelmann his data.—In the sixteenth and the first half of the seventeenth century the intellectual situation with regard to the colonists was better than in the eighteenth century, thanks to the Jesuit educators and their schools and institutions of higher learning.

[61] D. P. Kidder and J. C. Fletcher: *Brazil and the Brazilians* (Boston, 1879).

Brazil, "a voluminous wave of Africans came to install themselves in the lowest strata, nearly all of them from the most savage Kaffir tribes, having been brought here by the slave-traders from the coast of Africa." [62] This is an exaggeration, for the Sudanese were equally numerous; indeed, according to the researches of Nina Rodrigues, they were the predominating element in the formation of Bahian society, up to a certain point, at least. It was, thinks Nina Rodrigues, Spix and Martius [63] who were responsible for the mistake that lies in supposing the African colonists of Brazil to have been exclusively of Bantu origin; and it is to the distinguished professor of the medical faculty of Bahia that we are indebted for the first critical attempt to discriminate among the various stocks.

"In their valuable studies dealing with our country," writes Nina Rodrigues, in the pages of his as yet unpublished work, *The Problem of the Negro Race in Portuguese America*,[64] "these authors [Spix and Martius] reduce the origins of the Brazilian slave traffic to the Portuguese colonies of South Africa and the islands of the Gulf of Guinea. According to them, all the Africans that reached Brazil were Congos, Cabindas, or Angolas from the west coast, or Macuas or Angicos from the east coast. Also, they see Cacheo and Bissão as the points of origin for the Negroes of Pernambuco, Maranhão, and Pará, who are naturally better known through the history of the Commercial Company of Grão Pará and Maranhão, which held the contract for the transportation of the blacks. But they do not properly concern themselves either with these last mentioned Negroes or with those coming from the islands of Fernando Po, Principe, São Tomé, and Ano Bom, to whom they also allude. It is hard to understand how the Sudanese Negroes could have escaped the sagacious observation of Spix and Martius, who were interested in the Bahian slave traffic

---

[62] J. B. Sá de Oliveira: *Craniometria Comparada das Especies Humanas na Baía sob on Ponto de Vista Evolucionista e Médico-legal* (*Comparative Craniometry of the Human Species in Bahia from the Evolutionary and Medico-Legal Point of View*) (Bahia, 1895). See also his study: *Evolução Psíquica dos Baianos* (*Psychic Evolution of the Bahians*) (Bahia, 1898).

[63] The early nineteenth-century German travelers in Brazil (1817–20), J. B. von Spix and C. F. P. von Martius, whose work has been previously cited.

[64] *O Problema da Raça Negra na América Portuguesa.* For permission to read the original text, I am indebted to the kindness of Senhor Homero Pires, who threw open to me his excellent collection of Brasiliana. Later Nina Rodrigues's work was published under the title: *Os Africanos no Brasil* (*The Africans in Brazil*) (São Paulo, 1933), on the initiative of the same Senhor Pires.

and who were in the province precisely at the time the Sudanese were dominant there.

Unfortunately, researches having to do with the bringing of Negro slaves to Brazil have been rendered extremely difficult with regard to certain points of historical and anthropological interest ever since the eminent Bahian Councilor, Ruy Barbosa, Minister of the provisional government, following the proclamation of the Republic in 1889, had the archives of slavery burned (his motives were ostensibly economic, the order—No. 29—emanating from the Ministry of Finance, under date of May 13, 1891). It may be that precious genealogical data have been lost through these republican autos-da-fé.

Even without the valuable assistance that would have been afforded by the customs statistics of the port of entry for the slaves, Nina Rodrigues has been able to demolish the myth that the African colonizers of Brazil were exclusively Bantu. One has, indeed, but to look at the Portuguese policy with respect to the distribution of slaves in the colony, and one will doubt any such thesis. This policy was not to permit a preponderant number of slaves of the same nation or stock to be assembled in a single *capitânia*. "From which there might readily result pernicious consequences," as Dom Fernando José of Portugal put it in a letter to Luis Pinto de Sousa.[65] If the Sudanese predominated in Bahia and eastern Negroes of the Bantu group in Rio and Pernambuco, this does not signify that other stocks did not furnish their contingent to the three great centers where the slaves arrived and from which points they were distributed.

The letter written by Henrique Dias [66] to the Dutch, in 1647, contains some valuable information on this subject: "This regiment is composed of four nations: Minas, Ardas, Angolas, and Creoles.[67] These last are so malevolent that they know neither fear nor duty; the Minas so fierce that what they cannot come at with their brawn

---

[65] Citation by Nina Rodrigues, one supported by a variety of evidence in the manuscripts of the Historical Colonial Archives of Lisbon. It is a subject deserving of a separate study. Before Nina Rodrigues, a French observer, Adolphe d'Assier, had dwelt on the perspicacity of the Portuguese colonial policy in having Negroes brought from different "nations" that were even antagonistic to one another.

[66] Military leader of the period, in the era of the struggle against the Dutch; he commanded Negro troops. (Translator.)

[67] In Brazil ' the term *crioulo* (*creoulo*) signifies "originally the Negro born in America; today, any Negro; in Rio Grande do Sul, a native of any part of the state."—Lima and Barroso, op. cit. (Translator.)

they come at with their name; the Ardas so fiery that they would slash everything at a single stroke; and the Angolas so robust that no labor tires them." [68]

Now, the "Ardas," or "Adras," were Gêges or Daomanos of the ancient Kingdom of Ardia; the Minas were Nagôs; the Angolas alone were Bantus.

Barleus, Nina Rodrigues reminds us, had referred to the Ardrenses; and refer to them he does, but only to tell us that they were very bad agrarian slaves—they, the Calabrenses, and those from Guinea, Cape Verde, and Sierra Leone. The Congos, the Sombrenses, and the Angolas were good for labor in the field, while those from Guinea, Cape Verde, and Sierra Leone were bad slaves but comely of body. Especially the women, for which reason they were preferred for domestic service, for work in the Big Houses. [69] And, following out the chroni-

[68] Cited by Nina Rodigues (op. cit.).

[69] Gaspar Barleus: *Rerum per Octennium in Brasilien* (1660), a work recently (1940) translated into Portuguese and published in Brazil on the initiative of the Ministry of Education and Public Welfare, Rio de Janeiro. "The Ardrenses," wrote Barleus, "are very lazy, headstrong, stupid; they have a horror of labor, if we except a small handful who work very patiently and increase their value. . . ." He remarks on the "slackness and laziness" of the Negroes of Guinea, Sierra Leone, and Cape Verde, at the same time commenting on their delicacy and grace of form, chiefly in the women. He notes that the Congos and Sonhenses are apt at labor: "*aptissimi ad opera.*" He tells us that the most industrious of all were the Angolenses ("*laboriosissimi Angolenses*").—In the eighteenth century, André João Anotil (*Cultura e Opulência do Brasil*, etc., op. cit.) had this to say: "And inasmuch as they [the slaves] are commonly of diverse nations, and some are more ignorant than the others, being very different in physical appearance also, the selection and dividing up has to be done with great care and not blindly. Those that come to Brazil are the Ardas, Minas, Congos; from S. Thomé, Angola, Cape Verde, and some from Mozambique, who are brought in ships from India. The Ardas and the Minas are robust. Those from Cape Verde and S. Thomé are weaker. Those of Angola, reared in Loanda, are more capable of learning mechanical trades than those from other parts already mentioned. Among the Congos, there are some who are sufficiently industrious and are good not only for work in the cane fields, but for other tasks as well, household ones at any rate." With regard to the north, at the beginning of the nineteenth century, Koster gives us the following information: the majority of the slaves imported were those that came from Angola and the Congo, and those known as Moçambiques, Rebelos, Angicos, and Gabons. The Moçambiques came only in later times. (Henry Koster, op. cit.) Relying upon customhouse statistics that she had obtained in Rio de Janeiro, Maria Graham tells us that the Negroes most generally imported at the beginning of the nineteenth century were the Moçambiques, Cabindos, Benguelas, Quilumanos, and Angolas. —Maria Graham: *Journal of a Voyage to Brazil*, etc. (op. cit.).

cler's insinuation, it is easy to imagine that they were also employed as pleasing concubines or light-o'-loves in those relations between master and slave girl which were so common with our colonial patriarchs.

A valuable bit of evidence in favor of Nina Rodrigues's thesis, and one that does not appear to be known, is that afforded by Jan van Laet in his *History or Annals of the Accomplishments of the Privileged Company of the East Indies from Its Beginning until the End of 1636*, published originally in Leiden in 1644. Summing up the data provided by the political councilor Servacius Carpentier on the *capitânia* of Paraíba, Laet tells us that the Angola Negroes were largely employed in agricultural labor, but had to be "kept at it always with many lashes." He adds that "the Guinea Negroes are excellent, so that the majority of them are utilized for domestic service, for waiting on table, and the like; those of Cape Verde are the best and most robust of all and they are the ones that cost the most here." Regarding the *capitânia* of Pernambuco, the *Annals* report a great traffic annually between the port of Recife and "other regions of Africa" as well as Angola, although, it is true, the communication facilities with Angola were better than with other parts. The Count of Nassau wished to make of Recife the principal distributing center in furnishing slaves for American plantations and for the mines of Peru, with Angola remaining as an immediate dependency of the government of Pernambuco. As he saw it, Pernambuco had acquired rights over Angola, São Thomé, and Ano Bom inasmuch as it was the Brazilian-Dutch forces that had taken these African colonies from the Spaniards. It was, accordingly, from Recife and not from Amsterdam that the slave trade ought to be directed.[70] The Count's plan, however, had not won out, possibly because it was feared in Amsterdam that Nassau was preparing the ground for the founding of a tropical principality that should unite the African colonies with northern Brazil. In any event, it is certain that the importation of slaves was carried out on a big scale under Dutch rule; but what Laet tells us indicates that the blacks brought over did not come exclusively from Angola.

Historical evidence, together with the anthropological and linguistic researches of Nina Rodrigues among Bahian Negroes, thus reveals the weak basis of the idea that it was exclusively Bantus[71] who came

[70] Wätjen, op. cit. Wätjen also was recently translated into Portuguese and published in Brazil (1938), in the *Brasiliana* series of the Companhia Editora Nacional.

[71] "Term applied to the South African Negro race to which those slaves belonged who were known in Brazil

to Brazil.[72] Alongside the Bantu tongue, the "Quimbunda" or "Congoense" speech, other African languages were in common use among our Negroes: Gêge, Haussá, and Nagô or Yoruba—which, according to Varnhagen, was more widely spoken than Portuguese among Bahian Negroes in the early days,[73] while today it carries prestige by reason of its being the Latin of the Gegê-Yoruba cult.

Among the Brazilian Negroes whom he knew while slavery was still in existence, Nina Rodrigues speaks of the so-called "blacks of the white race," or Fuláhs; not only the Fula-Fulos, or pure Fuláhs, but mestizos from Senegambia, Portuguese Guinea, and adjacent coastal regions. These were a reddish-copper-colored people with wavy, almost straight hair. Negroes of this stock were looked upon by some as being superior to the others, from the anthropological point of view, owing to the admixture, in their case, of Hamitic and Arabic blood; they came principally to the *capitânias* (the later

as Angolas, Cabindas, Benguelas, Congos, Moçambiques, etc."—Lima and Barroso, op. cit. (Translator.)

[72] Silvio Romero, who appears at first to have been inclined to the idea that the Negro colonization of Brazil was limited to the Bantus, in his *Compendium of Brazilian Literary History*, written in collaboration with João Ribeiro, makes an intelligent distinction between the African stocks. "It was, however, not merely the numerous tribes of Guinea, of Nigritia or subtropical Africa, and those of the Bantu group that served as the breeding-ground for Brazilian slavery; the various branches of the Hottentots and Bushmen also furnished their contingents, and from them came—certain Ba-cancalas, Ba-cubais, Ba-corocas, Ba-cuandos, Ba-cassaqueres, and, probably, Ba-sutos and Bechuanas. Nor should we forget the contingent from the Nubian group. The Brazilian slaves who came from this last mentioned source were the most intelligent of all. Their number, however, was small compared to the others."—In his paper on the slave markets of Brazil and the imported tribes, read before the National History Congress (*Revista do Instituto*

Histórico e Geográphico Brasileiro, special volume, Part II), Braz do Amaral identifies the following stocks: Yorubas, Egbas, Gêges, Daomeianos, Ijejas, Angolas, Minas, Haussás, Krumanos, Filánios, Timinis, Bengos, Galinhas, Effans, Ashantis, Cabindas. The coast of Sierra Leone, Angola, and the Gulf of Guinea were the principal slave markets for Brazil. —In connection with the research for a study that I prepared for the *Diário de Pernambuco* collection, in collaboration with José Antônio Gonsalves de Mello Neto, I gathered from the "For Sale" and "Fugitive Slave" advertisements the following names of African "nations": Camundongo or Cambundongo, Angola, Moçambique, Caçanje, Congo, Rebolo, Benguela, Muxicongo, Mina, Cabinda, Calabar, Angico, Cabundá, Costa, Gabão (Gabon), Gegá, Quizamá, Beni or Benim, Costa de Nagou, Loanda, Quelimano, Songa or Songo, Magó, Baca, Mazango, Ubaca or Embaca, Ganguela, Malembá, Maçanganga, Costa de Caxéu, Senze or Senge, Ibanara, and Bude or Bufe.

[73] Nina Rodrigues, op. cit. Varnhagen: *História Geral do Brasil* (op. cit.).

provinces) of the north, and from there some of them must have emigrated to Minas and São Paulo. Those mystics who hold to a theory of racial superiority will perhaps discover in this fact the reason why the mestizo families of the north and of certain regions in Minas and São Paulo have made so large a contribution to Brazilian progress by furnishing a greater number of men of talent—statesmen under the Empire, writers, bishops, artists, presidents and vice-presidents of the Republic—than has the south, including Rio de Janeiro, the other regions of Minas and São Paulo, and Rio Grande do Sul. They might allege that we are here dealing with an element that has a large dose of Berber blood and that possibly is even of Berber origin. This African folk is regarded by Haddon [74] as being predominantly non-Negroid, and its true name according to him is Pulbe, the others (Fuláh, Fulani, Felava, Filani, Fube) being corruptions. Haddon describes the type as being tall, with a yellow or reddish skin, wavy hair, an oval face, and prominent nose.

The Haussás, who also came in large numbers to Brazil, notably to Bahia, are likewise a mixed-blood type, with Hamitic and possibly Berber strains, although the Negro characteristics are predominant in them; and the same is true of the Niam Niam, the Mangbatus, the Kanembus, the Bagirmis, the Bornús, and the Kanuris.[75]

Brazil received various contingents of Mandingos, who in their turn show traces of Arabic and Tuareg blood, while the Yorubas reveal a non-Negro strain that is yet to be identified, and the Bantus themselves, amid a great variety of types, exhibit a number of blends, chiefly Hamitic and Negrillo. As regards other physical characteristics, the Bantus are of a dark brown or chocolate color that differs from the dirty yellow or light-brown-reddish hue of the Fulos as much as it does from leather color of the Hottentots and Bushmen or the deep black of the natives of Guinea; they are dolichocephalic (with mesocephalic groups among them); and there is less prognathism with them than with those peoples looked upon as "pure" Negroes, the nose being more prominent and narrower.[76]

Various invasions and migrations have altered, in historic times, the cultural and anthropological aspects of the population of Angola, which was the point of origin of many of the slaves imported to Brazil. One of these invasions was that of the Jaggas, in 1490. No profound racial alteration could have been effected, however, given the similarity between the invading and the native stocks, all of them of a heterogeneous character from a remote period.

---

[74] A. G. Haddon: *The Races of Man and Their Distribution* (op. cit.).

[75] Ibid.

[76] Ibid.

Of the African peoples brought to Brazil, the Bantus—without taking into account certain exceptions, considering them only as large ethnic masses—may be included among the most characteristically Negro types; and by this I do not mean color, a convention of practically no importance, but rather ethnic traits of a more profound nature: the hair, in the first place. This latter, as is known, is extremely kinky in the *Ulotrichi africani*, a characteristic that is not so marked in individuals of the various stocks that show an admixture of Hamitic and even of Berber blood, as was the case with many of the slaves that came to us. The Fulos, on the other hand, and other peoples of east Africa who contributed to the formation of the Brazilian family are allied by their hair to the *Cynotrichi*. The hair in their case is straighter, the nose more shapely—physical traits that are nearer to those of Europeans. They are also more gentle, or "domesticated," as one would say in anthropological language.

But within the scope of this essay we are less interested in differences in physical anthropology than in African cultural anthropology and social history; for the physical differences, in my opinion, do not explain human inferiorities or superiorities when the terms of family heredity have been transposed for those of racial heredity. It is the anthropo-cultural and historico-social aspects of African life that seem to us to indicate that Brazil benefited from a better type of colonist from the "dark continent" than did the other countries of America. The United States, for example.

Nina Rodrigues was aware of the differences in African stocks in the colonization of the two Americas; but for him they were determined by the point of view which he had rigidly adopted: that of the inferiority of the Negro race. "The Haussás whom the slave traffic brought to Brazil were not ignorant Negroes," writes the professor of the Faculty of Medicine of Bahia.[77] And, dominated by his racial criterion, he triumphantly cites, along with the Haussás, who have an admixture of Hamite blood, the Fula-Fulos, or "Negroes of the white race," who did not come from Africa to the United States in any great stream as they did to Brazil.

In passing, we may remark that Professor Oliveira Vianna, the greatest exponent of a mystic Aryanism who has as yet arisen among us,[78] is less consistent than the Bahian scientist, when he writes, in one

---

[77] Nina Rodrigues, op. cit.

[78] Apropos of the controversy between Freyre and the well-known anthropologist Arthur Ramos on the one hand and Vianna on the other over the question of racial superiority or inferiority, Donald Pierson remarks: "An interesting fact in this connection, indicating the purely academic character of this question as

of his brilliant essays: "Even the North American Negroes—quite superior, so far as that goes, to our own, by reason of the selection imposed upon them by the contingencies of struggle with so formidable an enemy as the Anglo-Saxon—remained far below the average level of North American civilization," etc. Previously he had written that "the eugenic potentiality of *H. Afer*" not only "is reduced to begin with, but when called upon to function in a civilization organized by men of the white race, it becomes still further reduced." [79] The two statements of the Brazilian publicist are mutually contradictory. In the latter instance he asserts that the low capacity of the Negro for civilization becomes lower still in contact with the social organization of the superior race; and in the former, that the Negro's capacities are developed by such contact.

But on the whole it remains quite clear to the Aryanists, and much to their delight, that Brazil has been less affected than has the United States by the supposed evil of the "inferior race," owing to the larger number of Fula-Fulos and semi-Hamites—false Negroes and therefore, for every good Aryanist, of superior stock to the authentic blacks—among the slaves who came from Africa to the plantations and the mines of Brazil.

In a work that is already a classic [80] on the subject of African slavery in the United States, Phillips situates the principal sources of slaves for the plantations of his country in the following regions: Sierra Leone, or Leoa; the Grain Coast; the Ivory Coast; the Gold Coast; the Slave Coast; Rio do Eleo; Cameroons; Gabon; and Loango. In South Carolina, Negroes from Gambia, chiefly the Mandingos, were the preferred ones, but those from Angola were also quite acceptable. The Carromantes (of the Gold Coast), to judge from the statement of Christopher Codrington, Governor of the Leeward Islands, as transcribed by Phillips, must have been highly esteemed by the English in colonial America; and we also meet with references to Senegalese Negroes with their drop of Arabic blood as being favored for housework, by reason of their "greater intelligence." [81] There is no evidence, however, of Fula-Fulos being brought to the British colonies in America—at least, not in the same proportion as to Portuguese America; nor were the representatives of Mohammedan culture so

---

conceived in Brazil, is that Vianna is himself a mixed-blood; while both Ramos and Freyre are whites."— Donald Pierson: *Negroes in Brazil* (op. cit.), pp. 216–17. (Translator.)

[79] F. J. Oliveira Vianna: *Evolução do Povo Brasileiro* (op. cit.).

[80] Ulrick Bonnell Phillips: *American Negro Slavery, A Survey of the Supply, Employment and Control of Negro Labor as Determined by the Plantation Régime* (New York and London, 1929).

[81] Ibid.

numerous. It was only in Brazil that this culture found expression in schools and houses of prayer and gave rise to movements and organizations that reveal the presence of a true Malê élite among the African colonists of our country.

It would seem that for the English colonies the criterion for the importation of slaves from Africa was almost wholly an agricultural one. What was preferred was brute strength, animal energy, the Negro who was sturdy, with good powers of resistance, and who came cheap. In the case of Brazil there were other needs and interests to be taken into consideration: the lack of white women; and technical needs in connection with the working of metals as the mines were opened up. These were two powerful factors in the selective process.

Oliveira Vianna remarks that in Minas Gerais there are to be seen today, in the Negroes of that region, a "delicacy of features and a relative degree of beauty," contrasting with the "simian countenances . . . that are so plentiful in the eastern portion of the Rio de Janeiro lowlands"—indicating that some Negro tribe marked by ugliness of feature, possibly the "Bisagos" or "Yebus" or "Mandingos," had settled there in considerable numbers.[82] It should be noted that the former region attracted Negroes who were capable of working in metals and who accordingly possessed a higher degree of culture, while in the latter instance all that the sugar- and coffee-planters wanted was big strong blacks who were capable of giving a good account of themselves in the work of the fields. Even the Hottentots and Bushmen with their flaring nostrils and enormous buttocks would do here. As I see it, these circumstances account for the better Negro stock that was imported to the region of the mines. On the other hand, superior economic resources perhaps explain the fact that Pernambuco and Bahia received a higher grade of Africans than did Rio de Janeiro; for the northern plantation-owners could afford the luxury of importing slaves that brought a dearer price.

Oliveira Vianna has a quotation from Luis Vahia Monteiro, Governor of Rio de Janeiro in 1730, that favors the interpretation that we have given with respect to Minas Gerais: "and for the same reason there is not a Mineiro [83] who can live without a Negro Mina,[84] for they say that it is only with them that they were lucky." [85] It was

---

[82] Vianna: *Evolução do Povo Brasileiro* (op. cit.).

[83] A native or inhabitant of Minas Geraes.

[84] See Preface to the Second English-Language Edition, Note 10, p. xxx. (Editor.)

[85] Luis Vahia Monteiro, cited by Vianna: *Evolução do Povo Brasileiro* (op. cit.).

these Minas and Fuláhs—Africans who not only were lighter-skinned, but whose culture and "domestication" brought them closer to the whites—who were the preferred women in zones like that of Minas Gerais, where the foot-loose white colonists took them as "friends," as concubines (*mancebas*), and as "housekeepers." Prominent families of this state who today show Negroid features had their beginnings in such unions of whites with Negro Minas, who had come from Africa as slaves, but who, according to Vahia Monteiro, had been elevated to "mistresses of the house." Others remained slaves while continuing to have amorous relations with their white masters, being "preferred as maids and cooks." Araripe, Jr.,[86] observes that the Negro Mina always appears in Brazil as possessed of all the qualities for being "an excellent companion." She is wholesome, ingenious, sagacious, affectionate. "With such attributes," writes Araripe, "and under the precarious conditions with regard to the fair sex that prevailed in Brazil during the first and second centuries, it was impossible for the Mina not to have dominated the situation."[87] Dominate it she did, in various regions. Especially in eighteenth-century Minas.

In the middle of the nineteenth century Burton came upon a town of five thousand inhabitants in Minas Gerais with only two families of pure European descent. Along the seaboard the Englishman found that it was possible for the colonists to marry off their daughters to Europeans, but in the *capitânias* of the interior "mulattism[88] became a necessary evil." In the beginning—it is to be supposed—this "mulattism" was effected not so much through marriages as through irregular unions of whites with Negro women, who were often their slaves. Whence the "strange aversion to marriage" that Burton still found among the populations of Minas: the men "do not like to marry forever," preferring illegitimate unions or illicit affairs; while the Portuguese and Brazilian laws, which facilitated the adoption of bastard offspring, merely favored the tendency to concubinage and the forming of ephemeral bonds. The truth is that Brazilian moralists had already begun combating such irregularities, some even insisting that individuals living in open concubinage should not be eligible to public office.[89]

The slaves that came from the more advanced areas of Negro cul-

---

[86] Tristão Alencar de Araripe, Jr., prominent turn-of-the-century critic and novelist of the naturalist school. (Translator.)

[87] Araripe, Jr.: *Gregório de Mattos* (Rio de Janeiro, 1894).

[88] Burton's word. Cf. *mulattoism*. (Translator.)

[89] Richard F. Burton: *Explorations of the Highlands of the Brazil* (London, 1869).

ture were an active, creative, and, one might almost add, a noble element in the colonization of Brazil; if they occupied a lower rung, it was due simply to their condition as slaves. Far from having been merely draft animals and workers with the hoe in the service of agriculture, they fulfilled a civilizing function. They were the right hand in the formation of Brazilian agrarian society, the Indians and, from a certain point of view, the Portuguese being the left hand in the undertaking.

And not alone with respect to agrarian life. Eschwege stresses the fact that iron mining in Brazil was mastered by the Africans;[90] and Max Schmidt distinguishes two aspects of African colonization that afford us a glimpse of the technical superiority of the Negro over the native and even over the white man: his metal-working abilities and his skill at cattle-raising.[91] To these one might add a third: his skill at the culinary art, an art that in Brazil was enriched and refined by the African contribution.

Schmidt observed in Mato Grosso that many of the practices associated with cattle-raising were of African origin. The same was true of the blacksmith's tools. These must have been transmitted to Indian-white mestizos by Negro slaves. I have already referred to the interesting example, cited by Professor Roquette Pinto, of the civilizing effect of fugitive slaves upon the Indians of the Parecí Highlands. It may be stated in a general way that all the Negroes interned in the forests and the backlands played a useful part as bringers of civilization. Almost always they elevated the culture of the indigenous populations, and rarely did they permit themselves to be de-

---

[90] Eschwege, cited by J. Capistrano de Abreu: *Capítulos de História Colonial, 1500–1800 (Chapters of Colonial History*, etc.) (1928).—"In one instance they even served the Brazilians as tutors," says João Pandiá Calogeras; "theirs is the credit for the first process of working iron directly, in the rudimentary forges of Minas Gerais, a natural fruit of the practical science possessed by those born metallurgists, the Africans."—João Pandiá Calogeras: *Formação Histórica do Brasil (Historical Formation of Brazil*) (Rio de Janeiro, 1930). [M. C. von Eschwege was a German explorer who traveled in Brazil in the year 1811. For an account of his travels, translated from the Ger-

man, see *Diário de uma viagem do Rio de Janeiro á Villa Rica, na capitânia de Minas Gerais no anno de 1811 (Diary of a Journey from Rio de Janeiro to Villa Rica, in the Capitania of Minas Geraes, in the Year 1811*) (São Paulo: Imprensa Oficial do Estado; 1936). (Translator.)]

[91] Max Schmidt, article in *Koloniale Rundschau*, April 1909, summarized by Sir Harry H. Johnston: *The Negro in the New World* (London, 1910). Various studies by Max Schmidt, of considerable interest for Brazil, remain in manuscript form, manuscripts that I had an opportunity to see in the Barbero Museum at Asunción, Paraguay.

graded by the cultures with which they came in contact. So far as the *caboclos* were concerned, the Negroes were a Europeanizing force. They served as liaison agents with the Portuguese and with the Church. They were those plastic mediators between the Europeans and the natives to whom José Maria dos Santos alludes;[92] but in some cases their function was an original and creative one as well, and they contributed to the society in process of formation valuable elements of their own African culture and technique.

The more intimate contact that existed between certain of the advanced areas of Negro culture and Brazil explains, in my opinion, the circumstance observed by Professor Nina Rodrigues and by him attributed to the factor of *race* (that is to say, to the infusion of Hamite blood): namely, the superiority of the Negro colonizers of Brazil over those of the United States. This had previously been noted by an American, J. C. Fletcher,[93] and before him by the English naturalist George Gardner.[94]

Brazil not only took from Africa the topsoil of a black people that was to fertilize its cane fields and coffee groves, assuage its parched lands, and round out the wealth afforded by its patches of *massapé*;[95] there were to come to it also, from the same source: "mistresses of the house" for its colonists who were without white women; technicians for its mines; ironworkers; Negroes versed in cattle-raising and the pasturing of herds; cloth and soap merchants; schoolmasters, priests, and praying Mohammedans. The proximity of Bahia and Pernambuco to the African coast tended to give to the relations between Brazil and the Dark Continent an especially intimate character. These relations were more fraternal than those between Africa and the English colonies. From the British consul, O'Sullivan Beare, who, with Sir Roger Casement, was one of his best

---

[92] José Maria dos Santos: *Política Geral do Brasil* (*General Politics of Brazil*) (Rio de Janeiro, 1930).

[93] J. C. Fletcher, co-author with D. P. Kidder of *Brazil and the Brazilians* (Boston, 1879). (Translator.)

[94] Gardner was in Brazil in 1836 and visited Bahia. There he observed that the slaves were more difficult to control than in any other part of the country. "The cause of this," he writes, "is obvious. Nearly the whole of the slave population of the place is from the Gold Coast. Both the men and the women are not only taller and more handsomely formed than are those from Mozambique, Benguela, and the other parts of Africa, but have a much greater share of mental energy, arising perhaps from their near relationship to the Moor and the Arab. Among them there are many who both read and write Arabic."—George Gardner: *Travels in the Interior of Brazil*, etc. (op. cit.), p. 20.

[95] *Massapé* is clayey soil, usually black, which is very good for sugar cane. (Translator.)

sources of information in Brazil, Sir Harry Johnston gathered some extremely interesting data regarding the trade between Bahia and the African cities of Lagos and Dahomey at the beginning of the nineteenth century. This trade was a very active one, and was conducted by Fulos and Mandingos—in general, ex-slaves.[96]

Melville J. Herskovits's study of Africa,[97] based upon the concept of cultural areas, permits us to discover, in its high points and its low points, that African culture which by contagion was to enrich the Brazilian, through a prolonged importation of slaves of varied background and a frequent communication by trade channels with the African ports. By means of this criterion, we are enabled to distinguish the following principal areas:

(a) the Hottentot, characterized by cattle-raising, by the use of oxen for the transport of burdens, by the utilization of cowhides for clothing, by the extensive consumption of beef, etc.;

(b) the Bushman (Bosjesman), a culture inferior to the Hottentot, impoverished, nomadic, without any animal in the service of man, unless it be the dog,[98] without any organized agrarian or pastoral life; similar in its characteristics to the native culture of Brazil, but superior to the latter in artistic expression, at least in painting, as shown us by the examples brought forward by Frobenius;

(c) the cattle-raising area of East Africa (Bantu), characterized by agriculture with a superimposed pastoral industry, the possession of numerous herds rather than the ownership of extensive lands being the thing that confers social prestige upon the individual; iron- and wood-working; polygamy; fetishism;

(d) the Congo area (also that of the Bantu language, although on the eastern frontier Ibi, Fanti, etc., are spoken), studied by Leo Frobenius in his work *Ursprung der afrikanischen Kulturen*, in which he stresses the differences between the Congo and the circumjacent areas in the matter of clothing, type of habitation, tattooing, musical instruments, the use of the banana, etc., traits to which Herskovits adds others: an agricultural economy, in addition to hunting and fishing; the domestication of the goat, the pig, the hen, and the dog;

---

[96] Sir Harry H. Johnston: *The Negro in the New World* (op. cit.). —Nina Rodrigues also alludes to this traffic, as we shall see farther on.

[97] See the paper by Melville J. Herskovits: "A Preliminary Consideration of the Culture Areas of Africa," in the *American Anthropologist*, Vol. XXVI (1924).

[98] "The Bushmen are exceptions in language, race, habits, and appearance. They are the only real nomades in the country; they never cultivate the soil, nor rear any domestic animal save wretched dogs."—David Livingstone: *Missionary Travels*, Chapter ii, p. 55. (Translator.)

markets where agricultural and iron products, brooms, etc., are brought together for sale; possession of the land in common; and fetishism, an interesting artistic expression of which is to be found in the wood sculpture, artists occupying a place of honor in the community;

(e) the Eastern Horn region, one difficult to characterize, representing, already, the contact of the Negro culture of the south with the Mohammedan culture of the north; pastoral activity; utilization of numerous animals, the cow, the goat, the sheep, the camel; a form of social organization influenced by Islamism;

(f) Eastern Sudan, an area still more under the influence of the Mohammedan religion than the preceding one; Arabic language, abundance of animals in the service of man; pastoral activity; extensive use of camel's milk; nomadism; tents; cloth garments similar to those of the Berbers;

(g) Western Sudan, another area marked by the interpenetration of cultures, of Negro culture properly so called with that of the Mohammedans; a region of great monarchies or kingdoms: Dahomey, Benin, Ashanti, Haussá, Bornú, Yoruba; secret societies exercising a widespread and efficient domination over political life; agriculture, cattle-raising, and trade; notable artistic productions in stone, iron, terracotta, and tapestries; fetishism and Mohammedanism;

(h) the desert area (Berbers);

(i) the Egyptian area, whose characteristics I shall not outline here, since they are not of immediate interest in connection with the colonization of Brazil; I shall merely note the fact that they have exerted a large influence upon the African continent.[99]

---

[99] Sílvio Romero and João Ribeiro, in the *Compêndio de História da Literatura Brasileira* (op. cit.), do not fail to suggest the state of culture of the principal African tribes or "nations" that had a part in the colonization of our country. "They were not all of them, certainly, on the same rung of the cultural ladder; but as a result of their contact with the Arabians since the seventh century, with the Egyptians and the Berbers, the majority of the tribes had from time immemorial attained a notable degree of advancement." And they go on to mention, specifically: the Jalofos, "adapted to a seafaring life"; the Mandingas, "converted for the most part to Mohammedanism, intelligent and enterprising"; the Yorubuas or Minas, "almost all Mohammedans and quite as clever as the Mandingas"; the Haussás, "whose tongue is the most widespread in the Sudan"; the Felupos, "the most savage of the region"; the Fuláhs, "followers of Mohammed, the best-organized in the country"; the Balantas, "democratic heathen"; the Biafadas, "the lords of a regular empire, destroyed by the Visigoths"; the Ba-Congos, whose "vast kingdom" was "one of the most advanced in Africa in the fifteenth and sixteenth centuries"; the Cabindas, "excellent workmen"; the Ambaquistas, "astute, clever sophists, fond

From the foregoing description it may be seen that no area of Negro culture, not even the Bushman, suffers by contrast with the culture of the native peoples of Brazil. It may, however, be stressed that the African colonization of our country was effected chiefly with Bantu and Sudanese elements, with peoples from the agricultural and pastoral areas, well nourished on milk, meat, and vegetables.[100] The Sudanese of the western area made valuable contributions in the way of moral and material culture, some of which were their own, while others had been acquired and assimilated from the Mohammedans.

It is to the Sudanese that Nina Rodrigues assigns an "intellectual and social pre-eminence" among the Negroes imported to Brazil; and it seems to him that not only the Bahian movement of 1835 but other slave-hut revolts must have been affiliated with the religious organization of the Sudanese Mohammedans. He attributes a great importance to the influence exercised over the Yorubas (Nagôs) and the

of the written word"; the Maguiocos, "skilled at hunting"; the Guissamas, "good salt-miners"; the Libollos, farmers; the Bienos, artists; the Bagangelas or Ambuelas, iron-miners; the Guimbandes, artists; the Banhanecas and Ba-ncumbis, herdsmen and farmers; the Ajaus, who had had "relations for centuries with the Arabs"; the Sengas, ivory merchants; the Mozozuros, cattle-raisers and given to mining; the Vatuas or Zulus, warriors; the Tongas or Bitongas, "inferior in culture"; the Mabringelas, Machanganos, Macuacuas, Machopes, Mindongues, and Landins, herdsmen and agriculturists; the Nubians, source of the "most intelligent Brazilian slaves, imported in small numbers." They mention other tribes that must have had a share in the colonization of Brazil, but without pointing out their cultural significance.—Diogo de Vasconcellos, in his excellent *História Média de Minas Gerais* (*History of Minas Gerais in the Middle Period*) (Belo-Horizonte, 1918), and also in his *Older History* (*História Antiga*), notes the presence, among the African colonists of Brazil, of Negroes who had come from advanced cultural areas, "bordering on the Mohammedan countries." See also the paper

by Melville J. Herskovits: "On the Provenience of New World Negroes," *Social Forces*, Vol. XII, No. 2 (1933).

[100] Recent studies of Orr and Gilks show that the Masai, for example, are a superiorly nourished folk. So great is the abundance of their flocks of sheep and goats and their herds of oxen that, according to these authors, there would fall to each of them an average of twenty-five head of cattle and twice as many sheep and goats. The basic elements of their diet are milk, meat, and blood (this last being drawn from the animal by slitting its throat). Various roots and tree-barks are used in the making of infusions, which the men take with boiled meat and milk. According to these investigators, the quantity of proteins taken by the Masai amounts to: men, 300 gr.; women, 165 gr.—J. B. Orr and J. L. Gilks: "The Physique and Health of Two African Tribes," *Medical Research Council, Special Report Series*, 1932, No. 155, in Ruy Coutinho, work in preparation, previously cited.—On the diet of various African societies, see also Wilson D. Wallis: *An Introduction to Anthropology* (London, n.d.).

Ewes (Gêges) by the Mohammedan Fuláhs and Haussás, who appear to have led the various slave revolts; for they were by way of being the aristocrats of the *senzalas*. They came from the kingdoms of Wurno, Sokotô, and Gandô, which possessed an advanced form of political organization, a well-defined religious literature with native works composed in Arabic characters, and an art that was strong and original, superior to the anemic Portuguese imitations of Moorish models. Slaves such as these could not be expected to conform to the role of mere artistic puppets [101] for the Portuguese, nor could the holy water of Christian baptism all of a sudden extinguish the Mohammedan fire that was in them.

The Abbé Étienne noted that Islamism had branched out in Brazil in the form of a powerful sect that flourished in the dark of the slave huts, with teachers and preachers from Africa to give instruction in reading the books of the Koran in the Arabic, and with Mohammedan schools and houses of prayer functioning here.[102]

The atmosphere that preceded the movement of '35 in Bahia was one of intense religious ardor among the slaves. In Mata-Porcos Lane, on the Praça slope, at St. Francis' Cross, in the very shadow of the Catholic churches and monasteries and the niches of the Virgin Mary and St. Anthony of Lisbon, slaves who were schooled in the Koran preached the religion of the Prophet, setting it over against the religion of Christ that was followed by their white masters, up above in the Big Houses. They propaganized against the Catholic Mass, saying that it was the same as worshipping a stick of wood; and to the Christian rosary with its cross of Our Lord they opposed their own, which was fifty centimeters [nearly twenty inches] long, with ninety-nine wooden beads and with a ball in place of a crucifix on the end.[103]

As a result, Catholicism in Brazil could not but become imbued with Mohammedan influence as it had been with the animism and

---

[101] *Manés-gostosos dos portugueses.* *Mané-gostoso* is a term employed in the Brazilian northeast: "character of the *bumba-meu-boi* who appears on stilts to sing verses."—Lima and Barroso, op. cit. The *bumba-meu-boi* ("whack-my-ox"), or *boi-surubi* (the *surubi* or *surubim* is an edible fish), is defined by Lima and Barroso as a "popular dramatic dance (ballet) in the form of a procession, in which the principal characters are: the ox (*boi*); the sea-horse; Matthew, the physician; etc." It also means a puppet. This will serve to give the rich flavor of the term employed by Freyre, which cannot be carried over in direct translation. (Translator.)

[102] Abbé Étienne: "La Secte Musulmane des Malês du Brésil et leur révolte en 1835," in *Anthropos*, January-March 1909.

[103] Nina Rodriques, op. cit. Manuel Querino: "*A Raça Africana e os Seus Costumes na Baía*" (loc. cit.).

fetishism of the natives and the minor Negro cults. We find a trace of this influence in the prayer-papers, to deliver the body from death and the house from thieves and malefactors, which are still customarily hung about the neck or tacked up on the doors and windows of houses in the interior of Brazil. And it is possible that a certain predisposition of the Negroes and mestizos toward Protestantism, the enemy of the Mass, of saints, and of rosaries with the crucifix, is to be explained by the persistence of remote anti-Catholic prejudices of Mohammedan origin. Mello Moraes Filho describes a feast of the dead in Penedo (Alagoas),[104] which, as Nina Rodrigues sees it, is without a doubt Mussulman in character. Long prayers and fastings. Abstinence from alcoholic beverages. The relating of the feast to the phases of the moon. Sacrifice of sheep. Vestments consisting of long white tunics.[105]

In the course of my own observations of the practices and rites of the African sects in Pernambuco, I have frequently noted the fact that the devout remove their shoes or slippers before participating in the ceremonies; and in the *"terreiro"* [106] that I visited in Rio de Janeiro, I further noted the importance attached to the individual's treading or not treading on the old mat spread out in the middle of the room. In the center of this mat, legs crossed in Mussulman fashion, sat the aged "father of the *terreiro*." Beside him was an earthen vessel with

---

[104] Mello Moraes Filho: *"Festas e Tradições (Feasts and Traditions)* (Rio de Janeiro).

[105] With respect to the relation of the feasts to the phases of the moon and the use of white tunics during ceremonies, I observed the same thing in Pernambuco, among the members of the sect known as the "Worshippers of the Stars and the Water," in the Fundão quarter of Recife, a sect that was broken up a short time ago by the state police, which also closed the Xangô houses of Anselmo and others, referred to in the text. These "worshippers," also, were strict in their abstinence from alcoholic beverages. They worshipped chiefly the Morning Star, the Moon, and Running Water. The seat of the cult was a cottage painted all white, and the ceremony consisted mostly in dances in imitation of the "movements of the stars." The dances were per-formed by children, who also sang, now in Portuguese and now in "strange tongues" that appeared to be invented ones. A "sacred water" that received the "fluids of the stars" was distributed to the faithful in flasks or cups. They maintained a school, a "catechism class," and had an emissary in Pará. No one could watch the ceremonies who was not clad in white. The hymns sounded somewhat like those of Protestant churches:

> *A união das aguas*
> *Com as estrelas eu via,*
> *O círculo e o meu reino*
> *Que a Deus pertenecia.*

"I saw the union of the waters with the stars, the firmament and my kingdom which was God's."

[106] Name given to the place where the ceremonies of a fetishistic cult are held. (Translator.)

the sacred food—swimming in the blood of a black hen. In connection with the feasts of the African sects that I knew in Recife—one of them directed by Eloy, a lad of some seventeen years who was almost white and who had been brought up by aged Negro women; and another directed by Anselmo, a Negro of around fifty and the son of African parents, who frequently went to Bahia "in the interests of religion"—I observed the women dancing with a band of yellow cloth around their throats, exactly as in those Mohammedan fasts at Bahia which Manuel Querino describes,[107] celebrated during the week that the Church devotes to the feasts of the Holy Spirit. At the feasts of Anselmo, when a woman finished dancing, she would pass the yellow band to another, who, putting it around her own throat, would continue the dance. In other sects I have seen red bands, with functions that were obviously of a mystical nature. For among these adepts, as among the devout of the Church, colors are often associated in a mystical way with promises made to the saints. Manuel Querino also speaks of a "blue ink" imported from Africa of which the Malês made use in connection with their soceries or charms. With this ink they would make cabalistic signs on a blackboard; and then they would wash the board and give the water to drink to the one whose body they desired to charm; or else they spilled it in the path of the one on whom they wished to work their sorcery.[108]

Until a short time ago they imported from Africa a number of things for use in their cult: *tecebas,* or rosaries; sacred instruments such as the *heré* or *chéchéré*—a copper rattle that is shaken in the Xangô ceremonies by the "holy daughters"; and sacred herbs for aphrodisiac purposes or pure pleasure.[109]

---

[107] Manuel Querino: *"A Raça Africana e Seus Costumes na Baía"* Revista da Academia Brasileira de Letras, No. 70.

[108] Ibid.

[109] Among others, the herb known in Rio de Janeiro—according to Manuel Querino—as *pungo*, in Bahia as *macumba*, and in Alagoas as *maconha*. In Pernambuco, too, it is known as *maconha;* and according to what we have heard from the *aficionados*, or cult-followers, it also goes by the name of *diamba*, or *liamba*. Querino tells us that the use of macumba was forbidden by the Chamber of Rio de Janeiro in 1830, the one who sold it being liable to a fine of 20$000 while the slave who used it was to be condemned to three days' imprisonment. I have smoked macumba or diamba, and I disagree with Querino as to some of the qualities that he attributes to it. It really does produce visions, however, and a pleasing weariness; the impression is that of one who returns from a ball with the music still ringing in one's ears. It would seem, on the other hand, that its effects vary considerably with individuals. Inasmuch as its use has of late become general in Pernambuco, the police are rigorously prosecuting its venders and consumers—the latter smoke it in cigarettes and pipes, some of them even taking it in their tea. Professor

The Catholicism of the Big Houses was here enriched with Mussulman influences against which the padre chaplain was as powerless as was the padre schoolmaster against the corruption of the Portuguese language by native and African dialects. This matter of the interpenetration of cultural influences in the development of Brazilian Catholicism and the national tongue is one that I shall take up later on in more detail. At this point I merely wish to draw attention to the cultural effect upon the formation of Brazilian society that was exerted by an Islamism brought to Brazil by Malê slaves.

The Mohammedan Negroes in Brazil, once they had been distributed among the slave huts of the colonial Big Houses, did not lose contact with Africa, nor did the Negro fetishists fail to keep in touch with the advanced cultural areas of their native continent. The Nagôs, for example, from the Kingdom of Yoruba, as well as the Mohammedans, went to the trouble of importing religious objects and articles for personal use: kola nuts, cauris,[110] cloth and soap from the coast, and oil of the dendê palm.[111]

It is, moreover, a curious thing to note that down to the end of the nineteenth century the repatriation of Haussá and Nagô freedmen from Bahia to Africa took place, and it was such freedmen-repatriates who founded in Ardra a city by the name of Porto Seguro.[112] So intimate did the relations between Bahia and these cities come to be that heads of commercial houses in Salvador[113] received honorary distinctions from the government of Dahomey.[114]

Ulysses Pernambucano, director of the Psychiatric Clinic of the state of Pernambuco, is at present engaged in studying the effects of macumba or diamba upon many of those who use it. The plant is cultivated today in various parts of Brazil, and some attribute to it mystical properties; it is smoked, or "burned," with certain intentions, good or bad. Querino quotes Dr. J. R. da Costa Doria as assigning to it aphrodisiac qualities as well.

[The diamba, macumba, or maconha is "a variety of European hemp (*Cannabis sativa*, var. *indica L.*) whose leaves and flowers are impregnated with a narcotic the effects of which are similar to those of opium."—Lima and Barroso, op. cit. (Translator.)]

[110] *Cauris* (singular: *cauri, carim,* or *caril*) are small porcelain shells used as money on the African coast; worth the 130th part of a penny sterling. (Translator.)

[111] The dendê is an African palm, acclimated in Brazil (*Elæsis guineensis Jacq.*). (Translator.)

[112] Nina Rodrigues, op. cit.

[113] The city of Bahia. (Translator.)

[114] Nina Rodrigues, op. cit.—When a delegation of the Society of Friends (Quakers) arrived in Rio in 1852, it was received by a commission of Minas freedmen, seventy of whom had been repatriated to Benin. They presented the English visitors with documents written in Arabic. See John Candler and W. Burgess: *Narrative of a Recent Visit to Brazil* (London, 1853).

In Bahia, in Rio, in Recife, in Minas, African garb, showing the Mohammedan influence, was for a long time worn by the blacks. Especially by the black women who sold sweets and by the venders of *aluá*.[115] Some of these were the mistresses of rich Portuguese merchants and by them were clad in silks and satins and covered with trinkets, with jewels and gold chains, amulets from Guinea against the evil eye, objects of the phallic cult, strings of glass beads, trumpet-shell necklaces, and gold earrings. To this day, in the streets of Bahia, one may meet with these Negro women, peddling their wares, with their long shawls made of *pano da Costa*, or "cloth from the coast." [116] Over their many underskirts of white linen they wear a damasked one of lively hues. Their upstanding breasts appear to be bouncing out of their bodices as they walk. Trinkets, amulets, armbands. The *rodilha*[117] or the Mussulman turban on their heads. Sandals on their feet. Silver sea-shells. Gold bracelets. In the early years of the nineteenth century, Tollenare,[118] in Pernambuco, admired the all but queenly beauty of the Negro women, and Mrs. Graham [119] was surprised by their grace of figure and the rhythm of their gait.

These women, who are commonly known as "*baianas*," or "Bahians," are usually very tall. Heraldic-appearing. Aristocratic in bearing. Their stature, for that matter, is a characteristic that is worth noting; for the Sudanese are among the tallest people in the world. In Senegal one sees Negroes so tall that they seem to be walking on stilts. Indeed, in their long garments resembling an infant's nightgown, they impress one as being creatures from another world. Gaunt, big-toothed, angular, hieratic. It is in South Africa that one encounters a low, squat people. Big-hipped women. Aphrodisiac curves. The Hottentot and Bushman women are truly grotesque with their protruding buttocks (steatopygia).[120]

---

[115] "A refreshing drink made, in the north, of rice flour or toasted corn with water and fermented with sugar in clay vessels; in Minas Gerais it is made by the same process with the rind of the pineapple."—Lima and Barroso, op. cit. (Translator.)

[116] *Pano da Costa* is a blue-striped cotton cloth (Lima and Barroso, op. cit.). The term is also applied to a garment that Donald Pierson describes as a "long, heavy, striped cotton cloth, at times worn slung over the shoulder and pinned under the opposite arm, at times wrapped once

or twice in a wide fold about the waist and tied rather tightly" (*Negroes in Brazil*, op. cit., p. 246). (Translator.)

[117] "A roll of cloth on which burdens borne on the head are placed."— Lima and Barroso, op. cit. (Translator.)

[118] *Notas Dominicais*, etc. (op. cit.). Tollenare was the Frenchman who visited Brazil during the years 1816–17. (Translator.)

[119] *Journal of a Voyage to Brazil*, etc. (op. cit.). (Translator.)

[120] This disease, previously referred

It is interesting to trace the physical characteristics of the Negroes imported to Brazil through the picturesque language of the people as preserved in the advertisements for the purchase and sale of slaves for household or agricultural employment. In this respect the collection of the *Diário de Pernambuco*—the oldest daily paper in what is known as Latin America, having been founded in 1825—is of particular interest for the student of anthropology.[121] In the advertise-

---

to, is characterized by an excessive accumulation of fat in the region of the buttocks, especially in women, and is common among the Hottentots, Bushmen, and Pygmies. (Translator.)

[121] Following are some of the advertisements that impress me as being the more interesting from the point of view of anthropological characterization: "slave . . . tall, yellowish-black, bearded, head well back" (*Diário de Pernambuco*, March 7, 1828); "slave . . . yellowish-black, Massambique nation, with marks of the same nation on his face, widespreading feet" (March 13, 1828); "*ladino* [see Translator's note, following] of the Angola nation and the name of João, quite black, good appearance, not much beard, tall, big eyes" (August 6, 1828); "whatever bush-captain [see Translator's note, following] may be able to take the black called Benedicto, Gabon nation . . . short and lean of body, bearded, has whiskers, good-looking face and body . . ." (August 25, 1828); "Catarina, of the Benguella tribe, tall, heavy-set, upstanding breasts, broad face, thick lips, prominent teeth, very black, pretty figure" (October 9, 1828); Antônio, of the Coastal Tribe, aged 25, has three cuts on his head, the mark of his land, big toe on the left foot without a nail, well spoken, yellowish-black in color" (August 3, 1829); "slave of the Benguella nation, Manuel by name . . . slender of body, not much beard, nose rather slender" (September 6, 1828); "black slave woman of Angola with good and sufficient milk" (August 7, 1828); "Izabel, Congo nation, 30 years . . .

tall and heavy-set . . . little hair on the head" (January 22, 1835); "Bento, of the Camundá nation, tall, plump of body, without beard, big feet, walks with a slightly irregular gait" (July 9, 1850).—Many of the advertisements refer to Fulos: also to "tall Negroes . . . and with all the teeth in front"; some to black women with big buttocks. These characteristics are given as a means of identifying the fugitive slave. This shows the presence of Hottentots and Bushmen among the slaves of Pernambuco in the nineteenth century. That the male or female Negro who was ugly was of practically no worth on the slave market may be seen from various advertisements. This one, for example, from the *Diário de Pernambuco* of September 23, 1830: "For sale: a female slave at an incredibly low price for the present time; the said slave has no vice whatever and is a *quitandeira* [see Translator's note, following]; the only thing against her is an unpleasing figure, and it is for this reason that she is being sold; inquire in the city of Olinda at the second house above the embankment, or in Recife, rua do Crespo D. 3." The Negro who brought a good price, or who, when he fled captivity, was sought after as one would seek a family jewel, with promises to St. Anthony and the like, was the one who was strong and handsome. As late as 1882 the *Diário de Notícias* of Rio de Janeiro published an advertisement promising a reward of 200$000 to the one who should apprehend the slave Sabino: "good teeth . . . when he speaks, rolls his rr's a great deal . . . stutters a little . . .

ments for the years 1825, 1830, 1835, 1840, and 1850 we may see the well-defined preference for male and female Negroes who were tall and possessed of good figures—"comely of face and body" and "with all the teeth in front." Which shows that there was a eugenic and æsthetic selection of housemen and housemaids, the latter being the Negro women who were in closest contact with the white men of the Big Houses, the mothers of the young mulattoes who were rearered in the home, many of whom were to become learned doctors, bachelors of arts, and even priests of the Church.

Having considered these points, which appear to me to be of basic importance in studying the African influence on Brazilian culture and Brazilian eugenics, I now feel more inclined to undertake the task of discovering the more intimate aspects of this contagious influence.

Before beginning, however, there is a distinction that must be made: between the pure Negro influence (which, as I see it, is practically impossible to isolate) and that of the Negro in his condition of slave. "In the first place, the bad element of the population was not the Negro race, but that race reduced to slavery." So wrote Joaquim Nabuco, in 1881.[122] Admirable words to have been written in the same era in which Oliveira Martins, in weighty pages, was declaring: "There is, assuredly, an abundance of documents to show that the Negro is an anthropologically inferior type, frequently very close to the anthropoid, and little deserving to be called a man."[123]

When we are considering the influence of the Negro on the private life of the Brazilian, it is always the effect produced by the slave, and

---

intelligent and very handy" (July 10, 1882).—The subject was discussed by me in a lecture before the Felippe d'Oliveira Society in Rio in 1934, my topic being "The Slave in Newspaper Advertisements under the Empire." I also discussed it in a paper read before the First Afro-Brazilian Congress in 1935: "Bodily Deformities in Fugitive Negroes."

[Several of the terms employed in the foregoing note that are not readily translatable call for an explanation. A *ladino* was a slave who "already spoke Portuguese, had some notion of the Christian religion, and knew how to perform ordinary tasks in the house or the field."—Lima and Barroso, op. cit.—The "bush-captain" (*capitão-do-campo* or *capitão do mato*) was one

whose business was recapturing fugitive slaves.—A *quitandeira* is a maker and vender of home-made sweets. (Translator.)]

[122] Joaquim Nabuco: *O Abolicionismo* (op. cit.).—With regard to this and other of his points of view, which are intensely interesting for the present day, we are in need of a study of Nabuco that will integrate him with the best Brazilian traditions of intellectual vitality, traditions from which he was at times led astray by his cosmopolitanism, his Gallic propensities, and his Anglo-Americanism.

[123] J. P. de Oliveira Martins: *O Brasil e as Colônias Portuguesas* (*Brazil and the Portuguese Colonies*) (Lisbon, 1887).

not by the Negro *per se*, that we are evaluating. Ruediger Bilden undertakes to explain by the influence of slavery all the traits in the economic and social background of Brazil.[124] Together with the one-crop system, it was the force that most deeply affected our social plastics. At times what appears to be the influence of race is purely and simply that of the slave, of the social system of slavery, a reflection of the enormous capacity of that system for morally degrading masters and slaves alike. The Brazilian Negro appears to us, throughout the whole of our colonial life and the first phase of our independent life as a nation, as a being deformed by slavery, by slavery and by the one-crop system, of which he was the instrument, the firm point of support, unlike the Indian, who was always on the move.

Goldenweiser points out that it is absurd to judge the Negro, his capacity for work, and his intelligence by the effort that he put forth on American plantations under the regime of slavery. The Negro rather deserves to be judged by his industrial activity in the milieu of his own culture, where he had an interest in and an enthusiasm for his task.[125]

In the same way, it seems to me absurd to judge the morals of the Brazilian Negro by his deleterious influence as a slave. This was the mistake made by Nina Rodrigues in studying the African's effect upon our country: that of not realizing how the Negro's status drained his energies. "Aside, then, from their condition as slaves," he writes, in the opening pages of his work on the Negro race in Portuguese America, "the condition under which they were brought to Brazil, and judging their qualities as colonists as we would those who come from any other source. . . ." But this is impossible. It is impossible to separate the Negro who was brought to Brazil from the conditions under which he came.

If it is the habit that makes the monk, this is true of the slave; and the African was oftentimes obliged to divest himself of his Malê tunic, to don the *tanga*[126] of the filthy slave-ships. He had to put on the *tanga* or a pair of sackcloth trousers and become a bearer of the *"tigre,"*[127] or fecal urn. Slavery uprooted the Negro from his social and family environment and turned him loose among a strange and

---

[124] Ruediger Bilden, from a work in preparation. For Bilden, the study of the historical development of Brazil shows that the evils attributed by some critics to the racial composition of the country should, rather, be blamed on slavery.

[125] Alexander Goldenweiser: "Race and Culture in the Modern World," *Journal of Social Forces*, Vol. III.

[126] The *tanga* was a cloth that covered the body from the waist to the knees. (Translator.)

[127] See Preface to the First Edition, Note 20, p. xxv. (Translator.)

frequently a hostile people. In such surroundings, in contact with forces so dissolvent in their effect, it would be absurd to expect of the slave any other deportment than that immoral kind of which he is so commonly accused.

Eroticism, lust, and sexual depravity have come to be looked upon as a defect in the African race; but what has been found to be the case among the Negro peoples of Africa, as among primitive peoples in general, as I have pointed out in a previous chapter, is a greater moderation of the sexual appetite than exists among Europeans. African Negro sexuality is one that stands in need of constant excitation and sharp stimuli. Aphrodisiac dances. A phallic cult. Orgies. Whereas in the case of civilized man the sexual appetite is ordinarily excited without great provocation. Without effort. The vulgar idea to the effect that the Negro race, more than others, is given to sexual excesses is attributed by Ernest Crawley to the fact that the expansive temperament of Negroes and the orgiastic character of their festivals create the illusion of an unbridled eroticism. A fact that "indicates rather the contrary," demonstrating the need for them of an "artificial excitement." Havelock Ellis places the Negro woman among those who are cold rather than passionate: "indifferent to the refinements of love." And like Ploss, Ellis lays emphasis on the fact that the sexual organs among primitive peoples are "comparatively undeveloped." [128]

It is generally said that the Negro corrupted the sexual life of Brazilian society by precociously initiating the sons of the family into physical love. But it was not the Negro woman who was responsible for this; it was the woman slave. And what the African did not accomplish in this regard was accomplished by the Indian woman, likewise enslaved. In his *Life of Father Belchior de Pontes*, Padre Manuel Fonseca lays the responsibility for the easy seduction of colonial children upon the Indian. And it was from a region that was almost without a trace of Negro blood that the Bishop of Pará wrote, in the eighteenth century: "The wretched state of manners in this country puts me in mind of the end that befell the five cities, and makes me think that I am living in the suburbs of Gomorrah, very close indeed, and in the vicinity of Sodom." [129]

It is, I may say once again, an absurdity to hold the Negro re-

---

[128] Ernest Crawley: *Studies of Savages and Sex*, edited by Theodore Besterman (London, 1929). Havelock Ellis: "Analysis of the Sexual Impulse," *Studies in the Psychology of Sex* (Philadelphia, 1908).

[129] Frade João de São Joseph Queiroz: *Memórias* (Porto, 1868), p. 22.

sponsible for what was not his doing or the Indian's, but that of the social system in which they both functioned passively and mechanically. There is no slavery without sexual depravity. Depravity is the essence of such a regime. In the first place, economic interests favor it, by creating in the owners of men an immoderate desire to possess the greatest possible number of *crias*.[130] From a manifesto issued by slave-holding planters Nabuco quotes the following words, so rich in significance: "The most productive feature of slave property is the generative belly."[131]

It was so in Portugal, from where the institution of slavery, already opulent in vices, was brought to Brazil. "The Moorish slaves, and the Negro ones, in addition to those from other regions, to whom baptism was administered did not receive afterwards the slightest religious education." So we are informed by Alexandre Herculano. The masters of these slaves favored dissoluteness in order to "augment the number of *crias* and thus increase the herd."[132] In such an atmosphere, created by the economic interest of the masters, how hope that slavery—whether slave be Moorish, Negro, Indian, or Malay—could have any other effect than dissoluteness, lust, and licentiousness? Seeing that what was wanted was the productive female belly. Black bellies that would produce young slaves for their owners.

A point that is emphasized by Joaquim Nabuco is "the effect of African diseases upon the physical constitution of our people."[133] This was one of the terrible effects of the contact of Brazil with the Dark Continent. But it is essential to note that it was in Brazil that the Negro became syphilitic. One or another may have brought the disease with him, but it was in the colonial slave quarters that the contamination *en masse* occurred. The "inferior race," to which it is the custom to attribute everything that the present-day Brazilian finds to be a handicap,[134] had acquired from the "superior" one this great venereal malady which since the earliest colonial times has degraded us and diminished us as a people. It was the masters of the Big Houses who infected the Negro women of the *senzalas*. Very often these latter were virgins, girls of twelve or thirteen years, who were given to white lads already rotting with the syphilis of the towns. Whence the belief so long current in Brazil that there was no better purge for the disease than a young Negro virgin. It was Dr. João Alvares de

---

[130] *Cria*: a young Negro born and reared (*criado*) in the Big House. Cf. pp. 369, 399. (Translator.)

[131] Joaquim Nabuco: *O Abolicionismo* (op. cit.).

[132] Alexandre Herculano: *História da Origem e Establecimento da Inquisação em Portugal* (op. cit.).

[133] Joaquim Nabuco, op. cit.

[134] Word in English. (Translator.)

Azevedo Macedo, Jr., in 1869, who reported this strange custom, dating, it would seem, from colonial times, traces of which are still to be found in the old sugar-plantation areas of Pernambuco and Rio de Janeiro. According to Dr. Macedo, this "barbarous superstition" held that those suffering from gonorrhea would be cured if they contrived to have intercourse with a girl at the age of puberty: "the innocula-tion of a pubescent female with this virus is the surest means of ex-tinguishing it in oneself." [135]

It is similarly to be supposed that many a Negro mother who was a wet-nurse was infected by the infant at her breast, thus conveying from the Big House to the slave hut the blight of syphilis. In a study published in 1877 Dr. José de Góes e Siqueira gave it as his opinion that anyone who unscrupulously entrusted syphilitic children to the care of nurses who were in perfect health should be subject to fines and indemnities. "Breast nursing being one of the common means of transmission, it may readily be understood what favorable results for the population would be produced by a measure so simple and so easily carried out." The Negro wet-nurses "would not be permitted to hire themselves out without a health certificate or examination by a competent physician"; but on the other hand they "would have the right to claim damages of the parents or guardians of the young ones who had given them a syphilitic infection." [136]

It is to be expected that, once having been infected by their white masters—many of them before they had attained the age of puberty —these female slaves in their turn should have become, as adult women, the great transmitters of venereal disease between whites and blacks. Which explains why it is that our country in the days of slavery was overrun with syphilis and gonorrhea.

The same thing happened in the Southern United States. Janson, in his book *The Stranger in America*,[137] alludes to the veritable epi-demic of quack doctors pretending to cure venereal diseases, in the United States, during the first half of the nineteenth century. A sign

[135] João Alvares de Azevedo Ma-cedo, Jr.: *Da Prostituição do Rio de Janeiro e de Sua Influência sobre a Saúde Pública* ("On Prostitution in Rio de Janeiro and Its Influence on Public Health"), Thesis presented to the Faculty of Medicine of Rio de Janeiro, 1869. See also Evaristo de Moraes: *A Escravidão no Brasil (Slav-ery in Brazil)*.

[136] José de Góes e Siqueira: *Breve Estudo sobre a Prostituição e a Sifilis no Brasil (Brief Study of Prostitution and Syphilis in Brazil)* (Rio de Ja-neiro, 1877).

[137] Cited by Arthur W. Calhoun: *A Social History of the American Family from Colonial Times to the Present* (Cleveland, 1918). [*The Stranger in America*, by C. W. Janson, was published in 1807. (Trans-lator.)]

that many were suffering from the diseases in question. And Odum attributes alarming proportions to the spread of syphilis in the slave-holding states of the South.[138] In our own country, along the seaboard —that is to say, in the zone most affected by slavery—syphilis was always widespread and continues to be. To this day the advertising of remedies, elixirs, and nostrums for treating such ailments is carried on with an insistence that is nothing short of scandalous. There are even religious prints, showing the Infant Jesus surrounded by little angels, announcing that such and such an elixir will "cure syphilis"; that if "Christ Himself were to come back into the world today, He would be the one to raise His holy voice to recommend the use of the Elixir . . . to those suffering from any of the maladies that have their origin in an impurity of the blood." And the leaders in the field of Brazilian medicine recommend to their students in the clinic that they always "think syphilitically"—that is, that they consider first of all the possible syphilitic origin of the illness or disease with which they are dealing.[139]

Syphilis invariably had its own way in patriarchal Brazil. It killed, blinded, deformed at will. It caused women to abort. It took "little angels" [140] off to heaven. It was a serpent brought up in the house, with no one taking any notice of its venom. The poisoned blood then burst forth in sores; and the victims would proceed to scratch their ulcers or "giblets," would take quack remedies and suck on cashew nuts. As I have pointed out in the opening pages of this essay, the syphilization of Brazil—granted its extra-American origin—dates from the beginning of the sixteenth century; but in the voluptuous atmosphere of the Big Houses, filled with young Negro girls, with *mulecas* [141] and *mucamas*, it and kindred affections were propagated more freely through domestic prostitution, which is always less hygienic than that of the brothels. In 1845 Lassance Cunha wrote that

---

[138] Cited by Calhoun (op. cit.). [Howard W. Odum: *Social and Mental Traits of the Negro* (New York, 1910). (Translator.)]

[139] Oscar da Silva Araujo reminds us—and, for that matter, he is but repeating the words of the elder Silva Araujo—that the Baron of Lavrádio estimated at fifty per cent the number of syphilitic children that he encountered in the course of his service in the Hospital da Misericórdia of Rio; while Moncorvo and Clemente Pereira found the percentage of syph-

ilitic infections in the Pediatric and Polyclinic Service to be from forty to fifty, and Moura Brasil discovered that twenty per cent of the eye-patients in the Rio Polyclinic were affected by the disease.—Oscar da Silva Araujo: *Alguns Comentários sobre a Sifilis no Rio de Janeiro* (*Some Remarks on Syphilis in Rio de Janeiro*) (Rio de Janeiro, 1928).

[140] See p. 388 and Notes 302 and 303. (Translator.)

[141] *Muleca* (*moleca*): a young black girl. (Translator.)

the Brazilian attached no importance to syphilis, a disease that is "near to being hereditary and so common that the people do not look upon it as a scourge, nor do they stand in fear of it." A domestic disease, a family one, something like measles or the worms. And he strenuously protested against the frequency with which syphilitics married—marriages known to "us who are physicians and who are aware of the pathologic secrets of families." [142] In the early years of the nineteenth century, Manuel Vieira da Silva, later Baron of Alvaesar, in his *Reflexões sobre alguns dos meios propostos por mais conducentes para melhorar o clima da cidade do Rio de Janeiro. (Reflections upon Some of the Means Proposed as the Most Convenient for Ameliorating the Climate of the City of Rio de Janeiro)*, had noted the fact that "cutaneous affections" were "made little of in this city, popular superstition asserting that there was no need of treating them; and it is possible that the sickly constitution that the natives of the city appear to possess is due to such an attitude as this." [143] But Vieira da Silva was not the first who had the good sense to imply that what many regarded as the effect of climate or of the "heat" was in reality due to syphilis and the neglect of the disease. Before his time we find Luis dos Santos Vilhena, regius professor of the Greek language at Bahia at the end of the eighteenth century, refuting the idea that "the heat" was the principal cause of sensual vices and diseases in the colony. "Mere subterfuges," wrote Vilhena. The true cause appeared to him to be "the disordered sexual passion." Not only that of the streets, but that of the Big Houses as well, which had been contaminated by the slave huts. Contaminated by slaves. It was these latter who, as Vilhena saw it, had transformed the healthful climate of Brazil into a deadly one—a climate that "had been admirably wholesome, but which today differs little if at all from that of Angola. . . ." [144]

By the beginning of the eighteenth century Brazil had already come to be signaled out in books by foreigners as the land of syphilis *par excellence*. The author of the *Histoire générale des pirates* writes that

---

[142] Herculano Augusto Lassance Cunha: *Dissertação sobre a Prostituição em Particular na Cidade do Rio de Janeiro* ("Dissertation on Prostitution, Especially in the City of Rio de Janeiro"), Thesis Presented to the Faculty of Rio de Janeiro, 1845.

[143] Cited by Oscar da Silva Araujo (op. cit.), who supposes that among the "cutaneous affections" so tolerated by Brazilians were syphilitic ones. He recalls in this connection the superstition then prevalent to the effect that such diseases might "go inward, with great harm to the patient."

[144] Luis dos Santos Vilhena: *Recompilação de Notícias, Soteropolitanas e Brasilicas (Compendium of Bahian and Brazilian News)*, for the year 1802 (Bahia, 1921).

"presque tous les brésiliens sont atteints d'affections vénériennes." [145] And Oscar da Silva Araujo translates a curious passage on the subject of syphilis in Rio de Janeiro from the pen of John Barrow, an English traveler who in the 1700's made a voyage to Brazil, the island of Java, and Cochin China. According to Barrow, the "Gallic plague" had wrought devastation even in the monasteries. He goes on to tell the story of the Abbess of a convent who had received a box of mercurial ointment from a physician whom Barrow knew. The box was indiscreetly opened on the way by the bearer of it, a "jolly friar of St. Benedict"; and the traveler relates how the ecclesiastic in question, raising the box to his nose, winked his eye expressively and exclaimed: *"Ah! Domine! Mercurialia! Ista sunt mercurialia!"* And he added that the Abbess and the other ladies of Rio *"pronæ sunt omnes ac deditæ veneri."* [146]

I transcribe further from Silva Araujo these words of Bernardino Antônio Gomes, an old doctor of colonial times, in response to an inquiry by the Chamber of Rio de Janeiro, in 1798, the object of which was to ascertain what diseases were endemic in the city of the viceroys. The physician's reply was to the effect that "the familiar example of slaves, who know almost no other law than the stimuli of nature," had a great deal to do with prostitution and the venereal malady in Brazil. Dr. Bernardino might have pointed out that this animality in Negroes, their failure to restrain their instincts, and the prostitution that went on within the home were inspired by the white masters—in the interests of large-scale procreation on the part of some, while others were bent merely upon satisfying their sexual whims. It

[145] Cited by Oscar Clark: *Sifilis no Brasil e Suas Manifestações Vicerais* (*Syphilis in Brazil and Its Visceral Manifestations*) (Rio de Janeiro, 1918).

[146] Cited by Oscar da Silva Araujo (op. cit.)—According to the calculations of Góes e Siqueira (op. cit.), published in 1875, a sixth part of the army was found to be infected with syphilis in the year 1872, and at that rate, in six years' time, the entire army would have the disease. As to the civilian population, Góes e Siqueira wrote: "It is by no means an unknown fact that syphilis is invading all social classes."—Ruediger Bilden, in his studies of the formation of Brazilian society, attributes a great importance to syphilis as a factor in pauperizing the population. Modern studies of the disease and the success achieved in combating its effects in various countries indicate how comparatively easy it would be for Brazil to rid itself of this heritage of slavery. With reference to the fight against syphilis, the physician Durval Rosa Burges in a recent book remarks that it is a question of a campaign that would be "rewarding from the start," inasmuch as "we have all the weapons in hand." Durval Rosa Burges: *Estudos sobre sifilis, com especial referência a classe média paulistana* (*Studies of Syphilis, with Especial Reference to the Middle Class of São Paulo*) (Rio de Janeiro, 1941).

was not the Negro, however, who was the libertine, but the slave who was at the service of his idle master's economic interests and voluptuous pleasure. It was not the "inferior race" that was the source of corruption, but the abuse of one race by another, an abuse that demanded a servile conformity on the part of the Negro to the appetites of the all-powerful lords of the land. Those appetites were stimulated by idleness, by a "wealth acquired without labor," as Dr. Bernardino phrases it, by "idleness" or "laziness," as Vilhena would say; which means—by the economic structure of the slave-holding regime itself.

If it be true, as modern anthropologists would have it, that "irregularity in sexual relations has in general manifested a tendency to increase with civilization";[147] that in domesticated animals the sexual system is found to be more highly developed than in wild ones;[148] that among those domestic animals that have been rendered soft by a lack of struggle and competition the reproductive glands absorb a major quantity of nourishment;[149] and, further, that the reproductive power in man has been augmented with civilization in the same way that in animals it is increased by domestication—[150] if all this be true, then we may risk the conclusion that, under a regime such as that of a slave-holding monoculture, where a majority labors and a minority does nothing but command, there will of necessity develop in the latter, by reason of its comparative leisure, a greater preoccupation with sexual matters, a greater degree of erotic mania, and more amorous refinements than in the case of the former. There is the example of India, where the more elevated the social caste and the greater its leisure, the more refined, artistic, and even perversely cultivated is the rite of love.

There is nothing to authorize the conclusion that it was the Negro who brought to Brazil that viscous lustfulness in which we all feel ourselves ensnared the moment we reach adolescence. That precocious voluptuousness, that hunger for a woman, which at the age of thirteen or fourteen makes of every Brazilian a Don Juan, does not come from contagious contact with, or from the blood-stream of, the "inferior race," but rather from our economic and social system. The climate, perhaps, has something to do with it: the dense, heavy, enervating air we breathe, which early predisposes us to the prickings of love and at the same time deprives us of the inclination to any sustained exertion. For it is impossible to deny the effect of climate upon the sexual morality of societies. Without being a preponderant

---

[147] E. A. Westermarck: *The History of Human Marriage* (op. cit.).

[148] Havelock Ellis, loc. cit.

[149] G. Adlez, cited by Crawley (op. cit.).

[150] W. Heape, cited by Crawley.

one, it serves, nevertheless, to accentuate or to weaken existing tendencies, to harden or to soften social traits. We all know of cases of the voice becoming harsh and grating in hot climates; and under the influence of a greater or less degree of atmospheric pressure, an air that is drier or less dry, the temperature, circulation, and elimination of carbon dioxide in man undergo an alteration; and all this has a repercussion upon man's social deportment, upon his economic efficiency, upon his sexual morals. We may, then, conclude with Kelsey [151] that certain climates stimulate man to greater effort and consequently to greater productivity, while others drain his energies. In admitting this, it is not necessary to go along with the exaggerations of Huntington and other fanatics on the subject of the "influence of climate." Nor does this mean that we are to permit ourselves to be distracted from the enormous weight of responsibility that, when we come to look into the matter thoroughly, is to be attributed to social and economic forces; for it is within the sphere of these forces that cultures, forms of social organization, and types of society have been articulated. Very often there is something like a secret alliance between such forces and natural ones, while at other times they are practically independent of the latter.

The Negro, in his relations with the culture and the type of society here evolving, must be judged chiefly by the criterion of social and economic history. The criterion of cultural anthropology. Hence the impossibility—I insist upon this point—of separating him from his degrading condition as a slave, which stifled many of his best, his most creative and normal tendencies, to accentuate other artificial and even morbid ones. Thus it was that the African became, decidedly, a pathogenic agent in the bosom of Brazilian society. Owing to "racial inferiority," the Aryanizing sociologists will shout. But their shouts are drowned by the historical evidence, the cultural and, above all, the economic circumstances under which the contact of the Negro with the white man occurred in Brazil. The Negro *was* pathogenic, but by way of serving the whites, as the irresponsible part of a system that had been put together by others.

The principal causes of the abuse of Negroes by whites are to be looked for in those economic and social conditions favorable to masochism which were created by the process of colonization on the part of the Portuguese—with almost no women, to begin with—and are to be sought, also, in the slave-holding system of Brazil, with all-powerful masters and passive slaves; such factors will explain those

---

[151] Carl Kelsey: *The Physical Basis of Society* (op. cit.).

sadistic forms of love which are so prominent among us, and which are in general attributed to African lust.

It should be added that the cult of Venus Urania was brought to Brazil by the first colonists from Europe—Portuguese, Spaniards, Italians, Jews. Here it encountered, in the sexual code of the natives and in the jarring conditions attendant upon colonization, a cultural milieu favorable to the spread of this form of love and debauchery. Europeans with illustrious names figured as Sodomites in the trials that marked the *Visitation of the Holy Office to the Regions of Brazil.*[152] One of these, the Florentine nobleman Filipe Cavalcanti, was the founder of the family that bears his name. This is not to be wondered at, in view of the prevalance of sodomy in Renaissance Italy. It was from the Italy of that era that the principal terms for designating the peculiarities of the *unspeakable sin* became internationalized; and in the Spanish trials and judicial sentences of the sixteenth and seventeenth centuries Arlindo Camillo Monteiro encountered numerous cases of Italian Sodomites.[153] João Lúcio de Azevedo mentions specifically the Caorsinos, of whom there had come to be a considerable colony in Lisbon, and who must have been the propagators of Socratic love among the Portuguese.[154]

But among the Portuguese and Spaniards themselves, and among the Jews and Moors of the peninsula, this form of lust was intensely practiced at the time that Brazil was discovered and colonized. Among those who figure in the trials of this period are friars and other clerics, noblemen, chief magistrates, professors, and slaves. A number were exiled to Brazil, among others a certain Fruitoso Alvarez, Vicar of Matoim, who in Bahia confessed to the visitor of the Holy Office, on July 29, 1591: "that during the fifteen years that he had been in this *capitânia* of the Bay of All Saints,[155] he had had dishonorable relations

---

[152] The charge against Filipe Cavalcanti as a Sodomite will be found in the *Denunciations of Bahia (1591–1593)*, p. 448. He was denounced by Belchoir Mendes d'Azevedo, an inhabitant of Pernambuco, residing in the city of Olinda.

[153] Arlindo Camillo Monteiro: *Amor Sáfico e Socrático—Estudo Médico Forense (Sapphic and Socratic Love—A Medico-Forensic Study)* (Lisbon, 1922).

[154] João Lúcio de Azevedo: *"Organização Econômica"* (loc. cit.).

[The Caorsinos were inhabitants of Caorsa, or Cahors, in Gascony; they were of Italian extraction—*"del sangue nostro,"* as Dante puts it. A reference to them will be found in the *Paradiso,* XXVII, lines 58–9:

*Del sangue nostro Caorsini e Guaschi
S'apparecchian di bere . . .*

They also had the reputation of being great usurers. (Translator.)]

[155] The city of Bahia (the word means "Bay") is situated on All Saints' Bay. (Translator.)

with some forty persons, more or less, hugging and kissing. . . ." [156]

For such "hugging and kissing"—a euphemism to designate various forms of priapism—numerous individuals were shipped from Portugal to the colony; and it is to this white element rather than to the Negro that much of Brazilian lubricity is to be attributed. One element in the Portuguese colonization of Brazil that was apparently pure, but which as a matter of fact was a corrupting influence, was the young orphans brought over by the Jesuits for their schools. Monteiro informs us that in the "books of the unspeakable, they are cited with comparative frequency." [157]

It is known to be a fact that even Portuguese men of arms of the fifteenth and sixteenth centuries, possibly by reason of their long maritime crossings and their contact with the voluptuous life of Oriental countries, had developed all forms of lust. Heroes admired by all, they readily communicated to other social classes their own erotic vices and refinements. Lopo Vaz de Sampaio would have us believe that Affonso de Albuquerque himself—the "terrible Albuquerque"—had his libidinous pleasures of this sort. [158]

The frequent occurrence of sorcery and sexual magic among us is another trait that is looked upon as being exclusively of African origin; but meanwhile the first volume of documents relative to the activities of the Holy Office in Brazil records many cases of Portuguese witches. Their practices might have undergone an African influence, but in essence they were expressions of a European Satanism that to this day is to be met with in our country, mingled with Negro or Indian rites. Antônia Fernandes, known as Nobrega, stated that she was allied with the devil; and at her consultations the responses were given for her by "a certain thing that talked, kept in a glass." This is medieval magic of the purest European variety. Another Portuguese woman, Isabel Rodrigues, nicknamed "Wry-Mouth," furnished miraculous powders and taught powerful prayers. The most famous of all, Maria Gonçalves, whose sobriquet was "Burn-Tail," took the greatest familiarities with Satan. With much burying and digging up of kegs, Burn-Tail's witchcraft was almost wholly concerned with problems of impotence and sterility; for it would appear that the clientele of these colonial sorcerers was very largely made up of the lovelorn, those who were unhappy or insatiable in their passions.

In Portugal, for that matter, it is known that the most cultivated

---

[156] *Primeira Visitação do Santo Ofício as Partes do Brasil, Confissões da Baía* (op. cit.), p. 20.

[157] Monteiro, op. cit.
[158] Ibid.

and illustrious personages were involved in witchcraft. Júlio Dantas portrays Dom Nuno da Cunha himself, Grand Inquisitor of the realm in the time of John V, as swathed in his Cardinal's purple— "like a kind of silkworm," as the chronicler puts it—and trembling with fear of sorcerers and witches. And grave physicians, the advanced minds of their age, like Curvo Semedo, would recommend to their patients, as a remedy against conjugal infidelity, "a certain witches' brew made of the shoe-soles of the woman and her husband." "Crafty apothecaries in black-spotted capes and with big silver buckles on their shoes made a fortune selling the herb known as 'pombinha,' which was cast upon hot tiles and fumigated along with the teeth of a dead man—a strange practice, designed to awaken love in the decrepit organisms of old men and to thaw the disdainful frigidity of youths." [159]

Love was the great motive around which witchcraft revolved in Portugal. So far as that is concerned, it is not hard to understand the vogue of sorcerers, witches, and witch-doctors, specialists in Aphrodisiac spells, in a land that had been so drained of people and that only by an extraordinary effort of virility was still able to colonize Brazil. Witches and their art were one of the stimuli that, in their manner, contributed to the sexual superexcitation that was to result, legitimately or illegitimately, in filling the enormous gaps left in the scant population of the Kingdom by war and pestilence. As a result, the Portuguese colonists came to Brazil already imbued with a belief in spells. As for that variety of witchcraft which is of direct African origin, it was to develop here upon a European base of medieval superstitions and beliefs.

As was the case in Portugal, witchcraft or sorcery in Brazil, after it had come to be dominated by the Negro, continued to center in the love-motive and the interests of generation and fecundity. It was concerned with protecting the life of the pregnant woman and that of the child, threatened by so many things—by fevers, cramps, blood-ailments, snake-bite, fallen sternum, the evil eye. The pregnant woman, for her part, was to be prophylactically safeguarded from these and other afflictions by a set of practices in which African influences, frequently shorn of their original character, were mingled with traces of the Catholic liturgy and survivals of native rituals.

Brought here from Portugal, the various beliefs and forms of sexual magic proceeded to expand: the belief that the mandrake root attracts fecundity and undoes evil spells against the home and the

---

[159] Júlio Dantas: *Figuras de Ontem e de Hoje* (op. cit.).

propagation of families; the custom of pregnant women of hanging a small bag of "altar stones" [160] about their necks; the care taken by such women not to pass under ladders lest the child should fail to grow; their habit of donning St. Francis' girdle as they feel the pangs of parturition coming on; the promises made to Our Lady of Child-birth, of the Blessed Event, of Expectation, of the Conception, of the Pangs, in order that childbed may be easier or the child a comely one. And when Our Lady hears the request, the promise is kept. This consists, sometimes, in the child's taking the name of Maria; whence the many Marias in Brazil: Maria das Dores (of the Pangs); Maria dos Anjos (of the Angels); da Conceição (of the Conception); de Lourdes (Our Lady of Lourdes); das Graças (of the Favors). [161] At other times it consists in the child's going clad as an angel or a saint in some procession; in his studying for the priesthood; or in her be-coming a nun; in letting the hair grow in long clusters, which then are offered to the image of Our Good Lord Jesus of the Cross; or the child, up to the age of twelve or thirteen; may wear nothing but blue and white, or white alone, in homage to the Virgin Mary. [162]

I must also record the custom of votive offerings on the part of pregnant women: offerings of little wax or wooden dolls (children to the female saints and to those of Our Ladies who are known as the protectors of maternity. Some of the plantation chapels have numer-ous collections of these ex-votos.

But the bulk of the beliefs and practices of sexual magic as de-

---

[160] "Holy stones from the center of the altar."—Lima and Barroso, op. cit. (Translator.)

[161] A study should be made in Bra-zil of the promises to saints, as a re-flection of the æsthetic tendencies of our people, their predilections with regard to color, names, etc. Affonso Arinos has given us some exceedingly interesting pages on the "cult of Mary in the popular language of Brazil." "Each family," he tells us, "with rare exceptions, has one or many Marias." —Affonso Arinos: *Lendas e Tradições Brasileiras* (*Brazilian Legends and Traditions*) (São Paulo, 1917).—Many of these Marias are the result of promises made to Our Lady. Simi-larly, the names of many places in Brazil are the result either of such promises or of the cult of Mary in

general: names like Graça, Penha, Conceição, Monserrate, which render the geographic nomenclature of our country so much more picturesque than that of the United States, with its Minneapolises, its Indianapolises, and other names ending in *-polis*, which Matthew Arnold found to be so horribly inexpressive.

[162] This form of fulfilling promises is to be found also among the Negro fetishists, with respect to their deities known as Orixás. Fernando Ortiz found among the Cuban Negroes the custom of wearing only white in such cases, and Nina Rodrigues and Manuel Querino encountered similar observ-ances in Bahia, where the garments worn by the "holy daughters" vary in color to conform to the particular *orixá*.

veloped in Brazil were colored by the Negro's intense mysticism. Some of them were brought by him from Africa, while others, African in technique only, made use of native herbs and animals (*bichos*). Nothing is more characteristic than the use that is made of the toad in hastening the consummation of delayed marriages. In Afro-Brazilian sexual magic the toad also becomes the protector of the faithless wife, who, in order to deceive her husband, has but to take a needle threaded with green silk, make with it a cross on the face of the sleeping individual to be affected, and afterwards sew up the eyes of the toad. On the other hand, in order to hold her lover, a woman must live with a toad in a pot beneath her bed. In this case the toad is a live one, fed on cow's milk. They still employ the toad in sexual magic and witchcraft in Brazil, sewing up its mouth after it has been stuffed with the remains of a meal left by the victim. Other animals bound up with Afro-Brazilian sexual rites of this sort are the bat, the snake, the screech-owl, the hen, the dove, the rabbit, the tortoise. Various herbs are also employed, some of them native, others brought from Africa by the Negroes. Certain ones are so violent in their effect, Manuel Querino tells us, that they produce dizziness when they are merely crushed in the hand. Others are taken in the form of beverages or are chewed; and others again, like maconha, are smoked, the smoke being swallowed. Even the crayfish is an instrument of sexual magic. Prepared with three or seven peppers from the coast and dragged along the ground, it produces trouble at the domestic fireside.[163]

It was their skill in the preparation of aphrodisiac and other sexual incantations that gave the *macumbeiros*,[164] or love-sorcerers, so much prestige with those of the white gentry who were old and spent. In the coffee-growing region of Rio de Janeiro, Agrippino Grieco picked up traditional accounts of planters of seventy or eighty years

---

[163] Manuel Querino: "*A Raça Africana e os Seus Costumes na Baía*" (loc. cit.). See also Pereira da Costa: "*Folclore Pernambucano*" ("Pernambucan Folklore"), *Revista do Instituto Arquivístico, Histórico e Geográphico de Pernambuco*; Alfredo de Carvalho: "*A Magia Sexual no Brasil*" ("Sexual Magic in Brazil") (fragment), *Revista Arqueológico, Histórico e Geográfico de Pernambuco*, No. 106; Júlio Ribeiro: *A Carne* (*Flesh*) (São Paulo).
[With regard to the last mentioned work: Júlio Ribeiro was an end-of-the-century naturalist of the Zola school, and his novel *Carne* is by way of being, as the literary historian Ronald de Carvalho describes it, "a Dionysiac hymn to pleasure." (Translator.)]

[164] A *macumbeiro* is one who practices the magic art known as *macumba*, which Lima and Barroso (op. cit.) describe as a "fetishistic ceremony with a Negro base and showing Christian influence, accompanied by dancing and singing to the sound of the drum." (Translator.)

of age who, stimulated by the aphrodisiacs provided by the black *macumbeiros*, lived surrounded by young Negro girls who had not yet reached puberty and who were now giving their owners the last sensations of masculinity. Of a baron of the Empire, Grieco tells us that he died an octogenarian, caressing young teen-age *mucamas* and even younger ones. He was "a great crony of the witches and witch-doctors, who kept him supplied with aphrodisiacs."[165] In Portugal the Marquês de Marialva had the same kind of old age; Beckford tells us that he was surrounded by "little angels"—that is, by white-clad children—and that these young ones bestowed upon him every kind of caress.

Nor should we overlook the important role that coffee came to play in Afro-Brazilian sexual magic. We even have an expression: "witch's coffee" (*café mandingueiro*), coffee with a "spell" (*mandinga*) in it; it is taken with much sugar and "a few clots of the menstrual fluid of the sorceress herself."[166] This comes nearer to being a love-potion than a witch's spell; but it is a potion such as could not be conceived in any other country than Brazil: very strong coffee, much sugar, and the blood of a mulatto woman. There is another technique that is employed, which consists in straining the coffee through the lower portion of the nightgown in which a woman has slept for two consecutive nights; the coffee is then to be drunk twice by the man, once at breakfast and again at dinner.[167] A woman's soiled nightgown enters into many a love-spell, as do other nauseous things. Hairs from the armpits or the genital parts. Sweat. Tears. Saliva. Blood. Nail-parings. Sperm. Alfredo de Carvalho mentions yet another: "the menstrual mucus excreted by Bartholin's glands, and even stools." Give him such ingredients as these, and the sorcerer—*catimbozeiro*, *mandingueiro*, or *macumbeiro*—will tell you that he will "soften the heart" of the most indifferent persons.[168]

There are *catimbozeiros* who fashion dolls out of wax or cloth. This is a form of sorcery that is more hygienic from the point of view of the victim. Upon these *calungas*, as they are called, the magicians inflict whatever punishment they wish the individual in question to suffer; it is a matter of praying forcefully enough; the rest

[165] Agrippino Grieco: "*Paraíba do Sul*," *O Jornal*, Rio de Janeiro, special edition in commemoration of the coffee bicentennial. [Agrippino Grieco is one of the most distinguished literary critics of present-day Brazil. (Translator.)]

[166] Basílio de Magalhães: "*As Lendas em torno da Lavoura do Café*" ("Legends Having to Do with the Raising of Coffee"), *O Jornal*, Rio de Janeiro, special commemorative edition.

[167] Ibid.

[168] Alfredo de Carvalho: "*A Magia Sexual no Brasil*" (loc. cit.).

consists merely in doing various things to the figure, squeezing it, pounding it, stretching its arms, spreading its legs, all of which is reflected on the person of the distant victim.

Another form of sorcery consists in stealing a man's shirt from the laundry-bag and cutting a hole in it with a pair of scissors exactly in the middle of the bosom.

It was not merely for amorous purposes, but for those having to do with the newborn as well, that the two mystic currents, the Portuguese on the one hand and the African or Amerindian on the other, were united in Brazil. In the one case the representative is the white father, or father and mother; in the other it is the Indian or Negro mother, the wet-nurse, the foster-mother, the "black mammy," the African female slave. The prophylactic concerns of mother and nurse here mingle in the one stream of maternal tenderness. Whether it be a matter of bodily hygiene or of spiritual protection against witchery and the evil eye.

With regard to the mystic protection of the newborn, however, it is the African influence that is stressed. A number of Portuguese traditions were brought here by white colonists: that of dragging the umbilical cord through fire or the river in order that rats may not eat it and the child grow up to be a thief; that of hanging a penny or a key about the child's neck to cure it of "milk-curds"; [169] that of not putting out the light until the child has been baptized in order that no sorcerer, witch, or werewolf may come to suck its blood in the dark; that of giving the names of saints to children, by way of still further frightening the werewolves. All of these traditions were here modified or enriched through the influence of the African slave woman, the old Negro woman who was the child's nurse.

In the same way the Portuguese cradle songs were modified in the mouth of the Negro nurse, who altered the words and adapted them to regional conditions, associating them with her own beliefs and those of the Indians. Thus, the old song "Listen, listen, little one," in this country was softened into "Sleep, sleep, my little one," the Portuguese "fountain" (*fonte*) being transformed at Belem into the Brazilian "creek" (*riacho*).[170] This is the plantation creek. A creek with a *mãe-d'agua*, a "water-mother," [171] in it, in place of the enchanted

---

[169] *sapinhos do leite*: "white or yellowish patches existing in the mucous of the mouth and produced by a fungus, frequent in acidosis conditions, especially in children."—Lima and Barroso, op. cit. (Translator.)

[170] See the cradle song quoted in the Preface to the First Edition, p. xxviii. (Translator.)

[171] The well-known contemporary novelist of the Brazilian northeast, a close friend of Freyre, José Lins do Rego, has written a novel by the title of *Agua Mãe*. (Translator.)

Moorish damsel. The creek where the baby's clout was washed. The forest was inhabited by "a *bicho* called the *carrapatú*." [172] And in place of a goblin (*papão*) or a bogeyman (*coca*), the slave huts now began copying from the Big Houses the capering nanny-goats (*cabras cabriolas*), the will-o'-the-wisp (*boi-tátá*), the Negro with the Pouch (*negro de surrão*), the aged Negro as a stock character, the *papa-figos*, or liver-eaters—all of these being used to frighten ill-bred children who cried in their hammocks at night, or importunate ones who smeared themselves with guava jelly in the pantry.

They no longer rocked the young one to sleep, singing as in Portugal:

> *Go away, Coca, go away, Coca,*
> *Over the roof-top, go,*
> *And let the little one take a nap*
> *In quiet here below.*[173]

They preferred to sing:

> *See the old black man*
> *On top the roof;*
> *He's a-saying he wants*
> *Roast child on the hoof.*[174]

It was not that the *coca*, or *cuca*, had entirely disappeared from the cradle songs of Brazil. Amadeu Amaral (Sr.) is still able to collect this quatrain—obviously from the south:

> *Sleep, my little dear,*
> *The cuca hears my croon;*
> *Daddy's gone to the field;*
> *Mother is coming soon.*[175]

The *coca* had not vanished, but its prestige had faded before more terrible phantoms. New fears, and ghostly forms to embody them.

---

[172] See the verse quoted, p. 139. The "*carrapatú*" is a mythical "*bicho*." (Translator.)

[173]   *Vai-te, Coca, vai-te, Coca,*
    para cima de telhado:
    deixar dormir o menino
    um soninho descansado.

Leite de Vasconcellos: *Tradições Populares de Portugal* (op. cit.).

[174]   *Olha o negro velho*
    em cima do telhado.
    Ele esta dizendo
    quer o menino assado.

Lindolfo Gomes, in Amadeu Amaral, Jr.: "*Superstições do Povo Paulista*" ("Superstitions of the People of São Paulo"), *Revista Nova*, São Paulo, No. 4.

[175]   *Durma, meu benzinho,*
    que a cuca j'ei vem;
    papai foi na roça,
    mamãe logo vem.

Quoted by Amadeu Amaral Jr., loc. cit.—Luis da Camara Cascudo has in preparation a work on the Geography of Brazilian Myths.

New fears, brought over from Africa or assimilated from the Indians by the white colonists and by the Negroes, were now added to the Portuguese obsessions having to do with the bogeyman, the goblin, the werewolf, with the *olharapos*, the *cocaloba*, the *farranca*, the *Maria-da-Manta*, the *trango-mango*,[176] the man-with-the-seven-sets-of-teeth, and the souls-in-torment. The Brazilian child of colonial times was surrounded by a greater number of ghostly forms, and more terrible ones, than any other children in the world. On the beaches was the *homem-marinho*, the "man-of-the-sea," a terrifying creature that devoured people's fingers, noses, and private parts.[177] In the forest there are the *saci-pererê*,[178] the *caipora*, the man-with-his-feet-turned-backward, the *boi-tátá*.[179] And everywhere there are the capering nanny-goat, the she-mule-without-a-head, the *tutú-marambá*, the Negro with the Pouch, the *tatú-gambeta* the *xibamba*, and the *mão-de-cabelo*, the "goblin-with-hairs-for-hands." [180] In the creeks and lakes, the water-mother, the *mãe-d'agua*. On the banks of the rivers was the toad-goblin, the *sapo-cururú*. By night, the *almas penadas*, the souls-in-torment. These never failed to come and smear with "ghost-broth" ("*mingau das almas*") the faces of little children; and for this reason no child must neglect to wash his face or take a bath the first thing in the morning. Another great danger for the young ones lay in being caught in the street out of hours; white-clad phantoms that grew in size—the "grow-and-shrink" kind—were very likely to confront the daring one. Or else their hammocks would be haunted by creatures with pock-marked faces. And then, there was the *papa-figo*, the man who ate the child's liver. To this day they tell in Pernambuco the story of a certain rich man who could eat nothing but children's liver and who had his blacks go everywhere

---

[176] The untranslatable, or all but untranslatable, names of goblins, frequently used to frighten children. (Translator.)

[177] There are a number of Brazilian myths involving the suggestion or threat of castration. Among others, that of the *mão-de-cabelo*, or goblin-with-hairs-for-hands. In Minas, children who wet the bed are told: "Oia! if baby wets the bed, the *mão-de-cabelo* will come get him and cut off baby's little thing!"—See Basílio Magalhães: *O Folclore do Brasil* (op. cit.).

[178] The *saci-pererê*, or *saci*, is a

"mythical being, a little Negro with only one leg, who, according to popular belief, pursues travelers or lies in ambush for them along the road."—Lima and Barroso, op. cit. (Translator.)

[179] On this and other forest sprites, see Jorge Amado: *Terras do sem fim* (*The Violent Land*), Chapter ii. (Translator.)

[180] *mão-de-cabelo*: "a mythical being that popular superstition depicts as human inform, white-clad, and with hands made of long hairs."—Lima and Barroso, op. cit. (Translator.)

with gunny-sacks looking for young ones. And the Quibungo,[181] what of him? He came all in one piece from Africa. A horrible creature (*bicho*), half human, half animal, with an enormous head; and in the middle of his back was a hole that gaped open when he bent his head. That was the way he ate children, by bending his head; the hole in the middle of his back would open and the children would slip into it. And then, good-by! they were in Quibungo's maw. Quibungo would come up to the house where there was an ill-behaved child, saying:

> *Whose house is this,*
> *here by the way;*
> *do I eat a child, do I eat a child,*
> *do I eat a child today?* [182]

Cabeleira, bandit of the cane fields of Pernambuco, who was finally hanged, is another who became a ghostly figure. Almost a Quibungo. From the end of the colonial era to the beginning of the nineteenth century—the century of electric light, which did away with many a worthy ghost, to leave us only the banal ones of the spiritualistic seance—there was not a Pernambucan child who did not tremble with horror at the very name of Cabeleira. The old Negro woman had but to shout at the weeping young one: "Cabeleira's coming!" and the infant would at once stop crying and between its sobs would sing:

> *Shut the door, Rosa, do,*
> *Cabeleira is coming for you;*
> *for Cabeleira snatches women*
> *and little children, too.*[183]

In the rural regions of the south, the superstition of the *Turk* who eats children still persists,[184] a superstition that is not to be met with in the north. The old Negro with the Pouch, on the other hand, is one who has lost none of his ancient prestige. There are still young ones who shudder at hearing the story about him:

---

[181] In Minas Geraes, *quibungo* is the name given to a Negro dance.— Lima and Barroso, op. cit. (Translator.)

[182] Nina Rodrigues, op. cit.

[The stanza is very freely rendered, or paraphrased; the original reads:

> *De quem é esta casa,*
> *anê*

como gérê, como gérê,
como érá?

Literally: "Whose house is this? *Auê!* I eat *gérê*, I eat *gérê*. I eat *érá*." (Translator.)]

[183] *Fecha porta, Rosa,*
Cabeleira êh—vem
pegando mulheres,
meninos tambem!

[184] Amadeu Amaral, Jr., loc. cit.

Sing me a song, pouch, sing it quick,
Or I will let you have this stick.[185]

The old Negro with the Pouch is an individual whom children do not like to think about meeting, for they at once recall *the little girl who had some gold earrings.* She was a little girl who had a very wicked stepmother (stepmothers are always very wicked in Brazilian and Portuguese tales; see the one about the fig and the fig tree). One day the little girl went to take a bath in the river; and, as usual, she took off her gold earrings and laid them on top of a stone. When she came home, she found that her earrings were gone. Help me, Our Lady! Where are my pretty little earrings? My lovely little earrings! And my stepmother! My stepmother will kill me on account of those earrings. And so she went back to the river to look for them. When she came to the river—whom did she meet? An old Negro, and ugly, too, who seized the little girl and stuffed her in his pouch. Then the old fellow went away with the child, and when he came where he was going, he threw his pouch down on the ground and cried:

Sing me a song, pouch, sing it quick,
Or I will let you have this stick.

And then the pouch began to sing, in a sweet little voice:

In this pouch he put me,
In this pouch I'm going to die;
All on account of my earrings—
By the river I let them lie.[186]

Everyone liked the voice in the pouch very much, and gave the old Negro money. One day the Negro came to the stepmother's house. They invited him to rest himself, to have something to eat and drink and, since it was already late in the day, to sleep there as well. It appears, however, that the little girl's sisters had become suspicious of the voice in the pouch; and at night, when the old Negro was sound asleep, they went and opened it and took the little girl out. She was so weak there was little life left in her; for all that the Negro had given her to eat, poor thing, was an old shoe-sole. In place of the little girl, the sisters stuffed the pouch with *cocô* (excrement). The next morning the Negro rose, had some coffee, and departed—without noticing what had happened. When he came to the next house, he ordered his pouch to sing—but the pouch was silent. Thinking the

---

[185] *Canta, canta, meu surrão,*
    Senão te meto este bordão.

[186] *Neste surrão me meteram,*
    neste surrão hei de morrer,
    por causa de uns brincos de ouro
    que no riacho eu deixei.

little girl must be asleep, the Negro began beating it with his stick, and then the pouch split open and sprayed the old man all over with filth.

Portuguese tales in Brazil underwent considerable modification in the mouths of the old Negro women or wet-nurses. They were the ones who became our great story-tellers. For the Africans, Sir A. B. Ellis reminds us, possess their own raconteurs, and there are individuals who make a profession of telling stories and who go from place to place reciting tales.[187] There is the *"akpalô,"* maker of the *"alô,"* or story; and there is the *"arokin,"* who is the narrator of chronicles of the past. The *"akpalô"* is an African institution that flourished in Brazil in the person of the old Negro women, who would go from plantation to plantation telling stories to other black women, the nurses of white children. José Lins do Rêgo, in his novel *Menino do Engenho* (*Plantation Lad*), speaks of these strange old women who would put in an appearance at the *banguês*[188] of Paraíba; they would tell their tales and then be on their way. They made their living in that fashion, which is precisely the function and manner of life of the *"akpalô."*

Through these old Negro women and children's nurses, African stories, chiefly stories of animals—of animals fraternizing with human beings, talking like them, marrying, feasting, and so on—came to be added to the collection of Portuguese tales, by Trancoso,[189] that had been told by colonial grandmothers to their grandchildren—nearly all of them stories of stepmothers, princes, giants, princesses, Tom Thumbs, enchanted Moorish damsels, and Moorish hags.

The language of the young likewise grew softer through the contact of the child with the Negro nurse. Certain words that to this day are harsh or sharp-sounding when pronounced by the Portuguese are in Brazil much smoother, owing to the influence of the African palate. The African palate in alliance with the climate, that other corrupter

---

[187] Sir A. B. Ellis, cited by Nina Rodrigues, op. cit.

[188] *Banguê* is one of the most characteristic of Brazilian regional terms, with a number of meanings and shades of meaning. Sometimes it is a litter of one sort or another (see Preface to the First Edition, p. xxv and note 19). Here it is equivalent to *engenho*, or sugar plantation (*engenho de banguê*, from the brick-paved canal, or *banguê*, through which the sugar-foam drains off). (Translator.)

[189] Gonçalo Fernandes Trancoso (*c.* 1515–*c.* 1590), a writer of folk tales, published in the collection *Contos e Histórias de Proveito e Exemplo* (*Moral and Exemplary Tales*), which first appeared in 1569 and 1596; see the edition published at Paris in 1921. (Translator.)

of European tongues in the warmth of the tropical and subtropical Americas.

The process of reduplication of the tonic syllable, so characteristic of the speech of savages and children, had the effect, in the case of a number of words, of giving to our infantile vocabulary a special charm. The "*dói*" ("it hurts") of adults becomes the "*dodói*" of the little ones. A word that has much more of childish character.

The Negro nurse did very often with words what she did with food: she mashed them, removed the bones, took away their hardness, and left them as soft and pleasing syllables in the mouth of the white child. For this reason Portuguese as spoken in the north of Brazil, principally, is one of the most melodious forms of speech to be found anywhere in the world. Without double *r*'s or double *s*'s; the final syllables soft; the words all but chewed up in the mouth. The language of the Brazilian young, and the same is true of Portuguese children, has a flavor that is almost African: *cacá* (excrement); *pipí* (urine); *bumbum* (a buzz); *tenten* or *tem-tem* (the motions a child makes in learning to walk); *nenem* (a child); *tatá* (daddy); *papá*; *papato* (shoe); *lili* and *mimi* (personal pronouns); *au-au* (a dog); *bambanho* (bath); *cocó* (excrement); *dindinho* (godfather or grandfather); *bimbinha* (child's penis). This softening effect was largely due to the influence of the Negro nurse over the child, of the black slave over the white master's son. Proper names are among those that show this softening most; they lose their solemnity and are charmingly dissolved in the mouth of the slave. The Antônias become Dondons; Tonhinhas, Totonhas; the Teresas, Tetés; the Manuels: Nezinhos, Mandús, Manés; the Franciscos: Chico, Chiquinho, Chicó; the Pedros, Pepés; the Albertos: Bebetos, Betinhos. This is not to speak of the Iaiás, the Iaiós, the Sinhás, the Manús, Calús, Bembems, Dedés, Marocas, Nocas, Nonocas, Gegês.[190]

And it was not merely the language of children that was softened in this fashion, but the language in general, the serious, dignified speech of adults; the idiom as a whole in Brazil, through the contact of master with slave, went through a softening process, the results of which at times are extremely pleasant to the ear. The English and French languages, in other parts of America, were similarly influenced by the African Negro and by the hot climate, but principally by the Negro. In the Antilles and in Louisiana, "*bonnes vieilles négresses*" took away the harshness from the French, the unpleasing

---

[190] These are all familiar terms of endearment or personal nicknames. (Translator.)

nasal sound and the trilled *r*'s; while in the Southern United States "old mammies"[191] gave to the rough and grating English syllables an oily smoothness. In the streets of New Orleans, in its old restaurants, one may still hear the names of cakes, sweets, and other dishes in a French that is more lyric than that of France: *"pralines de pacanes," "bon café tout chaud," "blanches tablettes à fleur d'oranger."* The influence of those *"bonnes vieilles négresses."*

Caldcleugh, who was in Brazil early in the nineteenth century, was delighted with colonial Portuguese. A Portuguese grown fat and lazy. He quickly was able to distinguish it from that of the metropolis. The pronunciation of Brazilians impressed him as being less nasal than that of the Portuguese themselves, and "not so Jewish" in the manner of pronouncing the *s*'s; "and on the whole is a more agreeable language than in the mouth of a native."[192] A fact that Caldcleugh attributes wholly to the climate, the heat of the tropics. The climate appeared to him to confer upon the speech of Brazilians, as upon their mental activity, a high degree of lassitude. It is curious, however, that while he is so attentive to the influence of the Jews upon the pronunciation of the letter *s* in Portugal, Caldcleugh does not note the Negro influence upon the Portuguese of Brazil, although the blacks were greater enemies than the climate to the double *r*'s and double *s*'s and were greater corrupters of the tongue so far as its languid quality is concerned. Negro mothers and slave girls, allies of the lads and lasses, the young ladies of the Big Houses, created a Portuguese that was different from the stiff and grammatical tongue that the Jesuits endeavored to teach to the young Indian and semi-white pupils in their schools: the Portuguese of the Realm, which the padres dreamed of preserving intact in Brazil. After them, but with less rigor, the priestly schoolmasters and plantation chaplains sought to counteract the influence of the slaves by setting over against the latter's idiom what one might call a hothouse Portuguese. Their efforts were in vain, however.

While it may have failed, this attempt on the part of the Jesuits contributed, meanwhile, to that disparity to which I have already alluded between the written and the spoken language in Brazil, with the written idiom withdrawing like a scrupulous old maid from the slightest contact with the speech of the people, the language in current use. There were even, for a time, two spoken tongues: one of

---

[191] The words are in English. (Translator.)

[192] Alexander Caldcleugh: *Travels in South America during the Years* *1819–1820–21, Containing an Account of the Present State of Brazil, Buenos Aires and Chili* (London, 1825).

the Big Houses, the other of the slave huts. But the alliance of Negro nurse and white child, of slave girl and young mistress, of young master and slave lad, ended by doing away with this double character. For it was not possible to separate by the glass shards of the purist's prejudices two forces that were in the habit of fraternizing so frequently and so intimately. In the relaxed atmosphere of Brazilian slavery the African tongues, without any motive for continuing a separate existence in opposition to the language of the whites, became dissolved in the latter, enriching it with expressive modes of speech and with a whole set of delightfully picturesque terms that were new and untamed in flavor and that, many times, advantageously replaced Portuguese words that were worn and spoiled with usage. Let João Ribeiro tell it, for he is an authority on Portuguese and the history of the national idiom: "A large number of African words made their way into the Portuguese language, especially in Brazil, as a result of the relations set up with the Negro races." Nor was it merely single, disconnected words that were added to the tongue of the European colonizer; there took place also alterations "sufficiently profound, not only with respect to vocabulary, but even with regard to the grammar of the language." [193]

It is true that the differences that came to separate, more and more, Brazilian Portuguese from the language of Portugal were not, all of them, the result of the African influence, but of that of the native as well; that "of the gypsies"; that "of the Spaniards"; and, Ribeiro adds: "of the climate, of new necessities, new perspectives, new things, and new industries." But no influence was greater than the Negro's. The African words that are now in daily use, words in

[193] João Ribeiro: *Dicionário Gramatical contendo em resumo as materiais que se referem ao estudo histórico-comparativo* (*Grammatical Dictionary, Containing a Summary of Materials Relating to Comparative-Historical Studies*) (Rio de Janeiro, 1889). See also, regarding the influence of the African tongues on Brazilian Portuguese, the paper by A. J. de Macedo Soares: "*Estudos Lexicográficos do Dialeto Brasileiro*" ("Lexicographical Studies of the Brazilian Dialect"), *Revista Brasileira*, Vol. IV (Rio de Janeiro, 1880).—Among recent works may be noted: that of Jacques Raimundo: *O Elemento Afro-Negro na Lingua Portuguesa* (*The African Negro Element in the Portuguese Language*) (Rio de Janeiro, 1933); and the one by Renato Mendonça: *A Influência Africana no Português do Brasil* (*The African Influence in Brazilian Portuguese*) (Rio de Janeiro, 1933).—A notable contribution to these studies is one by Professor Mário Marroquim: *A Lingua do Nordeste—Alagoas e Pernambuco* (*The Language of the Northeast—Alagoas and Pernambuco*) (São Paulo, 1934). Mário Marroquim protests against "bilingualism within a single idiom" and against grammatical rules "based on linguistic facts isolated from man."

connection with which we are not aware of any unpleasant or exotic flavor, are innumerable. Those persons who are less puristic, when writing or when speaking in public, no longer have any feeling of shame in employing them as once was the case. It is just as if these words had come to us from Portugal, in dictionaries and in classics, with a Latin, Greek, or Arabic genealogy, with an illustrious father or mother. Yet all the while they are orphans, without definite parentage, words that we have adopted from the Negro dialects that have no history and no literature, words that we have permitted to come up, along with the slave lads and Negro women, from the slave huts to the Big Houses. What Brazilian—in the north, at any rate—is conscious of any exoticism in such words as: *caçamba, canga, dengo, cafuné, lubambo, mulambo, caçula, quitute, mandinga, muleque, camondongo, muganga, cafajeste, quibebe, quengo, batuque, banzo, mucambo, banguê, bozo, mocotó, bunda, zumbi, vatapá, carurú, banzé, jilo, mucama, quindim, catinga, mugunza, malungo, birimbau, tanga, cachimbo, candomblé?* [194] What better way could be found of saying a "bad smell" or "stench" than "*catinga*"? Or would one say "*garoto*" (wag or blackguard) in preference to "*muleque*"? Or "*trapo*" for "clout" or "rag" in place of "*mulambo*"? These are words that are better suited than the Portuguese ones to our experience, to our palate, to our senses, and to our emotions.

The padre schoolmasters and the plantation chaplains, who, after

---

[194] For those interested, the meanings of the words in this list are herewith given: *caçamba*, a bucket in a well; *canga*, a wallet or pouch; *dengo*, affected, presumptuous; *cafuné*, the gesture of snapping one's fingernails on the head of another person; *lubambo*, a fracas or plot; *mulambo*, a rag or clout; *caçula*, youngest son; *quitute*, a dainty confection; *mandinga*, sorcery or witchcraft; *muleque* (*moleque*), young Negro, comes to mean a wag or blackguard; *camondongo*, a mouse; *muganga*, (*moganga*), a grimace, contortion; *cafajeste*, person of low condition or with bad manners; *quibebe*, edible gourd paste; *quengo*, vessel made of half a coconut shell; *batuque*, Negro dance; *banzo*, the melancholy nostalgia typical of Negroes; *mucambo* (*mocambo*), a hut or shack; *banguê*, a litter, sugar canal, sugar plantation; *bozo*, a form of dice game; *mocotó*, a plant of the *Acanthaceæ* family (*Elytroria alagoana*); *bunda*, buttock; *zumbi*, a night-goblin; *vatapá*, paste made of manihot flour; *carurú*, one of the plants of the *Amarantaceæ* family; *banzé*, a rumpus; *jilo*, fruit of the *jileiro*, a garden plant of the *Solanaceæ* family (*Solanum melangena* Dum.); *mucama*, a favored slave girl employed in the Big House; *quindim*, amorous longing, also a sweetmeat made of egg-yolk, coconut, and sugar; *catinga*, a bad smell, stench; *mugunzá*, a dish made of corn and milk; *malungo*, comrade, playmate; *birimbau*, a despicable, low person; *tanga*, slave-garment worn from the waist to the knees; *cachimbo*, pipe (for smoking); *candomblé*, African fetishistic ceremony. (Translator.)

the Jesuits had withdrawn, became the principals responsible for the education of Brazilian children, attempted to react against the engulfing wave of Negro influence that was mounting from the slave huts to the Big Houses, exerting a more powerful effect upon the language of the young masters and young mistresses, the *sinhô-moços* and the *sinhazinhas*, than they, the padres, were able to do with all their Latin and with all their grammar, with all the authority of their quince-tree switches and their ferules of sicupira-wood.[195] Frei Miguel do Sacramento Gama was one of those who waxed indignant when he heard "gallant little girls" saying *"mandá," "buscá," "comé,"* in place of *mandar, buscar,* and *comer;* when he heard them saying *"mi espere," "ti faço," "mi deixe,"* instead of *"espere-me," "faço-te," "deixe-me";* when they said *"muler"* for *"mulher," "coler,"* for *"colher,"* or employed such expressions as *"le pediu," "cadê ele"* (for *"onde está ele"*), *"vigie," "espie,"* and the like.[196] And let some lad but utter in his presence a *"pru mode"* or an *"oxente,"* and he would see what a rap he would get from the knuckles of the angry friar.

For Friar Miguel—a padre schoolmaster if there ever was one—believed that it was from illustrious and polished Portuguese models that we should learn to speak, and not "with Aunty Rosa" nor "Mammy Benta," not with any black woman of the kitchen or the *senzala*. Young lads and young lasses ought to shut their ears to the *"oxentes"* and the *"mi deixe's"* and acquire a correct Portuguese, that of the Realm. He would have nothing to do with Bunda or Caçanje expressions.[197]

What happened, however, was that the Portuguese language neither yielded wholly to the corrupting influence of the slave huts in the direction of a greater spontaneity of expression, nor shut itself off completely in the drawing-rooms of the Big Houses under the stern eye of the padres. It was from an interpenetration of the two tendencies that our national language resulted; and it is to the "Mammy Bentas" and the "Aunty Rosas" that we owe it, as well as

---

[195] "Name common to two trees of the *Leguminosæ* family: *Ormosia* or *Rubinia coccinea* and *Ormosia coarctata* or *minor*."—Lima and Barroso, op. cit. (Translator.)

[196] Padre Miguel do Sacramento Lopes Gama: *O Carapuceiro* (Recife, 1832-4, '37, '43, and '47).

[Father Lopes Gama was a pamphleteer; cf. p. 270, Note 197. The modes of expression cited here were

looked upon as plebeianisms. Thus, *"pru mode"* was a vulgar form for *para;* "oxente" was a popular exclamation of surprise, mixed sometimes with disdain; etc.) (Translator.)

[197] *Bunda* is the language spoken by the natives of Angola; *Caçanje* is the Creole Portuguese dialect spoken by the same natives; comes to mean bad Portuguese. (Translator's Note.)

to the Padre Gamas and the Padre Pereiras. Brazilian Portuguese, linking the Big Houses to the slave quarters, the slaves to their masters, the slave girls to the young masters, became enriched with a variety of antagonisms that is lacking to the language as spoken in Europe. One example, and one of the most expressive, that occurs to me is in connection with pronouns. We have in Brazil two ways of placing them, where the Portuguese admits only one—the "stern and imperative mode": [198] *diga-me, faça-me, espere-me.*[199] Without contemning the Portuguese usage, we have created a new one, entirely new and characteristically Brazilian: *me diga, me faça, me espere.* A mild and pleasing way of phrasing a request. And we make use of both ways. Now, these two opposite modes of expression, depending upon the necessities of command or ceremony on the one hand, and, on the other, the degree of intimacy or of supplication, impress me as being typical of the psychological relations that, in the course of the formation of our patriarchal society, were developed between masters and slaves, between young ladies of the Big House and their Negro maids, between whites and blacks. *"Faça-me"* (do this or that) is the master speaking, the father, the patriarch. *"Me dê"* (give me) is the slave, the woman, the son, the housemaid. It is my opinion that the Brazilian way of placing pronouns is largely to be attributed to the slaves in alliance with the young ones of the Big House. This was the familiar, half-childish manner they had found of addressing the paterfamilias. By contrast, the Portuguese mode in the mouth of the master acquired a certain harsh emphasis that today is unpleasing: *"faça-me-isso"* (do this for me), *"dê-me-aquilo"* (give me that). The distinguished scholar João Ribeiro will perhaps permit me to add to his psychological examination of the question of pronouns this historico-cultural interpretation; and at the same time we may take his words as our own: "What interest have we, then, in reducing two formulas to one, in compressing two diverse sentiments into a single expression?"[200] No interest whatsoever. The strength or, better, the potentiality of Brazilian culture appears to me to lie wholly in a wealth of balanced antagonisms; and the case of pronouns may well serve as an example. Are we to follow only the so-called "Portu-

---

[198] João Ribeiro: *A Lingua Nacional* (*The National Tongue*) (São Paulo, 1933). "And this [the Brazilian] is a mode of speaking marked by great gentleness and suavity, whereas, the '*diga-me*' and the '*faça-me*' are stern and imperative."

[199] "Tell me," "do (for) me," "wait for me." (Translator.)

[200] João Ribeiro, op. cit.—The first edition of this essay appeared while João Ribeiro was still living and was received by him warmly and sympathetically in his literary-critical section of the *Jornal do Brasil*.

guese usage," regarding the Brazilian as illegitimate? That would be absurd. That would be to stifle ourselves, or at any rate to stifle the half of our emotional life and sentimental needs—the half of our intelligence, even—which only find a fitting expression in "*me de*" and "*me diga*." It would be to remain with one side of us dead, as we gave expression to but a portion of our being. Not that there exist in the Brazilian, as in the Anglo-American, two enemy halves: the white and the black; the master and the slave. By no manner of means. We are two fraternizing halves that are mutually enriched with diverse values and experiences; and when we round ourselves out into a whole, it will not be with the sacrifice of one element to the other. Lars Ringbom sees great possibilities of development in the mestizo's culture, but only when he reaches the point when one half of his personality no longer endeavors to suppress the other half.[201] Brazil may be said to have reached this point already; the fact that we say "*me diga*," and not exclusively "*diga-me*," is one of the most significant indications; just as is the fact that we now employ African words with the same naturalness as we do Portuguese. Without quotation marks or italics.

The pleasing figure of the Negro nurse who, in patriarchal times, brought the child up, who suckled him, rocked his hammock or cradle, taught him his first words of broken Portuguese, his first "Our Father" and "Hail Mary," along with his first mistakes in pronunciation and grammar, and who gave him his first taste of "*pirão com carne*," or manihot paste with meat, and "*molho de ferrugem*," or "rusty gravy" (a thick gravy made with meat juice) as she mashed his food for him with her own hands—the Negro nurse's countenance was followed by those of other Negroes in the life of the Brazilian of yesterday. That of the Negro lad, companion of games. That of the aged Negro, the teller of tales. That of the house-girl or *mucama*. That of the Negro cook. A whole series of varied contacts bringing new relations to the environment, to life, to the world. Experiences that were realized through the slave or under his influence as guide, accomplice, empiric healer, or corrupter.

I have already, in a previous chapter, referred to the young Negro playmate of the white lad—a playmate and a whipping-boy.[202] His functions were those of an obliging puppet,[203] manipulated at will by the infant son of the family; he was squeezed, mistreated, tormented just as if he had been made of sawdust on the inside—of cloth and

---

[201] Lars Ringbom: *The Renewal of Culture* (translation) (London, n.d.).
[202] See pp. 150–151. (Translator.)

[203] The author once more employs the term *mané-gostoso* (see note 101, preceding). (Translator.)

sawdust, like those Judases on Easter Saturday, rather than of flesh and blood like white children. "As soon as a child begins to crawl," writes Koster, who was so astute an observer of the life of the colonial Big Houses, "a slave of about his own age, and of the same sex, is given to it as a playfellow, or rather as a plaything. They grow up together, and the slave is made the stock upon which the young owner gives vent to passion. The slave is sent upon all errands, and receives the blame for all unfortunate accidents; in fact, the white child is thus encouraged to be overbearing, owing to the false fondness of its parents." [204] "There was not a house where there was not one or more *muleques*, one or more *curumins*, who were the victims specially devoted to the young master's whims." So writes José Verissimo in recalling the days of slavery. "They were horse, whipping-boy, friends, companions, and slaves." [205] And Júlio Bello reminds us of the favorite sport of the plantation lads of a former day: that of mounting horseback on sheep—and lacking sheep, it was the *muleque* who served. Their games were often brutal ones, and the Negro boys served every purpose; they were cart-oxen, saddle-horses, beasts for turning the millstone, and burros for carrying litters and heavy burdens. But especially cart-horses. To this day, in those rural regions that have been less invaded by the automobile, and where the plantation cabriolet still rolls along over the fertile topsoil, between the fields of sugar-cane, there may be seen small white lads playing horse-and-buggy, "with Negro boys and even little Negro girls, the daughters of their nurses," between the shafts.[206] A bit of packing-twine serves as the reins and a shoot of the guava tree as a whip.

It is to be presumed that the psychic repercussion upon adults of such a type of childish relationship should be favorable to the development of sadistic and masochistic tendencies. It was chiefly the child of feminine sex that displayed a sadistic bent, owing to the greater fixity and monotony in the relations of mistress and slave girl. It was even to be wondered at, as Koster wrote at the beginning of the nineteenth century, "that so many excellent women should be found among them," and it was "by no means strange that the disposition of some of them should be injured by this unfortunate direction

---

[204] Henry Koster: *Travels in Brazil* (op. cit.).

[205] José Verissimo: *A Educação Nacional* (*National Education*) (Rio de Janeiro).

[206] Antiogenes Chaves: "*Os Esportes em Pernambuco*" ("Sports and Games in Pernambuco"), Rio de Janeiro, *O Jornal*, special Pernambuco edition, 1928.

of their infant years." [207] Without contacts with the world that would modify in them, as in boys, the perverted sense of human relationships; with no other perspective than that of the slave hut as seen from the veranda of the Big House, these ladies still preserved, often, the same evil dominion over their housemaids as they had exercised over the little Negro girls who had been their playmates as children. "They are born, bred, and continue surrounded by slaves without receiving any check, with high notions of superiority, without any thought that what they do is wrong." It is again Koster speaking of the Brazilian senhoras.[208] What was more, they frequently flew into fits of rage, shouting and screaming from time to time. Fletcher and Kidder, who were in Brazil in the middle of the nineteenth century, attributed the strident, disagreeable voices of the women of our country to this habit of always shouting out their orders to slaves.[209] For that matter, they might have observed the same thing in the South of the United States, which underwent social and economic influences so similar to those that acted upon Brazil under the regime of slave labor. Even today, owing to the effect of generations of slave-holding ancestors, the young ladies of the Carolinas, of Mississippi and Alabama, are in the habit of shouting just as the daughters and granddaughters of plantation-owners do in northeastern Brazil.

As to the mistresses' being more cruel than the masters in their treatment of the slaves, that is a fact generally to be observed in slave-owning societies, and is one that is confirmed by our chroniclers, by foreign travelers, by folklore, and by tradition. There are not two or three but many instances of the cruelty of the ladies of the Big House toward their helpless blacks. There are tales of *sinhá-moças* who had the eyes of pretty *mucamas* gouged out and then had them served to their husbands for dessert, in a jelly-dish, floating in blood that was still fresh. Tales of young baronesses of adult age who out of jealousy or spite had fifteen-year-old mulatto girls sold off to old libertines. There were others who kicked out the teeth of their women slaves with their boots, or who had their breasts cut off, their nails drawn, or their faces and ears burned. A whole series of tortures.

And the motive, almost always, was jealousy of the husband. Sexual rancor. The rivalry of woman with woman.

"Among us," wrote Burlamaqui, in the early years of the last cen-

---

[207] Koster, op. cit.
[208] Ibid.
[209] J. C. Fletcher and D. P. Kidder: *Brazil and the Brazilians* (op. cit.).—

The same observation had been made by Saint-Hilaire, in the slave-holding zones of southern Brazil at the beginning of the nineteenth century.

tury, "the most common phrases, when a woman is suspicious of her husband or her lover, are: 'I'll have her fried, I'll roast her alive, I'll burn her, or I'll cut out such and such a part,' etc. And how many times are these threats even put into execution, and all because of a mere suspicion!" [210] Anselmo da Fonseca, writing half a century later, stresses the cruelty of the "slave-owning Brazilian women" who "take a delight in exercising an iron-handed tyranny over them [the female slaves], under the most afflicting of conditions; for the victims are obliged to be constantly at their mistress's side and to live at the feet of their executioner." As an example, Fonseca cites the case of D. F. de C., who carried her cruelty toward her women slaves to such an extent that legal proceedings were instituted against her, following the death of one of them, Joana by name.[211]

The Arabic isolation in which Brazilian women lived in former years, and, above all, the mistresses of the sugar plantations, with passive slave girls as practically their only companions, and the Mussulman-like submission of the woman to her husband, who was always timidly addressed as "Senhor," afforded, it may be, powerful stimuli to sadism, the *sinhás* revenging themselves on the *mucamas* and *mulecas* in the form of hysterical outbursts. What they were doing was "passing it along," as is done in certain brutal games; for, in the first place, it was the husbands who were sadists in their relations with their wives.

The padre schoolmaster Lopes Gama wondered quite as much as did the Englishman Koster at the fact that Brazilian women, growing up amid "the crudeness, the shamelessness, the licentiousness, and the disordered conduct of the slaves . . . the floggings, the blows that the latter received almost daily from our forebears," should still be as virtuous and as delicate as they were. "It may even be maintained that the Brazilian women are the most inclined of all to the virtues; since having viewed from their childhood so many examples of lubricity, there has still grown up among them so large a number of respectable, truly honorable ladies. What would they be like if they had had a delicate and careful upbringing?" [212]

It is true that there were cases of sexual irregularity between mis-

---

[210] F. L. C. B. (Frederico Leopoldo Cesar Burlamaqui): *Memória Analýtica Acerca do Commercio d'Escravos e Acerca da Escravidão Doméstica* (*Memoir on the Slave Trade and Domestic Slavery*) (Rio de Janeiro, 1837).

[211] L. Anselmo da Fonseca: *A Escravidão, o Clero e o Abolicionismo* (*Slavery, the Clergy, and Abolitionism*) (Bahia, 1887).

[212] Padre Lopes Gama: *O Carapuceiro* (op. cit.).

tresses and their male slaves. There was one said to have occurred in Pernambuco in the middle of the last century, and in the bosom of an important family. We are assured by an old plantation-owner that he himself saw a report of the matter in a private document replete with convincing details. But neither rural traditions, nor the accounts of trustworthy foreigners, nor the criticisms, which are frequently nothing more than libels, of cynical gossips of the stamp of Father Lopes Gama, would authorize us to accept the statement of M. Bomfim, in his *América Latina*, to the effect that "not infrequently the young mistress, who has been brought up to rub against the sturdy slave lads (*mulecotes*), yields herself to them when her nerves give way to her irrepressible desires. Then it is that paternal morality intervenes; the Negro or mulatto is castrated with a dull knife, the wound is sprinkled with salt, and he is then buried alive. As for the lass, with an increased dowry, she is married off to a poor cousin. . . ."[213]

It is not that paternal despotism in the days of slavery appears to me to have been incapable of such wickedness as this and even worse crimes; nor am I denying that the *iaiás*, the young ladies of the Big House, were often endowed with a morbid sensibility and lubricious desires; but the very environment in which they were reared rendered such adventures extremely difficult. That "not infrequently" of M. Bomfim sounds to me artificial, or at least exaggerated. We have but to recall the fact that during the day the white girl of whatever age was always under the eye of an older person or a trusted *mucama*, and this vigilance was redoubled during the night. A small room or bedroom was reserved for her in the center of the house, and she was surrounded on all four sides by her elders. It was more of a prison than the apartment of a free being. A kind of sick-room, where everyone had to keep watch. Do not misunderstand me: I am not praising the system; I am merely reminding my readers that it was incompatible with such adventures as those that M. Bomfim relates.

It may be objected that sex is an all-powerful thing, once it is unleashed; and this is something that I would by no means deny. The obstacle that I am recognizing is, rather, a physical one: that of the thick walls, the true convent bars behind which young ladies of the Big Houses were guarded. It was here that their bridegrooms would come for them in marriage when they reached the age of thirteen to fifteen years. There was, accordingly, no time for great passions to

[213] Manuel Bomfim: *América Latina* (1903).

develop in the young bodies of these little girls; and what passion they knew was to be quickly satiated, or simply stifled, in the patriarchal marriage-chamber. Stifled beneath the caresses of husbands ten, fifteen, twenty years older than their brides and very often utter strangers to them. Husbands who had been chosen solely to suit the parents' convenience. University bachelors, their mustaches glistening with brilliantine, a ruby on their finger,[214] and a political career ahead of them. Or Portuguese merchants, big and fat, with enormous whiskers and huge stones on their shirt-bosoms, their wrists, and their fingers. Officials. Physicians. Plantation-owners. Yet these marriages made by parents did not invariably result in domestic dramas or unhappiness. Possibly for the reason that the husbands of a riper age and with cool heads envisaged the problem with more realism and better practical sense than romantically impassioned young men would have been able to show.

True, the parents, in their choice of husbands for their daughters, were not always obeyed. There are traditions that tell of cases—rare ones, to be sure—of brides being abducted and of romantic elopements. Sellin asserts that, from the middle of the nineteenth century on, these cases became more numerous.[215] In them there always figured a Negro or *mucama*—an accomplice of either the abductor or the one abducted—whom it was the custom to set free for his or her services. It was through the complicity of an experienced *mucama* that a pretty young daughter of the C—— family in Pernambuco eloped in the early 1860's. The elopement occurred on the eve of her marriage to a distinguished gentleman of her parents' choice. The parents promptly offered the deceived bridegroom the hand of their other daughter, which was at once accepted, and as a result the marriage ceremony took place quietly enough, with no further incident to mar it.

It is a well-known fact that the *mucamas* attained an enormous prestige in the sentimental life of the *sinhazinhas*. It was through the trusted Negro or mulatto woman that the young girl was initiated into the mysteries of love. In the middle of the nineteenth century the celebrated novelist Joaquim Manuel de Macedo, author of *The*

---

[214] The university ring; see p. 233. (Translator.)

[215] A. W. Sellin: . *Geografia Geral do Brasil* (*General Geography of Brazil*), (translation) (Rio de Jeneiro, 1889).—This is confirmed, with respect to Pernambuco, by D. Flora Cavalcanti da Oliveira Lima, who is intimately acquainted with the social history of the region, and who supplied me with personal data on the subject.

Little Brunette,[216] observed that "the slave girl known as a *mucama*, although a slave, is at the same time more than the young lady's father-confessor or her physician; for the father-confessor knows only her soul, and the physician, in cases where her health has been seriously affected, knows only her ailing body, and that imperfectly; whereas the *mucama* knows her soul as well as the padre and her body better than the doctor."

On hot days the long hours of gentle lassitude would be filled with stories of love and marriage and other less romantic but equally fascinating tales told by the *mucamas* to the *sinhazinhas*, as the latter sat, Moorish fashion, upon a pipiri mat, sewing or engaged in lace-work; or else the young lady would lie stretched out in the hammock, her hair down, as the Negro maid snapped her fingernails through it, searching for lice; [217] or perhaps the girl would keep the flies away from her mistress's face with a fan. This made up for the lack of reading in an aristocracy that was practically illiterate. It was with the *mucamas*, too, that the white girls learned to sing the airs of the day, those colonial *modinhas* that were so imbued with the eroticism of the Big Houses and the slave huts—with the passionate longings of the young masters, or *ioiôs*, for the fragrant mulatto maids or for little white cousins—voluptuous songs, of which Eloy Pontes has given us one example that is highly expressive of the love between whites and blacks:

> *My little white charmer,*
> *Sweet master, my brother,*
> *Your captive adores you,*
> *You and none other.*
> *For you say "little sister"*
> *To a black girl like me,*
> *Who trembles with pleasure,*
> *So happy is she.*
> *At nightfall you go fishing,*
> *Little master, so sweet;*
> *You send piau and corvina*
> *For the little black girl to eat.*[218]

---

[216] The famous work *A Moreninha*, which has delighted generations of Brazilians and is still a best-seller today. (Translator.)

[217] The gesture known as *cafuné*. (Translator.)

[218] *Meu branquinho feiticeiro,*
Doce ioiô meu irmão,
Adoro teu cativeiro,
Branquinho de coração.
Pois tu chamas de irmãzinha
A tua pobre negrinha
Que estremece de prazer,
E vais pescar à tardinha
Mandí, piau e corvina
Para a negrinha comer.

Piau (*piaba*) is a river fish, the *Leporinus copelandi* Steind. The

In none of the other old *modinhas* does one so get the feeling of promiscuity in the relations of the young masters of the Big Houses with the little mulatto girls of the slave huts, relations that were at times marked by an unpleasant trace of incest; for it is possible that, in certain cases, the white son and the mulatto daughter of the same father made love to each other. Walsh, in his travels in Brazil, came upon one family that was openly incestuous: a brother who was having an affair with a sister.[219] And in Mantiqueira he witnessed a dance in which the members of a certain mestizo family revealed lamentably incestuous habits that scandalized the English priest.

The truth is that an extreme case of incest was not needed in order to scandalize him; those marriages, so common in our country since the first century of colonization, of uncle with niece and cousin with cousin were quite sufficient. These were marriages the obvious purpose of which was to prevent the dispersal of property and to preserve the purity of a blood-stream of noble or illustrious origin. Everything indicates that this was the objective of Jeronymo de Albuquerque, patriarch of the Pernambucan family of that name, in marrying off his first two sons—whom he had had by Dona Maria do Espírito Santo Arcoverde, the little Indian princess—to the sisters of their lawful mother, Dona Felippa de Mello, daughter of Dom Christovão de Mello.[220] Dona Felippa was the woman whom Her Majesty Dona Catherina, horrified at the polygamous, Mussulman-like way of life that was led by Duarte Coelho's brother-in-law, had recommended to him as his bride. However, these were not so much consanguineous marriages as they were unions on the part of individuals who, by so marrying, sought to draw tighter the bonds of family solidarity round the figure of the patriarch. That was the true purpose of the matings of uncles with nieces.

Maria Graham was charmed by certain aspects of family life in Brazil: by an affection, an intimacy, a solidarity between persons of the same blood that reminded her of the spirit of the Scotch clans. But she noted this unpleasant circumstance: that the marriages took place between relatives, and especially between uncles and nieces. These, she wrote, were marriages that, instead of broadening family

---

smaller varieties are commonly used only for bait. (*Piau* is the name given to the larger varieties.) *Corvina* (*corvo*, a crow) is the name of three fish of the Sciænidæ family, so called from their black fins. (Translator.)

[219] R. Walsh: *Notices of Brazil in 1828 and 1829* (London, 1830), p.

164. [An edition of Walsh's work was published at Boston in 1831. (Translator.)]

[220] José Victoriano Borges de Fonseca: *Nobiliarchia Pernambucana*, 1776–1777 (*Pernambucan Peerage*) (Rio de Janeiro, 1935), Vol. I, p. 9.

relationships and distributing property, tended to concentrate the latter in a few hands and to narrow and limit the former. In addition to being, as she observes, prejudicial to health.[221]

But the one who raises his voice in indignation against consanguineous marriages in Brazil, and against the Church and its priests for permitting them, is Captain Richard Burton. "Dispensations to commit incest," is what he calls the Church's rulings in this regard. He confesses, however, that he has not come upon cases in which the "terrible results" of this horrifying sin are revealed.[222] It is not that Burton—an English free-thinker, although he was married to a rock-ribbed wife with very strict ideas—harbored any belief in sin in the theological sense; it was merely that he was convinced of the ill effects, from the eugenic point of view, of marriages of this sort.

One thing that marriages between relatives, so common in Brazil in the days of slavery, did not succeed in preventing was those tremendous feuds that separated cousins and even brothers, sons-in-law and fathers-in-law, uncles and nephews, and made of them mortal enemies. They did not prevent great families from waging open warfare over questions of inheritance and lands, and at times from motives of honor or partisan politics: a stretch of canebrake, a woman, a slave, an ox, a disputed election. In the eighteenth century Andreoni (André João Antonil) wrote: "There are in Brazil many regions in which the plantation-owners are united among themselves by blood and but little united by charity, self-interest being the cause of all the discord; all that is needed is a stick of wood removed or an ox strayed into a cane field, and the slumbering hatred breaks out, leading to lawsuits and deadly quarrels." [223] But all this is inseparable from a system of private ownership, with its exaggerated sense of personal property, which begins by creating bloody rivalries between neighbors—the great landowners—and ends in the Balkanization of continents.

Colonial chronicles have preserved an account of the feuds in which the Pires and Camargos engaged in São Paulo; and in the nineteenth century the conflict between the Montes and the Feitosas in the northeast was a terrible one.[224] As for the slaves, they always fought loyally and valiantly on their master's side, giving their lives when necessary. In the time of the Empire, with its inter-party rival-

---

[221] Maria Graham: *Journal of a Voyage to Brazil*, etc. (op. cit.), p. 226.

[222] Burton: *Explorations of the Highlands of the Brazil* (op. cit.).

[223] André João Antonil: *Cultura e Opulência do Brasil*, etc. (op. cit.).

[224] These are all famous family names in Brazil. (Translator.)

ries, the Negroes of the slave huts as well as the whites of the Big Houses were divided into "liberals" and "conservatives" and participated in the election brawls by wounding, slashing, and clubbing one another.

The feud between the Pires and the Camargos broke out in 1640 and was prolonged for more than a century, other families being drawn into· it: the Taques, the Lemes, the Larus, on the Pires side; and the Buenos and the Rendons on the side of the Camargos.[225] In these great family struggles, Indians with bow and arrow took part, along with Negro slaves and *cabras*. It was in the course of such conflicts that our colored *bravi* were developed: the *cabras*, Negroes, *caboclos*, whose task at first was to defend the Big Houses against attacks by Indians, and who afterwards served in the wars against the Dutch, in the expeditions against the runaway-slave colonies, or *quilombos*, and in the war with Paraguay. It was they who gave force to the spirit of order represented by planters of the type of Morgado do Cabo, against the demagogy of the cities; to the spirit of Brazilian independence against the Portuguese who undertook to administer Brazil as a mere plantation colony. It was, however, not only the colored *bravi*—the "Swiss of America," as an Argentine official once called the Negroes of the *estâncias*[226] and slaughterhouses of southern Brazil[227]—it was not only the slaves who participated in these struggles; but their white masters as well, their fearless and fear-inspiring leaders. *Condottieri*, that is what they were. Leaders of the stamp of Pedro Ortiz de Camargo, who served notice on the Portuguese Governor of Rio de Janeiro that his presence in São Paulo was not needed. Leaders like those Pernambucan planters who in 1666 had the audacity to lay hands upon the fourth Governor and captain-general, in the rua de São Bento, and to expel him from the *capitânia* and send him back to the Realm. Leaders like Antônio Cavalcanti, Vidal de Negreiros, and Fernandes Vieira—men who won the war against the Dutch almost single-handed, with their own Negroes and *cabras* and without aid from the metropolis.[228]

---

[225] Affonso de E. Taunay: *Sob El-Rey Nosso Senhor* (op. cit.).

[226] An *estância* is a ranch or country estate. Cf. *fazenda*. (Translator.)

[227] Nicolau Dreys: *Noticia Descríptiva da Província do Rio Grande do São Pedro do Sul* (*Descriptive Account of the Province of Rio Grande do Sul*) (Rio de Janeiro, 1839).

[228] A seventeenth-century Dutch account stresses the resistance that was offered the invaders by the people of the land: "*Moradores, Mulatten, Mamalucquen, Brazilianen, als Negros*" ("Inhabitants, mulattoes, mamelucos, Brazilians, and Negroes"). —Account by Schonemburgh and Haecks: *Saken van Staet en Oorlogh, in ende Ontrent de Veroenidge Ne-*

But to come back to the plantation songs of Brazil—those songs that were an expression of patriarchal eroticism, of passionate longings for Negro women, mulatto girls, and white cousins—we may recall the fact that they created a furor in Portuguese salons of the eighteenth century, where they alternated with novenas, *laus perennes*,[229] and feasts of the Church. William Beckford, who had an opportunity to hear them in a nobleman's house that was frequented by the Archbishop of Algarve, Dom José Maria de Mello—a great fancier of *modinhas* and fond of hearing them sung to the strains of the viol—endeavored to give an interpretation of their haunting charm: "With a childish carelessness they steal into the heart, before it has time to arm itself against their enervating influence; you fancy you are swallowing milk, and are admitting the poison of voluptuousness into the closest recesses of your existence."[230]

Not all the *modinhas* celebrated the amorous longings (*quindim*) of the mulatto girls of the slave huts; many of them were devoted to praising the young ladies of the Big House, the planter's daughters. These were small lasses of twelve, thirteen, fourteen years. "Blonde angels." "Immaculate saints." "Pale Madonnas." "Heavenly Marias." "Marias of Grace." "Marias of the Pangs." "Marias of Glory." And they were, indeed, so many Our Ladies, and would step from their palanquin or litter, borne on the shoulders of liveried Negroes, as if they were descending from a processional bier. Gold earrings, jewels and trinkets, amulets. At times *mucamas* would go on before, bearing other earrings and other jewels of their young mistresses; and so great was the weight of gold that some of these slaves carried, in the form of chains, armbands, bracelets, and holy medals, that "without hyperbole," as Vilhena says, "it was enough to buy two or three Negro or mulatto women."[231] From the day of their first communion the little girls ceased to be children and became young ladies. It was a great day, greater than the day of their marriage. A long white gown, set off with flounces and pleats, the bodice likewise pleated. A fillet of blue ribbon with three long streamers behind that fell down over the robe. An alms-purse of taffeta. Lace veil. Orange-flower garlands on

---

derlanden, *Regions Beginnende met het Jaer 1645, nde enyndigende met het Jaer 1658* (The Hague, 1669).

229 *Laus perenne*: "the continual reading of psalms and other prayers in some churches; perpetual adoration of the sacrament."—H. Michaelis: *A New Dictionary of the Portuguese*

and English Languages (Leipzig, 1932). (Translator.)

230 William Beckford: *Italy, with Sketches from Spain and Portugal* (London, 1834).

231 Luis dos Santos Vilhena: *Recompilação de Notícias Soteropolitanas e Brasílicas* (op. cit.).

their heads. Satin slippers. Kid gloves. Prayerbook bound in mother-of-pearl. Rosary with a gold chain and crucifix of gold.

The prayerbook they were not always able to read. Early in the nineteenth century Tollenare observed that "there are many parents who do not wish their daughters to learn to read and write."[232] But the parents of others would entrust them to the retreats, where they learned to read, to sew, and to pray. In the retreat that the great Bishop, Azeredo Coutinho, founded in Pernambuco—that of Our Lady of Glory—they also learned to deal with slaves in a Christian manner, as "brothers and sisters of the same father." The "necessities of some and the slavery of others, imposed by human laws, or as a penalty for their crimes, or by way of preserving them from a greater evil" was the thing that set up this "accidental inequality."[233] Many Brazilian ladies, however, became baronesses and viscountesses under the Empire without ever having seen the inside of a retreat. Some of them were illiterate; others smoked like backwoodsmen, spitting on the ground; while others would have the teeth of female slaves pulled out upon the slightest suspicion that their husbands might be trifling with a Negro woman.

This in the nineteenth century. One can imagine what it must have been like in the other centuries, in the sixteenth, the seventeenth, and the eighteenth. In the eighteenth century an Englishwoman who had come to Brazil found the situation of women to be horrible there. They were ignorant and bigoted and did not even know how to dress. For to judge from what Mrs. Kindersley tells us, and she was no Parisienne herself, our feminine forebears of the seventeenth century must have been clad in a manner that would shame a female monkey: calico skirt, flower-embroidered blouse, velvet bodice, and fillet. And to crown these horrors, much gold, many necklaces, bracelets, combs. The young ladies and little girls were not ugly; but Mrs. Kindersley noted that Brazilian women aged quickly, their faces thereupon turning a sickly yellow.[234]

This, assuredly, was the result of the many sons they bore their husbands, of the morose, melancholy, indolent life they led inside the home; for when they went out, it was only in the hammock, under

[232] Tollenare: *Notas Dominicais,* etc. (op. cit.).

[233] *Estatutos do Recolhimento de Nossa Senhora da Glória* (*Statutes of the Retreat of Our Lady of Glory*), cited by Canon José do Carmo Baratta: "*Um Grande Sábio, um Grande Patriota, um Grande Bispo*" ("A Great Scholar, a Great Patriot, a Great Bishop"), lecture, Pernambuco, 1921.

[234] Mrs. Kindersley: *Letters from the Islands of Teneriff, Brazil, the Cape of Good Hope and the East Indies* (London, 1777).

heavy rugs—*modus gestandi lusitanus,* as Barleus described it in the sixteenth century; [235] or else in the *banguê* or litter, and, in the nineteenth century, in the palanquin or ox-cart. Some ladies even had themselves borne to church in their hammocks, and would enter, haughty and triumphant, carried by their slaves. This was a true affront to the saints, and it became necessary for the bishops to forbid such a show of indolence. "Inasmuch as it appears to us indecent for certain persons of the feminine sex to enter the church in *serpentinas* [236] or hammocks, we hereby forbid such entry." So wrote the Bishop of Pernambuco, Dom Frei José Fialho, in a pastoral letter of February 19, 1726. [237] To judge from what Dom Frei José says about the fashions of Pernambucan women, they did not dress in the apelike manner of those Bahian dames whom Mrs. Kindersley met. The Bishop, rather, saw in their clothes something that was diabolic: "It is not without great sorrow of heart that we behold the profane manner in which the majority of persons of the feminine sex clothe themselves, making use of devilish fashions and inventions; and we hereby admonish such persons that they abstain from such garments." The Pernambucan women in question were descendants of those "great ladies" whom Father Cardim knew in the sixteenth century: "great ladies" rather than devout ones. These latter, plantation mistresses, as far back as the time of the chronicler who wrote the *Dialogues,*[238] were in the habit of painting their faces red. They were the worthy "*iaiás,*" for love of whom the Dutch heretics of the seventeenth century adjured Calvinism to·embrace the Catholic faith.

The custom of women marrying young was general in Brazil. They married at twelve, thirteen, or fourteen years. With an unmarried fifteen-year-old daughter in the house, the parents already began to be worried and to make promises to St. Anthony and St. John. Before she had reached the age of twenty, the girl without a husband was a spinster. Today she would be green fruit, but in those days it was feared that the fruit would spoil from overripeness if no one plucked it in time. A seventeenth-century traveler tells us that in Salvador he found the belief prevalent that "*la fleur de virginité*

[235] Gaspar Barleus: *Rerum per Octennium,* etc. (op. cit.). An excellent Portuguese translation of this celebrated seventeenth-century chronicle dealing with Brazil has been published.

[236] *Serpentina:* "curtained palanquin, the body of which is a hammock."—Lima and Barroso, op. cit. (Translator.)

[237] This pastoral letter is unpublished. From a manuscript in the archives of the Cathedral of Olinda.

[238] The *Diálogos das Grandezas do Brasil,* referred to a number of times previously, attributed to Bento Teixeira Pinto. (Translator.)

doit se cueiller . . . dans les premières années, afin qu'elle ne se flétrisse pas. He also tells us that it was *"fort ordinaire aux mères de questionner leurs filles sur ce qu'elles sont capables de sentir à l'age de douze ou treize ans & de les inviter à faire ce qui peut émousser les aiguillons de la chair."* [239]

With regard to the belief that virginity might lose its flavor, the words of Coreal appear to be exact. Ever since the sixteenth century such a prejudice had prevailed in Brazil. Whoever had a daughter, let him marry her off as young as possible; for after a certain age women do not seem to possess the same attractiveness as virgins or damsels that they do at twelve or thirteen; they no longer have that provocative verdure of small girls which is appreciated by husbands of thirty or forty, and at times of fifty, sixty, or even seventy. Burton states that in the mid-nineteenth century it was still common to marry girls of fifteen to old men of seventy.[240]

Father Anchieta, who, like every sixteenth-century Jesuit, was a great marrying parson, was one day approached by a certain Alvaro Neto who had a daughter who was in a very sad situation: fifteen years old and still single. "Alvaro Neto, an inhabitant of the city of São Paulo, complained grievously to him," says Padre Simão de Vasconcellos, in his *Life of the Venerable Father Joseph de Anchieta of the Society of Jesus,* "stating that he had a daughter who was already fifteen years of age and that he had no way of marrying her." And there is another maiden who appears in the Jesuit chronicle in the same situation as Alvaro Neto's daughter: one Felippa da Matta. This girl had been betrothed to one Joseph Adorno, but the marriage had fallen through and the family was inconsolable. The unfortunate Felippa was perhaps not yet fifteen, and here she was, a pitiable old maid already. But the great missionary instantly consoled both her and her parents. Not only did he prophesy that she would soon be

---

[239] *Voyages de François Coreal, aux Indes Occidentales,* etc. (op. cit.), p. 153.

[240] "Unions between December of seventy and May of fifteen are common and the result is a wife coeval with her grandchildren by marriage," says Burton. This may be verified by the wills and inventories of the first half of the nineteenth century existing in plantation archives and old registry offices. It is also of interest to note the difference in age between husbands and wives in Pernambucan families as revealed in *Uma Estatística* (*A Statistical Study*), by João Francisco Paes Barreto, published in Pernambuco in 1857 and today a very rare item. Such differences as 40 and 20, 23 and 15, 31 and 21, 47 and 20, 57 and 22 are of frequent occurrence. And Walsh writes (op. cit., Vol. II, p. 90), in reference to the Brazil of 1828–9: "Men of sixty frequently marry girls of twelve, and have a family about them where the wife seems the daughter and the little ones the grandchildren."

married to a lad from Lisbon, but that she would live happily ever after: "so many sons that she would not know which shirt belonged to which." [241]

Even today, in the old rural regions, there are folklore reminiscences of these precocious marriages and of the idea that virginity loses its flavor when not plucked green. In the interior of Pernambuco they have a song that runs:

> St. John, marry me quick,
> while I am a lass, do you hear?
> For the corn that is split too late
> Yields neither straw nor ear.[242]

In other parts of Brazil the quatrain varies:

> Mother mine, marry us soon,
> while we are young in years;
> for the corn that is planted late, they say,
> never gives good ears.[243]

Nearly all the travelers who visited us in the days of slavery were in the habit of contrasting the charming freshness of our little girls with the wanness of countenance and the negligence of body of our matrons above the age of eighteen. We have already heard Mrs. Kindersley's opinion; speaking of the married ladies, she observed that "they look old very early in life." Their features lose their delicacy and charm. John Luccock made the same observation in Rio de Janeiro. Sparkling eyes, pretty teeth, sprightly manners—such is the picture that he gives us of the little girls of thirteen and fourteen years. At eighteen they are already matrons, having attained complete maturity. After twenty, a decline.[244] They become fat and flabby, develop a double chin, turn pale, or else they dry and wither. Some of them become as stout and corpulent as the original of a certain old portrait that today is to be seen in the gallery of the Historical Institute of Bahia: they grow more ugly, with down on their faces and with the air of a man or of a virago.

---

[241] Padre Simão de Vasconcellos: *Vida do Veneravel Padre Joseph de Anchieta da Companhia de Iesu* (op. cit.), p. 209.

[242] *Meu São Joao, casai-me cedo,*
enquanto sou rapariga,
que o milho rachado tarde
não dá palha nem espiga.

[243] *Minha mãe, nos casa logo,*
quando somos raparigas:
o milho plantado tarde
nunca dá boas espigas.

[244] John Luccock: *Notes on Rio de Janeiro and the Southern Parts of Brazil, Taken during a Residence of Ten Years in That Country from 1808 to 1818* (London, 1820), p. 112.

In the seventeenth century a Dutch observer noted that the Pernambucan women lost their teeth while they were still young; and owing to their custom of being always seated in the midst of their *mucamas* and Negro women, who did everything for them, they walked "as if they had chains on their legs." [245] They did not display the agility of the Dutch women. Mawe, in the course of his travels in the interior of Brazil, found the same tendency on the part of the women, and especially the young ones, to lose their vivaciousness.[246] Mrs. Graham in Bahia noted that they became "almost indecently slovenly after very early youth." [247]

In the mid-nineteenth century, in southern Brazil, Burton was enchanted witn the women of Minas; but those who impressed him were from thirteen to sixteen years of age. In Minas Geraes, he tells us, there is no "*beauté du diable*," [248] but little girls acquire the charms of young ladies without passing through the phase of puberty that is so unpleasing a one in Europe.

Another who let himself be seduced by the charms of the Brazilian small misses was von den Steinen, who was here in 1885. "An angel of a lass," the German scientist called one of them. An expression worthy of an Olinda bachelor of arts, writing verses to be recited in the ear of the Delilah in his cousin's house. "These Brazilian girls"—it is still the lyric von den Steinen who is speaking—"at the age of twelve to thirteen, when they have just attained puberty and their mother is beginning to think seriously of getting them married, are truly enchanting and ensnaring with their flowerlike beauty." For the man of science there emanated "from these tropical creatures, not yet wholly mature, so delicate, so delightful a fragrance of femininity as our own European rosebuds do not possess." [249] A pity that these half-opened buds had to be deflowered so soon, and their exotic beauty withered while they were yet so young. Too bad that their charms barely lasted until the age of fifteen.

For at that age they were already *sinhá-donas*, married ladies, and some of them were even mothers. They were to be seen at Mass, clad

---

[245] *Breve Discurso sobre o estado das quatro capitânias conquistadas,* etc. (op. cit.), Portuguese translation from the Dutch of a manuscript in the archives of The Hague, published in the *Revista do Instituto Arqueológico, Histórico e Geográfico de Pernambuco,* No. 31.

[246] John Mawe: *Travels in the In-* terior of Brazil (Philadelphia, 1816), p. 208.

[247] Maria Graham, op. cit., p. 135.

[248] Burton, op. cit.

[249] Herbert A. Smith: *Do Rio de Janeiro á Cuiabá (From Rio de Janeiro to Cuiabá),* with a chapter by Karl von den Steinen on the capital of Mato Grosso (Rio de Janeiro, 1922).

in black, weighted down with petticoats, and with their faces concealed by a veil or mantilla, only their eyes being visible—their big mournful eyes. But in the privacy of the home and the company of their husband and *mucamas* they let themselves go. A lace-embroidered smock; slippered feet, no stockings; breasts out, at times. Maria Graham hardly recognized at the theater those senhoras whom she had seen in their homes of a morning, so great was the difference between household dress and ceremonious attire.[250]

These were women who sometimes had nothing to do, unless it was to shout orders at their slaves or play with their parrots, their monkeys, and the little pickaninnies.[251] Others prepared fine desserts for their husbands or spent their time looking after their children. The devout ones would sew on tunics for the Infant Jesus or would embroider cloths for Our Lady's altar. In compensation for this, there were nuns who undertook to do the needlework on trousseaux and christening-robes for the Big Houses.

"Marriages are formed when the parties are very young," the Englishman Alexander Caldcleugh wrote from Brazil; "and it is by no means uncommon to meet with mothers not thirteen years old. The climate and the retired habits of the Brazilian woman have, early in life, a considerable effect on their appearance. When extremely young, the fine dark eyes and full person make them generally admired, but a few years work a change in their appearance, which long continued ill health could scarcely effect in Europe." [252] And Walter Colton, in his travel diary, tells us that they pointed out to him in Rio de Janeiro a child of twelve who was already a respectable married lady.[253] A mother as well! At an age when she should have been playing with her doll, she was laboring in childbirth.

A marriage was one of the most astonishing occasions in our patriarchal life. It was a festival that lasted six or seven days, and at times the abduction of the bride by her groom was simulated. They would prepare with great diligence the "bridal couch"—with pillow-cases,

---

[250] Mawe (op. cit.) likewise notes this disparity between street and house dress in Brazil. James Henderson is another, in *A History of the Brazil* (London, 1821).

[251] The Brazilian *mulequinhos* (diminutive of *muleque*) appears to be equivalent to our "pickaninnies."— The painter J. B. Debret has a picture showing a mistress of the house surrounded by her Negro servants, with two Negro infants playing on the

floor. It will be found reproduced in Donald Pierson's *Negroes in Brazil* (op. cit.), opposite p. 81. See also Debret's painting of a nineteenth-century Brazilian family on the way to church, ibid., opposite p. 76. (Translator.)

[252] Alexander Caldcleugh: *Travels in South America* (op. cit.), p. 65.

[253] Walter Colton: *Deck and Port* (New York, 1850).

counterpanes, sheets, all whimsically embroidered, generally by the hands of nuns; and on the wedding day all these gifts were laid out for the guests to view.[254] They would kill oxen, pigs, turkeys. They would make cakes, sweets, puddings of every sort. And the guests were so many in number that it was necessary on the plantations to erect tents to accommodate them. There would be dancing of the European variety in the Big House, African dances on the lawn. Certain Negroes would be freed as a sign of rejoicing, while others would be given to the bride as a present or a dowry: "so many blacks," "so many houseboys," "one young *cabra*."

It is sad to relate that many of the fifteen-year-old brides died shortly after their marriage, while they were still no more than little girls, almost as they had been on the day of their first communion, without their ever having had the chance to round out into obese matrons and develop a double chin, before they had had time to wither into little old ladies of thirty or forty years. They would die in childbirth—vain all the promises and supplications to Our Lady of Grace or of the Good Birth. Before they had had time to bring up their first son, even; without ever having known what it was like to rock a real child to sleep in place of the rag dolls made for them by the Negro women out of castaway clothes. The little one was then left for the *mucamas* to rear. It was a rare case in which a Brazilian lad was not suckled by a Negro nurse and did not become more accustomed to talking to her than to his own father and mother. It was rarely that he grew up without young Negro lads around him as his playmates. It was from them and from the Negro pantry-girls that he learned obscenity; and it was not long before he lost his virgin purity. Purity of body and purity of mind. His eyes would become two shameless blurs in his face, while his mouth was like that of Maria Sit-by-the-Fire's[255] sisters: nothing came out of it but dung. For all that the young ones talked of was filth—when not of horses and of fighting-cocks and canaries.

---

[254] In contrast to certain weaknesses and even a certain exhibitionism that marked the sexual life of the Brazilian of old, there were instances of an exaggerated discretion or modesty on his part that were truly morbid in character. Husband and wife, for example, never appeared before each other unclothed in the intimacy of the bedroom, and the sexual act took place between them through a coun-terpane with an opening in the center of it. Thus they avoided not only direct contact of body with body, but any show of nudity. One of these counterpanes has been preserved by a woman friend of mine among other relics of the patriarchal order in Brazil.

[255] Maria Borralheira, European folklore character, equivalent to our Cinderella. (Translator.)

This happened to many a lad while his mother was still alive; while she was still lively and energetic and kept busy having depraved Negroes or shameless Negro women punished for teaching her children such things. As for those who had no mother, no stepmother, no grandmother, it can be imagined how they fared; they were left to the *mucamas*, who were by no means capable always of taking a mother's place.

Writing in his journal, *O Capuceiro*, in 1837, the priestly schoolmaster Miguel do Sacramento Lopes Gama had this to say: "To begin with, I am persuaded that slavery, which has unfortunately been introduced among us, is the prime cause of our very bad education; for to tell the truth, who have our teachers been? Unquestionably, the African woman who suckled us, who did our thinking for us, who put the first ideas into our heads; and how many blacks were there, all in all, in the paternal household during our first years? With respect to manners, language, vices, we were wholly inoculated by this uncouth and brutal folk in whom rusticity and savagery are combined with an easy-going indolence and that servility which is the accompaniment of slavery. It was with ignorant blacks, male and female, and their offspring that we lived from the time we opened our eyes; and how, then, could our education have been a good one?" And he goes on: "The companions of our infancy were the pickaninnies born in our father's house, and their mothers were our first teachers; for, many times, the latter either nursed us at their bosoms or else served as our governesses; and what seeds of morality, what virtues would slaves be capable of implanting in our young and tender hearts?" Back in 1823, in his *Representation to the General Constituent Assembly*, José Bonifácio [256] had demanded to know: "What education could families have that make use of these unfortunate beings who are without honor, without religion, families that make use of slave women who prostitute themselves to the first comer? Everything in this life has its compensation. We tyrannize over the slaves, reducing them to brute animals, and they inoculate us with all their immorality and all their vices. And in truth, gentlemen, if the morality and justice of any people is founded partly on its religious and political institutions and partly on the domestic philosophy, so to speak, of each individual family, what picture can Brazil present to the outside world when we consider it from these two

---

[256] José Bonifácio Andrada was— as Freyre calls him a few lines farther on—the patriarch of Brazilian independence in the 1820's. He is one of the outstanding figures in Brazilian history. (Translator.)

points of view?" [257] Five years later the Marquis of Santa Cruz, Archbishop of Bahia, sounded the same note in a speech in Parliament: "Always I am persuaded that the word *slavery* awakens the idea of all vices and all crimes; and always, finally, do I pity the lot of those Brazilian lads of tender age who, being born and brought up among slaves, receive from them during the earliest years the sinister impression that is conveyed by the contagious example of these degraded beings. Oh, that I were mistaken! Oh, that the triumphs of the seducer and the shipwrecks of innocence were rarer than they are! Oh, that so many families did not have to deplore the infamy and the shame into which they have been hurled by the immorality of slaves!" [258]

Discounting, in the words of the patriarch of Independence, and especially in those of the Marquis Archbishop of Bahia, the exaggerations due to parliamentary overemphasis, and in those of Padre Lopes Gama the excesses of the moralist and pamphleteer, these words when shorn of their hypereloquence still reflect experiences that have been lived through, facts that have been observed, influences that have been undergone. It is to be noted that none of the three attributes to the Negro, to the African, to the "inferior race" those "sinister consequences" resulting from the influence of the slave quarters over the Big House. They attribute them to the social, not the ethnic factor. Their statements are material of the first order in support of those who, like Ruediger Bilden, would interpret the evils and vices in the formation of Brazilian society as being due not so much to the *Negro* or to the *Portuguese* as to the *slave*.

We cannot say whether José Bonifácio, in drawing up so strong an indictment against slavery, was conscious or not of the flaws in his own character, his own vices, which he had acquired through contact with slaves: his sadism, for example. This trait is revealed by his going to witness—out of pure pleasure and not out of any obligation—the patriarchal punishment that the Emperor Dom Pedro I once upon a time caused to be inflicted upon Portuguese soldiers in the Campo de Santana: fifty lashes each. The sort of punishment that a planter would inflict upon his thieving blacks. They drew the soldiers up in groups of five, according to height, and stripped them of their uniforms and shirts, the men being naked from their shoulders to their buttocks and bent over in front. Then the floggings began. Some of

[257] The *Representation* will be found among the documents brought together by Alberto de Sousa: *Os Andradas* (*The Andrada Family*) (São Paulo, 1922).

[258] *Parliamentary Annals*, Rio de Janeiro.

the soldiers ended by falling face-forward on the ground, overcome with the pain. But José Bonifácio looked on out of choice and stayed until the flagellation was at an end.[259] Stayed until nightfall, a sign that his dinner did not disagree with him. Evidence of various other traits in his character might be adduced that would point to the influence of slavery. If I mention him in particular, it is to convey an idea of how men of less consequence and less virile personality were affected by the same influence.

But admitting that the influence of slavery upon the morality and character of the Brazilian of the Big House was in general a deleterious one, we still must note the highly special circumstances that, in our country, modified or attenuated the evils of the system. First of all, I would emphasize the prevailing mildness of the relations between masters and household slaves—milder in Brazil, it may be, than in any other part of the Americas.

The Big House caused to be brought up from the *senzala*, for the more intimate and delicate service of the planter and his family, a whole set of individuals: nurses, house-girls, foster-brothers for the white lads. These were persons whose place in the family was not that of slaves, but rather of household inmates. They were a kind of poor relations after the European model. Many young mulattoes would sit down at the patriarchal board as if they were indeed part of the family: *crias* (those who had been reared in the house), *malungos* (foster-brothers), *muleques de estimação* (favorite houseboys). Some would even go out in the carriage with their masters, accompanying them on their jaunts as if they had been their own sons.

As for the "black mammies" (*mães-pretas*), tradition tells us that it was truly a place of honor that they held in the bosom of the patriarchal family. Granted their freedom, they would almost always round out into enormous black figures. These women were given their way in everything; the young ones of the family would come to receive their blessing, the slaves treated them as ladies, and coachmen would take them out in the carriage. And on feast-days anyone seeing them, expansive and proudly self-possessed among the whites of the household, would have supposed them to be well-born ladies and not by any means ex-slaves from the *senzala*.

This promotion of individuals from the slave quarters to the more refined service of the Big House was, of course, dependent upon their physical and moral qualities and was not done carelessly or at random.

[259] Tobias Monteiro: *História do Imperio—A Elaboração da Independência (History of the Empire—The Working-Out of Independence)* (Rio de Janeiro, 1927).

It was natural that the Negro or mulatto woman who was to suckle the master's son, rock him to sleep, prepare his food and his warm bath for him, take care of his clothing, tell him stories, and at times take the place of his own mother should have been chosen from among the best of the female slaves; from among the cleanest, the best-looking, the strongest; from among the less ignorant ones, or "ladinas," as they called them in those days, to distinguish the Negroes who had already been Christianized and Brazilianized from the ones who had only recently come over from Africa or who were more stubborn in clinging to their African ways.

In Brazil, a land whose historical background is profoundly Catholic, the religion of the slave mattered more than it did in the Antilles or in the Southern United States. "The Africans who are imported from Angola," Koster tells us, "are baptized in lots before they leave their own shores; and on their arrival in Brazil they learn the doctrines of the Church and the duties of the religion into which they have entered. These bear the mark of the royal crown upon their breasts, which denotes that they have undergone the ceremony of baptism, and likewise that the King's duty has been paid upon them. The slaves that are imported from other parts of the coast of Africa arrive in Brazil unbaptized, and before the ceremony of making them Christians can be performed upon them, they must be taught certain prayers, for the acquirement of which two years is allowed to the master before he is obliged to present the slave in the parish church." [260] It was Koster's belief that this law was not strictly enforced with respect to the length of time, but its essential provisions were carried out, inasmuch as there was no Brazilian government capable of betraying the precepts of the Church against paganism. "The slave himself wishes to be made a Christian; for his fellow bondmen will otherwise, in any squabble or trifling disagreement with him, close the string of opprobrious epithets with the name of *pagão* (pagan)." Pagan or Moor. Koster adds: "The unbaptized negro feels that he is considered an inferior being: and although he may not be aware of the value which the whites place upon baptism, still he knows that the stigma for which he is upbraided, will be removed by it; and therefore he is desirous of being made equal to his companions. The Africans who have been long imported, imbide a Catholic feeling, and appear to forget that they were once in the same situation themselves. The slaves are not asked whether they will be baptized or not. The entrance into the Catholic church is treated

---

[260] Koster, op. cit., p. 198.

as a thing of course: and indeed they are not considered as members of society, but rather as brute animals, until they can lawfully go to mass, confess their sins, and receive the sacrament." [261]

I shall not here undertake to discuss the degree to which the mass of slaves was Christianized—a subject with which I shall concern myself in a following essay; but it is certain that, as the result of contagious example and social pressure, the Negro slave in Brazil rapidly became infused with the dominant religion. It was the thing that brought him near to the master's culture and standards of morality. Some became as good Christians as their masters, being capable of transmitting to white children a Catholicism as pure as that which the young ones would have received from their own mothers.

Recalling his boyhood on a sugar plantation in the north, Sílvio Romero once remarked that he had never known anyone to pray so much as his old Negro nurse, Antônia. She it was who made him religious. "I owe it [religion] to the favorite *mucama* (*mucama de estimação*) who, in my grandparents' house, was entrusted with the task of caring for me in my infancy. This Antônia, whom I adored and whom I used to call mother, is still living today, a nonagenarian, with my own mother in Lagarto. . . . I never knew a human being so meek or one who prayed so much. She used to sleep in the same room with me, and when I awoke in the middle of the night, I would discover her there, on her knees . . . praying. I very soon learned the prayers and became so intensely accustomed to looking upon religion as a serious matter that even now I regard it as a basic and indestructible element in human upbringing. Unfortunately, woe is me! I no longer pray; but I am conscious within me of the religious sentiment, whole and unimpaired." [262] Other Brazilians of Sílvio Romero's generation might say the same thing. It may have been from his old Negro nurse on the plantation of Maçangana that Joaquim Nabuco learned the Lord's Prayer, which, at the close of his life, he was to recite once more in the Church of the Oratory in London. When his godmother died—that "scene of shipwreck" which he has evoked in the most deeply moving pages of his book *My Background* [263]—his one great consolation was the old Negro nurse who continued to serve him as before. The family friend who

---

[261] Ibid., p. 199.

[262] Sílvio Romero, in his reply to the symposium conducted by João do Rio among Brazilian intellectuals; the collected responses were published in volume form under the title *O Momento Literário* (*The Literary Moment*) (Rio de Janeiro, 1910).

[263] *Minha Formação*, a famous work in Brazilian literature; see the uniform edition of Nabuco's *Obras* (São Paulo, 1934). (Translator.)

was to take the young lad to court wrote to Nabuco's father: "The boy is better satisfied, now that I have told him that his nurse is to accompany him." [264]

But the point I would bring out is not the deep affection, almost that of mother and son, which in the days of slavery prevailed between the Negro wet-nurse and the young ones of the Big House; I am concerned rather with correcting the idea that it was through his nurse that the child received the evil influences of the slave hut, absorbing with his first nourishment the germs of all the African diseases and superstitions. The germs of diseases he oftentimes did receive, while he in turn transmitted others; but at the same time, through the caresses bestowed upon him by the *mucama*, there was revealed to him a human kindliness greater, perhaps, than that of which whites were capable, and a depth of tenderness of which Europeans do not know the like, along with an ardent, voluptuous, and contagious mysticism with which the sensibility, the imagination, and the religious feeling of Brazilians have been enriched.

What took place in our country was a deep-going and fraternal association of values and sentiments. Those that came up from the slave hut were predominantly collectivists, whereas the inmates of the Big House were inclined to individualism and private property. This was a kind of fraternization that could only with difficulty have been realized under any other type of Christianity than that which dominated Brazil during its formative period; a more clerical type, more ascetic, more orthodox, Calvinistic or strictly Catholic, would by no means have been so favorable as that mild brand of household religion, emanating from the chapels of the Big Houses, which presided over the development of Brazilian society, with family relations, one might say, prevailing between the saints and man and with churches that were always having feasts, baptisms, marriages, with banners, saints, chrisms, and novenas. It was this domestic, lyric, and festive Christianity, with its humanly friendly male and female saints and its Our Ladies as godmothers to the young, that created the first spiritual, moral, and æsthetic bonds between the Negroes and the Brazilian family and its culture. Those slaves who have become Christians make

---

[264] Carolina Nabuco: *Vida de Joaquim Nabuco* (*Life of Joaquim Nabuco*), (Rio de Janeiro, 1931).—On this subject—the relations of white children with their "Negro mammies" —the personal data that I was able to obtain through interviews with distinguished survivors of the slave-holding regime serve to confirm the statements of Joaquim Nabuco and Sílvio Romero. Among those interviewed were Dona Flora Cavalcanti de Oliveira Lima, Baronesa de Bomfim, Baronesa da Estrela, Senhor Raul Fernandes, Baronesea de Contendas, and Senhor Leopoldo Lins.

more progress in civilization, Koster observes. "No compulsion is resorted to, to make them embrace the habits of their masters: but their ideas are insensibly led to imitate and adopt them. The masters at the same time imbibe some of the customs of the slaves: and thus the superior and his dependent are brought near to each other. I doubt not that the system of baptizing the newly-imported negroes, proceeded rather from the bigotry of the Portuguese in former times than from any political plan: but it has had the most beneficial effects." [265]

That "system of baptizing Negroes" does not sum up the policy of assimilation and, at the same time, of compromise that was followed by the slave-owners in Brazil; this policy consisted chiefly in giving the Negroes an opportunity to preserve, alongside European customs and Catholic rites and doctrines, the forms and accessories of their African culture and mythology. João Ribeiro stresses the fact that Christianity in Brazil conceded the slaves a part in its rites; there were Negro saints like São Benedito and Our Lady of the Rosary who became the patrons of confraternities of blacks; and the slaves also formed groups that were true disciplinary organizations, with "kings of the Congo" exercising their authority over their "vassals." [266]

Before Ribeiro, Koster had noted that the institution of "kings of the Congo" in Brazil, in place of rendering the Negroes refractory to civilization, facilitated the civilizing process and aided in the disciplining of the slaves: "The Brazilian Kings of Congo worship Our Lady of the Rosary; and are dressed in the dress of white men. They and their subjects dance, it is true, after the manner of the country: but to these festivals are admitted African negroes of other nations, creole blacks and mulattos, all of whom dance after the same manner: and these dances are now as much the national dances of Brazil, as they are of Africa." [267] It may be seen from this how prudent and sensible was the social policy that was followed in our country with respect to the Negro. It was religion that became the point of contact and of fraternization between the two cultures, that of the master and that of the Negro, and there was never any stern and insurmountable barrier between them. The padres themselves proclaimed the advantage of conceding to the Negroes their own African pasttimes. One of them, a Jesuit writing in the eighteenth century,

---

[265] Koster, op. cit., p. 200–1.

[266] João Ribeiro: *História do Brasil*, higher course for schools (Rio de Janeiro, 1900).—See also Handelmann: *História do Brasil* (translation, op. cit.).

[267] Koster, op. cit., p. 20.

counseled the masters not only to permit but to "aid with their liberality" the feasts of the blacks. "Let them not be shocked when they [the Negroes] create their own kings and sing and dance for hours, in a respectable manner, on certain days of the year, or if they amuse themselves decently of an afternoon, after having in the morning observed the feasts of Our Lady of the Rosary, of São Benedito, and of the patron saint of the plantation chapel. . . ."[268]

This freedom of the slave to preserve, and even to display in public—at first on Epiphany Eve, and later on Christmas Night, New Year's Night, and during the three days of Carnival—the forms and accessories of his mystical, fetishistic, and totemistic culture affords a very good idea of the process of rapprochement between the two cultures in Brazil. It does not mean, however, that the Church ever ceased exerting a moral and doctrinal pressure upon the slaves. Koster observed, in Pernambuco: "the religion which the Brazilian slaves are taught, has likewise a salutary effect upon this point; for it tends to lessen or entirely removes the faith which was previously entertained by the Africans respecting the incantations of their countrymen. The superstitions of the native land are replaced by others of a more harmless nature. The dreadful effects of faith in the *Obeah*-men, which sometimes occur in the British colonies, are not experienced in Brazil from the *Mandingueiros*."[269] There was never any lack among us of those ready to admit the efficacy of magic spells; but the Englishman does not look upon this "superstition" as being either general or followed by "dreadful effects." The truth of the matter is that many a planter, without the strength left to take care of his harem of Negro and mulatto women, had his days cut short by the use of aphrodisiac beverages prepared by the black love-sorcerers, or *mandingueiros*. More than one died outright as the result of the African poison in these "concoctions." These, however, were rare and sporadic instances.

In treating of the subject of the Christianization of the Negro in Brazil, Nina Rodrigues in my opinion goes too far and falls into error when he looks upon the catechizing of the Africans as constituting a delusion.[270] Even in the face of the evidence brought together by the

[268] André João Antonil (João Antônio Andreoni), S.J.: *Cultura e Opulência do Brasil*, etc. (op. cit.), p. 96.

[269] Koster, op. cit., p. 214–15.

[270] Nina Rodrigues: *L'Animisme fétichiste des Nègres de Bahia* (Bahia, 1900). See also his *As Raças Humanas—Sua Responsibilidade Penal* (*The Human Races—Their Penal Responsibility*) (Bahia, 1894).—The studies of Nina Rodrigues are being intelligently carried on, from the psychological point of view, by Arthur Ramos in Rio and Ulysses Pernambucano de Mello and Gonçalves Fernandes in Pernambuco.

Maranhão scientist—a native of Maranhão, although the center of his intellectual activity was Bahia—in support of his thesis, the widespread educational, Brazilianizing, and moralizing (in the European sense of the term) effect of the Catholic religion upon the mass of slaves is not to be denied. What is more, I regard Nina Rodrigues's point of departure as being a false one: namely, the incapacity of the Negro race to rise to the abstractions of Christianity.[271] He was one of those who believe in the legend of the Negro's inaptitude for any kind of superior intellectual effort, and accordingly he could not admit the possibility of the black man's attaining the heights of Catholicism.

Yet it was in the fervor of the Catholic catechism that the harsher and more gross traits of the native culture were softened in the case of those Africans who came from the fetishistic areas—although, to be sure, this was a Catholicism that, in order to attract the Indians, had opulently decked itself out in fresh colors, with the padres even imitating the mummery of the native medicine-men. The catechism provided the first glow of warmth to which the mass of Negroes was subjected before being integrated in the officially Christian civilization that in this country was made up of so many diverse elements, elements whose force or harshness the Church sought to temper without wholly destroying their potentialities.

In the order of their influence, the forces within the slave-holding system of Brazil that were brought to bear upon the Negro were: first, the church (not so much the Church with the capital *C* as that other, with the small *c*, a dependency of the plantation or patriarchal estate); second, the *senzala*, or slave quarters; and third, the Big House, properly so called—that is to say, considered as a part and not as the dominating center of the system of colonization and the patriarchal society in process of formation in Brazil. The method of de-Africanizing the "new" Negro that was followed here was that of mingling him with the mass of "ladinos," or older ones, in such a manner that the slave huts became a practical school of Brazilianization.

---

[271] It may be of interest to compare what Euclides da Cunha has to say about the failure of the mestizo backlanders to grasp "the lofty ideology of a Catholicism that is beyond the comprehension of these backwoodsmen. . . ." *Os Sertões*, 16th edition, p. 142; *Rebellion in the Backlands* (op. cit.), p. 112. Da Cunha appears to look upon it as an exception, even though a not infrequent one (the exception that proves the rule?), when the mestizo "shows himself capable of broad generalizations and of grasping the most complex abstract relationships. . . ." *Os Sertões*, p. 109; *Rebellion in the Backlands*, p. 86. The author stresses Antônio Conselheiro's

The true initiation of the "new Negro" into the language, the religion, the morality, and the customs of the whites, or better, of the "ladinos," took place in the *senzala* and in the field, the newcomers imitating the old hands. It was the ladinos who initiated the "ignorant" ones into the technique and routine of sugar-planting and sugar-making. A Dutch chronicler of the seventeenth century praises the ladinos who had come from Angola as being the masters or initiators of the "new" blacks. This led him to advise that only Angola Negroes be imported.[272] Those of Arda were thick-headed and slow, hard to accustom to the routine of plantation life. They would frequently rise up against the overseers and shower them with blows.

There are other forces that may be specified as having acted upon the Negroes in the direction of their Brazilianization, by modifying their morals and, it is possible, their physique as well, conforming them not merely to the type and functions of the slave, but to the characteristics of the Brazilian and his type. The physical environment. The quality of the diet. Nature and the system of labor.

The repercussion of all these influences, some natural, others artificial and even perverse, upon the morality and physique of the Negro in Brazil is a subject to be studied minutely. Unfortunately, the materials are lacking for an anthropological investigation that would permit of a comparison of the Brazilian Negro—an extreme of racial crossing, strictly pure—with the African Negro.[273] The studies of Roquette Pinto reveal a surprising disparity, possibly to be attributed to the influence of *peristasis*, between the two types: with us, the brachycephalic type is general, in contrast to the African dolichocephalics. There are differences, likewise, in the nasal index—

---

inability to comprehend the true nature of Christianity. (Translator.)

[272] *Breve Discurso sobre o Estado das Quatro Capitânias Conquistadas*, etc. (op. cit.).

[273] It is curious to note that, in 1869, the Brazilian physician Nicolao Joaquim Moreira, in a study of racial crossings, brings out the fact that on the estate of Camorim, belonging to the Benedictine monks, there had been preserved without admixture for three centuries "a Negro population, homogeneous and vigorous . . . increasing in intelligence and undergoing a modification of the cranium that today brings it close to the Causasian

race. . . ."—"*Questão Ethnica-Anthropológica: o Cruzamento das Raças Acarreta Degradação Intellectual e Moral do Producto Hybrido Resultante?*" ("Ethnico-Anthropological Question: Does Racial Crossing Lead to the Intellectual and Moral Degradation of the Resulting Hybrid Product?"), in the *Anais Brasilienses de Medicina* (*Brazilian Medical Annals*), Vol. XXI, No. 10.—It is to be regretted that details are lacking with regard to this experiment in the segregation of the Negro race, made by the friars of St. Benedict—an experiment of great interest for anthropological studies of our milieu.

the Brazilian melanoderms, with a nose that is more flattened, approaching the bastard types of South Africa and the Philippines; which places them outside the great Negro group.[274]

Roquette Pinto attributes the differences in nasal index to the fact that really pure Negroes are rare in Brazil; as for the prevalence of brachycephalic types, he believes that is to be accounted for by "local differentiation that very possibly has its origin in old crossings." But he does not fail to admit the possibility of cases of imitation (Davenport) or the influence of *peristasis* (Boas).[275]

Interesting, furthermore, is the fact brought out by Professor Roquette Pinto that Brazilian mulattoes in the matter of stature are "in the neighborhood of the shortest whites";[276] whereas in the United States, where there would appear to have been a greater migration of tall Sudanese, the mulattoes are found to be of medium height. It may very well be a case of the diminution of stature as the result of diet, the native diet and nutrition of the Brazilian Negro differing from that of the Negro in the United States; or it may be simply the influence of crossings with whites, who in North America are better nourished.

Sá Oliveira, in a work published in 1895, pointed out various effects upon individuals of the Negro race of the new set of circumstances, what we might call the economic circumstances, of their domestic life and labor in Brazil, first as slaves and later as pariahs. For example: working long hours in the field each day, the Negro women were obliged to carry their young ones fastened to their backs, a custom followed in Africa, but only on journeys or during a small portion of the day; and as a result "their offspring later come to have faulty legs, so bowed as to form an elongated ellipse."[277] Again, nearly all of them, being compelled to engage in agricultural or domestic occupations, would cradle their young on a mat or in a hammock and leave them there for an entire day at a time; and this, in Sá Oliveira's opinion, was the reason why so many Negroes and mulattoes were

---

[274] E. Roquette Pinto: *"Notas sobre os Tipos Antropológicos do Brasil"* ("Notes on Brazilian Anthropological Types"), *Atas e Trabalhos* (*Proceedings and Papers*), First Brazilian Eugenics Congress, Rio de Janeiro, 1929.

[275] It is well to remember that in 1914 Alberto Torres, in *O Problema Nacional Brasileiro* (*The Brazilian National Problem*—where he, at that date, takes an anti-Weismann position —regarded Boas as having demonstrated "the alteration of somatic characteristics from one generation to another." But his assertions were marked by the lack of a rigorous scientific spirit, their value being prejudiced by a facile overemphasis in the statement of his convictions.

[276] E. Roquette Pinto, op. cit.

[277] J. B. de Sá Oliveira: *Craniometria Comparada das Espécies Humanas na Baía sob o Ponto de Vista Evolucionista e Médico-legal* (op. cit.).

to be met with in Brazil with the "occipital region projecting over the base of the skull as in the Africans, while in others it is flattened, the posterior cranium being in some manner diminished." This was the effect of unvarying and constant pressure on the occiput almost the whole day long.

F. A. Brandão, Jr., tells of an estate-owner of Maranhão who obliged his female slaves to leave their infants, some of them still at the breast, in the *tejupaba*, or field shack, with half of the body buried in a hole that had been dug in the ground for that purpose.[278] The idea, obviously, was to assure their immobility and avoid the danger of their creeping off into the jungle, the pasture, the barnyard, stable, etc. I am willing to believe that this custom was followed on a sugar plantation or other estate here and there; but I do not believe that it was the general practice, even in Maranhão, whose planters and *fazendeiros* were famous for their cruelty toward their slaves. Had the practice been general, it would have been another cause of pathological deformities in the Negro slaves and their descendants, who were so frequently handicapped in their physical, moral, and eugenic development by the circumstances of their economic situation, the necessities or abuses of the system of labor that prevailed on Brazilian plantations. It should be noted, on the other hand, that the Negro women in Brazil always preserved in so far as possible certain customs that to them were sacred, customs having to do with the deliberate deforming of the young, such as that of "kneading the head." It was in the slave huts that these customs were kept alive, but they must also, occasionally, have penetrated to the Big Houses, where some of the Negro nurses of the white children came to be very nearly omnipotent.

The matter of choosing a slave for the child's nurse brings up another highly interesting aspect of the relations between masters and slaves in Brazil: the hygienic one. The custom came to us from Portugal, where wealthy mothers did not suckle their own children, but intrusted them to the bosom of peasant women [279] or slaves. Júlio Dantas, in his studies of eighteenth-century Portugal, records this fact: "The place of the precious mother's milk was almost always taken by

---

[278] F. A. Brandão, Jr.: *A Escravatura no Brasil, precedida dum Artigo sobre Agricultura e Colonização no Maranhão* (*Slavery in Brazil, Preceded by an Article on Agriculture and Colonization in Maranhão*) (Brussels, 1865).

[279] The word in the text is *salóias*.

H. Michaelis (*A New Dictionary of the Portuguese and English Languages*, op. cit.) defines a *salóia* as a "countrywoman that lives within the district of Lisbon; especially one of those that supply the market with bread every day." (Translator.)

the mercenary milk of wet-nurses." [280] He attributes this to the fashion of the time. With respect to Brazil, however, it would be absurd to explain the apparent lack of maternal tenderness on the part of great ladies as due to the whims of fashion. In the case of these mothers it was a physical impossibility for them to attend to this, the first duty of motherhood. As we have seen, they were all of them married prematurely young, some of them being physically incapable of becoming mothers in the full sense of the word. Once married, one pregnancy succeeded another; one child came after another. It was a grievous and continuous effort to multiply the species. Many infants were born dead—"angels" who were promptly interred in sky-blue caskets. Others were saved from death only by a miracle. But in each case the mother was left a mere shred of a human being.

Our patriarchal grandsires were nearly always great procreators, and sometimes terrible satyrs, with a scapular of Our Lady dangling over their hairy bosoms; and these insatiable males, who got a weird sexual thrill from marrying small girls, rarely had the pleasure of the same wife's company until they reached old age; for the wives, despite the fact that they were much younger than their husbands, soon died, and the widower would then marry his first wife's younger sister or one of her cousins. These grandfathers and great-grandfathers of ours were, in a manner of speaking, Blue Beards. There were many cases in the old days of planters, captains-major of the province, big estate-owners, barons and viscounts under the Empire, who were married three and four times and who had a numerous progeny. These are facts that are pointed to with something like pride in their wills and testaments and on the tombs and gravestones of the old burying-grounds and plantation chapels. This multiplication of the species accordingly was accomplished at the cost of a great sacrifice on the part of the womenfolk, who were true martyrs in the cause of generation, consuming in the effort first their youth and, before long, life itself.

It is to this circumstance and not to any dictate of fashion that we are to attribute the importance that the wet-nurse came to assume in our family life, the slave nurse who had been summoned from the *senzala* to the Big House to assist the frail fifteen-year-old mothers in rearing their children. Imbert observes that in Brazil the white ladies, in addition to becoming mothers prematurely, suffered from "the incessant action of a subtropical climate," a climate that "exhausts their vital forces" and "irritates the nervous system"; whereas

---

[280] Júlio Dantas: *Figuras de Ontem e de Hoje* (op. cit.).

the Negro nurses were endowed with a "physical organization for living in hot regions, where their health prospers more than elsewhere; and under such climatic conditions they acquire a power of breast nourishment that the same region generally refuses to white women, for the reason that the physical organization of the latter is not so harmoniously adapted to the effects of the extreme temperature in these equatorial zones." [281] This is an observation that agrees with that of Bates regarding the melancholy of the Indian and the white man in the tropics as contrasted with the exuberant cheerfulness, the vivacity and splendid health of the Negro. The point that Imbert makes with regard to the greater power of breast nourishment on the part of the black woman as compared with the white in tropical countries is perhaps not wholly to be brushed aside. Brazilian tradition leaves us in no doubt on the subject: when it comes to a wet-nurse, there is none like a Negro woman.

But the principal reason for the greater vigor of the Negro women was, it may be, their better eugenic conditions, the explanation being social rather than climatic. In Portugal in the seventeenth and eighteenth centuries the masters of the "art of caring for and bringing up children" differed among themselves as to the color that was to be preferred in wet-nurses—which shows that the problem of blondes versus brunettes was one with which physicians were concerned long before those æsthetes whose task it is to pick the chorus girls for the theaters of Paris and New York. Dr. Francisco da Fonseca Henriques —a great medical celebrity in eighteenth-century Portugal—was opposed to dusky- and brown-skinned women, and recommended blondes.[282] The author of the *Poliantéia*,[283] on the other hand, was a great partisan of brunettes. He maintained that "in addition to being more full-blooded, they are better able to convert their nourishment into blood and milk, in the manner of the earth, which is the more fertile the blacker it is." [284]

The counsels of the author of the *Poliantéia* ought to have been favorably received by the Portuguese in America, for there were various circumstances that inclined them to have their children

[281] J. B. A. Imbert: *Guia Médico das Mães de Família, ou a Infância Considerada na Sua Hygiene, Suas Moléstias, e Tratamentos* (*Medical Guide for the Mothers of Families, or Infancy Considered in Its Hygiene and Its Diseases and Their Treatment*) (Rio de Janeiro, 1843), p. 89.

[282] *Socorro Délfico aos Clamores da Natureza Humana . . .* (*Delphic Response to the Cries of Human Nature*), by Dr. Francisco da Fonseca Henriques (Amsterdam, 1731), p. 126.

[283] The word has the sense of an *anthology* of writings; it commonly means a collection of tributes to a distinguished person. (Translator.)

[284] Júlio Dantas, op. cit.

suckled at the breast of a Negro slave. A Negro or a mulatto. The upstanding breasts of a healthy woman, the color of the best farming land in the colony. Women the color of *massapé* and dark red earth. Negro and mulatto nurses who had not only a better supply of milk, but other things to recommend them, who satisfied other conditions among the many laid down by the Portuguese hygienists of the time of John V. One of these was white, sound teeth; for among the white ladies it was rare to find one with good teeth, and on the basis of the colonial chronicles, anecdotes, and traditions it may be asserted that this was one of the principal causes of jealousy and sexual rivalry between the senhoras and the *mucamas*. Another condition was that they should not be with their first child. Another, that they should not have any skin affection. And finally, that they should be the mothers of healthy and viable offspring.

J. B. A. Imbert, in his *Medical Guide*, upon approaching the delicate problem of wet-nurses, begins a little pompously: [285] "The breasts should be suitably developed, neither rigid nor flaccid, the tips not too pointed and not too blunt, but adapted to the child's lip." [286] Imbert finds it fitting that wet-nurses should be slaves; for he will not admit that "as a general rule, Brazilian mothers, who are still very young, are able to endure the fatigue of a prolonged period of nursing without grave detriment to their own health as well as that of their children." But he stresses the need of their keeping a watch always over the wet-nurses whom they employ.

The *fazendeiros* had to be concerned with prenatal and infantile hygiene, not only in the Big Houses, but in the slave huts as well. Many a young Negro died as a result of his mother's ignorance. The author of the *Estate-Owner's Manual or Domestic Treatise on the Infirmities of Negroes* informs us that "the Negro women ordinarily cut the cord very far from the navel and are more and more inclined to follow the pernicious custom of putting pepper on it and fomenting it with castor oil or some other irritant. Having done this, the perverse creatures squeeze the child's belly to the point of suffocating it. This cuts the life-thread of many, many young ones and contributes to the development in the navel of that inflammation which in Brazil goes by the name of seven days' sickness." Moreover, the Negro

---

[285] Freyre's expression is *"acacianamente."* The Counselor Acacio is a sententious and ridiculous character in Eça de Queiroz's famous novel *O Primo Basílio* (*Cousin Basílio*). The word had passed into the language as the term for a pompous character; there is an adjective, *acaciano*, and a noun, *acacianismo* (Acacianism). (Translator.)

[286] Imbert, op. cit., p. 89.

women in the slave huts, "the moment the child is born, are accustomed . . . to knead its head, in order to give it a more pleasing shape; and without stopping to think of the weak digestive organs of the newborn, they sometimes give their infants, a few days after birth, coarse food such as the mothers themselves are used to eating." It was against practices of this nature that the white mothers were to be on their guard, with the object not only of preventing such crude habits as these from making their way up to the Big Houses, but of seeing to it also that they did not spread in the *senzalas*. For when all was said, "the Negro women that give birth," as Imbert says, "are augmenting their master's capital. . . ." [287] Infant mortality in the slave quarters meant a serious diminution of that capital.[288]

---

[287] J. B. A. Imbert: *Manual do Fazendeiro, Ou Tratado Doméstico Sobre as Enfermidades dos Negros* (Rio de Janeiro, 1839).—See also C. A. Taunay: *Manual do Agricultor Brasileiro* (*Brazilian Agriculturist's Manual*) (Rio de Janeiro, 1839).

[288] The infantile death-rate in the slave-huts came to be considerable. In Mata-Paciência, on the estate of Dona Marianna, eldest daughter of the Baron and Baroness of Campos—a plantation with, possibly, the first steam sugar-mill that was installed in Brazil, employing 200 slave laborers and around 100 oxen—Maria Graham was informed by the plantation mistress herself that "not half the Negroes born on her estate live to be ten years old." Mrs. Graham was greatly alarmed by this.—*Journal of a Voyage to Brazil*, etc. (op. cit.).— Eschwege had previously found that in Minas Gerais, among the mulatto slaves, the birth-rate was 4 to 105, the death-rate 6 to 100; among Negro slaves, the birth-rate was 3 to 103, the death-rate 7 to 102; while among the free whites, the birth-rate was 4 to 90, the death-rate 3 to 106; among the free Indians, the birth-rate was 4 to 99, the death-rate 4 to 108; among the free mulattoes, the birth-rate was 4 to 109, the death-rate 3 to 109; among the free Negroes, the birth-rate was 4 to 84, the death-rate 5 to 93. So

much for Eschwege's statistics, which led Oliveira Vianna to remark upon "the formidable destructive effect of ethnic and pathological selection within the *senzalas*," the Negro and mulatto, however, having "a death-rate lower than their birth-rate."

Meanwhile, the results of the census that was taken in Pernambuco in 1827, with reference to the population of Santo Antônio, show a minimum difference in the death-rate of Negroes, mulattoes (*pardos*), and whites. For example, for the year 1826, we have:

Births	*Deaths*
Whites, 192; mulattoes, 178; blacks, 294	Whites, 135; mulattoes, 60; blacks, 125

And with respect to preceding years, beginning with the year of Independence:

	Births		
Year	*Whites*	*Mulattoes (Pardos)*	*Blacks*
1822	279	197	239
1823	294	223	256
1824	281	209	276
1825	221	234	271

	Deaths		
1822	103	61	87
1823	108	49	95
1824	115	53	87
1825	124	70	119

(These statistics were kindly furnished me by Canon José do Carmo

Imbert is quite intolerant of anything having to do with the rearing and care of the child that savors of the unscientific or of the African medicine-man. He will not hear of any remedy, elixir, ointment, or pomade for buboes, ulcers, the itch, jaundice, erysipelas, abrasions of the groin, thighs, and buttocks of newborn infants due to infrequent changes of their diapers, milk-curds, mycosis, chickenpox, measles, tapeworm, and the like.[289] It is, accordingly, strange to hear him advising as an infallible remedy for children who wet the bed: the eating of roast meat and the drinking of a little good wine; or, again: "fear, the threat of punishment." "The threat of punishment and the fear of it sometimes produce a salutary effect, especially when the incontinence is the result of superstition or a bad habit. . . ."[290] From which it may be seen that physicians and medicine-men were not very far removed from each other, down to the second half of the nineteenth century.

The art of blood-letting was practiced in colonial Brazil and in the time of the Empire by African slaves, who were also barbers and dentists; and Negro women plied the trade of midwife alongside white ones and *caboclas,* all of them equally ignorant and all known by the name of *comadres.*[291] Besides officiating at childbirth, these "*comadres*" treated gynecological diseases by means of witchcraft, prayers, and invocations. The houses where they lived had a white cross on the door; and when they went out on professional business, they wrapped themselves in mantles or long hoodlike shawls, many of them "carrying beneath their mantillas love-missives, love-spells and brews." Many also took with them "the products of those illicit and criminal practices to which their profession lent itself and in which they unscrupulously engaged, to abandon them in the streets and hidden nooks."[292]

Baratta of the See of Olinda, with numerous other manuscripts from the archives of that See.)

[In concluding that the figures show a death-rate lower than the birth-rate, Vianna is obviously misinterpreting the statistics quoted. In a note to the translator Freyre remarks: "I am quoting from Oliveira Vianna. I think that he is wrong. But I am quoting him." (Translator.)]

[289] See also J. B. A. Imbert's brochure: *Uma Palavra sobre o Charlatanismo e os Charlatões* (*A Word on Charlatanism and the Charlatans*) (Rio de Janeiro, 1837).

[290] Imbert: *Guia Médico* (op. cit.) —The fear was to be inspired chiefly by talking to the bed-wetting child in a loud voice and telling him that the hairy-handed goblin (*mão-de-pelo*), the Quibongo, or the "old Negro" would eat his penis or cut it off. This was a fear that was also instilled in the child that masturbated.

[291] *Comadre* literally means a godmother or "gossip." (Translator.)

[292] Alfredo Nascimento: *O Centenário da Academia Nacional de Medicina de Rio de Janeiro—Primór-*

The ignorance of Brazilian mothers of a former day—inexperienced girls—did not find in the "*comadres*" the needed corrective. There is nothing, however, to justify the conclusion that these midwives and the African witch-doctors of colonial times exceeded in filthiness and false pretenses the official brand of European medicine of the sixteenth, seventeenth, and eighteenth centuries.

It is none other than the patriarch of medical literature in Brazil, Dr. Joam Ferreyra de Rosa, a seventeenth-century physician, whom we find prescribing for his patients: "powder of burnt crayfish taken in a cup of citronella water." [293] He further recommends their putting "under their armpits . . . orpiment paste" with "gum arabic"; and for "suppression of urine" he suggests the anointing of "the groins, the interseminal tube, and the belly" with copaiba oil. The plague that at the close of the seventeenth century laid waste Pernambuco appeared to him to be the work of the stars: "the air may receive . . . foulness or contagious qualities from the Stars." Or, again, it might be the work of Divine Justice "so long as we do not reform our very bad customs." The population ought to combat it with bonfires, burning "aromatic things," and going with "aromatic fruits in the hand." [294] This from the writings of Ferreyra da Rosa, who was by no means a quack doctor, but one of the most advanced of his age, drawing his remedies and his doctrines "not from the Empirics, but from the Methodics and the Rationals."

In Portugal in the eighteenth century Fonseca Henriques, an illustrious pediatrician, was still guided by the stars in his clinic. Whoever opens his celebrated *Delphic Response to the Cries of Human Nature* will come upon these solemn words regarding the moon: "The moon's light is harmful to the young." The infant's garments and cloths, even, were not to be left in the moonlight. Those children who were born wailing loudly would grow up to be robust, and "much more so those that are born with the scrotum wrinkled." [295]

In the *Doctrinal Observations* of Curvo Semedo, Luis Edmundo came upon prescriptions that in truth are not far removed from those

---

dios e Evolução da Medicina no Brasil (*Centenary of the National Academy of Medicine of Rio de Janeiro—Beginnings and Evolution of Medicine in Brazil*) (Rio de Janeiro, 1929).

[293] *Agua de herva cidreira*. The *erva cidreira* is a plant of the *Labiatæ* family (*Melissa officinalis Lin.*). In Pernambuco the name is also given to a plant of the *Verbenaceæ* family (*Lippia geminata H.B.K.*).—Lima and Barroso, op. cit. (Translator.)

[294] Joam Ferreyra da Rosa: *Trattado Unico da Constituiçam Pestilencial de Pernambuco Offerecido a Elrey N.S.* (*Treatise on the Pestilence in Pernambuco, Offered to His Majesty, etc.*) (Lisbon, 1694).

[295] Fonseca Henriques: *Soccorro Délfico*, etc. (op. cit.)

of the African or Indian medicine-men; and in a certain *Pharmacopéa Ulysiponense*, by one João Vigier, he found others that are still more repulsive. These are household remedies such as were common in Portugal and which from there were transmitted to Brazil: teas or infusions made of bedbugs and rat's excrement, for intestinal disorders; an ostrich's maw to dissolve gall-stones; the urine of man or donkey, burnt hairs, powdered dog-dung, the skin, bones, and flesh of toads, newts, crayfish, etc.[296]

A form of medicine that, through the voice of its most orthodox representatives, prescribed for patients such nauseous remedies as these could hardly make any pretensions to being superior to the healing art of the Africans and Amerindians. The truth of the matter is that from the medicine-men who were so looked down upon, official medicine absorbed much valuable knowledge and a series of curative processes: quinine, cocaine, ipecacuanha. It appears to me to be a just conclusion that in colonial Brazil the physicians, *comadres*, witch-doctors, and slaves who practiced blood-letting contributed almost equally to that high death-rate, especially of infants and mothers, which for successive epochs reduced by something like fifty per cent the production of human beings in the Big Houses and slave huts.

We have seen that the infantile death-rate was enormous among the indigenous populations from the sixteenth century on. This was naturally so, owing to the disturbing and unhygienic contact with the conquering race. There was likewise a high mortality of children among the families of the Big Houses; for child-hygiene was perhaps the sphere in which Europeans found it most painful and difficult to adapt themselves to the environment of the American tropics. They had brought with them strict notions as to how to safeguard their health, including a superstitious horror of bathing and fresh air—notions that, harmful to the young in a temperate climate, in a hot one oftentimes meant their death. One has but to contrast these concepts with the care that the *caboclos* gave their children, and one will

---

[296] Luis Edmundo: *O Rio de Janeiro no Tempo dos Vice-Reis* (op. cit.).—In the middle of the nineteenth century a daughter of Felix Cavalcanti de Albuquerque Mello came down with cholera, followed by a "suppression of urine . . . and all the remedies prescribed by the two systems of medicine were applied, but in vain. Five toasted house-flies dissolved in a spoon of lukewarm water caused her to urinate in thirteen minutes."—*Livro de Assentos* (manuscript cited). This manuscript by Felix Cavalcanti, rounded out with other notes left by the old Pernambucan, was recently published in book form, under the title *Memórias de um Cavalcanti* (*Memoirs of a Cavalcanti*), with an introduction by me.

conclude that the native method was superior. This was the conclusion reached by the Frenchman Jean de Léry, who was not a physician but simply a man of good sense.

The infant-hygiene of the native or the African—the greater freedom of the child from heavy garments and swaddling-clothes—was to be adapted by the Europeans through the mediation of the Indian or Negro slave woman; but only little by little and at the cost of a great sacrifice of human life.

Nieuhof lays stress on the high infantile death-rate in the first centuries of colonization, but he was sensible enough to attribute it not so much to the climate or the African nurse as to improper diet.[297] And Fernandes Gama practically repeats Nieuhof's words when he writes that "the Portuguese women at first reared very few children," adding that "two thirds of them died shortly after birth." He further tells us that "the daughters of these women who grew to maturity, and they themselves, adapting their methods of child-care to the climate, doing away with the heavy clothing of their infants, abandoning the custom of muffling the babies' heads, and forming the habit of bathing them in lukewarm water, were no longer to be heard complaining of the climate's being so destructive for the newborn." [298]

The death-rate of children in Brazil was lessened from the second half of the sixteenth century, that is certain, but it continued to be alarmingly high. In the eighteenth century Dr. Bernardino Antônio Gomes was concerned with it; and in the nineteenth century it was one of the problems that most disturbed the hygienists of the Second Empire—Sigaud, Paula Cândido, Imbert, the Baron of Lavrádio; until in 1887 José Maria Teixeira came to devote to it a truly notable study: *Causes of the Mortality of Children in Rio de Janeiro.*[299]

At the session of the Academy of Medicine of June 18, 1846, the subject was brought up for discussion and debate, under the following heads: (1) *To what cause is so high a death-rate of children in the first years of life to be attributed? Is the practice of having them suckled by slaves, selected with very little care, to be looked upon as one of the principal causes? (2) What diseases are most frequent in children?* The archives of the Academy contain, perhaps, no material

---

[297] John Nieuhof: *Voyages and Travels into Brazil and the East Indies* (translation, London, 1703). A Portuguese translation of Nieuhof's account of his voyage to Brazil has recently appeared.

[298] Fernandes Gama: *Memórias Históricas de Pernambuco (Historical Memoirs of Pernambuco)* (Recife, 1844).

[299] *Causas da Mortalidade das Crianças no Rio de Janeiro* (Rio de Janeiro, 1887).

that is more replete with social interest than the proceedings of that memorable session.

The most divergent opinions were expressed. Dr. Reis stressed the use and abuse of heavy foods, improper clothing, and suckling by wet-nurses as exerting a particularly harmful effect upon the health of Brazilian children; also the contagious diseases of the African nurses, many of whom were the bearers of syphilis and especially of buboes and scrofula. Dr. Rêgo laid the responsibility for the high infantile death-rate in Brazil not so much upon the slave nurses and the child's clothing as upon the habit of letting the little ones go naked. He emphasized another important factor: the lack of medical treatment to resist the invasion of diseases. Dr. Paula Cândido then rose to insist upon the danger associated with slave nurses who were chosen without a careful examination, and laid stress upon faulty dentition and worms. Various other physicians and hygienists spoke at this meeting. Dr. De Simone also dealt with the subject of nurses and improper alimentation. Dr. Jobim [300] reminded his listeners of the pernicious effects of the "dampness of dwellings." [301] Dr. Feital spoke of improper diet. Dr. Nunes Garcia stressed the same point, along with the feeding of children by wet-nurses, and was answered by Dr. Lallemant, who stated that, in his opinion, the Brazilian child was better nourished than the European. It was Dr. Marinho who had the last word, and he laid the cause of infantile mortality in Brazil to humidity, radical changes in temperature, clothing, premature feeding, and wet-nurses.

In 1847 the Baron of Lavrádio, in a series of articles in the journal of the Imperial Academy, under the title: "Some Considerations of the Causes of Mortality in the Children of Rio de Janeiro and the Diseases Most Frequent during the First Six or Seven Months of Life," went into the subject extensively, reaching the conclusion that the predominant causes were the following: faulty treatment of the umbilical cord; improper clothing; the little care that is given in the beginning to the diseases of female slaves and older children; disproportionate, insufficient, or improper diet; and the neglect at first of the diseases of early infancy, children not being brought to the

---

[300] Dr. José Martins da Cruz Jobim, previously referred to in this work. (Translator.)

[301] I shall endeavor to show in a forthcoming essay that many habitations in colonial days and in the time of the Empire were, indeed, horribly damp—not so much owing to the architecture of the houses as to the lack of care in the choice of material employed.

physician until they are already dying of gastroenteritis, hepatitis, and mesenteric tuberculosis.

The truth is that losing a young child was never for a patriarchal family the profound sorrow that it is for a family of today.[302] There would be another one. The "angel" had gone to heaven, that was all. Had gone to join Our Lord, who is insatiable in his quest of angels. Or else it was the evil eye. In any event, there was nothing to be done about it. It was witchcraft. Sorcery. The only remedies were amulets, alligator's teeth, prayers, and conjurations.

Dr. Teixeira states that he had frequently heard from parents these words: "The death of children is a blessing." [303] And the fact is that this interring of "angels" continued through the nineteenth century. Some of them were buried in sky-blue or carnation-hued caskets, their bodies painted with carmine like the tiny one whom Ewbank saw lying dead in Rio de Janeiro. The poorest were buried on wooden boards, laden with flowers; some even in big pasteboard boxes of the kind that are used for men's shirts.

If so many died young in Brazil in the days of slavery, the causes were chiefly social; and these causes have been set down with admirable clarity and critical sense by Dr. José Maria Teixeira, who attributes the high mortality principally to the economic system of slavery, or rather the social customs that derive from that system: the lack of physical, moral, and intellectual education on the part of the mothers; the disparity in the ages of married couples; and the frequency of illicit births.[304] He might have added: the unsuitable

---

[302] Burton observed that in Minas Gerais "an 'anjinho' or 'innocente,' a very young child, dies unregretted because its future happiness is certain."—*The Highlands of the Brazil* (op. cit.). It is likely that the superstition regarding the *"anjinhos"* derived from the fact that, in view of the alarming number of Indian children who were carried off by death in the sixteenth century, the Jesuits, to console the mothers and in the interests of the catechism, had spread the belief that death was "a blessing," inasmuch as the young ones were going to heaven.

[303] José Maria Teixeira: *Causa da Mortalidade das Crianças*, etc. (op. cit.).—Luccock (op. cit.) tells us that at the burial of an "angel" in Rio de Janeiro he overheard the infant's mother exclaiming: "Oh, how happy I am! Oh, how happy I am! When I die and go to the gate of Heaven, I shall not fail of admittance, for there will be five little children, all pressing toward me, pulling my skirts, and saying 'Oh, mother, do come in,—do come in.' Oh, how happy I am!"

[304] José Maria Teixeira, op. cit.— As to the disparity in ages between husband and wife, it is to be noted that Teixeira exaggerates the pernicious aspect of the marriage of mature men with girls of thirteen and fourteen. At that age, in tropical countries, the latter might be ready for procreation. There is no evidence of physical damage caused to the mothers of their offspring by the mere

diet; breast feeding by female slaves who were not always hygienically fit for their task; and syphilis in the parents or the nurses. It was obviously the effect of such influences that many confused with that of climate. Luccock observed in the Brazil of the early nineteenth century an "actual great neglect with regard to the welfare of children, to their life or death." [305]

The diseases that affected children in those days were numerous: the "seven days' sickness" (inflammation of the navel); mycosis; the itch in various forms; scurvy; measles; chickenpox; tapeworm—diseases that were combated with clysters, purgatives, leeches, cathartics, blood-lettings, emetics, mustard plasters. It is probable that some of the remedies and preventatives anticipated the effects of the diseases themselves, carrying off to heaven many a "little angel."

Some chroniclers attribute to the contact of white children with Negro lads the vice that many of the former acquired of eating earth, a vice that was the cause of the death of more than one slave in colonial Brazil, from the time of the Indians. "One of the means," writes Koster, "which it is very generally said that these miserable beings employ for the purpose of destroying themselves, is that of eating considerable quantities of lime and earth. . . . But it is strange that the habit of eating lime and earth should be contracted in some instances by African and likewise by Creole children, and as frequently by free children as by those who are in slavery. This practice is not treated as if it were a disorder, but it is accounted a habit, which, by

---

discrepancy in age. In various primitive societies, where individuals are strong and robust, girls are generally married immediately after puberty, their husbands being twice the age of the brides and sometimes even older. Under our patriarchal family system it is probable that in many cases the girls were not suited for marriage and procreation, and very grave harm resulted. The principal causes, however, for the death of so many frail mothers and so many children at the nursing age were social in character: the lack of physical education of the girls, who became mothers while still ignorant of sexual and maternal hygiene, and who, in addition, had been seriously handicapped in their physical development and in their health. "Diseases of the liver, of the organs

of respiration, and of the intestines, to which they were generally subject from infancy, had the effect of draining their strength," writes Luiz Corrêa de Azevedo, referring to Brazilian mothers.—*Annaes Brasileiros de Medicina* (op. cit.), Vol. XXI. He adds that another source of enervation was "exaggerated precautions against the effects of fresh air"; "tight clothing, prejudicial to the development of the viscera and consequently affecting the uterus"; and "leucorrhea, a disease more common than is supposed in our schools." On this subject see also Nicolao Moreira: *Discurso sobre a Educação Moral da Mulher* (*Discourse on the Moral Education of Woman*) (Rio de Janeiro, 1868).

[305] John Luccock: *Notes on Rio de Janeiro*, etc. (op. cit.), p. 117.

attention from those who have the charge of the children—in watching and punishing them, may be conquered without the aid of medicine. I know of some instances in which no medical treatment was deemed necessary: but the individual recovered by means of chastisement and constant vigilance. It is a subject upon which I was often led to converse: and I discovered that most of the free-born families were acquainted with the practice from experience among their own children, or those of their neighbours; and they always considered it as a habit and not as a disease. Among adults, however, slaves are infinitely more subject to it than free persons." [306]

It would seem that Koster did not have occasion to observe the treatment of young slaves and even white children who had contracted this vice of earth-eating, by means of a tin-plate mask. And certainly he was not familiar with the liana hamper: an enormous basket in which the Negro was hoisted all the way up to the roof of the improvised infirmary with the aid of ropes run through the rafters and caught on hooks in the doorway. These infirmaries existed down to the middle of the nineteenth century on plantations in the north. Phaelante da Camara saw them when he was a child: "The patient was isolated in an infirmary or hospital *sui generis* where it was quite impossible for him to keep up the abominable vice of geophagia." The slave having been placed in such a hamper and suspended above the ground, "they imposed upon him a quarantine of many days, meanwhile giving him jaracatiá [307] milk to correct his anemia and subjecting him to a substantial diet, which at certain hours was lifted up to him on the point of a stick when it was not possible to bring the hamper down under the eye of some person in whom the utmost confidence was reposed." [308]

It would appear that the child of those days forgot the hardships of his early infancy—diseases, punishments for bed-wetting, a monthly purge—to become, from the age of five to ten, a veritable little devil. His sports and games, as we have observed, reveal marked sadistic tendencies in him. And it was not only the plantation lad who in general played at "coachman," killing birds, and hectoring his Negro playmate, but the city lad as well.

Even in spinning his top or flying his kite the small boy of the Big House found a way of expressing his sadism through certain practices characterized by a pronounced childish cruelty that today are

---

[306] Koster: *Travels in Brazil* (op. cit.), p. 213.
[307] Plant of the *Caricaceæ* family (*Jaracatia dodecaphylla A.*). Also

known as the *mamoeiro* of the jungle.
[308] Phaelante da Camara: "*Notas Dominicais de Tollenáre*," *Cultura Acadêmica* (Recife, 1904).

still current in the north—such as "shivering the top" or "eating the parrot" (kite)[309] of another. In the case of the kite, it was a bit of glass or broken bottle that was hidden in the folds of the tail. In the colonial parlor games these sadistic tendencies are to be encountered: for example, in the game of "pinch-me," so beloved of Brazilian children in the eighteenth and nineteenth centuries. Inasmuch as it gave the lads a good opportunity to pinch their girl cousins and the household slaves, the popularity of so bestial a sport is no occasion for wonderment:

> *One two, little sprig,*
> *Put your foot upon the twig.*
> *Lad, I say, what game do we play?*
> *We are playing the capon's game,*
> *Capon, capon, 'tis all the same;*
> *Twenty, call each one by name.*
> *And now take back your little foot,*
> *Take it in your little hand;*
> *I'll pinch you as hard as you can stand. . . .*[310]

And the one who was reached with the line: "I'll pinch you as hard as you can stand," did indeed receive a stout pinch. A timid little pinch on the part of the slaves, a painful one when given by the white lads. But the greatest punishment came when all the other children fell upon the unfortunate one, threw him to the ground, and pommeled him, as they sang at the top of their voices:

> *And it's bing-bang-bong,*
> *Bing-bang-bong.*
> *Pound him neat;*
> *We'll have dried beef and beans to eat.*[311]

One can imagine how the slaves and little girls were tormented in the course of this game. On this point the documents that I have collected from survivors of the slave-holding order—one of them Leopoldo Lins—are highly expressive.

---

[309] "*comer-se o papagaio.*" *Papagaio* means "parrot," and also "kite." (Translator.)

[310]   *Uma duas, angolinhas*
      Finca o pé na pampolinha
      O rapaz que jogo faz?
      Faz o jogo do capão.
      O' capão, semicapão,
      Veja bem que vinte são
      E recolheu o seu pezinho

Na conchinha de uma mão
Que lá vai um beliscão. . . .
Sylvio Romero: *Cantos Populares do Brasil* (Rio, 1883). [The translation is freely rendered.]

[311] *E' de rim-fon-fon,*
E' de rim-fon-fon,
Pé de pilão,
Carne seca com feijão.

In another game, that of "pinch the little chick," [312] similar tendencies were displayed; the game began with pinches and ended with blows not unlike those that the overseer gave the poor Negro. And in the game of "hot-strap" (*peia queimada*) it is quite possible that very often the strap did serve as an imitation of the foreman's lash on the back of the fugitive slave; just as the guava-tree bough so many times fulfilled the role of buggy-whip in the game of "playing horse."

"And what," inquires Father Lopes Gomes, referring to the offspring of the plantation-owners, "are the sons of these sluggards like? Many do not even learn to read and write. . . . The inhumanities and the cruelties that they practice from early years upon the wretched slaves render them all but insensible to the sufferings of their neighbors. . . . And how, in truth, are the hearts of us Brazilians to acquire the social virtues if from the moment we open our eyes we see about us the cruel distinction between master and slave, and behold the former, at the slightest provocation or sometimes out of a mere whim, mercilessly rending the flesh of our own kind with lashes? How shall we be brought to appreciate modesty, we who have a poor slave girl stripped, or see her stripped, in order that she may be flogged? . . . No sooner do we acquire intelligence"—it is the same padre schoolmaster speaking, in one of his critical articles on Brazilian customs at the beginning of the nineteenth century [313]— "than we observe, on the one hand, the lack of delicacy, shamelessness, dissoluteness, and disorderly conduct of the slaves, and on the other hand the harsh treatment, the thrashings, the blows that these unfortunates receive almost every day from our elders, although the poor degraded creatures feel little more than a physical sensation, very rarely any moral sentiment. And what is the inevitable result of all this, if not to render us coarse, headstrong, and full of pride?" In his recollections of his infancy, the Viscount Taunay, [314] a man almost

---

[312] This is the game known as *belilisco de pintainho que anda pela barra de vinte e cinco*. In a note to the translator, Mr. Arthur Coelho describes it as follows: ". . . an old traditional game. No one ever thought of asking what the words stood for. The children sit in a circle and put their hands down on the floor. The leader repeats these words as he pinches the back of the hands, one at a time. The child with whom the leader finishes the phrase '*tira esta mão que já está fôrra* (take back this hand, it's out)' is considered 'free' and is out of the game by one hand, then perhaps by the other one. The child that is left alone at the end receives a '*bolo*' on his hand." As Coelho observes, Freyre's version appears to be a little different. (Translator.)

[313] *O Carapuceiro* (op. cit.).

[314] The famous nineteenth-century novelist. (Translator.)

as gentle and mild-mannered as a girl, confesses that he took pleasure in tormenting the Negro lads.[315] And there is a passage in one of Machado de Assis's novels in which that fine observer of Brazilian society in the time of the Empire portrays for us the type of sadistic child, the child who has been perverted by the social conditions of his upbringing, in the midst of passive slaves who were docilely responsive to his whims. There is not a Brazilian of the upper classes, even one born and brought up after slavery had been officially abolished, who does not feel a kinship with the young Braz Cubas [316] in the latter's maliciousness and fondness for teasing Negroes. The morbid pleasure of treating inferiors and animals rudely is one that is characteristic of us; it is characteristic of every Brazilian lad affected by the influence of the slave-holding system. "From the age of five I merited the nickname of 'little devil' . . ." confesses the hero of the *Posthumous Memoirs of Braz Cubas.* "For example, one day, I bashed the head of a slave girl for refusing me a spoonful of a coconut sweet that she was making; and not satisfied with this misdemeanor, I flung a handful of ashes into the kettle. Even this prank was not enough, but I had to go tell my mother that it was the girl who had spoiled the confection 'out of meanness.' And I was barely six years old at the time. Prudêncio, a Negro houseboy, was my horse every day; he would rest his hands on the ground, let me put a string through his mouth for a bridle, and I would then climb astride his back with a switch in my hand and would whip him soundly many, many times, on one side and on the other, and he would obey—he would groan, sometimes, but obey he would, without saying a word, or at the most an 'Oh, little master!'—to which I would retort: 'Shut your mouth, beast!' Hiding the hats of visitors, hurling paper darts at dignified individuals, pulling wigs off from behind, pinching the arms of matrons, and other exploits of this sort were the signs in me of a rebellious disposition, but I was led to believe that they were at the

---

[315] Visconde de Taunay: *Trechos da Minha Vida (Passages from My Life)* (posthumous edition, 1923). In a letter to a friend of mine, Professor Affonso d'E. Taunay states that he sees no basis for the generalization to the effect that his father was "almost as gentle and mild-mannered as a girl." He recalls that the elder Taunay, throughout his public life, exhibited attitudes that were strong and energetic.—With regard to this aspect of the relations between white and black lads, I gathered the statements and recollections of survivors of our agrarian aristocracy, almost all of whom spoke of sadism on the part of the whites.

[316] Hero of the famous novel by Machado de Assis: *Memórias Póstumas de Braz Cubas* (Rio de Janeiro, 1881). (Translator.)

same time the expressions of a robust turn of mind; for if my father now and then reproved me in company, it was out of mere formality; in private he would kiss me."

This attitude of toleration on the part of parents toward the stupidity, maliciousness, and even the braggadocio and defiance of their young ones was something that Father Lopes Gama could neither understand nor forgive. He could not understand why they should let the children of the family grow up like cats on the roof-tops or permit them to run wild, flinging stones and spinning their tops in the street "with the filthiest and most rascally riffraff." He was speaking here of the cities and suburbs. "In our backland districts (with few and honorable exceptions) the upbringing of the young is lamentable. There the first thing that they give them to play with is a sharp-bladed knife. Just as in the age of chivalry aristocratic fathers would equip their knightly sons with a suit of mail as soon as they were able to walk, while the pious would clothe their little ones like friars, so, many of our backwoodsmen are in the habit of furnishing their young knights-errant with a dagger the moment they are able to slip into a pair of drawers." And regarding the manner in which the planters rear their sons, the same writer adds: "There the lad is a cruel persecutor of innocent little birds, spying them out in their nests, and although he is not capable of handling a gun as yet, he is praised as if he were a notable marksman. From their tenderest years these children are perversely accustomed to blood, killing, and cruelty; for, out of sheer sport, to take the lives of small animals that do not harm us, but which rather give us pleasure and join in praising the works of the Creator—this, in my humble opinion, is to educate the heart to barbarity and inhumanity. With slaves as practically their only playmates, the lads acquire a coarse and vicious mode of speech and the rudest manners, and not a few of them form the terrible habit of eating earth." [317]

The planters' sons fell into other vices; and at times, owing partly

---

[317] *O Carapuceiro* (op. cit.).—To this day, in those rural regions that have been most influenced by the slave-holding regime, the small boy, in the sadistic tendencies that he displays, is very near the type described by Lopes Gama and Machado de Assis with respect to a precocious initiation into physical love and the vices acquired. See, in this regard, the regional novels: *A Bagaceira* (*The Bagaceira*), by José Américo de Almeida, and *Menino de Engenho* (*Plantation Lad*), by José Lins do Rêgo.

[The novels mentioned are two of the outstanding ones in modern Brazilian literature. *A Bagaceira*, in particular, is something of a literary landmark, between the generation of the 1920's and the contemporary one. (Translator.)]

to the effect of the climate, but chiefly as the result of conditions of life created by the slave-holding system, they would precociously engage in sadistic and bestial forms of sexuality. The first victims were the slave lads and domestic animals; but later came that great mire of flesh: the Negro or mulatto woman. This was a quicksand in which many an insatiable adolescent was hopelessly lost. But does this mean that we are to hold these women responsible for the precocious and disordered sexual life of the Brazilian young? With the same logic we might try to hold the domestic animals responsible, the banana stalk, the watermelon, or the fruit of the mandacarú with its clinging quality that is almost like that of human flesh. For all of these were objects upon which the sexual precocity of the Brazilian small boy was—and still is—exercised.

In the treatise known as the "General Idea of Pernambuco in 1817," an anonymous chronicler tells us of the "great lubricity" of the plantation Negroes; but he reminds us that this was stimulated "by the masters, eager to augment their herds." [318] It would not be at all far-fetched to conclude from this and other statements that our forebears, dominated by the economic interest of the masters of slaves, looked always with an indulgent and even a sympathetic eye upon the precocity of their sons in anticipating the generative functions and that they even made it easy for these young stallions to do so. Rural traditions tell of mothers, untrammeled by the morals of the case, who would thrust into the arms of their bashful and virginal sons young Negro and mulatto girls who were capable of awakening them from their apparent coldness or sexual indifference.

No Big House in the days of slavery wanted any effeminate sons or male virgins. In the folklore of our old sugar and coffee zones, whenever there is a reference to sexually pure youths, it is always in a tone of mockery, by way of holding the ladylike fellow up to ridicule. The one always approved was the lad who went with the girls at as early an age as possible. A *"raparigueiro,"* [319] as we would say today. A woman-chaser. A ladies' man. A deflowerer of maidens. One who lost no time in taking Negro women that he might increase the herd and the paternal capital.

If this was always the point of view of the Big House, how, then, are we to hold the Negro woman of the slave hut responsible for the

---

[318] "*Idéa Geral de Pernambuco em 1817,*" *Revista do Instituto Arqueológico, Histórico e Geográfico de Pernambuco*, 29.—See also Vilhena: *Cartas*, Vol. I, p. 138, on the relations of whites of good family with Negroes and mulattoes in Bahia.

[319] From *rapariga*, in Brazil a prostitute. (Translator.)

precocious depravity of the plantation lad in patriarchal times? All that the former did was to facilitate the latter's depravation by her docility as a slave, by opening her legs at the first manifestation of desire on the part of the young master. It was not a request but a command to which she had to accede. Brazilian publicists and even scientists who have concerned themselves with the subject of slavery have always been inclined to exaggerate the influence of the female Negro or mulatto, by holding her to be the corruptor of the son of the family. "Corruptors of the feminine and masculine offspring," F. P. do Amaral calls them.[320] And Burlamaqui states that they "corrupt the morals of their masters' sons." [321] Speaking of those mulatto women who succeeded in obtaining their freedom, Antonil observes that the money with which they purchased it "rarely comes out of any other mines than their own bodies, with repeated sins; and after they are freed, they continue to be the ruination of many." [322] Professor Moniz de Aragão, in a communication to the Medical Society of Paris, states that he looks upon the "great number" of unusual extra-genital chancres in the Negroes and mestizos of Brazil as a result of the "boundless apelike lubricity" of the Negro and mulatto women.[323] But there is nothing strange in this point of view: Nina Rodrigues believed the female mulatto to be an abnormal type, subject to sexual superexcitation.

A better sense of discrimination was shown by Vilhena, writing in the eighteenth century: "The Negro women and a large part of the mulatto women as well, for whom honor is a chimerical term signifying nothing, are ordinarily the first to begin the early corruption of the young masters, giving them their first lessons in libertinism, in which, from childhood on, they are engulfed; and from this there comes, for the future, a troop of young mulattoes and *crias* whose influence in the families is to be a most pernicious one." However, he

---

[320] F. P. do Amaral: *Escavações (Excavations)* (Recife, 1884).

[321] F. L. C. B.: *Memória Analýtica*, etc. (op. cit.). The reference is chiefly to agrarian regions of the south in the first half of the nineteenth century.

[322] André João Antonil: *Cultura e Opulência do Brasil*, etc. (op. cit.), pp. 92–3.

[323] Egas Moniz de Aragão: *Contribution à l'étude de la syphilis au Brésil*, in Oscar da Silva Araujo: *Alguns Comentários sobre a Sifilis no Rio de Janeiro* (op. cit.). Oscar da Silva Araujo arrives at conclusions wholly opposed to those of Egas Moniz de Aragao: "The number of syphilitic chancres," he says, in summing up his observations made in hospitals and out-patient clinics frequented by a large number of blacks, *pardos*, and mulattoes, "is not relatively high, and one does not find a major percentage among the Negroes or mestizos; a greater number is to be noted among the whites, and especially foreigners." —Op. cit.

at once adds: "But it often happens that those who are called the old masters in distinction from their sons are the very ones to set the example for their families, by their conduct with their own female slaves. . . ." [324] It was, rather, these masters who were the sexually superexcited ones, and not the women from the slave huts. Yet not even they were wholly to blame; it was the economic system of monoculture and slave labor in secret alliance with the climate that created an atmosphere of sexual intoxication. But the economic system and its social effects were preponderant over climate.

"*Les jeunes Brésiliens,*" wrote Alp. Rendu, "*sont souvent pervertis presque au sortir de l'enfance.*" This impressed him as being due in good part to the climate: "*la chaleur du climat hâte le moment de la puberté*"; but the principal causes were social and were bound up with the system of economic production: "*les désirs excités par une éducation vicieuse et le mélange des sexes souvent provoqués par les négresses.*" [325] No one denies that the Negro and the mulatto woman contributed to the precocious depravity of the white lad of the slave-owning class; but she in herself is not to blame, nor is this an expression of her race or of her mixed blood; it is part of a system of economy and family life: the Brazilian patriarchal system.

Speaking of the plantation youths of his time, Father Lopes Gama says: "They no sooner attain virility than they give free rein to the most swinish appetites; they are the stallions of those parts. . . ." [326] And when these young stallions were not functioning as such, their occupation was swapping horses and oxen and playing high-point and trumps down at the sugar-refining shed. But this—let me stress the fact once more—was after an infancy that had been marked by attacks of constipation, clysters, tapeworms, convalescences; by feminine blandishments and "crushes" on the *mucamas* and by maternal coddling; by caresses, craftiness, "*cafunés*" given by the hand of the mulatto looking for lice; milk taken at the breast of a Negro nurse who was frequently too old for the purpose; pancakes or manihot paste with meat (*pirão com carne*) eaten out of the "black mammy's" fat hand; sores scratched by the mulatto girl, fleas picked by the Negro nurse, naps in the housemaid's lap.

There were cases in which the caresses were prolonged through a second infancy, with mothers and *mucamas* rearing the young lads to be effeminates, more or less. Soft and languid, with no desire to ride horseback or play the rowdy with the young Negroes of the

---

[324] Vilhena: *Cartas* (op. cit.), Vol. I, p. 138.

[325] Alp. Rendu: *Études sur le Brésil* (Paris, 1848).

[326] *O Capuceiro* (op. cit.).

bagaceira. They would not sleep alone, but in the *mucama's* portable bed. They were always inside the house, playing priest and christening, or father to their sisters' dolls. Father Gama speaks of the young ones he knew as being always "bundled up in clothing" and surrounded with so many "precautions against the sun, the rain, fair weather, and everything, that the poor lads acquire from it all a weak constitution and are so susceptible that a breath of air constipates them, a little sun gives them a fever, any kind of food produces indigestion, and any kind of exertion tires them and makes them ill." [327] It was natural that many a lad, overwhelmed by all these caresses on the part of his mother and the Negro women, should grow up with a sallow complexion, the same pallor that marked the faces of his mother and sisters cloistered in the Big Houses. On the other hand, there were many "pickaninnies" from the slave hut who were brought up in their master's house and surrounded with the same affectionate care. Spinsters or women who were barren, having no child of their own to rear, would bring up a Negro or mulatto child, at times with an exaggerated degree of tenderness. Speaking of one of these privileged infants, Father Gama tell us: "The boy breaks everything he lays his hands on, and everything he does is 'cute.' He is seven or eight years old, yet he cannot go to bed at night until he has first slept awhile in the lap of his 'yayá' [328] who lulls him to sleep by rocking him on her knee and singing to him a whole string of monotonous songs and carols of the time of Captain Frigideira." [329] He goes on: "I am acquainted with a respectable sibyl who is bringing up a Negro girl who must now be around fourteen years of age. This girl never goes to bed at night without first climbing up into the lap of her fat *yayá*, who snaps her fingers through the young one's woolly mop (glistening like shoe-polish with pomade) and makes knots in the little simpleton's clothing for her to suck on until she falls asleep! All this is obscene and a very bad way to bring up a child." [330] The schoolmaster priest tells us, half seriously, half jestingly, of another curious instance: that of young lads, white ones and of good family in this case, who before they went to bed were in the habit of intoxicating themselves with the smell of their armpits, a vice that they possibly

---

[327] Ibid.

[328] *Yayá* is another spelling of *iaiá*, familiar terms used by slaves in addressing girls and young ladies of the Big House. (Translator.)

[329] A proverbial expression, some-

thing like "in the good old days." Frigideira is a name applied to a boastful or pompous individual. (Translator.)

[330] *O Carapuceiro* (op. cit.).

had acquired from their foster-brothers at the breast of their Negro nurse.

Vilhena was astonished at the number of pickaninnies—Negroes and mulattoes—brought up in the Big House "with the greatest affection." In one of his letters from Bahia he wrote: "There is here so dominant a passion for keeping Negroes and mulattoes in the house that, once a *cria* is born, he does not leave the house until death takes him; there are many families that have within doors sixty, seventy, and more unnecessary persons. I am here speaking of the city, for in the country this would not be surprising." [331]

The pickaninnies brought up in the Big Houses also attracted the attention of Maria Graham, on the sugar-cane plantations that she visited in southern Brazil. One of these was the plantation of the Affonsos, the property of the Marcos Vieira family; it was a good property, with 200 oxen and 170 slaves for work in the fields, and it yielded 3,000 arrobas [about 48 tons] of sugar and 70 hogsheads of brandy. It was there that Mrs. Graham saw children of all ages and all colors eating and playing within the Big House, and they were all treated as affectionately as if they had been members of the family.[332]

This excess of feminine caresses bestowed upon young whites, and mulattoes as well, and its opposite extreme—the freedom that was soon accorded the white boys to loaf around with the *bagaceira* hands, to deflower young Negro girls, to take slave women, and to abuse animals—represented vices in the upbringing of the child that were, perhaps, inseparable from the slave-holding regime under which the formation of Brazilian society took place. They are vices that explain, better than the climate and incomparably better than the doubtful effects of miscegenation upon the sexual organism of the mestizo, the precocious initiation of the Brazilian lad into the erotic life. I am not denying the effect of climate, however; for in the backland region of Brazil, a region free of the direct influence of slavery and of the Negro and mulatto woman, the adolescent is likewise sexually precocious. He forms the habit of abusing animals at an early age, and the watermelon and the mandacarú lend themselves to his perversions. He is a virgin only so far as women are concerned, in which regard he enjoys an enormous superiority over the plantation youth.

Certain tendencies in the character of the *sertanejo*, or backlander, that incline him to asceticism; a certain suspiciousness in his habits and

---

[331] Vilhena: *Cartas* (op. cit.), Vol. I, p. 139.
[332] Maria Graham: *Journal of a Voyage to Brazil*, etc. (op. cit.), p. 280.

attitudes; that air of a seminary student that he preserves all his life long; his extraordinary physical endurance; his angular Quixote-like frame, contrasting with the more rounded and sleeker figures of the marshland-dwellers [333] and the inhabitants of the seaboard; the purity of his blood, which only now is beginning to be contaminated with syphilis and other venereal diseases—these are traits that are bound up in the most intimate manner with the fact that the *sertanejo* in general, and particularly in those regions that are more isolated from the capitals and the cattle-fairs, does not know a woman until late and then almost always through marriage. Gustavo Barroso, in a study of the backlands populations of the northeast, states that lads of twenty who are still virginal are common in the *sertão*,[334] a circumstance that in the marshlands or on the seaboard would be the subject of jesting and fierce ridicule. Here is to be sensed the direct influence of slavery upon these two zones, whereas the *sertão* was influenced only indirectly and remotely. This antagonism in the matter of sexual conduct—it would be extremely interesting to make a statistical contrast, based upon an inquiry among students of higher schools coming from the two regions—has only begun to diminish during the last few years. Male virgins of more than twenty are now becoming rare in the backlands, and syphilis is spreading among the *sertanejos*. It is to the brothels of Itabaiana and the famous six hundred prostitutes of Campina Grande—the "two centers of contact of the *sertanejos* with newcomers from Recife and Paraíba"—that José Américo de Almeida attributes the recent rapid syphilizing of the Paraíban backlanders.[335]

Had the climate been the principal cause of Brazilian sensuality, it would have acted upon the *sertanejos* at the same time that it was acting upon the *brejeiros*, or marshlanders, and the populations of the littoral, and not three centuries later. Let us not be more naïve today than Vilhena was in the eighteenth century. In one of his letters from Bahia he criticizes those parents who, while they contribute to "destroying the innocence of their own sons," persist in attributing to the heat "certain inadvertencies that are nothing but the product of a bad upbringing and their own coarseness." [336]

---

[333] The *brejeiros* are the inhabitants of the *brejos*, a term that in northeastern Brazil is applied to a "terrain where the water of the rivers is more or less permanently conserved; generally fertile by reason of the annual overflows in the rainy seasons."—Lima and Barroso, op. cit. (Translator.)

[334] Gustavo Barroso: *Terra de Sol* (*Land of Sun*) (Rio de Janeiro, 1913). [The *sertão* is the backlands region of northeastern Brazil. (Translator.)]

[335] José Américo de Almeida: *A Paraíba e Seus Problemas* (*Paraíba and Its Problems*) (Paraíba, 1923).

[336] Vilhena: *Cartas* (op. cit.), Vol. I, p. 166. It is plain to be seen that for

Moreover, if we compare the moral or, better, the social effects of monoculture and the system of slave labor upon the Brazilian people with those produced by the same system upon peoples of a different race and under diverse conditions of climate and physical environment—in the Antilles and in the Southern United States, for example—the preponderance of economic and social causes (the slave-holding technique of production and the patriarchal type of family) over the influence of *race* or that of *climate* is verified.

In the South of the United States, there evolved, from the seventeenth to the eighteenth century, an aristocratic type of rural family that bore a greater resemblance to the type of family in northern Brazil before abolition than it did to the Puritan bourgeoisie of another part of North America, which was similarly of Anglo-Saxon origin, but which had been influenced by a different kind of economic regime. There were almost the same country gentlemen—chivalrous after their fashion; proud of their slaves and lands, with sons and Negroes multiplying about them; regaling themselves with the love of mulattoes; playing cards and amusing themselves with cock-fights; marrying girls of sixteen; engaging in feuds over questions of land; dying in duels for the sake of a woman; and getting drunk at great family feasts—huge turkeys with rice, roasted by "old mammies" [337] skilled in the art of the oven, jellies, puddings, dressing, preserved pears, corn-cakes.

In the Southern United States, as in Cuba, the child and the woman passively underwent the same influences as did the young lad and the *sinhá-dona* on the sugar plantations and other estates of Brazil. Just as, in our country, the plantation lads were more precocious than those of the backlands in their experiences with women, so those of the South in the U. S. A. had such experiences earlier than those in the North. Calhoun [338] tells us of a Southern business man who, on a journey to New York, remarked to his friends in that city that he had visited his brother's plantation not long before, that he had found all the household slaves there suffering from venereal disease, and that the planter's sons were not behind the others in this regard. "I told him he might as well have them educated in a brothel at once." Interesting, also, is the statement by an old slave-owner of Alabama, cited by Calhoun, to the effect that on his estate "every young man

---

Vilhena the causes of the idleness and sexual excesses of eighteenth-century Brazilians were social in nature; it was not "the food, climate, and natural inclination. . . ."

[337] Words in English. (Translator.)
[338] Arthur W. Calhoun: *A Social History of the American Family,* etc. (op. cit.).

. . . became addicted to fornication at an early age." The same thing was true on Brazilian plantations.

There was no necessity for the Negro women to rub up against the adolescent whites; for the latter, like the sons of Brazilian planters, had been reared from infancy to be stallions, just as the colored girls had been brought up to be "generative bellies." "Slave women were taught," says Calhoun, "that it was their duty to have a child once a year, and that it mattered little who was the father." [339] Thus the same economic interest of the masters in augmenting the herd of slaves that corrupted the family in Brazil and in Portugal was at work upon the family in the United States. Travelers who were there in the days of slavery tell us of incidents that sound as if they had happened in our country.[340] True, in that country as in ours there were those who, confusing cause and effect, held the Negro woman and her "strong sex instincts," and especially the mulatto, "the lascivious hybrid woman," [341] responsible for the depravity of white youths. Here at home we have seen that Nina Rodrigues considered the female mulatto an abnormal sexually superexcited type; and even José Veríssimo,[342] ordinarily so sober in his judgments, in speaking of the Brazilian mestizo woman, wrote that she was a "dissolvent of our physical and moral virility." [343] In other words, we are the little innocents, while they are a lot of devils, "dissolving" our morality and corrupting our bodies.

The truth is that it was we who were the sadists, the active element in the corruption of family life; the slave boys and mulatto women

---

[339] Ibid.

[340] Among other travelers may be mentioned: William Faux: *Memorable Days in America* (London, 1823); Harriet Martineau: *Retrospect of Western Travel* (London, 1838); Sir Charles Lyell: *Travels in North America* (London, 1845); Frances Trollope: *Domestic Manners of the Americans* (London, 1832). For the impressions that travelers in general gleaned of the South before the Civil War, see the excellent compilation by Allan Nevins: *American Social History as Recorded by British Travellers* (New York and London, 1923). With regard to life on a Jamaican plantation, see the *Journal of a West India Proprietor* (London, 1929), written by M. S. Lewis from 1815 to

1873; and for Cuba and the life of masters and slaves on its sugar plantations and in Havana, see the works by Fernando Ortiz: *Los Cabildos Afrocubanos* (Havana, 1921); *Hampa Afrocubana—los Negros Brujos* (Madrid, 1917); and especially *Los Negros Esclavos* (Madrid). Also the study by J. S. Saco: *Historia de la Esclavitud de la Raza Africana en el Nuevo Mundo* (Havana, 1893); and the one by Ramiro Guerra: *Azúcar y Población en las Antillas* (Havana, 1930).

[341] See Calhoun, op. cit.

[342] The distinguished turn-of-the-century literary historian, critic, and essayist. (Translator.)

[343] José Veríssimo: *A Educação Nacional* (op. cit.).

were the passive element. In reality, neither white nor Negro in himself was the active force, either as a race or under the preponderant effect of climate, in the sexual and class relations between master and slave that developed in Brazil. What was given expression in those relations was the spirit of the economic system that, like a powerful god, divided us into enslaver and enslaved. And it was from that system that the exaggerated tendency toward sadism was derived that is so characteristic of the Brazilian born and reared in the Big House, especially on the sugar plantation—a tendency to which I have time and again alluded in the course of this essay.

Imagine a country in which the children go armed with a double-edged hunting-knife! Yet that was Brazil in the time of slavery. In his *Histoire des Indes Orientales*, Monsieur Souchu de Rennefort, who visited us in the seventeenth century, says: "*Tous les habitans de ce Pays jusques aux enfants, ne marchent point en campagne, qu'ils ne portent de grands couteaux nuds, trenchans des deux côtez. . . .*" The French writer attributed the general use of the hunting-knife to the necessity on the part of children and adults alike of defending themselves against boa constrictors: "*pour couper ces serpens nommez cobre-veados. . . .*" But it was not always serpents that they killed; they killed men and women also.

As a matter of fact, the custom of carrying the hunting-knife dates from the earliest colonial times, when both children and grown-ups had to be constantly on their guard against surprise attacks by the Indians and by wild animals. This resulted in a certain precocity on the part of the colonial child, who at an early age was called upon to share the anxieties and concerns of adults. He came to share their joys and pleasures as well, which chiefly had to do with sex.

V

THE NEGRO SLAVE
IN THE SEXUAL AND FAMILY LIFE
OF THE BRAZILIAN (Continued)

THOSE travelers who visited our country in the nineteenth century are unanimous in emphasizing one ridiculous feature of Brazilian life: the fact that small boys were compelled to become little men from the age of nine or ten years. They were obliged to deport themselves like adults, their hair well combed, at times curled after the manner of the Infant Jesus; a stiff collar; long trousers; black clothing; black boots; a solemn gait; grave gestures; and the mournful air of one attending a funeral.

They were little devils only up to the age of ten. From then on they became young men. Their garments those of adults. Their vices those of men. Their concern: to syphilize themselves as soon as possible, thereby acquiring those glorious scars in the bouts of Venus that Spix and Martius were so horrified to see Brazilians proudly displaying.[1]

When Dr. Rendu, the French physician, visited Brazil in the early years of the nineteenth century, he was astonished at the precociousness of the young lads, which impressed him as being, above all, grotesque. The following remarks are from his *Études sur le Brésil*: "*A sept ans le jeune Brésilien a déjà la gravité d'un adulte; il se promène majestueusement, une badine à la main, fier d'une toilette que le fait plutôt ressembler aux marionettes de nos foires qu'à un être humain.*"[2] Some twenty years later Fletcher was to remark of the young Brazilian of the mid-century: "He is made a little old man before he is twelve years of age,—having his stiff black silk-hat, standing collar, and cane; and in the city he walks along as if everybody were looking at him, and as if he were encased in corsets. He does not run, or jump, or trundle hoop, or throw stones as boys in Europe and North America."[3]

The Brazil of our grandfathers and great-grandfathers came near

---

[1] Cf. p. 70. (Translator.)
[2] Alp. Rendu: *Études sur le Brésil* (op. cit.).
[3] Kidder and Fletcher: *Brazil and the Brazilians* (op. cit.).

to being a land without children. At the age of seven many a small shaver could repeat for you by heart the names of the European capitals, could tell you the "three enemies of the soul," could add, subtract, multiply, and divide, decline in Latin, and recite in French. We may picture him as he looked at his first communion: black top-coat and black boots or half-boots—all this funereal black contrasting with the sickly yellow of his anemic countenance. It was then that the child became a youth.

Luccock, who was in Brazil at the beginning of the nineteenth century, noted the lack of merriment on the part of small boys and of vivacity on the part of the older ones. The education of the child appeared to him to have been reduced to the melancholy function of destroying in the little ones all spontaneity. In the house, up to the age of five, he noted that they went naked like the Negro children; but later came the solemn and heavy garments, by way of distinguishing the sons of the family from the *muleques* of the slave hut. The garments of a grown man.

The English observer always retained a mournful impression of a school for small boys with which he became acquainted in Rio de Janeiro. He saw the little ones shut up in an air-tight room, reading their lessons aloud and all at the same time. Luccock also knew a school (*colégio*)[4] kept by priests in Rio: St. Joseph's Seminary. He saw groups of students in the recreation room, all of them clad in scarlet cassocks and some of them tonsured. The majority of them were mere children. He was not able to discover in them any mental elasticity or intellectual curiosity. They did not even have good manners. "They surveyed us with a stupid glare," says Luccock, who found them, in addition, none too neat in their personal appearance. Mattery eyes and dirty teeth, it might be. As to the instruction, it impressed him as being purely ecclesiastic in character, the teachers being little versed in science.[5] Yet in this same era, the illustrious Bishop Azeredo Coutinho was giving an imprint to the Seminary of Olinda that made it quite different from what the Englishman had observed at St. Joseph's.

Down to the middle of the nineteenth century, when the first railroads came in, it was the custom on the plantations to have the young ones study at home, with the chaplain or with a private tutor.

---

[4] *Colégio* (*collégio*) was the term applied to schools kept by Jesuits in colonial Brazil; today the word means a private school giving primary or secondary instruction. (Translator.)

[5] John Luccock: *Notes on Rio de Janeiro*, etc. (op. cit.), p. 71. ". . . No ray of science has penetrated here," says the English observer.

The Big Houses almost always had a schoolroom, and many of them had a dark closet as well, for the wayward one who did not know his lesson. Very often the Negroes of the household, the *crias* and *muleques*, studied with the white children and all together learned to read and write, to do sums, and to pray. In other cases the white and Negro lads grew up equally ignorant.

The Jesuit schools in the first two centuries, and afterwards the schools and seminaries kept by priests, were the great centers for the irradiation of culture in colonial Brazil. These institutions stretched out their tentacles even to the jungle and the backlands. The first missionaries who groped their way naked through the jungle came upon children who were almost white, the descendants of Normans and Portuguese, and they proceeded to gather these shaggy young ones into their educational fold. It was, indeed, a heterogeneous infantile population that was assembled by the padres in the sixteenth and seventeenth centuries: the sons of *caboclos* taken from their parents; the sons of Normans, encountered in the woods; the sons of Portuguese; mamelucos; young orphans from Lisbon. Blond children, freckled children, mulattoes (*pardos*), brown-skins, and cinnamon-colored ones.

Negroes alone appear to have been barred from the first Jesuit schools. Negroes and very dark *muleques* (mulattoes). For in the seventeenth century the voice of His Majesty had to be raised in favor of the *pardos*, in a document that does honor to Portuguese culture, while at the same time it casts an unfavorable light upon the Christianity of the Jesuits. It is to be regretted that a document of such significance should have remained unpublished all this time.

"Honored Marquis of Minas, my friend," wrote the King of Portugal, in 1686, to his representative in Brazil. "I, the King, send you hearty greetings, as to one whom I prize. On the part of our *pardos* of your city, it has been brought to my attention that, whereas for many years they have possessed the right to study in the public Schools at the College of the Religious of the Society, they have of late been excluded and refused admittance, although in the schools of Erva and Coimbra they are admitted, without the color of a *pardo* serving as an impediment. They have accordingly besought me to command such Religious to admit them to their schools of that State as they are admitted to the others of the Realm. And it has seemed good to me to order you (as I hereby do) to see to informing the Fathers of the Society that they are obliged to teach them in the schools of that State, and that they are further obliged not to exclude any of these our subjects generally, merely by reason of their quality as *pardos,* for schools of science ought to be common to all manner of persons, without any exception whatsoever—written in Lisbon, the 20th of November of the year 1686. The King." [6]

"For schools of science ought to be common to all manner of persons, without any exception whatsoever." We can hardly believe our ears when we hear these words coming to us out of the remote seventeenth century. They should be heeded by those who accuse the Portuguese of having always treated Brazil as a land of roustabouts and half-breeds, of *curibocas,*[7] Negroes, and Indians. There is, for example, the almost demagogic attitude of Luis Edmundo, in his recent work *Rio de Janeiro in the Time of the Viceroys.* The brilliant belle-lettrist endeavors to make the point that, if legitimate marriages were not of frequent occurrence in colonial Brazil—the place of marriage being often taken by concubinage and ephemeral liaisons, such as Burton found to be still common in Minas Gerais in the mid-nineteenth-century—a factor that had a powerful effect in bringing this about was "the prejudice of many Portuguese against the natives of the country, a prejudice instilled by Portuguese law, in accordance with which those who formed unions with the so-called despicable race of *caboclos* were to be looked upon as being beyond the pale." [8] Now, it is not my opinion that the frequency of concubinage is to be attributed to the prejudice, for that is what it amounts to, of Portuguese against Brazilians; for the *mazombos*[9] who here formed alliances with *caboclas* and black women, had, certainly, the same reasons for avoiding matrimony as did the white Brazilians of a later time, so many of whom, instead of marrying, took Negro Minas and mulattoes as their concubines. These were prejudices, not of those of the Realm against colonials, not even of whites against colored women, but of masters against their female slaves and the daughters of slaves. As to Portuguese law holding those who formed unions with *caboclas* and Negro women to be beyond the pale—when were such Portuguese and Brazilian prohibitions ever put into writing that they might be carried out to the letter? As for the Portuguese laws, they also prohibited individuals with Moorish or Negro blood from

---

[6] *Cartas Régias* (Letters-Royal), document no. 881 bis, Manuscript Section of the National Library, Rio de Janeiro.

[7] A *curiboca* (*cariboca*) is a mestizo, part Indian and part Negro. *Curiboca* is the form of the word employed in northern Brazil. (Translator.)

[8] Luis Edmundo: *O Rio de Janeiro no Tempo dos Vice-Reis* (op. cit.).

[9] *Mazambo*: one born in Brazil of European, and particularly Portuguese, parents; a depreciatory epithet. (Translator.)

being admitted to the priesthood; and Pandiá Calogeras [10] asserts that this was the practice, and that the priesthood in Brazil constituted a species of closed aristocracy on the part of the whites; [11] yet foreign observers worthy of credence—Koster and Walsh, for instance— make it clear that there were priests with Negro blood, and some of them very dark Negroes, in the nineteenth century at any rate. One priest whom Walsh saw celebrating High Mass was so dark that his "jet-black visage" afforded a striking contrast to the white lacework of the ecclesiastical vestments. Incidentally, the Englishman noted that his gestures were more decorous than those of white priests.[12]

Taking law for law, over against the one that declares "those Portuguese who form unions with *caboclas* to be beyond the pale" we ought to set the one promulgated by the Marquis of Pombal, whose intention is exactly the opposite, this decree being designed to encourage marriages with Indian women.[13] There is enough to criticize in the policy of the Portuguese colonizers of Brazil, so that if one wishes to accuse them of tremendous mistakes, there is no necessity of having recourse to the imagination and making of the most pliable and plastic of European types a ferocious exclusivist, filled with race prejudices which, as a matter of fact, he never harbored in the same degree as other peoples. Those Portuguese governors of Brazil were rare who had the harsh and intolerant attitude—I shall not say against

---

[10] Pandiá Calogeras is the author of an authoritative work on Brazilian history: *Formação Histórica do Brasil* (Rio de Janeiro, 1930). There is an English-language version by the late Professor Percy A. Martin: *History of Brazil* (Chapel Hill: University of North Carolina Press; 1939). (Translator.)

[11] "Among the privileges denied to colored people was that of the priesthood; and for this reason the more respectable families among our ancestors made a great effort to have some of their members become priests or religious, as this was a proof of the purity of their blood."—Pandiá Calogeras, op. cit.—It would appear that this exclusiveness was broken down after the founding of the diocese of Mariana, under John V. Capistrano de Abreu, in his *Chapters of Colonial History (Capítulos de História Colonial,* op. cit.), cites a document in

which it is set forth that the Governor of that bishopric, Oliveira Gondim, in less than three years had ordained a hundred and one candidates, dispensing them from the taint of being mulattoes and illegitimate sons. It is curious to note that Minas Gerais seems always to have taken the lead in movements having to do with the social democratization of Brazil, against prejudices in favor of the whites and legitimate offspring.

[12] Walsh: *Notices of Brazil* (op. cit.), p. 56.

[13] J. F. Lisboa transcribes the Pombal decree in his *Jornal de Timon* (op. cit.). There is in existence a contemporary copy of this decree, in the Manuscript Section of the Pernambucan Archæological Institute, where I first read it. It is to be regretted that the document is so little known.

the Indians, but against the Negroes—that was displayed by the eighth Viceroy, the Marquis of Lavrádio, who, in a decree of the 6th of August 1771, removed an Indian from his post of captain-major for having married a Negro woman and thus "having stained his blood and shown himself unworthy of the office." [14] For that matter, even after Brazilian independence there were priests who refused to marry white and black. Priests and judges. One of the latter was the Pernambucan Castello Branco. But all of these were sporadic attitudes; they did not genuinely represent the Portuguese and Brazilian tendency, which was always in the direction of favoring, in so far as possible, the Negro's social ascent. But we are here going beyond the limits of the present essay and invading the province of the one that is to follow.

Not only were blacks and mulattoes in Brazil the companions of the white lads in the Big House schoolrooms and in the *colégios;* there were also white boys who learned to read with Negro teachers.[15] Arthur Orlando tells us that his primary teacher in Pernambuco was a Negro named Calixto, who went about dressed in a gray top hat, black cutaway, and white trousers.[16] Dressed like a lord.

Like a lord, or like those learned doctors and gentlemen of colonial times who lived in dread of hemorrhoids, when they were not already suffering from the accursed malady, which ever since the sixteenth century seems to have so persecuted the rich or educated Portuguese and their descendants in Brazil. This is not to be wondered at, seeing that the colonists of the sixteenth, seventeenth, and eighteenth centuries wore clothes that were so unsuited to the climate: velvets, silks, damasks; and many of them went out in palanquins that were also of silk, velvet, or damask on the inside. These palanquins de luxe were, without exaggeration, ambulating furnaces, being covered with heavy blue, green, and scarlet drapes or with thick curtains. Within their hammocks and palanquins the gentry permitted themselves to be carried about by Negroes for whole days

[14] Cited by Alfredo de Carvalho: *Frases e Palavras—Problemas Históricos e Etimológicos (Words and Sentences—Historical and Etymological Problems)* (Recife, 1900).

[15] On Negroes in the teaching and other professions in present-day Brazil (Bahia), see Donald Pierson: *Negroes in Brazil* (op. cit.), pp. 186 f. "In a private elementary school," says Pierson, a class of boys ranging in age from seven to eleven years were being taught by a Negro teacher. Among the group were two whites, one *branco da Bahia,* one mulatto, and three blacks. Several substantial white citizens had received their training under this man." (Translator.)

[16] Arthur Orlando, in response to the inquiry conducted by João do Rio for the *Gazeta de Notícias,* afterwards published in book form: *O Momento Literáro* (op. cit.).

at a time, some of them traveling in this manner from one plantation to another, while others employed this mode of transport in the streets; when acquaintances met, it was the custom to draw up alongside one another and hold a conversation, but the masters would always remain stretched out or seated on a pile of steaming cushions. In the house, likewise, they were always seated, or lay at full length in their hammocks, stuffed with insufferably hot pillows.

As for the women, they spent so large a part of their lives sitting down that, as a Dutch chronicler of the seventeenth century remarks, they staggered when they tried to get to their feet. Even in church they would scatter out and sit, with legs crossed, upon the gravestones, which were sometimes very cold. It was within the house, at bedtime, that men and women did away with the excess of European clothing, while the young ones went nude or clad in their nighties. The adults would wear slippers without stockings or go barefoot. The lords of the manor would parade in calico dressing-gowns over their drawers, the women in smocks. "When they go out on ceremonious visits," writes Vilhena of the Bahian ladies, "they trig themselves out to such an extent that there is no doubt that they spend on a single gown four hundred milreis and more, just to appear at a single function. . . ." [17] Satins, Silks. Cambrics or embroidered muslins. Their *mucamas* also: "rich satin petticoats, gowns of the finest broadcloth, cambric blouses." With the good sense that he always displays, Vilhena defends the Brazilian ladies against their critics who would have it that they are "none too respectable, going about in their homes in their chemises, which are so open at the throat that at times they fall apart and you can see their breasts. . . ." These "evil-minded critics" appear to the 'Greek professor to have forgotten that they are not in Europe, but in Brazil, "just below the torrid zone, where the greatest cold that they experience corresponds to that which we have here [in Portugal] in the month of May." [18]

The lack of adaptation of Brazilian clothing to the climate continued through the nineteenth century and became still more pronounced.[19] Men, women, and even children continued to dress themselves for Mass, for social calls, or for school as if a perpetual state

---

[17] Vilhena: *Cartas* (op. cit.), Vol. I. p. 47.

[18] Ibid.

[19] In 1871 the statement was made in the Imperial Academy of Medicine of Rio de Janeiro by its titular member Luis Corrêa de Azevedo that "the black broadcloth cutaway and the huge and incomprehensible top hat from the courts of Europe have come in their turn to augment the temperature of this zone, which is already almost torrid as it is."—*Annaes Brasilienses de Medicina*, Vol. XXII, No. 11 (April 1872).

of mourning obliged them to this solemn and uncomfortable black. They traveled about in victorias and cabriolets on cushions that were quite as hot as those of the palanquins of old. The men were in top hat from seven o'clock in the morning; and down to the beginning of the twentieth century the law students of São Paulo and Olinda, the medical students of Rio and Bahia, physicians, lawyers, professors, all went about in beaver and black cutaway. Once in a while a light-colored sombrero would stand out daringly against the orthodox black of the toppers. Such compromise as the doctors and fidalgos made with the tropical climate was from the bottom up: with their white trousers. From the mid-century on, the proprietors of the sugar and coffee warehouses in Bahia and Recife, high public functionaries, physicians, lawyers, professors began wearing these latter. It may be seen, therefore, that Calixto in appearing before his pupils dressed in the manner described was merely following the approved fashion; this was, so to speak, the official garb of the upper and educated class of his day.

"He made an arrangement with my father," writes Arthur Orlando, in speaking of his Negro instructor, "to teach me to read in return for an ebony flute with silver keys." For the blacks were the musicians of the colonial era and in the time of the Empire. The altar-boys in the churches were Negro lads, and a number of plantation chapels had Negro choruses. Some of the Big Houses kept up the tradition of *Mangue la Bote* [20] by maintaining, for the pleasure of the whites, bands of musicians made up of African slaves. On the Monjope plantation, in Pernambuco—which for a long time was the property of some of the Carneiro-da-Cunhas, who ended by becoming barons of Vera Cruz—there was not only a Negro band, but a pony circus in which slaves took the part of clowns and acrobats. Musicians, circus acrobats, blood-letters, dentists, barbers, and even teachers of the young—Brazilian slaves were all of these things, and not merely the man with the hoe or the cook in the kitchen. Many a Brazilian lad must have had for his first hero, not any white physician, marine officer, or university man, but some acrobat from the slave hut whom he had seen executing difficult pirouettes in the plantation circuses and *bumbas-meu-boi;* [21] or it might be a Negro player of the trombone or flute.

---

[20] Cf. p. 275. (Translator.)

[21] On this form of entertainment, a dramatic ballet staged by Negroes, see Chapter iv, note 101, p. 315. See also Arthur Ramos: *O Negro Brasileiro* (*The Brazilian Negro*) (Rio de Janeiro, 1934), pp. 259–68; and the same author's *O Folk-lore Negro do Brasil* (*Negro Folklore of Brazil*) (Rio de Janeiro, 1935), pp. 103–14.

Happy were those youngsters who learned to read and write with Negro teachers, gentle and kind. They must have endured less than the others, less than those who went to school to the priests, to the friars, to "pecuniary professors," or to the public schoolmasters. These last were a terrible lot of old curmudgeons, ridiculous characters in buckled shoes who were forever taking snuff and who always had a quince-tree rod in their hands. A rod or a ferule. For it was by the grace of the rod and the ferule that "the old folks," our grandsires and great-grandsires, learned Latin and grammar, Church doctrine, and sacred history.

After independence had been achieved, private schools began to spring up, some of them kept by foreigners—pedagogues or charlatans; and these were attended by the sons of magistrates and high public functionaries, business men, and even plantation-owners. One can imagine the feelings of the plantation lads, accustomed to a life of loafing—bathing in the river, trapping birds, cock-fighting, playing cards with the Negroes down at the refinery, and chasing after their cousins and the colored girls—one can imagine their feelings upon leaving all these pleasures to travel, by boat or by horseback, to the schools where they were to study, stopping off en route at the plantations of relatives and friends of their parents. It might be a boarding-school or it might be a day school; in the latter case they would put up at the house of some sugar or coffee broker, who very often became a kind of second father to them. For these commission merchants were not always the terrible leeches, preying on the land-owners, that they have been made out to be. They were sometimes the loyal friends of the planters and *fazendeiros*.

With regard to the institutions conducted by foreigners, the schoolmaster priest Lopes Gama wrote in 1842: "Any Frenchman, any Englishman, any Swiss, etc., any cunning creature from those countries, coming to Pernambuco and having no other mode of livelihood, at once announces that he is going to share with us his great enlightenment." The sagacious padre anticipated the ill effects that were to accrue from such schools: "We shall soon see coming out of these centers of heterodoxy a lot of Socinians, Anabaptists, Presbyterians, Methodists, etc. . . ." [22]

After 1850 the railroads came to make it easier for the plantation youths to attend boarding-school in the capitals. The School of Our Lady of Good Counsel, founded in 1858 in Recife by the university

According to Donald Pierson, "the *bumba meu boi* is still to be seen in the Bahian interior" (*Negroes in* *Brazil*, op. cit., p. 103). (Translator.) [22] Padre Lopes Gama: *O Carapuceiro* (op. cit.).

bachelor Joaquim Barbosa Lima may be considered typical of this phase of broadened influence on the part of the convent schools. In these institutions they taught arithmetic, geography, Latin, French, penmanship, and music. The pupils would appear in the classrooms clad in black coats, brown trousers, shoes of carpet-weave or leather, and blue cravat. On feast-days and Sundays they were expected to present themselves in black swallowtail, black trousers, black hat, white vest, black silk cravat, and black shoes or pumps. They were obliged to wash their feet on Wednesdays and Saturdays and to take an all-over bath once a week.[23]

With the appearance of a larger number of schools, the hygienists of the era began to be concerned with conditions among the boarding pupils in particular. Many a lad from the interior died of fever or infection in these *colégios*. In his thesis, "Outline of a Hygiene for Schools, Applicable to Our Own," written in 1855, José Bonifácio Caldeira de Andrade, Jr., states: "Unfortunately, we can count a large number of schools in the heart of our city [Rio de Janeiro] located in narrow, winding streets that are none too clean for the most part, a circumstance that, in view of our hygrometric and temperature conditions and our slight degree of elevation above sea-level, cannot fail to exert a fatal influence upon the health of the pupils." Nor was this all: "The illumination in our schools is commonly with oil and gas; and these are, precisely, the least suitable means, especially the latter."[24] Another thesis on the subject of the convent schools, this one by a doctoral candidate of the Faculty of Medicine of Bahia, Fructuoso Pinto da Silva, turns by preference to the problem of morality and sexual hygiene among the students. The attention of parents, teachers, and school examiners is called to the perils of onanism, and this in alarming terms. The same with regard to pederasty. "Pederasty," wrote Pinto da Silva in 1864, "appears to go with crafty tread, making its pernicious conquests among the youth of our boarding-schools. . . ."[25] But even graver were the advances that gonorrhea and syphilis were making—an indication of the extent of sexual excesses among the pupils. Back in the eighteenth century, if we are to believe the account of Father Cepeda, now discreetly stored away in the archives of the Historical Institute of Rio de Janeiro, the royal gardens of São Cristovão, in the suburbs of the capital, where classes

---

[23] Colégio de Nossa Senhora do Bom Conselho, *Estatutos* (*Statutes*) (Recife, 1859).

[24] Thesis presented and sustained on the 12th day of December 1855 before the Faculty of Medicine of Rio de Janeiro (Rio de Janeiro, 1855).

[25] Thesis presented and sustained in November 1869 before the Faculty of Medicine of Bahia (Bahia, 1869).

in philosophy were then held, was a "Sodom." The pupils of Father Cardim and Father Fária, "with neither the fear of God nor the shame of men," would run around all day like a lot of he-goats, leaping fences and hedges as they chased the slave girls and "other women whom they had caused to be sent from the city for that purpose." [26]

In the schools of the old days, if there was on the one hand a certain laxity that was plainly to be seen in the excesses, the turbulence, and the perversions of the young, there was on the other hand a criminal abuse of childish weakness. The teachers took a real delight in humiliating the child, in doing him bodily violence. This was a reflection of the general tendency to sadism created in Brazil by slavery and the abuse of the Negro. The teacher was an all-powerful master. Looking down from his chair, which after Independence became something very like a royal throne, with the Imperial crown carved in relief upon the back, he delivered punishments with the terrible air of a plantation-owner castigating his runaway blacks. The one who did not apply himself as he should was stood up with his arms spread apart; the one caught laughing aloud was humiliated by having a dunce-cap stuck on his head, to make him the laughingstock of the entire school; another would be forced to crawl on his knees over grains of corn. This is not to speak of the ferule and the rod—the latter, often, with a thorn or a pin stuck in the end of it to permit the teacher to prick the calves of a pupil from a distance.

The pupil who did not know his Portuguese lesson, who made a mistake in Latin, or who blotted a page of his copybook—which was something like a missal in point of sanctity—ran the risk of a terrible punishment at the hands of the schoolmaster priest, the *mestre-régio*,[27] or the director of the school—one of those terrifying ogres in cutaway or cassock. In the old-time schools great attention was always paid to penmanship, and instruction in this branch had in it something of the liturgical. The writing was done with a quill pen. "The schoolmaster would spend hours and hours trying out the pen after having first sharpened the nib with a penknife," Father Autunes de Siqueira tells us.[28] When all was in readiness, the torture would begin—the child with his head on one side, the tip of his tongue sticking out of his cheek, in the attitude of one who is striving for

---

[26] Father Cepeda's account (*Relatório*), cited by Luis Edmundo: *O Rio de Janeiro no Tempo dos Vice-Reis* (op. cit.).

[27] Schoolmaster appointed by the crown. (Translator.)

[28] Padre Antunes de Siqueira: *Esboço Histórico dos Costumes do Povo Espírito-santense Desde os Tempos Coloniais até Nossos Dias (Historical Sketch of the Customs of the People of Espírito Santo from Colonial Times to Our Day)* (Rio de Janeiro, 1893).

perfection, while the master stands by, watching for the first Gothic letter that does not come out as it should. The slightest mistake—and thwacks on the knuckles, pinches over the body, ear-pullings, a horrible time. It was these lads with the fine handwriting that the Viscount of Cabo Frio [29] always preferred as secretaries of legation, rather than those with the "physician's hand," [30] and they were the ones who had been educated by these terror-inspiring schoolmasters who made a rite of instruction in penmanship—there was something religious about it for them, something sacred.

Another sacred study was Latin. As to spelling, it was learned "in a tiresome din," so Father Siqueira informs us. They spelled the syllables aloud, chanting:

B—a—ba
B—e—be
Ba! Be!

With the Valdetaro method, adopted by the middle of the nineteenth century, things improved somewhat. There came then *The Syllabic Charts, with Blackboard Exercises; Simão de Mantua, or the Merchant of the Fairs; the Sacred Poems* of Lopes Gama; and the *Synonyms* of Friar Luis de Souso.[31] The Latin grammar in use was Father Pereira's; the catechism, Montpellier's. Whoever may have the inclination, some day when he has nothing better to do, to run his eye over the compendiums, readers, and arithmetics from which our forebears of colonial times and those who lived under the Empire learned their lessons will be able to form an idea of how terribly melancholy a thing it was to learn to read in those days.[32] And then

[29] Joaquim Tomaz do Amaral, Visconde do Cabo Frio (1818–1901), was a Brazilian diplomat. (Translator.)

[30] The *letra bonita* versus the *letra de médico*, physicians being noted for their illegible handwriting. (Translator.)

[31] Padre Antunes de Siqueira: *Esboço*, etc. (op. cit.).

[32] I can recommend some of these texts to the more curious reader: the *Compêdio de Arithmética* (*Compendium of Arithmetic*), by Cândido Baptista de Oliveira (Rio de Janeiro, 1832); the *Educador da Mocidade* (*Educator of Youth*), by Alexandre de Mello Moraes (Bahia, 1852); the *Guia de Leitura e Maximas Geraes de Conducta* (*Guide to Reading and General Maxims of Conduct*), by Antônio Alves Branco Moniz Barreto (Rio de Janeiro, 1854); the *Lições Elementares de Arithmética* (*Elementary Lessons in Arithmetic*), by "Hum Brasileiro" (A Brazilian) (Rio de Janeiro, 1825). As for the sixteenth and seventeenth centuries, Alcantara Machado found in old São Paulo wills allusions to the following didactic works: *Epitome Historial* (*Historical Epitome*); *Floro Histórico* (*Historical Garland*); *Prosódia* (*Prosody*); *Tratado Prático de Arithmética* (*Practical Treatise on Arithmetic*); *Cartilha* (*Primer*); *Repertório* (*Repertory*); *Segredos da Natureza* (*Secrets of Nature*).—Alcantara Machado: *Vida e Morte do Bandeirante* (op. cit.).

imagine these horrifying manuals plus the crown-appointed school-masters and the convent teachers of the time—all of them stinking of snuff, blowing their noses every so often in big red handkerchiefs, and all of them with ferule and quince-tree rod in hand, and with an enormous nail like that of a Chinese Mandarin on the thumb or index-finger of the right hand.

The white child—and the black or mulatto one as well, when reared by the *iaiás* of the Big Houses—was subjected to yet other torments. "Society has its grammar, also." These words, written in 1845, are by the author of a certain *Code of Good Form*,[33] which enjoyed a great vogue among the barons and viscounts of the Empire, who, by way of assuming the air of Europeans, not only proceeded to line the roofs of their Big Houses—up to then the tiles had been left showing—but were bent on adopting the French and British rules of good form in the upbringing of their children. And adopt them they did, with many exaggerations and excesses.

The victim of this baronial snobbery was the son of the family. He might torment the Negro lads and young Negro girls; that was his right; but in the society of his elders he became the tormented. He it was who on feast-days must present himself in the garb of a grown man; he must be stern and correct and not wrinkle his black suit[34] by indulging in any childish play. It was he who, when older

---

[33] J. I. Roquette: *Código do Bom Tom* (Paris, 1845).

[34] It is true that, at the beginning of the nineteenth century, Joaquim Jerónymo Serpa, in his *Tratado de Educação Physico-moral dos Meninos* (*Treatise on the Physical-Moral Upbringing of the Young*), an adaptation of the pedagogical principles of one Mr. Garden, published in Pernambuco, advised parents to dress their sons in "colors that more nearly approximate white," while at the same time he condemned the practice on the part of certain parents, fearful of lice, of having "the heads of children close-shaved." This was a practice that perhaps was not wholly bad. Rebelling against the sadism of school-masters and parents alike, Serpa severely censures another custom: that of whipping children on the buttocks, a "pernicious practice," calculated to "foment sinister habits, the irritation that is occasioned upon this part communicating itself to the generative organs as soon as the sensation of pain is lessened somewhat." From which it might seem that those punishments of which Father Siqueira tells us were better: that of having the youngster kneel on grains of corn for two, three, and four hours; or the thwacks given with the several pedagogical and domestic varieties of ferule: the one made of fishskin, the one made of rosewood; and, for the really bad urchins, the one of grama-grass. In Minas they tell the story of a certain priest of Caraça, Padre Antunes, who "tied a handkerchief around his arm to give him greater strength in wielding the ferule."—Era Nigra: "*Histórias da Idade Media*" ("Tales of the Middle Ages"), in the *Revista do Arquivo Público* of Minas Geraes. Ano XII (1907). Brazilian pedagogy, like patriarchal discipline, rested upon

persons were present, must keep silent, with a seraphic look on his face as he received a blessing from each adult who entered the house and held out to him a hand filthy with snuff. He must always say "Senhor Pai" to his father and "Senhora Mãe" to his mother; for the freedom to say "Papa" and "Mamma" was only for his early childhood. This harsh custom, however, was modified in the nineteenth century; and women also ceased addressing their husbands solely with a "Senhor," the more daring ones employing the familiar "*tu*" (thou), while others used the more formal "*você*." Both wives and children became less ceremonious in speaking to the head of the house.[35] Up to then they had been practically on the same level as slaves.

---

a distinctly sadistic base. It was the result, in large part, of conditions surrounding its origins: a pedagogy and a discipline of conquerors over conquered, of masters over slaves. There is a study to be made of the various forms and instruments of punishment to which the child in Brazil was subjected, at home and in boarding-school: the various kinds of ferule; the quince-tree switch, at times tipped by a pin; the guava-tree bough; the thrashings; the blows on the nape of the neck; the ear-pullings; the pinchings and slappings; the knuckle-rappings; head-rappings; blows in the palm of the hand. The child as much as the slave was the victim of patriarchal sadism.

[35] The use even in present-day Portuguese of the third person singular in direct address—"*o senhor*" (the senhor), "*a senhora*" (the senhora), "*vossa senhoria*" (originally, "your lordship")—as well as the abuse of "*vossa excelencia*" (your excellency), may perhaps be looked upon as a heritage of the patriarchal slave-holding regime that dominated Brazilian life after having dominated that of the Portuguese. Miss Betham-Edwards observed in certain strata of French society, whose private life she undertook to study, a persistent use of the third person singular on the part of servants and subordinates in dealing with their employers, superiors, etc. A form of address in which she found a "survival of the *ancien régime* and caste."—*Home Life in France* (London, 1913).

Among us survivals of this nature are numerous and strongly marked. In contrast to such archaic forms of address as "*o senhor*," "*a senhora*," "*o senhor doutor*" (the senhor doctor), "*o senhor coronel*" (the senhor colonel), etc., there is to be observed in Brazil a great reluctance in the use of "*por favor*," "*por obséquio*" (if you please, etc.). It is with good reason that Tobias Monteiro remarks: "Our lack of politeness to those who serve us derives from the evils of slavery; we never ask anything of them as a favor and almost never thank them for anything, as is done among cultivated peoples."—*Funcionários e Doutores* (*Functionaries and Doctors*) (Rio de Janeiro, 1917).

Sousa Bandeira gleans the following traditional incident: the revolutionaries of 1817 having adopted the more familiar form, *vos*, one of the leaders was thus addressed by a Negro follower. The Pernambucan nobleman indignantly replied that he only permitted his equals to address him in such a manner. "For you ['*para ti*': familiar form used in addressing servants and intimates] it will always be '*Senhor Coronel, vossa senhoria*' "!

It is true that from a remote time the "Senhor" had been softened into "*Sinbô*," "*Nhombô*," and "*Ioiô*"; just as the word *Negro* had come to acquire in the mouths of whites a feeling of intimate and special tenderness or affection: "*meu nego*," "*minha nega*" (literally, "my Negro");[36] and we find colonial letters ending with "*Saudoso primo e muito seu negro*" ("Your affectionate cousin and very much your Negro"), "*negrinho humilde*" ("Your humble little Negro"), etc.[37]

Only after his marriage did the son venture to smoke in his father's presence; and his first shave was a ceremony for which the youth always had to have special permission. This was difficult to obtain, and was only granted when the down on the lad's face admitted of no further delay.

As for the girl, she was denied everything that savored in the least of independence. She was even forbidden to raise her voice in the presence of her elders. Should she be forward or impertinent in manner, it was a horrible thing and she would be properly slapped for it. Timid little girls with a humble air were the kind that were adored. That humble air which the Daughters of Mary display in processions and in the devout exercises of Holy Week formerly had to be preserved by young lasses all the year round. True, the bolder ones did a little flirting at the feast of São Gonçalo, others in church. But this was in the cities, in Rio, Recife, aBhia; and even these flirtations were carried on chiefly by motions with the fan, with almost no conversation or hand-holding.

Girls brought up in a strict patriarchal atmosphere lived under the

---

[36] ". . . *Meu negro* ('my Negro'), with its variation *meu nego* and diminutive *meu negrimho*, all spoken in soft tones, are terms of endearment used even by whites in speaking to other whites, especially in cases of great intimacy as, for instance, between lovers. Their use constitutes, as a Bahian put it, 'um modo de tratar bem' ('a way of being nice'). Occasionally one hears these expressions on the lips of a beggar asking alms of a white and, if he appears well to do, of a mulatto as well. Clerks sometimes employ them in addressing a customer. They appear to call up tender memories of intimate personal relations like those existent, for example between Mammy and Scarlet O'Hara in Margaret Mitchell's *Gone with the Wind*."—Donald Pierson: *Negroes in Brazil* (op. cit.), p. 139.

[37] Affonso de E. Taunay, in his *Sob El-Rey Nosso Senhor* (op. cit.), records various modes of address characteristic of the relations between husband and wife, brother and sister, etc., under the patriarchal regime. A sister to her brother, in a letter: "*Senhor Capitão*" (Senhor Captain), and at the end: "*De V.mce., irmã no amor e serva*" (Your Grace's loving sister and servant). And Padre José de Almeida Lara to his first cousin Diogo de Toledo Lara: "Your affectionate cousin and very much your Negro."

stern tyranny of their fathers—and later under the tyranny of their husbands.[38] and if the *mucamas* and houseboys were almost always the natural allies of the young people against their parents, the "*senhores pais*," and of wives of fifteen against the "*senhores maridos*," their husbands of forty, fifty, sixty, and seventy years, there were none the less cases of scheming slave girls who became informers, some of them out of vengeance, and who invented stories of love affairs on the part of the *sinhá-moças* or *sinhá-donas*. The womenfolk, accordingly, had to be always on their guard and could never consider themselves to be alone, not even for innocent flirtations with a fan, with a handkerchief, or through missives handed them by those Negro women who went about selling lace and similar trifles.

There was a saying in Portugal that served as a warning to those who were indiscreet in what they said or wrote, to the effect that behind every inkwell there lurked a friar. The eye or the ear of a friar of the Holy Office, beholding the acts and overhearing the words of those who were not so orthodox as they might be. In Brazil the eye of the plotting friar did not disappear from the houses; for it was an ecclesiastic who informed Verônica Dias Leite, a São Paulo matron of the seventeenth century, that her daughter had stood at the window for some little while. This was a horrendous crime and resulted—so tradition tells us—in the mother's having her daughter slain. Antônio de Oliveira Leitão, a patriarch if there ever was one, did not need any informer, whether friar or slave; having seen a handkerchief waving at the far end of the garden adjoining his home, a handkerchief that his daughter was drying in the sun, and thinking that it was a signal from some Don Juan who was out to stain his honor, he did not for a moment hesitate, but whipped out his long-bladed knife and with it ran the girl through her bosom.[39]

But usually in these stories of daughters or wives assassinated by the patriarchs, there was always a friar or a female slave involved. Especially the female slave. In Brazil, whoever had his love affair or his secret, let him beware not only of inkwells and the friars who might be hidden behind them, but, above all, of sweetmeat kettles, for behind these at times were the eyes of plotting Negro women.

---

[38] A tyranny that was carried to the extreme of shutting young married women up in convents. The husband was then free to go and live with the woman friend of his choice. —H. Handelmann: *História do Brasil* (op. cit.). In the court correspondence preserved in manuscript form in the Library of the State of Pernambuco will be found a number of petitions having to do with such cases, addressed to the authorities of the realm.

[39] Affonso de E. Taunay: *Sob El Ney Nosso Senhor* (op. cit.)

Dom Domingos de Loreto Coutto, the Dominican friar who, in his *Compensations of Brazil and Glories of Pernambuco*,[40] portrays so many interesting aspects of patriarchal life in our country, tells of some impressive instances of women who were assassinated because they were suspected of conjugal infidelity. These were crimes that were due to "false witness" on the part of individuals who, "free enough in their own lives, are very scrupulous where those of their masters are concerned." But the cap that Dom Domingos thus fashioned for slaves might very will have been fitted to the head of many an ecclesiastic.

Then there was Colonel Fernão Bezerra Barballo of Varzea, "a place that today is named for murder." A man of evil disposition, he let himself be taken in by the connivings of a slave whom the mistress of the house had ordered punished for offenses committed in his master's absence. The colonel had no hesitancy in assassinating his wife and daughters. "Accompanied by his first-born son and a few slaves, he hastily made his way to Varzea, and arriving at his own house and using the street door, he went on up. There was a horrible massacre. One daughter alone escaped death—and she was precisely the one on whom the scheming black wished most to avenge himself. It was another slave, possibly her Negro nurse, who prevented her from being slain. As for Fernão Bezerra, he "was arrested and brought before the court of higher appeals of Bahia and paid with his gray head for having so frivolously and madly yielded to his own mistaken judgment." [41] His fate was the same as that of Antônio de Oliveira Leitão.

It was a slave woman, in alliance with a terrible mother-in-law, who in Pernambuco was responsible for the assassination of Don' Ana, a young lady "of rare comeliness," the chronicler tells us, daughter of the sergeant-major Nicolao Coelho and wife of André Vieyra de Mello. The slave informed André Vieyra de Mello's mother that Don' Ana "was furtively admitting João Paes Barreto, who with a sacrilegious contempt for the sacrament and the constituted authorities was doing injury to the conjugal couch." The husband at first paid no heed to these stories; but so great was the insistence of his mother and his father as well that he had João Paes Barreto killed and his wife poisoned. Before taking the poison, Don' Ana begged them to bring her a priest to confess her and a Franciscan robe in which to be buried. She confessed herself and put on the robe.

[40] Domingos do Loreto Coutto: *Desaggravos do Brasil e Glórias de Pernambuco, Annals of the National Library of Rio de Janeiro*, Vol. XXIV.

[41] Ibid., Part II, p. 123.

Then they gave her the poison. Distrusting the efficacy of the potion, they gave her another. As a result, the second one undid the effects of the first, and Don' Ana did not die until "she had been choked to death by her mother-in-law.[42] . . . The story persists that, years afterwards, when they opened her grave, they found her body still fragrant and incorrupt." So says Loreto Coutto, who maintains that "chastity, a sense of shame, a retiring disposition, bashfulness, decorum, and modesty" were always "the distinctive mark of Brazilian women." It is true, he adds, that "in many black and mulatto women (*pardas*) composure is sometimes lacking and manners are altogether too free." He continues: "We do not deny that they [the colored women] serve as a temptation, but God permits this warfare in the world that the victors may deserve the crown of glory." These words constitute a great, even though an indirect, tribute to the beauty of the blacks and mulattoes, a beauty of which the Lord makes use in testing the steadfastness of white men.

But this same Dom Domingos also tells us of cases where mulatto women (the *pardas*) showed themselves to be extremely virtuous. The case of the saintly Joana de Jesús, for example. She flourished "in the new convent of the town of Iguarassú," where she distinguished herself as "a most sincere and devout follower of the Blessed Mary, Our Lady." She had begun life as a great sinner; she ended it near to being a saint. When she died, those who beheld her were surprised by "her beautiful colored face, from which there had disappeared all signs of death and all the ravages caused by the rigors of penance."

Another interesting case was that of Clara Henriques, a black woman and a slave belonging to Maria Henriques, who not only failed to instruct her in Christian doctrine, "but provoked her with bad examples." "According to Clara Henriques, the manners of her fourteen-year-old mistress were such as were conducive to a wanton life. . . ." From this life Clara was able to free herself, thanks to Our Lady of the Rosary, patron saint of Negroes. She thereupon became a holy woman. Taking advantage of her African leanings, the Lord bestowed upon her "the gift of prophecy, for she foretold many things that afterwards came to pass." [43]

The French travelers who in the seventeenth and eighteenth cen-

---

[42] For another mother-in-law incident, compare the legendary account that Euclides da Cunha gives of Antonio Conselheiro and his wife. See *Os Sertões,* 16th edition, pp. 165–6; *Rebellion in the Backlands,* pp. 130–1. (Translator.)

[43] Loreto Coutto: *Desaggravos do Brasil,* etc. (op. cit.), Part II, Book VI, Chapter v.

turies visited Brazil were not so credulous as the Benedictine Dom Domingos with respect to the chastity and conjugal fidelity of the Brazilian ladies; but as a compensation Dom Domingos has on his side the statements of English visitors. It is true that in matters of love and women the French are looked upon as being more deeply versed than the English; but as travelers the latter carry off the palm by the candor, faithfulness, and honesty of their accounts. A Rendu, a Saint-Hilaire, even a Pyrard are rare; on the other hand, those Frenchmen who exaggerate, who are none too scrupulous or are downright fantastic in their travel narratives, are by no means rare— a genre in which Thevet, Dabadie, and Expilly stand out.

It is Pyrard who tells us that he was swaggering through the streets of Salvador [44] one day, all dressed in silk and with the air of a fidalgo, when he was approached by a Negro woman. She asked him to accompany her, saying there was a gentleman who very much desired to speak with him. Pyrard followed her through the alleyways and narrow, unkept streets until he found himself, as in a *Thousand and One Nights* tale, in a very fine house, a real palace. And instead of a gentleman, there appeared before him a "young Portuguese dame," who not only bestowed her caresses upon the traveler, but made him a present of a felt hat fresh from Spain. All of which led Pyrard de Laval to indulge in the generalization that Brazilian women were more friendly to foreigners than were the men. [45]

No one, however, was bolder in his generalizations directed against the colonial ladies than Coreal—a traveler who has been as yet none too well identified. He found them more cloistered than in Mexico, but none the less licentious for all that. So great was the sexual fire in them that they would risk honor and life itself in a love adventure. The result was that some were stabbed to death by their husbands, while others became public courtesans, at the disposition of whites and Negroes alike. [46]

Frézier and Froger had much the same impression as Coreal of the Bahian women: these were very much cloistered and only left the house to go to church; but still they were "nearly all libertines" and were forever devising means of eluding the vigilance of their husbands or their fathers. In this, Frézier tells us, they were aided by their mothers; [47] but in the gallant episodes related by Pyrard and Coreal it

---

[44] The city of Bahia. (Translator.)
[45] Pyrard de Laval, op. cit., pp. 211–12.
[46] Coreal, op. cit., p. 192.
[47] Alluding to the colonial wives,

Frézier says: "*Les Portugais sont si jaloux qu'a peine leur permettent ils d'aller à la Messe les jours de Fêtes et Dimanches; neanmoins malgrès toutes leurs precautions, elles sont*

is the female slaves who assist the white ladies in their love affairs. It is likely that it was the Negro women who were the chief procuresses. Nevertheless, everything leads us to believe that such adventures were extremely difficult for colonial women, who at every hour were surrounded by indiscreet eyes. The eyes of friars. The eyes of Negroes. The eyes of mothers-in-law. Those of the more vigilant Negroes they might cause to be gouged out on some pretext or other, but those of the friars and mothers-in-law were more difficult to do away with.

To be sure, John Mawe, arriving in Brazil in the expectation of finding there a land where feminine morality was very lax and where travelers were approached by slave-women procuresses with missives and offerings from libidinous ladies, was led to form an entirely different impression. He tells us that neither in São Paulo nor in any other part that he visited did he find a single example of that levity which certain writers say is the most prominent trait of character in Brazilian women.[48] The same observation was made by the English physician John White, who was in Brazil at the end of the eighteenth century; after a month's residence in Rio de Janeiro he concluded that the women who did not deport themselves as they should were of the lower class.[49] It is true that, some years afterwards, at a party given in the home of Luiz José de Carvalho e Mello, in Botafogo—an affair graced with the presence of baronesses, the daughters of baronesses, viscountesses, young ladies speaking French, others speaking English, well-dressed matrons, and Negroes serving tea on silver trays —a compatriot of Mrs. Graham's told her, between sips of tea, scandalous things about the ladies of the court: in this gathering at least ten of those present—but looking about, the speaker stopped short: "Not here, no, but in Rio. . . ." Which shows that the generality was not easy to back up with concrete examples, at least not on the spur of the moment. This same Englishman remarked to Mrs. Graham that the cause of all the corruption in Brazil was the slaves.[50]

presque toutes libertines & trouvent le moyen de tromper la vigilance des pères & des maris, s'exposant à la cruauté de ces derniers qui les tuent impunément, des qu'ils découvrent leurs intrigues. Ces examples sont si frequens, qu'on comptoit depuis un an, plus de trente femmes égorgées par leurs maris. . . ."—Relation du voyage de la Mer du Sud aux côtes du Chily et du Pérou fait pendant les années 1712, 1713 et 1714 (Paris, 1716), p. 275.

[48] John Mawe, op. cit.
[49] John White: *Journal of a Voyage to New South Wales* (London, 1790), pp. 52-3.
[50] Maria Graham: *Journal of a Voyage to Brazil*, etc. (op. cit.), p. 225.—The incident related by Mrs. Graham, having to do with a lady of high society in Rio de Janeiro who was assassinated while in the company of her two little daughters, appears to be the same one with which Professor Assis Cintra deals in one of the

The female slaves. The Negro women. The *mucamas*. But were the ladies at the court of Brazil so much more corrupt than those of European courts? [51]

Loreto Coutto, who obviously has an exaggerated admiration for the women of slave-holding Brazil, wrote of the "sexual fire" as being a "hereditary evil" of the sons of Adam—one that might be fanned by the daughters of Eve—and not an evil peculiar to hot lands or climates. "The sensual influences" appeared to him to be active "in every part," and "in any place whatsoever their fire is always burning, if it be not extinguished with much prayer and much penance, and thus he who is the most devout and the most penitent shall be the most chaste." He could not understand why Brazil should be called, as it is by the author of a certain *History*, the land of a "hot climate, provocative of sensual vices." What example could the historian cite in support of his thesis? That of a certain individual "expelled from his Church for lewdness of appetite," who had been exiled to this country, and who here had grown in "lustful intemperance." As if the climate, comments the friar, could have augmented in the soul of this depraved being "the infernal conflagration." We have already seen, however, that Loreto Coutto beheld in the black and mulatto women of Brazil a temptation to be made use of in the perfecting of souls; all this was inflammable material, and that "infernal conflagration" was, consequently, always a danger. It was not the climate but the presence of these women that appeared to him to be an excitation to sin difficult to resist in our country. But it was those Negro and mulatto women who had been degraded by slavery; for the Benedic-

---

chapters of his book *As Amantes do Imperador* (*The Emperor's Mistresses*) (Rio de Janeiro, 1933). Mrs. Graham tells us that the crime was attributed to the jealousy of another woman, in love with the victim's husband; or else it was that she was found to be in possession of important political secrets. According to Assis Cintra, the crime was perpetrated by a madman who was put up to it by the Queen, Dona Carlota Joana; and she was indeed a wench capable of anything. Dona Carlota was supposed to be in love with the husband of the unfortunate lady, a certain Fernandes Carneiro Leão, a great dandy; and the victim is said to have complained of the affair to John VI him-

self. Cases of white men and women of quality being assassinated by Negroes or mulattoes on the order of their masters were not rare.

[51] Alexander Caldcleugh did not find that Rio de Janeiro in the early years of the nineteenth century was any more immoral than Paris, London, or Berlin: "I shall conclude with observing, and without wishing to extenuate anything, that taking into account the mixed nature of the inhabitants, the number of foreigners, and the mulatto and black population, no greater quantity of vice exists here than in the European cities of London, Paris or Berlin."—*Travels in South America*, etc. (op. cit.).

tine friar gives the Negro race its just dues by stressing its services to Brazil. Not alone services rendered in the execution of "difficult and laborious undertakings," but original enterprises marked by "valor and prudence."

What occurred in Brazil—I must emphasize this once again with respect to the Negro and mulatto women even more than with regard to the Indian women and the mamelucas—was the degradation of backward races through the domination of an advanced race. This from the first reduced the natives to captivity and prostitution, while between white men and colored women it set up the relationship of conquerors and conquered—always dangerous to sexual morality.

The Jesuits had succeeded in overcoming the repugnance of the first colonists to marrying Indian women. "Most of them here," wrote Father Nobrega from Pernambuco in 1551, "have had an Indian woman for a long time, by whom they have had children, and they have held it to be a great infamy to marry them. But now they are marrying and setting up the right kind of life." There were, however, a "great number of them who have wives in Portugal, while others are living here in a state of grave sin; some of them we send away and others we cause to bring their wives over." Of the mestizo women, he tells us: "if they did not marry before, it was because the men continued to live openly in sin, and some of them said that it was not sin, for the Archbishop of Funchal had given them license." That same supposed "license" on the part of the Archbishop was taken advantage of by lustful clerics that they might live in a state of regularized concubinage. Eight years later the great missionary wrote from Salvador: "with the Christians of this land there is little to be done, for we have closed to them the door of the confessional, on account of the slaves, with which they are loath to part, and for the reason that nearly all of them, married and unmarried alike, are living in concubinage withindoors, with their Negro women; and their slaves are all concubines, without their conscience troubling them in the one case or the other; and there are priests who are free with their absolutions and who live in the same manner. . . ." And from the same city of Bahia, in the middle of the sixteenth century: "The people of the land are living in a state of mortal sin, and there is no one but has many Negro women, who bear them many children, and this is a great evil." [52]

The African women having been brought to Brazil under irregular conditions of sexual life, the powerful voice of the fathers of the

---

[52] Padre Manuel de Nobrega: *Cartas* (op. cit.), pp. 119, 120, and 121.

Society was never once raised in their behalf as it was in behalf of the Indian women. As a result, the relations between the colonists and the Negro women were for long characterized by an undisguised animality; they represented a mere outlet for sexual feeling. Which does not mean that these women brought with them from their homeland —in their instincts, their blood, or their flesh—a sensuality any more violent than that possessed by their sex among the Portuguese or among the Indians.

Dampier, who was in Bahia in the seventeenth century, knew of a number of colonists who had illicit relations with Negresses: "*Plusieurs des portugais, qui ne sont pas merrez, entretennent de ces femmes noires pour leurs maitresses.*" [53] By that time the relations of the Portuguese with the black women were no longer purely animal in character as in the early days; for many a female African had succeeded in winning the respect of the white man, some through the fear inspired by their "*mandingas,*" or spells, and others, like the Minas, through their sexual allure [54] and womanly wiles. A minority had accordingly come to attain a position practically identical with that which the by no means impartial moralism of the Jesuits assured to the Indian woman. A position as "housekeepers" and "concubines" to the white males; they were no longer mere animals to be fattened up in the slave shed for the physical pleasure of their masters and for the purpose of increasing his human capital.

As life became easier and more leisurely for the colonists, with sugar selling in larger quantities and for better prices on the European market than at the beginning of the sixteenth century, there developed, at the end of that century and the early years of the one following, not only a lustful but an extravagantly luxurious mode of life among the sugar-planters of Brazil. In Pernambuco the production of sugar mounted from two hundred thousand arrobas [about 3,200 tons] in 1584 [55] to "more than a hundred and twenty shiploads"

[53] William Dampier: *Voyages . . . aux terres australes,* etc. (op. cit.).

[54] "*pelos seus quindins.*" The word *quindim* (plural, *quindins*) is really untranslatable; it is one of those that came into the "Brazilian language" with the African (see p. 346, note 194). (Translator.)

[55] This according to Father Cardim, who writes: ". . . the fertility of the cane fields is beyond estimate; there are sixty-six plantations, each with a fair-sized population; they raise, some years, two hundred thousand arrobas of sugar, and the mills cannot exhaust the supply of cane that, in the course of the year, is brought down for grinding; and for this reason they cannot keep up with the yield though they grind for three or four years; and each year there come to Pernambuco forty ships and they are unable to carry away all the sugar. . . ."— Fernão Cardim: *Tratados da Terra e Gente do Brasil* (op. cit.), p. 334.

for the year 1618.[56] The number of plantations rose from thirty in 1576 [57] to seventy-six in 1584 and 1590 and a hundred and twenty-one at the close of the first quarter of the seventeenth century.[58] This meant a corresponding increase in the number of African slaves; and it all contributed to a more leisurely life for the plantation-owners and a greater libertinism on their part. So leisurely, indeed, did life become in the sugar-raising zones that certain learned moralists of the era came to associate the slothfulness of the planters with the large consumption of sugar: "It is possibly from the abundance of this humor" – the phlegmatic, caused by an excess of sugar in the diet – "that there is derived that indolence which reduces so many to so wretched a state." So wrote one of the moralists in question, adding: "This humor, certainly, greatly predominates in many men in Brazil. There are many who spend their lives with one hand folded over the other; and although man is born for labor, all that they seek is rest. There are some who in an entire day do not stir so much as a single step." And he ends by advising that they eat less sugar – which, moreover, is a breeder of tapeworms.

But sugar, certainly, was not so directly responsible as all this for the sloth of the menfolk. It was, however, an indirect and potent cause, in that it necessitated slave labor and was inimical to a varied-crop system. It demanded slaves to be the "hands and feet of the plantation-owner," as Antonil puts it. And this was true not alone of the Portuguese planter, already vitiated by the institution of slavery,

[56] *Diálogos das Grandezas do Brasil* (op. cit.), p. 52.

[57] Cardim: *Tratados*, etc. (op. cit.), p. 329. See also Pero de Magalhães de Gandavo: *História da Província de Santa Cruz* (op. cit.)

[58] Senhor Rodolfo Garcia, note 1 to the Third Dialogue of the *Diálogos das Grandezas do Brasil* (op. cit.), states that when the squadron of Lonck appeared off Recife, they counted, in the *capitânias* of Pernambuco, Itamaracá, Paraíba, and Rio Grande, 166 sugar plantations, of which 121 were in Pernambuco. Frei Manuel Callado, in his *Valeroso Lucideno* (*Valorous Lucideno*) (Lisbon, 1648), provides us with interesting data regarding economic and moral conditions in Pernambuco prior to the Dutch occupation. The sugar produced by the Pernambucan plantations must have been of a superior quality, seeing that there was a rivalry among the skippers to obtain it, and they made "many gifts and did many favors to the planters and cultivators that they might give them their crates of sugar. . . ." For the sugar was transported in great wooden crates containing twenty arrobas [about 64 pounds] each. It was these crates, according to the friar, that tipped the scales of justice. For in the midst of all this prosperity, "usuries and illicit gains are a common thing," there being in the land many new-Christians. Common also were "public concubinage . . . thievery, robberies . . . brawls, wounds, slayings . . . rapes and adulteries. . . ." And "money led to the punishments being suspended. . . ."

but of the Dutch as well. The latter, when they installed themselves on the sugar-cane plantations of Pernambuco,[59] realized that it was necessary for them to rely upon the Negro; for without slaves they could not produce sugar. And a large number of slaves, at that: to plant the cane; to cut it; to bring it to the mills run by a water-wheel —the *"engenhos d'agua,"* as these mills were called—or to those that were turned by oxen or other animals, the so-called *"almanjarras"* or *trapiches;* and afterwards there was the sap to be purified in the kettles; and the heated sugar had to be congealed and then refined and whitened in clay forms and the *aguardente,* or sugar-brandy, drained off.

It was the slaves who literally became their masters' feet, running errands for their owners and carrying them about in hammock or palanquin. They also became their masters' hands—at least, their right hands; for they it was who dressed them, drew on their trousers and their boots for them, bathed and brushed them, and hunted over their persons for fleas. There is a tradition to the effect that one Pernambucan planter even employed the Negro's hand for the most intimate details of his toilet; and von den Steinen tells us that a distinguished nobleman of the Empire was in the habit of having a slave girl light his cigars for him and then pass them to the old fellow's mouth.[60] Every white of the Big House had two left hands, every Negro two right hands. The master's hands served only for telling the beads of Our Lady's rosary, for playing cards, for taking snuff from snuffboxes, or *"corriboques,"* and for playing with the breasts of young Negro and mulatto girls, the pretty slaves of his harem.

In the case of the slave-owner the body became little more than a *membrum virile.* A woman's hands, a child's feet;[61] the sexual organ alone was arrogantly virile. This was in contrast to the Negroes; for so many of those enormous giants had the penis of a small boy. Imbert, in his advice to the purchasers of slaves, makes a point of

---

[59] "Without such slaves it is not possible to do anything in Brazil; without them the sugar-mills cannot grind, nor can the land be cultivated, for which purpose slaves are necessary and can by no means be dispensed with; if anyone feels himself offended by this, his scruples will avail him nothing."—*Breve Discurso sobre o Estado das Quatro Capitânias Conquistadas* (op. cit.).

[60] Karl von den Steinen: *Unter den Indianern Zentral-Brasiliens* (op. cit.).

[61] Burton: *The Highlands of the Brazil,* etc. (op. cit.), noted in the "Anglo-American" as in the "Ibero-Brazilian" the "beauty, the smallness and delicacy of the extremities, which is so often excessive, degenerating into effeminacy," in contrast to the big hands and feet of the English and the Portuguese. He vaguely attributes this trait to an identity of local influences, but it appears to me to be chiefly the result of social causes.

this: the necessity of paying attention to the Negro's sexual organ in order to avoid acquiring individuals in whom it was undeveloped or ill-shaped;[62] for it was feared that they would prove bad procreators.

Slothful but filled to overflowing with sexual concerns, the life of the sugar-planter tended to become a life that was lived in a hammock. A stationary hammock, with the master taking his ease, sleeping, dozing. Or a hammock on the move, with the master on a journey or a promenade beneath the heavy draperies or curtains. Or again, a squeaking hammock, with the master copulating in it. The slave-holder did not have to leave his hammock to give orders to his Negroes, to have letters written by his plantation clerk or chaplain, or to play a game of backgammon with some relative or friend. Nearly all of them traveled by hammock, having no desire to go by horse; and within the house they permitted themselves to be jolted about like jelly in a spoon. It was in the hammock that, after breakfast or dinner, they let their food settle, as they lay there picking their teeth, smoking a cigar, belching loudly, emitting wind, and allowing themselves to be fanned or searched for lice by the pickaninnies, as they scratched their feet or genitals—some of them out of vicious habit, others because of a venereal or skin disease. Lindley tells us that in Bahia he saw persons of both sexes being searched for lice, while the men were always scratching their "syphilitic sores." [63]

The truth of the matter is, however, that these flabby males with the hands of a woman who were so over-fond of their hammocks and so voluptuous in their slothfulness, these aristocrats who were ashamed of having legs and of setting foot to the ground like any slave or plebeian, could still be stern and valiant in moments of danger; they could gird on their swords and defend themselves against the bold foreigner or against "buggers" and were able to expel from the colony His Majesty's captains-general. It was the Pernambucan planters who colonized Paraíba and Rio Grande do Norte, confronting the most savage and brave of Indian tribes in doing so; it was they who freed Maranhão from the French and who expelled the Dutch.

And this was true not alone of the men, but of the women, the ladies of the Big House, as well; they likewise had their outbursts of energy and stoicism. "They certainly did not display any less valor in this action than did our soldiers," says the Marquês de Basto of the

---

[62] Imbert: *Manual do Fazendeiro*, etc. (op. cit.)

[63] Thomas Lindley: *Narrative of a Voyage to Brazil . . . with General Sketches of the Country, Its Natural Productions, Colonial Inhabitants and a Description of the City and Provinces of St. Salvador and Porto Seguro* (London, 1805), p. 35.

Pernambucan women who took part in the retreat of Alagoas, leaving behind them plantations and Big Houses in ruins.[64]

But with the exception of these warlike exhibitions, the life of the sugar-raising aristocrats was a soft and languid one. It was a life broken now and again by a game of "reeds" or "rings," [65] by cavalcades or dancing; but these were rare occasions. Ordinarily the days went by, one like another, with the same lethargy, the same uneventful and sensual hammock-existence. Both men and women grew sallow-complexioned from living so much indoors and going about so much in hammock or palanquin. In the United States, where the hammock never attained the importance that it did here, where the ease-loving slave-owners were content with sofa or rocking-chair (later to be adopted by the Brazilian patriarchs), the males brought up under the influence of African slavery none the less impressed Europeans by their easy-going ways, their slouchy gait, the utter lack of any elegance in their carriage; they appeared as weak-chested individuals with narrow, stooping shoulders. Their voice alone was deep and imperious. Frances Trollope gives us a portrait of a North American Southerner of this period who might be a north Brazilian: "I never saw an American man walk or stand well. . . ." [66] And it was seldom that a European was not impressed by the sickly pallor of men and women in the ante-bellum South. The economic regime of production—slavery and the one-crop system—prevailing over the difference in climate, race, and religious morality, created in the Southern United States a type of frail, soft-handed aristocrat who was scarcely to be distinguished from the Brazilian type in his vices, his tastes, and even his physique. The ingredients were different, but the form was the same. The hot climate may have *contributed* to a greater lubricity and

---

[64] Duarte de Albuquerque Coelho: *Memorias Diárias de la Guerra del Brasil* (Madrid, 1654).

[For a plantation *sinhá-moça* who could be quite feminine and at the same time shoot it out with the men, see the portrait that Jorge Amado gives us of Don' Ana Badaró, in his *Terras do sem fim* (*The Violent Land*). In this case it was a cacao, not a sugar, plantation, but the spirit of the men and women was much the same in many ways. (Translator.)]

[65] The sports of "*canas*" and "*argolinhas.*" The former is defined by H. Michaelis (*A New Dictionary of*

the Portuguese and English Languages, op. cit.) as "a sport or exercise used by gentlemen on horseback representing a fight with reeds instead of lances." *Argolinha* is a sport that consists in running at rings. (Translator.)

[66] Frances Trollope: *Domestic Manners of the Americans* (London, 1832). See also John Bernard: *Retrospection of America* (*1797–1811*) (New York, 1887); William Faux: *Memorable Days in America* (London, 1823); and Anthony Trollope: *North America* (London, 1862).

languor on the part of the Brazilian, but it did not *create*, did not *produce* those qualities.[67]

Of the Pernambucan colonists, Souchu de Rennefort wrote: *"ils vivent dans une grande license. . . ."* A Levantine nonchalance, that of these slave-owners: *"ils dorment & fument & n'ont guères d'autres meubles que des brambes de cotton & des nattes; les plus somptueux ont une table & des chaises de cuir façonné; quelques-uns se servent de vaisselles d'argent, la plus grande partie de vaisselles de terre."* [68] It may be noted in passing that neither Pyrard in writing of Pernambuco nor Dampier and Mrs. Kindersley in writing of Bahia speak of any great luxury in the matter of furnishings or silverware. Dampier and Pyrard mention merely the size of the houses and the number of slaves; while all of them dwell on the soft and effeminate life led by the planters, who spent the entire day inside the house or being borne through the streets by their Negroes on the way to church. Dampier even came to the conclusion that the Portuguese colonists, like the Spaniards, attached little importance to furnishings or pictures; with them it was merely a question of large houses.[69] Large houses–Big

---

[67] Adolphe d'Assier, stressing the looseness of manners in slave-holding Brazil, states that the Brazilians were the first to admit this and that they attributed it to the effect of the climate. But travelers also, d'Assier notes, *"repètent cette excuse."* He himself does not do so, however: *"Il seriat peut-être plus exact de chercher dans l'exclavage la principale cause de la vie Licencieuse de l'Américain"* (he is referring principally to the Brazilian). Read the work of this excellent observer, who was here in the mid-nineteenth century: *Le Brésil contemporain — races — mœurs — institutions — paysage* (Paris, 1867).

[68] Souchu de Rennefort: *Histoire des Indies Orientales* (1688).

[69] It is problable that an exaggerated idea has at times been formed of the luxury of the northeasterners in the sixteenth and seventeenth centuries. Those houses with gold locks of which Frei Manuel speaks must have been rare; and only the richest displayed fine beds. Life in Pernambuco in this era, on the other hand, is not to be confused with that in São Paulo

—the latter being marked by simplicity and asceticism in the matter of furnishings and an almost Franciscan crudeness of utensils. Many of the Pernambucans were men of European origin and a higher social class, and had a larger capital with which to install themselves than was the case at São Vicente. Then, too, the returns from agriculture, from the raising and manufacture of sugar, were greater than in the south. Cardim, who traveled from the north to the south of Brazil in the sixteenth century, makes this distinction quite clear to us: there was much more ostentation in Pernambuco than in the south. Affonso de E. Taunay states that the "colossal returns from sugar" made possible "in Bahia and above all in Pernambuco" a large-scale importation of objects of luxury such as silks, velvets, and fine wines.—*S. Paulo nos Primeiros Anos* (op. cit.). As for the seventeenth century, we have among other statements those of the Italian Capuchins, Brother Michelangelo de Gattina and Brother Dyonisio de Piancenza, both of whom are quoted

Houses—and many slaves, feasts of the Church, women, slave girls.

Coreal in Bahia was impressed by the voluptuousness of the colonists. They were a lot of big loafers, always lying stretched out in their hammocks.[70] This was, however, a voluptuousness and an indolence broken in upon by the spirit of religious devotion, which only in the nineteenth century began to diminish in the menfolk, to find a refuge with women, children, and slaves. In the seventeenth and even in the eighteenth century there was not a white gentleman, however indolent, who would avoid the effort involved in the sacred duty of kneeling before the niches of the saints in prayer—prayers that were sometimes endlessly drawn out by Negroes and mulattoes. The rosary, the chaplet of Our Lord, the litanies. They would leap from the hammocks to go and pray in the oratories; for this was an obligation that must be fulfilled. They would go, rosary in hand, and with holy medals, reliquaries, scapulars, St. Anthony hung about their

by Taunay. These were two missionaries who in 1667 were in Brazil on their way to the Congo. As they entered the port of Recife, they observed eighty ships being loaded and unloaded. They disembarked and took part in the feast of Corpus Christi. There was a great throng and excellent music provided by harps, trumpets, and violins. Of the houses, we are told that they were "richly adorned." Visiting a sugar plantation, they carried away with them a gloomy impression of the grievous labor to which the Negroes were subjected; for they saw bands of them engaged in pushing the enormous wheel, at the risk, every step they took, of having their hands and arms caught in the mill. But the chief impression that these friars received was of the wealth of the Pernambucans. A wealth based on Negro labor. The Capuchins tell us with astonishment of the high prices paid for a Mass or a sermon.—Affonso de E. Taunay: *Non Ducor, Duco* (op. cit.).

[70] "*La mollesse des habitans de San Salvador & la pente des rues, que est fort roide, leur fait regarder l'usage de marcher comme une chose indigne d'eux. Ils se font porter dans une espèce de lit de coton à raiseau,* *suspendus à une perche longue, & épaisse, que deux Nègres portent sur leurs épaules. Ce lit est couvert d'une imperiale d'ou pendent des rideaux verts, rouges ou bleus. . . .*" These come near to being Frézier's words: "*Les gens riches . . . auroient honte de se servir des jambes. . . .*"

"*Je n'ai vu de lieu,*" adds Coreal, "*où le Christianisme parut avec plus d'éclat qu'en cette ville soit par la richesse & la multitude des Eglises, des Couvens & des Gentishommes, des Dames & des courtisannes & généralement des tous les citoiens de la Baie. On n'y marche point sans un Rosaire à la main, un chapelet au col & un Saint Antoine sur l'estomac. On est exact à s'agenouiller au son de l'Angelus au milieu des rues; mais en même tens on a la précaution de ne point sortir de chez soi sans un poignard dans le sein, un pistollet dans la poche & une épée des plus longues au côté gacuhe. . . .*" The exceedingly large number of persons confessing themselves appeared to Coreal to indicate an excessive number of sins: "*la confession y est fort commune, sans doute à cause de la multitude des péchés. . . .*"—François Coreal: *Voyages aux Indes Orientales,* etc. (op. cit.).

necks, everything that was needed for their prayers and devotions. Maria Graham speaks of hearing litanies sung at nightfall in the streets of Bahia, with whites, Negroes, mulattoes, all praying to the same God and the same Our Lady. Some of the more devout women would accompany the sacrament to the homes of the dying. Within the house they prayed in the morning, at mealtimes, at midday; and at night they prayed in the room set aside for the saints, slaves accompanying the whites in the rosary and the Salve Regina. If there was a chaplain, he would intone the *Mater purissima, ora pro nobis.* In Cantagalo, in the Big House of the *fazendeiro* Joaquim das Lavrinhas, Mathison was charmed with the patriarchal character of the master of the house kneeling in front of all those on the plantation—relatives, tenants, slaves—to ask God's blessing and the protection of the Virgin Mary. It seemed to the Englishman that there was nothing more praiseworthy in the colonial Brazilian than the fact that in his house he always set aside a place for divine worship. The sign of a "respect for religion," the visitor concluded. And he does not forget to stress the observance of the rites of the Church by the Negroes.[71] One chronicler tells us that at dinner the patriarch would bless the table and each would put his food on his plate in the form of a cross.[72] Others would bless the water or the wine, first making in the air the sign of the cross with the goblet.[73] Finally, they would say grace in Latin:

> *Per hæc dona et cœtera data*
> *Sit Sancta Trinitas semper laudata.*[74]

Upon going to bed, the whites in the Big House and, in the slave huts, the older Negroes would pray:

> *With God I lay me down, with God I rise,*
> *with the grace of God and of the Holy Spirit. May Thine eyes*
> *watch over me as I sleep this night;*
> *and if I should die, then wilt Thou light*
> *me with the tapers of Thy Trinity*
> *into the mansion of Eternity.*[75]

---

[71] Gilbert Farqhar Mathison: *Narrative of a Visit to Brazil, Chili, Peru and the Sandwich Islands during the Years 1821 and 1822* (London, 1825).

[72] Padre Antunes de Siqueira: *Esboço Historico*, etc. (op. cit.).

[73] A custom still observed today in certain places in Brazil. When a child, I saw this rite performed by an elder of my family.

[74] Padre Antunes de Siqueira, op. cit.

[75] Ibid. The Portuguese original is

Com Deus me deito, com Deus me levanto,
com graça de Deus e do Espírito Santo.
Se dormir muito, accordai-me
se eu morrer, alumiai-me
com as tochas de vossa Trinidade
na mansão da Etermidade.

And in the morning, when they rose, it was also with the name of Our Lord in their mouths: "My God, it is thanks to Thy goodness that I again see the light of day. Wilt Thou see that I walk safely, guided by Thy unfailing providence!" When anyone sneezed, he was greeted with a "God save you!" Negroes would receive a blessing from their master, saying: "Praised be the name of Our Lord Jesus Christ!" And the master would reply: "Forever!" or "Praised be!"

When it thundered loudly, whites and blacks would gather in the chapel or the sanctuary to sing the Benedicite, intone the Magnificat, and recite the prayers of St. Braz, St. Jerome, and St. Barbara. They would light candles, burn holy boughs, and recite the Credo. Certain ailments were treated with prayers and anointings with oil as in apostolic times—erysipelas, for example:

> *Peter and Paul went to Rome*
> *and met Jesus Christ on the way,*
> *who to them did say:*
> *"Well, and what brings you here?"*
> *" 'Tis the erysipelas, Lord, we fear."*
> *"Bless it with olive oil*
> *And it will disappear.*[76]

They would tack up prayer-papers to the windows and doors of houses to protect the family from thieves, assassins, lightning-bolts, and tempests. Prayers to Jesus, Mary, and Joseph. And on the old patriarchal plantations they would sing hymns to the Holy Family. Among the papers and manuscripts of the captain-major Manoel Thomé de Jesús—a Pernambucan patriarch who flourished at the end of the eighteenth and during the first half of the nineteenth century—I came upon the following devout lines in praise of St. Anne, "mother of Mary and grandmother of Jesus":

> *Let us all sing,*
> *Let our praises ring*
> *To the good St. Anne*
>
> . . . . .
> *And the Holy Family.*
>
> *St. Anne was born*
> *Christ's grandmother to be;*
> *God the Father chose her*
>
> . . . . .
> . . . . .

[76] *Pedro e Paulo foi a Roma* / *e Jesus Cristo encountrou.* / *Este lhes perguntou:* / —*Então que ha por lá?* / —*Senhor, erisipela má.* / —*Benze-a com azeite* / *E logo te sarará.*

Blessed St. Anne,
Pray for each one
Of us wretched sinners
To God, thy grandson.

Praised be St. Anne,
Praised be her spouse, and then
All of the Trinity,
Forever, Amen.[77]

On the plantations they fasted and observed the precepts of the Church. They adjusted such observances, it is true, to the exigencies of work in the fields and the diet of the slaves, the "persons engaged in labor." The same Manoel Thomé de Jesús, a very devout man who gave to his Big House the aspect of a convent—a kind of rustic Escurial, as Luis Cedro remarked, with a large cross in front and a chapel at one side [78]—did not hesitate to address himself to Dom João, Bishop of Pernambuco, petitioning His Excellency the Right Reverend to grant the plantation Negroes the privilege of eating meat on days of abstinence:

"Manoel Thomé de Jesús, master of the plantation of Noruega, sets forth that, having on the said Plantation a large number of slaves and other persons in his service, and it not being possible to provide all of them on days of abstinence with that diet which is needful for laboring persons, and wishing to conform to the Precepts of Holy Mother Church and the obedience that is due Her, for this reason and with the most profound respect he does beseech Your Right Reverend Excellency, by the faculties that Your Excellency has from the Holy See, to deign to dispense the suppliant and all the family of his Plantation and the persons of his service from the precept of abstinence from meat, with the exception of a certain few days which Your Excellency will note."

---

[77] Manuscript in the archives of Manoel Thomé de Jesús, Noruega plantation, Pernambuco. A portion of the manuscript was illegible, being greatly moth-eaten.
The Portuguese original reads:

Descantemos todos
Em lírios divinos
Os dons de Sta. Anna
. . . . .
Na Santa família.

Sta. Anna nasceo
Para avó de Christo
Deus Padre eschlheo
. . . . .
. . . . .
Sta. Anna bemdita

Rogai com affecto
Por nos miseraveis
A Deos vosso neto.

Louvores a Sta. Anna
E ao Esposo tambem
E toda a Trinidade
Para sempre, Amen.

[78] In the words of Luis Cedro: "the Big House . . . an enormous convent-like country house whose massive construction is somewhat reminiscent of the Escurial. An immense cross in the patio, dominating the landscape with a taciturn and mystic air."—"*O Dr. Geróncio de Noruega*" ("Dr. Geróncio of Noruega"), *Diário de Pernambuco*, July 26, 1925.

This request Dom João saw fit to grant:

"In accordance with the faculties that the Holy See has reposed in us, we grant the suppliant permission to use meat on all those days on which the Holy Church has prohibited its use, even in Lent, and this permission is granted to all his family and slaves. We except, however, Christmas Eve, Ash Wednesday, Holy Week, and the Vigil of the Ascension of Jesus Christ into the Heavens, as well as the Saturday preceding the Sunday which is the Feast of the Holy Spirit and the 14th day of August or the 13th of the same month, the Vigil of the Assumption of Our Lady. The suppliant shall deliver to the Poor Box one hundred milreis to be divided among the needy for his intention. Palácio da Soledade, 16th of December of the year '18.—João, Bishop of Pernambuco." [79]

On the day on which they began grinding the cane, the priest never failed to be there to bless the sugar-mill, and the labor was undertaken with the Church's benediction. Mass was first said, and then they all made their way to the mill, the white males in their sun-hats, slow-paced and solemn, and the fat senhoras in their mantillas. The Negroes were happy, thinking of the *batuques*, or dances, they would have that night. The young Negro lads shouted *vivas* and set off fireworks. The priest made the sign of the cross in the air with the hyssop and sprinkled the mill with holy water, many of the slaves taking good care to be sprinkled also. There followed other slow gestures on the part of the priest. Latin sentences. At times a sermon.[80] It was not until all this ceremonial had been completed that the first

---

[79] Manuscript found in the archives of Manoel Thomé de Jesús.

[80] The noted nineteenth-century preacher, Padre Lino do Monte Carmello Luna, in blessing the Maçauassú sugar-mill on the 4th of November 1868, delivered a sermon that was greatly applauded and later published in pamphlet form, copies of which today are extremely rare: *A Benção do Engenho Maçauassú* (*The Blessing of the Maçauassú Mill*) (Recife, 1869). In this sermon praise is bestowed upon the patriarch who owned the plantation: "A family gathering composed of the father and husband, of sons and brothers, is always a fine and pleasing thing." Such was the manner in which the schoolmaster priest began. But at the same time he praised the machine itself and industrial progress as represented, at the moment, by "the system adopted in this mill-house; that is to say, the ease with which an ordinary cart on iron tracks receives all the cane trash that comes out of the mill and, with a mere push of the arm, is propelled to the proper place for depositing its load." The new system meant a great economy in the matter of slaves. The number of slaves required for the service of a good mill in this era was one or two hundred. Back in the sixteenth century Cardim had observed that in the mills of Bahia there was needed a minimum of sixty; "but most of them have a hundred and two hundred slaves from Guinea and from this land."—*Tratados*, etc. (op. cit.). What Father Luna was praising was two irreconcilable things: the patriarchal family and the machine.

of the ripened cane was placed in the mill, in bundles tied with green, red, or blue ribbons. Only then did the labor begin on these patriarchal plantations. That was the way it had been ever since the sixteenth century. As far back as Father Cardim's day that priest, speaking of the plantation-owners, had observed: "They are accustomed, the first time they go to grind, to have the mills blessed, and on that day they make a great feast, inviting those from round about. The priest, upon being requested to do so, blesses some of those present, a thing that is very much esteemed." [81] The blessing of the mill was followed by a banquet in the Big House, with revelry and dancing by the slaves on the terrace, and the merrymaking would last until dawn. At the banquet they would serve young calves, pigs, hens, turkeys. All of this with the blessing of the Church, which, however, did not officially number "among its rites an ecclesiastical ceremony vulgarly known as the Litanies of May, which are nothing more than prayers to God for a prosperous harvest." [82]

When they felt death drawing near, the planters would think of their goods and slaves in relation to their descendants, which meant their sons in lawful wedlock. The wills that have come down to us show the economic concern of the patriarchs thus to perpetuate their property through their legitimate heirs. But occasionally, in opposition to this attitude, they also display a lively Christian sentiment of affection toward bastards and Negro women. There is the last will and testament of Jerónymo de Albuquerque, dated from Olinda, "on the third day of the month of November in the year of the birth of Our Lord one thousand five hundred and eighty-four"; and in this document we find the following provision: "I order that there be given to all my natural sons who are unmarried five hundred thousand reis, to be divided among them fraternally." And, addressing himself to the legitimate sons, the testator continues: "In the second place, I commend to them all their natural Brothers and Sisters, and in this regard let it be enough for them to know and understand that these are my children. . . ." Concerned for the peace of his soul, Jerónymo, great sinner that he was, then beseeches the "Virgin, Our Lady, and all the male and female saints of the Court of Heaven that when my soul leaves my body, they will conduct it it into the presence of Divine Majesty." He goes on to petition "the Sr. Superintendent and Brothers of the Santa Misericórdia" to accompany his body "to the Church which I have on my Plantation of Our Lady of Succor, where I have my tomb." He then indicates the various ways in which

---

[81] Cardim, op. cit.
[82] Introduction to the *Benção do*   *Engenho Maçauassú*" (op. cit.). Family archives.

his money is to be divided: bequests of fifty thousand reis to the Brothers of the Misericórdia; twenty cruzados for the poor; Masses for his soul; thirty thousand reis for a large silver candlestick for the plantation chapel; twenty cruzados to the Confraternity of the Most Blessed Sacrament; from three to six thousand milreis to other confraternities. All this represented a great dispersion of money, to the prejudice of a patriarchal perpetuity and cohesion of goods in the hands of legitimate sons.[83]

Rarely did a plantation-owner die without freeing, in his will, some of the Negroes and mulatto women on his estate. True, "the freedman," as Alcantara Machado remarks in reference to the slaves on São Paulo plantations in the sixteenth and seventeenth centuries, "is very often a bastard, fruit of the testator's amours or the offspring of some member of the family and a Negro woman of the household."[84] Bastards, natural sons—what sugar-planter did not have them in large number? Rarely was there a patriarch in those days who, at the moment of "unburdening his conscience," could seraphically declare as did Manoel Thomé de Jesús in Pernambuco: "In God's name, Amen. Father, Son, and Holy Ghost. Three distinct Persons and one true God. Know all men by these presents that in the year of the Birth of Our Lord Jesus Christ one thousand eight hundred and fifty-five, on the tenth day of the month of October of the said year, I, Manoel Thomé de Jesús, being in sound mind and in my home on the new plantation of Noruega, parish of Our Lady of the Stair, etc. . . . do hereby make my solemn testament in the form, mode, and manner following. . . ." This exceedingly devout and scrupulous Catholic then goes on to commend his soul to Our Lord Jesus Christ, "my Redeemer, Saviour, and Glorifier," to Most Holy Mary, Our Lady, to the Archangel Michael, "Prince of the Court of Heaven, and to his principal companions who are there in the presence of God and who carry out His orders, St. Gabriel, St. Raphael, St. Uriel, St. Theatrieal, St. Barakiel"; following which comes the impressive statement: "I declare that I have been married three times, always with the blessing of the Church . . ." and "that I have no natural son or bastard. . . ." This last is truly a sensational declaration for the epoch.

Manoel Thomé further directed that, attendant upon the death of

---

[83] Transcribed by Antônio José Victoriano Borges da Fonseca: *Nobiliarchia Pernambucama* (1777) (op. cit.).

[84] Alcantara Machado: *Vida e Morte do Bandeirante* (op. cit.). Professor Alcantara Machado's book is an excellent study of the inventories filed in São Paulo from 1578 to 1700.

his grandson André, a number of slaves should be freed, one of them being Felippa, the mulatto, wife of Vicente, "for having given me sufficient *crias*." [85] The glorification of the "generative belly" again. There follow numerous donations to confraternities and churches.

In 1866, in his "historico-juridico-social essay" entitled *A Escravidão no Brasil (Slavery in Brazil)*, Perdigão Malheiro wrote: "In testaments and codicils the granting of freedom is common; I may even state, as Procurator of Deeds in this court, that it is rarely that a person possessing slaves does not liberate some of them, and there is no better evidence of this than the records of the Registry Office." The same may be said of those nineteenth-century wills that I was able to examine in Pernambuco, not only in plantation archives, but in the old registry offices of the slave-holding regions.[86]

From the time of Jerónymo de Albuquerque, brother-in-law of the founder of the *capitânia* of Pernambuco, down to that of Manoel Thomé de Jesús, captain-major by the grace of John VI, a patriarch who died of a wound in the leg at the age of eighty-one after a life that had been as austere as that of Jerónymo had been dissolute and licentious—during all this time it was the custom to bury the masters and members of their family almost inside the house, in chapels that were in reality annexes of the patriarchal dwelling. The dead thus kept company with the living, until, in the days of the Second Empire, hygienists began to raise the question: "How long are the dead to continue to enjoy the unhappy prerogative of poisoning the lives of living persons?" [87]

---

[85] Will of Manoel Thomé de Jesús. Manuscript in the archives of the Noruega plantation. On this point I examined numerous wills in the registry offices of Recife and Ipojuca.

[86] Chiefly in the registry office of Ipojuca, the municipality where many members of the Sousa Leão family were concentrated. Also in Minas Gerais I examined the inventories and wills of colonial times in the Public Archives collection in Belo Horizonte, where I had the pleasure of being assisted by Luis Camillo de Oliveira, a young and enlightened investigator of the history of Minas.

[87] Inaugural address delivered by José Martins da Cruz Jobim at the Public Installation Ceremonies of the Medical Society of Rio de Janeiro, published in Rio de Janeiro, 1830. In 1808 Manuel Vieira da Silva, in his *Reflections on Ameliorating the Climate of Rio de Janeiro* [see p. 327] had emphasized the necessity of forbidding burial inside the churches. And in 1812 José Corrêa Picanço, in his monograph *Essay on the Perils of Burial within the Cities and Their Environs*, had made the same point. It was not until 1838, however, that the Municipal Code of Rio de Janeiro absolutely prohibited interments "within the churches, or sacristies, the cloisters of convents," etc.—Antônio Martins de Azevedo Pimental: *Subsídios para o Estudo da Higiene do Rio de Janeiro (Contributions to the Study of Hygienic Conditions in Rio de Janeiro)* (Rio de Janeiro, 1890).

Burials were at night and were marked by a great expenditure of wax candles, much chanting in Latin by the padres, and much wailing on the part of the ladies and the Negroes. The blacks did not know just what kind of new master the fates had in store for them, and wept not alone out of grief for the one who had died but from uncertainty as to what the future held for them.

Ewbank describes for us the luxurious burials of the nobility in Rio de Janeiro, the ostentatious toilets of the dead—the regimentals, uniforms, silks, religious robes, decorations, medals, jewels; the little ones all painted with rouge, clusters of blond hair, angels' wings; the virgins dressed in white, a garland of orange flowers, sky-blue ribbons.[88] And amid all this luxury of gilt, rouge, silks, the deceased were carried to their tombs in the churches, churches that on damp days had so horrible a rotting smell that it was a wonder the dead did not burst forth from their graves.[89]

For the Negroes, naturally, there were no silks and flowers, nor were they buried inside the church edifices. Their corpses were wrapped in mats and their graves were in the cemetery near the plantation chapel that was set aside for slaves, with black wooden crosses to serve as markers. In the case of Negroes who had been in the house for a long time, it was different; they died like white persons, confessing themselves, receiving communion, and entrusting their souls to Jesus and to Mary, to St. Michael, St. Gabriel, St. Raphael, St. Uriel, St. Theatriel, St. Barakiel—blond archangels who were supposed to receive the aged blacks as St. Peter did the Negress Irene in Manuel Bandeira's [90] poem: "Come in, Irene! Come in, Cosme! Come in, Benedito! Come in, Damião!" Some masters would have Mass said for the souls of their favorite slaves,[91] would decorate their graves

Elsewhere in Brazil the unhygienic practice continued for long years.

[88] Thomas Ewbank: *Life in Brazil, or a Journal of a Visit to the Land of Cocoa and the Palm,* New York, 1856.

[89] "The catacombs of the Carmelite Church, St. Peter's, and the Church of St. Francis of Paola, as well as other churches, contaminate the surrounding places; for the emanations from them filter through the walls. Those exhalations that escape from the catacombs of the last mentioned edifice are perceptible to the smell of anyone going through the rua do Cano, alongside the foundations of the church."—*Report of the Commission on Public Health of the Medical Society of Rio de Janeiro, on the Causes of Infection of the Atmosphere of the Court* (Rio de Janeiro, 1832).—In this connection, see R. Walsh: *Notices of Brazil* (op. cit.).

[90] Manuel Bandeira is one of the leading poets of present-day Brazil. (Translator.)

[91] "They [many masters] are accustomed to have the last sacraments administered to them [the Negroes] and prayers said for their souls after they are buried." Agostinho Marquês Perdigão Malheiro: *A Escravidão no Brasil* (op. cit.).

with flowers, and would weep for them as they would for a friend or beloved relative. But there was also many a stony-hearted one; and in the city, owing to a lack of cemeteries in colonial times, it was not easy even for charitable and Christian masters to give their Negroes the same pious burial as on the plantations. Many of the blacks were buried along the edge of the beach, in level graves where the dogs and the vultures would have little difficulty in finding them. Along the seashore between Olinda and Recife, Maria Graham was horrified to see a dog digging up a Negro's arm. According to the Englishwoman, not even these leveled graves were accorded to the "new Negroes"; the bodies of these latter were bound to pieces of wood and sent out with the tide. This is one respect in which the Church, the priests, and the Misericórdias, or charitable societies, in Brazil may be accused of having failed in the strict performance of their duty.[92]

A source of conflict for a long time between the doctrines of the Church and the interests of the slave-owners was the question of keeping the Sabbath. In his book *Compensations of Brazil and Glories of Pernambuco*, Loreto Coutto devotes an entire chapter to this subject, reaching the conclusion that it is not a "mortal sin for overseers and slaves to labor on Sundays and holy days on the sugar plantations of Brazil." This conclusion is based on the circumstances alleged by every planter and manufacturer of sugar, that the grinding must be done in the summer season: "for when the winter comes with its rains, either the mills are choked and the cane remains in the fields, or else the cane fails to yield on account of the moisture and turns green, from which it is clearly to be seen that there will be no yield." And "in addition to this necessity," adds one Dom Domingos, in defending the sugar-planters, "there are various other reasons why labor on such days is excused from being a mortal sin, such as custom, utility, the fear of losing a great deal of money, and other similar ones which the Doctors point out, all of which, or almost all, are to be

---

[92] When the first cemeteries for Negroes, paupers, and heretics were established by the Misericórdia, the situation improved; but these cemeteries were filthy places. A document of the year 1832 informs us that in the Misericórdia na Corte cemetery the corpses were "thrown in heaps in a huge trench," being "barely covered over with earth, the layers of earth that were cast upon them being poorly pressed down." When premature exhumations were made, "the bones would come out with the ligaments and membranes still clinging to them, and the soft and rotting tissues would adhere like mire to the mattocks."—From the report mentioned in note 89.

found combined in our case." [93] It should be noted in passing that the friars of the order to which Dom Domingos belonged—that of St. Benedict—together with the Carmelites, were great landed proprietors and slave-owners in Brazil. Sugar-planters in a monk's robe. The Benedictines treated their Negroes very well; they allowed the young ones to play the greater part of the day, they took care of the aged ones, arranged marriages between the fourteen- and fifteen-year-old girls and the lads of seventeen or eighteen, and made it easy for those who labored diligently to obtain their freedom.[94] The Carmelites, on the other hand, would seem not to have been noted for their good treatment of their slaves; and one of them, in Bahia, was assassinated in a barbarous manner, being slashed to bits by the Negroes.

Not all the slave-owners were in a position to appeal to their bishops —as the captain-major of Noruega had appealed to Dom João da Purificação Marquês Perdigão—to dispense them and their blacks from days of abstinence. For some of them the fast-days must have represented an element of equilibrium in a precarious existence: days of economy, not merely with regard to the outlay for meat, but with respect to food in general; days of dried fish and meal. Ensnared by the peninsular tradition—were they not the descendants of those *radish-eaters* whom Clenardus so cruelly portrays for us? [95]—many of our less opulent grandsires must have sacrificed home comforts and the diet of their families and their Negroes to vanity and a simulated grandeur. Some would cover their patron saints and their black mistresses with jewels; others would display their silks and velvets in the streets and in the churches. Meantime the Negroes engaged in the work of the plantation, and sometimes those employed in the house as well, would be going in rags or practically naked—especially after the Treaty of Methuen made all cloth very dear in Portugal and in Brazil. The Bishop of Pernambuco, Dom Frei José Fialho, finally had to advise his curates to forbid semi-nude Negresses from entering the churches inasmuch as he looked upon them as being in a state of "deplorable indecency." "We further admonish the masters of these slaves not to consent to their going naked as they commonly are accustomed to do, but rather covered with such apparel as shall be sufficient to conceal the provocations of sensuality. . . ." This in a pastoral letter of the 19th of February 1726.[96] On the 16th of August 1738, in a new letter to his curates, the Bishop came back to the sub-

---

[93] Loreto Coutto: *Desaggravos do Brasil*, etc. (op. cit.), pp. 182, 183.

[94] Henry Koster: *Travels in Brazil* (op. cit.).

[95] See p. 256 and note 160. (Translator.)

[96] Manuscript from the archives of the Cathedral of Olinda.

ject, this time reproving the slave-owners not only for the nudity of certain Negro women, but for the fact that others "had great openings in their skirts, commonly known as *maneiras.* . . ." [97] Ornaments were forbidden "under pain of major excommunication." [98]

A hundred years later we have the fugitive slave advertisements in the *Jornal do Comércio* of Rio de Janeiro and the *Diário de Pernambuco* to enlighten us as to the kind of clothing worn by the domestics of Pernambucan families. Some of them went about semi-nude, that is to say, "only with the *tanga*," or loin-cloth; most of them, however, wore a "shirt of flesh-colored baize and cotton drawers," "rough linen shirt and trousers," or "coarse cotton shirt and nankeen trousers." The mulatto girls were dressed in "*pano da Costa* with red stripes," while the old Negresses wore "garments of violet-colored calico print, lilac-colored skirt black at the top, blue *pano da Costa* with white gores, and a blue kerchief about the head." [99] Some of the Negroes wore earrings, an ornament brought from their native land which they were permitted to retain.

Le Gentil de la Barbinais remarked that if it had not been for their saints and mistresses, the Brazilian colonists would have been very rich.[100] For money did not go far when it came to cutting a figure at the feasts of the Church, which were occasions of great pomp, with processions, rockets, wax candles, incense, comedies, sermons, dances; and it similarly took a great deal of it to make a showing with the Negro and mulatto women, laden with their *balangandans* and golden trinkets.

There was high revelry on the occasion of these feasts; but on ordinary days the diet was deficient and many a false lord went hungry. Such was the situation of a good part of the aristocracy and,

[97] The *maneira* was "a posterior opening in the skirts from the waist down to permit their being slipped over the shoulders and buttocks."—Lima and Barroso, op. cit. (Translator.)

[98] Pastoral letter of Dom Frei José Fialho, "given in this city of S. Antonio do Recife . . . on the 16th day of the month of August 1738."—Manuscript in the archives of the Cathedral of Olinda.

[99] Collection of the *Diário de Pernambuco.* The period from 1825 to 1880 is the most interesting one for a study of the fugitive-slave advertisements and those concerned with the sale and purchase of slaves.

[100] La Barbinais writes of the Luso-Brazilians: "*Ils dépensent le revenu d'une année en courses de Taureaux, Comédies, en Sérmons, en ornemens d'Église & ils meurent de faim le reste de l'année. Si on otoit aux Portugais leurs Saints et leurs maitresses, ils deviendroient riches.*"—*Nouveau Voyage au tour du monde par M. Le Gentil enrichi de plusieurs plais. Vues & perspectives des principales villes & ports du Pérou, Chily, Brésil & de la Chine* (Amsterdam, 1728).

above all, of the colonial bourgeoisie in Brazil, a state of affairs that was prolonged under the Empire and the Republic. It was the same old trait derived from our Portuguese ancestors, who, though they might be reeling from hunger, were always dressed in their silks and velvets, with two, three, as many as eight slaves following after them, carrying brush, sunshade, and comb. In India Pyrard found a trio of Lusitanian noblemen with only one suit of clothes among the three of them; one would show himself in the street while the other two remained at home in their underwear. Even to this day one discovers in the Brazilian a great effort to simulate grandeur in the matter of clothing and other externals, at the sacrifice of domestic comfort and daily diet. Up to not long ago the students of our higher schools were irregularly nourished, some going hungry from the fifteenth to the end of the month, while nearly all of them lived in "republics" [101] that were utterly lacking in comfort—nothing but hammocks hung from the walls, racks for their clothes, and kerosene crates for their three or four indispensable books. But in the street they were so many princes, in dress coat and top hat, smoking cigars, and showing off their favorite mistresses as if they owned the world.

What neither the Portuguese nor the Brazilian ever sacrificed to any other interest whatsoever was the pleasurable cult of Venus. And particularly that of the dusky Venus. *"Est etiam fusco grata colore Venus."* Frézier, exaggerating, goes still further: *"Matres Omnes filiis in peccato ad-jutrices,"* [102] etc. This is not merely exaggeration; it is, very likely, calumny.

And Froger, in speaking of the Brazilians: *"Ils aiment le sexe à la folie. . . ."* [103]

---

[101] A *"república"* is a group of students living together in the same house. (Translator.)

[102] *Rélation du voyage de la Mer du Sud aux côtes du Chily et du Pérou, fait pendant les années 1712, 1713 et 1714 . . . par M. Frézier, Ingenier ordinaire du Roy* (Paris, 1715), p. 275.

[103] *Rélation d'un voyage fait en 1695, 1696 et 1697 aux côtes d'Afrique, Détroit de Magellan, Brésil, Cayenne & les Isles Antilles par une Escadre des Vaisseaux du Roy commandée par Monsieur de Gennes, faite par le Sieur de Froger . . .* (Paris, 1700), p. 142.—With regard to Recife, Pierre Moreau writes that at the time of his residence in that tropical city—in the middle of the seventeenth century—it was a place where ". . . *tous les vices y estoint en vogue. . . .*" During the Dutch rule, Moreau tells us that Christians and Jews *"faisoient commerce non seulement des enfans esclaves qu'ils permettoient aux nègres de venir abuser en leurs maisons mais encore de ceux que avoint esté engendrez de leur propre san gavec les negrines lesquelles debauchoient & tenoient comme concubines, vendoint & acheptoint, comme l'on fait ici avec les veaux & les moutons."* He adds that everyone, and not merely the Portuguese of the realm or the creoles, here led a lascivious and a

This was true not merely of ordinary Christians, but of friars and ecclesiastics as well, many of whom led the same life of Turkish debauchery as did the plantation-owners, under the provocation of the young Negro and mulatto girls of the household who were filling out into young women, *mulecas* whose breasts were becoming those of a women—and all within easy reach of the most indolent hand. This, assuredly, was one of the considerations that led Antonil to recommend to his chaplains that they take up their dwelling "outside the house of the master of the plantation." Outside the Big House, that den of perdition. And even though they dwelt in a cottage apart, let them not have a slave woman in their service, unless it was an aged Negress or one well along in years. This latter was the same recommendation that Dom Frei José Fialho made to his reverend curates of Pernambuco: that they should not have in their houses female slaves of "less than forty years." Over forty the Negro women were looked upon as not being dangerous.[104]

It was in fixing the dangerous age for female slaves that Dom Frei José possibly erred. For it would appear that Negro women do not age so quickly in the tropics as do white women; at forty they impress one as resembling those women of thirty that we hear of in the cold and temperate climates. A black woman of forty is in the prime of life and still capable of temptations and intrigues.

Le Gentil de la Barbinais, who visited us in the early years of the eighteenth century, noted the almost morbid preference of the colonists for women of color: "*Les portugais naturels du Brésil préfèrent la possession d'une femme noire ou mulâtre à la plus belle femme. Je leur ai souvent demandé d'où procedait un gout si bizarre mais ils l'ignorent eux-mêmes. Pour moi je crois qu'élevez & nourris par ces Esclaves, ils en prennent l'inclination avec le lait.*" This is none other than the theory that Calhoun applies to the Anglo-Americans of the Southern United States—blond gentry who have developed the same pronounced taste for Negro and mulatto women. The octoroon and mulatto balls of New Orleans are famous, and are attended by youths of the best white families, who go there to find colored mistresses.

Le Gentil de la Barbinais mentions in particular a curious case that

---

scandalous life: ". . . *Juifs, Chrestiens, Portugois, Hollandois, Anglois, François, Allemands, Nêgres, Brésiliens, Tapoyos, Molates, Mammelus & Crioles habitoint pesle-mesle, sans parler des incestes & pechez contre nature pour lesquels plusieurs Portugois convaincus furent exécutez à mort.*"—Pierre Moreau: *Histoire des derniers troubles du Brésil* (Paris, 1651).

[104] Manuscript of the Pastoral Letter of Dom Frei José Fialho, preserved in the archives of the Cathedral of Olinda.

came under his observation in eighteenth-century Brazil: that of a charming woman of Lisbon who was married to a Luso-Brazilian. Within a short time a profound difference arose between them, the Brazilian casting the Lisbon lady aside for love of a Negress who, we are told, would not have merited "the attentions of the ugliest black in all Guinea." This is the Frenchman's opinion—homesick, it may be, for his fair-haired and freckled Parisiennes.

The sexual intercourse of whites of the best stocks [105]—including ecclesiastics, undoubtedly one of the most select and eugenic elements in the formation of Brazilian society—with Negroes and mulattoes attained formidable proportions, and the result was a great multitude of illegitimate offspring, in the form of young mulattoes, who very frequently were brought up with the children of lawful wedlock in accordance with the liberal attitude of the patriarchal Big Houses. Others were reared on the plantations conducted by friars, or in foundling-asylums (*"rodas"*) and orphanages.

The outstanding problem in connection with the Portuguese colonization of Brazil—that of people—led to the attenuation among us of scruples concerning irregularities in moral or sexual conduct. Perhaps in no other Catholic country have illegitimate sons, especially those of priests, received so kind a treatment or grown up in circumstances so favorable. Writing of the illegitimate children gathered in the numerous colonial orphanages, La Barbinais says: *"Ces sortes d'enfants sont fort considerez dans ce Pais: le Roi les adopte, & les Dames les plus qualifiées se font un honneur de les retirer dans leurs maisons, & de les élever comme leurs propres enfans. Cette charité est bien louable mais elle est suyette à bien des inconvenens."* [106] More worthy of admiration, however, were the children born in the slave huts and reared in the house, where they mingled with the white and legitimate young ones.

In the sixteenth century, with the exception of the Jesuits, who remained uncompromisingly virginal in their attitude, a large number of priests and many friars belonging to those orders that were more relaxed in their discipline took up with Indian or Negro concubines. Father Nobrega was shocked by the clergy of Pernambuco and

---

[105] Word in English. (Translator.)

[106] La Barbinais, op. cit.—It should be noted that at times infants were abandoned at the door of persons who then undertook to bring them up with the aid of grants from the Municipal Chambers. Such was the case of the little girl left at the door of Surgeon-Major Manuel da Costa Bacellar, of Sabará, in 1782.—Manuscript from the archives of the Municipal Chamber of Sabará, 1782, in the manuscript collection of the Public Archives of Minas.

Bahia. Throughout the seventeenth and eighteenth and a good part of the nineteenth century, cassocks were freely tucked up that the wearers might fulfill quasi-patriarchal functions, when they did not also imitate the patriarchs' sexual excesses. Very often, behind the most seraphic-sounding names in the world—"Divine Love," "Assumption," "Mount Carmel," "Immaculate Conception," "Rosary"—if we are to believe what certain chroniclers tell us, in place of ascetics austerely concerned with their vows of virginity there flourished formidable stallions in clerical garb. Father La Caille was horrified at the libertinism of the monks of Rio de Janeiro.[107]

Froger, who was in Rio before La Caille—in the seventeenth century—tells us that not only the burghers but the religious made a show of their mistresses. Le Gentil de la Barbinais states that in Bahia religious and secular friars openly maintained relations with women; and he adds: *"on les connoit plutôt par le nom de leurs Maitresses que par celui qu'ils ont."* Further: *"Ils courent pendant la nuit travestis les uns en femmes en habits d'Esclaves, armez de poignards & d'armes encore plus danzereuses. Les couvens mêmes . . . servent de retraite aux femmes publiques."* The author of the pamphlet *Revolutions of Brazil*, in speaking of the eighteenth century, has horrors to relate of the convents: "centers . . . of ignorance, impudence, and licentious manners." Carmelites, Benedictines, Franciscans, Marists, Italian Barbinos, Oratorians—he accuses them all of obscenities. There must be an element of exaggeration in this pamphlet, however, just as there is in the account of Father Bento José Cepeda regarding the Jesuits, a document preserved in the archives of the Brazilian Historical Institute. It was from this document that Luis Edmundo took his anecdote of the Jesuit who, during a solemn religious ceremony, is supposed to have asked of the congregation "a Hail Mary for the Bishop's woman, who is in labor"; as well as that other story regarding one Victor Antônio, who, it is said, was in the habit of taking the wig from the crucifix of Our Lord and disguising himself in it when he went a-junketing. Father Lopes Gama, in his *Carapuceiro*, does not spare the monks, but portrays or, better, caricatures them in a cruel manner.

Maria Graham, at the beginning of the nineteenth century, received a bad impression of the Brazilian clergy; but she speaks largely from hearsay, picked up in Pernambuco. She could not forgive the

---

[107] La Caille, op. cit. E. Froger, apropos of Rio in the seventeenth century, had spoken "d-*une autre* Sodome."—*Rélation du voyage*, etc. (op. cit.), p. 75.

priests for the state of abandonment of the convent school and library of Olinda.[108]

It cannot be said, however, that the eccelesiastical libertines – those priests and friars who, forgetful of God and their books, scandalously kept company with prostitutes – constituted a majority; there were priests who impressed English Protestants like Mathison with their pure and saintly lives; who impressed a Koster with their learning and lofty interests, or a Burton with their goodness of heart and their education.[109] There were others who kept concubines (*"comadres"*) it is true, but discreetly, without sin, as it were, living the life of a married man and rearing and educating with care their "godsons" or "nephews."[110]

Many of these unions were with colored women, slaves or exslaves; others, however, were with white or light-skinned mulatto girls, true types of beauty, the Aryan would say.[111] If I insist on the

[108] Maria Graham: *Journal of a Voyage to Brazil*, etc. (op. cit.), p. 111.—See also the report of the Bishop of Pernambuco, Dom Frei Luis de Santa Thereza, to His Holiness with regard to the state of the clergy in the eighteenth century.—Canon José do Carmo Baratta: *História Ecclesiástica de Pernambuco* (Recife, 1922). The report of Dom Frei Luis de Santa Thereza, a copy of which is preserved in the archives of the Cathedral of Olinda, is an extremely interesting document. It is to be regretted that it has not as yet been published or translated into Portuguese.

[109] Richard Burton, who is not to be suspected of favoring the Church, remarked that foreigners were generally inclined to exaggeration in their criticisms of Brazilian priests: "As a rule they are grossly and unworthily abused by foreigners, especially by English Catholics, who as a rule are Ultramontanes." Burton found them "sufficiently elevated in point of education above their flocks." In addition to this, they were liberal, good-hearted, hospitable. He recalls that Liais was of the same opinion; the Frenchman wrote: *"J'ai eu occasion, à Olinda, surtout, de voir souvent des prêtres très recommendables sous tous les rapports.*—Richard Burton: *The Highlands of the Brazil*, etc. (op. cit.).

[110] Richard Burton notes the fact that parishioners made little of the curates' keeping a woman or "housekeeper." "The climate," he writes, "is not favorable to chastity; the race, especially where the blood is mixed, is inflammable material, and the sayings and doings of slaves do not comport with early modesty. It is hardly necessary to state that clerical celibacy is purely a question of discipline. . . . On the other hand," he adds, with the prejudices of a nineteenth-century liberal, but at the same time with an accurate feeling for Brazilian necessities, "the superior worth of asceticism, of a sterile virginity, whether forced or voluntary, is a concept that is repugnant to reason and to good sense, especially in a new country, where polygamy morally justifies itself, the evils being more than compensated for by the benefits."—*The Highlands of the Brazil* (op. cit.).

[111] Alexander Caldcleugh knew in Minas an old priest, Antônio Freitas, whose "housekeeper" was a strikingly beautiful woman, with lovely black eyes.—Caldcleugh: *Travels in South*

point I have been making here, it is not with the object of stressing the weak vocation that the colonial celrgy had for the ascetic life—a deficiency that, in the case of those parish priests who entered into unions with *"comadres,"* was largely compensated by the patriarchal virtues which they developed and cultivated. My insistence has, rather, another purpose: that of bringing out the fact that in the formation of Brazilian society there was not lacking a superior element recruited from the best families and capable of transmitting to its progeny major advantages from the point of view of eugenics and social heritage. Hence the fact that so many illustrious families in Brazil were founded by priests or have a priest in their lineage; the fact that so many sons and grandsons of priests have been distinguished in letters, politics, jurisprudence, and administration.

Basing himself upon Lapouge, Alfredo Ellis, Jr., includes "religious selection" among the forces or influences that he sees as having diminished the "eugenic potentiality" of the Paulista.[112] The Church is seen as having taken away from the task of procreation those individuals endowed with the highest spiritual qualities, thereby contributing to its own decadence. The writer in question pictures to himself still "more sinister" results of this religious selection as exerted by Catholicism with regard to the Brazilian family: "it also kept from reproducing themselves those elements of greatest value from the cerebral point of view, thus diminishing the strength of intellect in the population, seeing that it was the custom among São Paulo families to dedicate to a priestly career the son who showed the greatest inclination toward intellectual things. The best elements of the family accordingly failed to reproduce themselves, this function being left to those who displayed the least aptitude for things of the mind." This is a point on which I must disagree with the São Paulo sociologist. Granted that a very large number of priests and friars came from the best colonial homes—they were, in general, the flower, the finest intellectual expression of each family—I still do not feel

America, etc. (op. cit.).—Years later Burton visited the Big House of Father Freitas and there learned that not only was the padre's ghost accustomed to put in an appearance, but it would provide itself with food from the pantry. One of the priest's old slaves, Pedro, his locks now white, took care to leave meat on the table for his master's spirit, which gave signs of not yet being surfeited with earthly delights.—Gardner found in Ceará a vicar, from seventy to eighty years old, who with his six sons was a perfect patriarch. One of the sons, also a priest, was Chief Magistrate of the province and a Senator of the Empire. He lived with a woman cousin by whom he had ten children. And he was the father of still others here and there.—George Gardner: *Travels in the Interior of Brazil,* etc. (op. cit.).
[112] Alfredo Ellis, Jr.: *Raça de Gigantes* (op. cit.).

that this superior intellectual potential was stifled or sterilized by "religious selection." Lapouge is alluding to the influence of the Church in those milieus in which asceticism or celibacy is strictly observed by the clergy. This was by no means the case in Brazil. With us it was rare for ecclesiastics to remain sterile; the great majority of them contributed liberally to the increase of the population, by begetting sons and grandsons of superior quality. As for the circumstance alleged by Alfredo Ellis, Jr., that the Paulistas have been "in the past very mediocre as regards cerebral functions," this appears to me to be due to other causes, undetermined as yet. The truth of the matter is that the "religious selection" of which Lapouge speaks was scarcely perceptible in Brazil, for there are numerous cases of notable Brazilians who were the sons or grandsons of priests.

Notable not alone for their talent or culture, but for their excellent moral conduct. To this day these descendants of the clergy are prominent in literature, politics, and diplomacy. I might cite the name of a distinguished novelist of the time of the Empire; that of a learned jurisconsult who is still living; that of a famous hygienist of the early days of the Republic; that of an eminent diplomat, co-worker of Rio Branco; [113] that of a minister of state in the Vargas government; along with various physicians, advocates, instructors in higher schools. It is not merely a matter of two or three families; there are many in Brazil who have a priest in their family tree or who can trace their descent from a vicar or curate. This is true of one of our finest families, the Andradas. Here, according to Alberto de Sousa, we may meet with the respectable figure of an old colonial priest, the Right Reverend Father Patrício Manuel Bueno de Andrade, a wealthy landowner of Santos, whose daughter, Dona Maria Sabinda, was married to her cousin, Francisco Xavier da Costa Aguiar, thus bringing to the legitimate branch of the family the fortune that had belonged to the old minister of the Church.[114]

Luis dos Santos Vilhena, the erudite regius professor of the Greek

---

[113] The Visconde do Rio Branco was a statesman of the Second Empire. (Translator.)

[114] Alberto de Sousa: *Os Andradas* (op. cit.).—Pedro P. de Fonseca, in an unpublished work that I was permitted to read: *Fundação de Alagoas —Apuntamentos Históricos, Biográficos e Genealógicos* (*Founding of Alagoas—Historical, Biographical, and Genealogical Notes*) (1886),

mentions the names of some distinguished priests who were among the founders of Alagoas families. According to this investigator, the curate Manuel José Cabral (eighteenth century) was one of those who had numerous descendants; among his sons were three who were ordained to the priesthood, and one of these, Father Joaquim, left a numerous progeny.

language in colonial days, discovered a serious drawback to the distorted patriarchalism of the clergy. Inasmuch as many of them formed unions, not with white women or very light-skinned mulattoes, whose descendants might readily be reabsorbed into the old and legitimate branch of the family, but with Negresses or darker-colored girls, this led to a dispersal of property in the hands of mulattoes. "There are ecclesiastics, and not a few of them," Vilhena tells us, "who, out of old and evil habit, without giving a thought to their character and station, live disorderly lives with mulatto and Negro women, by whom they have sons who upon their death become their heirs; and in this and other ways many of the most valuable estates in Brazil have come to pass into the hands of mulattoes who are presumptuous, haughty, and vain, as is the case here with those sugar plantations which within a short time are broken up, to the very grave damage of the State. . . ." So serious did this situation impress Vilhena as being, so widespread the instances of wealthy priests living with Negro and mulatto concubines, that the Greek professor saw fit to call the circumstance to the attention of John VI: "this being a matter well deserving of His Majesty's Royal attention; for if these Plantations and Estates are not prevented from falling into the hands of these bastard *pardos*—profligate individuals, ordinarily, who only hold these incomparable properties to be worth what they cost them—then in the course of time we shall see the properties in question slipping from their hands and, consequently, being lost, which is what has happened to the major part of those that have come into the possession of owners of this sort." [115] It is possible that Mestre Vilhena was exaggerating; however this may be, we may see in the frequency of these unions of well-to-do individuals—merchants, ecclesiastics, rural proprietors—with Negresses and mulattoes one of the causes of the rapid and easy dispersion of wealth in colonial times, to the undoubted prejudice of the patriarchal system of economy and the capitalist State, but with decided advantages for the development of Brazilian society along democratic lines.

In addition, the patriarchal activity of the priests, even though exercised very frequently under unfavorable moral conditions, contributed to the formation of Brazil an element that was socially and eugenically superior, in the form of individuals of the best families and of the highest intellectual capacity, reared and nourished as was no other class, who as a rule transmitted to their white and even their mestizo descendants this ancestral superiority due to social advantages

---

[115] Vilhena: *Cartas* (op. cit.), Vol. I, p. 139.

that included culture and wealth. This goes to explain the rapid social rise of so many sons of priests, when they were whites or light-colored mestizos, a rise that is always accomplished with great ease, the noblest professions and careers being open to them as well as marriages into the bosom of the most exclusive families. It is not without reason that the popular imagination is accustomed to attribute to the sons of priests an exceptional lot in life. To the sons of priests in particular and to bastards in general. "Happier than the son of a priest" is a saying commonly heard in Brazil. "There is none that's not . . ." is a saying prevalent among the people; which means: "There is no illegitimate son, especially the son of a priest, who is not happy."

The same may be extended to apply to bastards in general, though without the same degree of emphasis, it is true. It may be applied to those mestizos who almost always resulted from the union of the best masculine element—the socially elevated whites of the Big Houses—with the best feminine element of the slave huts: the prettiest, healthiest, and freshest of the Negro and mulatto women.

Comte—not the philosopher of the rue Monsieur-le-Prince, but the other one, Charles, who unfortunately has never attained the same vogue among us as has Auguste—Comte emphasizes this fact, which is of great significance for the study of the formation of Brazilian society: namely, the ample opportunity that the masters in slave-holding societies have of choosing the most beautiful and the healthiest slave women for their mistresses: *"les plus belles et les mieux constituées."* This was an opportunity that the Portuguese colonizer of Brazil did not have with respect to the Indian women.

From such unions, Charles Comte believed, there almost always resulted, in the lands of slavery, an element of the best sort; and it is my opinion that he would have said "the most eugenic" sort if, instead of writing in 1833, he were writing today, a hundred years later. *"Les enfans nés de ces alliances"*—these are Comte's words—*"n'out pas tous été affranchis; ce n'est cependant que par mieux qu'il y a eu de nombreux affranchissemens. Les personnes de cette classe aux-quelles la liberté n'a pas été ravie, ayant été soustraites aux fatigues et aux privations des esclaves, et n'ayant pu contracter les vices que donne la domination, ont formé la classe la mieux constituée et la plus énergique."* [116] Instead of looking upon the sons born of masters and slave women as socially dangerous, combining the vices of both ex-

[116] Charles Comte: *Traité de légis-lation ou exposition des lois générales suivant lesquels les peuples prospèrent,* dépérissent ou restent stationnaires (Paris, 1835).

tremes,[117] Charles Comte regards them as being, rather, free from the drawbacks of either class and constituting a happy middle term.

In Brazil many a *cria* and young mulatto, illegitimate son of the master, learned to read and write sooner than did the white lads, leaving them behind as he went on to higher studies. Rural traditions tell us of many such cases, cases of *crias* who made their way upward, socially and economically, by making good use of the instruction that was given them, while the white youths, upon reaching maturity, were interested only in horse-racing and cock-fighting. It was in the hands of these legitimate white sons, and not in those of the "bastard *pardos*," so despised by Vilhena, that many estates were dispersed; it was in such hands that fortunes that had been accumulated for two, three, and four generations were squandered.

Meanwhile, there are certain reservations to be made with respect to Charles Comte's statement concerning the advantages possessed by the mestizo offspring of master and slave. For there were disadvantages, too: in the form of the inevitable prejudice against mixed-bloods. Color prejudice on the part of some; a prejudice against those of slave origin on the part of others.

Under the pressure of such prejudices there developed in many a mestizo that obvious inferiority complex that even in Brazil, a land so favorable to the mulatto, is to be observed under a number of forms. One of these is a pronounced attitude of climbing (*arrivismo*) on the part of those mulattoes who have attained a superior position with respect to culture, power, or wealth. Of this restless *arrivismo* we may note two characteristic expressions: Tobias Barreto,[118] the type of newly educated man, who in so many of his aspects recalls the figure of Lucian studied by Chamberlain; and in politics, Nilo Peçanha.[119] On the other hand, no one could be more reticent than was Machado de Assis,[120] nor more subtle than the Baron of

---

[117] This was the opinion commonly held in Brazil, as Mathison found. The mulattoes "seem to unite the vices of savage and civilized life, without opposing to them any stock of characteristic virtues: and the women, as well as men, are remarkable for the indulgence of violent passions, unregulated by any principle of religious or natural morality." —Gilbert Farquhar Mathison: *Narrative of a Visit to Brazil*, etc. (op. cit.), p. 158. On the subject of miscegenation, in the proper sense of the term, the reader may be referred to my *Sobrados e Mucambos* (*Town House and Slums*), the chapter on the "Ascent of the University Bachelor and the Mulatto."

[118] Prominent literary figure at the turn of the century. (Translator.)

[119] One of the Presidents of the Brazilian Republic (1909-10); as Vice-President he succeeded Alfonso Penna. (Translator.)

[120] The nineteenth-century novelist —Brazil's greatest novelist, many

Cotegipe.[121] It is my purpose to study this and other aspects of miscegenation in my next essay.

Some chroniclers of slavery attach a great importance to Negro prostitution—the prostitution of Negro and mulatto women exploited by whites. La Barbinais asserts that even ladies of standing engaged in such nefarious commerce. They would deck their slave girls out in gold chains, bracelets, rings, and fine lace and then share in the profits of the day.[122] The male and female Negroes, known as *negros de ganho*, or "Negroes for hire," were to be found throughout Brazil, selling castor oil, cakes, couscous, mangoes, bananas, transporting burdens, and carrying well-water to the homes of the poor. At night they would bring the profits home to their masters; and if we are to credit La Barbinais, they served another purpose as well. But, granting an exception here and there, it was not ladies of good family but déclassée white women who thus exploited the slave girls. At times little Negro girls ten and twelve years old were to be seen in the street offering themselves to the big, strapping, ruddy-complexioned English and French sailors who were just off the boat and starving for women; and these blond giants in their superexcitation would vent their bestial impulses upon the young mulattoes. What was more, many of these seafaring men were rotting with syphilis and other diseases picked up in the four corners of the globe, in international ports of call.

In the mid-nineteenth century His Majesty the Emperor Dom Pedro II was reigning over Brazil, a chaste man and pure, the ideal type of husband for a Queen Victoria. In this respect he afforded a contrast to his august sire,[123] who, very much a Brazilian, even took and deflowered young Negro girls. Yet during Pedro II's reign the rua do Sabão and the rua da Alfândega were even worse than the Mangue district of today;[124] and slave girls of ten, twelve, or fifteen years would here show themselves half-naked at the windows—slaves who, we are told by a writer of the epoch, were obliged by their masters and mistresses (the latter usually *maîtresses de maison*) "to sell their favors, deriving from this cynical commerce the means of subsistence." [125] Referring to the last years of colonial life, Vilhena

would say—who was of part Negro descent. (Translator.)

[121] Politician and diplomat of the Second Empire.—See the chapter, "The Rise of the Mixed-Blood," in Donald Pierson: *Negroes in Brazil* (op. cit.), Chapter vi. (Translator.)

[122] Le Gentil de la Barbinais, op. cit.

[123] Dom Pedro I. (Translator.)

[124] "Segregated district" of the Brazilian capital. (Translator.)

[125] João Alvares de Azevedo Macedo, Jr.: *Da Prostituição no Rio*

tells us that conditions were horrible in the streets of Bahia: "Libidinous, vagrant, and idle persons of one and the other sex who as soon as night falls fill the streets and wander up and down them, without shame or respect for anyone, but glorying in their lewdness. . . ." The Greek professor then goes on to speak of the "fathers of poor families"—our "poor whites"—who, with no other inheritance to leave their daughters than that of idleness and a prejudice against manual labor, "after they become adults, take advantage of them for their own livelihood. . . ."[126] But the great majority of prostitutes were those Negro women exploited by the whites. It was their bodies —at times, tiny ten-year-old bodies—that, in the moral architecture of Brazilian patriarchalism, constituted a formidable block of defense against bold attacks by Don Juans on the virtue of the white ladies.

Burton reminds us of the relation between Agapemone [127] and the purity of the domestic hearth: the more prosperous the former, the freer the latter of Don-Juanism. The theory of Bernard Mandeville.[128] Applied to patriarchal Brazil, it leads to this conclusion: the virtue of the white woman of the upper classes rested largely upon the prostitution of the Negro slave girl. The mother of a family, the unmarried girl, women in general, not alone in Minas but in Brazil as a whole, impressed Burton as being "exceptionally pure." For the Brazilian woman was not to be judged by the customs of the court and the cities, but by the manners of her sex in the interior of the country. In the provinces women lived under a system of Oriental semi-seclusion, that is true; but they were exceptionally pure, for all that. This purity the English traveler does not hesitate to contrast with the "flirtations" of young women in the British Isles before marriage, and with the comparative freedom that Canadian and North American women enjoy both before and after wedlock.[129] But before accepting in any self-congratulatory spirit Burton's eulogies of the purity of Brazilian women in the days of slavery, we are compelled to recall the fact that much of this chastity, much of this purity, rested upon slave prostitution and was at the expense of the much maligned mulatto woman; it was at the cost of a promiscuity and lax-

---

de Janeiro e da Sua Influência Sobre a Saúde Pública (*On Prostitution in Rio de Janeiro and Its Influence upon Public Health*), thesis sustained on the 6th day of December 1868, in the august presence of His Majesty the Emperor (op. cit.).
[126] Vilhena, op. cit., p. 166.

[127] The term is employed here, euphemistically, for prostitution. (Translator.)
[128] Bernard Mandeville was an English philosopher and satirist, born in Holland, 1670 (?)-1733. (Translator.)
[129] Burton, op. cit.

ness of morals stimulated in the slave hut by the white masters themselves.

"Some masters are opposed to the marriage of male and female slaves," wrote the Jesuit Andreoni, "and not only think nothing of free unions, but consent to them more or less openly, saying: 'You, So-and-So, will in due time marry So-and-So'; and from then on the thing is taken for granted, as if they were already man and wife; and it is said that the reason why they do not marry is the fear that, tiring of the match, they may kill one another with poison or with witchcraft; for there are among them notable masters of the art." Alluding to slave-owners at the close of the seventeenth century, the priest continues: "Others, after having married off their slaves, separate them for years in such a manner that they remain as if unwed; and this is something that they cannot in conscience do." [130]

A distinction should be made, however, between those slaves engaged in work in the fields and those employed in the house; for the latter benefited from a moral and religious training that the former often lacked.[131] In a majority of the Big Houses they always made it a point of baptizing Negroes, for there was something like a superstitious repugnance to having "pagans" or "Moors" within the home, even though they were but slaves. The nineteenth-century wills and inventories frequently allude to Negro marriages, to Such-and-Such a woman as being the wife of So-and-So. Perdigão Malheiro tells us that there were plantation mistresses so interested in the well-being of their slaves that they even suckled at their own aristocratic white bosoms little pickaninnies whose mothers had died in childbirth; and that on plantations and estates many Negroes would unite in marriage, "thus setting up a family with certain privileges that the masters bestowed upon them." [132]

These baptized Negroes thus living in wedlock generally took the family names of their white masters; whence the many Cavalcantis, Albuquerques, Mellos, Mouras, Wanderleys, and individuals called Lins, Carneiro Leão, and so on, who have no trace of the illustrious blood to which their names would seem to point. In Brazil, even more than in Portugal, there is no more uncertain and precarious

---

[130] Antonil: *Opulência do Brasil,* etc. (op. cit.), p. 93.

[131] Letters-Royal of 1663, 1701, 1704, and 1719 indicate that many masters did not give their slaves the necessary rest or time to work for themselves, that some of them neglected the spiritual needs of the blacks, to the point of not baptizing the newborn or sending the last sacraments to the dying. See Perdigão Malheiro: *A Escravidão no Brasil* (op. cit.). But it is obvious that the reference is to field laborers rather than to household servants.

[132] Perdigão Malheiro, op. cit.

means of determining a person's social origin than his name. I was told by a lady of a distinguished Pernambucan family, widow of an eminent diplomat and historian, that once upon a time in London or in Washington there appeared as military attaché of the Brazilian legation an army officer with the same family name as her own. Who could tell?—possibly they were relatives. She investigated and found that the name in question had been adopted out of purely æsthetic motives; the officer had liked the sound of it and had adopted it. The same thing was done by certain sons of priests and others born out of matrimony. Many not content with pretty-sounding or noble names of their own land proceeded to ransack the history of Portugal and Spain for those of still greater resonance and glory, the more exquisite not forgetting to add a "da" or a "de" as a suggestion of nobility: So-and-So da Alba, de Cadaval, da Gama, etc. This is what the writer Antônio Torres once referred to as "letter-head nobility," or hotel-register nobility, one might call it.[133]

In the case of the slaves who had set up Christian families in the shadow of the plantation Big Houses, there was less foolish vanity on their part in connection with the adoption of noble names; it was, rather, the natural influence of patriarchalism, inducing blacks and mulattoes, in their efforts to climb the social ladder, to imitate their white masters by taking over the outward forms of superiority. It is worthy of note, moreover, that very often the illustrious or noble name of the white master was absorbed in the native and even the African one [134] that was given to the rural estate, the land thus re-creating the names of its owners in its own image and likeness. Thus in Pernambuco one branch of the old Cavalcanti de Albuquerque family came to be known by the name of Suassuna; and more recently the name of a branch of the Carneiro Leão family was trans-

---

[133] Adolphe d'Assier writes that he frequently encountered in Brazil "*les plus grands noms du Portugal portés par des* tropeiros. . . ." And he adds: "*L'explication est cependant des plus simples: tout affranchi prend à volonté le nom de son patron, de son parrain ou de tout autre protecteur. . . .*" Adolphe d'Assier: *Le Brésil contemporain*, etc. (op. cit.). [A *tropeiro* is a mule-driver. (Translator.)]
[134] The following names of plantations in the north appear to be of African origin: Qualombo, Malemba,

Mamulunga, Inhama; and the following names of places or plantations are assuredly African: Zumbí, Macangano, Catucá, Cafundó. In Minas, Senhor Nelson de Senna believes, numerous place names are of African derivation: Angola, Bengo, Cabinda, Fubá, Mumbaça, Zungú, etc.—"*Toponímia Geográfica de Origem Brasilico-indígena em Minas Gerais*" ("Geographical Place Names of Native-Brazilian Origin in Minas Geraes"), *Revista do Arquivo Público Mineiro*, Ano X (1924).

formed into Cedro. Suassuna and Cedro—these were the names of plantations in which the distinguished European names of landowning families had been extinguished.[135]

Immediately following Independence, there was a great craze for things Indian throughout Brazil, and many of the gentry then changed their Portuguese family names for the indigenous ones that were associated with their estates, which at times were confirmed by titles of nobility bestowed under the Empire. Many individuals of European origin and others with African forebears thus came to bear Indian names, which led some of them to imagine themselves *caboclos* rather than being predominantly of Portuguese or African descent. Whence such arrogantly indigenous names as Burití, Murití, Jurema, Jutaí, Araripe.[136] The man who was to become Viscount of Jequitinhonha transformed into Gê Acaiaba Montezuma the exceedingly Portuguese name of Francisco Gomes Brandão. Certain Brazilians, less given to Indian associations but none the less nativist [137] in their tendencies—some of them, even, being *bairristas*, or enthusiasts for their own city or quarter of the town—would interpolate in their names a "Brasileiro" (Brazilian), a "Pernambucano" (Pernambucan), a "Paraense" (of Pará), or a "Maranhão" (of the city of Maranhão), by way of emphasis, thereby proclaiming their Brazilian or specifying their regional origin. Such was the case with old José Antônio Gonsalves de Mello, who gave to one of his sons the name of Cicero Brasileiro and to another that of Ulysses Pernambucano, names that have been handed down in the family for three or four generations now. Another patriarch of the same family, of the branch connected with the Fonseca Galvão's, changed his legitimate Portuguese name to that of Carapeba; and a son bearing this horrible appelation [138]

---

[135] The indigenous plantation names are many in number: Tibirí, Una, Cacaú, Catende, etc., while some, like Luango, are African. Sousa Bandeira recalls a number of instances of family names being absorbed in those of the estates: Chico do Caxito, Casusa do Quisenga, Ioiô de Cursai, Joca de Pindobal.—J. C. Sousa Bandeira: *Evocações e Outros Escritos* (*Evocations and Other Writings*) (Rio de Janeiro, 1920). See also the biography of the Baron of Goiana, by João Alfredo Correia, *Revista do Instituto Arqueológico, Histórico e Geográfico de Pernambuco*, Vol. XXVII, where there will be found a list of estates and their owners.

[136] Theodoro Sampaio: *O Tupí na Geografia Nacional* (op. cit.); Alfredo de Carvalho: *Frases e Palavras* (op. cit.).

[137] The terms *nativista* ("nativist") and *nativismo* ("nativism") have a special meaning in South America; there are "nativist" movements in literature, politics, etc. (Translator.)

[138] *Carapeba* (*Acarapeba*) is the name of a fish (*Diapterus rhombeus* Cuv. and *Val.*). It is applied jestingly to a very thin person. (Translator.)

died a hero's death in the war with Paraguay. He, moreover, received from his father (who, it may be, was an ardent freemason) the name —can one call it a Christian name?—of Voltaire. Voltaire Carapeba.

Many times the names of plantations were joined to the Christian names and occasionally to the surnames of their owners: Joaquim de Lavrinha; Sinhôzinho (Sousa Leão) de Almecega; Orico do Vena (Eurico Chaves do Venus); Sebastião (Wanderley) do Rosário; Seraphim (Pessoa de Mello) de Matarí; Pedrinho (Paranhos Ferreira) de Japaranduba; Zezinho (Pereira Lima) do Brejo; the Pinheiros of Itapeçoca; the Coelhos and Castanhos de Macaranduva; the Vieiras of Calugí; the Pedros (Wanderleys) of Bom-Tom; and the Lulús (Pessoa de Mello family) of Maré.

As to Christian names, it would seem that for a long time there was little difference between those of whites and Negroes, all being taken from the Church calendar.[139] Names of saints—with that of João (John) predominating; if a child bore this name, the devil would not come to dance at the door of the house. Names like Antônio, Pedro, José (Anthony, Peter, Joseph), powerful saints who kept the seventh son of the family from turning into a werewolf. But still, without any ostensible difference, certain names such as Benedito, Bento, Cosme, Damião, Romão, Esperança, Felicidade, Luzia, may be looked upon as being characteristically Negro.

There is one important aspect of the infiltration of Negro culture into the domestic life and economy of the Brazilian that remains to be stressed, and that is the culinary aspect. The African slave dominated the colonial kitchen, enriching it with a variety of new flavors. "If from the rude cooking of the *caboclo*," writes Luis Edmundo, "we go on to the praiseworthy kitchen of the *mazombo*, we shall see that the latter was nothing more than an assimilation of the Portuguese cuisine, subject merely to environmental contingencies."[140] This is an unfair statement, in that, as always, the influence of the Negro on Brazilian life and culture is overlooked.

In connection with Brazilian diet, the chief contributions of the African were the following: the introduction of oil of the dendê palm and malagueta pepper,[141] so characteristic a constituent of the

---

[139] In the nineteenth century the tradition of bestowing saints' names began to be broken, and there appear names inspired by "profane history, by mythology, by novels, and by geography."—Lopes Gama: *O Carapuceiro* (op. cit.). The names in the Felix Cavalcanti de Albuquerque Mello family reflect this tendency: Demócrito, Heraclito, Thales, Lycurgo, Lisbella, Ranuzia, etc.—Manuscript memorandum book.

[140] Luis Edmundo, op. cit.

[141] What is known as "grains of paradise." (Translator.)

Bahian cuisine; the introduction of the quiabo, or okra plant; greater utilization of the banana; a greater variety in the preparation of poultry and fish. A number of Portuguese or native dishes were modified in Brazil by the Negro mode of spicing food or by African culinary technique; some of those that are most typically Brazilian are the result of that technique, such as *farofa*; [142] *quibebe*, or gourd paste; and *vatapá*, a manihot paste with oil and pepper and fish or meat.

The slaves employed in the Big Houses had highly specialized functions, and two or sometimes three of them were always reserved for work in the kitchen. Ordinarily these were enormous black women, but occasionally they were male Negroes who were unsuited for hard labor but who were without a rival in the preparation of culinary sweets and confections. These latter were always very effeminate; and some of them even wore beneath their man's clothing a woman's lace-trimmed smock set off with a rose-colored ribbon, while about their necks were strung feminine trinkets. They were the great chefs of colonial times, as they still are today.

In Rio de Janeiro nobles of the realm for long kept cooks brought over from Lisbon. In those kitchens that were typically Brazilian, on the other hand, those of the great patriarchal landowning families, the one who, from the sixteenth century on, prepared the ragouts and desserts was the male or female African slave. "The gentry of times past," Manuel Querino tells us in *The Culinary Art in Bahia*,[143] "very often, in expansive moments, would grant freedom to slaves who had satiated their gullets with a variety of dishes, each more tempting than the others; or they might prefer to give vent to their philanthropic feelings by remembering these servitors in certain clauses of their wills. . . . It was a common thing, at dinners of the bourgeoisie, to drink a toast to the cook, accompanied by songs in her honor, and she was invited to come into the dining-room and receive the homage of the guests." [144]

A number of foods in use in Brazil are purely or predominantly African in origin. This is true in the north especially, in Bahia, Pernambuco, and Maranhão. Manuel Querino has noted those of Bahia,[145]

---

[142] *Farofa* is manihot meal mixed with hot butter or fat; at times mixed with eggs, meat, etc. (Translator.)

[143] *A Arte Culinária na Baía* (Bahia, 1928).

[144] See also Richard Burton, op. cit. Burton refers to these after-dinner songs of greeting to the cook as being one of the most interesting and joyful features of the patriarchal feasts of yesteryear.

[145] Op. cit.

Nina Rodrigues those of Maranhão,[146] and I have attempted the same thing with regard to those of Pernambuco.[147]

Of these three centers of Afro-Brazilian cooking, Bahia is without a doubt the most important. The sale of confections in the street there developed as in no other Brazilian city, with a true civil war prevailing between the cakes sold on trays and those made at home. The street commerce in the old days was conducted by Negro women so expert in the confectioner's art that they managed to get together quite a little money by selling their wares. The fact is that the ladies of the Big House and the abbesses of convents at times engaged in this occupation, the nuns accepting orders even from abroad for dried sweets, gumdrops, marchpane, sugarplums, and other dainties. Vilhena speaks of these sweets and other dishes—confections made at home and sold in the street, the trays containing them being borne on the heads of Negro women, but the profits going to the white ladies: *mocotós*, or calves' feet; *vatapá; mingau; pamonhas*, or corncakes; *canjica* or corn paste; *acaçá*, a confection made of rice flour and Indian corn; *abará*, a dish consisting of cooked beans spiced with pepper and dendê oil; *arroz de coco* (rice with coconut); *feijão de coco* (beans with coconut); *angú* (dough made of corn, manihot, or rice flour with water and salt); *pão-de-ló de arroz* (spongecake with rice); *pão-de-ló de milho* (spongecake with Indian corn); *rolete de cana* (sugar-cane roll); *queimados*, or bonbons; etc. "Unattractive viands," Vilhena calls them; "and the most scandalous of all is a drink made with honey and certain other ingredients to which they give the name of *aloá*, and which serves as a lemonade for the Negroes." [148] The truth of the matter is that the Bahian Greek professor was homesick for the vegetable-broth [149] of his native Portugal.

But the real sweets or confections as sold on the sweetmeat-trays were those made or prepared by Negro freedwomen who were expert at their art, their wares being set off by blue or red paper flowers that they themselves had fashioned, cutting them into the shape of hearts, ponies, little birds, fish, hens, and the like—figures that were at times reminiscent of the old phallic or totem cults.[150]

---

[146] Nina Rodriques: *O Regime Alimentar no Norte do Brasil (Diet in Northern Brazil)* (Maranhão, 1881).

[147] Paper read at the Regionalist Congress of the Northeast, Recife, 1925.

[148] Vilhena: *Cartas* (op. cit.), Vol. I, p. 131.

[149] *Caldo verde*, made of turnips or cabbage chopped very fine and seasoned with salt or oil. (Translator.)

[150] In Portugal to this day it is the custom, in Bragança, on the occasion of marriages, to prepare two cakes, one representing the sexual organs of the male, the other those of the fe-

Spread over the top would be fresh banana leaves; and on the inside, the trays, which were almost liturgical in character, would be lined with towels white as altar-cloths. The *"mães Bentas"* (small cakes made of wheat flour and eggs) of these venders became famous; and to this day at Garanhuns, in the interior of Pernambuco, they sell "cornbread [151] made by the Negresses of Castainho." All this was the work of the African woman.

Some of these venders went about through the streets, while others stationed themselves at certain definite points, such as the corner of some large town house or in the courtyard of a church, beneath the aged gameleiras.[152] Here they would rest their trays on a wooden stand in the form of an X, the Negresses being seated on stools beside them.

In these courtyards or on these corners Negro women with a chafing-dish would take their stand and there would prepare such dishes as: fried fish; *mungunzá;* [153] roast corn; popcorn; *grude;* [154] and *manuê.*[155] In São Paulo, which at the close of the eighteenth century became the great coffee-growing country, the black women of the chafing-dish undertook the sale of the drink that resembled their own skins in color, "at ten reis the cup, accompanied by slices of the unfailing couscous with fish, baked rolls, popcorn, kneaded-corn or manihot cakes, *"purva,"* [156] fish-cakes made of the piquira or the

---

male. Upon leaving the church, the bridegroom raises his cake and the bride does the same. The lads and lasses then try to take the cakes away from the wedded pair; the one that succeeds will be married shortly. And in Azurei, near Guimarães, they sell cakes with the name of *"sardões,"* (popular name given to the masculine genital organs); in other places, they use the name *"passarinhas,"* applied to the genital organs of the female. See also, on this subject, the work by Emmanuel Ribeiro: *O Doce Nunca Amargou . . . Docaria Portuguesa, História, Decoração, Receituário (The Sweet Never Grew Bitter— Portuguese Sweet-Making, History, Ornamentation, Recipes)* (Coimbra, 1928). In Brazil, as has already been remarked [see pp. 259–260] a number of cakes and sweets have suggestive names. As for recipes, I have gathered a number of these and published them

in my book *Açucar (Sugar)* (Rio de Janeiro, 1939).

[151] *"broas das negras do Castainho"*: *broa* is cornbread made with rice or tapioca and beaten eggs. (Translator.)

[152] The *gameleira (gamelleira)* is a tree of the *Moraceæ* family, of which there are various species. (Translator.)

[153] *Mungunzá (munguzá, mugunzá)* is a sugared broth made of grains of corn, and at times with coconut milk or cow's milk. (Translator.)

[154] Dish made of dried tapioca and grated coconut, baked in the oven and wrapped in banana leaves. (Translator.)

[155] Variety of cake made of corn flour, honey, and other ingredients. (Translator.)

[156] None of the many Brazilians whom the translator has consulted, in this country and in Brazil (including

lambari,[157] *quitunga* (the peanut toasted and pressed with cumari pepper),[158] *pé-de-muleque*[159] with manihot flour and peanut, toasted *içá*,[160] *quentão*,[161] *ponche*,[162] and other such delights, all of them directly out of the African or the native kitchen." [163] At night the trays were lighted, liturgical-fashion, with black wax tapers, tin-plate candelabra, or paper lanterns.

One still sees, now and again, one of these black women with sweetmeat-tray or chafing-dish in Bahia, in Rio, or in Recife; but they are becoming rare. Traces still exist, however, of the ancient rivalry between their more definitely African sweets and those of family make. In the preparation of various confections such as *acaçá*, *acarajé*,[164] and *manuê* the Negro women greatly outdistance their competitors. And it is my opinion that even in the preparation of *arroz doce* (milk-rice), traditionally a Portuguese dish, there is none like that sold by Negresses in the street, in huge porringers from which the greedy may sup it without need of a spoon. Similarly, there is no creamed tapioca like that of these venders, served in the African manner, on a banana leaf. I know only one exception: this dish as prepared by a distinguished Pernambucan lady of the Andrade Lima family.[165]

In the preparation of *acaçá* and other African confections, the orthodox procedure is to use: first, the *grating-stone*, which also is African in origin and which has been triumphantly incorporated into Afro-Brazilian culinary technique; then the *wooden spoon;* and fi-

---

the author), has been able to identify this dish. (Translator.)

[157] The *piquira* is a scaly fish of the *Caracinidæ* family (*Bryconops alburnus*). *Lambari* is a name common to a number of varieties of river fish. (Translator.)

[158] On the peanut, see Chapter i, note 82, p. 34. The *cumari* (*cumarim*) is a plant of the *Palmaceæ* family (*Astrocaryum vulgare Mart.*). (Translator.)

[159] The *pé-de-muleque* (literally, "black boy's foot") is a cake made out of fermented manihot dough. (Translator.)

[160] Dish made from the *içá*, or female of the large reddish ant known as the *saúba* (or *saúva*, the *Œcodoma cephalotes*). Mr. Arthur Coelho provides this note: "When fattened with their eggs, these ants are eaten by the country people. I have been told that they are delicious. In the north they are called *tanajuras*." (Translator.)

[161] Sugar-cane brandy with ginger or a fruit drink. (Translator.)

[162] *Ponche* is a drink consisting of tea or coffee mixed with brandy or rum, lemon juice, sugar, etc. (Translator.)

[163] João Vampré: "*Fatos e Festas na Tradição*" ("Facts and Feasts in Tradition"), *Revista do Instituto Histórico de São Paulo*, Vol. XIII.

[164] *Acarajé* (*acará*) is a dish consisting of beans fried in dendê oil. (Translator.)

[165] Dona Angelina Barros de Andrade Lima. Also her sister, Dona Angelita Ferraz. The recipe is a traditional one in the family.

nally, when it is ready, to serve the cream or the cake on a smooth layer of banana leaf. The grating-stone measures fifty centimeters [19.6 inches] in height [166] and readily pulverizes corn, beans, rice, etc. With the aid of this stone *acaçá* is prepared. This corn with water is put into a clean vessel until it is softened, and is then grated, run through the *urupema*, or wickerwork sieve, and refined. When the corn adheres to the bottom of the vessel, the water is drained off, and it is then put on the fire in some more water and boiled until done. While on the fire, it is stirred with the wooden spoon, and with the same spoon it is dipped out in small portions and laid in rolls upon the banana leaves.

Arroz de auçá (rice with dried fish and pepper) is another African delicacy, which is prepared by placing boiled rice in water without salt and mixing it with the wooden spoon; after which it is mixed with a sauce containing malagueta pepper, onions, and shrimps, all grated on the stone. The sauce is then placed on the fire with dendê oil and a little water. Thoroughly African, likewise, is the *acarajé*, which is one of the fine offerings of the Bahian kitchen. It is made of beans (*feijão fradinho*) grated on the stone, with a dressing of onions and salt. It is heated in a clay frying-pan, into which is poured a little dendê oil. With certain Bahian dishes of African origin one eats a sauce prepared with dried malagueta peppers, onions, and shrimps, all ground on the stone and fried in oil of the dendê palm.

But the two African dishes that achieved the greatest triumph on the patriarchal table in Brazil were *carurú* and *vatapá*, both of them made with an intimate and special skill in Bahia. The *carurú* is prepared with okra or leaves of the capeba,[167] the taioba,[168] or the oió,[169] placed on the fire with a little water. The water is later drained off, the mass is pressed out, and then is placed once more in the vessel, with onions, salt, shrimps, and dried malagueta peppers, the whole being grated on the stone and sprinkled with dendê oil. To this is added the garoupa[170] or other baked fish. This is the same process of

[166] Manuel Querino: *A Arte Culinária na Baía* (op. cit.).

[167] The *capeba* (*caapeba*) is a plant of the *Piperaceæ* family (*Piper rohrii DC*), also known as the *pariparoba*. The *capeba-do-norte* is the *Piper pettatum L.* (Translator.)

[168] Herbaceous plant of the *Araceæ* family (*Colocasia antiquorum* and *Xanthosoma violaceum Schott.*), also

known as *talo, tarro, jarro,* and *pé-de-bezerro.*—Lima and Barroso, op. cit.

[169] No botanical authority, Brazilian or American, has been able to identify this plant. (Translator.)

[170] The *garoupa* is a sea-fish of the *Serranidæ* family (*Cerna gigas Brunn.*), also called *garoupa-verdadeira.* (Translator.)

efô-making [171] in which that great black woman named Eva, discovered in Bahia by the poet Manuel Bandeira, was skilled. The good Eva died in the fateful year 1930, which also saw the death in Pernambuco of the cook José Pedro, a Fuláh Negro, son of an African mother, nephew of a love-sorcerer (*macumbeiro*), and possibly the greatest specialist of his time in dishes prepared from Indian corn and coconut milk: *mungunzá*, couscous, *pamonha*, *canjica*, corn-cakes. He was cook for the Baltars in Poço da Panela and for the Santos Dias, Pessoa de Queiroz, and Pessoa de Mello families, ending his days in the casa do Carrapicho as chef to some bachelors who are now scattered.[172] Mammy Eva, we are told, was also highly skilled in the preparation of the dish known as *xin-xin*—a hen with dried shrimps, onions, jerimum kernels,[173] and dendê oil.[174]

The hen, moreover, figures in a number of African religious ceremonies and aphrodisiac potions in Brazil. Dampier had noted this in the seventeenth century, alluding in particular to a form of grill known as "Macker," employed in the making of love-philters.[175] Certain Afro-Brazilian dishes still keep something of a religious or liturgical character as regards the manner of their preparation. In order to prepare them as they should be prepared, in all their fine points, the Negroes for a long time brought over from Africa, in addition to the oil of the dendê palm, a number of exquisite condiments: bejerecum, ierê, urú, ataré. Manuel Querino speaks of certain rice-cakes made with dendê oil or with honey which the black Mussulmans at Bahia were accustomed to consume at religious ceremonies.[176]

Some of the Southern Negro dishes with which I became acquainted in the United States, in the South Carolina home of Dr. E. C. Adams, in that of Mrs. Simkins, and in Mr. Clint Graydon's

---

[171] The *efô* is "a kind of ragout made of shrimps and herbs, seasoned with dendê oil and pepper."—Lima and Barroso, op. cit.

[172] The bachelors referred to are the author and his brother, the owner, Ulysses de Mello Freyre. (Translator.)

[173] On the jerimum, see p. 135. Plant of the *Cucurbitaceæ* or gourd family. (Translator.)

[174] Unfortunately, in Bahia there is no restaurant that is up to the culinary traditions of the region, none to compare with the Afro-French restaurants of New Orleans. But anyone wishing to find a worthy substitute for Mammy Eva may go to the home of Dona Valéria, in the rua da Assembléia, and see if he can succeed in persuading her to prepare him a lunch or dinner.

[175] Dampier, op. cit.

[176] Manuel Querino: *A Arte Culinária na Baía* (op. cit.). Querino notes a number of other Afro-Bahian dishes: *eran-patetê*, *efun-oguedê*, *ipetê*, *ebó*, *abará*, *aberén*, and many others.

home in Charleston are very like those prepared in the Brazilian kitchen. The home of Dr. Adams, the physician and folklorist, author of extremely interesting studies of Carolina Negroes, was a real north-Brazilian plantation manor, being full of young Negro lads and lasses (*mulecas* and *muleques*) and aged Negroes as well, and with the best kitchen in the environs of Columbia. In New Orleans, also, I tasted sweets and confections with the pleasing flavor of Africa, putting me in mind of those of Bahia and Pernambuco. Especially the dishes prepared from chicken with rice and okra.

The Brazilian cusine with its predominant African influence, alongside enthusiasts and worthy apologists such as Pereira Barreto [177] and John Casper Branner,[178] has had its severe critics and even its detractors. Sigaud, who was possibly the first to concern himself with the scientific criticism of the food that Brazilians ate, looked upon the Bahian kitchen—which is to say, the characteristically Afro-Brazilian one—as being "*la véritable cuisine nationale*"; and he mentions in particular *matapá* (*sic*),[179] which he takes to be a variety of East Indian Kari. He was agreeably impressed by the luxury of the Brazilian table, the table of the Big House on feast-days; for he stresses the fact that "*ce luxe . . . ne se déploie qu'à l'occasion des fêtes nationales ou de famille*." But what made the chief impression upon him was the luxurious desserts, the sweets and sugared candies—the latter of Pernambucan rather than Bahian creation. Berthelemot, Sigaud tells us,[180] was astonished "*de tout ce que le génie peut extraire du coco, des amandes de menduby, de sapotille, et des palmiers. . . .*" The genius involved was that of the African slave woman rather than that of the white mistress. Sigaud goes on to refer to baked breadfruit and to certain sweet-tasting cactuses, also cooked, as well as other pleasures of the Brazilian dessert. If all these delicate dishes escape the attention of foreign visitors who leave Brazil speaking ill of the food, it is for the reason that many are only acquainted with the bill of fare of the worst inns and hostelries. Had they enjoyed the hospitality of a Big House on a sugar plantation or a fazenda, they would

---

[177] L. Pereira Barreto: "*A Higiene da Mesa*" ("Table Hygiene"), *O Estudo de São Paulo*, September 7, 1922.

[178] John Casper Branner: "*O Que Faria Se Fosse Estudante Brasileiro nos Estados-Unidos*" ("What I Should Do, If I Were a Brazilian Student in the United States"), *El Estudiante Latino-Americano*, New York, January 1921. This article by the North American geologist was written at my request.

[179] Author's note to translator: "He probably—almost certainly—means *vatapá*." (Translator.)

[180] J. F. X. Sigaud: *Du climat et des maladies du Brésil* (Paris, 1844). (Translator.)

have left the country with quite another impression of its culinary art. Had they sampled the confections of a good black cook in a patriarchal family, it would have been another story. Let Mawe, Spix, Martius, Saint-Hilaire give their testimony. As for Sigaud, he had nothing but praise for Brazilian food, although he noted that it had been undergoing a perceptible process of modification since the beginning of the nineteenth century, due to English influence, which brought a greater use of tea, wine, and beer. It was modified also by the introduction of ice, in 1834, brought to Brazil for the first time on a North American boat, the *Madagascar*.[181] Great water-drinkers —possibly because of the large amount of sugar and African condiments in their food—Brazilians were enormously pleased with this novelty. Our delightful sherbets—delightful to the smell and to the taste—made of tropical fruits, date from this time, those sherbets that were so appreciated by Max Radiguet,[182] who must have been a gourmet of the first order.

Other critics have been a good deal less sympathetic to the Afro-Brazilian kitchen than was the French scientist. We have seen the repugnance that Vilhena felt for colonial food, a repugnance that was, in a manner of speaking, an æsthetic one. Others severely criticized our cuisine from the hygienic point of view. As Antônio José de Sousa saw it, the immoderate use of condiments "such as dendê oil, pepper, and especially blites (*carurús, quibebes*)" was the cause of the various infirmities that were common to masters and slaves in Brazil, all of whom used to excess these "aphrodisiacs of the palate." "Food of this sort" had a great deal to do with "indigestion, diarrhea, dysentery, hemorrhoids and all the diseases of the digestive tract." [183] In 1850 José Luciano Pereira, Jr., in making a study of the diet of the well-to-do classes, took great satisfaction in stressing the fact that the "Brazilian cuisine, represented today by Bahia and Pernambuco," was being "gradually modified." The "altogether too stimulating diet of another day has been changed for another, simpler one under the influence of foreign cooking." *Feijoadas* (dishes with beans, plus bacon, sausage, etc.) were no longer so common; the use of "pepper" and other "stimulating condiments" in ragouts was also becoming "much rarer today." So wrote this enthusiastic supporter of culinary

---

181 Ibid.

182 Max Radiguet: *Souvenirs de l'-Amérique espagnole* (op. cit.).

183 Antônio José de Sousa: *Do Regime das Classes Pobres, e dos Escravos, na Cidade do Rio de Janeiro em* *Seus Alimentos e Bebidas; Qual a Influência desse Regime sobre a Saúde* (op. cit.), thesis presented to the Faculty of Medicine of Rio de Janeiro (Rio de Janeiro, 1851).

progress, in the direction of de-Africanizing the Brazilian table. "The immoderate use of fats, which entered into the ragouts of a former day, has been curbed, and in many cases French butter has been substituted." The place of aluá, tamarind juice, and cane juice was to be taken by English tea; and in place of manihot paste or gourd paste, the so-called English potato. Added to all this was the luxury of ice, "which goes so well with a hot climate like ours." [184] French butter, the English potato, tea (also English), and ice—all with the object of doing away with that major influence represented by Africa and native fruits, an influence that, since the first years of independence, had presided over our table.

Bread was another novelty that came in with the nineteenth century. In place of bread in colonial times they use the *beijú*, or tapioca cake, for breakfast or lunch, and for dinner *farofa*, parched pirão,[185] or manihot dough in a fish or meat broth. The bean was in daily use, and as I have said, *feijoadas* were common, made with salt meat, pig's head, sausage, and much African dressing; and greens and vegetables, so characteristic of the African diet, were more common than during the nineteenth century. It was with the Europeanization of his table that the Brazilian became an abstainer from vegetables. At the same time he began to be ashamed of his most typical desserts: honey or cane juice with meal; the *canjica*, or green-corn paste, seasoned with sugar and butter. The only thing saved was sweetmeats with cheese. From the time of independence on, French recipe and etiquette books began their work of undermining the real Brazilian cuisine, and those African Negro women who presided over the oven and the hearth commenced to undergo the European influence to a considerable degree.

I am not denying that the African influence on Brazilian diet, with its excessive use of spices and condiments, stood in need of certain restrictions or correctives. This was especially true of the poorer classes, who, insufficiently nourished as they were, did not, for all that, leave off their overuse of the most stimulating spices along with the wretched salt fish that constituted a good portion of their daily

---

[184] José Luciano Pereira, Jr.: *Algumas Considerações Sobre . . . o Regime das Classes Abastadas da Cidade do Rio de Janeiro em Seus Alimentos e Bebidas* (op. cit.), thesis presented to the Faculty of Medicine of Rio de Janeiro (Rio de Janeiro, 1850). See also José Maria Rodrigues Regadas: *Regime das Classes Abastadas no Rio de Janeiro em Seus Alimentos e Bebidas*, etc., thesis presented to the Faculty of Medicine of Rio de Janeiro (Rio de Janeiro, 1852); and Ferdinand Denis: *Brésil* (Paris: Collection l'Univers; 1839).

[185] A paste made from manihot flour. (Translator.)

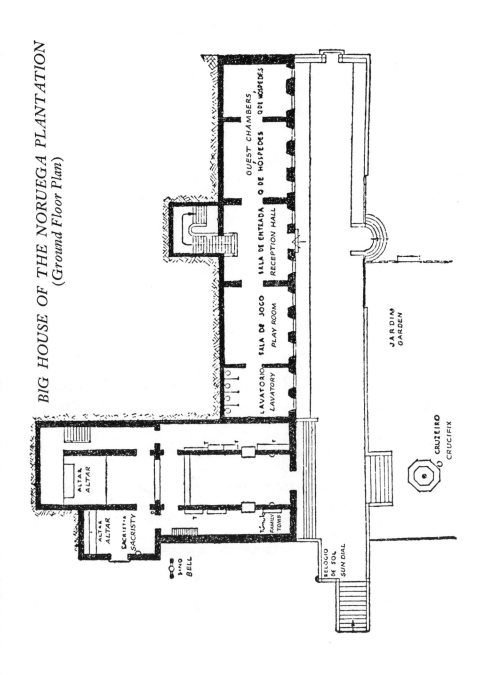

BIG HOUSE OF THE NORUEGA PLANTATION
(Ground Floor Plan)

ALTAR
ALTAR

ALTAR
ALTAR

SACRISTIA
SACRISTY

SINO
BELL

GUEST CHAMBERS
Q DE HOSPEDES

SALA DE ENTRADA
RECEPTION HALL

SALA DE JOGO
PLAY ROOM

LAVATORIO
LAVATORY

FAMILY TOMB

RELOGIO
DE SOL
SUN DIAL

JARDIM
GARDEN

CRUZEIRO
CRUCIFIX

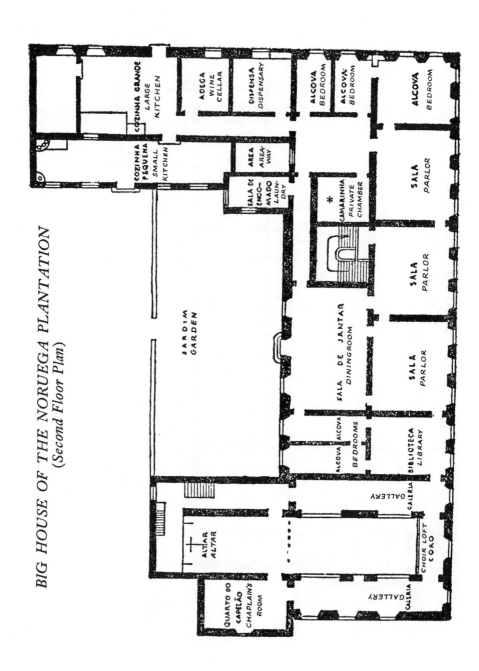

BIG HOUSE OF THE NORUEGA PLANTATION
(Second Floor Plan)

fare. "Highly spiced desserts, with all those articles of diet that are excessively stimulating, and that pernicious oil from the African coast which our poorer population uses to such an extent, the result being that on the one hand it has a diet insufficient in quantity and on the other hand one deficient in quality." [186] Half a century after Sampaio Vianna, another critic of the Brazilian cuisine in general and of the Afro-Bahian one in particular pointed out that, besides being deficient, our diet still showed the effects of the "abuse of pepper and oleous substances such as enter especially into the highly praised *moquecas* (fish ragouts with oil and pepper), *carurús, vatapás, et reliqua*, dishes that show the sinister influence of those Africans whom our colonizers brought into the country." By Santos Sousa, the Afro-Bahian kitchen is seen as being not only *insufficient*, but *harmful*. For, since it is insufficient, "a large amount of food is necessary for sustenance, resulting in a dilatation of the stomach and the consequences that ensue from this." It is further harmful by reason of the "abuse of pepper, whose causticity is greater than that of mustard, giving rise to gastritis and gastroenteritis (intestinal infections), so frequent with us," and also by reason of the "abuse of palm oil and other condiments that later bring on disturbances of the liver, due to a superexcitation of the bile through the irritating action of such condiments." Then there is the use, when not the abuse as well, of "overcooked foods which, containing a large amount of calcium and xanthic bases (the sources of uric acid, according to Fawel), are the principal cause of those arthritic manifestations so common among us." [187]

Eduardo Magalhães, in his study entitled *Alimentary Hygiene*,[188] is quite as severe as Santos Sousa in his criticism of the Afro-Bahian kitchen: "dyspepsia, stomach ulcer, diseases of the liver, intestinal disorders, affections of the kidneys, cardiac syncope, aneurism, apoplexy, and other ills are the epilogue to all this abuse and sensuality." He goes on to apply to Brazil Rasforil's words: "the indigestion of the rich offsets the hunger of the poor." He might have added that the slaves, who prepared for the tables of their white masters the meat and fish so overseasoned with pepper and spices, had a more nourish-

---

[186] Azevedo Cesar de Sampaio Vianna: *Qual a Causa da Freqüência das Ascites na Baía? (What Is the Cause of the Frequent Occurrence of Ascites in Bahia?)*, thesis presented to the Faculty of Medicine of Bahia (Bahia, 1850).

[187] Francisco Antônio dos Santos Sousa: *Alimentação na Baía—Suas Consequências (Diet in Bahia—Its Consequences)*, thesis presented to the Faculty of Medicine of Bahia (Bahia, 1910).

[188] Eduardo Magalhaes: *Higiene Alimentar* (Rio de Janeiro, 1908).

ing diet of their own in the slave huts; for they had preserved in Brazil the African's wholesome fondness for vegetables, whereas in the diet of the whites leguminous and other vegetables had practically disappeared. "There are among us those who never in their lives have tasted salad or a dish of vegetable broth, but who limit themselves to a diet merely of meat with bread or meal." [189] Such was the observation of Magalhães, in 1908. We shall see, in a following essay, that vegetables played a leading part in the diet of the Negro slaves [190] and were in daily use with them. It is one of the characteristics of the orthodox Afro-Brazilian kitchen that delicacies prepared with fish, meat, and poultry are accompanied by greens—by okra, cabbage, taioba, jerimum.

As for pepper, so prominent a feature of Afro-Bahian *vatapás* and *carurús*, it has found defenders even among foreigners. Prince Maximilian considered it "excellent for the digestion," and Burton called it an "excellent stomachic." Burton, so far as that goes, was a voluptuary of the Brazilian kitchen; he was delighted with the *tutú de feijão*, or pork and beans,[191] of Minas, proclaiming it a hygienic dish that combined carbon and nitrogen, even though it might be indigestible when eaten daily.[192]

It does not impress one as just to accuse the Negro cook, sweet-maker, or pantry girl of being slovenly or careless in the preparation of food or in domestic hygiene. A cake-tray of one of the Negro women venders simply glistens with cleanliness and white towels. The kitchen of the Big House in colonial days, it is true, was far from being a model one from the hygienic point of view. Mawe, Luccock, Mathison, all speak with repugnance of the dirtiness of the ones they knew. This lack of cleanliness, however, which was characteristic not alone of the homes of the poor, but of those of the wealthy planters as well, was the fault not so much of the slaves as of the white masters.

The Negro in those days was obliged to perform the filthiest of

---

[189] Eduardo de Magalhães, op. cit. —Koster observed that among the inhabitants of the *sertão*, or backlands— the region least influenced by the Negro—almost no green vegetables were eaten: "they laugh at the idea of eating salad," he says, in speaking of the *sertanejos.—Travels in Brazil* (op. cit.).

[190] At the First Afro-Brazilian Congress of Recife (November 1934), Dr.

Ruy Coutinho read an interesting paper on the diet of the Negro slave in Brazil.

[191] *Tutú de feijão* is "a dish composed of salt pork, bacon, beans, and manihot flour."—Lima and Barroso, op. cit.

[192] Burton, op. cit. Burton, further, expresses the opinion that meat is a food that is more easily digested than vegetables, in the tropics.

tasks in connection with both household and public sanitation. One of these was to carry on his head, from the house down to the waterfront, the barrels of excrement commonly known as "tigers" (*tigres*). In city mansions these barrels would remain for days at a time inside the house, under the stair or in some other nook, as their contents piled up. By the time the Negro came to carry them out, they were overflowing with filth and could hold no more. Sometimes the bottom would drop out, drenching the bearer from head to foot. These and other functions were fulfilled by the African slave with an animal-like passivity. And while we are on the subject, it was not the Negro who brought lice to Brazil, nor the "scratching-hand" (*mão de coçar*),[193] nor the bedbug. It is to be presumed that the African slave, especially the one of Mohammedan origin, very often experienced a genuine repugnance at the unclean habits of his master.[194]

One can hardly accuse those Negroes of spreading filth who, once they had obtained their freedom, became barbers, dentists, manufacturers of piaçava-palm [195] brooms, and importers of African soap (*sabão da Costa*); and the same goes for the Negro women, those sweetmeat venders so insistent upon the cleanliness of their caketrays, or the laundresses, who were equally neat. Such professions, obviously concerned with hygiene, in part remove the disgrace of having had to be the bearers of the "tiger." It is true that certain Negro barbers had a macaiba-palm [196] contrivance which they in-

---

[193] Reference is to the "*mãozinhas de coçar*" (little scratching-hands), made of ivory, which were formerly much used in Portugal by aristocratic families, complacent victims of the louse. (Visit the Portuguese Ethnographic Museum.) The fact should also be reported that in Brazil the ladies and gentlemen of the Big Houses were in the habit of growing an enormous nail, Chinese fashion, on one of their fingers, a custom that Thomas Lindley observed among the colonists of Bahia, in the eighteenth century (Lindley, op. cit.). This was obviously for the purpose of scratching for lice, and for scratching their sores as well. I have known old people with nails of this sort.

[194] In his paper on "*As Tribus Negras Importadas*" ("The Imported Negro Tribes"), in the *Revista do Instituto Histórico e Geográfico Brasileiro*, special volume for the Congress of National History, Part II, Affonso Claudio writes: "With regard to one point, that of hygiene, it is necessary to stress the instinctive care that the African took to avoid epidemics. From this point of view, that of preventive hygiene, there is no doubt that he is far above the native of Oceania and the American native as well."

[195] The *piaçava* (*piaçaba, piaça*) is the name given to two varieties of palms: the *Attalea funifera Mart.* and the *Leopoldinia piassaba Wal.* Their fibers are employed in the manufacture of brooms.—Lima and Barroso, op. cit. (Translator.)

[196] The *macaiba* (*macahiba*) is a species of palm, the *Acrocomia scelerocarpa Mart.* It is also known as the *macaúba, côco-de-catarro, macajá,* and *macajuba.*

serted in the mouths of white customers to make their cheeks stand out and render them easy to shave, and, this being used in common, was anything but hygienic. It was only employed in the case of customers with unclean habits, however; the more fastidious ones merely filled their mouths with air at the moment when the African said to them: *"Ioiô, fazê buchichim"* ("Master, puff out your cheeks").[197]

It was the Negro who gave to household life in Brazil its cheerful note. The Portuguese, naturally inclined to melancholy, in our country became gloomy and sullen. As for the *caboclo*, we need not speak of him; he was silent, distrustful, all but a sick man in the somberness of his disposition. Contact with him only added to the melancholy of the Portuguese colonizer. It was the Negro's hearty laugh that broke in upon the "dull, abject mournfulness" that tended to stifle the life of the Big Houses. He it was who cheered the plantation hands, who inspired the *bumbas-meu-boi*, the *cavalos-marinhos* (carnival "horses" with men inside them), the carnivals, the festivals. As a tolerant Church looked on, he filled the popular feast-days of Brazil with reminiscences of his own totemistic and phallic cults: on the eve of the Feast of Epiphany, and afterwards, at Carnival time, with the crowning of its kings and queens. At such a time, with mystic canopies and banners and with lights that were almost like those of a religious ceremony, he would appear with the members of his *rancho*, or club, along with the animals that were their patrons—eagles, peacocks, elephants, fish, dogs, rams, ostriches, canaries—each club having its own *bicho* made of tin plate and borne triumphantly at the head of the procession, the Negroes all the while singing and dancing, exuberantly, expansively. Only a year or so ago, at the Carnival in the Praça Onze in Rio de Janeiro, I had an opportunity to view these totemistic societies; and at the carnivals of Pernambuco I have seen the Negroes any number of times dancing happily behind their banners, some of which are very fine, embroidered in gold, emblems vaguely reminiscent of the trade guilds mingling with totemistic ones: the gilded shovel of the Shovel Club, the broom of the broom-makers, the brush of the wall-and-roof-cleaners,[198] the dog of the association known as the Cachorro do Homem do Miudo,[199] etc.

---

[197] *Baía de Outrora (Bahia of Former Times)* (Bahia, 1916).

[198] The *vasculhadores* (*basculhadores*) were those who made a business of cleaning roofs and high walls.

The *espanador* was the special brush they used. (Translator.)

[199] The name of the association means literally: "the dog of the man who sells the internal small parts of an ox." (Translator.)

On the plantations as inside the house, in the clothes-vats, in the kitchens, washing clothes, drying dishes, making sweets, grinding coffee; in the cities, carrying bags of sugar or transporting the pianos and jacarandá-wood [200] sofas of their white masters, the Negroes always sang as they labored; and their work-songs as well as those of the Xangô cult, their feast-day melodies, and their cradle songs filled Brazilian life with an African joyfulness.[201] At times they suffered a little from *banzo*, or nostalgia; but for the most part they were gay. Never in the old days did the Negroes hoist a piano on their backs but that they sang: *"E' o piano de ioiô, é o piano de iaiá"* ("It is the master's piano, it is the mistress's piano"). Refined persons found this custom an objectionable one, and it became the object of severe measures of repression on the part of the administrative officers of the municipal chambers.

In Maria Graham's time the masters of the Big Houses would send for the Negroes to sing their African songs whenever a visitor arrived.[202] Work-songs. Religious songs. Possibly the same songs that in Pernambuco the Negroes of Anselmo's sect still sing on their feast-days, now partially suppressed by the police:

> *Xéco, xéco, xéco, O ni—ba—rá*
> *Xéco, xéco, xéco, O ni—ba—rá*
> *Xéco, xéco, xéco, O ni—ba—rá.*

Anselmo alone:

> *Ogunmanjô, marnô.*

---

[200] The *jacarandá* is a tree of the *Leguminosæ* family, *Papillonaceæ* division (*Machoerium villosum Vog.*); it is also known as the *jacarandá-paulista.*—Lima and Barroso, op. cit. (Translator.)

[201] As they went about selling sugar-candy, coconut-bars, and other sweets, the Negroes would sing:

> *Chora, menino, chora*
> *chora porque não tem*
> *vintem.*

"Weep, little one, weep; he weeps because he does not have a cent."

In Rio, Fletcher beheld enormous mountains of coffee moving as if of their own accord; but underneath them were gigantic Negroes—real giants; and the song that such Negroes sang was:

> *Maria, rábula auê*
> *Calunga auê.*

For the influence of the Negro on the popular music of Brazil, see Mario de Andrade: *Compêndio de História da Música* (*Compendium of Musical History*) (São Paulo, 1929); also his *Ensaio sobre Música Brasileira* (*Essay on Brazilian Music*) (São Paulo, 1928); and the *História da Música Brasileira*, by Renato Almeida (2nd edition, Rio de Janeiro, 1942), a book that is not merely of technical but of historical-social interest also.

[202] Maria Graham: *Journal of a Voyage to Brazil*, etc. (op. cit.), p. 282.

All together:

> *Colé marnô, ogunmanjo marnô, ocólangê*
> *Ogunhô!!!*
> *E' cun dô dô. E' cun gé gé.*

Anselmo alone, addressing the deity, Orixá:

> *Ogunni tôcôbá, oni, ômaroli, rolé*
> *Ó dê, ó dê, panilé, ó dê, ó dê, panilé.*[203]

But the lives of the Negro slaves who served the white *ioiôs* and *iaiás* was not altogether a merry one. There were those who committed suicide by eating earth, by hanging themselves, or by consuming the poisonous herbs and brews of the sorcerers. *"Banzo"* put an end to many of them—*"banzo"*: the melancholy longing for Africa, as a result of which some became crack-brained, idiotic. These latter did not die, but lived to endure their torment; with no taste for a normal mode of life, they would indulge in all sorts of excesses: brandy; the use of the narcotic herb maconha; masturbation. African diseases also followed them to Brazil, wreaking havoc in the slave

---

[203] This song is a prayer for corn, beans, etc., at the festivals of fecundity. The music, along with other pieces, was gathered from the African sect led by the Negro Anselmo, by an assistant of the Psychiatric Clinic of Pernambuco, whose director, Professor Ulysses Pernambucano, during the years 1930 to 1935, did so much to persuade the police to recognize as religious sects these associations of Negroes that had been indiscriminately classed as *"catimbó"* (witchcraft) gatherings and unjustly persecuted by police officials. This persecution, however, was resumed with greater intensity than ever by the present government of Pernambuco, due, it is said, to pressure brought to bear by the Portuguese Jesuits, who today are extremely powerful in this northern state.

I have in my possession various other songs, some of them obtained from *"menino Eloy"* (little Eloy), others from the sect of "star-worshippers." In this work, I had the assistance of Dr. Pedro Cavalcanti. I also obtained from Eloy a mystic vocabulary, and an extensive one was got together by the Institute; this vocabulary, which would appear to be Nagô, was organized with the assistance of Anselmo. The words appear to be extremely mutilated, but some of them may be identified as being of the Yoruba tongue.

[According to the author, in a note to the translator, the words of the African cult song given above are in reality untranslatable. Freyre states: "Anselmo, whom I knew personally, was very ignorant. Unlike 'Pai Adão' (also a personal friend of mine until he died in 1936—both died as old men), who, though born in Brazil, had studied religion in Africa, he was quite unlettered, and what he says here seems to be a caricature of African words. He himself probably did not know the exact meaning of every word, though he knew that he was engaged in thanking his god for corn, asking for rain, etc." (Translator.)]

huts.[204] Buboes, among others. These diseases at times were communicated to the whites of the Big Houses; and in this manner did Africa take vengeance for the ill treatment she had received from Europe. On the other hand, there were not a few diseases of whites that the household blacks acquired; not to speak of those that laid hold of them as a consequence of the unhygienic conditions under which they had been brought from Africa to America and the new manner of living and the forced labor that they encountered here. In the cities this labor was almost always "out of proportion to the nutrition." This is the assertion of José Martins da Cruz Jobim, who, in 1835, noted the following maladies as being prevalent among the workers and household slaves of Rio de Janeiro: syphilis; cardiac hypertrophy; rheumatism; bronchitis; affections of the respiratory passages; pneumonia; pleurisy; pericarditis; encephalic irritations and inflammations; tetanus; hepatitis; and erysipelas, commonly in the lower members and the scrotum, leading to hypertrophy and fibrolardaceous degenerescence of the subcutaneous cellular tissue, extravasations in the various sonorous cavities, rarely in the joints but frequently in the abdomen, the pleura, the pericardium, the testicular membrane, and the cerebral ventricles, where it gave rise to paralysis. Still other affections were pulmonary tuberculosis, intermittent fevers, and ancylostomiasis.[205] "Worms, especially the tapeworm and lumbricoid roundworms, are to be found in great abundance," Jobim adds.[206]

---

[204] According to Professor Octávio de Freitas, in a paper read before the First Afro-Brazilian Congress of Recife, in November 1934, the following were the maladies and afflictions brought to Brazil by the *"negros bichados"* (infected Negroes): *"bicho da Costa"* (a parasite), dysentery (*maculo*), buboes, bony excrescences on the nose and cheek-bones (*gundú*), chills, thickening of the skin (*ainhum*), fleas, and nematode worms (*filárias*). As another physician, Eustáquio Duarte, has observed, the subject of the origin of these and other diseases formerly common in Brazil is one that calls for a more extended study.

[205] The term in the original is *"opilação,"* which Brazilian physicians of the old school employ in a very loose sense; in some cases, but not in all, it has reference to the effects of ancylostomiasis, as it probably does here. (Translator.)

[206] José Martins da Cruz Jobim: *Discurso Sobre as Moléstias Que Mais Affligem a Classe Pobre do Rio de Janeiro* (op. cit.) (paper read at the public session of the Medical Society, June 30, 1835) (Rio de Janeiro, 1835). See also Sigaud, op. cit.; Roberto Jorge Haddock Lobo: *Discurso Recitado em Presença de S.M. o Imperador na Sessão Solemne, Anniversário da Academia Imperial de Medicina do Rio de Janeiro, Rio de Janeiro, 1847, Seguido de Reflexões Acerca da Mortalidade da Cidade do Rio de Janeiro,* (op. cit.) (Rio de Janeiro, 1847); *"Resposta ao Inquérito da Comarca do Rio de Janeiro entre Médicos*

Sobre o Clima e a Salubridade da Corte dos Vive-Reis" ("Response to the Inquiry by the District of Rio de Janeiro among Physicians Regarding the Climate and Healthfulness of the Court of the Viceroys) (1798), in the *Annaes Brasilienses de Medicina*, Vol. II, No. 5 (1846); and Antônio Martins de Azevedo Pimental: *Quais os Melhoramentos que Devem ser Introduzidos no Rio de Janeiro*, etc. (op. cit.), thesis presented to the Faculty of Medicine of Rio de Janeiro (Rio de Janeiro, 1884).

GLOSSARY

OF BRAZILIAN, PORTUGUESE, AMERICAN INDIAN, AND AFRICAN NEGRO EXPRESSIONS, INCLUDING BOTANICAL AND ZOOLOGICAL TERMS

abacaxí.——Pineapple. Fruit of a cultivated plant of the *Bromeliaceæ* or pineapple family (*Ananas sativus Schult.*).

abalcoado.——A Moorish balcony.

abará.——Culinary preparation consisting of beans with pepper and dendê (palm) oil.

abarén (aberém).——Variety of baked or fried corn or rice cake wrapped with banana leaves.

abati-i.——A fermented drink made from corn.

abatiuí.——Indian term for flour made from maize.

Abrilada.——The April Revolution (from *abril*, April) or restorationist revolt in Pernambuco in 1832. Cf. *Cabanada.*

abuñã.——Smoked turtle or tortoise eggs. See p. 132.

acaçá.——Dish prepared from corn flour or rice flour; for a description of the process by which it is prepared, see p. 464. The name is also applied to a drink made of rice or fermented corn with sugar and water.

acanijic.——Indian term for corn paste; modern form: *canjica* (q.v.).

acará.——See *acarajé.*

acarajé (acará).——Dish consisting of beans fried in dendê (palm) oil.

Achantis (Axantes).——Well-known African tribe.

administrados.——The "help" on a plantation.

aficionados.——The followers of a cult.

agua de erva cidreira.——Infusion of citronella. Cf. *erva cidreira.*

aguardente.——An inexpensive alcoholic beverage most commonly made from sugar-cane juice. Similar to brandy.

ainhum.——"Disease that attacks Negroes and mestizos, characterized by a progressive thickening of the skin and the consequent formation, about the base of one or more of the toes, of a fibrous ring that mutilates them."—Lima and Barroso: *Pequeno Dicionário Brasileiro da Lingua Portuguesa.*

Ajaus.——African tribe.

akpalô.——An African raconteur. Cf. *alô.*

albinágio.——A law providing for the seizure by the State of the property of aliens who had died in the country. Such laws did not figure in the Portuguese codes. See p. 193. Cf. *detração* and *naufrágio.*

aldeia (aldea).——An Indian village; a village.

almanjarra.——A sugar-mill (*engenho*) propelled by oxen or other beasts of burden. Cf. *trapiche.*

almas penadas.——"Souls in torment." Souls that, having left this world without atoning for their sins, are condemned to come back to expiate them. Expression used to frighten the young. See *mingau das almas.*

alô.——With African Negroes, a tale told by an *akpalô,* or raconteur.

aloá.——See *aluá.*

alqueire.——Land measure varying in different regions, from 24,200 to 48,400 square meters, or, roughly, from 6 to 12 acres. (*Alqueire* originally signified a bushel measure.)

altéia.——Medicinal plant of the *Malvaceæ* or mallow family (*Althæa officinalis L.*).

aluá.——"A refreshing drink made, in the north, of rice flour or toasted corn with water, and fermented with sugar in clay jars; in Minas Geraes, made with pineapple rinds, by the same process."—Lima and Barroso, op. cit.

Ambaquistas.——African tribe.

Ambuelas.——African tribe; see *Ba-gangelas.*

amendoim.——Peanut plant of the *Leguminosæ* family (*Arachnis hypogæa Lin.*). With this plant Freyre identifies the *midubi.* See p. 34, note 82.

angico.——Name common to various trees of the *Leguminosæ* family, *Mimosaceæ* division, genus *Piptadenia.*

Angicos.——African "nation."

Angolas.——Well-known African "nation."

angú.——Dish consisting of corn, manihot, or rice flour with water and salt.

anta.——A tapir. Mammifer of the *Tapiridæ* family (*Tapirus americanus Briss.*).

arabú (arabu).——Dish made from the yolk of turtle or tortoise eggs and flour. Freyre states that these are the only ingredients. Lima and Barroso (op. cit.) give the ingredients as turtle eggs, flour, and sugar. See p. 132 and note 162.

araça.——Guava tree. Tree of the *Myrtaceæ* family (*Psidium araça Raddi*).

arara.——Bird of the *Psitaci* or parrot family.

araribá.——Tree of the *Leguminosæ* family (*Centrolobium tomentosum Benth.*).

arokin.——African narrator of chronicles.

arrivismo.——Social climbing.

arroba.——Portuguese measure of weight equivalent to thirty-three pounds. (Cf. the Spanish *arroba,* equivalent to a little over twenty-five pounds.)

arroz de auçá.——Rice with dried fish (meat) and pepper. For description, see p. 464.

arroz de coco.——Dish consisting of rice with coconut.

arroz doce.——Milk-rice, prepared with rice, coconut milk or cow's milk, sugar, cloves, and cinnamon.

ataré.——Afro-Brazilian condiment; a variety of pepper.

au-au.——Childish expression for dog; cf. our "bow-wow."

auto.——Ancient Portuguese term for a dramatic piece; it was applied to the old farces; comes to mean a solemnity.

azeite.——Most commonly means olive oil, but may refer to cooking oils made from other plants, e.g. corn and peanuts.

azeitona.——An olive.

azenha.——A mill (often a sugar-mill) propelled by water-power.

Ba-cancalas.——African people.

Bacas.——African "nation."

Ba-cassoqueres.——African people.

Ba-congos.——African tribe.

Ba-corocas.——African people.

Ba-cuandos.——African people.

Ba-cubais.——African people.

bagaceira.——The place on a sugar plantation where the bagasse, or "cane trash," was stored.

Ba-gangelas (Ambuelas).——African tribe.

Bagirmis.——African people.

bairrista.——Literally, a person who lives in or frequents a *bairro*, or particular quarter of a town; one who defends the interests of his *bairro* or is especially loyal to it.

baito.——Indian name for a secret society, or house, something like a Masonic lodge, among the natives. See pp. 123 and 149.

Balaiada.——Term applied to the civil war in Maranhão, 1838–40. See p. 153 and note 255.

balangandã.——See *balagandan.*

balangandan (balangandã).——Set of feast-day ornaments, often of silver, used by Bahians. For description, see p. xxxi, note 31.

Balantas.——African tribe.

bambanho.——Childish word for bath (*banho*).

Ba-ncumbis.——African tribe.

bandeira.——Armed band in colonial days, composed of adventurers, particularly those of the São Paulo region, who made their way into the backlands in search of gold, silver, diamonds, emeralds, etc., and of the Indian as a slave. See p. xxxii, note 37.

bandeirante.——Member of a *bandeira* (q.v.).

banguê.——In northeastern Brazil, a variety of litter with leather top and curtains. Term for a sugar plantation (*engenho de banguê*). The brick-paved canal through which the sugar-foam drains off. See p. 342, note 188.

Banhanecas.——African tribe.

banzo.——The melancholy nostalgia characteristic of Negroes.

barí.——Indian term for medicine-man.

basculhadores.——See *vasculhadores.*

Ba-sutos.——African people.

batuque.——A Negro dance, usually with drum accompaniment.

Bechuanas.——African tribe.

beijú.——Name of a number of varieties of cake made of manihot flour. See pp. 127 f. Cf. *mbeiu.*

beijú-açú (beijú-guaçu).——Variety of manihot cake. See p. 127.

beijú-cica.——Variety of manihot cake. See p. 127.

beijú-ticanga (beijú-ticuanga).——Variety of manihot cake. See p. 127.

bejerecum.——Afro-Brazilian condiment.

Bengos.——African tribe.

Benguelas.——African tribe.

Benins (Beni, Benim).——African people.

Biafadas.——African tribe.

bicho.——A worm, insect, or wild animal. A rather vague term. See p. 139, note 197. ——A game of chance. See p. 147.

bicho da Costa.——An African parasite brought to Brazil by the Negroes.

bicho de pé.——A type of flea that burrows beneath the skin of the foot and lays its eggs there.

Bienos.——African tribe.

bimbinha.——Infantile expression for a child's penis.

birimbau (birimbao).——A mean, despicable person; a Jew's-harp.

Bisagos.——African tribe.

Bitongas.——African tribe; see *Tongas.*

Bodoque.——Double-stringed Indian bow for shooting clay pellets hardened in the fire, or a small spherical fruit.

boi-surubi.——See *bumba-meu-boi.*

Boi-tatá (Boitatá).——A mythical being; popular name of the *ignis fatuus,* or will-o'-the-wisp; the spirit that protects fields from fire.

Bornús.——African people.

boto.——Cetacean of the dolphin family (*Stena tucuxi*), which the Amazonian Indians believed to be enchanted; its form was supposed to be assumed by the generative demon, *uauiara* (q.v.). See p. 121, note 116.

bozo.——A form of dice game.

brancarão.——A very light-skinned mulatto, so light as to appear almost white.

bravi.——Term (meaning brave or fierce) applied to Brazilian Negroes and *caboclos*—the "*cabras*" (q.v.)—who fought the battles of the whites. See p. 358.

brejeiro.——Native or inhabitant of the *brejos* (q.v.), or marshland river district.

brejos.——Name given in northeastern Brazil to the marshland river district. See p. 400, note 333.

broa.——Bread made with rice or tapioca and beaten eggs.

Budes (Bufes).——African "nation."

budum.——". . . the body odor, the so-called *catinga,* or *budum,* reputedly characteristic of the African."—Donald Pierson: *Negroes in Brazil,* p. 175. Cf. *catinga.*

Bufes.——See *Budes.*

bugre.——A bugger, or sodomite; sometimes, simply, an Indian. See pp. 33 f., note 81, and p. 124.

bumba-meu-boi.——A popular dramatic ballet in northeastern Brazil, organized in the form of a procession, with a number of stock characters. Also known as *boi-surubi.*

bumbum.——Onomatopoetic term for a buzzing sound.

bunda.——Buttock. As an adjective, *bunda* refers to the language spoken by the natives of Angola.

caaguaçú.——Plant of the *Eriocaulaceæ* family (*Ericaulon sellowianum* Kth.).

caapeba.——See *capeba.*

Cabanada.——Term applied to the revolt that broke out in Pernambuco in 1832, with the object of restoring Pedro I.

Cabindas.——African tribe.

cabocla.——Feminine of *caboclo* (q.v.).

caboclo.——Term (literally, "copper-colored") applied to an Indian or mestizo (mixture of Indian and white). Also a rural person or "hillbilly." Cf. *cabocla.* On the laudatory use of *caboclo* in Brazil, see p. 67, note 187.

caboré (caburé).——Offspring of Negro and Indian. Cf. *cafuso.*

cabra.——A brave mestizo of African, white, and Indian ancestry.

cabra-cabriola.——An imaginary "*bicho,*" or goblin character, the "capering nanny-goat."

cabrocha.——A feminine dark-skinned mestizo type. See p. xxiv, note 11.

Cabundás.——African tribe.

cacá.——Childish term for excrement. Cf. *cocô.* Cf. the French *caca,* "*faire caca,*" etc.

caçamba.——A bucket used for drawing water from a well.

Caçanje (Caçange).——The Creole dialect of Portugal spoken in Angola; comes to mean bad Portuguese.

Caçanjes (Caçanges).——African tribe.

cachimbo.——A pipe for smoking.

caçula (caçulo).——The youngest son of a family.

cafajeste.——An infamous person or one with bad manners.

café mandingueiro.——"Witch's coffee." Consisting of strong coffee, much sugar, and the menstrual blood of the (mulatto) sorceress; for description, see. p. 336.

cafuné.——Name applied to the custom of snapping with the fingernails on the head of another person.

cafuso.——Offspring of Indian and Negro parents.

Caiapós.——An Indian tribe of the linguistic family Gê. See p. 259, note 170.

caipira.——Inhabitant of the *campo,* or open country; an uncouth rustic; a "hick."

caipora.——A traditional mythological being among the Indians, variously described. See pp. 99–100 and note 59.

caiporismo.——As used by Freyre, the cultural complex that in Brazil has grown up around the traditional *caipora* (q.v.) of the Indians. See pp. 99–100 and note 59.

Cairiris.——See *Cariris.*

Calabars.——African tribe.

caldo verde.——Broth made of turnips or cabbage chopped very fine and seasoned with salt or oil; popular in Portugal.

calunga.——The small doll upon which a sorcerer works; a secondary divinity of the Bantu cult or its fetish.

camondongo.——A mouse.

campo.——Open country, land without forests or only scattered trees.

Camundás.——An African people or "nation."

Camundongos (Cambundongos).——African tribe.

candomblé——Fetishistic ceremony of African provenience. See p. lxiv, note 13.

canga.——A sack or pouch for carrying things on one's back. Also a yoke for oxen.

cangaceiro.——A bandit, one laden down with the *cangaço,* or bundle of weapons that bandits carry in northeastern Brazil.

canindé.——Bird of the *Psitaci* or parrot family (*Ara ararauna Lin.*).

canjica.——Paste made from grated green corn, with various added ingredients such as sugar, salt, cinnamon, and coconut milk. See p. 130, note 148. Cf. *acanijic.*

capanga.——A professionally brave man, often a personal bodyguard. Cf. *cabra.*

capeba (caapeba).——Plant of the *Piperaceæ* family (*Piper robrii DC*), also known as the *paripoba.* The *capeba-do-norte* is the *Piper pettatum L.*

capitânia.——Jurisdictional division or fief corresponding to a province, in colonial Brazil. See p. xliv, note 56.

capitão-do-campo.——See *capitão-do-mato.*

capitão-do-mato.——A "bush-captain," one whose profession it was to recapture fugitive slaves. Also known as a *capitão-do-campo.*

capivara.——Species of rodent (*Hydrochoerus capybara.*)

capoeira.——A pastime in which the participant, "armed with a razor or a knife, with rapid and characteristic gestures goes through the motions of criminal acts." (Lima and Barroso, op. cit.) ——One who takes part in this pastime.

cará.——A tuberous plant, the starchy roots of which are used for food. Name given to various plants of the *Dioscoreaceæ* or yam family.

caraguatá.——Agave. Name given to various plants of the *Bromeliaceæ* family.

Caraibas.——Term applied by the Brazilian Indians to Europeans; also the Carib linguistic stock to which many of the Brazilian tribes belonged. See p. 13, note 28.

caraiurú (carajurú).——Amazonian plant of the *Bignoneaceæ* or trumpet-flower family (*Arribadæa chica Verlot*). It yields a red dye.

Carajás (plural).——Indians of the state of Goiás.

carapeba (acarapeba).——Fish of the *Encinostomidæ* family (*Diapterus rhombeus Cuv.* and *Val.*).

caribé.——Variety of manihot cake. See p. 127.

cariboca (curiboca).——A mestizo, part Negro and part Indian; cf. *mameluco.* The form *curiboca* is employed in northern Brazil.

carimã.——Cake made for children, of manihot dough dried in the sun.

Cariris (Cairiris).——Tribe of Indians inhabiting the highlands of Borborema, on the boundaries of Pernambuco and Piauí; also applied to a linguistic division of the Brazilian tribes.

carrapatú.——A mythical *bicho* (q.v.) used to frighten children. See pp. 139–40.

carrapeta.——A children's top or whirligig.

Carromantes.——African tribe of the Gold Coast.

carurú (caruru).——Name given to various plants of the *Amarantaceæ* family. Identified as the *Amarantus oleracea.*—"A variety of salad prepared from the *carurú* or *okra* (q.v.) to which are added shrimps, fish, etc., the whole seasoned with dendê (palm) oil and much pepper."—Lima and Barroso, op. cit. For Freyre's description, see p. 464.

catimbó (catimbau).——Practice of sorcery or spiritualism in its grosser forms.

catimbozeiro.——A sorcerer.

catinga.——A bad smell or stench; sometimes applied to the reputed body odor of Negroes—cf. *budum.*

cauaba.——Vessel for containing the drink known as *cauim* (q.v.).

cauim.——"Kind of drink prepared from cooked and fermented manihot. Originally it was prepared by the Indians from cashew nuts and various other fruits, and also from crushed Indian corn and manihot." —Lima and Barroso, op. cit. See *cauaba.*

cauri (carim, caril).——Porcelain shell used as money on the east coast of Africa, worth $\frac{1}{130}$th part of a penny sterling.

cegonha.——Device, of Moorish origin, for drawing water from a well. Cf. *picata.* Cf., also, *nora.*

chéchéré.——See *heré.*

chicha.——Fermented drink among the Indians, generally made of corn, but also of sweet potatoes, manioc, sugar-cane juice, etc.

Coajerucu.——See *Pijericú.*

Coca (Cuca).——Bogeyman; fanciful being used to frighten children.

cocaloba.——A mythical monster.

cocô.——Childish word for excrement; cf. *cacá.*

côco-de-catarro.——See *macaíba.*

coivara.——Pile of brush and wood that was not burned during the initial burning of a piece of land. This is burned subsequently.

colégio (collégio).——In colonial times, a school kept by Jesuits; in modern times, a private school offering primary or secondary instruction.

comadre.——Godmother; "gossip"; name given to midwives. Also, a concubine.

compadrismo.——Political system of oligarchic nepotism and patronage (from *compadre*: godfather, sponsor, friend, etc.).

Congos.——Prominent African tribe.

conomis-miri.——Young Indians (a native term).

coqueiro.——Commonly the coco tree, but applied in general to palms producing edible fruit or in wide use industrially.

corregedor.——In colonial times, a magistrate with functions corresponding to those of the modern judge.

corriboque.——Receptacle for snuff.

corrução.——See *maculo*.

Coruqueama.——A mythical monster of terrifying aspect, feared by the Indians.

corvina.——Name given to three fish of the *Sciænidae* family; so called (from *corvo*, a crow) because of their black fins.

Costa.——The West Coast of Africa, or, in general (in various expressions), Africa.

cria.——A young Negro, born and reared (*criado*) in the Big House.

cruzado.——Coin worth four hundred reis.

cuca.——See *coca*.

culumim (culumi, curumí, curumim, curumbim).——An Indian lad; in modern usage, a small boy, a lad, a servant.

cumari (cumarim).——Plant of the *Palmaceæ* family (*Astrocaryum vulgare Mart.*).

cunhã.——Tupí-Guaraní word meaning woman.

cunhatain.——Tupí-Guaraní word meaning a young girl, corresponding to the masculine *culumim* (*curumí*). Cf. *cunhã*.

curadá.——Variety of manihot cake. See p. 128.

curandeiro.——A medicine-man among the Indians; in modern usage, one who practices the healing art without a license; a medical charlatan.

curape.——See *ticuna*.

curiboca.——See *cariboca*.

curumi.——Brazilian plant, the *Muntingia calabura L.* Cf. *kurumikáa*.

cururupeba.——Indian sobriquet, meaning "little toad."

cutia.——Rodent of the *Caviidæ* family, which includes the guinea-pigs, etc. (*Dasyprocta aguti Lin.*).

Daomeianos.——An African people, of Dahomey.

dendê.——African palm acclimated in Brazil (*Elæis guineensis Jacq.*).

dengo (dengue).——Affected, presumptuous, boastful, effeminate, fond of women, etc.

detração.——Law by which the State might deduct a quarter part of the possessions of dead foreigners when the property in question was sent out of the country. Portugal had no such laws. See p. 193. Cf. *albinágio* and *naufrágio.*

diamba.——See *macumba.* Cf. *liamba.*

dindinho.——Familiar term for godfather or grandfather.

ebó.——Afro-Brazilian culinary preparation. See p. 465, note 176.

Effans.——An African people.

efô.——Dish composed of shrimps and herbs seasoned with dendê (palm) oil and pepper.

efun-oguedé——Afro-Brazilian culinary preparation. See p. 465, note 176.

Egbas.——An African people (Yoruba subgroup).

Embacas.——See *Ubacas.*

embaiba (umbaúba).——Tree of the *Moraceæ* family (*Cecropia palmata*). It has a number of other names as well.

embira.——Term applied to a number of Brazilian plants with fibrous bark of which ropes are made.

emboaba.——Nickname given in colonial times to the *bandeirantes* (q.v.) and their descendants, then to the Portuguese in general.

encoêma.——Tupí expression meaning "good day."

engenho.——A sugar plantation; a sugar-mill.

engenho d'agua.——A sugar-mill propelled by a *roda d'agua* (q.v.), or water-wheel.

eran-pateté.——Afro-Brazilian culinary preparation. See p. 465, note 176.

erva cidreira.——Citronella. Plant of the *Labiatæ* family (*Melissa officinalis Lin.*); in Pernambuco the name is given also to a plant of the *Verbenaceæ* family (*Lippia geminata H.B.K.*).——The cedrat, or citron.

espanador.——Brush used by the *vasculhadores* (q.v.) in cleaning high walls and roofs.

estância.——A ranch or country estate, particularly in southern Brazil. Cf. *fazenda.*

Fanti.——African language spoken on the eastern frontier of the Congo area.

farofa.——Manihot meal mixed with melted butter or fat, at times mixed with eggs, meat, etc.

farranca.——A mythical monster.

farrapos (plural).——Term applied by the legalists to the insurrectionists of Rio Grande do Sul in 1835.

fazenda.——A large estate, ranch or plantation. Cf. *estância.*

fazendeiro.——Owner of a *fazenda* (q.v.).

feijão de coco.——Dish consisting of beans with coconut.

feijão fradinho.——Variety of bean.

feijoada.——A stew of beans plus some meat, preferably fatty, such as bacon, sausage, pork, etc.

Felupos.——African tribe.

fidalgo.——A Portuguese nobleman, gentleman; cf. the Spanish *hidalgo*.

figa.——An amulet. "Small object in the form of a closed fist, with the thumb between the index and middle finger, of which superstitious use is made in warding off evil spells, sickness, etc."—Lima and Barroso, op. cit.

filárias.——Nematode worms.

fojo.——A trap for catching game; it is concealed by tree boughs.

fonte.——Fountain or spring; source.

freirático.——One who likes and admires monastical customs. One enamored of a nun (*freira*) in a convent.

fruta-pão.——The breadfruit tree (*Artocarpus incisa*), of the *Malvaceæ* or mallow family.

Filanis.——One of the names of the Fuláh people of Africa. Cf. *Fulanis*. See *Fuláhs; Fulas; Fulos; Fula-Fulos; Felavas; Fubes; Pulbes*.

Fubes.——One of the names of the Fuláh people of Africa. See *Fuláhs; Fulas; Fulos; Fula-Fulos; Fulanis; Filani; Felavas; Pulbes*.

Fuláhs.——See *Fulas; Fulos; Fula-Fulos; Fulanis; Filanis; Felavas; Fubes; Pulbes*.

Fulanis.——Fulanins; a name for the Fuláh people of Africa. Cf. *Filanis*. See *Fuláhs; Fulas; Fulos; Fula-Fulos; Felavas; Fubes; Pulbes*.

Fulas.——An African people, the Fuláhs, Cf. *Fulos; Fula-Fulos*.

Fula-Fulos.——An African stock—"pure Fuláhs (Fulas)," according to Freyre (see p. 304). Cf. *Fulas; Fulos*.

Fulos.——An African people, the Fuláhs (Fulas). Cf. *Fula-Fulos*.

Gabão.——Gabon, or Gabun, region in French Equatorial Africa.

Galinhas.——African tribe.

gameleira (*gamelleira*).——Tree of the *Moraceæ* family, of which there are various species.

gandú-açú.——Indian name for the hedgehog.

Ganguelas.——African "nation."

garoupa.——Sea-fish of the *Serranidæ* family (*Cerna gigas Brunn.*), also called *garoupa-verdadeira*.

Gegás.——African tribe.

Gêges.——Well-known African tribe.

genip tree (*jenipapeiro*).——Tree of the *Rubiaceæ* family (*Genipa americana Lin.*), known in English as genipa, or genip tree, its fruit being known as genipap.

girão (*girau*).——A platform between the floor and the roof, raised on wooden stakes and used for storing provisions; or a food-cage suspended from the ceiling.

gravatá.——Same as *caraguatá* (q.v.).

grude.——Dish made of dried tapioca and grated coconut, baked in the oven and wrapped in banana leaves.

guaçu.——See *beijú-açú*.

guaiazi.——An indescribable, mythical monster that terrified the Indians.

guará.——Bird of the *Ibides* family, which includes ibises and spoonbills (*Eudocismus ruber Lin.*).

Guaraní.——"Ethnographic division of the great Tupí-Guaraní family [of Indians] which includes the Tupís of the south."—Lima and Barroso, op. cit. See *Tupí.*

Guimbandes.——African tribe.

guiraquinguira.——Indian sobriquet, meaning "bird's behind."

Guissamas.——African tribe.

gundú.——"Osseous excrescences that develop in a symmetrical manner on the bone of the nose and the superior maxillary."—Lima and Barroso, op. cit.

Haussás.——Members of an African tribe.

heré (*chéchéré*).——Copper rattle used in the African fetishistic ceremony known as *xangô.*

hipupiara (*hupupiara*).——Among the Indians, a mythical marine monster in the form of a man that came up from the sea and devoured the bodies of human beings. For a description, see p. 153 and note 249. The *hipupiara* was used to frighten children.

homem-marinho.——The "man of the sea," a mythical monster supposed to haunt beaches and to devour the fingers, nose, and private parts of his victims; see p. 339.

hupupiara.——See *hipupiara.*

iaiá (*yayá*).——Familiar term employed in addressing girls and young women. Much used in the days of slavery, it has now fallen into disuse. Cf. *ioiô.*

iambú.——Indian name for partridge. Cf. *ianhambí.*

ianhambí.——Indian name for partridge. Cf. *iambú.*

ian-ou-are.——An animal (*bicho*) supposed to devour savages.

Ibanaras.——African "nation."

Ibi.——African language spoken on the eastern frontier of the Congo area.

içá.——The edible female (bloated with eggs) of the *saúba* ant.

ieré.——Afro-Brazilian condiment.

igara.——Small boat or canoe.

Ijejas.——African tribe.

ioiô.——Term used by slaves in addressing their masters. Cf. *iaiá.*

ioó.——Brazilian plant, the leaves of which are used in making the salad known as *carurú* (q.v.).

ipeca.——Indian name for a variety of ducks.

ipeté.——Afro-Brazilian culinary preparation. See p. 465, note 176.

irara.——Carnivorous animal of the *Mustelidæ* family, which includes weasels, skunks, badgers, etc. (*Tayra barbara Lin.*).

jacami (*jacamim*).——Bird of the *Psophiidæ* family, or South American trumpeters.

jacarandá.——Tree of the *Leguminosæ* family, *Papillonaceæ* division (*Machoerium villosum Vog.*); also known as the *jacarandá-paulista.*

jagunço.——Originally, a back-country ruffian. The term comes to be practically synonymous with *capanga*, or hired assassin.

Jalofos.——African tribe.

jaracatiá.——Plant of the *Caricaceæ* family (*Jaracatia dodecaphylla A.*).

jararaca.——Poisonous snake of Brazil (*Bothrops jararaca*).

jarro.——See *taioba.*

jequiá.——A trap for game.

jerimum.——Plant of the *Cucurbitaceæ* or gourd family.

jilo.——Fruit of the *jileiro*, a garden plant of the *Solanaceæ* family (*Solanum megalena Dum.*).

judinga.——A kind of Jewish dance, staged in connection with feast-day processions in fifteenth-century Portugal. See p. 258, note 168.

juquitaia.——Hybrid condiment composed of salt and pepper mixed. For a description of the manner in which it is made, see p. 132.

jurupari.——Demon of the Tupí Indians.

Kanembus.——African people.

Kanuris.——People of Africa.

Krumanos.——African tribe.

kurumikáa (curumí).——Indian name for the plant from the leaves of which the *puçanga* (q.v.) of the medicine-men was prepared. See p. 128. The *Mutingia calabura L.*

ladina.——Feminine form of *ladino* (q.v.).

ladino (feminine: ladina).——A slave who "spoke Portuguese, had some notions of the Christian religion, and knew how to perform ordinary tasks in the house or the field."—Lima and Barroso, op. cit.

lambari.——Name common to a number of varieties of river fish.

Landins.——African tribe.

laus perenne.——Perpetual adoration of the sacrament or similar rites.

liamba.——See *macumba*. Cf. *diamba.*

Libollos.——African tribe.

lili.——Childish form of the personal pronoun *lhe* (third person, dative).

lubambo.——A fracas; a plot.

Mabringelas.——African tribe.

macahiba.——See *macaíba.*

macaíba (macahiba).——Species of palm, the *Acrocomia scelerocarpa Mart.* It is also known as the *macaúba*, *côco-de-catarro*, *mocajá*, and *macajuba.*

macajuba.——See *macaíba.*

Maçanganas.——African "nation."

macapatá.——In northern Brazil, a cake made out of soft manihot dough; for description, see p. 128.

macaúba.——See *macaíba*.

macaxeira.——The sweet manioc (*Manihot aipi*).

Machanganaos.——African tribe.

Machopes.——African tribe.

"Macker."——Name given by the French writer Dampier to a form of grill used in the making of love-philters; see p. 465.

macobeba.——A mythical *bicho* (q.v.), creation of a child's imagination. See p. 140.

maçoca.——Manihot dough of which various cakes are made. For description, see p. 129.

maconha.——An aphrodisiac herb employed by sorcerers in the Alagoas region; also known as *diamba, liamba, riamba*. "A variety of European hemp (*Cannabis sativa* var. *indica* L.) whose leaves and flowers are impregnated with a narcotic the effects of which are similar to those of opium."—Lima and Barroso, op. cit.

Macuacuas.——African tribe.

maculo.——Disease common to Negroes just brought over from Africa in the days of the slave traffic. A diarrhea with relaxation of the anal sphincter. Also known as *corrução* and *mal-de-bicho*.

macumba.——"Fetishistic ceremony with a Negro base and showing Christian influence, accompanied by dances and songs to the sound of the drum; sorcery in general."—Lima and Barroso, op. cit. Cf. *macumbeiro*.

macumbeiro.——A love-sorcerer, one who practices the art of *macumba* (q.v.).

mãe.——Mother. ——*mãe preta*: "black mammy."

mãe d'agua.——"A fanciful being, a sort of fresh-water siren or mermaid, also known as *uiara* and *iara*."—Lima and Barroso, op. cit.

Magós.——African "nation."

Maguiocos.——African tribe.

mão (maõzinho) de coçar.——An artificial (ivory) hand for scratching the person. See p. 471, note 193.

maõzinho de coçar.——See *mão de coçar*.

mal-de-bicho.——See *maculo*.

Malembás.——African "nation."

malungo.——A young Negro playmate of the white lads of the Big House. Meaning "comrade," the word, an African one, was employed by Negroes in addressing one another on the slave-ships that brought them to Brazil. It was also used by the *quilombolas*, or runaway slaves, in the *quilombos*, or colonies, that they set up.

mamão.——Papaw or papaya. Fruit of the *mamoeiro* (q.v.).

mameluca.——See *mameluco*.

mameluco (feminine: *mameluca*).——Offspring of white and Indian; sometimes employed as a generic term, embracing all varieties of mestizo, including the offspring of Negro and white, of Negro and Indian, etc. Cf. *cariboca*.

manceba.——A concubine.

mamoeiro.——Papaw or papaya tree. Of the *Caricaceæ* or papaw family (*Carica papaya Lin.*); its fruit is known as *mamão.*

mandacarú.——Variety of fig tree, vernacular name in Brazil for a species of *Cereus* in general. See p. xix, note 3.

mandioca.——Plant of the *Euphorbiaceæ* family (*Manihot utilissima* Pohl), known in English as the manihot, manioc, or cassava.

mandinga.——Sorcery or witchcraft. Cf. *mandingueiro.*

mandingas.——An African people.

mandingueiro.——One who practices *mandinga*, or sorcery.

mandiopuba.——Indian sobriquet, meaning "rotten manihot."

mané-gostoso.——A puppet; also a character in the *bumba-meu-boi*, or *boi-surubi*, a popular dramatic performance in the Brazilian northeast. The *mané-gostoso* appears on stilts, to sing couplets.

maneira.——"Posterior opening in skirts, from the waistband down, to permit their being slipped over the shoulders and buttocks."—Lima and Barroso, op. cit.

mangaba tree (mangabeira).——The *mangaba* is the fruit of the *mangabeira* (*Hancornia speciosa Gomez*); it is a round orange-colored fruit that is eaten when over-ripe. The tree yields a milky juice from which so-called "Pernambuco rubber" is produced.

mangangá.——Term applied in northeastern Brazil to a species of large wood-gnawing beetles.

Mangbatus.——African people.

manja.——A children's game, somewhat like our hide-and-seek, with certain sadistic variations. See p. 151, note 236. Also known as *temposerá* (q.v.).

mamoeira.——The papaya tree (*Carica papaya Lin.*).

manuê.——Variety of cake made of corn flour, honey, and other ingredients.

mão-de-cabelo.——"A fanciful being that, according to popular superstition, has a human form, goes clad in white, and whose hands are made of long hairs."—Lima and Barroso, op. cit.

mão-de-pelo.——Hairy-handed goblin, used to frighten children.

maracatú.——A carnival dance.

Maria-da-Manta.——A mythical apparition.

Masai.——African people.

mascate.——Originally, a peddler. Nickname given to the Portuguese of Recife by the inhabitants of Olinda. See p. 80, note 217.

massapé.——Clayey soil, usually black, which is very good for sugar cane.

mata-mata-marinheiro.——A riotous disturbance in the early days of Brazil, directed by the Brazilians against the Portuguese, known as "*marinheiros*," or "sailors." "*Marinheiro*" is here roughly equivalent to "*gringo*," and "*mata-mata-marinheiro*" to "kill-kill-the-*gringo*."

mata-naariti.——A form of ball-game among the Parecí Indians. See p. 147.

mate.——Name applied to a tea-like drink—"Paraguayan tea," "South Sea tea," "yerba"—and to the tree (*erva-mate*) from the leaves of which it is made. This tree belongs to the *Aquifoliaceæ* family (*Ilex Paraguariensis Hil.*).

matuto.——A backwoodsman, one who lives in the *mato*, or jungle backlands.

mazombo.——One born in America of European, especially Portuguese, parents; a depreciatory epithet.

Mazangos.——African "nation."

mbeiu.——See *beijú*.

midubi.——Freyre identifies this plant with the peanut. Cf. *amendoim*. See p. 34, note 82.

miguiguaçú.——Indian sobriquet, meaning "big buttocks."

mimbaba.——Indian term for domestic animals kept as pets.

mimi.——Childish form of the first person singular personal pronoun, dative and objective.

Mina.——Name derived from Forte de el Mina on the west coast of Africa and applied to highly respected Negro women of Bahia. See p. xxiv, note 10.

Minas.——Prominent African tribe.

Mindongues.——African tribe.

Mineiro.——Native or inhabitant of Minas Geraes.

mingau.——Porridge made of manihot. An edible paste made of manihot (or wheat) flour and water, with or without sugar and eggs.

mingau das almas.——"Broth of souls," with which the faces of children are supposed to be smeared by the *almas penadas* (q.v.).

mixiria (mixira).——Fish or turtle preserved in oil. See p. 131 and note 157.

mocajá.——See *macaíba*.

Moçambiques.——Africans from Mozambique.

mocotó.——Plant of the *Acanthaceæ* family (*Elytroris alagoana*). Foot of a bovine animal used for edible purposes.

modinha.——Formerly, a variety of drawing-room ballad, in the vernacular; today, a variety of urban popular song. (Lima and Barroso, op. cit.) The word is a diminutive of *moda*: originally a new song, one in the *mode*.

mokaen.——Indian form of the modern *moquem* (q.v.).

moleque.——See *muleque*.

mocambo.——See *mucambo*.

molho de ferrugem.——"Rusty gravy." A thick gravy made with meat-juice; so called on account of its color.

moqueca (muqueca).——Ragout of fish or shellfish, with oil and pepper. Cf. *pokeka*.

moquem.——Process of preparing fish or meat by roasting it over the coals or upon a gridiron; the gridiron itself. See p. 130 and note 152.

mourejar.——To work or labor a great deal; from *mouro*, a Moor. See p. 212.

Mouro.——A Moor.

Mozuzuros.——African tribe.

mucama (*mucamba*).——A favorite Negro maid employed as house servant and personal attendant. Sometimes a wet-nurse. ——*mucama de estimação*: a favorite *mucama;* often applied to the nurse who suckled the white child.

mucamba.——See *mucama*.

mucambo (*mocambo*).——A fugitive-slave settlement (*quilombo*, q.v.) or a hut in such a settlement (see p. 69, note 193).

muganga (*moganga*).——A grimace, contortion.

mugunzá.——See *mungunzá*.

mujanguê (*mujangüê*).——Dish made from turtle or tortoise eggs, with sugar and fermented manihot flour. See p. 132 and note 163.

mulambo.——A rag or clout.

muleca (*moleca*).——A young Negro girl, maid in the Big House. Cf. *mucama; mucamba*.

mulecote (*molecote*).——A sturdily built *muleque* (q.v.), or Negro lad.

muleque (*moleque*).——A young Negro; comes to mean a wag or a blackguard. ——*muleque de estimação*: a *muleque* who was given the run of the Big House.

mulequinho.——Small Negro lad; "pickaninny."

mundéu (*mundé*).——Trap for catching game.

mungunzá.——Dish of the Brazilian north consisting of grains of corn in a broth sweetened at times with coconut milk or cow's milk.

munguzá.——See *mungunzá*.

muqueca.——See *moqueca*.

murubixaba (*morubixaba*).——Temporal chief of an Indian tribe. See p. 33, note 81. See *pajé*.

Muxicongos.——African tribe.

naufrágio.——The law of shipwreck, which gave kings and lords the right to take possession of the persons and cargoes of shipwrecked vessels. Portugal did not have such a law. See p. 193. Cf. *albinágio* and *detração*.

negro de ganho.——In the days of slavery, a Negro slave engaged in a gainful occupation who gives the proceeds to his master.

Negro de Surrão.——The Negro with the Pouch; for the story of this mythical character, see pp. 338 f.

nenem (*nenen, nenê*).——A newborn child or one a few months old.

Niam Niam.——Name of an African folk.

nora.——Moorish device for raising water. Cf. *picata* and *cegonha*.

Nubians (*Nubios*).——Well-known African people.

oca.——Communal (Freyre calls it "communistic") dwelling of certain Brazilian Indians, housing from eighty to a hundred persons. It was built of rafters covered with palm fronds or straw. See p. 145.

ochente.——Plebeian expression of surprise, mixed sometimes with disdain. Probably a corruption of the exclamation "*O'gente!*"

olharapos.——A goblin.

oliva.——An olive.

olival.——Terrain planted with olive trees. Cf. *olivedo.*

olivedo.——Terrain planted with olive trees. Cf. *oliva* (*olival*).

Orixá.——A secondary divinity of the African *gegê-nagô* cult; an African idol or anthropomorphic representation of an Orixá.—Lima and Barroso, op. cit.

pacoba sororca (*pacova sororoca*).——The Brazilian banana. In the north *pacoba* is a term for banana in general; in the south it is applied to a large-sized variety.

pacoca.——Dish made of roasted and pounded cashew nut kernels with fermented manihot flour and sugar. Cf. *paçoka.*

paçoka.——Indian form of the modern *pacoca* (q.v.).

pacova sororoca.——See *pacoba sororoca.*

padre.——A priest; literally, father. Freyre employs the term especially with reference to the fathers of the Society of Jesus.

pagé.——See *pajé.*

pajé (*pagé*).——"Spiritual chief of the aborigines, a mixture of priest, prophet, and medicine-man." (Lima and Barroso, op. cit.) The *pajé* was the spiritual and the *murubixaba* (q.v.) the temporal leader of the tribe.

pamonha.——Cake made of green corn, coconut milk, butter, cinnamon, anise, and sugar, baked in corn leaves. Cf. *pamuna.*

pamuna.——Indian term for cake made of green corn and other ingredients; modern form: *pamonha* (q.v.).

pano (*panno*) *da Costa.*——A garment of African origin worn by certain Negro women in Brazil. It consists of a "long, heavy, striped cotton cloth, at times worn slung over the shoulder and pinned under the opposite arm, at times wrapped once or twice in a wide fold about the waist and tied rather tightly." (Donald Pierson: *Negroes in Brazil,* p. 246.)

pão-de-lo de arroz.——Spongecake with rice.

pão-de-lo de milho.——Spongecake with corn.

papá.——Father, papa.

papa-figo.——A goblin who eats the livers of children.

papão.——Imaginary monster or goblin used to frighten children.

papato.——Childish form of *sapato,* shoe.

pardavasco.——Dark-skinned individual approaching the mulatto type; offspring of Negro and mulatto.

pardo.——General and somewhat vague term for mulatto.

Parecís (*Paricís*) (plural).——Indian (Aruak) tribe of Mato Grosso.

paripoba.——See *capeba.*

Paulista.——Inhabitant of the state of São Paulo of Brazil.

paxicá.——Ragout made of turtle's liver, seasoned with salt, lemon, and Indian pepper.

pé-de-bezerro.——See *taioba.*

pé-de-muleque.——Cake made of fermented manihot dough. (Literally: "black boy's foot.")

peia queimada.——"Hot-strap," a game played by Brazilian children, described by Freyre as sadistic.

peipetaba.——A plant (*Scoparia dulcis*) commonly known in Brazil as "*vassourinha*" ("little broom").

peitica.——Bird with a monotonous, annoying song, object of superstition among the Indians. The *Tapera nævia nævia.* See p. 140, note 203.

peixe-boi.——Mammifer of the order *Sirenidae* of the *Trichechidæ* family (*Trichechus inunguis*). See p. 131, and note 158.

peteca.——A plaything made of hide and feathers and batted in the air with the palms of the hands; in Alagoas, the game is played with a cornstalk and a head of Indian corn and is called "*bola de milho,*" or "corn-ball."—Lima and Barroso, op. cit.

petume (*petum*).——Tupí Indian name for tobacco. Also written *petema* and *petima.*

pexorim.——See *pixurim.*

piá.——A young Indian or *caboclo* child (term of endearment).

piaçá.——See *piaçava.*

piaçaba.——See *piaçava.*

piaçava (*piaçaba, piaçá*).——Name given to two varieties of palm: the *Attalea funifera Mart.* and the *Leopoldinia piassaba Wal.* Their fibers are employed in the manufacture of brooms.

piau.——A river fish; name given to the larger varieties of *piaba* (*Leporinus copelandi Steind.*).

picado.——Ragout of chopped fish or meat.

picata.——Device for drawing water from a well; introduced by the Moors into the Hispanic peninsula. Cf. *cegonha.* Cf., also, *nora.*

pichana.——Indian name for cat.

pijericú (*pijerecu*).——Plant of the *Anonaceæ* family (*Xylopia fructescens*), also known as *coajerucu.*

pindoba.——Plant of the *Palmaceæ* family (*Attalea compta Mart.*).

pinhão (Plural: *pinhões*).——Plant of the *Euphorbiaceæ* family (*Jatropha curcas L.*).

pipí.——Childish word for urine.

pipiri.——Herbaceous plant of the *Ciperaceæ* family (*Rhynchospora storea*).

piquira.——Scaly fish of the *Caracinidæ* family (*Bryconops alburnus*).

piracuí.——Flour made from dried fish. See p. 130 and note 151.

piranha.——River fish of the *Caracinidæ* family, fear-inspiring by reason of its voracity.

pirão.——Manihot paste.

pirão com carne.——*Pirão* with meat, the *pirão* being a thick paste made of parched manihot flour.

pirarucú.——Large Amazonian fish (*Arapaima gigas*) of the *Osteoglossidæ* family. (Spanish: *paiche.*)

pixurim.——Medicinal plant of the *Lauraceæ* family (*Acrodiclidium puchury-major*), also called *pexorim* and *puxuri.*

pokeka, poqueca.——Indian form of the modern *moqueca* (q.v.).

pombinha.——An aphrodisiac herb used by Portuguese sorcerers, for stimulating old men and frigid young ones.

ponche.——Drink consisting of tea or coffee mixed with brandy or rum, lemon juice, sugar, etc., or even mixed fruit without alcohol.

pru mode.——Plebeian form of the preposition *pará*, meaning "for."

puçanga.——A remedy prepared by Indian medicine-men; comes to be a term for household remedy.

Pulbes.——The correct name of the Fuláh people of Africa, according to A. G. Haddon (*The Races of Man and Their Distribution*); see p. 305. See *Fuláhs; Fulas; Fulos; Fula-Fulos; Fulanis; Filanis; Felavas; Fubes.*

pungo.——Aphrodisiac herb employed by sorcerers in the Rio de Janeiro region.

pupunha tree (pupunheira).——Tall prickly palm of the genus *Guilielma* (*Guilielma speciosa* Mart.). The tree is known as *pupunheira;* the *pupunha* is its fruit.

"purva."——Popular form of *puba*, a dish prepared from fermented manihot.

puxuri.——See *pixurim.*

quati.——Coati. Carnivorous mammifer of the *Procionidæ* family (*Nasua narica*).

Quebra-quilos.——Name given to those who participated in the seditious movement in Paraíba in 1875. See p. 156 and note 256.

queda de braço (quebra de braço).——The "arm-breaking" game of the Brazilian Indians, a game in which the players endeavor to bend each other's forearm over the horizontal support on which their elbows rest.

queimado.——Caramel-like candy made with molasses.

quengo.——Vessel made of half a coconut shell.

quentão.——Sugar-cane brandy with ginger.

quiabo.——The okra plant (*Abelmoschus esculentus*).

quibebe.——Edible gourd paste.

quibungo.——A character in African Negro mythology supposed to swallow children through a hole in his back. For a description, see p. 340. In Minas Geraes, *quibungo* is the term applied to a Negro dance.

quilombo.——A fugitive-slave settlement in the backlands in the days of slavery. See p. 68, note 190.

quilombola.——A slave who had run away to a *quilombo* (q.v.).

Quilumanos.——African tribe.

quindim.——Sexual longing; also, a confection made of egg-yolk, coconut, and sugar.

quitandeira.——A woman who makes and sells home-made sweets and pastries.

quitunga.——Peanuts toasted and pressed with *cumari* (q.v.) pepper.

quitute.——A dainty confection.

quizamas.——African tribe.

rancho.——A carnival club or society. (The word has a number of other meanings.)

raparigueiro.——A woman-chaser, ladies' man, "lady-killer," etc. From *rapariga*, in Brazil a prostitute; in Portugal a girl, a lass.

Rebolos.——African tribe.

reconcavo.——Strip of land outside the city of Salvador (Bahia), bordering All Saints Bay, some sixty miles long and up to thirty miles in breadth, formerly the seat of the landowning, slave-holding rural aristocracy.

reduções (plural of *redução*).——Term applied to places where Indian converts were gathered by the Jesuit missionaries.

reisado.——A popular dramatic dance staged in honor of Epiphany.

república.——Group of students living together in the same house (literally, a "republic").

riacho.——A creek or small stream.

ribeira.——Name applied to the women of Leiria in Portugal (women of the people).

roda.——A foundling-asylum.

roda d'agua.——Water-wheel for propelling an *engenho*, or sugar-mill.

rodilha.——A fold of cloth on the head where a burden rests.

rolete de cana.——Sugar-cane roll (culinary preparation).

rotula.——A latticed or Venetian blind. Also a small opening in a door through which a person in the house can see and speak with a visitor before opening the door.

rua.——A street.

sabão da Costa.——A variety of soap imported by Brazilian Negroes from their native Africa.

Sabinada.——Term applied to the separatist revolution of Bahia in the time of the Regency.

Saci-pererê (Saci).——"A mythical being, a little Negro with one leg, that, according to popular belief, pursues travelers or lies in ambush for them."—Lima and Barroso, op. cit.

sairé.——An Indian children's dance, described by Father João Daniel.

Salóia.——"Countrywoman that lives within the district of Lisbon; especially one of those that supply the market with bread every day."

—H. Michaelis: *A New Dictionary of the Portuguese and English Languages.*

samburá.——An Indian basket made of liana or bamboo.

sapé.——Often refers to long grass used for thatching. Name given to plants of the *Graminea* or grass family (*Imperata exaltata Brogn.* and *Imperata brasiliensis Trin.*).

sapinhos de leite.——"Milk-curds" in an infant's mouth, white or yellowish splotches due to an acidosis condition.

sapo-cururú.——An imaginary animal supposed to haunt the banks of rivers.

sarará.——A light-colored Negro with red (sandy) kinky hair.

saúba (saúva).——Species of leaf-cutting ant (*Œcodoma cephalotes*); for description, see p. 251, note 150.

Senzes (Senges).——African "nation."

senzala.——The quarters where the slaves lived on a plantation.

senzes.——See *senges.*

serpentina.——Curtained palanquin, the bed of which is a hammock.

serralha.——Plant of the *Composta* family (*Sonchus lævis*).

sertanejo.——Inhabitant of the *sertão* (*sertões*), or backlands.

sertanista.——Sometimes, a pioneer or explorer of the backlands, or *sertão;* at other times, a student of or authority on the subject. Not to be confused with *sertanejo,* a native of the backlands.

sertão (plural: *sertões*).——The backlands. *Sertão* is applied in particular to the backland region (Bahia and neighboring states) of northeastern Brazil.

sertões.——See *sertão.*

sicupira.——"Name common to two trees of the *Leguminosa* family: the *Ormosia* or *Robinia coccinea* and the *Ormosia coarctata* or *minor.*— Lima and Barroso, op. cit.

simiavulpina.——Among the Indians, a terrifying mythical monster.

sinhá.——Term employed by slaves, in place of *senhora,* in addressing ladies of the Big House. Cf. *sinhá-dona; sinhá-moça; sinhazinha.*

sinhá-dona.——Term applied to the mistress of the Big House, *sinhá* being the slave's rendering of *senhora,* and *dona* meaning lady or mistress.

sinhama.——Affectionate term for a Negro nurse or "mammy."

sinhá-moça.——Term applied to a young lady of the Big House. *Sinhá* for *senhora; moça:* a young woman or girl.

sinhazinha.——Term of endearment employed by slaves in addressing their mistress's daughter. Diminutive of *sinhá,* which the slaves employed for *senhora.*

sinhô-moço.——Young master; familiar form of address by slaves.

solar.——A Portuguese (as distinguished from a Brazilian) country house.

Songas (Songos).——African "nation."

Songos.——See *Songas.*

taba.——An Indian village.

tabatinga.——Clay used in pottery-making. May be white, red, blue, or yellow.

tabuá.——Plant of the *Typhaceæ* family (*Typha dominguensis Pers.*), also known as *partazana.* It is used in making mats.

taioba.——Herbaceous plant of the *Araceæ* family (*Colocasia antiquorum* and *Xanthosoma violaceum Schott.*), also known as *talo, tarro, jarro,* and *pé-de-bezerro.*

talo.——See *taioba.*

tambaquí.——Various species of fish of the *Caracinidæ* family. See p. 131, note 156.

tanga.——Garment worn by a slave or worker, reaching from the waist to the knees.

tapitim.——See *tipiti.*

tapuia (tapuya).——Generic term for Brazilian Indian (cf. *caboclo*); commonly refers to a linguistic stock.

taquara.——Tough-fibered bamboo that grows wild in Brazil (*Guadua spp.; Chusquea spp.*).

tarubá.——A sweet-perfumed drink in the far north of Brazil. For description, see pp. 128, 129.

tarro.——See *taioba.*

tatá.——Daddy.

tatajuba (tatajiba).——Plant of the *Moraceæ* family (*Bagassa guianensis Aubl.*), also known as *jataíba.*

tatú-gambeta.——A goblin.

teceba.——African rosary, with a string of ninety-nine wooden beads and a ball in place of a crucifix on the end.

tejupá.——An Indian habitation smaller than the *oca* (q.v.).

tejupaba.——A shack, hut, or cabin in the fields. Cf. *tejupá.*

tenten (tem-tem).——Motions of a child when learning to walk.

terreiro.——Place where an African fetishistic ceremony is held.

ticanga (ticuanga).——Variety of manioc cake. See *beijú-ticanga.*

ticuna.——The Indian poison known as curare. Also called *curape.*

tigre.——Vessel for fecal matter. Literally, "tiger."

timbo.——Variety of liana.

Timinis.——African tribe.

tinguí (tingui).——Method of catching fish by poisoning them with the juice of the *tingui-de-peixe,* a shrub of the *Theophrastaceæ* family (*Jacquininia tingui*). This method is "employed in the north to poison the fish in the water (the fish thus poisoned do not harm those who eat them."—Lima and Barroso, op. cit.

tipití (tapitim).——Cylindrical basket made of palm leaves in which the manihot is placed for pressing, to rid it of moisture. For description, see pp. 126 f.

tipóia.——The band of cloth by which the Indian woman secures the child to her back.

Tongas (Bitongas).——African tribe.

tracajá.——Fresh-water tortoise of the genus *Emys.* (Spanish: *terecai.*)

trango-mango.——A goblin.

trapiche.——A sugar-mill (*engenho*) propelled by oxen or other beasts of burden. Cf. *almanjarra.*

tricana.——Countrywoman or woman of the people (in Portugal).

trova.——A poetic form (song) stemming from the love songs of the medieval troubadours of the Iberian Peninsula.

tucanaré.——Fish of the *Cyclidæ* family (*Cichla oscellaris*).

tucum.——Species of palm (*Bactris setona Mart.*) from the leaves of which fiber is extracted.

tucupí.——Indian term for the water drained off from the pressed manihot root.

Tupí.——One of the four principal linguistic families of Brazil; the *lingua geral*, or common tongue, spoken down to the sixteenth century on the seaboard and today in Amazonas under the name of *nheengatu;* generic designation for certain tribes of the seaboard.—Lima and Barroso, op. cit. See *Guaraní.*

Tupinambá.——"Generic designation of various Tupí tribes that, in the sixteenth century, inhabited the seacoast of Brazil."—Lima and Barroso, op. cit.

tutú.——Goblin with which children are frightened.

tutú (tutu) de feijao.——Dish composed of salt pork, bacon, beans, and manihot flour.

tutú-marambá.——A goblin.

uauiara.——Indian name of a demon supposed to interfere in the process of generation; it took the form of a fish, the *boto* (q.v.). See p. 121, note 116.

Ubacas (Embacas).—African "nation."

umbauba.——See *embaiba.*

uru.——Bird of the *Odontophorinæ* family, which includes the American quails (*Odontophorus guiannensis Gm.*).

urú.——Afro-Brazilian condiment.

urucú.——Tropical American dye-yielding shrub of the *Bixaceæ* or Indian plum family (*Bixa orellana*), widely used by the Indians for dyeing purposes and body paint. It is orangish red in color. Known in English by the name *arnotto*, it produces the annotto of commerce.

urupema (urupemba).——Wicker-work sieve for use in cooking. See p. 464.

urupemba.——See *urupema.*

valentão (plural: valentões).——Literally, a valiant man; comes to mean a "bad man" in our wild west sense.

valentões.——See *valentão.*

vaqueiro.——Cowboy of northeastern Brazil.

vasculhadores (*basculhadores*).——Workers who make a specialty of cleaning roofs and high walls.

vatapá.——Dish made of manihot flour with dendê (palm) oil and pepper mixed with fish or meat.

Vatuas.——African people, also known as Zulus.

Vinagrada.——Term applied to the revolt in Pará in 1836. See p. 157, note 258.

Xangô.——Deity of an African fetish cult. See p. lxiii, note 11.

Xianos.——Term applied by the Indians to the Portuguese invaders.

xibamba.——A goblin.

xibé.——A food paste the base of which is flour and water. See p. 49, note 123.

xin-xin.——Dish consisting of a hen with dried shrimps, onions, jerimum kernels, and dendê (palm) oil.

xique-xique (*chique-chique*).——Plant of the *Opuntia* or cactus family, the *Opuntia brasiliensis* or the *Opuntia* in general. Euclides da Cunha identifies it as the *Cactus peruvianus*. See p. xix, note 3.

yayá.——Form of *iaiá* (q.v.).

Yebus.——African tribe.

Yorubas.——An African Negro people.

Zulus.——See *Vatuas.*

zumbí.——A ghostly apparition that wanders at night (Afro-Brazilian superstition).

BIBLIOGRAPHY

THE published items and manuscript documents included in this bibliography are, almost without exception, those to which reference is made in the text. The source-material is given first (manuscripts and other documents, lithographs, photographs, maps, plans of the Big Houses and sugar plantations, etc.), and following this the auxiliary or secondary material. In connection with the latter, books are listed first, followed by periodicals. As for those items, including documents and manuscripts, that provided the author with concrete and at times original and unused material, the majority of these sources have been indicated as accurately as possible in the notes accompanying the text, page-numbers being cited in the case of books. In addition there will be found listed below the books and periodicals of general interest that were most helpful in verifying the subject-matter of the present essay and in affording suggestions for the interpretations that are here attempted; this material has also been made use of for purposes of sociological comparison.

I

SOURCES: MANUSCRIPTS, DOCUMENTS, Etc.

Actas da Cámara de São Paulo, Vols. I–XXXII (Publications of the Prefecture of the Municipality of São Paulo).

"A discours of the West Indies and South Sea written by Lopez Vaz a Portugal borne in the citie of Elvas continued unto the yere 1587, etc.," *in the Principal Navigations Voyages Traffiques & Discoveries of the English Nation . . .* by Richard Hakluyt. New York, 1926; London, 1927.

Album Brésilien. Ludwig & Briggs (lithographs).

Album Carl (lithographs, with drawings by Schappriz).

Albums of photographs of the nineteenth century, from the collections of the following families: Sousa Leão (Pernambuco-Rio); Cavalcanti de Albuquerque (Pernambuco-Rio); Sousa-Bandeira (Pernambuco-Rio); Rocha Wanderley (Pernambuco); Albuquerque Mello (Pernambuco); Cunha Figueiredo (Pernambuco); Pereira de Lyra-Bivar (Ceará); Pires Albuquerque (Bahia); Albuquerque Maranhão (Rio Grande do Norte).

Almanack Administrativo, Mercantil, Industrial e Agricola da Provincia de Pernambuco. Rio de Janeiro.

Almanack de Lembranças Luso-Brasileiro. Lisbon.

Almanack do Brasil. Rio de Janeiro.

Almanack do Rio Grande do Sul (Ferreira Rodrigues).

Almanack dos Negociantes do Império do Brasil. Rio de Janeiro.

Almanacs, *see under* Pequeno.

ALMEIDA, J. M.: *Algumas Notas Genealógicas.* São Paulo, 1886.

Anais do 1°. Congresso Brasileiro de Eugenia. Rio, 1929.

ANCHIETA, PADRE JOSEPH DE: "Informação da Provincia do Brasil para Nosso Padre" (1585).

——: *"Informações e Fragmentos Históricos 1584–1586"*; in *Achegas para a História e Geographia,* by order of the Ministry of Finance, No. 1, Rio de Janeiro, 1886.

ANDRADE, JOSÉ BONIFÁCIO CALDEIRA DE, JR.: *Esboço de uma Higiene dos Colégios aplicavel aos nossos.* Thesis presented and sustained December 12, 1855, before the Faculty of Medicine of Rio de Janeiro. Rio de Janeiro, 1855.

ANTONIL, ANDRÉ JOÃO: *Cultura e Opulência do Brasil por suas Drogas e Minas.* With a bio-bibliographical study by Affonso de E. Taunay. São Paulo and Rio de Janeiro, 1923.

Archives of the Municipal Chamber of Sabará, 1782, in the manuscript collection of the Public Archives of Minas Geraes.

Arquivo do Distrito Federal (Publications of the Prefecture of the City of Rio de Janeiro). 1895–7.

ASSIER, ADOLPHE D': *Le Brésil contemporain—races—mœurs—institutions —paysages.* Paris, 1867.

Autobiography (MS.) of Dr. Cassio Barbosa de Resende. (Minas Geraes.)

Autobiography (MS.) of Higino Cunha. (Maranhão.)

Autobiography (MS.) of José Supertino Dantas. (Unha do Gato plantation, Sergipe.)

Autobiography (MS.) of Júlio de Albuquerque Bello. (Queimadas plantation, Pernambuco.)

Autobiography (MS.) of Leopoldo Lins. (Pernambuco.)

BARLEUS, GASPAR: *Rerum per Octennium in Brasilien.* 1660.

BARRETO, ANTÔNIO ALVES BRANCO MONIZ: *Guia de Leitura e Máximas Geraes de Conducta.* Rio de Janeiro, 1854.

BARRETO, JOÃO FRANCISCO PAES: *Uma Estatística.* (On the difference in ages between husband and wife in Pernambucan families.) Pernambuco, 1857.

BATES, HENRY WALTER: *The Naturalist on the River Amazon.* London, 1864.

BECKFORD, WILLIAM: *Excursion to the Monasteries of Batalha and Alcobaça.* London, 1835.

——: *Italy, with Sketches from Spain and Portugal.* London, 1834.

BELLO, JULIO: *Memórias de um Senhor de Engenho.* Rio de Janeiro, 1939.

BILDEN, RUEDIGER: "Race Relations in Latin America, with Special References to the Development of Indigenous Culture." Institute of Public Affairs, University of Virginia, 1931. (MS. of lecture.)

British and Foreign State Papers. London, 1825–41.

BURLAMAQUI, FREDERICO LEOPOLDO CESAR: *Memória Analýtica acerca do commércio d'escravos e acerca da escravidão doméstica.* Rio de Janeiro, 1837.

BURTON, RICHARD F.: *Explorations of the Highlands of the Brazil.* London, 1869.

Cake recipes, *see under* Modinhas, below.

CALDCLEUGH, ALEXANDER: *Travels in South America in the Years 1819, 1820, 1821. Containing an Account of the Present State of Brazil, Buenos Ayres and Chili.* London, 1825.

CALLADO, FREI MANUEL: *O Valeroso Lucideno.* Lisbon, 1648.

CANDLER, JOHN, and W. BURGESS: *Narrative of a Recent Visit to Brazil.* London, 1853.

Carapuceiro, O. (Recife, 1837–42.)

CARDIM, FERNÃO: *Tratados da Terra e Gente do Brasil.* Introduction and Notes by Baptista Caetano, Capistrano de Abreu, and Rodolfo Garcia. Rio de Janeiro, 1925.

Cartas de Datas de Terra, Vols. I–III. Publications of the Prefecture of the Municipality of São Paulo.

Cartas Jesuíticas (1550–68). Rio de Janeiro, 1887.

Cartas Syllábicas com Exercícios Paritaes (Nineteenth-century school text).

CEPEDA, PADRE: *Relatório,* in Luis Edmundo's *O Rio de Janeiro no Tempo dos Vice-Reis* (q.v., under Secondary Material: Books).

Chronicle of the Society of Jesus by Padre Jacinto de Carvalho. Manuscript in the Library of Evora. Cited in João Lúcio de Azevedo's *Os Jesuítas no Grão-Pará* (q.v., under Secondary Material: Books).

COELHO, DUARTE DE ALBUQUERQUE: *Memórias Diarias de la Guerra del Brasil.* Madrid, 1654. (Rare copy in the Oliveira Lima collection of the Library of the Catholic University of Washington.) *See under Letter, below.*

Collection of Manuscripts of the Historical Institute of Alagoas.

Collection of plants, drawings, and photographs of plantation Big Houses of the Serviço do Patrimônio Histórico e Artístico Nacional. Rio de Janeiro.

Collection of newspaper clippings in the private archives of Alberto Lamego of Campos, State of Rio.

COLTON, WALTER: *Deck and Port.* New York, 1850.

COREAL, FRANÇOIS: *Voyages aux Indes Occidentales . . . depuis 1666 jusqu'en 1697.* Amsterdam, 1722.

Correspondência da Corte. MS. in the Library of the State of Pernambuco.

COSTA, ANTONIO CORRÊA DE SOUSA: *Qual a alimentação de que vive a classe pobre do Rio de Janeiro e sua influencia sobre a mesma classe*. Rio de Janeiro, 1865. (Thesis.)

CREARY, REVERENDO: "Brasil under the Monarchy—A Record of Facts and Observation." MS. in the Library of Congress, Washington, D. C.

——: "Chronicas Lageanas." MS. in the Library of Congress, Washington, D. C.

CRÉVAUX, JULES: *Voyages dans l'Amérique du Sud*. Paris, 1883.

CUNHA, AUGUSTO LASSANCE: *Dissertação sobre a prostituição, em particular na Cidade do Rio de Janeiro*. Thesis presented to the Faculty of Medicine of Rio de Janeiro, 1845.

CUNHA, FRANCISCO: *Reminiscências*. Rio, 1914.

DAMPIER, WILLIAM: *Voyages . . . aux Terres Australes, à la Nouvelle Hollande &c., fait en 1699* (translation). Amsterdam, 1705.

DEBRET, J. B.: *Voyage pittoresque et historique au Brésil ou séjour d'un artiste française au Brésil depuis 1816 jusqu'en 1831 inclusivement, époques de l'avènement, et de l'abdication de S. M. D. Pedro Ier., fondateur de l'Empire brésilien*. Firmin-Didot, 1834–39. 3 vols.

DÉNIS, FERDINAND: *Brésil. Collection l'Univers*, Paris, 1739.

Diálogos das Grandezas do Brasil. Introduction by Capistrano de Abreu and Notes by Rodolfo Garcia. Edition of the Brazilian Academy of Letters, Rio de Janeiro, 1930.

Diario da Bahia (1835–38, 1877 —).

Diario do Rio de Janeiro (1821–78).

Diario de Pernambuco (1825 —).

DIAS, CICERO: *Jundiá*. MS. of an autobiographical novel in preparation.

Documentos Históricos (correspondence of governors-general, letters-patent, etc.). Publications of the National Library of Rio de Janeiro.

Documents in the *Revista do Arquivo Público* of the State of Rio Grande do Sul, Porto Alegre.

Documents in the *Revista do Arquivo Municipal* of São Paulo.

Documents in the *Revista do Arquivo Público Mineiro*, Belo-Horizonte.

Documents in the *Revista do Instituto Archeologico, Histórico e Geographico* (later, the *Revista do Instituto Arqueológico, Histórico e Geográfico Pernambucano*).

Documents in the *Revista do Instituto Histórico do Ceará*.

Documents in the *Revista do Instituto Histórico e Geográfico Brasileiro*, Rio de Janeiro.

Documents in the *Revista do Instituto Histórico*. Bahia.

Documents in the *Revista do Instituto Histórico* of Mato-Grosso.

Documents in the *Revista do Instituto Histórico de São Paulo*.

Documents in the *Anais do Arquivo Público da Baía*. Bahia.

Documents in the *Anais da Biblioteca Nacional do Rio de Janeiro*. Publications of The National Library, Rio de Janeiro.

Documents in the *Anais Brasilienses de Medicina* (Journal of The Imperial Academy of Medicine of Rio de Janeiro). Rio de Janeiro, 1835 —

Documents in the *Anais do Parlamento*. Rio de Janeiro.

Documents in the *Publicações do Arquivo Nacional*. Rio de Janeiro.

Documents in the *Revista Trimensal do Instituto Histórico e Geográfico da Santa Catarina*.

Documents in the *Anais do Museu Paulista*. São Paulo.

Documents (unpublished) found by Professor Roquette Pinto in the Archives of the Brazilian Historical and Geographic Institute (Archives of the Ultra-marine Council, Correspondence of the Governor of Mato Grosso, Codex 246).

Documents relating to Brazil in the period of the Dutch Invasion, in the Royal Archives of The Hague, published in the *Revista do Instituto Arqueológico, Histórico e Geográfico de Pernambuco*, No. 33, Recife, 1887; also, documents in the manuscript section of the Archeological Institute of Recife.

DUARTE, JOSÉ RODRIGUES DE LIMA: *Ensaio sobre a higiene da escravatura no Brasil*. Rio, 1849 (thesis).

Estatutos of the Colégio Nossa Senhora do Bom Conselho. Recife, 1859.

EVREUX, IVES D': *Voyages dans le nord du Brésil*. Leipzig and Paris, 1864.

EWBANK, THOMAS: *Life in Brazil, or a Journal of a Visit to the Land of Cocoa and the Palm*. New York, 1856.

FIGUEIRA, PADRE LUIS: *Relação do Maranhão, documentos para a história do Brasil especialmente do Ceará, 1608–1625*. Fortaleza, 1904.

FONSECA, BORGES DA: "Nobiliarchia Pernambucana." MS. in the Instituto Arqueolígico, Histórico e Geográfico de Pernambuco.

FONSECA, JOAQUIM MOREIRA DA: "Casamento e Eugenia," *Atas*, First Brazilian Eugenics Congress, Rio de Janeiro, 1929.

FONSECA, PEDRO P. DA: "Fundação de Alagoas—apontamentos históricos, biográficos e genealógicos." 1886 (unpublished paper).

"Fragmentos de uma Memória sobre as Sesmarias da Baía" (copy of a manuscript that appears to have been the property of the late Marquês de Aguiar, and which is possibly from his pen), in the *Livro das Terras ou Collecção da Lei, Regulamentos e Ordens Expedidos a respeito desta matéria até ao presente. . . .* 2nd edition, Rio de Janeiro, 1860.

FRÉZIER: *Rélation du voyage de la Mer du Sud aux côtes du Chily et du Perou, fait pendant les années 1712, 1713 et 1714*. Paris, 1716.

FROGER: *Relation d'un Voyage fait en 1695, 1696 et 1697, aux côtei d'Afrique, Détroit de Magellan, Brésil, Cayenne et les Isles Antilles par une escadre des vaisseaux du Roy commandée par Monsieur de Gennes*. Paris, 1700.

GAMA, PADRE MIGUEL DO SACRAMENTO LOPES: *O Carapuceiro*. Recife, 1832–7, 1843, 1847.

——: *Poesias Sacras*.

GANDAVO, PERO DE MAGALHÃES DE: *História da Provincia de Santa Cruz e que vulgarmente chamamos Brasil.* Rio de Janeiro, 1924.

GARDNER, GEORGE: *Travels in the Interior of Brazil, Principally through the North of Provinces.* London, 1846.

Gazeta do Rio de Janeiro (1808–22).

Genealogical data on some of the most important families of Minas, collected by Luis Pinto. (MS. in the private collection of the family, Minas Geraes.)

GRAHAM, MARIA: *Journal of a Voyage to Brazil and Residence There during the years 1821, 1822, 1823.* London, 1824.

HAKLUYT, RICHARD: *The Principal Navigations Voyages Traffiques & Discoveries of the English Nation.* New York, 1926; London, 1927.

HENRIQUES, DR. FRANCISCO DA FONSECA: *Soccorro Delfico aos Clamores da Natureza Humana . . .* Amsterdam, 1731.

"Historia Profana, pela Mithologia, pelas Novellas e pela Geographia," cited by Padre Gama: *O Carapuceiro* (see *Carapuceiro*, above).

Idade de Ouro do Brasil (Bahia, May 14, 1811).

IMBERT, J. B. A.: *Ensaio Hygienico e Medico sobre o Clima do Rio de Janeiro e o Regime Alimentar de seus Habitantes.* Rio de Janeiro, 1837.

——: *Guia Medico das Mães de Familia, ou a Infancia considerada na sua hygiene, suas molestias e tratamentos.* Rio de Janeiro, 1843.

——: *Manual do Fazendeiro ou Tratado Domestico sobre as enfermidades dos Negros.* Rio de Janeiro, 1839.

——: "Uma palavra sobre o charlatanismo e os charlatães." Rio de Janeiro, 1837.

Inventories and Wills, Archives of the State of São Paulo, 1920–1.

Inventories, Archives of the Registry Office of Ipojuca.

JOBIM, JOSÉ MARTINS DA CRUZ: "Discurso inaugural que na sessão publica da installação da Sociedade de Medicina do Rio de Janeiro recitou. . . ." Rio de Janeiro, 1830.

——: "Discurso sobre as molestias que mais affligem a classe pobre do Rio de Janeiro (lido na sessão publica da Sociedade de Medicina a 30 de Junho de 1835). . . ." Rio de Janeiro, 1835.

Jornal do Comercio (Rio de Janeiro), 1827 —.

KIDDER, D. P., and FLETCHER, J. C.: *Brazil and the Brazilians.* Boston, 1879.

KINDERSLEY, MRS.: *Letters from the Islands of Teneriff, Brazil, the Cape of Good Hope, and the East Indies.* London, 1777.

KOCH-GRUNBERG, THEODORE: *Zwei Jahre unter den Indianern.* Stuttgart, 1908–10.

KOSTER, HENRY: *Travels in Brazil.* London, 1916.

KRAUSE, FRITZ: *In den Wildnissen Brasiliens.* Leipzig, 1911.

LA BARBINAIS, LE GENTIL DE: *Nouveau Voyage autour du mond par M. Le Gentil enrichi de plusieurs plais, vues et perspectives des principales villes et ports du Perou, Chily, Brésil et de la Chine.* Amsterdam, 1728.

LA CAILLE, ABBÉ DE: *Journal historique du voyage fait au Cap de Bonne Espérance.* Paris, 1763.

LAET, JOÃO DE: *História ou Annaes dos Feitos da Companhia Privilegiada das Indias Occidentaes desde o seu começo até o fim de 1636.* Leyden, 1644.

LAVRÁDIO, MARQUÊS DO: Portaria de 6 de agosto de 1771, cited by Alfredo de Carvalho: *Frases e Palavras—Problemas Históricos e Etimológicos.* Recife, 1900.

Letter of Amerigo Vespucci, in Capistrano de Abreu's *O Descobrimento do Brasil.* Rio de Janeiro, 1883.

Letter of Duarte Coelho to His Majesty, in *História da Colonização Portuguesa do Brasil.* Lisbon, 1924. *See under Coelho, above.*

Letter of Pero Vaz de Caminha, in Manuel de Cazal's *Chorographia Brasilica.* 2nd edition, Rio de Janeiro, 1833.

Letter Royal of September 3, 1709, and Proclamation of 1740, in Maranhão, in Agostinho Marquês Perdigão Malheiro's *A Escravidão no Brasil, ensaio jurídico-histórico-social.* Rio de Janeiro, 1866.

Letters and dispatches of Richard Gumbleton Daunt (MS. in the Archives of the Brazilian Historical and Geographic Institute).

Letters, decrees, and patents, 1711–1824 (MS. in the Library of the State of Pernambuco).

Letters Royal, document No. 881-bis, MS. section of the National Library, Rio de Janeiro.

LÉRY, JEAN DE: *Histoire d'un voyage faict en la terre du Brésil* (nouvelle édition avec une introduction et des notes par Paul Gaffarel). Paris, 1770.

Lições Elementares de Arithmetica by "Hum Brasileiro." Rio de Janeiro, 1825.

LINDLEY, THOMAS: *Narrative of a Voyage to Brazil . . . with General Sketches of the Country, its Natural Productions, Colonial Inhabitants and a Description of the City and Provinces of St. Salvador and Porto Seguro.* London, 1825.

LOBO, ROBERTO JORGE HADDOCK: "Discurso recitado em presença de S. M. o Imperador na sessão solemne anniversaria da Academia Imperial de Medicina, Rio, a 30 de Julho de 1847, seguido de reflexões acerca da mortalidade da cidade do Rio de Janeiro." Rio de Janeiro, 1847.

LUCCOCK, JOHN: *Notes on Rio de Janeiro and the Southern Parts of Brazil, Taken during a Residence of Ten Years in that Country from 1808 to 1818.* London, 1820.

LUNA, PADRE-MESTRE LINO DO MONTE CARMELLO: "A Benção do Engenho Maçauassú." Recife, 1869.

MACEDO, JOÃO ALVARES DE AZEVEDO, JR.: *Da Prostituição do Rio de Janeiro e de sua Influencia sobre a Saude Pública.* Thesis presented to the Faculty of Medicine of Rio de Janeiro, 1869.

MAIA, MANOEL A. VELHO DA MOTTA: *O Conde de Motta Maia.* Rio de Janeiro, 1937.

MANSFIELD, CHARLES B.: *Paraguay, Brazil and the Plate.* Cambridge, 1856.

Manuscript of Max Schmidt, in the Barbero Museum, Asunción, Paraguay.

Manuscript of Memoirs of the Guimarães Peixoto family (1800–50).

Manuscript of the intimate diary of L. L. Vauthier (1840–46).

Manuscript on conversions, in the Archives of the Archæological, Historical and Geographic Institute of Pernambuco.

Manuscript in the private collection of M. de Oliveira Lima (Washington).

Manuscripts of the family archives of the Engenho Itapuá (Paraíba do Norte).

Manuscripts of the family archives of the Fazenda Forquilha (Rio de Janeiro).

Manuscripts on the English, in the Archives of the Archæological, Historical and Geographic Institute of Pernambuco.

Manuscripts in the archives of the Capitão-Mor Manoel Thomé de Jesus, Engenho Noruega (Pernambuco).

Manuscripts. *See also under Collection.*

Map (topographic) showing the demarcation made in the year 1779 of the lands belonging to the Engenho da Aldeia de Serinhaem (Pernambuco). (Author's collection.)

MARCONDES, MOYSÉS: *Pai e Patrono.* Rio, 1926.

MARTIUS, C. F. P. VON: *Beiträge zur Ethnographie und Sprachenkunde America's zumal Brasiliens.* Leipzig, 1867.

—— and SPIX, J. B. VON: *Travels in Brazil* (translation). London, 1824.

MATHISON, GILBERT FARQHAR: *Narrative of a Visit to Brazil, Chili, Peru and the Sandwich Islands during the years 1821 and 1822.* London, 1825.

MAWE, JOHN: *Travels in the Interior of Brazil.* Philadelphia, 1816.

MELLO, FELIX CAVALCANTI DE ALBUQUERQUE: "Livro de assentos particulares" (book of special memoranda), begun in Olinda, March 1, 1843. (MS.)

MENDONCA, MARCOS DE: *O Intendente Câmara* (1764–1835). Rio de Janeiro, 1936.

Modinhas, book of, formerly the property of Cicero Brasileiro de Mello. (MS. in the private collection of the family, Recife.)

Modinhas and cake recipes, book of, formerly the property of Geroncio Dias de Arruda Falcâo. (MS. in the private collection of the family, Recife.)

Monitor Campista (1834–1929; 1931 —), Campos, State of Rio.

MOREAU, PIERRE: *Histoire des derniers troubles du Brésil.* Paris, 1651.

NIEUHOF, JOHN: *Voyages and Travels into Brazil and the East Indies* (translation). London, 1703.

NOBREGA, PADRE MANUEL DA: *Cartas do Brasil (1549–60)*. Rio de Janeiro, 1931.

OLIVEIRA, CÂNDIDO BAPTISTA DE: *Compêndio de Arithmética*. Rio de Janeiro, 1832.

Ordenações Filipinas, L. V, tit. III.

PADILHA, FRANCISCO FERNANDES: *Qual o regime das classes pobres do Rio de Janeiro?* (thesis). Rio, 1852.

Parliamentary Papers (London), especially *Reports from Committees, Sugar and Coffee, Planting, House of Commons, Session 1847–8.*

Pastoral letter (unpublished) of Dom Frei José Fialho, of February 19, 1726. (MS. in the Archives of the Cathedral of Olinda.)

Pastoral letter of Dom Frei José Fialho, "Given in the City of Santo Antônio de Recife . . . on the 16th day of the month of August 1738. (MS. in the Archives of the Cathedral of Olinda.)

Pequeno Almanack do Rio de Janeiro. Rio de Janeiro.

PEREIRA, JOSÉ LUCIANO, JR.: *Algumas considerações sobre . . . o regime das classes abastadas do Rio de Janeiro em seus alimentos e bebidas.* Thesis presented to the Faculty of Medicine of Rio de Janeiro, 1850.

Photographs. *See under Albums; see under Collection.*

PICANÇO, JOSÉ CORRÊA: *Ensaio sobre os perigos das sepulturas dentro das cidades e seus contornos.* 1812.

PIMENTEL, ANTÔNIO MARTINS DE AZEVEDO: *Quais os melhoramentos que devem ser introduzidos no Rio de Janeiro*, etc. Thesis presented to the Faculty of Medicine of Rio de Janeiro, 1884.

PINTO, E. ROQUETTE: "Notas sobre os Tipos Antropológicos do Brasil," in the *Atas e Trabalhos*, First Brazilian Eugenics Congress, Rio de Janeiro, 1929
——: *Rondônia*. Rio de Janeiro, 1929.

PISONIS, G.: *História Naturalis Brasiliæ*. Amsterdam, 1648.

Plants of the Grujaú de Baixo and Grujaú de Cima (Pernambuco) and other plantations, comprising the lands formerly in the possession of Arnau d'Olanda. (MS. dating from the end of the eighteenth century, formerly in the archives of the Engenho dos Bois (Noruega) and now in the author's collection.)

POMBAL, MARQUÊS DE: Decree relating to the marriage of Portuguese colonists and Indian women, contemporary copy in the manuscript section of the Archæological, Historical and Geographic Institute of Pernambuco.

Primeira Visitação do Santo Ofício às Partes do Brasil pelo Licenciado Heitor Furtado de Mendonça; Confissões da Baía—1591–2. São Paulo, 1927 (in the Eduardo Prado series, edited by Paulo Prado, with an Introduction by Capistrano de Abreu).

Primeira Visitação do Santo Ofício às Partes do Brasil, etc.; *Denunciações da Baía*—1591-3. São Paulo, 1925 (Eduardo Prado series, with an Introduction by Capistrano de Abreu).

Primeira Visitação do Santo Ofício às Partes do Brasil, etc.; *Denunciações de Pernambuco*—1593-5. Sãn Paulo, 1929 (Eduardo Prado series, with an Introduction by Rodolfo Garcia).

PURSER, THOMAS GRIGS: "Certain Notes of the Voyage to Brazil with the Minion of London . . . in the yere 1580," *in The Principal Navigations Voyages Traffiques & Discoveries of the English Nation . . .* by Richard Hakluyt. New York, 1926; London, 1927.

RADIGUET, MAX: *Souvenirs de l'Amérique Espagnole.* Paris, 1848.

REBOUÇAS, ANDRÉ: *Diário e Notas Autobiográficas*, annotated by Ana Flora and Ignácio José Veríssimo. Rio de Janeiro, 1940.

REGADAS, JOSÉ MARIA RODRIGUES: *Regime das Classes Abastadas no Rio de Janeiro e seus Alimentos e Bebidas.* Thesis presented to the Faculty of Medicine of Rio de Janeiro, 1852.

Recipes. *See under Modinhas; see under Sweetmeat recipes.*

Register of Land Grants and Allotments, 1689-1730. MS. in the Public Library of the State of Pernambuco.

Register-General of the Chamber of the City of São Paulo, Vols. I-XXIII (Publications of the Prefecture of the Municipality of São Paulo).

Relatório da Commissão de Salubridade Geral da Sociedade de Medicina do Rio de Janeiro sobre as Causas de Infecção da Athmosphera da Côrte. Rio de Janeiro, 1832.

RENDU, A.: *Études sur le Brésil.* Paris, 1848.

RENNEFORT, SOUCHU DE: *Histoire des Indes Orientales.* Paris, 1688.

Report of Schonemburgh and Haecks: *Sacken van Staet en Oorlogh in Ende Ontrent de Veroenidge, Nederlanden, Regions Beginninde met het Jaer 1658.* The Hague, 1669.

Reports of consuls (MSS. in the Archives of the State of Pernambuco).

Reports of consuls (MSS. in the Archives of the State of Bahia).

REUTER, E. B.: *The American Race Problem.* New York, 1927.

REYNAL, ABBÉ: *Histoire philosophique et politique des établissements et du commerce des Européens dans les deux Indes.* Geneva, 1775.

RODRIGUES, NINA: *Regime Alimentar no Norte do Brasil.* Maranhão, 1881.

ROQUETTE, J. I.: *Código do Bom Tom.* Paris, 1845.

RUGENDAS, MAURICE: *Voyage pittoresque dans le Brésil, par Maurice Rugendas, traduit de l'allemand par M. de Golbery, conseiller à la court royale de Colmar, correspondant de l'Institut, membre de plusieurs sociétés savantes, Chevalier de la Légion d'Honneur. Publié par Engelmant et Cie.*, Paris et Mulhouse, 1835.

SAINT-HILAIRE, AUGUSTE DE: *Voyages dans l'intérieur du Brésil.* 1852.

SAINT MARTIAL: *Au Brésil.* Paris, without date.

SALVADOR, FREI VICENTE DO: *História do Brasil,* edition revised by Capistrano de Abreu. S. Paulo and Rio de Janeiro, 1918.

SANTA THEREZA, D. FREI LUIS DE: Relatorio à Sua Santidade (MS., a copy of which is preserved in the Archives of the Cathedral of Olinda). *See, also, under Manuscript.*

SCHMIDT, MAX: *Indianerstudien in Zentralbrasilien.* Berlin, 1905.

SERPA, JOAQUIM JERÔNYMO: *Tratado de Educação Physica-Moral dos Meninos.*

SIGAUD, J. F. X.: *Du climat et des maladies du Brésil.* Paris, 1844.

SILVA, FRUCTUOSO PINTO DA: Thesis on the problem of morality and sexual hygiene in boarding-schools, presented to the Faculty of Medicine of Bahia, to be sustained there in November 1869.

SILVA, MANUEL VIEIRA DA (Barão de Alvaesar): *Reflexões sobre alguns dos meios propostos por mais conducentes para melhorar o clima na cicade do Rio de Janeiro.* 1808.

Simão de Mantua ou o Mercador de Feiras.

SIQUEIRA, JOSÉ DE GOES E: *Breve Estudo sobre a Prostituição e a Sífilis no Brasil.* Rio de Janeiro, 1877.

SMITH, HERBERT S.: *Do Rio de Janeiro à Cuiabá* (with a chapter by Karl von den Steinen on the capital of Mato-Grosso). Rio de Janeiro, 1922.

SOUSA, ANTONIO JOSÉ DE: *Do Regime das classes pobres e dos escravos na cidade do Rio de Janeiro, em seus alimentos e bebidas. Qual a influencia desse regime sobre a saude.* Thesis presented to the Faculty of Medicine of Rio de Janeiro, 1851.

SOUSA, FRANCISCO ANTÔNIO DOS SANTOS: *Alimentação na Baía—Suas Consequências.* Thesis presented to the Faculty of Medicine of Bahia, 1910.

SOUSA, GABRIEL SOARES DE: *Tratado Descriptivo do Brasil em 1587,* edition of F. A. Varnhagen, *Revisto do Instituto Histórico e Geográfico Brasileiro,* tomo XIV. Rio de Janeiro, 1851.

SOUSA, THOME DE: Prescript (MS. in the Public Library of the State of Pernambuco).

STADEN, HANS: *Warhaftig Historia vnd beschreibung eyner Landtschafft der Wilden, Nacketen, Grimmigen, Menschfresser Leuten, in der Newenwelt America gelegen, vor und nach Christi geburt in Land zu Hessen vnbckant, biss uff dise ij. nechstvergangene jar, Da sie Hans Staden von Homberg auss Hessen durch sein eygne erfarung erkant, vnd yetzo durch den truck an tag gibt,* etc. Marburg, 1557.

——: *Viagem ao Brasil.* Portuguese version of the Marburg text of 1557, by Alberto Löfgren, revised and annotated by Theodoro Sampaio. Rio de Janeiro, 1930.

——: *Duas Viagens ao Brasil. Arrojadas aventuras no século XVI entre os antropófagos do Novo Mundo,* based upon the modern German text of Fouquet and translated by Guiomar de Carvalho Franco, with an Introduction and Notes by Francisco de Assis Carvalho Franco. São

Paulo, 1942 (Publications of the Sociedade Hans Staden of São Paulo, Vol. III).

NOTE.—Staden's work, commonly known as the "True History," is the first book published on Brazil. Eleven Portuguese editions have appeared, 1892–1942, all of them printed in Brazil. There are two English translations, one by Richard Burton and one by Malcolm Letts (see p. xl, note 53). For a complete bibliography to date, see the article by C. Fouquet: "Bibliografia da 'Verdadeira Historia' de Hans Staden," *Boletim Bibliográfico* (Biblioteca Pública Municipal de São Paulo), No. 4, 1944, pp. 7–31.

Statutes (*Compromissos*) of the Confraternity of Nossa Senhora de Guadalupe de Sergipe.

Statutes of Confraternities (Pereira da Costa MSS. in the Public Library of the State of Pernambuco).

STEINEN, KARL VON DEN: *Unter den Indianern Zentral-Brasiliens.* Berlin, 1894.

Sweetmeat recipes of Dona Angelina Barros Andrade Lima (MS.)

"Synopsis de Sesmárias registradas nos livros existentes no Archivo da Thesouraria da Fazenda da Bahia" (Publications of the National Archives, XXVII), with a preface by Alcides Bezerra.

TAUNAY, C. A.: *Manual do Agricultor Brasileiro.* Rio de Janeiro, 1839.

Theses. (See under Andrade, Jr.; José Bonifácio Caldeira de; Cunha, Augusto Lassance; Duarte, José Rodrigues de Lima; Macedo, Jr., João Alvares de Azevedo; Padilha, Francisco Fernandes; Pereira, Jr., José Luciano; Pimentel, Antônio Martins de Azevedo; Regadas, José Maria Rodrigues; Silva, Fructuoso Pinto da; Sousa, Antônio José de; Sousa, Francisco Antônio dos Santos.)

THÉVET, ANDRÉ: *Les Singularitez de la France antarctique autrement nommée Amérique. . . .* Paris, 1878.

VASCONCELLOS, PADRE SIMÃO DE: *Chrónica da Companhia de Jesus do Estado do Brasil,* etc. with an Introduction by Canon Fernandes Pinheiro. 2nd edition, Rio de Janeiro, 1864.

——: *Vida do Parde Veneravel Ioseph de Anchieta da Companhia de Iesu, Taumaturgo do Novo Mundo na Província do Brasil . . .* Lisbon, 1672.

VESPUCCI, AMERIGO. (See under Letter.)

"Viagem a Portugal dos Cavaleiros Trom e Lipomani" (1580), translated by Alexandre Herculano, *Opusculos.* Lisbon, 1897.

VIANNA, AZEVEDO CESAR DE SAMPAIO: *Qual a causa da frequência das ascites na Baía?* Thesis presented to the Faculty of Medicine of Bahia, 1850.

VILHENA, LUIS DOS SANTOS: *Recompilação de Noticias Soteropolitanas e Brasílicas* (for the year 1802). Bahia, 1901.

Voyage du Marseille à Lima et dans les autres Indes Occidentales. Paris, 1720.

WALLACE, ALFRED R.: *A Narrative of Travels on the Amazon and Rio Negro.* London, 1852.
WALSH, R.: *Notices of Brazil in 1828 and 1829.* London, 1830; Boston, 1831.
WHITE, JOHN: *Journal of a Voyage to New South Wales.* London, 1790.
Will of the Capitão-Mor Manoel Thomé de Jesus. (MS. in the archives of the Engenho Noruega, Pernambuco.)
Wills (MSS. in the archives of the Ipojuca registry office).

II

SECONDARY MATERIAL: BOOKS

ABREU, J. CAPISTRANO DE: *Capítulos de História Colonial.* 1928.
——: *O Descobrimento do Brasil,* Rio de Janeiro, 1922.
ALENCAR, JOSÉ DE: *Mãe.* Rio de Janeiro, 1862.
——: *Lucíola.* Rio de Janeiro, without date.
——: *Senhora.* Rio de Janeiro, without date.
——: *O Demônio Familiar.* Rio de Janeiro, without date.
——: *O Tronco do Ipê.* Rio de Janeiro, 1871.
——: *Sonhos d'Oiro.* Rio de Janeiro, without date.
——: *Pata da Gazela.* Rio de Janeiro, without date.
ALMEIDA, JOSÉ AMÉRICO DE: *A Bagaceira.* Paraiba, 1927.
——: *A Paraíba e Seus Problemas.* Paraíba, 1923.
ALMEIDA, MANUEL ANTÔNIO DE: *Memórias de um Sargento de Milicias.* Rio de Janeiro, 1863.
ALMEIDA, PIRES DE: *L'Instruction publique au Brésil.* Rio de Janeiro, 1889.
ALMEIDA, RENATO: *Historia da Música Brasileira.* 2nd. ed., Rio de Janeiro, 1942.
ALTAMIRA, RAFAEL: *Filosofia de la Historia y Teoria de la Civilización.* Madrid, 1915.
AMARAL, AZEVEDO: *Ensaios Brasileiros.* Rio de Janeiro, 1930.
AMARAL, F. P. DO: *Escavações.* Recife, 1884.
AMADO, GILBERTO: *Grãos de Areia.* Rio de Janeiro, 1919.
ANDRADE, MARIO DE: *Compêndio de História da Música.* São Paulo, 1929.
——: *Ensaio sobre Música Brasileira.* São Paulo, 1928.
"Annual Production of Animals for Food and per capita Consumption of Meat in the United States." U. S. Department of Agriculture (1905), in Ruy Coutinho: *O Valor Social da Alimentação.*
Anuário Estatístico de Pernambuco. Recife, 1929–1930.

APERT, EUGÈNE: *La Croissance*, in Sorokin: *Social Mobility*.

AQUINAS, THOMAS: *Summa Theologica*.

ARAGÃO, EGAS MONIZ DE: *Contribution à l'étude de la syphilis au Brésil*, in Oscar da Silva Araujo: *Alguns Comentários sobre a Sífilis no Rio de Janeiro*.

ARARIPE, J.: *Gregório de Matos*. Rio de Janeiro, 1894.

ARAUJO, OSCAR DA SILVA: *Alguns Comentários sobre a Sífilis no Rio de Janeiro*. Rio de Janeiro, 1928.

——: *Subsídios ao Estudo da Framboesia Trópica*. Rio de Janeiro, 1928.

ARINOS, AFFONSO: *Lendas e Tradições Brasileiras*. São Paulo, 1917.

ARMITAGE, F. P.: *Diet and Race*. London, 1922.

ARROYO, ANTONIO: "O povo português," in *Notas sobre Portugal*. Lisbon, 1908.

ASSIS, MACHADO DE: *Memórias Póstumas de Braz Cubas*. Rio de Janeiro, 1881.

——: *Helena*. Rio de Janeiro, 1929.

——: *Iaiá Garcia*. Rio de Janeiro, without date.

——: *D. Casmurro*. Rio de Janeiro, without date.

ATHAYDE, TRISTÃO, DE: *Estudos*, 1st series. Rio de Janeiro, 1927.

AZEVEDO, JOÃO LÚCIO DE: "Algumas Nôtas relativas a pontos de história social," in *Miscelânea de Estudos em Homenagem de D. Carolina Michaelis de Vasconcellos*. Coimbra, 1930.

——: *Épocas de Portugal Econômico*. Lisbon. 1929.

——: *História dos Cristãos-Novos Portugueses*. Lisbon, 1922.

——: "Organização Econômica," in *Historia de Portugal*, edição monumental, Vol. III. Barcellos, 1931.

——: *Os Jesuitas no Grão-Pará, suas Missões e a Colonização*. 2nd edition, Coimbra, 1930.

AZEVEDO, PEDRO DE: "Os Primeiros Donatários," in *História da Colonização do Brasil*. Lisbon.

BAENA, ANTONIO LADISLAU MONTEIRO: *Ensaio Chorográphico sobre a Província do Pará*. Pará, 1839.

BAKER, JOHN: *Sex in Man and Animals*. London, 1926.

BALBI, ADRIEN: *Essai statistique sur le Portugal*. Paris, 1822.

BALLAGHE, J. C.: *A History of Slavery in Virginia*. Baltimore, 1902.

BANDEIRA, J. C. SOUSA: *Evoluções e Outros Escritos*. Rio de Janeiro, 1920.

BAPTISTA, V.: *Vitaminas e Avitaminoses*. São Paulo, 1934.

BARATTA, CÔNEGO JOSÉ DO CARMO: *Historia Eclesiastica de Pernambuco*. Recife, 1922.

BARROS, GAMA: *Historia da Administração Pública Moderna em Portugal nos séculos XV e XVI*. Lisbon, 1896.

BARROS, J. J. SOARES DE: "Memorias sobre as Causas da Diferente População de Portugal em Diferentes Tempos da Monarquia Portuguesa," in *Memórias Econômicas da Academia Real das Ciências*. 2nd edition, Lisbon, 1885.

BARROS, PAULO DE MORAES: *Impressões do Nordeste*. São Paulo, 1923.
BARROSO, GUSTAVO: *Terra de Sol*. Rio de Janeiro, 1913.
BAUR, ERWIN, EUGEN FISCHER and FRITZ LENTZ: *Human Heredity* (translation, with additions by the authors). London, 1931.
BEAN, R. R.: *The Races of Man*. New York, 1932.
BELL, AUBREY F. G.: *Portugal of the Portuguese*. London, 1915.
BELLO, JÚLIO: A comedy (see p. 268, note 191), special edition of the *Revista do Norte*, edited by José Maria Carneiro de Albuquerque e Mello.
BÉRINGER, EMILE: *Estudos sobre o Clima e a Mortalidade da Captial de Pernambuco* (translated by Manuel Duarte Pereira). Pernambuco, 1891.
BERNARD, JOHN: *Retrospection of America (1797–1811)*. New York, 1887.
BEVILAQUA, CLOVIS: "Instituições e Costumes Jurídicos dos Indígenas Brasileiros no Tempo da Conquista," in Martins, Jr.: *História do Direito Nacional*. Rio de Janeiro, 1895.
BOAS, FRANZ: *Anthropology and Modern Life*. London, 1929.
——: *Changes in Bodily Form of Descendants of Immigrants*, Senate Documents, Washington, 1910–11.
——: *The Mind of Primitive Man*. New York, 1911.
BOGART, ERNEST LUDLOW: *Economic History of the United States*. New York, 1913.
BOLDRINI, M.: *Biometrica, Problemi della Vita, della Specie e degli Individui*. Padua, 1928.
BOMFIM, MANUEL: *América Latina*, 1913.
——: *O Brasil na América*. Rio de Janeiro, 1929.
——: *O Brasil na Historia*. Rio de Janeiro, 1931.
BONIFÁCIO, JOSÉ: *Representação à Assembléia Geral Constituinte*, in Alberto de Sousa: *Os Andradas*. São Paulo, 1922.
BORGES, DURVAL ROSA: *Estudos sobre Sífilis com especial referencia à classe media paulistana*. Rio de Janeiro, 1941.
BOTSFORD, JAY BARRETT: *English Society in the Eighteenth Century as Influenced from Oversea*. New York, 1924.
BOULE, MARCELLIN: *Les Hommes fossiles*, in Mendes Corrêa: *Os Povos Primitivos da Lusitania*. Porto, 1924.
BRAGA, THEÓPHILO: *O Povo Português*. Lisbon, 1885.
BRANDÃO, ULYSSES: *A Confederação do Equador*. Pernambuco, 1924.
BRANDÃO, F. A., JR.: *A Escravatura no Brasil, precedida de um artigo sobre agricultura e colonização no Maranhão*. Brussels, 1865.
BRIFFAULT, ROBERT: *The Mothers*. London and New York, 1927.
BROWN, ISAAC: *O Normotipo Brasileiro*. Rio de Janeiro, 1934.
BROWN, W. LANGDON: *The Endocrines in General Medicine*. London, 1927.
BRUCE, P. A.: *Economic History of Virginia in the Seventeenth Century*. New York, 1895.
BRUNHES, JEAN: *La Géographie humaine*. Paris, 1912.

BRYCE, JAMES: *The Relations of the Advanced and Backward Races of Mankind.* Oxford, 1902.

——: *South America—Observations and Impressions.* London, 1911.

BUCKLE, HENRY THOMAS: *Bosquejo de una Historia del Intelecto Español* (translation). Madrid, without date.

BURET, F.: *La Syphilis aujourd'hui et chez les anciens.* Paris, 1890.

CALHOUN, ARTHUR W.: *A Social History of the American Family from Colonial Times to the Present.* Cleveland, 1918.

CALMON, PEDRO: *Historia da Civilização Brasileira.* Rio de Janeiro, 1933.

CALOGERAS, JOÃO PANDIÁ: *Formação Histórica do Brasil.* Rio de Janeiro, 1930.

——: *Os Jesuitas e o Ensino.* Rio de Janeiro, 1911.

CANNON, WALTER B.: *Bodily Changes in Pain, Hunger, Fear and Rage.* New York and London, 1929.

CAPTAIN, L., and HENRI LORIN: *Le Travail en Amérique avant et après Colomb.* Paris, 1930.

CARDOSO, FONSECA: "Anthropologia Portuguesa," in *Notas sobre Portugal.* Lisbon, 1908.

CARPENTER, EDWARD: *Intermediate Types among Primitive Man.*

CARVALHO, ALFREDO DE: *Frases e Palavras—Problemas Históricos e Etimológicos.* Recife, 1900.

CASTRO, JOSUÉ DE: "O Problema Fisiológico da Alimentação Brasileira." Recife, 1933.

CAZAL, MANUEL AYRES DE:—*Chorographia Brasilica.* 2nd edition, Rio de Janeiro, 1833.

CEREJEIRA, M. GONÇALVES: *O Humanismo em Portugal—Clenardo.* Coimbra, 1926.

CÉU, SOROR VIOLANTE DO: *Parnaso de Divinos e Humanos Versos.* Lisbon, 1733. In Leite de Vasconcellos: *Ensaios Etnográficos.* Lisbon, 1910.

CHAMBERLAIN, ALEXANDER FRANCIS: *The Child and Childhood in Folk-Thought.* New York, 1896.

——: *The Child.* 3rd edition, London, 1926.

CHAMBERLAIN, HOUSTON STEWART: *The Foundations of the Nineteenth Century.* London, 1911.

CHAVES, LUIZ: *O Amor Português—O Namoro, o Casamento, a Familia.* Lisbon, without date.

——: *Lendas de Portgual.* Porto, 1924.

——: *Páginas Folclóricas.* Lisbon, 1929.

CHILD, C. N.: *Physiological Foundations of Behaviour.* New York, 1925.

CINTRA, ASSIS: *As Amantes do Imperador.* Rio de Janeiro, 1933.

CLARK, OSCAR: *Sífilis no Brasil e suas manifestações viscerais.* Rio de Janeiro, 1918.

COMTE, CHARLES: *Traité de Législation ou Exposition des Lois Générales suivant lesquelles les peuples prospèrent ou restent stationnaires.* Paris, 1735.

CONSIGLIERE, PEDROSO: *As Mouras Encantadas.*

CORNILLI, J. J. J.: *Recherches chronologiques et historiques sur l'origine et la propagation de la fièvre jaune aux Antilles.* Paris, without date.

CORRÊA, GASPAR: *Lendas da India.*

CORRÊA, MENDES: *A Nova Antropologia Criminal.* Porto, 1931.

——: *Os Criminosos Portugueses.* Lisbon, 1914.

——: *Os Povos Primitivos da Lusitania.* Porto, 1924.

——: *Raça e Nacionalidade.* Porto, 1919.

COSTA, PEREIRA DA: *Origens Históricas Modernas da Industria Açucareira de Pernambuco.* Recife, 1905.

COUTINHO, RUY: *Valor Social da Alimentação.* São Paulo, 1935.

COUTY, LOUIS: *L'Esclavage au Brésil.* Paris, 1881.

COWAN, ANDREW REID: *Master Clues in World History.* London, 1914.

COWDRY, EDMUND V., ALES HRDLICKA, and others: *Human Biology and Racial Welfare.* New York.

CRAWLEY, ERNEST: *Studies of Savages and Sex,* edited by Theodore Besterman. New York, 1927.

——: *The Mystic Rose,* edited by Theodore Besterman. New York, 1927.

CRULS, GASTÃO: *A Amazonia Que Eu Vi,* Rio de Janeiro, 1930.

CUNHA, EUCLIDES DA: *Os Sertões.* Rio de Janeiro, 1902.

CUNNINGHAM, J. P.: *Modern Biology, a Review of the Principal Phenomena of Animal Life in Relation to Modern Concepts and Theories.* London, 1928.

DALGADO, D. G.: *Lord Byron's Childe Harold's Pilgrimage to Portugal.* Lisbon, 1919.

——: *The Climate of Portugal.* Lisbon, 1914.

DANTAS, JÚLIO: *Figuras de Ontem e de Hoje.* Lisbon, 1914.

DAVENPORT, F. B.: *Heredity in Relation to Eugenics.* New York, 1911.

—— and MORRIS STEGGERDA: *Race Crossing in Jamaica.* Washington, 1929.

DEBBANÉ, NICOLAS J.: "L'Influence arabe dans la formation historique, la litterature et la civilization du peuple brésilien." Cairo, 1911.

DELAFAGE-BREHIER, JULIE: *Les Portugais d'Amérique (Souvenirs historiques de la guerre du Brésil en 1635).* Paris, 1847.

DELPECHE, ADRIEN: *Roman brésilien.* Paris, 1904.

DENDY, ARTHUR: *The Biological Foundation of Society.* London, 1924.

DEODATO, ALBERTO: *Senzalas.* 1919.

DETLEFSEN, J. A.: *Our Present Knowledge of Heredity.* Philadelphia, 1925.

DEXTER, EDWIN GRANT: *Weather Influences.* New York, 1904.

DIAS, CARLOS MALHEIRO: *História da Colonização Portuguesa do Brasil, Introduction.* Lisbon, 1924.

——: "O Regime Feudal dos Donátarios anteriormente à Instituição do Governo Geral," *História da Colonização Portuguesa do Brasil,* III.

DIAS, GONÇALVES: *O Brasil e a Oceânia.* São Luiz, 1869.

"Discurso sobre as cousas da India e da Mina." Lisbon, 1573.

DODD, W. E.: *The Cotton Kingdom.* New Haven, 1916.
DREYS, NICOLAO: *Notícia Descriptiva da Província do Rio Grande de S. Pedro do Sul.* Rio de Janeiro, 1839.

EAST, EDWARD MURRAY, and D. F. JONES: *Inbreeding and Outbreeding* (1919), in G. H. Lane Fox Pitt-Rivers: *The Clash of Cultures and the Contact of Races.* London, 1927.
EDMUNDO, LUIS: *O Rio de Janeiro no Tempo dos Vice-Reis.* Rio de Janeiro, 1932.
EDWARDS, M. B. BETHAM-: *Home Life in France.* London, 1913.
EHRENREICH, PAUL: *Beiträge zur Völkerkunde Brasiliens.* Berlin, 1891.
ELLIS, HAVELOCK: *Studies in the Psychology of Sex.* Philadelphia, 1908.
ELLIS, ALFREDO, JR.: *Raça de Gigantes.* São Paulo, 1926.
ENGELHARDT, C. A.: *The Missions and Missionaries of California.* Santa Barbara, 1929.
ENGRACIA, PADRE JULIO: *Relação Cronológica do Santuario e Irmandade do Senhor Bom Jesus de Congonhas no Estado de Minas Gerais.* São Paulo, 1908.
Essai historique sur la colonie de Suriman . . . le tout redigé sur des pièces authentiques y joustes, et mis en ordre par les Regens et Représentans de ladite Nation Juive Portugaise. Paramaribo, 1788.

FAITHFUL, THEODORE: *Bisexuality.* London, 1927.
FANFANI, AMINTORE: *Cattolicismo e Protestantismo nella Formazione Storica del Capitalismo.* Milan, 1934.
FARIA, MANUEL DE SEVERIM DE: *Noticias de Portugal.* Lisbon, 1655.
FAURE, ÉMILE: *Trois Gouttes de sang.* Paris, 1929.
FAUX, WILLIAM: *Memorable Days in America.* London, 1923.
FEHLINGER, H.: *Sexual Life of Primitive People.* London, 1921.
FERRAZ, ALVARO, and ANDRADE LIMA, JR.: *A Morfologia do Homem do Nordeste.* Rio de Janeiro, 1939.
FIGUEIREDO, FIDELINO DE: *Crítica do Exilio.* Lisbon, 1930.
FISCHER, EUGEN: *Rasse und Rassenentstehung bein Menschen.* Berlin, 1927.
——: *Die Rehobother Bastards und das Bastardierungsproblem bein Menschen.* Jena, 1913.
FISCHER, MOLLISON, SCHWALBE, HOERNES, GRAEBNER, and PLOETZ: *Anthropologie.* Leipzig and Berlin, 1923.
FLEMING, E. K., and others: *Report of Committee on Nutrition, Supp. to the British Medical Journal,* 1923, Vol. II.
FLEURY, CLAUDE: *Historia Ecclesiastica,* in Henry Thomas Buckle: *Bosquejo de uma História del Intelecto Español* (translation).
FONSECA, JOSÉ VITORIANO BORGES DA: *Nobiliarchia Pernambucana* (1776–7). Rio de Janeiro, 1935.
FONSECA, L. ANSELMO DA: *A Escravidão, o Clero e o Abolicionismo.* Baía, 1887.
FONSECA, PADRE MANUEL: *Vida do Padre Belchior de Pontes.* Lisbon, 1752.

Frades julgados no Tribunal da Razão, Os, posthumous work of Frei,
——, Doctor of Coimbra. Lisbon, 1814.

FREEMAN, E. A.: *Historical Geography of Europe.* London, 1882.

FREER, ARTHUR S. B.: *The Early Franciscans and Jesuits.* London, 1922.

FREITAS, JOÃO ALFREDO DE: "Algumas Palavras sobre o Fetichismo Religioso e Político entre nós." Pernambuco, 1883.

——: "Lendas e Superstições do Norte do Brasil." Recife, 1884.

FREITAS, JOSÉ ANTONIO DE: *O Lirismo Brasileiro.* Lisbon, 1873.

FREUD, SIGMUND: *Psychologie Collective et Analyse du Moi* (translation). Paris, 1924.

FREYRE, GILBERTO: "A Agricultura da Cana e a Industria do Açucar," in *Livro do Nordeste.*

——: *Açucar,* Rio de Janeiro, 1939.

——: "Introdução" a *Memórias de um Cavalcanti.* São Paulo, 1940.

——: *Sobrados e Mucambos.* São Paulo, 1936.

——: *Social Life in Brazil in the Middle of the 19th Century.* Thesis presented to the Faculty of Political and Social Sciences of the University of California, 1923.

——: "Vida Social no Nordeste," in *Livro do Nordeste* (commemorating the centenary of the *Diário de Pernambuco,* Recife, 1925).

FROBENIUS, LEO: *Und Africa Sprach,* "Unter den Unstraflichen Athiopen." Charlottenburg, 1913.

——: *Ursprung der afrikanischen Kulturen,* in Melville J. Herskovits: "A Preliminary Consideration of the Culture Areas of Africa," *American Anthropologist,* Vol. XXVI, 1924.

FRIEDERICI, GEORG: *Die Europäische Eroberung nad Kolonisation America.* Vol. I, 1930; Vols. II and III, 1937; Stuttgart.

GAFFAREL, PAUL: *Histoire du Brésil français au sizième siècle.* Paris, 1878.

GAMA, FERNANDES: *Memórias Históricas de Pernambuco.* Recife, 1844.

GANIVET: *Idearium Español.* Madrid, without date.

GENER, POMPEYO: *Herejias.* Barcelona, 1888.

GILLESPIE, JAMES E.: *The Influence of Oversea Expansion on England to 1700.* New York, 1920.

GRANT, MADISON: *The Passing of a Great Race.* New York, without date.

GREGORY, J. W.: *The Menace of Colour.* Philadelphia, 1925.

GUERRA, RAMIRO: *Azúcar y Población en las Antillas.* Havana, 1930.

GÜNTHER, KONRAD: *Das Antlitz Brasiliens.* Leipzig, 1927.

GÜNTHER, H. F. K.: *Rassenkunde des Deutschen Volkes.* 11th edition, Munich, 1927.

GUIMARÃES, FRANCISCO PINHEIRO: *História de Uma Moça Rica.* Rio de Janeiro, 1861.

——: *Punição.* Rio de Janeiro, without date.

HADDON, A. G.: *The Races of Man and Their Distribution.* Cambridge, 1929.

HALL, J. S.: "A Study of Fears," in Alexander Francis Chamberlain: *The Child, a Study in the Evolution of Man.* 3rd edition, London, 1926.

HAMBLY, W. D.: *Origins of Education among Primitive Peoples.* London, 1926.

HANDELMAN, H.: *História do Brasil* (translation). Rio de Janeiro, 1931.

HANN, JULIUS: *Handbuch der Klimatologie.* Stuttgart, 1897.

HARTLAND, EDWIN SIDNEY: *The Science of Fairy Tales.* 2nd edition, London, 1925.

HAYES, RICARDO SÁENZ: Introduction to *Casa Grande y Senzala* (Spanish Edition). Buenos Aires, 1942.

HEARN, LAFCADIO: *Two Years in the French West Indies.* New York and London, 1923.

HENDERSON, JAMES: *A History of the Brazil.* London, 1821.

HERCULANO, ALEXANDRE: *Controvérsias, in Opúsculos.* Lisbon, 1887.

——: *Estudos Históricos, in Opúsculos.*

——: *História da Origem e Estabelecimento da Inquisição em Portugal.* Lisbon, 1779.

——: *História de Portugal.* Lisbon, 1853.

——: Introduction to *O Bobo,* (Era of Dona Thereza, 1128). Lisbon, 1897.

——: *Opúsculos.* Lisbon, 1897.

HERRICK, A. J.: *Neurological Foundations of Animal Behavior.* New York, 1924.

HERTWIG, OSKAR: *Das Verden der Organismen, 1916,* in Erik Nordenskiöld: *The History of Biology.*

HERTZ, F.: *Rasse und Kultur.* 1925.

HESS, A. F.: *Rickets, including Osteomalacia and Tetany.* London, 1930.

——: *Histoire générale des pirates,* cited by Oscar Clark: *Sífilis no Brasil e suas manifestações viscerais.*

HOBEY, C. W.: *Bantu Beliefs and Magic* (Introduction by J. G. Frazer). London, 1922.

HOBHOUSE, L. T., G. C. WHEELER, and M. GINSBERG: *The Material Culture and Social Institutions of the Simple Peoples.* London, 1915.

HOLMES, S. J.: *The Trend of the Race.* New York, 1923.

HOOTON, E. A.: *Up from the Ape.* New York, 1931.

HRDLICKA, ALES: *The Old Americans.* Baltimore, 1925.

HUNTINGTON, E.: *Civilization and Climate.* New Haven, 1915.

HUNTINGTON, ELLSWORTH, and LEONARD WILLIAMS: *Business Geography.*

JANSON: *The Stranger in America,* cited by Calhoun: *A Social History of the American Family.*

JENNINGS, H. S.: *Prometheus.* New York, 1925.

JOHNSTON, SIR HARRY H.: *The Negro in the New World.* London, 1910.

KAMMERER, P.: *The Inheritance of Acquired Characteristics.* New York, 1924.

KARSTEN, RAFAEL: *The Civilization of the South American Indians.* New York, 1920.

KEITH, A.: *Ethnos*. London, 1931.

KELLER, A. G.: *Colonization*. New York, 1908.

KELLER, C.: *Madagascar, Mauritius and Other East African Islands*. London, 1901.

KELSEY, CARL: *The Physical Basis of Society*. New York and London, 1928.

KIDD, BENJAMIN: *The Control of the Tropics*. London, 1898.

LAHKOWSKY, GEORGE: *La Civilisation et la folie raciste*. Paris.

LAMEGO, ALBERTO: *A Terra Goitacá*. Rio de Janeiro, 1913–25.

LAMEGO, ALBERTO, *fils: Planicie do Solar e da Senzala*. Rio de Janeiro, 1933.

LAVAL, FRANÇOIS PYRARD DE: *Voyage contenant sa navigation aux Indes Orientales, Maldives, Molugues et au Brésil, etc*. Paris, 1679.

LEÃO, A. CARNEIRO: "Oliveira Lima." Recife, 1913.

LEÃO, DUARTE NUNES DE: *Descripção Geral do Reino de Portugal*. Lisbon, 1610.

LEITE, PADRE SERAFIM: *História da Companhia de Jesús no Brasil*. Lisbon, 1938.

LEITE, SOLIDONIO, *fils: Os Judeus no Brasil*. Rio de Janeiro, 1923.

LEGENDRE, M.: *Portrait de l'Espagne*. Paris, 1923.

LEROY, BEAULIEU, PAUL: *De la colonisation chez les peuples modernes*. Paris, 1891.

LÉVY-BRUHL, LUCIEN: *La Mentalité primitive*. Paris, 1922.

LEWIS, M. S.: *Journal of a West India Proprietor*. London, 1929.

LIMA, OLIVEIRA: "A Nova Lusitania," in *História da Colonização Portuguesa do Brasil*.

———: *Aspectos da Literatura Colonial Brasileira*. Leipzig, 1895.

LIPPMANN, EDMUNDO VON: *História do Açucar*, translated by Rodolfo Coutinho. Rio de Janeiro, 1941.

LISBOA, JOÃO FRANCISCO: *Jornal de Timon* (edited by Luis Carlos Pereira e Castro and Dr. A. Henriques Leal). São Luiz do Maranhão, 1864.

LOBO, COSTA: *A História da Sociedade em Portugal no século XV*, Lisbon, 1904.

Lois Genitales, de Jacobus X-. Paris, 1906.

LOPES, CUNHA, and HEITOR PÉRES: *Da Esquizofrenia—Formas Clínicas—Ensaio de Revisão da Casuística Nacional*. Rio de Janeiro, 1931.

LOPES, RENATO SOUZA: *Regime Alimentar nos Climas Tropicais*. Rio de Janeiro, 1909. (Thesis.)

LOURO, ESTANCO: *O Livro de Alportel—Monografia de uma Freguesia Rural*. Lisbon, 1929.

LOWIE, ROBERT H.: *Are We Civilized?* London, without date.

LYCEL, SIR CHARLES: *Travels in the United States*. London, 1845.

MACEDO, FERRAZ DE: *Bosquejos de Antropologia Criminal*. Lisbon, 1900.

MACEDO, JOAQUIM MANUEL DE: *Vitimas Algozes*. Rio de Janeiro, 1869.

———: *O Moço Loiro*. Rio de Janeiro, 1876.

———: *As Mulheres de Mantilha.* Rio de Janeiro, 1870.

———: *A Moreninha.* Rio de Janeiro, 1929.

MACEDO, RIBEIRO DE: *Sobre a Introdução das Artes, 1675,* in Antonio Sergio: *Antologia dos Economistas Portugueses.* Lisbon, 1924.

MACHADO, ALCANTARA: *Vida e Morte do Bandeirante.* São Paulo, 1930.

MACHADO, BRAZILIO: Paper in *Terceiro Centenário do Veneravel Joseph de Anchieta.* Paris and Lisbon, 1900.

MacIVER, R. M.: *Community.* New York, 1928.

MADUREIRA, (S. J.), J. M. DE: *A Liberdade dos Indios e a Companhia de Jesús, sua Pedagogia e seus Resultados.* Rio de Janeiro, 1927. Special volume of the International Historical Congress of the Americas (Vol. IV).

MAGALHÃES, COUTO DE: *O Selvagem.* Rio de Janeiro, 1876.

MAGALHÃES, BASÍLIO DE: *O Folclore no Brasil.* Rio de Janeiro, 1928.

MAGALHÃES, EDUARDO: *Higiene Alimentar.* Rio de Janeiro, 1908.

MALHEIRO, AGOSTINHO MARQUÊS PERDIGAO: *A Escravidão no Brasil, Ensaio Jurídico-histórico-social.* Rio de Janeiro, 1866.

MALINOWSKI, BRONISLAW: *The Sexual Life of Savages in North Western Melanesia.* London, 1929.

MARROQUIM, MÁRIO: *A Lingua do Nordeste (Alagoas e Pernambuco).* São Paulo, 1934.

MARTIAL, RÉNÉ: *Vie et constance des races.* Paris, 1938.

MARTIN, R.: *Lehrbuch der Anthropologie.* Berlin, 1914.

MARTINEAU, HARRIET: *Retrospect of Western Travel.* London, 1838.

MARTINS, J. IZIDORO, JR.: *Historia do Direito Nacional.* Rio de Janeiro, 1895.

MARTINS, J. P. DE OLIVEIRA: *O Brasil e as Colonias Portuguesas.* Lisbon, 1887.

———: *A História de Portugal.* Porto, 1882.

McCARRISON, R.: "Relative Value of the National Diets of India," Transactions of the Seventh Congress, British India, 1927, Vol. III, in Ruy Coutinho: *Valor Social da Alimentação.*

McCAY: "The Relation of Food to Physical Development," *Scientific Memoir by Officers of the Medical and Sanitary Department of the Government, of India,* New Series, No. 37 (1910), Vol. V, Part II, cited in Ruy Coutinho: *Valor Social da Alimentação.*

McCOLLUM, E. V., and NINA SIMMONDS: *The Newer Knowledge of Nutrition, the Use of Foods for the Preservation of Vitality and Health.* New York, 1929.

McDOUGALL, WILLIAM: *National Welfare and National Group.* London, 1921.

———: *The Group Mind.* Cambridge, 1920.

MELLO, ANTÔNIO JOAQUIM DE: *Biografias* (ordered published by governor Barbosa Lima). Recife, 1895.

MENDES, JOÃO, JR.: *Os Indígenas do Brasil—Seus Direitos Individuais e Políticos.* São Paulo, 1912.

MENDONÇA, RENATO: *Influencía Africana no Português do Brasil.* Rio de Janeiro, 1933.

MERCADAL, J. GARCIA: *España Vista por los Estranjeros; Relaciones de Viajeros y Embajadores (Siglo XVI).* Madrid, without date.

MERÊA, PAULO: "Organizacão Social e Administração Pública," in *Historia de Portugal.*

MIRANDA, PONTES DE: *Fontes e Evolução do Direito Civil Brasileiro.* Rio de Janeiro, 1928.

MOLL, ALBERT: The Sexual *Life of the Child* (translation). New York, 1924.

Momento Literário, O, Symposium conducted by João do Rio among Brazilian intellectuals. Rio de Janeiro, 1910.

MONTEIRO, ARLINDO CAMILLO: *Amor Sáfico e Socrático—Estudo Médico-forense.* Lisbon, 1922.

MONTEIRO, TOBIAS: *Funcionários e Doutores.* Rio de Janeiro, 1917.

——: *Historia do Imperio—A Elaboração da Independencia.* Rio de Janeiro, 1927.

MORAES, ALEXANDRE J. DE MELLO: *Educador da Mocidade.* Bahia, 1852.

——: *Chorographia.* Rio de Janeiro, 1859.

MORAES, MELLO, *fils: Festas e Tradições.* Rio de Janeiro, without date.

MORAES, PADRE JOSÉ DE: *Memória sobre o Maranhão,* in A. J. de Mello Moraes: *Chorographia.*

MOREIRA, NICOLAO: "*Discurso sobre a Educação Moral da Mulher.*" Rio de Janeiro, 1868.

MUCKERMANN (S. J.), H.: *Rassenforchung und Volk der Zukunft.* Berlin, 1932.

MYERSON, A.: *The Inheritance of Mental Disorders.* Baltimore, 1925.

NABUCO, CAROLINA: *Vida de Joaquim Nabuco.* Rio de Janeiro, 1931.

NABUCO, JOAQUIM: *O Abolicionismo.* London, 1883.

——: *Minha Formação.* Rio de Janeiro and Paris, 1900.

——: Paper in *III Centenario do Veneravel Joseph de Anchieta.* Paris and Lisbon, 1900.

NASCIMENTO, ALFREDO: *O Centenario da Academia Nacional de Medicina do Rio de Janeiro—Primordios e Evolução da Medicina no Brasil.* Rio de Janeiro, 1929.

NASH, ROY: *The Conquest of Brazil.* New York, 1926.

NEIVA, ARTHUR: *Esboço Histórico sobre a Botânica e Zoologia no Brasil.* São Paulo, 1929.

NEUVILLE, HENRI: *L'Espèce, la race et la métissage en anthropologie.* Paris, 1933.

NEVINS, ALLAN: *American Social History as Recorded by British Travellers.* London, without date.

NEWTON, A. P.: *The Colonizing Activities of the English Puritans.* New Haven, 1914.

NICEFORO, A.: *Les Classes pauvres.* Paris, 1905.

524 *The Masters and the Slaves*

NORDENSKIÖLD, ERIK: *The History of Biology, a Survey* (translation). New York and London, 1929.
NORDENSKIÖLD, ERLAND: *Indianerleben.* Leipzig, 1912.

OCTAVIO, RODRIGO: *Direito do Estrangeiro no Brasil.* Rio de Janeiro, 1909.
OLIVEIRA, J. B. DE SÁ: *Craniometria comparada das especies humanas na Baía sob o ponto de vista evolucionista e médico-legal.* Bahia, 1895.
———: *Evolução Psíquica dos Baianos.* Bahia, 1898.
ORLANDO, ARTHUR: Response to the Symposium conducted by João do Rio among Brazilian intellectuals in *O Momento Literário*, 1910.
ORTIGÃO, RAMALHO: *As Farpas.* Lisbon, 1887–90.
———: *Culto da Arte em Portugal.* Lisbon, 1896.
ORTIZ, FERNANDO: *Los Cabildos Afrocubanos.* Havana, 1921.
———: *Los Negros Esclavos.* Madrid, without date.
———: *Hampa Afrocubana—Los Negros Brujos.* Madrid, 1917.
———: *Contrapunteo Cubano del Tabaco y el Azucar.* Havana, 1940.
Our Present Knowledge of Heredity (a series of lectures given at the Mayo Foundation. Philadelphia and London, 1923–4.

PAIVA, TANCREDO DE BARROS: *Bibliografia do Clima Brasílico.* Rio de Janeiro, 1929.
PALACIOS, A.: *El Islan Cristianizado.* Madrid, 1931.
PALACIOS, PADRE ASIN: *La Escatologia Musulmana en la Divina Comedia.* Madrid, 1919.
PASCUAL, A. D. DI: *Ensaio Crítico sobre a Viagem ao Brasil em 1852 de Carlos B. Mansfield.* Rio de Janeiro, 1861.
PAVLOV, IVAN PETROVICH: *Conditioned Reflexes* (translated by Professor G. V. Anrep of Cambridge University). London, 1927.
PAYNE, J.: *History of European Colonies.* London, 1878.
PECKOLT, THEODORO: *Historia das Plantas Alimentares e de Gozo do Brasil.* Rio de Janeiro, 1871.
PEDROSO, SEBASTIÃO JOSÉ: *Itinerário de Lisboa e Viana do Minho, etc.*, in Leite de Vasconcellos *Ensaios Etnográficos.* Lisbon, 1910.
PEIXOTO, AFRÂNIO: *Minha Terra e Minha Gente.* Rio de Janeiro, 1916.
———: *Uma Mulher como as Outras.* Rio de Janeiro, 1927.
PENTA, PASCALE: *I Pervertimenti Sessuali.* Naples, 1893.
PEREIRA, J. M. ESTEVES: *A Industria Portuguesa (Séculos XII a XIX)*, with an introduction on the trade guilds in Portugal. Lisbon, 1900.
PFISTER, OSCAR: *Love in Children and Its Aberrations* (translation). London, 1924.
PHILLIPS, ULRICK BONNELL: *American Negro Slavery, a Survey of the Supply, Employment and Control of Negro Labor as Determined by the Plantation Regime.* New York and London, 1929.
———: *Plantation and Frontier Documents.* Cleveland, 1909.
PIMENTEL, ANTÔNIO MARTINS DE AZEVEDO: *Subsídios para o estudo da higiene do Rio de Janeiro.* Rio de Janeiro, 1890.

———: *O Brasil Central.* Rio de Janeiro, 1907.
Pinto, E. Roquette: *Seixos Rolados.* Rio de Janeiro, 1927.
Pitta, Rocha: *Historia da América Portuguesa.* Lisbon, 1730.
Pitt-Rivers, G. H. Lane Fox: *The Clash of Cultures and the Contact of Races.* London, 1927.
Plekhanov, George: *Introduction à l'histoire sociale de la Russie* (translation). Paris, 1926.
Ploss, Hermann Heinrich: *Das Weib in der Natur- und Völkerkunde,* revised and edited by Max Bartels. Leipzig, 1935; Berlin, 1927.
Poinsard, Léon: *Le Portugal Inconnu,* Paris, 1910.
Pompéia, Raul: *O Ateneu,* Rio de Janeiro, 1905.
Prado, Caio, Jr.: *Evolução Política do Brasil* (attempt at a materialistic interpretation of Brazilian history). São Paulo, 1933.
Prado, Eduardo: Paper in *III Centenário do Veneravel Joseph de Anchieta.* Paris and Lisbon, 1900.
Prado, Paulo: *Paulística.* 2nd edition, Rio de Janeiro, 1934.
Price, A. G.: *White Settlers in the Tropics.* New York, 1939.

Queiroz, Eça de: *A Ilustre Casa de Ramires.* Porto, 1904.
Queiroz, Frei João de S. José: *Memórias.* Porto, 1868.
Querino, Manuel: *A Arte Culinária na Baía.* Bahia, 1928.
———: *Baía de Outrora.* Bahia, 1916.
Quetelet, Adolphe: *Physique social.* Brussels, 1869.

Raimundo, Jacques: *O Elemento Afro-negro na Lingua Portuguesa.* Rio de Janeiro, 1933.
Rangel, Alberto: *Rumos e Perspectivas.* Rio de Janeiro, 1914.
Rebello, Silva: *Memoria sobre a população e a agricultura em Portugal desde a fundação da Monarquia até 1865.* Lisbon, 1868.
Rego, José Lins do: *Menino de Engenho.* Rio de Janeiro, 1932.
Ribbing, Seved: *L'Hygiène sexuelle et ses conséquences morales.* Paris, 1895.
Ribeiro, Emmanuel: *O Doce Nunca Amargou . . . (Doçaria Portuguesa), Historia. Decoração. Receituario.* Coimbra, 1928.
Ribeiro, João: *Dicionário Gramatical contendo em resumo as materias que se referem ao estudo histórico-comparativo.* Rio de Janeiro, 1889.
———: *História do Brasil,* higher course for schools. Rio de Janeiro, 1900.
———: *A Lingua Nacional.* São Paulo, 1933.
Ribeiro, Júlio: *A Carne.* São Paulo, 1888.
Ricardo, Cassiano: *Marcha para Oeste.* Rio de Janeiro, 1939.
Richarding, Edmond: *La Cuisine française du XV.e au XVI.e Siècle.* Paris, 1913.
Ringbom, Lars: *The Renewal of Culture* (translation). London, without date.
Rios, A. Morales de los: "Resumo Monográfico da Evolução da Arquitetura do Brasil," in *Livro de Ouro Comemorativo do Centenário da*

Independência e da Exposição Internacional do Rio de Janeiro. Rio de Janeiro, 1934.

RIPLEY, W. Z.: *The Races of Europe.* London, without date.

ROBERTSON, W. R.: *Aspects of the Rise of Capitalism.* Cambridge, 1929.

RODRIGUES, DOMINGOS: *A Arte de Cozinha.* Lisbon, 1692.

RODRIGUES, NINA: *Os Africanos no Brasil.* São Paulo, 1933.

——: *L'Animisme Fétichiste des Nègres de Bahia.* Bahia, 1900.

——: *As Raças Humanas—Sua Responsabilidade Penal.* Bahia, 1894.

ROMERO, SÍLVIO: *Cantos Populares do Brasil.* Rio de Janeiro, 1883.

——: *História da Literatura Brasileira.* Rio de Janeiro, 1888.

——: *Provocações e Debates.* Porto, 1916.

——: Response to the Symposium of João do Rio, in *O Momento Literário.* Rio de Janeiro, 1910.

—— and JOÃO RIBEIRO: *Compêndio de História da Literatura.* 2nd edition, revised, 1909.

ROSA, JOAM FERREYRA DA: *Trattato único da Constituiçam Pestilencial de Pernambuco Offerecido a Elrey N. S.* Lisbon, 1694.

ROSENAU, MILTON T.: *Preventive Medicine and Hygiene.* 5th edition, New York and London.

ROSSELI Y VILAR: *La Raza.* Barcelona, 1930.

ROSTAND, JEAN: *Hérédité et racisme.* Paris.

ROWER, FREI BASÍLIO: *Páginas da História Franciscana no Brasil.* Rio de Janeiro, 1941.

RUSSEL, ROBERT: *Atmosphere in Relation to Human Life and Health,* Smithsonian Institution, Miscellaneous Collection, Vol. XXXIX.

SÁA, MARIO DE: *A Invasão dos Judeus.* Lisbon, 1924.

SACO, J. S.: *História de la Esclavitad de la Raza Africana en el Nuevo Mundo.* Havana, 1893.

SAMPAIO, ALBERTO: *Estudos Históricos e Econômicos.* Lisbon, 1923.

SAMPAIO, THEODORO: "S. Paulo no tempo de Anchieta," in *III Centenário do Veneravel Joseph de Anchieta.* São Paulo, 1900.

——: *O Tupi na Geografia Nacional.* 3rd edition, Bahia, 1928.

SANT'ANNA NERY, BARÃO DE: *Folk-Lore brésilien.* Paris, 1889.

SANTOS, JOSÉ MARIA DOS: *Política Geral do Brasil.* Rio de Janeiro, 1930.

SARMENTO, MORAIS: *D. Pedro I e sua época.* Porto, 1924.

SAY, HORACE: *Histoire des rélations commerciales entre la France et le Brésil.* Paris, 1839.

SCHAFER, H.: *Geschichte von Portugal.* Hamburg, 1836–54.

SCHAFFER, RITLER VAN: *Brazilian als Unabhaengiges Reìch.* Altona, 1924.

SCHEIDT, W.: *Allgemeine Rassenkunde.* Berlin, 1926.

SCHMIDT, W., and W. KOPPERS: *Völker und Kulturen.* Regensburg, 1924.

SCHWEINFURTH, GEORG: *Im Herzen von Africa.* 3rd edition, Leipzig, 1908.

SELLIM, A. W.: *Geografia Geral do Brasil* (translation). Rio de Janeiro, 1889. Preface by Capistrano de Abreu.

SEMEDO, CURVO: *Observações Doutrinarias,* in Luis Edmundo: *O Rio de Janeiro no Tempo dos Vice-Reis.*

SEMPLE, ELLEN CHURCHILL: *Influences of Geographic Environment.* New York, 1911.

SEQUEIRA, GUSTAVO DE MATOS: *Relação de varios casos notaveis e curiosos sucedidos em tempo na cidade de Lisboa,* etc. Coimbra, 1924.

SEQUEIRA, PADRE ANTUNES DE: *Esboço Histórico dos Costumes do Povo Espírito-santense desde os tempos coloniais até nossos dias.* Rio de Janeiro, 1893.

SERGI, G.: *Europa.* Turin, 1908.

SÉRGIO, ANTÔNIO: *Antologia dos Economistas Portugueses.* Lisbon, 1924.

——: *Bosqueja da História de Portugal.* Lisbon, 1923.

——: *A Sketch of the History of Portugal* (translation by Constantino José dos Santos). Lisbon, 1928.

SIEMEN, HERMANN WERNER: *Théorie de l'hérédité.* Paris, without date.

SEVERO, RICARDO: *A arte tradicional no Brasil (a casa e o tempol).* São Paulo, 1916.

SILVA, O. B. DE COUTO: "Sobre a lei de Rubner-Richet" (thesis). Rio de Janeiro, 1926.

SIMKIN, FRANCIS BUTLER, and ROBERT HILLIARD WOODY: *South Carolina during Reconstruction.* Chapel Hill, 1932.

SIMÕES, J. DE OLIVEIRA: "A evolução da industria portuguesa," in *Notas sobre Portugal.*

SMITH, MAYO: *Statistics and Sociology.* New York, 1907.

SOROKIN, PITIRIM: *Contemporary Social Theories.* New York and London, 1928.

——: *Social Mobility,* New York, 1927.

SOUSA, ALBERTO DE: *Os Andradas.* São Paulo, 1922.

SOUSA, FREI LUIS DE: *Synonimos,* cited by Padre Antunes de Sequeira: *Esboço Histórico dos costumes do povo espírito-santense,* etc.

SOUTHEY, ROBERT: *History of Brazil.* London, 1810–19.

SPENGLER, OSWALD: *La Decadencia de Occidente* (translation). Madrid, 1927.

STEPHENS, H. M.: *The Story of Portugal.* New York, 1891.

STILES, PERCY GOLDTHWAIT: *Nutritional Physiology.* Philadelphia and Boston, 1931.

SUMNER, WILLIAM GRAHAM: *Folkways.* Boston, 1906.

TAUNAY, AFFONSO DE E.: *História Geral das Bandeiras Paulistas.* São Paulo, 1924–9.

——: *Non Ducor, Duco.* São Paulo, 1924.

——: *Sob El-Rey Nosso Senhor—Aspecto da Vida Setecentista Brasileira, sobretudo em São Paulo.* São Paulo, 1923.

——: *São Paulo no século XVI.* Tours, 1921.

——: *São Paulo nos primeiros tempos, 1554–1601.* Tours, 1920.

Taunay, Visconde de: *Trechos de Minha Vida*. Published posthumously, 1923.

Tawney, R. H.: *Religion and the Rise of Capitalism*. London, 1926.

Taylor, Griffith: *Environment and Race*. Oxford, 1926.

Teixeira, José Maria: *Causas da mortalidade das crianças no Rio de Janeiro*. 1887.

Terman, L. M.: *Genetic Studies of Genius*. 1925–30.

Thomas, W. I.: *Sex and Society*. Chicago, 1907.

Thomaz, Pedro Fernandes: *Canções Populares da Beira*. Lisbon, 1896.

Thompson, R. Lowe: *The History of the Devil*. London, 1929.

Thorpe, M. R. and others: *Organic Adaptation to Environment*. New York, 1918.

Torres, Alberto: *O Problema Nacional Brasileiro*. Rio de Janeiro, 1914.

——: *A Organização Nacional*. Rio de Janeiro, 1914.

Trollope, Anthony: *North America*. London, 1862.

Trollope, Frances: *The Domestic Manners of the Americans*. London, 1832.

Tylor, Edward B.: *Primitive Culture*. 5th edition, London, 1929.

Unamuno y Jugo, Miguel de: *Por tierras de Portugal y de España*. Madrid, 1911.

Vasconcellos, Diogo de: *História Media de Minas Gerias*. Belo Horizonte, 1918.

Vasconcellos, Leite de: *Ensaios Etnográficos*. Lisbon, 1910.

——: *Tradições Populares de Portugal*. Porto, 1882.

Verissimo, José: *A Educação Nacional*. Rio de Janeiro.

Vianna, Oliveira: *Evolução do Povo Brasileiro*. Rio de Janeiro, 1929.

——: *Populações Meridionais do Brasil*. São Paulo, 1933.

——: *Raça e Assimilação*. São Paulo, 1932.

Vieira, Padre Antônio: *Obras Varias*. Lisbon, 1856–7.

Vigier, João: *Pharmacopéa Ulysiponense*, in Luis Edmundo, *O Rio de Janeiro no Tempo dos Vice-Reis*.

Viterbo, Sousa: *Artes e Artistas em Portugal (Contribuição para as Artes e Industrias Portuguesas)*. Lisbon, 1892.

Walles, Wilson D.: *An Introduction to Anthropology*. London, without date.

Ward, Robert De Courcy: *Climate Considered Especially in Relation to Man*. New York, 1908.

Wätjen, Hermann: *Das Judentum und die Anfange der modernen Colonisation (in Das hollandische Kolonialreich in Brasilien)*. Gotha, 1921.

Weber, Max: *Gesammelte Aufsätze zur Religionsoziologie*. Berlin, 1922.

——: *General Economic History* (translation). New York.

Webster, Hutton: *Primitive Secret Societies*. New York, 1908.

WERNECK, AMÉRICO: *Graciema*. Rio de Janeiro, 1920.
WERTENBAKER, T. J.: *Patrician and Plebeian in Virginia*. Virginia, 1912.
WESTERMARCK, E. A.: *The History of Human Marriage*. London, 1921.
——: *The Origin and Development of the Moral Ideas*. London, 1926.
WHIFFEN, THOMAS: *The North-West Amazon*. London, 1915.
WISSLER, CLARK: *The American Indians*. New York, 1922.
——: *Man and Culture*. New York, 1923.

ZIEGLER, H. E.: *Die Vererbungslehre in der Biologie und in der Soziologie*. Jena, 1918.

III

SECONDARY SOURCES: PERIODICALS, YEARBOOKS, REPORTS, BULLETINS

Africa (African Institute of African Languages and Cultures), England.
American Anthropologist. United States.
American Journal of Physical Anthropology. United States.
American Journal of Sociology. United States.
Annaes de Medicina. Rio de Janeiro.
Annales, Museo de la Plata. La Plata, Argentina.
Annual Report, Smithsonian Institution. United States.
Annual Reports, Bureau of Ethnology. Washington, D. C.
Anthropos. Austria.
Anuário Estatístico. State of Pernambuco, Recife.
Arqueólogo Português, O. Portugal.
Archiv fur Ethnographie. Germany.
Archivio per l'Antropologia e la Etnologia. Italy.
Archivos e Boletim, Museu Nacional. Rio de Janeiro.

Boletim, Museu Goeldi. Pará.

Folk-Lore (A Quarterly Review of Myth, Tradition, Institution and Custom). London.

Journal of Anthropology. England.
Journal of the African Society. London.

L'Anthropologie. France.

Man. England.
Memoirs, Peabody Museum of Archeology and Ethnology. Cambridge, Massachusetts.

Scientia (Rivista Internazionale de Sintesi Cientifica). Italy.
Smithsonian Contributions to Knowledge. United States.

The Sociological Review. London.
Trabalhos, Sociedade Portuguesa de Antropologia e Etnologia. Portugal.

IV

SPECIAL REFERENCES (ARTICLES IN REVIEWS, Etc.)

ALMEIDA, A. OZÓRIO DE: "A Ação Protetora do Urucú," separata of the *Boletim do Museu Nacional*, Vol. VII, No. I. 1931.
——: "O Metabolismo basal do homem tropical de raça branca," in the *Journal de Physiologie et de Pathologie Générale*.
AMARAL, AMADEU, JR.: "Superstições do povo paulista," in the *Revista Nova*, No. 4. São Paulo.
AMARAL, BRAZ DO: Paper presented to the Congress of National History, published in the *Revista do Instituto Histórico e Geográfico Brasileiro*, special volume, Part II.
Anais Brasilienses de Medicina, No. 5, Vol. II, Ano II.
ANCHIETA, PADRE JOSEPH DE: "Informação dos casamentos dos indios do Brasil," in the *Revista do Instituto Histórico e Geográfico Brasileiro*, Vol. VIII.
ANDRADE, ANTONIO ALFREDO DE: "Alimentos brasileiros," in the *Anais da Faculdade de Medicina do Rio de Janeiro*, Vol. VI, 1922.
ARARIPE, TRISTÃO DE ALENCAR: "Pater-familias no Brasil nos tempos coloniais," in the *Rev. do Inst. Hist. e. Geog. Bras.*, Vol. LV.
ARAUJO, H. C. DE SOUSA: "Costumes paraenses," in *Boletim Sanitário*, Ano 2, No. 5. Rio de Janeiro, 1924.
Article in the newspaper *O Sete de Setembro*, of Recife, Vol. I, No. 34. (1846), concerning the manuscript of the "Nobiliarchia Pernambucana," of Borges da Fonseca.
AZEVEDO, LUIS CORRÊA DE: Paper presented to the Imperial Academy of Medicine of Rio de Janeiro, published in the *Anais Brasilienses de Medicina*, Vol. XXII, No. 11 (April 1872).
——: Article in the *Anais Brasilienses de Medicina*, Vol. XXI.

BALFOUR, A.: "Sojourners in the Tropics," in *The Lancet*, 1923, Vol. I.
BARRETO, L. PEREIRA: "A higiene da mesa," in *O Estado de São Paulo*, September 7, 1922.
BEAM, R. R.: "The Negro Brain," *Century Magazine*, 1906.
BEZERRA, ANDRÉ: Discussion conducted at the Rotary Club of Recife (*Diário de Pernambuco*, April 2, 1933).

Bibliography 531

BILDEN, RUEDIGER: "Brazil, Laboratory of Civilization," in the *Nation*, New York, 1926.

Boletim do Museu Goeldi (Museu Paraense) *de Historia Natural e Etnografia*, Vol. VII. Pará, 1913.

BOTELHO, ADAUTO: Study of dementia præcox among Negroes and mulattoes, made in Rio de Janeiro in 1917, and cited in the *Boletim de Eugenia*, No. 38 (April-June 1932).

BOWDITCH, H. P.: "The Growth of Children," *8th Annual Report of the State Bureau of Health of Massachusetts*.

BRANNER, JOHN CASPER: "O que eu faria se fosse estudante brasileiro nos Estados-Unidos," *El Estudiante Latino-Americano*. New York, 1921.

"Breve discurso sobre o estado das quatro capitanias conquistadas, de Pernambuco, Itamaracá, Parahyba e Rio Grande, situadas na parte septentrional do Brasil," translation of a Dutch manuscript in the Archives of The Hague, published in the *Revista do Instituto Arqueológico, Histórico e Geográfico de Pernambuco*, No. 31.

British Medical Journal, August 11, 1923, in Arthur Dendy: *The Biological Foundation of Society*.

BRYANT, A. T., and C. G. SELIGMAN: "Mental Development of the South African Native," in *Eugenics Review*, Vol. IX.

CAMARA, PHAELANTE DA: "Notas dominicais de Tollenare," in *Cultura Acadêmica*. Recife, 1904.

CAMPOS, J. DA SILVA: "Tradições baianas," in the *Revista do Instituto Histórico e Geográfico da Baía*, No. 56.

CARVALHO, ALFREDO DE: "O Zoobillion de Zacharias Wagner," in the *Revista do Instituto Arqueológico, Histórico e Geográfico de Pernambuco*, Vol. XI (1904).

——: "Magia Sexual no Brasil," (fragments), in the *Revista do Instituto Arqueológico, Histórico e Geográfico de Pernambuco*, No. 106.

——: Uncompleted paper on sexual magic in Brazil, in the *Revista do Instituto Arqueológico, Histórico e Geográfico de Pernambuco*, No. 102.

CEDRO, LUIS: "O doutor Gerôncio de Noruega," in the *Diário de Pernambuco*, July 26, 1925.

CHAVES, ANTIOGENES: "Os esportes em Pernambuco," in *O Journal*, Rio de Janeiro, special Pernambuco edition, 1928.

CHAVES, NELSON: "Aspecto da fisiologia hipotálamo-hipofisiario—interpretação da precocidade sexual no Nordeste," in *Neurobiologia*, Vol. III, No. 4. Recife, 1940.

CLAUDIO, AFFONSO: "As tres raças na sociedade colonial—contribuição social de cada uma," in the *Revista do Instituto Histórico e Geográfico Brasileiro*, Vol. III (special volume), 1927.

——: "As tribus negras importadas," in the *Revista do Instituto Histórico e Geográfico Brasileiro*, special volume devoted to the National Historical Congress, Part II.

Corrêa, Padre J. Alves: Critical article on *Casa-Grande & Senzala*.

Costa, Lúcio: "O Aleijadinho e a arquitetura tradicional," in *O Jornal*, special Minas Geraes edition, Rio de Janeiro.

Costa, Pereira da: "Folclore Pernambucano," in the *Revista do Instituto Arqueológico, Histórico e Geográfico de Pernambuco*.

Coutinho, Ruy: Study of the nutrition of the Negro slave in Brazil, paper presented to the First Afro-Brazilian Congress of Recife, November 1934.

Coutto, Domingos do Loreto: *Desagravos do Brasil e Glorias de Pernambuco*, in the *Anais da Biblioteca Nacional do Rio de Janeiro*, Vol. XXIV.

Couty, Louis: "L'Alimentation au Brésil et dans les pays voisins," in the *Revue d'Hygiene*, Paris, 1881.

Cunha, Alberto da: "Higiene mental," in the *Arquivos de Higiene*, No. 11, Rio de Janeiro.

Dantas, Pedro: "Perspectivas," in the *Revista Nova*, No. 4, São Paulo, 1931.

Dessoir, Max: "Zur Psychologie der Vita Sexualis," in the *Allgemeine Zeitschrift fur Psychischgerichtliche Medicin*, cited by Westermarck: *The Origin and Development of the Moral Ideas*.

Diário de Noticias, Rio de Janeiro, July 10, 1882 (runaway-slave advertisements).

Diário de Pernambuco: Runaway-slave advertisements in the issues of March 3, March 27, August 3, August 25, October 9, 1828; August 3, 1829; September 23, 1830; January 22, 1835; June 9, 1850.

Engelman, G. J.: "First Age of Menstruation in the North American Continent," *Transactions of the American Gynecological Society*, 1901.

Escudero, Pedro: "Influencia de la alimentacion sobre la raza," *La Prensa*, March 27, 1933.

Étienne, Abbé: "La Secte Musulmane des Malés du Brésil et leur révolte en 1835," in *Anthropos*, January-March 1909.

Fazenda, José Vieira: "Antigualhas e Memorias do Rio de Janeiro," in the *Revista do Instituto Histórico e Geográfico Brasileiro*, Tomo 95, Vol. CXLIX.

Ferreira, Costa: "La Capacité du crâne chez les portugais," in *Bulletins et Mémoires de la Société d'Anthropologie*, Paris, Series V, Vol. IV.

Francisco, Martim: "Jornal de viagens por diferentes vilas da capitânia de São Paulo," in the *Revista do Instituto Histórico e Geográfico Brasileiro*, No. 45.

Franco, Affonso Arinos de Mello: "Mundo imaginário," article in *A Manhã*, April 12, 1942.

Frank, Waldo: "La Selva," in *Sur*, No. 1 (Buenos Aires, 1931).

Freitas, Octávio de: Paper on diseases brought to Brazil by infected

Negroes (*"negros bichados"*), read before the First Afro-Brazilian Congress of Recife, November 1934.

FREYRE, GILBERTO: "A proposito de um livro em 3.ª edição," in the *Revista do Brasil*, July 1938.

——: "O escravo nos anúncios de jornais do tempo do Império," lecture before the Sociedade Felipe d'Oliveira, Rio de Janeiro, 1934.

——: Paper on the diet of Pernambuco, read before the Regionalist Congress of the Northeast, Recife, 1925.

GOELDI, EMILIO: "O estado atual dos conhecimentos sobre os indios do Brasil," in the *Boletim do Museu Paraense de Historia Natural e de Etnografia*, Vol. II, No. 4.

GOLDENWEISER, ALEXANDER: "Concerning Racial Differences," in the *Menorah Journal*, Vol. VIII (1922).

——: "Diffusionism and the American School of Historical Ethnology," in the *American Journal of Sociology*, Vol. XXXI (1925).

——: "Race and Culture in the Modern World," in the *Journal of Social Forces*, Vol. III (1924).

——: "Sex and Primitive Society," in *Sex and Civilization*, edited by Calverton and Schmalhausen. London, 1929.

——: "The Significance of the Study of Culture for Sociology," in the *Journal of Social Forces*, Vol. III (1924).

GRIECO, AGRIPPINO: "Paraíba do Sul," in *O Jornal*, Rio de Janeiro, special edition commemorating the Coffee Bicentennial.

HANKINS, F. H.: "Individual Differences and Their Significances for Social Theory," publications of the *American Sociological Society*, Vol. XVII (1922).

HERSKOVITS, MELVILLE J.: "A Preliminary Consideration of the Culture Areas of Africa," in the *American Anthropologist*, Vol. XXVI, No. 1 (1924).

——: "On the Provenience of New World Negroes," in the *Journal of Social Forces*, Vol. XII, No. 2 (1933).

"Histórias da Idade Media," in the *Revista do Arquivo Público Mineiro*, Ano XII (1907).

"Idea geral de Pernambuco em 1817," article by an anonymous author in the *Revista do Instituto Arqueológico, Histórico e Geográfico de Pernambuco*, No. 29.

IVANOVSKY, A.: "Physical Modifications of the Population of Russia under Famine," in the *American Journal of Physical Anthropology*, No. 4 (1923).

KEITH, ARTHUR: "On Certain Factors Concerned in the Evolution of Human Races," in the *Journal of the Royal Anthropological Institute*, London, Vol. XLVI.

KEYSERLING, COUNT HERMANN VON: "Portugal," (translation from the German by Herta Oppenheimer and Osório de Oliveira), in *Descobrimento*, No. 2. Lisbon, 1931.

LAVRÁDIO, BARÃO DE: ."Algumas considerações sobre as causas da mortalidade das creanças no Rio de Janeiro e Molestias mais frequentes nos seis ou sete primeiros mezes de idade," articles published in the *Journal of the Imperial Academy*, 1847.

LEAL, ANTONIO HENRIQUES: "Apontamentos para a história dos Jesuitas, extrahidos dos Chronistas da Companhia de Jesus," in the *Revista do Instituto Histórico e Geográfico Brasileiro*, Vol. XXXIV, Rio de Janeiro, 1871.

LEITE, PADRE SERAFIM: critical article on *Casa-Grande & Senzala* in the review *Broteria*.

LIMA, J. F. DE ARAUJO: "Ligeira contribuição ao estudo do problema alimentar das populações rurais do Amazonas," in the *Boletim Sanitario*, Rio, Ano II, No. 4 (1923).

LINS, DR. SINVAL: "Fundamentos científicos modernos da alimentação racional nos climas quentes," in *Brasil Médico*, Ano XLV, No. 40.

LOPES, CUNHA: "Psicoses nos selvagens," communication to the Brazilian Psychiatric Society, 1927.

LYDE, L. W.: "Skin Color," in *The Spectator*, London, May 16, 1931.

MAGALHÃES, BASÍLIO DE: "As lendas em torno da lavoura do café," in *O Jornal*, Rio de Janeiro, special edition commemorating the Coffee Bicentennial.

MANCHESTER, ALAN P.: "The Rise of the Brazilian Aristocracy," in the *Hispanic American Historical Review*, Vol. XI, No. 2.

MARIANNO, JOSÉ: "As razões da arquitetura brasileira," in *O Jornal*, Rio de Janeiro.

MARIANNO, JOSÉ, *fils*: lecture in the School of Fine Arts of Recipe, April 1933.

MASON, O. T.: "Cradles of the American Aborigines," in *Report of the United States Museum*, 1886–7.

MILLIET, SÉRGIO: "Psicologia do Cafuné," in *Planalto*, January 9, 1941. São Paulo.

MONTOYA: "Manuscripto Guaraní da Bibliotheca Nacional do Rio de Janeiro sobre a Primitiva Catechese dos Indios das Missões," in the *Anais da Bibliotheca Nacional*, Vol. VI.

MORAES, EUGÉNIO VILHENA DE: "¿Qual a influência dos jesuitas em nossas letras?" in the *Revista do Instituto Histórico e Geográfico Brasileiro*, special volume for the National Historical Congress, Part V. Rio de Janeiro, 1917.

MOREIRA, NICOLAO JOAQUIM: "¿Questão ethnico-anthropológica: o cruzamento das raças acarreta a degradação intelectual e moral do producto hýbrido resultante?" in the *Anais Brasilienses de Medicina*, Vol. XXI, No. 10.

OLIVEIRA, JOÃO ALFRE O CORRÉIA DE: Biography of the Baron of Goiana, in the *Revista do Instituto Arqueólogico, Histórico e Geográfico de Pernambuco*, Vol. XXVII.

OLIVEIRA, J. J. MACHADO DE: "Notícia racionada sobre as aldeias de indios da Província de São Paulo," in the *Revista do Instituto Histórico e Geográfico Brasileiro*, VIII.

ORR, J. B., and J. L. GILKS: "The Physique and Health of Two African Tribes," in *Medical Research Council*, Special Report Series, 1932, No. 155, in Ruy Coutinho: *O Valor Social da Alimentação*.

Panorama, O, Lisbon, Vol. II (1938).

PEREIRA, ASTROGILDO: "Sociologia ou Apologética," in *A Classe Operária*, Rio de Janeiro, May 1, 1929.

PERNAMBUCANO, ULYSSES: Paper on "As Doenças Mentais entre os Negros," in *Arquivos da Assistência a Psicopatas de Pernambuco*, No. 1 (April 1932).

PINHEIRO, CANON FERNANDES: "Ensaio sobre os Jesuitas," in the *Revista do Instituto Histórico e Geográfico Brasileiro*, Vol. XVIII.

QUERINO, MANUEL: "A raça africana e seus costumes na Baía," in the *Revista da Academia de Letras*, No. 70.

RENDON, JOSÉ AROUCHE DE TOLEDO: "Memórias sobre as aldeias de indios da Província de São Paulo," in the *Revista do Instituto Histórico e Geográfico Brasileiro*, VI.

Responses to the inquiry conducted among physicians by the District of Rio de Janeiro, regarding the climate and healthfulness of the Court of the Viceroys (1798), published in the *Anais Brasilienses de Medicina*, Vol. II, No. 5 (1846).

Revista do Instituto Arqueológico, Histórico e Geográfico de Pernambuco, No. 33, Recife, 1887; Vol. XI, 1904.

Revista do Instituto Histórico e Geográfico Brasileiro, Vol. XIV (containing Gabriel Soares de Sousa's *Tratado Descriptivo do Brasil em 1587*, edited by F. A. Varnhagen); Vol. LXXVIII, Part II.

RIBEIRO, JOÃO: critical article on *Casa Grande & Senzala*, in the *Jornal do Brasil*, Rio de Janeiro, 1933.

ROSA, FRANCISCO LUIZ DA GAMA: "Costumes do Povo nos Nascimentos, Batizados, Casamentos e Enterros," in the *Revista do Instituto Histórico e Geográfico Brasileiro*, special volume, No. 1, National Historical Congress, Part V. Rio de Janeiro, 1917.

ROTH, H. LING: "On the Significance of the Couvade," in the *Journal of the Anthropological Institute of Great Britain and Ireland*, Vol. XXII (1893).

Roth, Walter E.: "An Inquiry into the Animism and the Folklore of the Guiana Indians," 13th Annual *Report*, Bureau of American Ethnology. Washington, 1915.

Sampaio, Theodoro: "São Paulo de Piratininga no fim do século XVI," in the *Revista do Instituto Histórico de São Paulo*, Tomo IV, Vol. II.

Schmidt, Max: article in *Koloniale Rundschau*, April 1909: résumé by Sir Harry H. Johnston: *The Negro in the New World*.

Schuller, R. R.: "A Couvade," in the *Boletim do Museu Goeldi*, Vol. VI (1910).

Senna, Nelson de: "Toponimia geográfica de origem brasílico-indígena em Minas Gerais," in the *Revista do Arquivo Público Mineiro*, Ano X (1924).

Soares, A. J. de Macedo: "Estudos léxico-gráficos do dialeto brasileiro," in the *Revista Brasileira*, Vol. IV. Rio de Janeiro, 1880.

Spencer, Frank Clarence: "Education of the Pueblo Child," *Columbia University Contributions to Philosophy, Psychology and Education*, Vol. VII, No. 1. New York, 1899.

Statutes of the Retreat of Nossa Senhora da Gloria, cited by Canon Antônio do Carmo Baratta: "Um grande sabio, um grande patriota, um grande bispo" (lecture). Pernambuco, 1921.

Stevenson, T. E.: "The Religious Life of the Zuñi Child," *Bureau of Ethnology Report*, Vol. V. Washington.

Taunay, Affonso de E.: "A Fundação de São Paulo," Vol. III, special volume for the First International Historical Congress of the Americas, of the *Revista do Instituto Histórico e Geográfico Brasileiro*. Rio de Janeiro, 1927.

"Thesouro descoberto no Máximo Rio Amazonas," beginning of Part II, which treats of the Amazon Indians, their religious faith, life, customs, etc.; copied from a manuscript of the Public Library of Rio de Janeiro, published in the *Revista do Instituto Histórico e Geográfico Brasileiro*, Vol. II, No. 7. Rio de Janeiro, 1858.

Tollenare, L. F.: *Notas Dominicais Tomadas Durante uma Viagem em Portugal e no Brasil em 1816, 1817 e 1818* (part relative to Pernambuco translated from the unpublished French manuscript, by Alfredo de Carvalho), in the *Revista do Instituto Arqueológico, Histórico e Geográfico de Pernambuco*, Vol. XI, No. 61.

Torres, Heloisa Alberto: "Cerâmica de Marajô" (lecture). Rio de Janeiro, 1929.

Uchoa, Samuel: "Costumes Amazônicos," in the *Boletim Sanitário* (National Department of Public Health), Rio de Janeiro, 1923.

Vampré, João: "Fatos e Festas na Tradição," *Revista do Instituto Histórico de São Paulo*, Vol. XIII.

Bibliography 537

VIANNA, ARAUJO: "Das artes plasticas no Brasil em geral e da cidade do Rio de Janeiro em particular," in the *Revista do Instituto Histórico e Geográfico Brasileiro*.

V

WORKS CITED BY THE TRANSLATOR

ALMEIDA, JOSÉ AMÉRICO DE: *A Bagaceira*. Rio de Janeiro, 1928.
AMADO, JORGE: The Violent Land, translated by Samuel Putnam. New York, 1945.

BELMONTE: *No Tempo dos Bandeirantes*. São Paulo, 1939.

CASCUDO, LUIS DA CAMARA: *Vaqueiros e Cantadores*. Porto Alegre, 1939.
CUNHA, EUCLIDES DA: *Os Sertões*. 16th edition, Rio de Janeiro, 1942.
——: *Rebellion in the Backlands (Os Sertões)*, translated with an Introduction and Notes by Samuel Putnam. Chicago, 1944.

FREYRE, GILBERTO: *Região e Tradição*. Rio de Janeiro, 1941. (With a Preface by José Lins do Rego.)

Glossary of Brazilian-Amazonian Terms, Compiled from the Strategic Index of the Americas. Washington, D. C.: Coordinator of Inter-American Affairs; 1943.

KIRKPATRICK, F. A.: *Latin America, A Brief History*. Cambridge (England) and New York, 1939.

LIMA, HILDEBRANDO DE and GUSTAVO BARROSO: *Pequeno Dicionário Brasileiro da Lingua Portuguesa*, fifth edition, revised by Manuel Bandeira and José Baptista da Luz. Rio de Janeiro, São Paulo, and Bahia, 1944.

MACHADO, ALCANTARA: *Vida e Morte do Bandeirante*. São Paulo, 1930.
MICHAELIS, H.: *A New Dictionary of the Portuguese and English Languages*, etc. Leipzig, 1932.

PIERSON, DONALD: *Negroes in Brazil, A Study of Race Contact at Bahia*. Chicago, 1942.

TAUNAY, AFFONSO D' E.: *História Geral das Bandeiras Paulistas*. São Paulo, 1924-9.
TAUNAY, ALFREDO D'ESCRAGNOLLE: *Inocência*, translated by Henriqueta Chamberlain. New York, 1945.

VERÍSSIMO, ERICO: *Brazilian Literature, An Outline*. New York, 1945.

INDEX OF PERSONS

i

Index

v

Index

INDEX OF SUBJECTS

xliv *Index*